This book brings together under the heading of business history an account of the development of leading American financial, commercial, agricultural, transportation, and manufacturing enterprises during the period from the settlement of the colonies to the beginning of the twentieth century.

At the outset, all enterprises were undifferentiated functions of general entrepreneurs. After the Revolution one after another of these functions was spun off to become institutions of American business life. The process of institutionalization was largely completed by 1860. After the Civil War the dominant trend in business development was the combination, and in some cases integration, of small units into big business as we know it today, facilitated by new forms of business organization such as the trust and holding company. During this latter period the typical businessman gradually evolved from the commercially oriented entrepreneur of the traditional type to the specialist characteristic of business leadership today. Around 1900, as the outlines of these various patterns of business development became fully apparent, American business could be said to have come of age.

This important study incorporates into a single narrative a tremendous volume of monographic and periodical literature devoted to the multifarious and usually mutually exclusive, aspects of business, industrial, commercial, and financial history.

As a pioneering work, this volume should be of interest to students, American historians in general, and business and economic historians in particular. It will also be of value to businessmen since it traces the development of their specialties.

The Coming
of Age
of American Business

The Coming
of Age
# of American Business

Three Centuries of Enterprise, 1600–1900

by Elisha P. Douglass

The University of North Carolina Press
Chapel Hill

Manufactured in the United States of America
Printed by The TJM Corporation
ISBN 0–8078–1170–X
Library of Congress Catalog Card Number 78–132254

For Louisa

Contents

Preface

If there be any truth to the contention of a dour president of the United States that the business of America is business (and who can doubt that there is), it would seem that the record of this ubiquitous activity should occupy an important place in our historical literature. Far more people have been engaged in business than in politics, diplomacy, or warfare, and business has perhaps had more to do with the material success of the American experiment than any of these. If the test of historicity is the capacity of events to produce change, business history deserves an important position in the circle of historical studies.

In the last three or four decades interest in the subject has rapidly increased. General textbooks in American history have given more attention to it and courses in business history have been inaugurated at some colleges and universities. An increasing number of fine monographs on industries, corporations, and functional aspects of business have come from the university presses, and the examination of business careers has become an important segment of biographical studies. Following World War II, articles on business history have appeared more frequently in the journals of economics, and today *Business History Review* is devoted entirely to the subject. Numerous articles on business history are also to be found in *Explorations in Economic History*.

My purpose in this book is to bring together as much of the widely varie-

ix

gated literature of American business history as possible into a single narrative covering the formative period of American business. Such a task poses many difficult problems, few if any of which can be solved to the satisfaction of all readers. Probably the first is the question of theme. Since business in its broadest sense covers such a broad range of human activities it is difficult to deal with its many segments within the same conceptual framework. The development of banking, for instance, seems to follow a quite different course than the history of manufacturing, and likewise the relationship between life insurance and retailing appears to be only tangential. Yet throughout the course of American history one pattern of development has been shared by many, if not most types of business. In their initial condition, as described in the first part of this book, all were part of the undifferentiated functions of the entrepreneur. This venerable type of businessman, whose ancestry stretched back into antiquity, might combine in various configurations the functions of importing and exporting, wholesaling and retailing, banking and brokerage, and even manufacturing on the small scale usual in colonial America. Of course business organizations in the form of partnerships and joint stock companies also extend back into antiquity, but these too were essentially entrepreneurial and bore little resemblance to the modern corporation with its specialization of function and carefully organized management.

Progress toward our modern business system was initiated when entrepreneurial functions became separate entities and embarked on courses of individual institutional development. Thus banking, insurance, and textile manufacturing became businesses rather than part-time activities of general entrepreneurs—to take three random examples. This stage of institutional development proceeded rapidly during the antebellum period, and by the 1870s American businesses had assumed substantially their modern forms. The second stage of development, which reached its apogee at the turn of the century, was combination and integration—the reorganizing of business units to provide more strategies of defense and opportunities for profit in a rapidly changing and highly competitive economy. The conclusion of this first wave of combination seems to be a convenient terminal point for this study because it marks the end of the formative period of American business.

In following the institutional development of business I have tried to keep the focus of this study on the continuing specialization of business operations. Therefore, I have dealt with such matters as finance, procurement, management, operations, technology, and marketing. Unfortunately the monographic literature available does not make it possible to deal with these matters in an equally comprehensive manner throughout the wide spectrum of American business. Some industries, like the oil industry, for example, have been the subject of intensive research and excellent scholarly work. Yet much remains to be done in other areas. Such enterprises as public utilities, construction, and coal mining—to take only a few random examples—have been given so little attention that it is difficult to deal with them at all. Also, some less important businesses have been treated with such fine scholarship that there is danger of exaggerating their importance in the over-all story. A too great reliance on the better corporate histories emphasizes the particular at the expense of the general. In view of these limitations it scarcely needs to be said that this volume can make no pretension to being definitive. It is my hope, however, that it can to some degree summarize the existing work which has been done on American business history during the formative period.

In describing the development of business, with which this book is mainly concerned, I have tried to stand in the shoes of the men conducting the manifold enterprises described herein and see the business world as they saw it, taking note of their problems and their opportunities, and keeping pace with them as they struggle toward success or failure, or—in the great majority of cases—toward the gray zone in between which holds small rewards and small losses. I have attempted no extended economic analysis, and I have used quantitative materials primarily for purposes of illustration. Also, I have had relatively little to say about the relations of business to society at large, mainly because this aspect has received much more attention from historians than internal development.

Since the present volume is based entirely on secondary materials, footnotes have been considered unnecessary. The annotated bibliographical note reviews and analyzes all of the materials used in the text.

This study has been made possible through the generosity of the Smith Richardson Foundation, Incorporated, and the co-operation of the late Arthur W. Page. The foundation made a substantial grant to the history department of The University of North Carolina at Chapel Hill to subsidize studies in the operation of the free enterprise system. Mr. Page, a retired vice-president of the American Telephone and Telegraph Company and personally interested in the project, acted as co-ordinator of it. Some time later I was asked to start the program with a short survey of the subject within the field of my speciality—intellectual history. I soon discovered that I could write nothing significant about free enterprise until I understood more about American business and its internal operations—subjects which were to me at the time terra incognita. I thereupon began a program of reading which extended much beyond my original expectations and eventuated, finally, in this book. The institutional development of major business enterprises interested me particularly, and upon starting a course in American business history I found that students shared this interest, if only because this aspect has been largely ignored in the historical surveys of a more general nature.

During the development of this study I have received valuable assistance from others at times when it was particularly needed. Gustavus G. Williamson helped me organize and write a section on the colonial period which since that time has been much condensed for reasons of space and balance. John H. Jensen, who saw the need for a comprehensive treatment of American business history, gave constant encouragement for me to proceed with my work long before I could see light at the end of the tunnel. Eugene D. Genovese shortened my labors considerably in one aspect of this study by providing me with an extended bibliography of the literature devoted to the plantation system. I owe a particular debt of gratitude to Ralph W. Hidy and Thomas C. Cochran, who read a preliminary draft of this book. Their incisive and detailed criticisms led to a complete reorganization of the work. I am equally indebted to George Rogers Taylor whose suggestions at a later date enabled me to further rework the manuscript into the form in which it here appears. It is only fair to emphasize, however, that the conclusions and interpretations in the book are my own and do not necessarily reflect those of the individuals who have helped me. In the last analysis I owe the most to the hundreds of historians listed in the bibliographical note whose work is represented in this volume. I hope I have done justice to them in return for the education they have given me.

Part One

The Formation of American Business Institutions

I. Entrepreneurship and American Economic Growth

As the twentieth century advances, the ability of the American economy to produce and distribute wealth becomes continually more striking. With about 7 percent of the world's population, the nation enjoys some 42 percent of the world's income. There is one automobile in use for every two or three persons, over 85 percent of American homes contain television sets, and the people collectively own one-half of all the telephones in the world. According to the economist Seymour Harris, "In 150 years [ending in 1947] the income of the country [grew] from half a billion to more than 200 billion dollars, an increase of four hundred times or more. In the same period, population rose by twenty-six times and the supply of money by 1,150 times. It is a striking fact that this country now supports twenty-seven times as many people at a standard of living ten or more times as high as in 1820." All the statistics of wealth relative to the rest of the world are equally impressive, but—like the measurements of a beauty queen—they only emphasize the obvious.

What is less obvious is the explanation of America's phenomenal economic growth. Certain factors, of course, come readily to mind—abundant, strategically located, and readily available natural resources; a large market unrestricted by internal tariff barriers; peaceful neighbors, and until recently, at least, relative security against attack from abroad; fertile soil; salubrious climate; good natural communications. To these may be added favorable institutional factors. One of the most important of these is a free government which has protected property rights without freezing the existing distribution of wealth, which has in many ways, direct and indirect, fostered economic growth, and which has applied economic controls sparingly, and for the most part only where they were needed. In the United States politics has seldom made war on economics, as it has so often done in other societies. During the nineteenth century, economic advance was also stimulated by the unrestricted immigration of millions of Europeans who demonstrated their enterprising spirit by seeking better opportunities in a faraway land. Urbanization, industrialization, and the construction of transportation and communications networks brought specialization of functions, vastly increased employment and productivity, and economies of scale in nearly all categories of production. From these developments the American people were able to reap the fruits of growth in rising standards of living.

Merely to state these factors, however, imparts a deceptive simplicity to economic growth. In recent years the study of the process has absorbed the attention of an increasing number of economists, sociologists, and psychologists, and as a result the output of scholarly literature and quantitative analysis devoted to the subject has ballooned to massive proportions. As is so often the case, however, increase of knowledge serves more to bring problems into focus than to provide precise answers on which observers can agree. Like organic growth, economic growth becomes baffling in its complexity. As the economist Evsey Domar has pointed out, no one of the factors pertinent to it "could properly be taken as an independent variable." Simon Kuznets, whose work on the quantitative aspects of the subject is of monumental significance, has declared that so ambitious an objective as a general theory of growth may be "forever beyond reach."

The problem is further complicated by the fact that the causes of economic growth probably lie outside the realm of economics, and are therefore difficult to isolate and analyze by quantitative methods. Presumably most observers would agree that social characteristics are more important than material circumstances in determining the rate of advance. Nations may lack critically needed resources, but they can prosper if their citizens exhibit a willingness to work; an interest in science and technology and a readiness to accept innovations in these fields; an acceptance of social mobility and a desire for personal advancement; a corresponding freedom from arbitrary restraints of custom, tradition, and status; respect and desire for wealth; and the ability and willingness to create an educational system which will rationalize and promote the attainment of these objectives. The development of such nations as Holland, Switzerland, Sweden, and Japan illustrates the primacy of these human qualities over natural resources in explaining economic growth. The manifold difficulties encountered by the so-called underdeveloped nations in getting the growth process underway, even with abundant help from outside, shows that underdeveloped people can be an insurmountable handicap regardless of the material means available.

The origin of the characteristics conducive to economic growth is as obscure as all ultimate historical causation. Sociologists, like Talcott Parsons, may neatly categorize characteristics of successful societies in general terms, and while the categories provide a useful analytical tool, they tell us little about the beginnings of the process. The historians Marx, Toynbee, and Oswald Spengler, and the psychologist Sigmund Freud, by treating history as a process of rise and fall taking place within time, implicitly or explicitly postulate theories of growth, but none of these can be verified empirically. The contemporary psychologist David McClelland has identified "achievement motivation" as a basic cause of economic growth and has attempted to provide empirical verification by devising and applying tests to measure degrees of motivation. His research, conducted on a world-wide basis, has revealed that societies characterized by economic growth almost invariably show high levels of achievement motivation, and that the reverse is true of static and backward societies. When applied to historical materials, the tests yield the same results for societies of the past. Yet when dealing with causation of motivation itself, McClelland's findings can be only inferential.

As far as the United States is concerned, "the free enterprise system" constitutes for many a satisfying explanation of American economic growth. Actually, "free enterprise," or "private enterprise," is an emotion-laden phrase nearly pillaged of its meaning by generations of political controversy. For those who look upon themselves as guardians of the conservative tradition (whatever that may be), free enterprise is an honorific term representing an economic system in which government and business are carefully separated and business is allowed to conduct its affairs in an atmosphere of laissez-faire. For some professed liberals, free enterprise is a delusive euphemism appropriated to give a mask of respectability to a selfish, monopolistic type of capitalism which rewards the few and exploits the many. For practical businessmen who think free enterprise is a good thing, but do not ponder deeply about its meaning, it is, according to Albert Lauterbach, "a well-developed, satisfying belief system, which gives desirable status and meaning to many different kinds of discrete business activities. . . . It is an ideology that integrates the strivings for personal wealth and power, with the culturally accepted ideas of democracy, freedom, and service to one's fellow men." Quite apart from considerations of definition, however, it should be apparent that free enterprise is not a cause of growth as much as a description applied to some of the institutional processes which apparently have contributed to it in this country. The term also serves as a subjective, varying standard of judgment for evaluating the "proper" relations of business and government.

Considerations of definition aside, many conclusions about economic growth appear to have been derived largely from the American experience; so much so, in fact, that one wonders whether the process might be a unique aspect of Western culture as difficult to transfer to underdeveloped societies as the transplantation of a vital organ from one human being to another. Japan has indeed been strikingly successful in adopting western culture and values, but with this exception the question remains as to whether the material success of America and the West is a unique event in history or a process which can be shared by all peoples.

INTERPRETATIONS OF ENTREPRENEURSHIP

American economic growth has always been accompanied by a high degree of entrepreneurial activity which some economists have considered to be the major cause of the process. The functions performed by the various types of business institutions today were, during the eighteenth and early nineteenth centuries, combined in the manifold, undifferentiated activities of ubiquitous entrepreneur-businessmen. Throughout the development of American business, while these activities were spun off to become discrete business institutions and were later combined into larger units, entrepreneurial activity was very much in evidence. Since entrepreneurship appears to be such a close concomitant to development, therefore, a history of American business may well begin with an examination of the various conceptions of the role.

As the conductors of business, businessmen acting as entrepreneurs have been described as innovators, as the makers of creative (or destructive) decisions, and as combiners. The entrepreneurial role has also been sharply distinguished from that of the "manager" and the "risk taker." The manager is pictured as an administrator who devotes his efforts to keeping a business unit running smoothly rather than seeking to alter it for some creative purpose or to combine it with other units. The risk taker, according to this analysis, is the investor pure and simple who provides financing but assumes no responsibility for the conduct of business.

Historically the entrepreneur was first conceived as the combiner. As described by J. B. Say, the early nineteenth-century economist who helped to develop the concept, he is the functionary who "united all means of production—the labor of one, the capital or land of the others—and who finds in the value of the products which result from their employment the reconstitution of the entire capital that he utilizes, and the value of the wages, the interest, and the rent which he pays, as well as the profits belonging to himself." The more modern conception of entrepreneurship as innovation stems from the formulation by the influential Harvard economist Joseph Schumpeter. According to his description, the entrepreneur is the creative individual who in some manner breaks the habitual, circular flow of demand, production, and consumption, perhaps by producing new and attractive articles or services, or by creating new markets for articles or services already in production, or by devising more efficient and less costly production methods. As a result of the entrepreneur's efforts, a new configuration of demand-supply then comes into being, the innovator makes an extraordinary profit, and imitators rush into the field to share in the new source of weath. As supply mounts, profits decline, marginal firms fail, and business cycles begin. Schumpeter thus insisted that fluctuations in the economy are not caused primarily by supply and demand operating under market conditions, as the classical economists had maintained, but rather by the activities of entrepreneurs.

Throughout history the forms of entrepreneurship have differed both in relation to types of enterprises and to chronological period. Say perhaps had the "outputter" of seventeenth- and eighteenth-century Europe in mind when he based his definition on combination. Schumpeter, concerned with innovation, might well have been thinking of the industrial giants of the late nineteenth century. Yet it is obvious that the creative role of the businessman, evolving over the years in response to economic and cultural stimuli, has come to embrace many kinds of activity not directly related to the act of combining elements of production or to innovation. The modern executive conducting the affairs of a giant corporation from a suite of offices in a New York skyscraper performs a multitude of functions completely unforeseen by Say, and only a very few of these men are innovators in the Schumpetrian sense. Most entrepreneurs are imitators, and many fail in business.

Because of the inadequacies of these two definitions, therefore, modern conceptions of entrepreneurship focus on the function of decision making. This is not to say that decision making has replaced combining and innovation as the operating principle of entrepreneurship; rather, it has absorbed them. Throughout the nineteenth century, as we will often see in the following pages, creative businessmen devoted their most intense efforts to the combining of business units, and the most successful of them were innovators at various points over a wide spectrum of business activities. But if we are to include within a definition the great number of creative businessmen who have labored unnoted by history and by recognized business leaders, we must define the entrepreneur as the maker of decisions which have consequences, and result in a new configuration of business relationships. As expressed more specifically by G. Herberton Evans, Jr., entrepreneurship is exercised by "the person or group of persons [who] determine what kind of a business . . . is to be operated." In this connection entrepreneurs decide upon "the kinds of goods and services to be offered, the volume of goods and services, and the clientele to be served." Questions of technological methods, marketing, relation to the public and to government, and labor policy must also come within the purview of entrepreneurs if the over-all purpose of the business enterprise is to be successfully achieved. In all of these areas successful entrepreneurs discern some opportunities for innovation and combination, and determine their courses of action accordingly.

As far as personality is concerned, it would be impossible to say that an "entrepreneurial type" exists, although biographers tend to present successful businessmen in stereotyped form as aggressive, forceful, courageous, far-seeing, and decisive—men of action rather than of contemplation. But businessmen, like men in other fields, are men first and men of business second. Some do indeed correspond to the stereotype, although one suspects that biographers often distort the characters of their subjects by allowing the fact of success or failure to dictate the traits with which the subjects are endowed. Many successful businessmen may be timid, retiring, occasionally indecisive, prone to reach objectives by indirection. Most, however, share certain attitudes associated with their role which exist independently of personality. McClelland has found from his tests that entrepreneurs rate high in achievement motivation, and as a result respond positively to challenges, willingly accept moderate business risks, desire "feedback" from their efforts in the form of recognized results, value the satisfaction of a job well done more than public acclaim, feel anxieties that their performance may not be adequate, tend to become frenetically active in times of crisis, and desire long-range planning.

From the historical point of view entrepreneurs also seem to share more generalized attitudes. One of the most important of these has been the acceptance of change as desirable, and faith that change, through human effort, can be transformed into material progress. All entrepreneurs have varying abilities to envision opportunities in this direction and plan accordingly. Most, acting upon a personal calculus in which they balance desires against effort and risk, settle for limited, though significant objectives, the attainment of which constitutes their personal conception of success. A few, with grander dreams, more compulsive personalities, and greater physical and mental capacities for sacrifice and effort, make the great successes which provide the material for the rags to riches stories that have done so much to support faith in the free enterprise system. In order to reach their goals all entrepreneurs are willing in some measure to defer present enjoyments. Some have reinvested a part of their incomes in productive enterprises. Others, while acting in managerial positions, have reinvested a part of their time and effort in outside entrepreneurial ventures. Entrepreneurs seldom carry saving and sacrifice to the point of asceticism. Many have had a propensity for ostentatious display of wealth, but their spending for luxuries has usually proceeded at a rate considerably slower than the rate at which they accumulate capital, either for themselves or for others.

Entrepreneurial attitudes toward profit are somewhat different today than they were during the nineteenth century. For preindustrial entrepreneurs profit maximization was the most important and sometimes the only goal of business enterprise. Captains of industry during the late nineteenth century professed a wider variety of motives, among which the desire to meet and master challenges was particularly important. Today the widespread conviction that entrepreneurial behavior should promote public welfare, and the considerable amount of legislation on the books designed to achieve this objective, have pushed the profit motive further into the background. Also, the separation of ownership and management in larger corporations and the professionalization of management have contributed to this development by sharply limiting management's participation in profit. Profit is of course indispensable for the firm, but for many corporate executives it has become a kind of academic grade indicating proficiency, one way among many of achieving status and acceptance.

Studies of the origins of entrepreneurs confront the student with something of a paradox. On one hand, many of the most successful businessmen in America came from relatively humble backgrounds that provided little impetus toward a business career. The careers of such well-known figures as Astor, Girard, Vanderbilt, Swift, and Carnegie seemed to give documentary proof of the rags to riches story and thereby verify the contention of Social Darwinists that the challenge of adversity produced the character of tempered steel. On the other hand, recent statistical studies indicate that most businessmen came from substantial business or professional backgrounds, and began life with advantages greater than those enjoyed by the population generally. The merchant and planter class of the eighteenth century, which constituted the business community, was recruited from the upper ranks of society. From independence until about 1820 the number of businessmen coming from humble origins increased markedly, but after that time the trend was reversed, and continues unabated today. Of a test group examined for the decade 1900–1910, for example, about 80 percent came from business and professional families. Of these families, 50 percent could be designated as upper class, 45 percent as middle class, and only 5 percent as lower class. "It is plain," concludes the compiler of these figures, William Miller, "that the men who had the most advantages to start with made the most rapid business ascent." Entrepreneurs tend to breed entrepreneurs—a not surprising situation—and doubtless the accumulation of wealth by an increasing number of entrepreneurial families and kinship groups has enabled a continually larger proportion of recruits into the world of business to begin their careers on the middle- and upper-class level.

The recruitment of entrepreneurs from middle- and upper-class origins has undoubtedly contributed much to American economic growth. From the beginning of our history the active, influential aristocracy in American life has been drawn from entrepreneurial groups, and this aristocracy has been able to impress its values upon a society uniquely free from the remnants of feudalism. Trade carried no stigma, upward mobility was unobstructed by arbitrary privilege, and achievement—particularly in the acquisition of wealth—was the highway to status. Of course America has also had aristocracies which sought exclusiveness in "society" and have attempted to imitate the class-conscious attitudes and values of the European aristocracy. These groups have always been rather small, however, and have been subjected to criticism because of deviation from the egalitarian ideals of American life. Any influence they might bring to bear in order to gain general acceptance of their values was further lessened by financial dependence upon entrepreneurial leadership and by the fact that successful entrepreneurs who gained acceptance from these groups usually refused to renounce their entrepreneurial values. In this regard American entrepreneurs, as a group, differed markedly from many of their European counterparts, who often considered the acquisition of a title and abandonment of the life of trade to be an ultimate goal.

On the following pages entrepreneurs acting as combiners, innovators, and decision makers will play important roles, but the roles themselves will undergo progressive evolution as they are affected by the institutionalization of business functions. At the outset of our story business history and entrepreneurial history are one and the same thing since all business is carried on in undifferentiated fashion by general entrepreneurs. But as specialization of function results in the formation of discrete business institutions, the creative role of the entrepreneur will be increasingly channeled and directed by the specialized needs of business organizations characterized by growing size and complexity. Under these circumstances many entrepreneurial functions merge into managerial specialities, and the firm or the industry becomes the focus for business history.

II. Business and Businessmen in Colonial America

The preoccupation with business which has characterized our national career was plainly evident in the colonial period. From the outset America was envisaged and developed as a business enterprise. Paraphrasing Lincoln one might say that the nation was conceived in a counting house and dedicated to the proposition that most, if not all men, should have an equal opportunity to make a profit. The first settlements, as attempted by Gilbert and Raleigh, were private ventures backed by considerable capital and designed to bring wealth and power to their promoters. Virginia was founded by a large corporation whose stockholders anticipated a handsome return on their investment. Another corporation, the Massachusetts Bay Company, established a Puritan commonwealth as much for profit as for the glory of God. Carolina was a purely commercial enterprise despite the proprietors' dream of a new feudal empire. William Penn and George Calvert had noble visions of their provinces as havens for the persecuted, but it is apparent from their correspondence that they were at least equally interested in making money out of their colonizing enterprises. Unfortunately for all these founding fathers, their efforts uniformly turned out to be better business for America than for themselves. Their heavy losses were roughly equivalent to our foreign aid programs today, which strive to create social overhead capital and viable economies, but generate profits only for the recipients.

The first businessmen in America were the agents of colonial promoters resident in England. The function of these agents was to import into the infant settlements the food supplies and the tools and building materials so desperately needed by the pioneers of the early seventeenth century, and to dispatch to England the paltry amounts of furs, skins, and staple products collected in payment. But as the controls of the English promoters weakened because of heavy financial losses, interlopers made their way into the colonial trade. At the outset these were ship captains, whole or part owners of their vessels and cargoes, but sometimes agents of English mercantile houses. Forefathers of the tramp traders of a later period, these peddlers of the sea visited the coastal towns of Massachusetts and the settlements ringing Chesapeake Bay, exchanging supplies, manufactured goods, and in some cases slaves and servants, for whatever the local people had to offer.

When Virginians turned to the production of tobacco, even the small farmers became caught up in a capitalist economy spanning the Atlantic. Owning their own land, producing a cash crop for sale in a distant market, and using the proceeds plus credit extended to them by the purchasers to buy farming supplies and farm labor, they were released from the peasant economies of Europe and operated as primitive agribusinessmen. The larger farms devoted to capitalized agriculture came into existence in a variety of ways. In Virginia some stockholders of the Virginia Company pooled or purchased the hundred-acre dividends periodically distributed. The relatively few gentlemen who emigrated to Maryland and the southern counties of Pennsylvania (today Delaware), utilized the manorial privileges extended by the Calverts and the Penns to form plantations operated by unfree labor.

Although most first generation Americans lived in a condition of social and economic equality, here and there appeared the nabobs who were to form a small, but very powerful class that was to become a feature of frontier life. William Claiborne established a petty barony on Kent Island, where he not only grew tobacco and raised cattle but conducted a trading post that became the commercial center of the northern Chesapeake. Sometimes sea captains like Samuel Mathews in Virginia and Robert Keayne in Massachusetts settled down to become sedentary rather than traveling merchants. In William Pyncheon Massachusetts produced a tycoon similar to Claiborne. From a fort on the Connecticut River near the present site of Springfield he came to dominate the trade of the entire region.

From each successive generation on the westward moving frontier emerged similar figures. For example, during the Revolutionary period the organization of government in the transmontane areas of Virginia and North Carolina was largely the work of three pioneer businessmen— Richard Henderson, William Blount, and John Sevier. Henderson also formed the colonizing company that employed Daniel Boone as a trail blazer, and all hastened the pace of settlement by their activities in land speculation. Examples of similar leading frontier businessmen could be multiplied almost indefinitely, but the breed culminated, probably, in the post Civil War cattle kings of the prairies and the silver and copper barons of the western mining regions. Although specific economic activities varied with the potentialities of various regions, all of these businessmen, from the early seventeenth to the late nineteenth centuries, performed certain similar functions. They organized production, created markets and secured the credit necessary for market operations, improved methods of communication and transportation, and in many other ways enabled the frontier to merge into the mainstream of American life.

Of course, during the seventeenth century creative entrepreneurship of this type was limited by the very slow rate of economic growth which necessarily resulted from the cessation of direct British investment in the colonies. Almost the only capital beside funds brought in by immigrants came in the form of long-term commercial credits advanced by British merchants. But by the beginning of the eighteenth century the pace of economic growth speeded somewhat. Increased production of tobacco in the Chesapeake region and a growing surplus of food and provisions in the northern colonies brought greater earning power. Markets for colonial products widened as the West Indies, specializing in sugar production, came to depend on the Atlantic colonies for supplies of all kinds. Colonial staples, particularly tobacco, began reaching European markets when Britain, replacing Holland as the world's foremost maritime nation, became an effective marketing agent for colonial products she did not herself need.

Enhanced opportunities attracted the able and aggressive young men who from Massachusetts to South Carolina were to found first families. Almost without exception they came from backgrounds in commerce or in guild manufacturing. For example, the sire of the Byrd family of Virginia was a London goldsmith. The Ludwells were descended from mercers and the Blands from skinners. William Fitzhugh, one of the most successful businessmen of his generation, was the son of a London draper. Nearly all of the great merchant-landholders of New York—Schuylers, Livingstons, Van Rensselaers, Verplancks, Bayards, De Lanceys, and Beekmans—came from similar origins. The same can be said for most of the leading families of Boston, Philadelphia, and Charleston. All members of this first generation, including those settled in the South on plantations, owed their rise to trade. Moreover, they retained their entrepreneurial orientation throughout their lives, and most passed it on to succeeding generations.

In every phase of colonial life this business aristocracy was dominant. As members of assemblies they acted as trustees for the mass of the people, and those few who became royal councillors manipulated to their own advantage the sovereign power of the motherland, chiefly in the acquisition of large land grants. Seated on the benches of county courts and installed as administrative functionaries, they constituted the judiciary and the civil service. In the vestries of the Church of England they administered not only the ecclesiastical establishment but local government and community services as well. As leaders of the militia they were the top military brass, and military rank was usually equated with social rank. No inconvenient doctrines of separation of powers or conflict of interests existed to interfere with their manifold, interlocking activities. Probably at no time in our history have business and government been so closely linked. Indeed, it is no exaggeration to say that at this time they were one and the same thing—as illustrated by the fact that in England the most active policy making body for the colonies was the Board of Trade.

BUSINESS FUNCTIONS OF COLONIAL ENTREPRENEURS

The economic activities of the business aristocracy were so all-embracing that one can characterize these men only by saying that during the eighteenth century they constituted the directors and supervisors of colonial economic life. The Chesapeake planters were not only growers of tobacco but purchased large amounts from farmers and marketed it through London correspondents via the consignment system. The large planters were also wholesale and retail merchants. They invested part of the proceeds from tobacco sales in manufactured goods of all kinds, some of which they sold in their own retail stores, and some of which they dispatched to merchants in the interior. They were also the bankers of their localities. As the recipients of long-term book credits from British merchant correspondents, they were in a position to extend accommodations on somewhat shorter terms to farmers and lesser planters. Aubrey C. Land's recent research in tax and probate records of the Chesapeake area reveals that large planters often carried a hundred or more debtors. Planter businessmen also purchased and sold bills of exchange and the many types of currency and coins in use in the colonies. Servants and slaves were shipped to them on consignment from London and Liverpool correspondents, and the merchant planters marketed the unfree labor in the same manner that they sold store truck—usually on credit. Slave trading carried none of the stigma it acquired during the antebellum period. As a matter of fact, among Charleston merchant planters participation in it brought greater prestige than any other branch of commerce. Ironically enough, these same traffickers in human flesh considered it demeaning personally to tend their own retail stores.

Merchant planters built and operated mills, tanneries, blacksmith shops, forges, and other community services in connection with their plantation enterprises. Many plantations had spinning and weaving shops. At Monticello Jefferson not only had the equipment for carrying on all of the home industries, but a nail shop as well which he tried unsuccessfully to operate as a commercial venture. At Shadwell he built two flour mills. Robert Carter of Nomini Hall constructed a bakery for ship biscuit and provisioned ships as part of his plantation operations. Larger manufacturing undertakings invariably were started and operated by merchant-planters. Governor Spotswood operated a profitable iron works on the upper James, largely with imported German labor, and shipped bar and cast iron to London along with tobacco. Augustine Washington, father of George, supplied ore for the largest iron works in the colonies, the Principio Company, of which he was a partner. Members of the Carroll family and other leading Marylanders built and operated the profitable Baltimore Iron Works, located on the upper Chesapeake near Principio.

But by far the most attractive enterprise for merchant planters was land speculation. Because of their large families they were more or less compelled to engage in it in order to avoid dissipation of landed estates within a few generations by partible inheritance. But equally important, land speculation, like stock speculation today, offered an opportunity to make a lot of money in a hurry. Merchants who sent surveyor-partners ahead of the westward moving pioneer farmers with the purpose of spying out the best land could get five to sometimes tenfold increment on funds invested in these tracts. Throughout the whole of our frontier experience the farmer, upon reaching the land of his dreams, found that Kilroy, in the form of the speculator, had already been there.

But during the colonial period land speculation east of the Appalachians was carried on under restrictions, and speculators needed patience, tact, and influence to acquire large tracts. The Board of Trade constantly forbade royal governors to make extensive unconditional grants because land engrossment dispersed population and kept land out of cultivation, thereby obstructing the proper operation of the mercantile system. But this limitation was widely evaded by large planters who had the political power to do so. Headrights, granting fifty acres for every immigrant above the age of sixteen brought into the colonies, were often fraudulently issued and could be purchased in commercial centers. Royal governors and favored councillors, particularly in New York, often built up large estates for themselves by making a multitude of small grants to dummies who by prearrangement reconveyed to the grantor. But the Board was always willing to confer large acreages upon merchant planters who would contract to import and settle farmers on the land. Thus Spotswood, by bringing in German families, came to own as much as 80,000 acres, including the valuable ore properties. William Byrd received 131,000 acres contingent upon his settling at least one family on every thousand acres. But since the promotion of settlement under these circumstances was an expensive and unpredictable process, many planters were not able completely to fulfill the terms of their contracts, and as a result much land reverted back to the crown. Nevertheless, most speculators managed to keep a considerable portion of their grants. Although Byrd, for example, failed to bring in enough Swiss and Scotch-Irish immigrants to acquire title to all of his holdings on the upper Roanoke, at the end of a lifetime of speculation he had 179,000 acres to show for his pains.

Remoteness and the Indian menace made settlement in the Appalachians and beyond a much more difficult process. Faced with these problems planters adopted the solution for colonization of distant areas used by the English promoters of the early seventeenth century—the joint stock company. The first of these organizations was the Ohio Company of 1748, made up of some twenty Virginia planters headed by Lawrence Washington, half-brother of George. The company was granted 500,000 acres on the upper Ohio under the condition that it ultimately settle 500 families in the region. In the next year the Loyal Company received 800,000 acres and in 1754 Governor Dinwiddie promised 200,000 acres to volunteers in the opening campaign of the French and Indian War. When the French were finally expelled from the Mississippi Valley in 1763, the pace of speculation mounted. Petitions for grants poured in upon the British government, and companies formed on a shoestring proposed to build empires west of the Appalachians. Typical of these was the Mississippi Company established by thirty-eight Virginia and Maryland planters, among them five Lees, three Washingtons, and three Fitzhughs. The promoters expected jointly to establish fifty proprietaries of 50,000 acres apiece in the area bounded by the Mississippi, the Wabash, and the Tennessee Rivers.

Of course, none of these imperial projects brought the returns expected from them, but the fascination of western lands continued to arouse the vaulting ambitions of merchants and planters throughout the rest of the century—nearly always to their sorrow. Operating on borrowed money, overestimating the speed at which they could sell off their tracts, most speculators of the early republic ended in bankruptcy. Yet the limited and carefully conducted speculations, more in the nature of land development, were often successful. Washington early demonstrated his business acumen by surveying, patenting, and distributing the land granted to the volunteers of 1754. By combining his own claim with others which he purchased from fellow volunteers he came to own 24,000 choice acres.

The merchant-planters of Charleston were if anything even more commercially oriented than those of the Chesapeake region. Actually Charleston during the decade preceding the Revolution was one of America's first boom towns. Nearly all of the great merchants combined rice production with overseas trade, and in the process escalated their profits until they became by far the wealthiest group of businessmen in the colonies. The degree of Charleston's prosperity is indicated clearly by the course of the slave trade. While the Virginia House of Burgesses was attempting, against the opposition of the Board of Trade, drastically to curtail the importation of slaves—thus reflecting the soggy condition of the tobacco economy—three to four thousand Negroes per year entered South Carolina at Charleston. This of course represented a large capital import and was both a cause and a result of the rapid growth of the rice and indigo economy. Marketing the slaves for the London and Liverpool slave trading houses at the usual commission of 10 percent could bring gross commissions on single cargoes of from 500 to 700 pounds. On the eve of the Revolution a few merchant planters had developed such financial muscle that they were able to purchase entire cargoes at wholesale prices and market the Negroes on their own account.

The preceding description of the activities of southern merchant planters makes any extended description of the functions of northern merchants unnecessary. Like the merchants of the Chesapeake and Charleston, those of Boston, Newport, New York, and Philadelphia imported manufactured goods and exported native produce, sold at wholesale and retail, and engaged in banking, brokerage, and land speculation. One of the largest operations in this latter category was the Vandalia promotion. In 1768 a group of merchants and Indian traders led by the frontier mogul, Sir William Johnson, and members of the Wharton family of Philadelphia—for whom the Wharton School of Business is appropriately named—purchased a sizable chunk of the Old Northwest from Indians, organized the Indiana Company, and dispatched Samuel Wharton to London for the purpose of inducing the Board of Trade to validate the Indian title. The promoters hoped to have their proprietary set off as a fourteenth colony. But since the purchase lay within Virginia's western claims, stockholders of the Ohio Company immediately protested. Then ensued a long tug of war during which wealthy Englishmen were brought into the Indiana promotion and the company was reorganized as the Vandalia Company. But even though the Board of Trade came very near to sanctioning the project, in part because of the astute lobbying for it by Benjamin Franklin, a leading stockholder, the company died on the eve of the Revolution for political reasons and the promoters lost the 10,400 pounds they had paid for the Indian title. Yet the promotion established a precedent for large-scale land speculation which was to reappear in the activities of similar organizations in the new republic—the Ohio Company of Associates, the Scioto Company, and the Yazoo Companies.

TRIANGULAR TRADE AND WARTIME ACTIVITIES

The trading patterns of the northern merchants differed from those of their southern counterparts. While southern merchants carried on a direct trade with England, the northern merchants had to acquire their English goods indirectly by the familiar triangular route. The sloops and other small vessels in the West Indies trade, averaging forty to fifty tons in weight, were loaded in ports from Salem to Philadelphia with such local products as flour and bread, fish and oil, beef and other salt meat, corn, peas, cattle and sheep, lumber, staves, and shingles. Sailing orders to the captains sometimes specified ports to be visited and transactions to be made, but more often the disposal of the cargo and the obtaining of a return lading was left to the captain's judgment. Most captains, therefore, were entrepreneurs in their own right. Under these circumstances the voyages usually followed the tramping pattern.

On the way to the West Indies captains sometimes put into southern ports such as Norfolk and Charleston in order to investigate the opportunities of turning over a portion of the cargo at a profit. The first ports of calls in the West Indies were in the Windward Islands, from which the vessels could make their way eastward with the trade winds through the

Leeward Islands and onward to Jamaica. Exchanges were conducted in a variety of ways. Some parcels of cargo were handed over as remittances; others were delivered to commission merchants for sale at a commission of 10 to 12 percent. The captains personally sold to the large merchants and planters. Prices for both incoming and outgoing goods fluctuated widely because of the inelasticity of the island markets, the lack of storage facilities, and the frequent convergence of several ships with similar cargoes upon the same port. Wherever possible goods were sold for cash or for bills of exchange on London, but more often the transactions were on a barter basis with prices hiked upward in accordance with the amount of credit granted and the time allowed for payment.

The collection of return ladings, which usually consisted of sugar, molasses, indigo, and dyewoods, was a slow and laborious process and involved the same multiple transactions as the disposal of the cargo. When fully loaded, some vessels set out for the Atlantic ports from which they had come, with stopovers along the way, but more continued their tramping voyages by visiting southern Europe, the Wine Islands, or even Africa. Eventually, goods collected in the latter course of trade found their way into the warehouses of London merchants, where they served as remittances for the English manufactures which were carried back to home ports.

The fact that annual exports from the Atlantic colonies worth about 500,000 pounds were valued at about 725,000 pounds in the West Indies would seem to indicate that the trade was profitable when taken as a whole. But since individual outgoing cargoes were seldom worth more than a few hundred pounds, and since a voyage between east coast ports, the West Indies, and England required almost a year to complete, the returns to merchants participating must have been of modest proportions. Moreover, in many cases, losses were sustained because of the lack of market reports and the widely fluctuating prices in the West Indies.

Losses could be limited, however, by taking advantage of the many hedges available to general entrepreneurs. Most merchants owned shares in several vessels and collected cargoes in partnership arrangements. Some participated in marine underwriting syndicates. Since the cost of shipbuilding was 25 percent less in the colonies than in England because of the ubiquity of good ship timber, merchants could add shipbuilding profits to trading profits by entering into partnerships with shipbuilders and selling ships as well as cargoes in England after initial trading voyages to the West Indies. Many merchants had shares in ironworks, distilleries, and potasheries, as well as in fishing and whaling vessels.

Since the New England traders served markets outside the British empire, they were more easily drawn into illegal trade than the merchants of the South. In time of war some merchants covertly gave aid to the French by shipping supplies to the Dutch Island of St. Eustatius or to Monte Christi, a Spanish town near the border of Santa Domingo, fully aware that these goods would be taken to France or the French West Indies. Privateering offered a stimulating opportunity to get these goods back for free. By 1759 forty-eight privateers had been commissioned in New York alone. About one-third of the adult males of Newport, including slaves, were afloat and looking for prizes. In order to spread the risk the capital outlay of the expeditions was divided into sometimes as many as thirty-two or even sixty-four shares, and documents representing these were bought and sold in the merchants' exchange of the seaport towns. Many handsome prizes were taken, of course, usually by the most heavily armed vessels which represented the largest investments. But losses were heavy among the smaller vessels outfitted on a shoestring by merchants with little financial resources. Newport lost so many ships during the French and Indian War that its merchant community was in serious straits after 1763. In the long run losses and profits probably balanced each other out, and privateering in effect operated as a device for redistribution of wealth among the merchants engaged in it.

A less risky source of profit, but one which laid heavy responsibilities on the investors, was military contracting. In the absence of a central quartermaster organization, individual British commanders contracted with American merchants to provision their armies. The lion's share of the contracts went to some twoscore merchants of New York, Boston, and Philadelphia, and some of these men—particularly Oliver De Lancey and John Watts of New York, and Thomas Hancock and Charles Apthorp of Boston, made impressive fortunes from the business. Merchants also sometimes "bought" soldiers' wages. Since the British Treasury was very dilatory in paying troops, necessitous soldiers often sold to merchants at a discount the orders for payment which they received from their commanders. Connecticut merchants invested many thousands of pounds in these orders and they circulated in trade as merely another type of scarce but polyglot colonial currency.

BACK-COUNTRY MERCHANTS AND RESIDENT FACTORS

A significant development in the colonial business world during the quarter century before independence was the rise of the interior merchant. Since the first days of settlement storekeepers in the back country had operated with credit advanced by seaport merchants, but since the store-keepers never had the capital to engage in entrepreneurial activities outside retailing, they could not claim the prestigious title of "merchant." But with the rise of the population in the back country, some energetic storekeepers became independent entrepreneurs and founded wealthy family dynasties. Thus Jonathan Trumbull of Lebanon, Connecticut, began his career as a drover, gathering herds of cattle from neighboring farmers and driving them to Boston for sale. With his profits he branched out into retailing, wholesaling, and banking. He also sold goods on consignment from Boston merchants, collected debts for them, speculated in cargoes of whale oil dispatched to London, purchased soldiers wages, and operated a large farm, fulling mill, flour mill, and brewery. Although he failed because of over-extension of credit, his liberality as a banker paid off handsomely in political coin. For over fifty years he continuously held high office in Connecticut and was so revered as Revolutionary governor that during the nineteenth century school children were taught that he was the man whom Washington had helped to win the war. The Dwight family of Springfield established a wealthy dynasty by extending their small retail business forward into chain stores and backward into wholesaling and warehousing. In South Carolina many "country factors," originally no more than agents of the great Charleston merchant planters, worked into independent entrepreneurial positions by the same methods used in the North. Because of slender resources, however, the back-country merchants tended to operate in myriad, temporary partnerships, striving to collect by pooling the capital few individually possessed in adequate amounts. Seaboard merchants, blessed by financing from England, could conduct their business with a smaller number of more or less regular correspondents.

In the Chesapeake region the functions of back-country merchants were often performed by resident English or Scottish factors representing large mercantile houses of London and Glasgow. During the decade prior to the Revolution Glasgow merchants came to handle much of the tobacco re-shipped to France, Holland, and Germany—which amounted, incidently, to about 85 percent of total English imports. In order to guarantee adequate supplies the factors opened stores in Virginia and Maryland which purchased tobacco direct from planters and farmers and advanced the credit formerly given by English correspondents. Many planters apparently considered this method of marketing preferable to consigning tobacco on their own account to London. For generations planters had felt themselves to be exploited by the consignment system, and Jefferson reflected a commonplace sentiment when he referred to planters as "a species of property attached to certain mercantile houses of London." Because of charges for inspection, handling, freight, insurance, and customs, and a commission of 2½ percent charged by English merchants for selling tobacco and a similar commission charged for purchasing goods for the planters, the net return on leaf which sold in England at about twelve pence per pound was not much more than a penny.

By dealing with resident factors planters might have been able to avoid some of the risks and charges of the consignment system, but probably lower prices offered in the Chesapeake wiped out most of the savings which might be anticipated from direct marketing. In any event, the large planters continued to send tobacco to London for sale, and the aggregate debt they owed to British merchants continued to mount. Low tobacco prices were partially responsible for their plight, but more important, as a conscious aristocracy they had come to consider as obligatory an extravagant mode of life which few could really afford. When crops were short, quality poor, or prices below average, they did not decrease their purchases from England proportionally, but requested advances from their merchant correspondents, promising to make up the debt on a future crop. Often as not the next crop did not eliminate the debt, yet the planters, fervently voicing further promises to pay, requested even more credit. The merchants could have stopped this pyramiding of debt quickly enough if they had dared to, but they were dependent upon the planters for tobacco and for commissions, and in any event interest payments gave the debts the character of investments.

Diversification of enterprises and an intensified drive for self-sufficiency was one response on the part of the planters toward the inadequacies of the tobacco economy. Another was the growing of wheat as a major crop and the entrance into processing where possible. As previously indicated, Robert Carter operated a bakery for ship biscuit. Washington produced a superfine flour which he sold in the West Indies under his own name. As a result of agricultural changes in the Chesapeake region, Baltimore and Norfolk grew rapidly as flour exporting centers during the decade before the Revolution.

FINANCIAL RESOURCES OF MERCHANTS AND ACCOUNTING
PROCEDURES

By this time a well-defined mercantile hierarchy had come into being. At the top were the very few moguls like Charles Carroll, Robert Carter, or Henry Laurens possessing property worth 50,000 to 100,000 pounds, of which perhaps 30 percent was represented by debts owed to them. Beneath them on the ladder were the "large" planters, whom Aubrey Land defines as individuals who had estates of at least 1,000 pounds. These men constituted only a small proportion of the population—perhaps 2 or 3 percent—yet Jackson T. Main finds from his investigation of Charleston probate records that 30 percent of the merchant planters of the city possessed estates worth 1,000 pounds or more. One thousand five hundred pounds was the median value of merchant estates in the northern cities, and one merchant out of eight was worth 5,000 pounds or more.

But perhaps more important for business development than the large merchants was the growth of the class of merchants with fortunes of from 500 to 1,000 pounds. These men were coming increasingly to share with the large merchant planters the control of the political and economic life of the colonies. From their number came assemblymen, justices of the peace, judges, and militia officers. Below this group were storekeepers and farmers, sometimes listed on the records as merchants or planters, but because of their lack of risk capital not businessmen in the entrepreneurial sense.

It is much more difficult to determine the income of merchants and planters than their property holdings because income was not a matter of public record. Moreover, the relatively small number of business records which have come down from the colonial period usually do not give an adequate accounting of profit and loss. Although most merchants and planters had some dim understanding of double-entry bookkeeping, in practice—according to the historian of accounting, William T. Baxter—"crude single entry was overwhelmingly the rule." Since cash and currency were very scarce, particularly in the back country, merchants ran the equivalent of charge accounts for their customers in which they entered credits and debits under a system of "barter bookkeeping." By this procedure, for example, a merchant might accept two sheep in part payment for a bolt of cloth, and the debit and credit would be entered on the ledger in current monetary values. Merchants also acted as bankers by allowing customers with credit balances to draw bills of exchange against these, or the merchants upon order might transfer goods to third parties and debit the customer's account. Day to day transactions were recorded in a "day book," or "waste book." Periodically the accounts were consolidated into a ledger. A letter book and an invoice book completed the business records of a store. But since merchants were involved in myriad small ventures outside of retail and wholesale transactions, few—according to Baxter—ever attempted a trial balance from which over-all profit or loss could be computed. Jackson Main estimates that established merchants considered wealthy netted on the average about 500 pounds per year.

For plantation enterprise the problem of determining profit was practically impossible not only because most planters kept inadequate books, but because they were unaware of the accounting concepts which must be taken into consideration for such an undertaking. The hidden income in the form of food and provisions produced on the plantation was never adequately evaluated, and the personal living costs of the planter and his family were never segregated from the costs of running the plantation. The planter could have only the foggiest notion of the capital value of his plantation against which to compute percentage return, and such factors as depreciation were never taken into consideration. From scanty available evidence, however, it appears that when profit is considered as purchasing power, then the great majority of plantations were unprofitable.

One illustration will have to suffice. George Washington was one of the best planter businessmen of his generation. Because of his meticulous bookkeeping, his interest in scientific farming and in organizing the work on his plantations, he became a veritable forerunner of the "scientific management" clique of the late nineteenth century. Yet not until his last years did he even try to determine annual profit. In 1798 he computed the "gain" from all of his manifold operations to be 898 pounds. Apart from the fact that this "gain" doubtless included capital increment as well as disposable income, it represented only a very small return on property estimated to be worth in the aggregate about 200,000 pounds. Often Washington was so short of ready cash that he had to borrow to meet current expenses. Rent collections from his numerous tenants usually did not amount to simple interest on the investment because of many defaults and arrearages, and as a moneylender he lost heavily during the Revolution because of repayments in depreciated currency. In 1789 he was in such straitened circumstances that he had to borrow 250 pounds to pay off some debts and cover his traveling expenses to his inauguration in New York. Throughout his life most of his income came from the land speculation with which he was constantly occupied. The desperate financial straits into which Jefferson, Madison, Monroe, and Jackson fell during the last years of their lives tell us something about the ability of the slave plantation to produce income in the form of purchasing power. But actually, since so much of plantation income is not of this variety, profit as an accounting concept cannot realistically indicate the returns from plantation operations.

The wealthiest planters, nevertheless, had impressive incomes. Charles

Carroll's was about 1,800 pounds per year and incomes of 1,000 pounds were not uncommon in tidewater South Carolina. In all of these cases, however, it is likely that the bulk of cash income came from banking and commercial rather than agricultural operations.

SUCCESS FACTORS IN AN UNSTRUCTURED BUSINESS MILIEU

The differences between the colonial and the modern businessman are striking. As general entrepreneurs operating without benefit of business institutions, colonial businessmen were spared the grueling routine and the pressures imposed by large modern corporations. Few worked as hard as successful modern executives. Even the largest merchants made no more than a dozen or so transactions a day. Large planters, if they so desired, could be busy men, as the plantation routine of Washington and Jefferson indicates. Yet William Byrd's diary testifies that he led a very relaxed life at Westover and during the years spent in London passed much of his time in gentlemanly dissipation. Eighteenth-century observers often spoke of the "indolence" of Virginia planters. With no telephones, no daily flood of mail, no problems churned up by an administrative staff, no conferences to be constructively led, no deadlines to be met, no competitors to be out-distanced, it is understandable that gout and not stomach ulcers was the occupational disease of the eighteenth-century businessmen.

But the cost of operating without structured business institutions was the inability to delegate responsibility. Because of the shortage of skilled, responsible labor, merchants and planters had to personally carry out nearly all tasks connected with their enterprises. Even large northern merchants tended their retail stores. Enforced absences of owners from their plantations usually entailed large losses, and this is one reason for the chronic financial difficulties of the members of the Virginia dynasty who occupied the White House. Without the financial reserves and informational services of modern business organization, all business risks were greater. Furthermore, until the eve of the Revolution co-operation among merchants outside of partnership relations was rare. In 1761 merchants of Boston, Newport, and Providence dealing in whale products and spermaceti candles formed a pool to peg prices and restrict output—the first such organization in America—but this initial experiment to restrict competition was no more successful than similar attempts during the nineteenth century. The periodic boycotts of British goods from 1765 to 1774 brought temporary unity of action among the merchants of Whig persuasion, yet many neutral and all Troy merchants refused to join, and there were constant charges of evasion among even active members of the associations.

The most substantial form of co-operation was the New York Chamber of Commerce, chartered in 1770, but similar organizations were not formed in other cities until after the Revolution.

In view of the high risks and unstructured characteristic of the business world of the colonies, what was the formula for a successful career? As suggested before, except in plantation enterprise, hard work and the practice of the prudential virtues were less important than in later generations because of the slow pace of business. Specialized knowledge was likewise an unimportant factor simply because not much of it was necessary to carry on the mercantile transactions of the day. Aspiring youngsters began their careers by learning office routine in apprenticeship to an established merchant. Apprentices headed for the overseas trade then acquired a knowledge of markets and distant commercial communities by serving as supercargoes on trading voyages. Nearly all the wealthy merchants of Salem and many in other small ports became ship captains as well. The universal practice of setting aside a portion of cargo space for the private ventures of the ship's company sharpened entrepreneurial motivation. The period of training came to an end when the novice struck out for himself, usually as an agent or correspondent for an established merchant. Some merchant planters sometimes studied law as a preparation for business. Many of the Charleston merchants active in the Revolution had attended the Inns of Court in London. Of course, some merchants combined their commercial activities with the practice of law, much to their financial advantage.

Certain personal qualities were more important than formal training in smoothing the highway to success, among them the ability to envisage commercial opportunities, the courage to act upon them, and the willingness to accept high business risks while distinguishing between business risk and gambling. Yet access to credit was as important as any of these and was the most important external circumstance making for success or failure. In a region without banks or large accumulations of capital credit was never easy to acquire, and because of the usual absence of security for loans was extended by creditors largely on the basis of personal confidence in borrowers. Under these circumstances a reputation for financial integrity was the greatest asset a merchant could have. Without it his operations would be sharply circumscribed or brought to a halt entirely. The beginning of a successful career for a young merchant came when he received credit from an established merchant, and the young merchant could consider himself arrived when he could secure similar accommodation from a wide range of correspondents. Importing merchants were able to stay in business only because of continuing ability to draw upon leading English mercantile houses. Although merchants might accumulate tidy fortunes, they carried on their business as much as possible with borrowed funds. This explains why merchants with estates of 1,000 pounds could enjoy incomes of 500 pounds a year.

Of course, a large proportion of the merchant planters of the Revolutionary generation inherited wealth, so initial credit for members of first families starting out on their careers was not so much of a problem. Main estimates that seventy-nine or eighty of the wealthiest men in Virginia acquired their fortunes in this manner. A somewhat smaller proportion would doubtless be found in Charleston because it was a newer commercial community. Yet only 45 percent of the members of the New York Chamber of Commerce came from old families, and about 25 percent of the Boston merchants were in this category.

Many ambitious young merchants not fortunate enough to be born into first families solved their financial problems by marrying into them. Fair fortunes have throughout American history been found at the altar, but marriage into a wealthy family was even more advantageous in the colonial period than today because it was the only way in which outsiders could gain entree into the kinship groups which exercised real muscle in the business world. Here the capital for the larger, more far-reaching enterprises could be found, and family ties formed a stronger bond for partnerships than any available in the outside commercial world. The list of distinguished merchants who obtained their start by fortunate marriages is a long one. Robert Livingston, for example, an ambitious Scottish immigrant to New York, founded a first family when he married into the Schuyler clan. Another young man in a different line of work also entered upon a distinguished career when he married a Schuyler—Alexander Hamilton. William Bingham laid the basis for what became probably the greatest merchant fortune in America during the 1790s when he married the daughter of the Philadelphia merchant prince, Thomas Willing.

The vigorous entrepreneurship of merchants and planters constituted a fortunate cultural characteristic for the young nation which can only be appreciated when we compare our colonial and Revolutionary periods with that of other peoples around the world who are having such difficulty attaining economic independence. The United States was once an undeveloped nation, but it never had undeveloped people, and this was what made all the difference. The recent study of economic development has made it plain that entrepreneurial talent is a vital ingredient of the process. The first American businessmen were no doubt unaware that they were building better than they knew, but in the ramifications of their entre-preneurship they were in fact creating a dynamic force without which the great material growth of America would have been impossible.

THE ROLE OF MERCHANTS DURING THE REVOLUTION

It is unnecessary to review here the course of the struggle between Parliament and the colonial legislatures over the imperial legislation of 1764 to 1774. But it should be emphasized that although the actual tax burden laid on the colonies was miniscule, every piece of British legisla-tion threatened vital interests already in trouble because of the slump fol-lowing the French and Indian War. The "customs racketeering" practiced under the strengthened revenue acts was an annoyance at best and a kind of extortion at worst. Customs officials, entitled to one-third of all con-fiscations made according to law, revived without notice long-dormant rules and juggled interpretations to suit their purposes. The Stamp Act overreached all traditional forms of taxation, at least for the colonies. The cry so often heard in mercantile communities, "If Parliament has the right directly to tax us one penny, she has the right to seize our estates," testified to the conviction that the Act was an assault upon colonial property rights masquerading as a tax bill.

The fact that the various measures of imperial reorganization forced colonial merchants and planters to take collective action in the form of nonimportation agreements indicates how deeply these grievances were felt. As the two sides drifted toward open warfare, merchants like everyone else, were forced to re-evaluate their positions in the light of the coming struggle. In general, merchants with strong family and business ties in England supported the mother country; those whose roots were more firmly attached to American soil tended toward the Whig cause. In every community, however, there were so many exceptions to the rule that generalization is difficult. For the merchants taking the Whig side the Rev-olution completed the work of co-operation begun by the nonimportation movement and brought them into national politics as a cohesive group with common interests and a common outlook regarding economic policy.

Without an administrative bureaucracy of any kind, Congress was com-pelled throughout the war to rely upon the mercantile community for supply of armies. In order to prevent profiteering the contract system of supply was rejected and merchants were commissioned as procurement agents who bought and sold on government account and were paid by commission. Nevertheless, the procurement agents were able to utilize the arrangement to their advantage by mingling public and private business.

As one student of this period, E. James Ferguson has expressed it, "They bought goods from themselves or their partners and employed their own ships in the public service. They used public wagons to carry private commodities, and mixed public and private goods in overseas shipments. They engaged the government as a shareholder in privateering cruises, and, alternatively, allotted themselves shares in voyages fitted out with public money. . . . Government officers sometimes sold public goods in the civilian market to raise funds to buy other goods they thought more urgently needed. In guarding against personal loss arising from debts incurred in behalf of the government, they were known to seize and hold goods which they had purchased as government agents."

The pattern of mercantile conduct was set by Robert Morris. Affable, energetic, tremendously talented in commercial skills, young Morris, as the leading member of the Secret Committee of Trade, appointed most of the commissaries, strove to open sources of supply abroad, and formed merchant combines which bought and sold to the government the material needed by the armies. He made no secret of his intention to use his public position to benefit his private affairs. ". . . there never has been so fair an oppert'y of making a large Fortune since I have been conversant with the world, . . ." he wrote enthusiastically to Silas Deane, his partner in many speculative ventures. From 1775 to 1777 nearly one-third of all disbursements on government contracts—about $850,000—went directly to the firm of Willing and Morris or to other partnerships in which Morris was involved. Although his abilities were undoubtedly of great service to Congress, he nevertheless used public funds in his own business. Twenty years after the war, when his accounts were finally settled, it was found that he still owed the government $93,000.

Under Morris's tutelage scores of merchants made fortunes by utilizing their knowledge of governmental needs as a guide to speculation. Among the most successful were: Jeremiah Wadsworth of Connecticut, who managed combines that supplied Washington's troops on the Hudson and the French Navy at Newport; General Philip Schuyler, who organized the supply for the troops in southern New York; Silas Deane, purchasing agent of Congress in Paris; and William Bingham, purchasing agent in Martinique.

The profiteering of the merchants in government employ, coinciding as it did with the ruinous inflation that drove the value of currency down to almost nothing, produced a chorus of condemnation from agrarian interests. But despite the uproar, few prosecutions were made. In the absence of a central auditing agency there were few men who had the time, skill, or inclination to examine thoroughly the confused accounts of the procurement officers. In the second place, no legal or ethical sanctions existed to prevent the merchants from carrying on their trading activities in conjunction with their public duties. Because of the lack of an administrative bureaucracy and laws compelling the separation of public and private functions, they were usually free to make their own rules as they went along. Finally, there was a pervasive conviction that the welfare of the business class and the welfare of the country at large went hand in hand. Government, according to the views of most merchants, should therefore in its own interest adopt policies which would leave the businessman unfettered in his search for profit and protect his capital against raids from debtors and the unpropertied. If this were done, as Morris once pointed out in one of his infrequent excursions into the larger questions of public policy, the wealthy members of the community would give financial support to the government and thereby insure its success as a going organization. This point of view is a significant adumbration of the Hamiltonian conception of the proper relation of business and government which has had such great influence in American history.

After Morris resigned from Congress in 1778 to devote his full time to his private affairs, continental finances drifted into indescribable confusion and the flow of supplies diminished dangerously. In 1781, faced with disaster, Washington and leading members of Congress begged Morris to accept the post of superintendant of finance, which in effect would make him the financial Czar of the United States. His acceptance, upon condition that he be free to conduct his private business in conjunction with his public duties, marked a definite victory for the mercantile program of wartime finance. Merchants had long maintained that administration of finance and procurement by congressional committees was inefficient, and that the price controls imposed by Congress and the state governments were drying up the sources of goods needed by the army. Already in 1780 continental currency had been devalued at a rate of forty to one—a figure fairly close to its market value—and thereafter the punitive statutes designed to force its acceptance at artificially high levels were repealed. Morris jettisoned the commissary system of supply and inaugurated the contract system as it had existed during the French and Indian War. At Morris's urging the Bank of North America was established in1781 which —like the later Bank of the United States—mobilized private credit for public needs. Thereafter the financial situation improved, although the political weakness of Congress and the lack of an adequate system of public finance made impossible a permanent solution to the nation's economic difficulties.

All in all, the mercantile community contributed considerably to the success of the Revolutionary movement. Certainly the cost of the war had been inordinately high (as has been the case with all the wars of the United States), certainly there had been a good deal of embezzlement by even the lax standards of the times, but before harsh judgments are made these factors should be viewed in their proper perspective. The United States had entered a war against the greatest empire of the day without a central government, an army, a navy, or an administrative bureaucracy. Furthermore, only one-third of all Americans supported the Continental cause; the rest were either Tory or neutral. The supply of the armies was handled entirely by the voluntary co-operation of the mercantile community. That merchants did their job imperfectly is surely not as significant as the fact that under such trying circumstances they were able to do it at all. Since government service carried no regular stipend or adequate means of financial support, merchants could scarcely be expected to abandon their private business while they administered public affairs. The war brought no change in business methods or organization, but military procurement did widen the acquaintance of the seaboard merchants with each other and for the first time brought many of them into direct contact with the European business community.

The American Revolution is an important event in business history as well as in political and military history because it signaled the end of the long period during which all business enterprise was carried on in undifferentiated fashion by general entrepreneurs. The Bank of North America represented the first specialization of an entrepreneurial function. With its establishment, therefore, banking became a business institution. Henceforth the number of banks in the nation multiplied rapidly; a similar growth of insurance companies and other financial institutions also took place. During the 1790s transportation improvement came within the purview of entrepreneurs and necessitated the formation of progressively larger corporations. Manufacturing underwent a similar process of specialization and eventually came to be perhaps the most important business institution of the latter nineteenth century.

The rise of business institutions by no means brought about the demise of general entrepreneurship. For half a century in urban areas general entrepreneurs performed the same functions as business institutions, and on the advancing frontier operated in substantially the same manner as their ancestors during the colonial period. Moreover, for an equally long period managers of business units were dominated by entrepreneurial procedures, values, and goals.

III. Business Seeks Independence in a Wider World

As American businessmen surveyed the postwar world of 1783 and evaluated opportunities for the expansion of commerce, they saw causes for both satisfaction and concern. Foremost among factors stimulating optimism was the release from the British mercantile system. No longer were merchants and planters compelled to send export staples to England, but now had their choice of world markets. Manufactured goods from continental Europe need no longer funnel through British middlemen but could come direct to American ports. Favorable trade treaties, based on the principle of reciprocity, had been signed with France and the Netherlands, and were soon to be signed with Sweden and Prussia.

Although direct trade with Europe was inaugurated even before the end of the war, the most spectacular expansion of commercial frontiers occurred with the opening of trade with the Far East. At the outset the risks appeared large and the profits uncertain. The routes around Africa and

South America were unknown and American mariners had only second-hand information about what goods would be salable in eastern ports. They had no way of knowing whether their reception there would be friendly or hostile, and they were completely unfamiliar with the conditions of trade. Nevertheless, in the same year that peace was signed, Captain Hallet of Hingham, Massachusetts, sailed for China in a fifty-ton sloop with a cargo of ginseng, a root reportedly prized in the Far East as a medicine. Stopping at the Cape of Good Hope, he sold the cargo to British traders for double its weight in Hyson tea. Late in 1783 Robert Morris and a group of partners who had made money in army contracting fitted out the 350-ton *Empress of China* for a voyage to the Far East with a mixed cargo of ginseng, brandy and wine, tar and turpentine, and specie. The total cost came to $120,000—an almost unheard of investment in a single trading voyage. One of the partners, the noted speculator, William Duer, considered going along as supercargo, but the post ultimately fell to young Samuel Shaw, who later became a noted China merchant and American consul at Canton. After a two-year voyage the *Empress* returned with a cargo of teas, silks, nankeens, and chinaware which brought a profit of $37,000—a modest return under the circumstances but sufficient to inaugurate the China trade on a regular basis.

Within a few years American vessels could be found in all the major ports of the Far East open to westerners. Elias Hasket Derby, the very wealthy Salem merchant who had made a fortune in privateering during the war, spent three years cruising Far Eastern waters in command of his own ship, familiarizing himself with markets and procuring reliable correspondents. So heavy did his commitment to this commerce become that at one point during the 1780s four Derby vessels lay at anchor simultaneously in the harbor of Canton. In the developing pattern of the trade, American vessels sailed for the Far East via Europe or the Cape of Good Hope with cargoes of provisions, ginseng, Yankee notions of all kinds, and specie. The provisions would be traded en route for goods more acceptable in the Far East, or for bills of exchange on London, Canton, or Calcutta. Sometimes cargoes would be turned over several times in tramping voyages lasting two or three years before full cargoes of exotic Eastern goods could be obtained. These were returned to Salem, Boston, or New York, or were often exchanged in European ports for the bills of exchange, specie, or manufactured goods necessary to repeat the trade cycle. The value of return cargoes sometimes ran into hundreds of thousands of dollars, and profits were high.

Yet the volume of this trade remained very small. As late as 1809 it absorbed no more than 2 percent of the exports of the United States. But the importance of the Far Eastern trade lay primarily in the manner in which it symbolized the imagination, vigor, and ingenuity of American commercial enterprise. It also projected Salem into a brilliant, but short-lived career as an entrepôt for a world-wide commerce.

Despite the expansion of commerical frontiers, the United States was unable to take full advantage of the enhanced opportunities confronting it because, as an exporter of raw and semifinished products, it remained a colonial economy, now set adrift in an indifferent, if not hostile world. But the wars of the French Revolution brought a welcome and unexpected windfall. Demand for American foods and staples rose rapidly both in Europe and in the West Indies, and with high agricultural prices the terms of trade tipped in favor of the United States. With much of the shipping of the continental powers driven from the seas, the United States, as a neutral, became a major carrier for these nations. Between 1790 and 1801 the value of exports rose from $20.2 million to $108.3 million, and net freight earnings rose from $6 million to nearly $30 million. The most dramatic statistic was the rise in the value of the re-export trade from $539,000 in 1790 to $60.3 million in 1806.

During the dramatic reversal of economic fortunes during the 1790s the metropolitian trading centers showed a sharp rise in population and wealth. Between 1790 and 1810 the population of Baltimore rose from 13,500 to 35,580; Boston from 18,000 to 33,250; Philadelphia from 42,520 to 91,874; and New York from 33,130 to 96,373. "A new era was established in our commercial history," wrote the careful observer, Adam Seybert. "The individuals who partook of these advantages were numerous; our catalogue of merchants was swelled much beyond what it was entitled to be from the state of our population. The most adventurous became the most wealthy, and that without the knowledge of the principles which govern commerce under ordinary circumstances. No one was limited to any one branch of trade; the same individual was concerned in voyages to Asia, South America, the West Indies, and Europe. We seemed to have arrived at the maximum of human prosperity; in proportion to our population we ranked as the most commercial nation, in point of value, second only to Great Britain."

A more enduring source of profit, which played a most important part in American economic development, was the burgeoning cotton trade. The development in England of power spinning and weaving machinery during the second half of the eighteenth century had inaugurated a textile revolution. Cotton gradually replaced wool and linen as the foremost clothing fabric. The invention of the cotton gin in America and the subsequent expansion of cotton production from 500,000 pounds in 1793 to 48,000,-000 pounds in 1807 gave the United States a major role in the revolution as the world's foremost supplier of the raw material. Since cotton production came to be financed to a large extent by merchants in the northern seaboard cities after 1820, much of the crop funneled through northern ports—chiefly New York—and provided balances in England and on the continent from which these merchants paid for the rapidly rising volume of imports.

During the piping years of neutral trade many fortunes were made. William Gray of Salem, reputed to have owned or shared ownership in 155 vessels before 1815, was worth three million dollars at the time of his death. Elias Hasket Derby, Joseph Peabody, and Simon Forrester—also of Salem—and Israel Thorndike of Beverly likewise became millionaires. William Sturgis and Thomas Handasyd Perkins were among the Boston merchants who made fortunes in the China trade. Archibald Gracie of New York not only gained great wealth, but also built a magnificent mansion that is today the home of New York's mayors.

Another large fortune, made by Robert Oliver of Baltimore, illustrates how trading profits could take primacy over even military objectives during the wars of the eighteenth and early nineteenth centuries. In 1795 the Oliver firm recorded profits of $111,898 on a working capital of $11,000. But this achievement was small compared with the returns from the Mexican trade opened up by an improbable partnership of the Spanish crown, Napoleon, the Hope banking firm of Amsterdam, and the Barings of London. When the Spanish crown found it impossible to raise from European sources the annual subsidy of 72 million francs demanded by Napoleon upon resumption of the war in 1803, the Hope firm, acting as agent for the crown, brought the Barings into a syndicate which recruited British and American merchants to carry silver from Vera Cruz to Amsterdam with which to pay the subsidy. The British ministry, at the request of the Barings, obligingly opened the blockade for passage of the ships carrying the silver, even though everyone knew that the bullion was destined to aid Napoleon's war effort. The *quid pro quo* for this amazing concession was permission by the Spanish government for licensed British and American traders to visit Vera Cruz, which at all times in the past had been tightly closed to foreigners. David Parish, an energetic and bold young English merchant established in Amsterdam, son of the great Hamburg banker John Parish, was the agent sent by the Barings to Philadelphia to recruit American merchants to transport the silver. For their services the Americans received a 5 percent commission plus two-thirds of the profits from the new Mexican trade. The remaining one-third went to the Hope-Baring syndicate. The Oliver firm was one of five or six American houses which participated in the operation. Total profits to the syndicate and the merchants came to about £862,000, of which Parish received about $1 million and Oliver $775,000.

With the imposition of the embargo Robert Oliver retired from trade, having made between one and two million dollars since the beginning of the wars in Europe. He invested his money in land, urban real estate, and corporate and government securities. Later he became one of the chief promoters of the Baltimore and Ohio Railroad. One of his daughters married Nicholas Biddle, thus forming an impressive family alliance.

FOREIGN TRADE PRODUCES THE FIRST AMERICAN OF GREAT
WEALTH—STEPHEN GIRARD

Perhaps the merchant most adept, and certainly the most success-ful in manipulating the risky strategies of foreign trade during the war years was Stephen Girard. Born in 1750, the son of a substantial merchant of Bordeaux, young Stephen at the age of twenty-three commanded his own ship on a voyage to the West Indies which unfortunately proved to be a financial failure. Unable to pay the debts owed to his backers, he conducted a tramping business in the West Indies for two years, trying with indifferent success to recoup his losses. During the course of a voyage to New York in 1776 he was forced into Philadelphia by the British blockade. It was here, in the city of brotherly love, as an adopted American, that Stephen Girard made his great fortune. During the Revolution his familiarity with trading conditions in the French West Indies brought him modest profits, but he did not become really wealthy until the 1790s, when he eagerly seized the opportunities open to neutral traders.

By 1805, with six large ships named after the principal philosophers of the Enlightenment, he was conducting a trade that was world-wide in scope. Like the outgoing cargoes of the Salem merchants, his exports of American provisions and staples constituted merely the beginning of a series of exchanges which often ended with cargoes from China, India, or Malaya worth as much as $250,000, bringing net profits often ranging be-tween 60 and 300 percent. The unique opportunities of the time account in part for his success, but Girard's admiring and envious contemporaries ascribed more weight to his almost uncanny ability to foresee the fluctua-tions of markets. Doubtless a mercantile background more cosmopolitan than that of the average American helped in this regard. Again, the fact that he was an accomplished seaman and designed his own ships may help explain why his voyages were more efficiently managed than most, his turnabouts faster, and the losses he suffered in common with all neutral traders smaller.

When legal access to nearly all foreign ports was cut off by Napoleon's Continental System, the British Orders in Council, and the resulting American Embargo, Girard gradually liquidated his trading capital and deposited much of it with Baring Brothers in London. In 1811, when war between the United States and Britain became an imminent possibility, he repatriated about $1 million of his funds to the United States, largely in the form of goods, government securities, and United States bank stock. When subsequent liquidation of the bank forced him again to seek new opportunities for investment, he utilized his large holding of stock to buy the bank's Philadelphia building, take over its business, and continue operations as the Girard Bank—by far the largest private bank in the nation. In 1813 he participated in a syndicate which inaugurated investment banking in this country by purchasing $10 million of a government loan of $16 million. Because of the unfavorable course of the war, the hostile attitude of New England merchants toward the Republican administration, and high interest rates brought on by wartime inflation, the market price of the securities sagged badly during the next year and a half. But with the coming of peace security prices moved upward toward par, and the syndicate eventually disposed of its holdings at a profit.

By now fully aware of the value of a central bank in maintaining national financial stability, Girard became one of the most active promoters of the Second Bank of the United States. He also no doubt recollected that the First Bank, by providing a market for government securities, had built a floor under prices. As events turned out, the stipulation in the Second Bank's charter that four-fifths of the sums tendered for bank stock must consist of government securities not only pulled the market prices of the securities upward, but allowed Girard and the syndicate to exchange the low yield 3 percent bonds for an equity investment of rising value which could be expected to yield at least 6 percent. Yet although Girard was successively a commissioner to float the stock of the Second Bank and a government director, he took little interest in day-to-day management, and within a few years resigned his directorship even though he continued to be a large stockholder. In typical entrepreneurial fashion he appeared to consider his proper role to be promotional and financial rather than managerial. In the latter part of his career he abandoned his overseas trade and built up a diversified portfolio of investments with emphasis on un-developed land, urban real estate, and bank stock.

Cold and forbidding, Girard's was not a pleasant personality. Clamorous in defense of his rights, vituperative when things did not turn out well, bitterly antagonistic to all organized religion, he was further soured by domestic unhappiness and family quarrels which harrassed him through-out his life. Associates admired his ability, but few considered him a friend. His business morality was typical of the time. Aware of the great value of a reputation for probity—as were all merchants—he was scrupulously hon-est in his dealings with colleagues, correspondents, and associates, but he practiced whatever fraud or falsification was necessary in order to avoid inconvenient trade restrictions. During his last years, as a "lonely Midas," he gave generously for philanthropic purposes, but so little credit did he receive for his benefactions that not one word of regret appeared in the Philadelphia newspapers to mark his passing in 1831. When it became known that he had left the bulk of his six million dollar fortune for public purposes and two million dollars specifically to found a school for orphan boys, indifference suddenly turned to acclaim, and a mythology was over the years created to place the benefactor in proper perspective with his benefactions.

As an entrepreneur, Girard was much more in the style of the eighteenth than of the nineteenth centuries. His concentration on foreign trade and banking, and his diversified investment program were typical of merchants of earlier generations. Yet in some ways he was a bridge between two eras. In joining the syndicate that bought the government loan of 1813 he anticipated the "finance capitalism" of the late nineteenth century. An interest in transportation improvement, although relatively slight, was also typical of nineteenth- rather than eighteenth-century financiers. Girard's benefactions were equally important as an innovation in entrepreneurial behavior. The philanthropy of wealthy, public-spirited men was nothing new, but never before had it been practiced on such a scale. Girard's frugal life, his allegedly humble origins, his dramatic endorsement of the gospel of self-help by the establishment of Girard College were the raw material out of which the image of the self-made man was created.

The last decade of Girard's life marked the end of a golden era in foreign trade which was not to be repeated. Because of mercantilistic restrictions, competition from foreign bottoms, and falling freight rates, shipping earn-ings ran much below the record of $42 million set in 1807. Henceforth as the re-export trade died and the tramping pattern declined, a larger proportion of goods carried was of American rather than foreign origin. Under the circumstances much capital formerly employed in overseas trade was shifted into industry and transportation improvement. It was Boston mercantile capital, for example, which financed the Middlesex Canal and built the industrial city of Lowell.

Perhaps the most striking aspect of the great boom in overseas trade from 1793 to 1807 had been the ability of American commercial enterprise to respond so strongly to opportunities for profit opened up by the extraordinary international market conditions of the times. But in the future, American entrepreneurs, trained to commerce by generations of experience, would find profits harder to come by in manufacturing and transportation enterprise.

IV. Beginnings in Banking and Insurance

COLONIAL ORIGINS OF BANKING AND THE BANK OF NORTH AMERICA

Banking has occupied a unique place in American history because of its involvement in politics and its position as a focal point for struggle on class, sectional, and party lines. Nearly every generation of Americans during the late eighteenth and nineteenth centuries passed through a political and economic crisis in which banking was a major ingredient; then suddenly, and rather dramatically, the controversies came to an end with the passage of the Federal Reserve Act in 1913.

The struggles grew out of the fact that bankers combined the public function of regulating credit with the private function of providing credit in individual cases. By expanding credit they could stimulate the economy and create apparent abundance; by contracting credit they could bring about depression and business failure. It is understandable, therefore, that in the early republic the feeling was widespread that banks were an anomaly in a democratic society. Such oracles as Thomas Jefferson, John Adams, and Andrew Jackson fortified this belief. "I sincerely believe with you," wrote Jefferson to his friend, John Taylor, "that banking establishments are more dangerous than standing armies." Jefferson's political enemy and philosophical friend, John Adams, vowed that he would "die abhorring banks." Declared Jackson, that improbable historical scholar, ". . . ever since I read the history of the South Sea Bubble I have been afraid of banks."

To the unsophisticated, the process by which credit was created by banks was a legerdemain something less than honest. When a group of men could subscribe $100,000 to form a bank, and then drew interest on loans several times this amount, outsiders felt that someone was being cheated. Yet the popular distrust of banks and bankers was balanced by a deeply held conviction that these were indispensable for the economic welfare of the country. In unconscious ambivalence, many of the loudest critics were equally vociferous in specifying the benefits banks could bring to commerce, industry, and agriculture. Preambles of some early bank charters proclaimed that the institutions were designed to increase the circulating medium, promote promptness in paying debts, and provide a source of loans for government. For every argument against banks there was a counterargument in favor of them. In times of prosperity the number of banks multiplied, with the general approbation of the community at large. When a downturn in the business cycle caused bank failures, with accompanying losses to depositors, noteholders, and investors, banks were loudly denounced as corrupt conspiracies.

Actually, bankers were more sinned against than sinning. In inflating credit beyond safe levels they were for the most part responding to community pressures, and were pulled into financial crises by forces they could hardly have withstood. Furthermore, knowledge about business cycles and the intricacies of the credit system was slight, and could be gained only by often bitter experience. Finally, in most states an attitude of laissez-faire made it difficult for governments to secure control over public credit. Alone among the great nations of the world, the United States, after the demise of the Second Bank of the United States, had no central bank during the rest of the nineteenth century. Considering the general lack of guidance in the banking system, its performance under the trying conditions of a rapidly growing economy was remarkably good.

In England, through the operations of the goldsmiths, banking had its origins in surpluses of money seeking profitable utilization; in America, banking began when surpluses of goods and land sought the credit in the form of paper money to promote exchange in the marketplace. The agencies were the colonial land banks and loan offices which issued currency in return for mortgages. "Making a bank," therefore was simply the issuing of paper money, and had no relation to the other functions of deposit, discount, and transfer which are the main purpose of modern banks. Colonial land banks and loan offices established certain banking precedents which lasted well into the nineteenth century. The notion that the major purpose of banks was to increase the circulating medium was reflected in the lavish note issues by "country banks" before the Civil War, and their reluctance to redeem notes in specie. Public sentiment no less than bankers' necessity dictated that banknotes be kept in circulation. The tendency to allow specie reserves to diminish to a dangerously low level was justified for some bankers by the dictum of Sir James Steuart, the celebrated eighteenth-century political economist, that a banking stock "might consist indifferently of any species of property."

Commercial banks whose major function was the discounting of commercial paper and dealing in exchange simply did not exist in colonial America, mainly because there was no need for them. As general entrepreneurs, most merchants were also bankers, lending at interest and buying and selling exchange as part of their normal routine. The fact that London merchants were the major source of credit relieved the colonial merchants of the necessity of undertaking any more extensive banking operations. Also, the lack of industries and the indifference to internal improvements obviated a need for developmental capital.

As we have seen, the Revolution produced the first chartered bank in the United States—the Bank of North America—designed by Robert Morris to be the major instrumentality through which he was to handle the financial affairs of the faltering republic. Three days after assuming office as financier, Morris submitted to Congress a plan for a bank which was in effect the offer of a bargain. The mercantile community, as represented in the bank, would assume responsibility for government finances in return for the use of government funds deposited in a private bank immune to governmental control. Private profit and public welfare were to go hand in hand. "It is not to be doubted," Morris wrote, "but every subscriber to the bank stock will increase his capital in the bank so soon as he finds not only the national advantage it will produce, but sees clearly his private interest advanced beyond his most sanguine expectations."

Congress was in no condition to quibble about the terms of the offer. Shortly thereafter it granted a "blue sky" charter to the Bank of North America. By this document the bank was allowed a capitalization of $10 million and was given an indefinite monopoly of the banking business. All questions of banking practice and procedures were left to the directors and stockholders to decide by bylaws. Massachusetts and New York followed the lead of Congress by granting a monopoly, but only for the duration of the war. No specie reserve was stipulated, but Morris perhaps created one, in effect, by depositing in the bank $254,000 in specie received from France.

Although Morris did not specifically say so, the major precedent for the Bank of North America was the Bank of England, established in 1694, also the concession of a necessitous government. In order to gain the support of the London mercantile community at the onset of war with France, the British government had created a private banking monopoly with the exclusive privilege of note issue in London, and gradually relinquished to it a large amount of control over the financial affairs of the kingdom.

The Bank of North America managed finances of the United States during the remainder of the war with a success that contrasted strongly with the miserable record of Congress. Loans from France, and other lesser sources of revenue, were fed into the bank, and payments for the government were made in the bank's notes, or in Morris's personal notes. The fact that both types of notes circulated at par testified to the confidence of the business community in the new dispensation. In addition to functioning as a fiscal agent of Congress, the bank carried on a private business, using the government revenues as part of its working capital. By 1783 it was paying a dividend of 14 percent per year.

But the very success of the bank proved to be a threat to its existence. Restricting the scope of its business to merchant banking, it aroused the antagonism of farmers by refusing to make mortgage loans. When the bank's officers and stockholders petitioned against an emission of paper money by which the Pennsylvania House of Representatives attempted to alleviate the postwar depression, and then, when the appeal was denied, refused to accept the state bills of credit at par, the back country rang with denunciations against the griping usurers of Philadelphia. Although Morris and the supporters of the bank replied with well-reasoned pamphlets and newspaper articles citing the many benefits the institution conferred upon the government and the community, the House vacated the charter in 1785. It was restored in 1791, however, after the mercantile group came back into power under a new and much more conservative state constitution.

The early career of the Bank of North America is very important in several respects. In the first place the bank was the prototype of the commercial banks which constituted our first banking system. Established by leading merchants, who, in Morris's phrase, "clubbed their capital together," it was not only designed to be a profitable business, but also served the directors and stockholders as a source of personal loans and as a credit rating agency on the people with whom they did business. Essentially the bank centralized under one management the merchant banking operations which most of the directors had carried on previously as individuals. When merchants of New York and Boston, respectively, considered establishing banks in their own cities, they wrote to Thomas Willing, president of the Bank of North America and long-time business partner of Robert Morris, asking for advice on administrative procedures and other technical matters. The Bank of New York and the Bank of Massachusetts, both formed in 1784 by Willing's correspondents, were closely modeled after the Bank of North America. The bank was also important because the charges which had led to the vacating of the charter anticipated the back-country hostility to the First and Second Banks of the United States. The back country never had adequate credit, to be sure, but the mercantile banks never had the resources to supply it, and quite rightly restricted their loans to short-term paper and collateral loans. Finally, the Bank of North America served as a model for the relationships between private enterprise and public function embodied in the First and Second Banks of the United States, and in the various state banks similar to these two.

THE COMING OF THE CORPORATE FORM IN BUSINESS

One notable and precedent-setting aspect of the formation of the Bank of North America was the adoption of the corporate form. Today incorporation for business is so ubiquitous and seems so natural that it is easy to forget that this type of organization, while very ancient, was only rarely applied to business enterprise before 1800. Since the Middle Ages, if not before, partnerships, individual proprietorships, and the many types of joint stock companies had been the usual methods of organization. Yet incorporation had been extended to many charitable, philanthropic, educational, ecclesiastical, and municipal bodies. Those individuals seeking charters from the crown simply wanted royal sanction to pursue some form of organized activity under a common name, and to hold and manage property in accordance with their own plan. Usually there was an implied bargain in the grant; in order to receive a charter the incorporators felt it necessary to demonstrate that the activities they intended to pursue would redound to the welfare of the realm as well as to themselves. Business incorporations became important with the chartering of the overseas trading and colonizing enterprises of the sixteenth and seventeenth centuries. Here the *quid pro quo* was quite definite. For their risks and labors in expanding the commerce of the realm the incorporators demanded a monopoly of any trade which they brought into existence.

During the seventeenth and eighteenth centuries a scattering of charitable, educational, and ecclesiastical bodies in the colonies received charters from royal governors or assemblies. The only business enterprises so endowed were two companies organized to build wharfs in the harbors of New Haven and Boston, respectively, a few water companies, and a copper mine in Connecticut. By the time of the Revolution it was apparent that incorporation for business was considered appropriate only when the enterprise was intended to perform a public service and when, as a result, the incorporators felt entitled to ask for special privileges to enable them to fulfill their objectives. Consistent with precedent, the major privilege desired was often monopoly in some form. It has often been maintained that a major reason for incorporation was the gaining of limited liability. Yet it is far from clear that this was the case; limited liability was not automatically given to early business corporations, and was sometimes denied to them by law. But it is probably true that incorporation made the collection of capital easier because corporate charters granted other privileges not available to nonincorporated businesses.

Under the circumstances it is not difficult to understand why from the outset banks were incorporated. In issuing a circulating medium they provided a public service, and one which promised a considerable profit to themselves. Obviously the grant could not be extended to an indefinite number of applicants, and just as obviously the terms of the grant must be made specific and the grantees made to account for their administration of the privilege. The incorporators of the Bank of North America no doubt felt that the request for a monopoly of note issue in Philadelphia, New York, and Boston was reasonable and in accordance with precedent. The element of monopoly in note issue was short-lived in America. The state grants to the Bank of North America were terminated by the treaty of peace, and new banks were soon chartered in New York and Boston. Because of the insatiable demand for circulating medium, subsequent groups of incorporators could get bank charters by merely demonstrating an unfilled need for bank services and for note issue.

The same logic applying to the incorporation of banks led to the incorporation of insurance and transportation improvement companies. The fact that turnpike companies needed the right of eminent domain was another reason for requesting charters. The Insurance Company of North America—the nation's first marine insurance company—and the nearly contemporaneous Philadelphia and Lancaster Turnpike Company, were both conceived at the outset as semipublic enterprises (see below, pp. 56, 73). Incorporation came to be applied to manufacturing enterprises when they, like banking and transportation improvement companies, became invested with the larger purposes of public policy.

During the first half of the nineteenth century the states slowly relaxed charter controls and by 1850 limited liability was generally allowed. Meanwhile, the monopoly aspects of charters and the questionable means by which these were purchased from legislatures brought corporations increasing public criticism. Banks in general, and the Second Bank of the United States in particular, became the main targets for opprobrium primarily because of a growing realization of the power wielded through private control of public credit. But with the demise of the BUS, the coming of "free banking" (p. 133), and particularly the passage of general incorporation laws beginning with a New York enactment of 1811, the volume of criticism decreased. Since general incorporation laws specified the terms under which all companies within a certain segment of the business world would be formed, they removed the suspicion, often justified in the past, that during the back room negotiations which had always accompanied the requests for individual charters, lawmakers had bargained away rights belonging to the public in return for secret and valuable consideration. By 1900, as one category of business enterprise after another had been brought under general incorporation laws, the corporation became the dominant form of business organization in the western world, the major instrumentality of the capitalist system.

THE FIRST BANK OF THE UNITED STATES

In the new republic the public creditors constituted an elite group of businessmen who could contribute much to the success of the new regime and who expected a suitable reward in the form of a national debt funded at par. Alexander Hamilton, the new secretary of the treasury, worked out his famous financial plans with the interests of this group constantly in mind. Funding both the national and state debts at par would give the holders an impressive capital gain, and would in addition create in the form of new government bonds attractive investment opportunities which would bring timid savings out of hiding. Hamilton was quite justified in saying that his funding plans "created a capital" for the business community. To cap his financial system and make it viable, Hamilton then proposed a national bank in the tradition of the Bank of England and the Bank of North America.

In his *Report on a National Bank*, Hamilton had argued that such an institution would increase the country's active or productive capital by lending more money in the form of notes than it kept on hand in specie. It would also facilitate the collection of taxes and serve as a source of loans for the government. The opponents of the bank, repeating the argument heard in Pennsylvania six years before, charged that a privileged institution such as Hamilton had in mind would export specie in the form of dividends, divert capital from agriculture, and create a new moneyed aristocracy. The Bank Bill, as passed by Congress, called for a capitalization of $10 million, the stock to be subscribed one-fourth in specie and three-fourths in the funded debt. This provision was designed to secure a 25 percent specie reserve and at the same time provide a price support for the market value of the new government securities. The bank might not issue notes to a greater amount than its capitalization, but nothing was said about a limit to the deposit credit it could create. The government was to subscribe for $2 million worth of stock, and in return receive the proportionate right to appoint one-fifth of the board of directors. The bank was to have two very important privileges. It was to be the main depository for government funds, and its notes alone among those of other banks would be receivable for public dues. The sectional vote in the House of Representatives which brought the bank into being demonstrated the harmony of the business community and the national administration. Only three southerners voted for the bank, and only one northerner voted against it. When the subscription books were opened in July, 1971, the stock was oversubscribed within one hour.

Hamilton's financial program was a brilliant tour de force. With the funding of the debt and the establishment of the Bank of the United States he had overnight transformed a hopelessly bankrupt nation into one with an excellent credit rating on foreign bourses. From the outset United States securities and bank stock sold at premium. By 1809 nearly 50 percent of the funded debt and 75 percent of the bank stock were held abroad. The partnership of government and business seemed to promise a glowing future for the new nation.

Meanwhile the bank fulfilled the fondest expectations of its founders. To its stockholders it paid annual dividends averaging 8 percent and its stock sold for as high as $45 above par. Total deposits rose from approximately $3 million in 1793 to a high of $17 million in 1809; in the same period discounts rose from $5 million to $14 million. Throughout its career the bank was managed in a very conservative manner, and was well-integrated into the commercial community. Its president from 1791 to 1807 was Thomas Willing, former president of the Bank of North America. The presence on the board of William Bingham, Rufus King, and Samuel Breck provided interlocking directorates with the major banks of

New York and Boston, as well as with the Bank of North America. The bank discounted only double-name paper, with a time limit of sixty days, and firmly refused to lend on the security of land or stored agricultural products. Throughout its career it suffered a loss of less than one-half of one percent of its funds by bad debts. By 1811 branches had been established in eight of the major towns of the Union. The directors of the parent bank appointed the directors and cashiers of the branches, fixed a limit on capital, discounts, and note circulation, and demanded weekly statements of condition.

The bank's services to the national government were as impressive as those provided to the mercantile community. By 1795 it had loaned to the treasury a total of $6,200,000. When Secretary Oliver Wolcott sold the government's bank stock to reduce this debt, the treasury made a clear profit of $671,860 over and above dividends of slightly over $1 million received since 1791. The bank transferred government funds without charge and made payments on behalf of the treasury—a very valuable service at the time considering the slowness of communications and the scarcity of other financial institutions. The services to the economy were no less important. Notes of the bank, circulating at par, constituted a uniform currency, and the bank was able to police institutions chartered by the states by presenting their notes for redemption promptly. Notes of the BUS were also a convenient medium for the payment of customs duties.

Yet, even more than in the case of the Bank of North America, the success of the Bank of the United States was its undoing. A privately controlled, privileged corporation was now in a position to exercise a good deal of influence over public credit, and thereby indirectly manipulate the distribution of wealth itself. Soon the preachments of Jefferson and Madison began to be repeated by the interests associated with the multiplying state banks, who resented the privileged position of the BUS and the discipline it imposed upon its competitors. Eventually partisan clamor overrode reasoned argument; the bank's petition of 1808 for renewal of the charter was rejected in Congress by one vote, and the institution came to an end in 1811.

POLICIES AND OPERATIONS OF THE FIRST STATE-CHARTERED BANKS

The initial success of the Bank of North America, its obvious benefit to the Philadelphia business community, and the ending of its monopoly of note issue in Massachusetts and New York following the Revolution resulted in the formation of the Massachusetts Bank and the Bank of New York in 1784. Closely modeled on the Bank of North America, both were designed to serve a commercial and professional clientele exclusively. Operations of the Massachusetts Bank tended to typify those of other commercial banks to be founded during the next two decades. Management was in the hands of a board of directors whose chief duty was to meet regularly to consider applications for loans, usually in the form of short-term notes offered for discount. The notes were secured by one or two endorsers and in most cases by goods as well. Voting on the applications was done secretly by placing white or black balls in a jar, and one black ball was sufficient to turn down an application. The directors, considering their institution in the traditional sense as a money bank, made no effort to acquire deposits, and paid no interest on the few they carried. Since promoting punctuality in the payment of debt was one of the purposes in founding the bank, every effort was made to avoid long-term collateral loans and renewals on commercial loans. Yet since stockholders, directors, and other influential people continually sought accommodations of this sort, exceptions to established policy were often made. Day-to-day management was carried on by individual directors "sitting" at the bank in rotation and supervising the three or four clerks who comprised the staff. Accounting methods, copied from those of the Bank of North America, were those of mercantile bookkeeping supplemented by entries in a discount book and a specie book.

Although the directors might on occasion deviate from a conservative loan policy, they seldom allowed loans and circulation to exceed double the bank's capital. The bank prospered from the outset. Average annual dividends were about 12 percent from 1784 to 1792, and average weekly discount income rose from $340 during the eighties to $955 in 1791. Yet growth was slow because the directors made no attempt to build up reserves or attract a clientele outside the commercial community. The bank's most important service during its first two decades was creating a market for commercial paper.

The Bank of New York, whose charter was drafted by Alexander Hamilton, operated in much the same fashion, except that after 1790, limiting its services to deserving Federalists, it took on a strong political coloration. Since the first banks were looked on as regional monopolies, and since Federalists usually controlled the New York legislature, it appeared that deserving Republicans might be indefinitely deprived of bank credit until Aaron Burr, by a clever stratagem, secured the establishment of a second bank in 1799. A short time previously, in company with other Republican politicians and a group of wealthy merchants, he organized The Manhattan Company to bring pure water to New York City—the nation's first public utility. Since this would be a very expensive undertaking, the legislature obligingly inserted in the charter a clause permitting the company to use its "surplus capital," not further defined, "in the purchase of public or other stock, or in any other monied transactions . . . for the sole benefit of said company." The business community immediately got the point, and as interest in pure water was rapidly replaced by interest in pure profit, a revived promotional effort resulted in the chartering of The Bank of the Manhattan Company.

Started in the midst of a boom, the bank was immediately profitable and became a bastion of the Republican party. Operated in a much more liberal fashion than the Bank of New York or the Massachusetts Bank, it brought several innovations into banking practice—not all of them favorable. The shady methods by which the charter had been secured inaugurated the corruption of legislatures by groups desiring incorporations. Henceforth the building of canals and railroads was often to become a pretext for securing a bank charter which otherwise might not have been granted. Burdened by almost no restrictions of any kind in its charter, the bank did not confine itself to commercial discounts but extended funds to tradesmen, artisans, manufacturers, land speculators, and the state government in return for a wide range of collateral including the bank's own stock. The stock had been floated in such small denominations that ownership of the bank was spread beyond the business community. These innovations strengthened the bank's political position and funneled some money into developmental enterprise, but at the cost of inaugurating the inflationary practices and loss of liquidity which became a characteristic of wildcat banking.

POLICIES AND OPERATIONS OF COUNTRY BANKS

The utility and profits of banking, the desire of the back-country inhabitants for cheap money, and the demise of the BUS in 1811 all stimulated a rise in the number of banks from six in 1791, capitalized at $4.6 million, to approximately 232 in 1816, capitalized at $123,977,000. Banknote circulation rose to $99 million during the period. In the early republic, banking, without question, was the fastest growing business institution. Although small, most of the early banks were so successful that states began reserving in bank charters the rights for educational and philanthropic institutions to subscribe for stock. Transportation enterprises and other institutions in the nature of public utilities supplemented their income by operating banks, and in these instances the making of banking profits became the object of greater attention than the providing of public services. Southern and western state governments increasingly after 1816 bought bank stock, paying for their subscriptions with state securities. In part the states were motivated by a desire to make profitable investments; more important, the governments were responding to the almost universal demand for developmental capital made by the people in rapidly growing areas. The example of the First and Second banks of the United States stimulated experiments in central banking on the state level. The needs of special groups for credit were met by the creation of "mechanics' banks," "farmers' banks," "merchants' banks," "plantation banks," and the like. Before 1830 some 64 private banks had made their appearance, but most of these disappeared or abandoned their private status shortly thereafter because of the insistence of state governments that banks of issue operate under corporate charters.

The banks serving special interest groups and "country" banks outside of commercial centers were from the outset somewhat less cautious in their policies than the first banks in eastern seaports, partly because their purpose was developmental as well as commercial, and partly because they served areas where money was scarce and pressures for generous emissions of bank notes correspondingly high. Equally important, banks were a source of loans to their promoters. As the economist Amasa Walker wrote in 1857: "It has come to be a proverb that banks never originate with those who have money to lend, but with those who wish to borrow." Many country banks were a kind of operation bootstrap whereby leading men of a community created purchasing power for their own enterprises by mobilizing the savings and credit of their friends and neighbors. In the words of Paul B. Trescott, banks of this type were in reality "a sort of committee for the economic development of the community." In Cincinnati between 1815 and 1822 the eighty-eight men who served as bank directors during the period were as a body simply the leading businessmen of the community. The largest proportion were merchants, as might be expected, but there were also many farmers, some professional men, and even a few mechanic-manufacturers. The major function of the Cincinnati banks was to grant credit in the form of bank notes or deposits which enabled the products of the area to be grown, gathered, processed, shipped to markets as far away as New Orleans, and sold. The banks also financed land purchases and the importation of goods from the East, contributed to industrial development, and made various kinds of transfers for the state and federal governments.

The organization of the small country banks was simple and varied little from generation to generation because the functions the banks were expected to perform remained essentially the same during the nineteenth century. Most were capitalized at between $10,000 and $100,000. Before the coming of general incorporation laws in the forties and fifties, the provisions of charters varied widely, even within the same state, but always included a stated maximum capitalization and requirements of regular reports. Restrictions on bank note issue in relation to specie reserves became more rigorous as time went on. Usually the ratio was two or three to one, but here, as in all other requirements, there was no uniformity. In the early period legislatures sometimes failed to realize that deposits were not merely funds paid into banks for safekeeping, but represented loans to borrowers as well and amounted therefore to the creation of money no less than the printing and issuing of bank notes. When legislatures omitted bank debts in the form of deposits from the over-all ratio of bank debts to reserves, they left a loophole for inflationary adventures.

The affairs of small country banks were carried on in much the same way as those of the first commercial banks except that policies reflected the needs of diverse artisan and agricultural interests as well as commercial interests. While the entire board of directors, meeting at regular intervals, was theoretically responsible for decisions on loan applications, in practice small groups or even single individuals particularly interested in the banks' affairs came to dominate the process. The amount of business done was small, and since the banks were considered to be regional or vocational monopolies, there was little competition between them. Professionalization and specialization of function emerged when cashiers, at first little more than clerks, began to relieve board members of the probably unwelcome duties of management. A second step toward specialization was taken when standing committees of directors were appointed for specific tasks such as preparing reports and buying land. In informal fashion, then, those individuals who demonstrated an interest in the banks' affairs and an ability to conduct them came to the fore as managers.

The discounting of short-term bills and notes continued to be the major function of country banks, yet—particularly in rapidly developing regions —these banks were almost invariably driven by inflationary pressures to undertake riskier operations. "Accommodation loans," in the form of long-term, indefinitely renewed notes secured by collateral of doubtful or fluctuating value, were often made to directors and stockholders, or other favored individuals. Needless to say, such favoritism helped fan hostility against banks. Accommodation paper and loans to transportation and industrial companies for expansion were obviously less safe than commerical discounts, and in times of depression left banks with considerable amounts of depreciated securities and defaulted mortgages on their hands. In ante-bellum America there was always a crying need for developmental capital, but the attempts of commercial banks to supply it often ended in disaster for all concerned.

In attempting to maximize profits by expanding loanable funds beyond safe limits, many banks evaded their charter stipulations regarding capital and reserves. Actual reserves of country banks were usually no more than 10 to 20 percent of liabilities, and worse, there was seldom a central bank mechanism or co-operative organization through which banks could borrow reserves in time of need. Most charters stipulated that banks could not start business until a certain portion of their specified capital had been paid in. Yet many stockholders, after a small down payment, received their stock and gave their personal notes, secured by the stock, for the rest of the purchase money. Since these notes were indefinitely renewed, they represented only a fictitious capital. When bank examiners arrived to inspect specie reserves, the necessary bullion was sometimes borrowed for the occasion, and returned after the examiners had departed. Stories were current that in some parts of the country wagonloads of specie sometimes preceded the examiners on their rounds, and at every bank the officials viewed merely the same money. Notes for as small denominations as six cents and a quarter, called "shinplasters," were sometimes circulated in the confidence that holders would never find it worthwhile to redeem them. Through brokers and sometimes by agreement with distant banks, notes were often put into circulation so far from the place of issue that redemption was practically impossible. In attempts to evade their creditors, banks sometimes sought inaccessible locations. One enterprising Wisconsin banker established his headquarters on an Indian reservation which was off-limits to whites. To make doubly certain that he would have no unwelcome callers requesting specie, he placed a man with a gun before the door. Banks of this kind were called "wild cats," because, like these furtive felines, the banks disappeared into the woods before the hunter. In times of stringency banks often issued "post notes," which deferred redemption until a future date. Sometimes banks issued notes to borrowers under agreements, enforced by penalties, that the notes would not be presented for redemption.

Far from feeling defrauded by the chicanery of inflationary banking, country people tended to agree with the bankers that paper should flow generously and that specie should never see the light of day unless absolutely necessary. For example, in Windsor County, Vermont, an indictment was sought against a Boston citizen who had obliged the state bank to pay specie for $9,000 worth of its notes. According to the charge, the culprit was "an evil-disposed person . . . not minding to get his living by truth and honest labor but contriving how he might injuriously obtain . . . money to support his idle and profligate way of life and diminish and destroy the resources of the state of Vermont and render it difficult and impossible for the good citizens thereof to obtain money."

Yet, with due allowance for the great variety of charter provisions, the haphazard nature of regulation, the absence of standards for sound banking, and the unfamiliarity of many country bankers with the techniques of their profession, the banks performed tolerably well. Historians, focusing on the monetary difficulties and the stimulation of business cycles brought about by the banking of this period, have tended to overlook the service performed by the system in providing rapidly expanding bank credit. Between 1790 and 1860 the quantity of money in the nation, largely in the form of bank notes and deposits, increased fortyfold from $15 million to $600 million and was not accompanied by the price inflation so often promoted by rapid increases in currency supply. The importance of this contribution to economic development would seem to be quite obvious. Furthermore, despite the hazards of antebellum banking, many of the nation's strongest banks were established in that period. Although about 1,000 of the some 2,500 banks founded by 1860 closed within ten years of opening, more than one-third formed before the War of 1812 reached the twentieth century.

BEGINNINGS OF MARINE INSURANCE

During the latter part of the eighteenth century, marine and fire insurance, like banking, detached themselves from the undifferentiated functions of the general entrepreneur and became independent financial institutions. Because of the hazardous condition of the seas marine insurance is nearly as old as commerce itself and was a well-developed institution in the Roman world. During the colonial period it was a collective enterprise in which merchants underwrote each other's voyages. "Agents" wrote policies for merchants, determined premiums, and secured underwriters from the commercial community. The underwriters collectively pledged the face value of the policies and left cash or notes for their individual subscriptions in the hands of the agents. If a voyage so insured were successful, the underwriters shared the premium proportionally to their commitment; if a loss occurred they paid off claims in the same manner. The agents—or more properly, brokers—received a small commission for the limited part they played in the operation.

Little is known about the process of ratemaking in this early period. To some degree rates no doubt reflected the collective judgment of the business community on risks to be encountered, and varied rather widely in accordance with the length of voyages, the condition of ships, ports to be visited, and the existence of war or the rumors of war. By the end of the Revolution underwriters had become more or less permanently grouped together under a number of brokers, and by running open accounts with these brokers constituted loose business units for the sale of marine insurance.

THE INSURANCE COMPANY OF NORTH AMERICA

The marine insurance business entered a new phase with the establishment of the Insurance Company of North America in 1792. Promoted by Samuel Blodgett, Jr., a pioneer developer of Washington, D.C., and the well-known Philadelphia merchants John M. Nesbitt and Ebenezer Hazard, the company offered 60,000 shares of stock at $10 per share, thus creating the enormous stated capitalization for the time of $600,000. The project aroused great enthusiasm in the Philadelphia business community, partly because of the favorable profit record of marine underwriting, but more importantly because concentrated reserves in a large company would make insurance more reliable and permit the assumption of large risks which previously could be underwritten only in London. In eleven days after the stock had been placed on the market, over 5,000 individuals had subscribed for 40,000 shares. The wide ownership of the company not only testified to the confidence of the public in the profitability and stability of the insurance business but also reflected the patriotic desire for economic independence and material progress associated with the inauguration of banks and manufacturing associations. As demonstrated in the formation of banks, businessmen were aware of the possibilities of expansion inherent in the rationalization and specialization of what had previously been a function of merchant capitalism.

Although the company was empowered to write fire and life insurance, at the outset it concentrated its efforts in the marine insurance field. Its profit record justified the most sanguine hopes of its founders. Incorporated in 1794 along with a company promoted by Thomas Willing, the Insurance Company of the State of Pennsylvania, it paid dividends of 28¾ percent in 1796 and ushered in 1797 with a half-year dividend of 20 percent. These large profits doubtless were the result of the greatly expanded neutral trade. But the onset of the Naval War with France in 1798 brought heavy losses. Careful management, a large award from the joint committee on claims established by the Jay Treaty, and the shifting of some capital into fire insurance enabled the company to survive this difficult time, however, and by 1808 it was recouping its capital losses and was paying 10 to 12 percent per year. From that time until the present the company has maintained its position as one of the country's leading insurance institutions.

The business procedures of the company were much more efficient than those of the informal underwriting syndicates. Applications for insurance were acted upon within several hours of their presentation. Ebenezer Hazard, secretary and the full-time executive, carefully examined applicants' papers and all particulars relating to intended voyages, and had ships "surveyed" for seaworthiness by a retired sea captain employed by the company. A committee of directors then passed upon the applications, usually accepting Hazard's recommendation. Premiums were usually paid in the form of well-secured notes payable after sale of the cargo. Rates were still not set in any systematic manner, but, as in the period of private underwriting, tended to reflect the state of the money market and the judgments of the commercial community regarding risks. The inflated initial profit of the company would seem to indicate that rates were higher than necessary during this period. Although the premium for a voyage to the French West Indies reached 30 percent in 1794, and other schedules were raised proportionally, the losses suffered after 1797 suggest that the increase still was not commensurate with extraordinary war risks. Even with more flexibility in the rate structure the rapid changes in the commercial policies of the belligerent nations must certainly have added enormously to the difficulty of ratemaking.

The company apportioned its funds in three separate accounts: capital, surplus, and reserve. The capital account was invested and maintained at $600,000. Surplus represented net earnings, and reserve the premiums on "undetermined" risks, that is, premiums on policies still in effect. Claims were paid out of reserve, and if this was not sufficient for the purpose, then successively out of surplus and capital. In normal times nearly the whole of the surplus was distributed semiannually in dividends. During the first several decades of the company's history no need was felt to build up a permanent reserve capable of meeting all contingencies, nor was a part of net earnings fed into the capital account to provide for growth. Like the merchants of an earlier day, the directors regarded capital as stock-in-trade, and surplus as profits to be distributed. Shortsighted as such financial procedures might seem today, they were standard practice for banks as well as insurance companies during the early nineteenth century. Yet the Insurance Company of North America was so conservatively managed that capital was broken into only twice during the first thirty-two years of the company's existence.

Consistent with its conservative management, the firm followed a generally prudent investment policy. By 1807 it had invested about half of its capital in public securities, and kept a large cash balance at interest in commercial banks. During the coming years it bought shares in toll roads, bridge companies, and canal companies—equity investments which would be considered inappropriate for insurance companies by modern standards and which must have brought disappointing returns. Purchase of blocs of stock in other insurance companies led gradually to a system of interlocking directorates among the organizations.

The success of the Insurance Company of North America during its early years promoted a wave of similar incorporations. By 1800 the nation was served by thirty-two marine insurance companies. Every seaport town of commercial importance had at least one.

FIRE INSURANCE

Fire insurance is of much more recent origin than marine insurance. The need for it was probably not as keenly felt as for marine insurance, and underwriters were reluctant to make the long-term commitments inherent in fire insurance. Continuous growth of the business began in America with the founding in 1752 of the Philadelphia Contributorship for Insurance of Houses from Loss by Fire. This organization was the outgrowth of a campaign initiated by Benjamin Franklin to provide Philadelphia with organized fire protection. In 1735, after publishing an article on fire prevention, Franklin and four friends formed the Union Fire Company, the first fire fighting organization in America. The some thirty members who were ultimately recruited equipped themselves with leather buckets, fire hooks, and linen bags, and pledged themselves to fight fires in any part of the city. Convivial dinners held once a month lent attractiveness to the organization, and soon others like it appeared bearing names such as "Fellowship," and "Heart-in-Hand," which indicate the fraternal feeling that bound the members together. In 1750 the members of the Union company established a mutual fund with which they insured their own houses. Two years later this organization was expanded to become the Philadelphia Contributorship.

From the outset the members regarded fire prevention as an objective of equal importance as fire insurance, and this view was to continue throughout the development of mutual fire insurance companies. Fire losses are immediately reflected in rising premium rates and diminution of dividend payments; hence there is a strong incentive among members to reduce losses to the absolute minimum. The Contributorship established an important precedent, therefore, when it "surveyed" the houses of applicants for insurance, ordered the removal of fire hazards before the insurance was granted, and maintained high standards of fire prevention by means of periodic inspections. Flexible premium rates proportional to risk were another innovation. Upon joining, members were assessed $17.50 to $25 per thousand valuation for a seven-year premium. In accordance with the mutual principle, the premium constituted not only a payment covering the cost of insurance, but also an investment in the reserves of the company as well.

The company was an immediate success. At the end of its first year it had $108,360 of insurance outstanding. In 1763 the company strengthened its financial structure by uniting all deposits and all payments of interest and carrying the two in separate accounts. Losses were paid out of the interest account, and deposits were broken into only after the interest account was exhausted. Henceforth the Contributorship's growth was uninterrupted. By 1781 it had $2 million of insurance in force. When in that year the company refused to write policies on houses surrounded by trees because of a conviction that they were likely to be struck by lightning, the Mutual Assurance Company was formed to meet the needs of householders who wished shade and insurance at the same time. The new organization inaugurated perpetual, one-payment fire insurance, a type which had the advantage of giving the company a firm financial position from the outset. Both companies identified the houses they insured by placing on the front of the buildings the lead plates which are today prized collectors' items. The Contributorship's plates contained a clasped hands design, showing its close relation to the Union Fire Company. The Mutual Assurance indicated its reason for existence by display of a green tree. The identifications were intended to increase the ardor with which the fire companies performed their duties. The Contributorship and the Mutual Assurance both paid gratuities for the fighting of fires in the houses which they respectively insured—a sometimes unfortunate policy because of the tendency of rival companies to fight each other for the remuneration with greater ardor than they exhibited in fighting fires. In the main, however, the policies followed by the two companies proved to be very sound, as indicated by the fact that both are still in existence and are in flourishing condition.

After the formation of the federal government, fire insurance companies multiplied rapidly. The Insurance Company of North America entered the fire insurance business in 1794. In an attempt to increase the volume of business and reach areas free from the competition of the two intrenched Philadelphia companies, it offered to write insurance anywhere in the United States, and advertised its services in some 5,000 pamphlets circulated throughout the nation. In deciding to expand, the company may well have realized the advisability of spreading risks—a most important consideration for fire insurance companies. Time and again during the coming years conflagrations which destroyed sections of cities would bankrupt companies which had concentrated their risks in the devastated areas. The display of enterprise by the Insurance Company of North America brought gratifying results. Within two years it was receiving over $10,000 per year from fire insurance premiums, and was firmly established in the business. This success was no doubt partially responsible for the appearance of seven new companies in Philadelphia between 1797 and 1804. By 1810, according to a contemporary estimate, there were forty companies in the nation with a capitalization of $10 million. The fire insurance business grew rapidly in Connecticut, starting Hartford on its career as an insurance center. Since the late eighteenth-century merchant partnerships there had written marine and fire insurance policies, and in 1810 Jeremiah Wadsworth incorporated the Hartford Fire Insurance Company, today the oldest company in the state.

An important instrumentality promoting growth of the larger companies was the agency system, inaugurated in 1797 when the Insurance Company of North America appointed an agent in Baltimore. The first agents acted for their principals only on a part-time basis. Not empowered to write policies, they could only solicit business and forward to the companies applications for insurance which met the companies' conditions. The obvious drawbacks of this procedure induced companies in a short time to grant agents the power to write policies, but fees remained so low that the agents could not afford to devote all their time to their insurance business. The professional agent first made his appearance in life insurance, and for reasons to be discussed in a later chapter.

The nation's banks and insurance companies were founded with surprising ease, primarily because the techniques of merchant capitalism thoroughly understood for hundreds of years were sufficient for the purpose. Furthermore, no large injections of capital were necessary, and what little was needed could be manufactured in the form of credit instruments. Competition was minimal because of the constantly growing demand for financial services of all kinds. Although failures of banks and insurance companies were not uncommon, the sound institutions in both categories were among the most stable business enterprises in the nation. The existence today of so many of the early banks and insurance companies, either in merged form or as they were originally established, testifies to the entrepreneurial skill of their founders.

V. "The Animating Pursuit" —Land Speculation in the Early Republic

The American Revolution intensified land speculation by bringing to an end the restrictions imposed by the British government, by throwing on the market confiscated loyalist properties, and by opening promising new markets in France and Holland. Also, speculators had reason to believe that state legislatures and the Continental Congress would be more responsive to their importunities for grants than was Parliament and the Board of Trade. Almost without pausing to breathe the lobbyists of the Ohio Company turned their attention to the Virginia House of Delegates, and those of the Indiana and Vandalia interests went to work on the members of Congress. Robert Morris, as secretary of the Committee of Finance, included big chunks of land in the inventory of goods he and his partners offered abroad. "Indeed," writes Thomas P. Abernethy, "it is almost impossible to separate the trading and land interests, so closely were they intertwined, for usually the merchants and the speculators were identical.

To those of commercial bent the West was not a great public resource to be used for the benefit of the people, but a commodity to be used in trade."

Silas Deane, Morris's agent in Paris, after buying into the Vandalia Company concocted a lottery scheme to dispose of 20 million acres on the Ohio and Mississippi rivers, and put together an organization to conduct it. During the war the speculators with contacts in Europe bought huge areas with reckless abandon, certain that they could find moneyed investors among the tired and disillusioned of the Old World who yearned to carve Elysiums out of the American wilderness. In this connection the appeals to natural rights and equality in the Declaration of Independence, and the iteration of the pristine republican virtues, had considerable advertising value for land speculators. As the fever heightened in intensity, Morris and two partners formed the first trust in American history—the North American Land Company—which at one time claimed nearly 6,000,000 acres in several states. The company assigned a nominal value of fifty cents an acre to the land, and issued 30,000 shares of stock against it at a par value of $100 per share. Since the lands were heavily encumbered, the partners turned them over to three trustees who granted title to purchasers and protected the interests of creditors. The partners reserved a large amount of stock for themselves, and guaranteed minimum dividend payments of 6 percent per year from the proceeds of land sales. Ultimately 22,265 shares were sold, representing about 4,500,000 acres. The documents representing the shares came to be called "scrip," and when fed into the market became a part of the circulating medium. Until after the middle of the nineteenth century the many types of land scrip were as much an object of speculation as any other credit instruments.

Not all investment in land was designed merely to secure a profit on a quick resale. Judge Richard Henderson of Hillsboro, North Carolina, acting in the tradition of Raleigh, Calvert, and Penn, bought much of what is today eastern Tennessee and eastern Kentucky from Cherokee Indians in 1775 and formed the Transylvania Company to sponsor settlement there. After employing Daniel Boone to cut a road through the mountains to the new country, Henderson led a group of settlers to the purchase, sold land on a quitrent basis, assisted the settlers in writing a constitution, and petitioned Congress to recognize his domain as a new state. Henderson's plans for a republican proprietary collapsed, however, when Virginia refused to relinquish its claim to the Kentucky area. The Transylvania Company was later recompensed by a grant of 200,000 acres farther west.

After independence was declared the rival claims in the Northwest based on Indian titles procured by speculators from Virginia and from states with no putative western extensions came into collision in Congress and postponed the adoption of the Articles of Confederation for five years. Pennsylvania and Maryland speculators called loudly for the abandonment of all state claims of sovereignty to Congress, for only if that body exercised jurisdiction could they hope to validate their Indian titles dating from the cessions to the Indiana and Vandalia companies. Virginia at first refused to give up a seemingly indisputable claim to the Northwest based on both charter rights and conquest. But when it became clear that no state by its own efforts alone could provide the military protection necessary to give value to the land, the Virginia legislature reluctantly agreed to cede jurisdiction to Congress. Now that equality of opportunity was assured to speculators of all the states, the Maryland legislature, by ratifying the Articles of Confederation in 1781, allowed the United States to have its first constitution. This was not the last time that a major political issue was to be determined by the course of land speculation.

THE OHIO COMPANY OF ASSOCIATES

The pressure exerted by speculators upon Congress intensified after the war. One of the most interesting promotions of the period was the Ohio Company of Associates and its shadow organization, the Scioto Company. The Ohio Company was formed in Massachusetts by two Revolutionary veterans, Generals Rufus Putnam and Benjamin Tupper, who raised $250,000 from a large group of prospective settlers as down payment on a grant in the Ohio region surveyed by Congress. Although in the Land Ordinance of 1785 Congress had decided against large grants to speculators in favor of direct sales to small settlers under the New England township system, the desperate need for money made Congress receptive to the importunities of the Ohio Company's lobbyist, the Reverend Manasseh Cutler. Yet when Cutler arrived in Philadelphia in 1787 to close the deal, he found it impossible to get the terms he wanted until the veteran speculator, William Duer, a member of Congress from New York, offered his aid.

Duer was a remarkable man, an epitome of the plungers of this period. Born in England, the son of a West Indies planter, young William was educated at Eaton and served as aide-de-camp to Lord Clive in India in 1764. After the death of his father he went into business and came to New York in 1768 to fill a contract for masts for the Royal Navy. At the suggestion of Philip Schuyler he erected a sawmill near Saratoga and shortly after taking up residence there became a local nabob. Affable, cosmopolitan, and energetic, he established a firm position for himself in society by marrying the daughter of William Alexander (self-styled "Lord Stirling"), a member of the Royal Council of New York. At the beginning of the Revolution he took the Whig side and became one of the principal contractors of the army. An inveterate speculator, with contacts among important men everywhere, he was a natural leader of that small group of merchant capitalists who made fortunes for themselves by supplying the needs of the military forces. For the rest of his life he was constantly involved in speculative schemes of some sort. On one occasion he participated in a syndicate with Swiss and Dutch bankers to purchase the American debt held by France, but the project fell through. For seven months he served as assistant secretary of the treasury under Hamilton, but resigned to devote his full time to speculating in the funded debt and in bank stock. Meanwhile he speculated heavily in land, and played an important part in the formation of The Society for Useful Manufactures (see below, pp. 84–85).

As the price of his support for the Ohio Company grant, Duer proposed to form a secret partnership called the Scioto Company including Cutler and others from the Ohio Company, which would participate in an enlarged land grant and help finance the Ohio Company's undertaking. Duer was aware that without a "front" he had very little chance of getting Congress to grant land for what would undoubtedly be speculative purposes. By the terms of the final contract with Congress, the Ohio Company, for a down payment of $500,000 in depreciated currency and securities, obtained an option on an ultimate five or six million acres at two-thirds of a dollar per acre in the same coin. Title to the first portion would pass with the payment of an additional $500,000. With the help of the silent Scioto partners the Ohio Company made its down payment and dispatched its first settlers to the Ohio, who founded the town of Marietta.

Duer, uninterested in settlement, planned to market Ohio lands in Europe. As its agent the Scioto Company chose young Joel Barlow of Connecticut, a budding poet. Barlow went to France but had little success in finding purchasers until he fell in with William Playfair, an English engineer, author, and adventurer. At Playfair's suggestion, Barlow formed a third partnership, La Compagnie de Scioto, which brought into the enterprise Frenchmen interested in settlement. With the grudging aid of Duer, who now was desperately trying to raise the money to complete the purchase, some four hundred French immigrants were by 1791 precariously settled on Scioto Company lands. But disillusionment brought about by Indian attacks and by Duer's inability to provide title and suitable facilities for settlement discouraged further immigration, and in the next year, as a result of his bankruptcy, the Ohio and Scioto companies disintegrated.

John Cleves Symes, a New Jersey speculator, had somewhat more success in settling the Ohio region. Purchasing a tract of eventually 311,862 acres on the Ohio between the Miami and Little Miami rivers, he moved to the area and was instrumental in founding Cincinnati. Although the region filled rapidly with settlers and land values rose precipitantly, Symes, like nearly all other contemporary land speculators, died in poverty.

But the relatively few speculators who became more interested in land development than in the mere making of a middleman's profit often conferred great benefits upon the areas they controlled. Some younger members of first families in New York moved to the frontier and grew up with the country, among them Ogdens, Parishes, and Van Rensselaers. The Platts founded Plattsburgh, the Lows Lowville, the Duanes Duanesburg. James Fenimore Cooper was the son of the princely William Cooper, founder of Cooperstown and lord of a huge estate with hundreds of tenants. Through the marketing efforts of Robert Morris three million acres of land in western New York came into the hands of Dutch capitalists organized as the Holland Land Company, and an additional three million was likewise acquired from him by the English Pulteny Association. The association spent $1,375,000 on its tract between 1792 and 1799, building roads and mills, and constructing the town of Bath complete with theatre, racetrack, and hotel. The Holland Land Company likewise invested a considerable sum in the facilities necessary to attract and keep settlers, laid out the town of Buffalo, and in 1817 donated 100,000 acres to New York State to aid in the construction of the Erie Canal. Both organizations sold land on easy terms with deferred payments. Yet the companies were not outstandingly successful financially. Many years were required for the sums invested in social overhead capital to bring significant returns, and administrative costs were high. When the companies finally wound up their affairs—the Holland Land Company in 1836 and the Pulteny Association about 1890—it appeared doubtful that they had earned 6 percent on their total outlay. Yet they had plainly hastened the pace of economic development in the areas they controlled.

LAND SPECULATION IN THE SOUTHWEST

In the Southwest the erratic course of political and military affairs was in many ways a reflection of all-encompassing land speculation. After the Revolution, Virginia, North and South Carolina, and Georgia reasserted their colonial boundaries stretching to the Mississippi south of the Ohio, and in order to reduce the Revolutionary debt and pay soldiers' bonuses printed millions of dollars worth of land warrants giving claims in this territory. Virginia speculators like George Rogers Clark, Patrick Henry, and members of the Breckinridge and Nicholas families; and North Carolina speculators such as Richard Caswell, John Sevier, James Robertson and members of the Blount family, accumulated these warrants in large amounts. Such a course was not difficult for men of a little capital and credit because the warrants circulated as currency at very depreciated figures and in North and South Carolina could be purchased with the depreciated paper money of state issue.

In the usual manner the speculators formed partnerships whereby the partner in the West located land and the partner in the state capital patented it. Agents were sometimes sent to Europe to market the tracts, but more often the land was sold to merchant syndicates in Philadelphia, New York, and Boston, who were usually in a better position to undertake this kind of transaction. Also in the usual manner the speculators bought titles to huge areas from Indians, and then called loudly for Congress to assert sovereignty over the Southwest and provide the military protection necessary to give the land any value. Fraud and corruption in the land system was all but universal, taking the form of forged or altered warrants or land acquired through the various forms of pressure and bribery on legislatures. An investigation of the affairs of William Blount, first governor of the Southwest Territory, made by a hostile committee of the North Carolina legislature in 1798, revealed what Blount's biographer calls "one of the most comprehensive records of fraud and land thievery in the history of the public lands."

Blount, incidently, had a career which in many respects paralleled that of Duer. Born to a planter-mercantile family in North Carolina engaged in commercial activities of all types, Blount was active in procurement for the army, speculated in land and currency, and began a promising career as a member of the North Carolina Assembly. Inevitably he was drawn into speculations in the Southwest, which he pursued from the vantage point of increasingly important political positions. Appointment as governor of the Southwest Territory in 1790 enabled him to redouble the scope of his operations. Moving to what is today Tennessee, he founded Knoxville and became the most important nabob of the area. In 1796, when Tennessee entered the union, Blount was elected to the United States Senate.

THE YAZOO SCANDAL

The most notorious speculation in the Southwest was the Yazoo scandal, which implicated leading figures as far north as New England, rocked Congress with angry controversy, and for a period split the Democratic-Republican party. In 1789 the Georgia legislature tentatively granted an aggregate 25 million acres in its western claim to the Yazoo Companies of South Carolina, Virginia, and Tennessee at a price of less than one cent per acre. Actually the grants were meaningless and were never completed because Spain claimed the region and Choctaw Indians occupied it. But by 1794, when there were strong indications that Spain might abandon its claim and allow Americans to navigate the Mississippi and market goods in New Orleans, the area in which the Yazoo Companies were interested became much more valuable. Now reorganized with strong financial support from the Northeast, the Yazoo speculators offered Georgia $500,000 for grants containing not less than thirty-five million acres, with one fifth of the purchase price to be paid as down payment. Since the speculators obviously intended to market the land abroad, the proposal got a stormy reception from a Georgia legislature which was naturally loath to alienate to foreigners a domain consisting of what is today a large part of Alabama and Mississippi. The proposal was at first rejected, but was then passed after the companies reportedly offered 50,000 acres for each favorable vote.

Grand juries in every Georgia county but two immediately protested what appeared to be a gigantic steal, and Congress adopted a resolution condemning it. Nevertheless, the companies immediately flooded the land market with scrip, and dispatched agents abroad to expedite the sales campaign. But to the consternation of company members, a newly elected Georgia legislature, responding to the outrage of Georgia voters, rescinded the sale, and Yazoo scrip plummeted in the market. Thousands of small investors lost heavily, but canny speculators, sensing the possibility of a reversal of the legislature's action in the federal courts, began buying up the scrip. They were rewarded for their farsightedness when Chief Justice Marshall, in the famous case of Fletcher *vs.* Peck (1810), ruled the repudiation of the sale to be an impairment of the obligation of contract. The Yazoo claimants were finally in 1815 awarded $4,282,151 by an angry Congress which still rang with charges of criminal conduct. John Randolph mercilessly castigated the administration for what he considered to be invasion of states' rights and collusion in fraud. In the course of the debates on the Yazoo issue in the Senate he would cavort about the chamber, pointing to prospective beneficiaries of a settlement, and screaming at the top of his lungs, "Yazoo! Yazoo!"

The Yazoo scandal brought the era of the large grants to an end. After Virginia, North and South Carolina, and Georgia abandoned their western claims, which resulted in the formation of Kentucky, Tennessee, Alabama, and Mississippi, the federal government alone controlled the distribution of the western domain. Federal land offices were established and the course of land legislation after 1800 made it progressively easier for the small farmer to buy directly from the government without the services of the middleman. The fact that land was surveyed in advance and sold at public auction made it harder but by no means impossible for speculators to engross large areas.

The specialization of entrepreneurial functions inherent in the establishment of banking and insurance companies between the Revolution and the War of 1812 did not take place to a comparable degree in land speculation during the period. The land companies of that era moved no farther toward rational organization than did the companies of the colonial period. On the surface the land companies formed during and after the Revolution were similar to the colonial land banks established half a century before. But the purposes of the two types of organization were different. The object of the land banks had been to increase the circulating medium in times of depression by issuing a currency secured by mortgages upon urban and farm properties. But the land companies of the early national period were merely speculative marketing operations designed to sell off huge areas of wild land in the thousands of small acreages represented by scrip. The purchase of options and the occasional use of trustees to hold titles were financial innovations, but whatever value they may have had was dissipated by their speculative purpose. The attitude of Congress and the state governments toward land speculation during the Confederation period was vastly different from the attitude of the Board of Trade before the coming of independence. The Board of Trade was interested exclusively in settlement, and made large grants only in return for commitments to get the land into production. Congress and the state governments, on the other hand, hoped to ease perennial financial difficulties by selling chunks of their public domains for the highest price possible.

The speculators, or more properly land brokers, who purchased the wild land in wholesale lots for retail distribution via the issuance of scrip, were perhaps the most unsuccessful group of businessmen in American history devoted to a single enterprise. Duer, Morris, Alexander Macomb,

James Greenleaf, and James Wilson—the leading speculators of the Northeast—all were ruined by the Panics of 1792 and 1796 which they precipitated. William Blount was expelled from the United States Senate in 1797 because of his fraudulent land deals in the Southwest and died shortly thereafter, his once vast landed empire gone. Greatly overestimating the demand for the wild lands of the back country, these men borrowed to the ultimate limit of their credit in order to acquire options to hugh areas which they were not able to sell off at a fast enough rate to meet interest payments and the installments necessary to acquire title. Selling lands they did not own and could not pay for not only brought them to grief but also created generations of litigation. Moreover, having sunk all of their funds in options, they had nothing left with which to build roads, schools, and other community facilities which would make their areas attractive.

Actually, the speculators of the early national period deserve the epithet "robber baron" more than do the industrial titans of the late nineteenth century. Although the latter served themselves well and on occasion were ruthless with small competitors and the public, they created great wealth for the nation at large in the form of the industries they brought into being. But the land brokers left behind them only financial wreckage and a lengthy record of fraud and corruption. Their careers illustrate the fact, repeatedly to be demonstrated down to our own time, that land speculation unconnected with land development is usually an arid enterprise which creates no real wealth but only business cycles of boom and bust.

VI. Turnpike Fever

The building and operation of transportation facilities has been one of the most vital of all American businesses. Transportation is an important element in any economy, but under American conditions of the late eighteenth and early nineteenth centuries its role was crucial. The market area of the nation in 1790 stretched westward in irregular arcs from the seaport towns and navigable rivers and on the approaches to the frontier diminished rapidly, particularly for bulky agricultural commodities. Perhaps 50 percent of all Americans were locked in the deep backwoods, doomed to a primarily subsistence livelihood because the prohibitive cost of transportation without improved roads, canals, or railroads made impossible any significant exchanges with the market economy to the east. The businessmen and statesmen of the new nation could plainly see that widening the area in which exchanges would be economically feasible was indispensable for economic development. Furthermore, transportation improvement brought with it a host of fringe benefits of immediate interest to speculators and merchants in the seaboard towns such as enhanced land values, an increased volume of commodities for export, and a widened market for imports from Europe.

Apart from these considerations, the conviction became widespread at the outset that the building of better roads, and later the construction of

71

canals and railroads, would almost invariably be profitable in itself. Albert Gallatin, in his celebrated *Report on the Subject of Public Roads and Canals* of 1808, provided a formula by which these gains could be calculated: "It is sufficiently evident that whenever the annual expense of transportation on a certain route in its natural state exceeds the interest on the capital employed in improving the communication, and the annual expense of transportation (exclusively of the tolls) by the improved route, the difference is an annual additional income to the nation." In the sanguine expectations of many of Gallatin's contemporaries, the cost of transportation on an unimproved route was bound to exceed the interest on capital invested in its improvement by a wide enough margin to justify the imposition of a considerable toll.

Doubtless all economists would agree with the main precept of the transportation doctrine—that lower cost of transportation promotes specialization, raises the prices of land and commodities produced on the land, and in many other ways plays an important part in economic advancement. But time has proved false the corollary that almost any *particular* improvement is bound to be profitable. Profit might well be anticipated over strategic routes already in existence where a heavy volume of traffic would be guaranteed, but in developmental transportation projects the possibility of profit was considerably less. Here promoters had to create traffic as well as the means of carrying it, and the former task often assumed staggering proportions. Yet in the minds of most enthusiasts for transportation improvement the sanctity of the transportation doctrine extended to its corollary. The problems of developmental enterprises were seldom investigated sufficiently and were usually ignored. Costs of completion were almost invariably underestimated, and were increased by a consuming desire for speed in construction. Hence although the United States had more miles of canals in 1850 than the British Isles, and more miles of railroad in 1890 than all of Europe, the social cost of the transportation system in the form of individual failures, bankruptcies, and reorganizations—with concomitant political disturbances—was unnecessarily high. Yet these shortcomings should not detract from the achievement itself. The conceiving and construction of the American transportation network was one of the finest examples in modern times of entrepreneurial vision and the application of creative innovation. And more than any other single enterprise the building of the transportation network stimulated the thousands of other economic and technological advances which have created the nation as we have it today.

TRANSPORTATION IMPROVEMENT AS A FUNCTION OF PRIVATE ENTERPRISE

It seems something of a paradox that despite the enthusiasm for transportation improvement at the end of the eighteenth century there was little interest in bettering the condition of existing public roads. In the back country the problem was insuperable. Because of sparse population the labor, capital, and engineering skill were unavailable to carry out the extensive ditching, draining, filling, and stump pulling necessary to keep the roads in good condition. Most farmers preferred to devote their energies to the obviously more profitable task of clearing new land and tending their crops. Most within reach of the market area could manage to get their produce to a country storekeeper and exchange it for the articles required by their simple existence. In the spring all of the rivers flowing into the Atlantic from the Kennebec on the north to the St. Mary's on the south became highways of commerce as a year's production of wheat, corn, peas, pork, beef, flour, potash, and other commodities was rafted down on the freshets to the seaport towns. Through traffic by road was almost unknown.

The movement for better roads was therefore not a grass roots affair springing up from the back country. On the contrary, it originated among the merchants of the seaboard towns. Transportation improvement had almost from the beginning of settlement been taken over as an entrepreneurial function. Ferries had been established by individuals under the authority of franchises which prescribed in general terms the manner in which the business was to be conducted and established maximum charges. Until the late nineteenth century nearly all of the important bridge structures in the nation were private undertakings.

The building of toll roads, or turnpikes, began with the chartering of the Philadelphia and Lancaster Turnpike Company in 1791. Amid great public enthusiasm the 1,000 shares of stock offered at $300 apiece were subscribed for within a few hours after the subscription books had been opened. Like the Insurance Company of North America, which was to be ushered into the world in the next year with a similar demonstration of confidence, the Lancaster Turnpike Company represented the dynamic desire for expansion, a balanced economy, and economic independence which was becoming so prominent in the cities of the eastern seaboard. In the following decades the turnpike movement gained momentum. By 1821, 278 companies chartered in New York capitalized at over $11 million had completed about 4,000 miles of roads and had planned 2,000 miles more. By 1831 Pennsylvania had 2,500 miles of improved roads built by private enterprise and in New England by the end of the decade 135 turnpike corporations had constructed 3,764 miles of roads at a cost of $6.5 million. Enthusiasm for turnpikes was considerably less in southern and western states, mainly because financial means was not yet available for extensive transportation improvement. The greatest concentration of turnpikes naturally developed in the vicinity of seaport cities whose merchants were increasingly eager to expand urban hinterlands. Elsewhere in the nation these roads exploited strategic transportation routes between commercial centers or acted as feeders for navigable rivers.

SOURCES OF CAPITAL FOR TURNPIKES

Capital for turnpikes was gathered from a wide variety of sources. Initial stock subscriptions tapped the savings of a wide cross section of society from merchant princes like Stephen Girard to humble artisans. Bank credit was also funneled into turnpike companies in the form of loans and stock subscriptions. Early insurance companies, as we have seen, sometimes had turnpike stock in their portfolios. Despite the enthusiasm indicated by the proliferation of companies, financing in most cases proved to be a difficult matter. Initial payments on stock of 5 or 10 percent enabled companies at the beginning to construct only short stretches of road, and unless profits were forthcoming further assessments on the stock were difficult to collect. If the stock were issued in small denominations, as was often done in order to attract small investors, successive issues were necessary in order to complete additional sections of road. Because of the general unprofitability of turnpikes the limits of equity capitalization were reached in a relatively short time, and companies then tried to finance construction and operations by acquiring a floating debt, mortgaging whatever property they possessed, or even farming out tolls.

Difficulties of raising capital forced turnpike companies almost at the outset to turn to state governments for financial assistance. Some governments responded generously. Pennsylvania, through stock purchases, contributed almost one-third of the some $6 million invested in turnpikes throughout the state. Virginia, through its Board of Public Works, by 1860 acquired a portfolio of turnpike and bridge company stock nominally valued at $5 million. After 1830 western state legislatures offered increasing amounts of aid. Only the New England states refused to contribute public funds, perhaps because a greater availability of mercantile capital after 1793 made such a course unnecessary.

Stock subscriptions by state governments inaugurated the policy of "joint enterprise" which in various forms was to be a vital feature in the financing of internal improvements throughout the first half of the nineteenth century. At first sight it might seem a paradox that a nation so devoted to private enterprise would accept with so little reservation government intervention into the affairs of private corporations. But upon examination the paradox becomes more apparent than real. In the first place, public participation in the financing, construction, and even operation of internal improvements was looked upon as a supplement and stimulus to private enterprise, not a substitute for it. In practice public participation was usually limited to projects which were considered to have developmental significance but which did not have prospects of profit sufficient to entice private capital from the normal channels of trade. The state, therefore, stepped in where private investors feared to tread.

A second reason for the illusory nature of the paradox was that government assistance, as contrasted with government control, has always been an implicit corollary of free enterprise. The American free enterprise system has never been divorced from government and sequestered in its own autonomous world by the dictates of classical laissez-faire economics. From the colonial period until the present, sympathetic assistance from government has been expected, and whenever such assistance has not been forthcoming, complaints have been bitter and prolonged. The recipients of mail subsidies, government loans, land grants, or parity payments, or the beneficiaries of protective tariffs, have seldom, if ever, felt that the intervention of government in their behalf militated against free enterprise. Such a threat was only felt when such special benefits were focused upon individuals or groups in such a way as to foster monopoly, or were conferred upon groups with interests which conflicted with those of business. Government controls, rather than government largesse, very early came to be looked upon as the hallmark of collectivism. As long as decision-making was relatively unfettered, businessmen saw no reason to fear for the future of the free enterprise system.

The circumspection with which state governments used the powers of control which accompanied their investment in joint enterprise was a third factor in reconciling private business to government participation. Public members on boards of directors usually allowed themselves to be guided by the representatives of private stockholders. The fact that the federal government seldom participated in joint enterprise also no doubt helped remove any objections which could be raised against the system. To be sure, Albert Gallatin, foreseeing the inability of private enterprise to undertake large-scale transportation improvements, had advocated in his *Report* a gridwork of canals and turnpikes linking east and west to be built by the federal government. But although the specific routes he recommended were all later traversed by canals, turnpikes, or railroads, the proposal for federal construction aroused little enthusiasm. Congress did authorize the Cumberland Road, which reached Wheeling, Virginia, in 1818 and by mid-century had been completed to Vandalia, Illinois. Federal aid of other sorts reached substantial proportions even before 1860, and John Quincy Adams was an enthusiastic advocate of federally sponsored improvements, but most presidents during the antebellum period foresaw that large-scale federal involvement would produce logrolling, intra-party squabbles, and a "stockjobbing interest." The doubtful constitutionality of federally sponsored internal improvements gave presidents a convenient pretext for veto of programs likely to cause trouble. The land-grant policy inaugurated in the 1850s obviated many of the difficulties associated with other forms of assistance and seemed to be more firmly justified by national interest.

CONSTRUCTION AND OPERATION OF TURNPIKES

Turnpike charters were quite restrictive, indicating a strong desire on the part of legislatures to protect citizens against possible exploitation by monopolies. Rates of toll, the number of toll gates, and maximum capitalization were always specified, and often the amount of stock which could be held or voted by a single individual was limited. Details of construction and requirements of maintenance were included in the documents. In order to protect stockholders' enjoyment of monopoly of route, public or private roads paralleling turnpikes—often called "shunpikes"—were forbidden.

Turnpike construction varied widely. Many companies merely took over and improved existing public roads. The minimum improvement consisted of ditching and crowning the roads in order to provide better drainage, and pulling stumps. In the absence of power machinery the latter task was so onerous that companies were often allowed by charter to leave the larger stumps standing in the roadways. The more elaborate roads, such as the Philadelphia-Lancaster or Albany-Schenectady turnpikes, were given a hard "macadamized" surface of small stones overlaid with gravel resting on a base of larger stones. The paved strips were usually about twenty feet wide and were flanked on both sides by dirt shoulders of equal width called "summer roads." In good weather these were used in preference to the pavement because the soft dirt surface was easier on the feet of horses and livestock. Costs varied as widely as the care given to construction. Expenditures for the Cumberland road amounted to $13,000 per mile, for the Albany-Schenectady turnpike $10,000 per mile, and for the Lancaster turnpike $7,500 per mile, yet most roads, built without hard surfacing, cost no more than $1,000 per mile. Estimated costs often proved to be quite erroneous because of unanticipated difficulties of construction such as rock excavations and drainage problems. Poor whites living along the routes were the principal source of labor. Contractors provided food and lodging. Wages ranged up to 75 cents per day—a relatively high figure for the times.

The reduction of transportation costs brought about by turnpikes was disappointingly small, mainly because maintenance was often haphazard and because companies usually would not undertake the heavy cost of reducing grades to the point that heavier loads could be drawn by fewer horses than over public roads. Actually, the cost of transportation over turnpikes seldom dipped under twenty cents per ton mile, a figure more than ten times greater than the cost of canal or rail carriage during the 1880s. Turnpikes were more important in providing year-round, through service than in increasing transportation efficiency. Tolls varied considerably and were based on the principle of charging what the traffic could bear which was to cause so much controversy when applied by railroads at a later date. Under these circumstances private carriages paid a heavy toll, but the large freight wagons carrying heavy, low value commodities could travel over turnpikes for a cost of about one cent per mile.

From the outset turnpikes yielded little profit to their owners. The 2 or 3 percent annual dividends paid by the Lancaster Turnpike Company was about average for the returns from the more heavily traveled roads. Many turnpikes could be operated only at a loss. Among the reasons for poor profit records were: high construction costs, floating debt, poor management, diversion of traffic during the summer months to public roads and shunpikes, and ultimately competition from canals and railroads. Yet, somewhat surprisingly, the unprofitability of the roads did not diminish enthusiasm for further building until the coming of competing types of transportation. The reason may well have been that investors in turnpike stock were often more interested in fringe benefits such as enhanced land values and business opportunities than in dividends.

Although little is known about the management of the companies, it probably involved tasks of the simplest kind which required little specialized skill. Directors were drawn from among the merchants, bankers, and farmers who promoted the roads. Small executive staffs, no doubt working on a part-time basis, handled financial affairs. Toll receivers were probably the only full-time employees in the smaller companies. The large organizations may have had engineers and maintenance crews, but in many instances maintenance as well as tolls was farmed out under contract.

The failure and eventual abandonment of most turnpikes to the states, in contrast to the later failures of canal and railroad enterprises, caused no tremors to the financial stability of the nation. Unlike railroads and canals turnpike companies did not create the mountains of debt built up at a later date by successive issues of railroad and canal bonds. Furthermore, states do not appear to have gone deeply into debt in order to make contributions to turnpike companies. Wide distribution of stock minimized losses to individuals and frequent requirements that contractors accept part of their remuneration in stock reduced cash outlays. Also the progressive forfeiture of a large amount of stock by failure to pay assessments probably spread losses over a longer period of time. Finally, the expenditures by companies for construction and maintenance were all made locally. Stone and gravel were obtained from local sources and the roads in the Northeast were built by farmers along the routes who contracted for short stretches of construction. By contrast, railroads were later compelled to make large expenditures for rails and equipment in England, thus causing an outflow of funds and an increase in the amount of debt held abroad.

As with river traffic in the Mississippi Valley, the transportation business on turnpikes was carried on by thousands of small operators. Wagons and horses were usually owned by their drivers, who, as often as not, were farmers living along the route who hauled freight in slack seasons. Towns and cities connected by turnpikes were served by many small stagecoach lines, all in sharp competition with each other, particularly for the mail contracts which constituted perhaps the most profitable part of their business. Every type of business organization could be found in stagecoaching: some coaches were owned by their drivers, some lines were operated as partnerships, and a few were even incorporated. The coaching network put together by Levi Pease, "father of New England stagecoaching," probably represents the most usual form of the large organizations. The component lines were owned jointly by Pease and individual proprietors who met regularly as a "company" to decide such matters as rates and the division of fares, the terms of mail contracts, and rules regarding "conductors"—the first carriers of express. By the 1830s a few companies even rivaled railroads of a later date in the magnitude of operations. The Eastern Stage Company, for example, which ran coaches between Boston and outlying points, was capitalized at $100,000. Drovers were often independent businessmen who bought livestock from farmers in the hinterland of major port cities, often on credit, and drove it to the cities for sale to butchers.

The roads from the Midwest converging on east coast centers performed a very important service by enabling stock breeders to walk corn to market, thus by the conversion increasing the value of basic farm crops and reducing transportation charges.

Apart from their economic impact turnpikes contributed to the aura of romance which has surrounded American transportation. Just as the river traffic in the Mississippi Valley developed the tough, brawling breed which manned rafts, arks, and keelboats, so the turnpikes brought into being the professional wagoners and drovers whose exploits contribute richly to folklore and literature. Busy turnpikes presented a vivid panorama of movement. Wheeled vehicles of every type from huge Conestoga wagons with their white canvas "sails" to pony chaises mingled with cattle, hogs, and even geese in the polyglot traffic of the more important through routes. Inns were frequent and of different varieties which catered to drovers, wagoners, or the carriage trade. Night after night the more plebian hostelries re-echoed with bibulous celebration as wagoners and drovers sought to authenticate their reputations as hard drinkers and hard fighters.

Although the turnpike movement died out in the eastern states, nevertheless, in rapidly developing regions further west it reappeared, and—following the cyclical pattern in the eastern states—declined as public funds became adequate for the construction of roads. In our own day, after a long period of dormancy, the movement has unexpectedly revived. Because of the massive cost and bright profit prospects of modern superhighways, many have been built with private funds raised and administered by state turnpike commissions. But if the past is any guide, we may expect that in the future an increasing proportion of these roads will be constructed by public authority.

VII. Inauguration of the Textile Industry

Manufacturing was a late addition to the circle of business activities coming within the purview of entrepreneurs. Since the beginning of recorded history they had bought and sold manufactured goods, but not until the coming of the putting-out system in the late Middle Ages did they participate in the control over production exercised by guilds and independent artisans. In the sixteenth century a few English artisans with entrepreneurial drive began gathering other workmen together under the same roof. In the course of planning and supervising production, procuring raw materials, and selling the final product, these artisan-entrepreneurs became the precursors of modern industrial capitalists.

In colonial America the sparse and scattered population, poor transportation, and the commitment to agriculture prevented the development of outputting and the factory system to any appreciable extent. Yet frontier conditions stimulated certain types of manufacturing. Because of ubiquitous and readily available raw materials, colonial America had a competitive advantage over western Europe in some forest industries—particularly in shipbuilding and the production of iron, naval stores, and potash. Moreover, the absence of a market economy in much of the back country fostered the growth of home industries and thereby developed the basic skills which could be adapted at a later date to the operation of automatic machinery. Perhaps 90 out of 100 farm families spun linen and woolen yarn from home-grown flax and from native fleeces, wove fabrics, and made their own clothes. They also tanned leather, made shoes and nails, did their own carpentry, boiled soap, and preserved meat by smoking. Community services such as lumbering and milling brought familiarity with the design and use of water power.

The inventive talent to produce automatic machinery and the skilled labor to operate it were lacking, but "ingenius mechanicks" could be found who were capable of copying and improving imported prototypes and training for new and special tasks a native labor force familiar with the techniques of home industry. Actually the scarcity of skilled labor was in one way an advantage because it obviated the formation of the entrenched artisan groups who strove so bitterly in England to prevent the spread of automatic machinery. Finally, American entrepreneurs, as jacks of all commercial trades, were ready, willing, and able to perform the marketing, procurement, and financial services necessary to conduct industrial enterprise. Thus it was that the infant United States, although undoubtedly a primarily agricultural nation, had the potential in both human and natural resources to develop rapidly into an industrial society.

After the Revolution an "industrial consciousness" which had materialized first during the period of the nonimportation agreements and had been greatly stimulated by wartime necessity, began to exercise a palpable influence upon the nation. Now a twofold question emerged; would industrial development be desirable for the United States, and if so, would it be possible? The public debate over the issues became spirited, and occasionally bitter. An agrarian position, developed by Thomas Jefferson and John Taylor, of Caroline, appealed not only to economics, but to moral philosophy. According to the argument the United States was naturally an agricultural country, with neither the capital nor the labor to create an industrial system. Its economy was complementary to that of Europe, particularly Britain, to whom it could export foodstuffs and extractive products and from whom it could purchase the manufactures it needed. Industry brought with it large cities with their vice, luxury, mobs, and political corruption. Republics could maintain their virtue only in an agrarian environment with the widespread land ownership which alone could give the degree of economic security and equality necessary for the cultivation of political responsibility.

The argument for manufactures was cogently presented by Tench Coxe and Matthew Carey. Coxe was an able pamphleteer and perennial political placeman who had a much clearer understanding of the nation's economic welfare than his own. Carey, publisher of the *American Museum*, was the nation's first political economist. In writings during the eighties and nineties the two, with occasional assists from likeminded businessmen, emphasized the advantages of a balanced economy. They insisted that only an industrial system could bring economic independence from Britain, and so complete the work of the patriots of '76. Also, they pointed out that domestic manufactures on an extensive scale would stem the drain of specie which chronically depressed prices, made debts hard to collect, and slowed the pace of the whole economy. Capital, Coxe and Carey felt, could be secured by lotteries held for the benefit of manufacturing firms and by borrowing abroad against securities representing a funded national debt. Abundant raw materials and water power would in part compensate for the cheaper labor of Britain, and in any event the growth of manufacturing would attract immigration and so swell the supply of labor. Coxe met the moral problem by pointing out that whole families, including children, would be put to work and thereby placed out of reach of the devil. In an era in which all members of farm families worked from dawn to dusk and few children received more than a rudimentary education, this argument did not carry the opprobrious connotations it would have today. The fact that an industrial system would hold families together was considered a strong argument in its favor. Many of Coxe's and Carey's arguments found their way into Hamilton's famous *Report on Manufactures* of 1791, which in view of the preceding years of debate was more a summary of the position taken by the advocates of manufactures rather than an original work.

In order to give substance to the doctrine of manufactures, societies were formed in the late eighties and early nineties which were at once propaganda agencies and pilot textile manufacturing plants. Although spinning and weaving was a ubiquitous family art, the manufacture of textiles by automatic machinery was unknown in the new nation. Yet to many advocates of industrialization it was the most important branch of manufacturing which could be undertaken. Considerably more than half of the value of imports was represented by textiles, and business and professional men were dressed entirely in imported fabrics. Acute observers were aware that textile manufacture was the greatest single source of British prosperity, and the lack of it the major reason for American dependency. Actually, to the advocates of industrialism in the era, "manufacturing" implied, first and foremost, textile manufacturing.

The first, and most characteristic of the industrial societies was The Pennsylvania Society for the Encouragement of Manufactures and the Useful Arts. Founded in 1787, it boasted Benjamin Franklin as principal patron and Thomas Mifflin, Tench Coxe, Matthew Carey, and Samuel Wetherill as principal sponsors. Membership was open to all citizens for a payment of ten shillings annually. Stock was also issued at ten pounds per share. By 1788 a capital fund of 1,800 pounds had been raised, and the state subscribed 1,000 pounds in 1789. By cloak and dagger methods the company appears to have gotten from England spinning jennies, or the plans for their construction, in spite of stringent prohibitions against the export of either. Reproducing with crude, hand-operated machinery some of the processes of hand spinning, jennies were the first in the series of inventions in the field of textile machinery which eventually mechanized textile manufacture. By 1790 the society had in operation four jennies with a total of 224 spindles. It also operated 26 hand looms and had produced 11,367 yards of cloth. The directors proudly claimed that profits were running at the rate of 30 percent per year. But in 1790 the building was destroyed by fire, perhaps by an incendiary motivated by the same fear of competition which in future years was to lead to the burning of textile mills in England.

Organizations similar to the Pennsylvania society were founded in New York and Baltimore, and were even planned in such unlikely areas as South Carolina and Ohio. None was financially successful, probably because of the lack of efficient machinery, the scarcity of skilled labor, and the overwhelming superiority of British cloth. But the societies performed a real service by focusing public attention upon the concrete problems of textile manufacture rather than upon abstractions regarding the feasibility of industrialization, and by mobilizing community support for the mechanization of textile manufacturing.

THE SOCIETY FOR ESTABLISHING USEFUL MANUFACTURES

The culmination of the movement to stimulate industrialization by pilot project supported by government and private enterprise jointly reached its culmination in the ill-starred career of The Society for Establishing Useful Manufactures, the first large industrial corporation in American history. Hamilton considered it to be a specific application of his recommendations in the *Report on Manufactures*, and an integral part of his system of economic nationalism. The original plan, worked out by Tench Coxe with the assistance of Hamilton, contemplated the establishment of an industrial town at the falls of the Passaic River in northern New Jersey by a large corporation which would develop a water power complete with canals and raceways, and build factories for the manufacture of a wide range of goods including textiles, beer, liquor, iron and paper. The capital to finance the project would be imported by allowing stock subscriptions to be made in the funded debt, which would then be pledged abroad for loans to carry out the construction program. Interest on the pledged government securities would pay the interest on the incurred debt, thus relieving the corporation of overhead charges. Investors could be sure that whatever capital gains they may have already secured from the funding of the national debt and from the subsequent advance in price of the new securities would be further enhanced by an increase in the value of corporate stock. The promoters embodied this vision of industrialization and escalating profits in a glowing prospectus. The corporation, by demonstrating to the country at large the benefits of manufactures, and to entrepreneurs, landowners, and artisans the profits to be derived from them, would formally inaugurate the industrial revolution in the United States.

On the first wave of enthusiasm $650,000 was subscribed to the SUM, $10,000 coming from the New Jersey legislature. The stockholders were mostly New York and Philadelphia businessmen, many of them seasoned speculators. No one connected with the enterprise had had any previous experience with manufacturing, and probably many, if not most, were more interested in escalating their already considerable profits in the funded debt than in presiding over the industrialization of the nation. William Duer was elected governor, a choice reflecting the orientation of the stockholders and directors.

The rest of the unhappy history of the SUM is soon told. The company selected a site at the falls of the Passaic River, retained the famous Major L'Enfant, architect of the National Capitol, to design the factory buildings, appointed a superintendent, and recruited workmen. But the Panic of 1792 gave what eventually proved to be a fatal blow to the enterprise. Duer and many prominent stockholders went to the wall, payments on stock subscriptions fell in arrears, and the pace of construction at the falls of the Passaic slowed. Newspaper critics, correctly identifying the SUM with the speculative excesses which had brought on the panic, denounced it as a monopoly in words which were to be heard again in the fulminations against the Second Bank of the United States.

Despite these discouragements a water power installation and a cotton mill were completed, and the mill went into intermittent production on a small scale. After the Panic of 1796 all operations were brought to a halt. By this time the company had received $250,000 on stock subscriptions, and spent $30,000 for land, $67,150 for buildings, and retained a cash balance of $19,540.

The panic and stockjobbing were by no means the only reasons for the collapse of the SUM. More important was an abysmal failure in management and an inability to solve technological difficulties. Money was no problem. Even though the company lost some $60,000 through defalcations of Duer and a director to whom funds had likewise been entrusted, at all times during the first two or three years the treasury had adequate funds on hand in the form of government securities to finance a reasonable building program and operate a cotton mill. The supervisor, Peter Colt of Hartford, appears to have been an able mechanic, but his efforts were constantly frustrated by the inappropriate planning of Major L'Enfant, who was much more adept at designing heroic classical edifices than practical factory installations. Ostensibly skilled workers imported from England proved to be lethargic, sullen, and inept; the poorly designed machinery did not operate properly; and top management was uniformly inaccessible. Directors seldom visited the work site, and so distracted were they by their commercial affairs and financial problems that it proved impossible for months at a time to get together the quorums required for directors' meetings.

As the money drained away, wasted on amateurish improvisations or on visionary projects like a seven-mile cut stone aqueduct which could never conceivably be completed with the funds at hand, final decision making, by default, devolved upon Alexander Hamilton. Actually, he had been responsible for much of the confusion in the first place. It was he who had retained Major L'Enfant, hired the workmen, and recommended Duer as governor after the latter had been thoroughly discredited by his speculation in the funded debt. Nearly overwhelmed by his duties as secretary of the treasury while the company coasted downhill, Hamilton had neither the time nor the training to run an industrial enterprise in Passaic from a desk in Philadelphia.

But even if management had not been so uniformly incompetent, thirty-five to fifty years of technological experience would be necessary before any enterprise on the scale of the SUM could be successful. During the 1820s and 1830s Lowell, Massachusetts, evolved into a manufacturing center quite like the vision of the SUM promoters. Chicopee and Holyoke were built by the method which the SUM had hoped to inaugurate. Even with the much greater accumulation of capital and technological know-how then available, however, the construction of industrial towns and water power installations strained the engineering and financial resources of the capitalists who undertook the enterprises.

The suspension of the company's operations was an important event in American business history because it marked the end of attempts to start manufacturing enterprises on a large scale by joint public and private participation and by the granting of extensive corporate privileges. As we have seen, joint enterprise was to continue in the field of transportation, where large initial investments were required, but in manufacturing, where capital needs could be much smaller, there existed no such justification for government participation. Moreover, because of the smaller capital-output ratio for manufacturing than for canals or railroads, profits could be expected even before projects were completed, and expansion could therefore be increasingly financed internally without resort to successive bond issues which could not be absorbed by the private sector of the economy alone.

SAMUEL SLATER AND THE INTRODUCTION OF AUTOMATIC SPINNING MACHINERY

While Coxe, Hamilton, and Duer in the early 1790s were building their castles in the air, the firm of Almy, Brown, and Slater inaugurated a more humble but much more practical approach to manufacturing in Providence, Rhode Island. Moses Brown and his son-in-law, William Almy, were members of the venerable Brown family which for generations had been engaged in a variety of overseas and domestic trades and small-scale manufacture. Slater was an English artisan who had served an apprenticeship in a cotton mill equipped with Arkwright spinning machinery. Seeking wider opportunities for his considerable skill, he familiarized himself with the machinery with the intention of reproducing it, sailed for America, and in 1789 found employment in The New York Manufacturing Society, an organization similar to the Pennsylvania Society for the Encouragement of Manufactures. Aware that the lack of water power made it impossible to build an Arkwright frame in New York, Slater offered to construct the machine for Moses Brown, who he had heard was conducting experiments with textile machinery.

Slater's offer came at an opportune time. Brown had built a spinning jenny and a carding machine, and had copied a model of an Arkwright frame constructed on order of the Massachusetts government. But the jenny and card did not work well, and the spinning frame was a complete failure.* Now feeling hopeful that a successful spinning mill could be built, Brown and Almy negotiated a contract with Slater whereby in return for building two carding machines and a spinning frame Slater was to receive half the profits of the business and half-interest in the machinery. As merchants, Almy and Brown were to act as purchasing and sales agents for the mill on a commission basis. One year after signing of the contract the mill was in operation, powered by an old fulling mill wheel. Because of the simplicity of the Arkwright machinery only nine children, supervised by Slater, were required to run the mill.

As a business venture the Slater mill was successful for several reasons. The first, and most important, was Slater's mechanical skill. All other attempts to spin yarn by machinery had foundered because of lack of technical know-how. Second, there was an immediate, nearby market for the product of the mill. Because hand spinning was a slower process than hand weaving, home weavers were compelled to reduce the pace of their work to that of the spinners, or buy imported yarn. The Slater mill helped remove this bottleneck. Furthermore, since Slater did not attempt to produce cloth he did not have to face British competition and the deeply-rooted preference for British textiles. Slater's yarn was designed for the weavers who produced the rough cloth worn by the rural population. Since the capital invested in the mill was relatively small, the firm had no heavy overhead charges and could easily adjust output to meet market demands. With a work force of only nine children, operating costs were obviously low, doubtless somewhat lower than the cost of producing yarn on home spinning wheels. Later, as the mill expanded, Slater kept operating costs to a minimum by hiring families, as was done in England, and paying them partly in due bills on Almy and Brown's store. The aggressive marketing by the merchant firm was another reason for the success of the mill. Almy

---

* Carding is the preparatory operation in textile manufacturing by which cotton, wool, or flax fibers are combed parallel to each other and then are loosely formed into the hanks for spinning which are called roving. Carding machines of the nineteenth century consisted essentially of drums covered with wire teeth which rotated slowly through a mass of fiber, cleaning it and combing it out into roving. Spinning is the operation by which fibers are attached to each other by twisting and drawing, then wound on a bobbin as yarn. The Arkwright spinning frame, a vast improvement over the spinning jenny, drew the fibers by passing them through three sets of rollers, the second revolving faster than the first, and the third revolving faster than the second. The fibers were twisted while being wound on bobbins. In contrast to the jenny the Arkwright frame was a continuous action, fully automatic machine which could easily be harnessed to water power.

and Brown advertised extensively in newspapers and by 1801 were supplying retailers throughout New England and even in New York and
Philadelphia.

The Slater mill was vitally important not only as a pilot enterprise but
also as a seedbed for the spread of the textile industry northward through
the Blackstone River valley and westward into Connecticut. Ambitious
young mechanics, trained in the mill, picked out likely water power sites,
and formed partnerships with local merchants, landowners, and professional men to build and operate other Arkwright mills. Often these partnerships were kinship groups, and widening family alliances formed channels
through which expansion was effected. As in so many other nascent industries in early America, capital outlay was greatly reduced by contributions of land, labor, skills, materials, and equipment by the various partners
as their share of the investment. Labor was secured very cheaply from farm
families eking out a precarious living on the rocky, infertile countryside.
Merchant partners, in addition to sending yarn on consignment to correspondents in market centers, sometimes put a part of the yarn out to
neighborhood weavers, and then sold cloth as well. Some of the larger
mills brought weavers into the plants, and with the adoption of the automatic loom after 1820 integrated weaving into factory operation. Finishing, however—bleaching and dyeing—was put out for a much longer
period and until modern times was usually a function separated from cloth
manufacture. Directly or indirectly, Almy, Brown, and Slater fathered
most of the twenty-seven cotton mills which Secretary of the Treasury
Albert Gallatin found in southern New England in 1809. Slater himself
married into the Wilkinson family of Pawtucket, which had produced many
ingenious mechanics. Expanding his interests through the family's kinship connections, he entered into a series of partnerships whereby he
designed mills and provided part of the capital while other partners completed construction and supervised operations. Slater thus became one of
the first of a new breed of enterprisers in America—the industrial capitalists. At the outset of his career he had worked as an artisan dependent
upon the procurement and marketing services of a mercantile house of the
traditional type. But by the end of his career he was independent of any
such connection and derived his large income from the promotion, design,
and management of industrial operations.

THE BOSTON MANUFACTURING COMPANY AND THE BUILDING OF LOWELL

The third approach to textile manufacturing, which proved to be
the most successful and which foreshadowed the future course of indus-

trial development, was inaugurated by the formation of the Boston Manufacturing Company. The moving spirit of the organization was Francis Cabot Lowell, an energetic young merchant with kinship connections in wealthy Salem and Boston families and widespread acquaintance with the commercial community generally. On a trip to England in 1811, supposedly for his health, he utilized personal and business contacts to visit textile mills, and, like Samuel Slater some twenty-two or twenty-three years earlier, tried to commit to memory the design and construction of the machinery he saw with the object of reproducing it in the United States. He was particularly interested in the power loom, the most advanced piece of machinery in operation in Britain.

Returning to Boston in 1812, Lowell prevailed upon Patrick Tracy Jackson to join him in constructing an integrated, automatic textile mill which would combine spinning and weaving. Like Lowell, Jackson was a young merchant with extensive kinship connections in prominent mercantile families. The two brought together a group of prominent businessmen who subscribed for $100,000 worth of stock and in 1813 incorporated the Boston Manufacturing Company. Much of the original investment—much smaller than the total subscription—probably represented mercantile profits made in overseas trade during the halcyon period of 1792 to 1807. The coming of the War of 1812 threatened to bring a total stoppage of trade, which had been curtailed since 1807. Most of the some 210 small spinning mills in operation by 1811 were quite successful, and the cessation of imports would not only increase the market for yarn but create a market for domestically manufactured cloth as well.

The project of an integrated mill might well have gone the way of the SUM had not Lowell and Jackson secured the services of Paul Moody as construction engineer and supervisor of the plant. Moody was an artisan with better than average education who had taken full advantage of the opportunities for training in practical mechanics offered by the many types of mills and shops in Massachusetts. Moody and Lowell spent a year in constructing a power loom while a mill and water power installation were being built at Waltham, on the Charles River several miles west of Boston. By the end of 1813 the mill was in working order, although no cloth was placed on the market until 1815. The success of the Boston Manufacturing Company was immediate, and all the more remarkable in the years after the War of 1812 when so much nascent American industry succumbed to British competition. A second mill was begun in 1816. By 1822 annual sales reached $345,000, and in the next year total assets, valued at $39,000 in 1814, amounted to $771,000.

Meanwhile, Patrick Jackson, chief executive officer of the company, and the directors had purchased a large water power site on the Merrimack River twenty-five miles north of Boston. In 1823 the Boston Manufacturing Company moved to this location in order to obtain additional power needed for expansion, and was renamed the Merrimack Company. Backers of the enterprise, their number swelled by other merchants seeking profitable industrial investments for their capital, now proceeded to realize the dream of Hamilton and Coxe by building an industrial city. Aware that the problems of building a water power installation were quite different than those of operating a textile plant, the directors spun off the construction activities to a company known as The Proprietors of the Locks and Canals on the Merrimack River. Under Moody's direction, this organization also fathered a textile machinery company still in existence—the Saco-Lowell Shops.

At an initial cost of $120,000 the proprietors constructed a dam and canals, and plotted fifty factory sites, each with a fall of water from the feed canal sufficient to drive 3,584 spindles. Companies settling on the sites paid $4 per spindle for use of the water power plus an annual rent of $300 for the land. Appropriately named Lowell, the town grew rapidly as new mills—the Hamilton, Appleton, Lawrence, Suffolk, Tremont, and Middlesex—were built. Dwellings, boarding houses, and stores were constructed to house and maintain workers. The entire enterprise was carried out by an expanding group of merchant capitalists with widely ramified and interlocking interests who came to be known as "the Boston Associates." Fortified by the experience and the profits gained from the development of Lowell, the group was to play a prominent part in the building of many other industrial communities, among them Lawrence, Chicopee, Holyoke, Manchester, Dover, and Nashua.

Many factors contributed to the success of the Boston Manufacturing Company and its successors on the Merrimack. First, probably, was the ability of the leading figures. Francis Lowell was not only a capable merchant, but, in contrast to the promoters of the SUM, he was an able self-taught engineer as well. Recognizing the primacy of technological problems he devoted intense efforts to reproducing the British power loom. In the course of this task he made intricate mathematical calculations, drafted blueprints, and drew patterns for individual parts. Paul Moody made the parts to specification, assembled the loom, and by modifications and adjustments made it into an efficiently operating machine. The merchants Nathan Appleton and Abbot Lawrence played key roles in rounding up the capital for the enterprise even though Appleton, at least, was highly dubious of its success. Kirk Boote, first agent (chief executive officer) of the Merrimack Company, deserves much credit for the later success of the organization. A trained engineer who had served in Wellington's army, he was able and imperious, and thoroughly dominated the little empire under his control until his death in 1837.

The ample financial resources of the Lowell companies constituted another reason for their success. Appleton insisted that no more then two-thirds of a capital fund be spent in constructing production facilities; the remainder he felt should be retained as working capital. Violation of this excellent rule has led to hundreds of thousands of business failures from that day to this. Agents and supervisors were expected to devote their full time to their jobs, and were proportionally well paid. Directors, appointed from among the large stockholders, were close at hand and participated in procurement, marketing, and finance; but it appears that they increasingly delegated decision making in production matters to the salaried personnel. The decision of the Boston Manufacturing Company to limit its production to rough sheetings was also a success factor. This was an article in broad demand, not only in New England but also in the southern states where it was used for slave clothing. Since the low cost of sheetings was increased proportionally more by transatlantic freight charges than the cost of more expensive materials, British competition was minimal. When some Rhode Island mills, shut down in 1815 because of British competition, installed power looms on Appelton's advice, they soon recovered their prosperity by turning out the rough fabrics for which there was a large market. To add to the advantages of American producers, Francis Lowell lobbied successfully in Washington for an increase in tariff rates on sheetings in the tariff bill of 1816.

The methods of labor recruitment and maintenance also contributed to the success of the Lowell companies. With the building of powered mills companies could no longer settle in urban areas, but were forced to locate on waterfalls often far removed from readily available labor. Slater, as we have seen, had solved the labor problem by settling families near his mills and using principally the labor of children. But by leaving fathers often unemployed and dependent, this system had bad social consequences. Lowell, who had seen the degradation of English mill villages brought about by this practice, was determined not to introduce it into the United States. Also, reverberations of Jeffersonian dogma concerning the corruption of populations brought about by industrialization may have sharpened the sensitivity of Lowell and the associates to moral issues implicit in their enterprise. Therefore Lowell adopted at the outset a policy of recruiting teenage girls from farm families and establishing them in decent boarding houses built near the mills. Earnings of $2.00 to $3.25 per week, of which $1.25 was deducted for board, were abysmally low by our standards today, but were greater than women could make in any other occupation and were generous in comparison with the returns from farm labor. Kept under close supervision, the girls were given religious instruction and rudimentary education and were exposed to cultural influences by lyceums. Lowell's labor policy removed objections to mill work by parents solicitous for the moral welfare of their daughters, and the low cost of board allowed the girls to accumulate small dowries by a few years of work. In slack times they could go back to the farms and return to the mills when conditions were better. The "Lowell System," while falling short of the romantic panegyrics of some of its advocates, became known and admired throughout the United States and England, and certainly brought better working conditions than those in industrial centers elsewhere.

Finally, the Lowell firms had a very advantageous location. The Middlesex Canal, and later the Boston and Lowell Railroad promoted by Patrick Jackson, provided competing transportation links with Boston, a major distributing center and home port for much shipping engaged in the cotton trade. The moist climate of Lowell aided mill operations, and the clear river water made bleaching and dyeing possible.

The inauguration of the industrial revolution in America was easier than could have been expected, primarily because of good timing and a fortunate combination of all the factors making industrial production possible. The boom in overseas trade beginning in 1793 created surplus capital which could be fed into industry as the profits from trade declined after 1807. The curtailment and final cessation of imports during the War of 1812 revealed a market for rough fabrics in which domestic producers would have a comparative advantage over English producers. Technological problems were solved by imitation and improvement of British machinery. Labor with adequate skills could be found throughout the New England countryside, and entrepreneurs to handle financing, procurement, and marketing operated in all seaport towns. Finally, the raw material, cotton, was being produced in volume more than adequate to meet the mounting needs of the mills.

Actually, the inauguration of the cotton textile industry was not as easy as the above summary would indicate, but perhaps the greatest oversimplification lies in the implicit assumption that the process merely *happened* as a response to external stimuli such as market conditions. Actually the cultural heritage of the American people was an indispensable element, and without its fortunate configuration of motivations, values, and skills, the happening could not have taken place.

VIII. Overseas Shipping and Commerce

After the boom and bust cycle of 1816 to 1820 the American economy began to grow rapidly, favored by nearly all of the factors necessary for economic expansion. During the antebellum period the merchant marine rose from 1,299,000 tons to 5,354,000 tons, and the value of exports from $65,000,000 to $400,000,000. The large seaboard cities, with their multifarious commercial, financial, and transportation services were at once a cause and an effect of growth. New York was by far the most important in this regard. With a populous hinterland, and trade contacts reaching back via the Hudson River to the fertile areas upstate, the city was able to reap greater advantages from the European wars of the nineties than its rivals on the seaboard. Also, its merchant class was considered particularly aggressive. With a population which tripled between 1790 and 1810 it passed both Boston and Philadelphia and emerged, with 96,000 people, as the largest city in the nation. By 1860 its population was nearly one million.

A series of business and commercial developments combined with natural advantages to stimulate this growth. After completion of the Erie

Canal, New York became a major entrepôt for western produce and a major distributor of imported goods in the West. As a great emporium of goods, it was a focus for wholesalers and retailers from all over the country, who made annual trips to the metropolis to buy their year's stock. When the charter of the Second Bank of the United States lapsed, New York became without question the financial center of the nation, and its mounting ability to finance commerce drew more and more of it away from disappointed rivals. By advancing long-term credit to southern planters New York merchants were able to secure nearly one-third of all cotton produced, and shipped much of this to England on the second leg of the "cotton triangle" in payment for imported manufactured goods. Large earnings from ocean commerce and its ancillary services swelled the profits already gained from merchandising and banking. New York's shipping also made it a focus of the immigrant trade and of transoceanic and coastal steamship lines. As financial functions became rapidly specialized, an increasing amount of public and corporate securities gravitated to its stock market, and it naturally became a center for brokerage and insurance. By 1855 the city had twenty millionaires, and one individual out of 500 could be accounted wealthy. With 838,000 tons of shipping on its register in 1860, about two-thirds of the nation's total, it had a foreign trade six times greater than that of all New England.

Businessmen of Boston, Philadelphia, and Baltimore viewed the burgeoning prosperity of their arch rival with envy and anxiety. For a wide variety of reasons, some imperfectly understood even today, these seaports did not grow at the rate maintained by New York. Yet, judged by a less exalted standard their progress was impressive, and in all cases the proliferation and specialization of commercial institutions was marked.

BRITISH FINANCE IN AMERICAN COMMERCE

This specialization did not bring about the financial independence from Britain which might be expected, however. On the contrary, London merchant bankers, continuing to finance American importations by advance of long-term credit, exerted nearly as much financial control over Anglo-American trade as during the colonial period.

The measure of British influence could be seen in the spread of auction selling after the War of 1812. Anxious to work off overstocks of goods and "stifle American manufacturing in the cradle," British merchants dumped large amounts of goods on the American market, chiefly in New York. Here the goods were sold at auction to jobbers and wholesalers, thus bypassing the American importer. The importer's profit, often as high as 100 percent, was in effect split between the exporter and the American whole-sale purchaser. Quick turnover and cash payments reduced the cost of sales at least two-thirds. By systematically undercutting the general importing merchant, the auction system brought about the virtual demise of this venerable type of entrepreneur.

But after 1830 the amount of goods distributed by auction declined. American merchants began to specialize in their importations, and with the financial assistance of the "American" banking houses of London, gained direct contact with the British merchant middleman. Agents of American firms resident in England opened credit accounts with "American" houses such as the Barings, Rothschilds, Browns, or the houses of Thomas Wilson, Timothy Wiggin, or George Wilde. English manufacturers could be paid in bills drawn against these accounts, and payment to the bankers ultimately made in the form of cotton or other American goods dispatched to them. Often an American importer wishing to buy from a British manufacturer would secure a letter of credit from the American agent of a British banker. Upon notification of the grant of credit the British banker would accept bills drawn upon him by the British manufacturers, and would send the invoices and bills of lading to the American agent to be held until payment for the goods by the importer. Variations of this new system of exchange were an improvement over the traditional way of making remittances by purchase of bills on London in the open market. Under the old system fluctuations in the price of exchange made it difficult for the importer to determine in advance the cost of any single transaction. Financing by the "American" houses, however, was uniform, quick, and relatively inexpensive. As London became a major financial center for the entire trading world, American importers of oriental or Latin American goods were able to make their payments by bills drawn on their London bankers.

The effects of British credit extended deep into the internal market. Since the London bankers allowed very liberal credit terms, American jobbers and wholesalers were able to grant corresponding benefits to their own customers. Of course, membership in this vast British credit union had its drawbacks. A money panic on the London market could send shock waves rolling to the most secluded country store in the American West, bringing bankruptcies all along the way. Yet despite these periodic crises reliance on British commercial credit was inevitable. Rapid American economic growth absorbed surplus funds so quickly that importers and exporters would have found it very difficult to finance their operations without outside aid.

WOODEN SHIPBUILDING AND SHIPPING OPERATIONS

An important factor stimulating the expansion of overseas commerce before 1860 was the superiority of American ships and the rapid growth of the shipbuilding industry. Although a third-rate nation in terms of military and naval power, the United States by 1800 was second to Britain in merchant tonnage and equaled Britain in this respect by 1860. During the antebellum period shipbuilding continued to be carried on in small yards not markedly different from those of the colonial era. The industry produced no monopolists or financiers, and surprisingly enough, in practically no instances made fortunes for even the most skillful builders. Most ships were built on contract for merchants, acting singly or in groups. Often seafaring men themselves, they worked closely with master shipwrights in the design and construction of the vessels. Between 1820 and 1860 the cost per ton of conventional brigs and ships was about $34, as compared with $55 to $65 in Britain, Holland, or France. The greater availability and lower cost of ship timber in the United States provided a competitive cost advantage which more than offset higher wages in American yards.

Other economies made United States shipping a strong competitor in world trade. Until the 1850s masters and crews came from a more stable stratum of society than those of European countries and were often considered to be more skillful in their profession. As a result, American ships could be operated with .5 to 1.5 fewer men per hundred tons than European vessels. Generous allowances of cargo space for private ventures and small commissions on proceeds of the voyages helped attract high quality officers. In Boston's China trade, for instance, a master could easily multiply his wages of $300 per year ten times by astute utilization of these advantages. Better built, American ships generally outlasted those constructed by European competitors, and therefore permitted the initial cost to be spread over a longer period of use.

The career of the American wooden shipbuilding industry came to a dramatic climax with the building of the great clipper ships. Their beauty and speed evoked admiration the world over, yet for all their glamour the clippers were by no means as economical or practical as the bluff-bowed freighters of a generation before. Requiring the finest ship timber and a multitude of metal fastenings, their construction cost varied from $55 to $100 per ton, and could amount to $125,000 for a full rigged ship—twice the cost of even the largest vessels of the twenties. Carrying capacity was not proportionally increased, however, and the complex rigging and multiple sails required a crew twice as large as needed on ships of 300 to

400 tons. Under hard-driving masters depreciation was rapid as spars were carried away and sails often split. As one captain complained, a clipper was "a thousand-ton ship in capacity and a two-thousand-ton ship to keep in repair." Yet in the booming days of the early fifties when the passenger traffic to California was heavy and shippers of Oriental goods would pay double rates for swift carriage, clippers could sometimes earn their cost in a few round-the-world voyages from east coast cities to San Francisco, and from there to Canton for a load of exotic wares destined for Liverpool. But the halcyon days of the clippers ended when freight rates plunged as a result of the Panic of 1857. Passengers to California increasingly used the Panama route, now dominated by steamship companies. First wooden, and then iron steamships emerged clearly as the ocean carriers of the future. No more clippers were built after 1857, and those in service, denuded of their mountainous rigging, often ended their days ignominiously as coal scows or lumber schooners.

The ownership and operation of ships were carried on in a wide variety of ways. Some merchants owned vessels in connection with their business, and a few of the most wealthy—among them William Gray, Elias Hasket Derby, and Joseph Peabody of Salem; Archibald Gracie, Daniel Ludlow, and John Jacob Astor of New York; and Stephen Girard of Philadelphia—possessed veritable fleets. Some large-scale owners regularly sold carrying space to others. Ownership of individual ships was often divided into fractions as low as sixty-fourths, and widespread participation was common even among smaller vessels. Sometimes owners appointed "ships' husbands" who managed vessels in return for a commission on their earnings. Although there were a few large shipping firms before 1850, like Leroy Bayard and Company, and Grinnell and Minturn—both of New York—the corporate form did not become common in the business until after this time, and then mostly for steamboat lines. Captains often invested in the ships they commanded, and merchants, hoping to secure profits on the transportation as well as the sale of their goods, often bought shares in the vessels which regularly carried these goods. Shippers, insurers, brokers, and owners made their arrangements with each other at daily meetings on the floor of the New York Merchants' Exchange. The westbound rate from Liverpool to New York was traditionally $10 per ton; eastbound rates were somewhat less and more varied because the commodities which made up the bulk of the carriage fluctuated in price and could not afford to pay the rate charged for "fine freight."

The organization of the shipping business changed little from the Middle Ages to the nineteenth century, but in 1817 came a major innovation when the Black Ball Line, the nation's first transatlantic packet service, began regular, scheduled trips between New York and England. Inauguration of the service, with ships which ran loaded or in ballast, in fair weather or foul, was a bold and revolutionary business venture which, after many centuries of merchant shipowning, finally began the separation of the mercantile from the ocean transport function. Soon capturing the bulk of the high rate "fine freight" and passenger business, the Black Ball Line was a shining success. Imitators followed, and by 1822 four liners a month sailed for Liverpool from New York. Attempts to establish packet lines in the other port cities were not as successful. The maintenance of the service required a heavy flow of freight relatively unaffected by seasonal variations into the ports for transshipment. None of the east coast cities could match New York in this regard. On the westward run the packets carried large numbers of immigrants.

Packet lines were usually profitable. The ships, costing about $50,000 to $70,000 apiece, were not large by even the standards of the day, but were fast, well-built, and economical to operate. In keeping with the traditions of merchant shipowning, the lines were not capitalized by the issuance of stock but by the sale of shares in ships. Each vessel was considered an entity in itself, of which investors could purchase eights, sixteenths, or in some cases even sixty-fourths. Some twenty-five or thirty major owners in the lines investigated by the historian of packets, Robert G. Albion, left fortunes of between $100,000 and $500,000—very substantial ones for the antebellum period. The packets competed successfully with the first steamships, but declined with the coming of the large, subsidized lines such as Cunard and Collins.

THE BEGINNINGS OF A STEAM MERCHANT MARINE AND
EXPERIMENTS WITH GOVERNMENT SUBSIDIES

Building and operating steamships proved to be more difficult than the construction and operation of sailing vessels. At the outset Great Britain possessed a competitive advantage in the machine shops, heavy industry, and skilled labor necessary to turn out engines and iron reinforced hulls. The first American ocean steamship, the *Savannah*, launched in 1819 in an ambitious attempt by Georgia capitalists to inaugurate direct packet service to Europe, used her paddle wheels only about eighty hours during the twenty-seven-day maiden voyage from Savannah to Liverpool. So unsuccessful was the power plant that it was later removed and the ship consigned to the coasting trade. Other ventures with steamships were tried sporadically during the thirties, but because of breakdowns, rapid depreciation, and high operating costs, these vessels simply could not compete with the sailing packet lines. From 1847 to 1860, however, registered steam ocean tonnage rose from 5,631 tons to 97,296 tons.

In part the advance was due to the rapid increase in the size of the ships. But equally important were government subsidies to important lines in the form of heavily inflated payments for carrying mail. Since the Middle Ages, in the Western world, merchant shipping had been owned and operated by thousands of small entrepreneurs and a lesser number of large merchants. Because of its strategic significance in maritime and naval policy, all nations had protected their shipping from foreign competition by discriminatory navigation acts. Nevertheless, within the circle of this legislation the shipping business was carried on under conditions of free competition. But the building and operation of steamships required the resources and organization of big business, and—at the early stage of development—government assistance. In a few short years, therefore, both here and in Europe ocean steamship lines became the large government-sponsored enterprises, few in number and heavily freighted with national interest, which they remain today.

The policy of subsidizing steamship lines was inaugurated in 1836 by the nation which was shortly to profess undying devotion to the principles of laissez-faire—Great Britain. By 1850 Britain was the center of a network of steamship lines, subsidized at $3.7 million per year, radiating outward to all parts of the world. One of the most successful was the Cunard Line, capitalized at over $1 million, operating six large ships between Boston, New York, and Liverpool, and subsidized in 1848 at $705,600 per year. Congress, fearful that Britain would choke off opportunities for American steam navigation, agreed to subsidize a line to be founded by E. K. Collins, principal owner of the Dramatic Packet Line and an experienced operator of passenger ships. In return for an initial subsidy of $385,000 per year (later increased to $858,000), Collins contracted to form a company which would construct and operate five large steamships making twenty round trips annually between New York and Liverpool. Determined to outdo the Cunard Line, Collins constructed ships that were larger, faster, and more luxurious than those of this principal competitor. They were also much more expensive to build and operate, and required a complete overhaul after every voyage. One vessel, the huge *Adriatic*, 4,144 tons burden, cost over $1 million, yet was so inefficient that it was laid up after one year of operation.

When Congress, under the leadership of southerners jealous of New York's control of southern trade and finance, abandoned the subsidy policy in 1858, the Collins Line collapsed. In part the failure was due to the loss of the *Arctic* by collision in 1854, with heavy casualties, and the *Pacific*, which disappeared with all hands in 1856. Bad planning and mismanagement added to the gravity of these disasters. All voyages showed hopeless deficits, even though the Collins Line carried 50 percent more passengers westbound and 30 percent more eastbound than the Cunard line. Britain's competitive advantages in construction also played a part in bringing about the demise of the Collins Line. Large wooden steamers cost 25 percent less to build there, and had better engines and fittings, thanks to the more advanced state of British heavy industry. Two other subsidized lines were more fortunate than the Collins Line. The United States Mail Steamship Company, running between New York, Havana, and Panama, and the Pacific Mail Line, connecting Panama and San Francisco, were both started on government subsidies, and were able to operate at a profit after the subsidies were withdrawn.

After the Civil War the American shipping business went into the doldrums, and remained there until World War I. Tonnage remained practically stationary, and at no point in the late nineteenth century equaled the figure of 1861, the peak year. American ships had carried 92 percent of American trade in 1807, but the figure drifted downward with increasing rapidity to 10 percent in 1914. One reason for the plight of shipping was the restriction of registry to American-built ships. As long as American builders had a competitive advantage over those of Europe because of cheaper raw materials, this policy was not disadvantageous, but when the cost differentials were reversed during the transition from sailing vessels to iron steamships, American shipbuilding suffered a real blow. High labor and maintenance costs merely compounded the difficulties. As capital gravitated toward the industrial, railroad, and mining sectors of the economy, the United States yielded its position as a great maritime nation to European competitors such as Britain, the Netherlands, Norway, and Greece.

IX. Steamboats Revolutionize River Transportation

STEAMBOATS ON EASTERN WATERS

Steamboating on coastal and inland waters was a transportation innovation which American entrepreneurs conducted much more successfully than the operation of transoceanic steamship lines. No competition from foreigners had to be faced, the relative lack of good roads created an immediate need for improved river transportation, and steamboats were far less costly to build and maintain than ocean liners. Steamboats revolutionized transportation on the river systems of the Mississippi and its tributaries by inaugurating fast and cheap service upriver as well as downriver, and thereby contributed tremendously to the growth of the Midwest.

In contrast to the free competition which characterized the operation of packet lines and the sailing merchant marine, steamboating on eastern waters from the outset was conducted by powerful monopolies which fought each other with all the strategies of rate wars, political manipulation, and outright violence used later during the period of railroad consolidation. As innovators of a transportation service which plainly offered great benefits to the nation, early steamboat entrepreneurs felt that they had a claim upon the public for reimbursement of their considerable expenditures and encouragement for their future efforts. Thus they not only sought patents on their mechanical inventions, but, like turnpike companies, also demanded monopolies of specific routes—in this case the major rivers of the nation. Since most of the early steamboat promoters were men of wealth and influence, they usually got what they wanted.

Work on steam engines had been in progress in England since the early eighteenth century, and experiments with steamboats were undertaken in the United States by Oliver Evans, James Rumsey, John Fitch, and John Stevens, among others. Fitch was the first to get a practical steamboat in operation. An itinerant clock repairer with a suspicious, contentious nature but extraordinary mechanical ingenuity, Fitch—like other inventors who lacked entrepreneurial skills—was doomed to see the rewards of his considerable skill go to others. In 1785, while temporarily residing in Philadelphia, he became interested in steam engines. With his accustomed fervor he plunged into the task of designing a steamboat even though he had never seen one, nor even a steam engine, for that matter. To finance construction he formed a joint stock company from among petty tradesmen of Philadelphia whom he had come to know through pursuit of his craft of clock repairer, and by 1787 had a steamboat in operation which performed for the members of the Constitutional Convention. Receiving further financing from Dr. William Thornton, a former West Indies planter who later became the first superintendent of the United States Patent Office, he obtained fourteen-year monopolies for steamboat operation from the legislatures of New Jersey, New York, Pennsylvania, Delaware, and Virginia. Although he constructed a second boat which ran on regular schedule between Philadelphia and Burlington, New Jersey, the enterprise was a commercial failure apparently because the craft was so small and uncomfortable that it could not compete with the established means of transportation. After a decade of further unsuccessful efforts to establish steamboat service, Fitch committed suicide, a confirmed alcoholic, bitter over his manifold failures.

Like Fitch, Robert Fulton, who developed the first commercially successful steamboat, came from a humble background and early exhibited mechanical skill. But in contrast to Fitch he had a warm, outgoing personality, a talent for friendship, and considerable entrepreneurial ability. Also, like Samuel F. B. Morse, and the famed Leonardo da Vinci, he combined engineering and artistic talent. Beginning his career in Philadelphia as a miniaturist, he moved to London in 1786 to study and work with his celebrated compatriot, Benjamin West. But during the next few years his interests were drawn more and more toward engineering projects. He designed a spinning machine for flax, a mill to saw marble, and wrote a treatise on canal construction. Moving to Paris in 1793 where he shared quarters with Joel Barlow—the wealthy Connecticut merchant, poet, dedicated republican and agent of the Scioto Company—Fulton designed and built a workable submarine and crude torpedoes, and vainly tried to interest the French government in subsidizing the development of undersea warfare.

Fulton's attention was focused on steamboats by Robert R. Livingston, who had been appointed American minister to France in 1801. Member of a great landed family of New York and chancellor of equity jurisdiction, Livingston had enjoyed a distinguished career in state and national politics since the beginning of the Revolution. Interested in mechanics and no doubt aware of the revolutionary potentialities of the steamboat, he acquired Fitch's monopolies after Fitch's death. Livingston's brother-in-law, John Stevens, a landed magnate of New Jersey with influence as great as Livingston's and with an even keener interest in mechanics which he later demonstrated by building the first railroad locomotive in America, had also become vitally interested in steamboats as a result of Fitch's experiments. In 1800 Livingston, Stevens, and Nicholas Roosevelt had entered into a partnership to build steamboats. Roosevelt was a valuable addition to the enterprise because he owned a foundry on the Passaic river capable of forging the components for engines. All that was lacking was an engineer to design and build the boat. Livingston solved this problem in 1802 by persuading Fulton to join the combine. In the next year Fulton and Livingston built a steamboat on the Seine, which operated successfully. In 1806 the two returned to the United States with a Boulton and Watt engine, purchased in England after protracted negotiations. Fulton then constructed the *Clermont*, which, by its dramatic thirty-two hour run from New York to Albany in 1807, firmly established the steamboat as a means of transportation. Livingston had assumed the financing of the vessel— much faster and much more commodious than Fitch's boat. Stevens had pulled out of the combine before completion of the *Clermont*—an action he later regretted.

Steamboat service between New York and Albany was an immediate financial success in contrast to Fitch's venture on the Delaware because the voyage by water between New York and Albany was faster, cheaper, and more comfortable than the trip by stage. By 1810 Fulton and Livingston were making $50,000 a year from two boats on the Hudson. Their total investment at this time was probably no more than $60,000 to $70,000.

Despite these returns, steamboating brought no wealth to Fulton, nor did it increase the chancellor's fortune. Construction of new boats and endless litigation undertaken to protect the Hudson monopoly against vigorous and determined interlopers drained off most of the profits from operations. In view of the rapidly increasing popularity of steamboat travel, the two men would probably have done better by abandoning the monopoly and concentrating all their funds in the improvement of service. Commodore Vanderbilt was to show that competition itself can become a more effective instrument for diminishing competition than can legal privilege.

The profits and bright future of steamboating brought many eager entrants on the major rivers of the seaboard. Stevens, pushed out of New York harbor by the monopolists, recapitalized a small packet company of Philadelphia and with it secured a monopoly of steamboat travel on the Delaware similar to that enjoyed by Livingston and Fulton on the Hudson. Steamboats quickly achieved a near-monopoly of passenger service on heavily traveled routes such as New York–Albany and New York-Philadelphia, in the latter case with a New Brunswick-Trenton stage connection between the Raritan and the Delaware legs of the trip. Moreover, since the urban population of the Northeast was increasing so rapidly, the steamboat companies by creating tourism as a popular diversion further increased the volume of their business. From the outset steamboats in the East had carried far more passengers than freight, and patronage of the boats multiplied as they became more luxurious and commodious. Stevens estimated that a vessel on the New York–New Brunswick run which cost $75,000 to build would yield a net return of 33 1/3 percent per year. But if Stevens in his accounting utilized a realistic figure for depreciation, net returns of this magnitude would not necessarily indicate large profits. Depreciation of steamboats was always much more rapid than for sailing vessels and the incidence of accidents was greater. As a result the life span of steamboats over which the capital investment had to be returned was short.

CORNELIUS VANDERBILT

Although Stevens had been expelled from the profitable New York–New Brunswick route, future interlopers were more difficult to dislodge. In 1813 Colonel Aaron Ogden, governor of New Jersey and a man whose wealth and influence equaled that of Livingston, attempted to operate a line terminating in New York harbor. After a lively legal skirmish, Ogden bowed to the monopoly and bought a license for his operations. But in a second interloper, Thomas Gibbons, a former Savannah planter with large interests in New York real estate and in turnpike and banking companies, the monopoly found a more formidable rival. Belligerent and vengeful, Gibbons ran two vessels on the New York–New Brunswick route in direct competition with Ogden. The intensity of the rivalry greatly increased when Gibbons employed Cornelius Vanderbilt as captain of one of his boats.

Vanderbilt is a very significant figure in the history of entrepreneurship, primarily because he was the first individual in the United States to make a great fortune out of a service rather than some form of merchandising or banking. Also, he is notable for the manner in which he refined and expanded the various practices of cutthroat competition which became standard for big business later in the century.

Born to a poor farm family which had lived on Staten Island for generations, young "Cornele" began his career at the age of sixteen by operating a small sailing ferry between Staten Island and Manhattan. Foreshadowing his later emphasis on efficiency, he was said to have adhered to such rigid schedules of sailing, even in the bitterest weather, that his patrons could set their watches by the time of his arrivals and departures. During the War of 1812 he carried supplies for the garrisons in the harbor, and after the coming of peace invested his savings in an oyster boat and coasting vessels. In 1817, at twenty-three years of age, he was a successful businessman with assets at $15,000.

Aware of the bright opportunities in the steamboat business, he sold most of his interests in sailing vessels, invested the proceeds in a New Brunswick tavern catering to New York-Philadelphia travelers, and—at a considerable sacrifice—became captain of Gibbons's steamboat. The two men were admirably suited to the bracing, bare-knuckle business of battling the monopoly controlling the New York–New Brunswick run. While Gibbons fought the monopoly in the courts, and carried on a particularly virulent personal vendetta against Ogden, Vanderbilt managed to cut costs, improve service, and elude process servers by bold and imaginative stratagems. This latter phase of the warfare was brought to an end by the decision in the famous case of Gibbons *vs.* Ogden, delivered in 1824, in which the Supreme Court declared the Hudson River traffic to be interstate trade over which Congress, and not the states, had plenary power. In the next year the New York legislature repealed the Hudson River monopoly. Other states almost immediately took similar actions, and the monopolies of use came to an end.

In the era of monopolistic competition which followed, Vanderbilt swept ahead of all rivals. The secret of his success was simply offering at lowest cost the fastest and best steamboat service available. With military precision Vanderbilt and Gibbons combined stage lines across the neck of New Jersey with a steamboat line on the Delaware, and thereby cut the time of the New York–Philadelphia run via New Brunswick and Trenton to a single day. In 1829 Vanderbilt challenged the Hudson River Association (the allied companies formerly enjoying the legal monopoly), by placing his own vessel on the New York–Albany run and cutting fares.

During the following decade he built up a small fleet of steamboats on the Hudson, and steadily accumulated the competitive advantages of efficiency. With his most unusual perception, adaptability, and drive, he mastered every aspect of his business, from the design of hulls and engines to the cuisine in his restaurants. He spared no expense for the improvement of service. By 1839 the association had had enough, and rid themselves of Vanderbilt by persuading him to abandon the Hudson in return for a lump sum of $100,000 plus an annual subsidy of $5,000 per year.

The remainder of Vanderbilt's career was an unqualified record of success. Thriving on competition, fair or otherwise, he placed several splendid steamboats on Long Island Sound. Later he entered the coastal lanes by operating boats between Boston and Portsmouth, and Wilmington and Charleston. He also bought the Staten Island Ferry. Vanderbilt was quick to seize the opportunities for steamboat operators offered by the California gold rush. With a group of associates he formed a company to operate steamboats between New York, Nicaragua, and Panama, but the two lines already established on this run—the United States Mail and the Pacific Mail—were so alarmed by the fearsome prospect of competition with Vanderbilt that between 1856 and 1858 they paid him $1.2 million to transfer his operations elsewhere.

Meanwhile, Vanderbilt entered the transatlantic run with two liners, one a magnificent vessel costing $500,000, the largest and most luxurious afloat and therefore appropriately named after himself. But although he operated at a profit he realized after the collapse of the Collins Line that the withdrawal of mail subsidies placed American-owned lines at a competitive disadvantage to those of Britain. Aware of the greater profit potential in railroads, he took advantage of high wartime shipping prices to sell off his fleet in 1864 and thereby prepared, at the age of seventy, to enter a new career in which he was to make a dazzling success.

Historians usually award Vanderbilt a prominent position in the fraternity of the robber barons. Yet except for his suppression of competition, his guilt was by association rather than actions. In contrast to men like Jay Gould and Daniel Drew, with whom he was to come to grips at a later date, he never used his enterprises as a mere springboard for financial manipulations. All of his life he had strong proprietary feelings of responsibility which had characterized an earlier generation of entrepreneurs. Under his direction the New York Central, no less than his steamboats at an earlier date, offered constantly improved service, and at his death was considered by many to be the finest railroad in the world as far as equipment was concerned. He expected to make his money in the transportation business rather than out of it. The unofficial title "Commodore," bestowed upon him by friends and the press, symbolically expressed his role as he saw it: that of a commander personally directing the palpable power of a transportation system.

As a personality Vanderbilt was no more typical of his peers than was Girard. A bluff, direct, self-made man whose distinguished appearance contrasted sharply with vulgar tastes, he had no desire for social or political eminence, and no use at all for any of the finer things of life. Although honest according to the lenient standards of the day, he did not hesitate to exploit anyone who stood athwart his highway to success, and he destroyed rivals without compunction simply because they were rivals. Although he drove himself unmercifully in times of crisis, he was not a consistently hard worker. He left business routine to a trusted subordinate or to his son or sons-in-law. The few letters he wrote were marred by execrable spelling and usage, and after he achieved success he never kept regular business hours. His recreation was as competitive as his career: racing steamboats with himself at the helm, driving spanking bays on a harness track, or playing all night games of whist with cronies. Business also was a game, and Vanderbilt valued winning for its own sake as much as the financial rewards of the victory. He owed his great success to his ability to comprehend every aspect of his business, to see clearly the main chances for advancement in terms of service and combination of units, and to push his plans forward with confidence and courage undiminished by setbacks.

STEAMBOATING ON WESTERN RIVERS

Steamboating developed quite differently on western than on eastern waters. Before the coming of steam, swift currents in the Mississippi River and in its tributaries had made river transportation primarily a one-way affair. Produce from the upcountry, loaded on large flatboats called "arks," was slowly rowed or poled down the river systems to New Orleans, where the boats—often put together with wooden pegs—were dismantled and sold as lumber. High-value, low-bulk goods were taken upriver in "keelboats"—sharp, double prowed, light draft vessels driven with great labor by crews which set poles in the river bottoms and then walked the boats against the currents. Sometimes keelboats required three or four months to make the trip from New Orleans to Louisville, and nearly six months from New Orleans to Pittsburgh.

Because of the enormous difficulties of upriver travel and the almost complete lack of adequate land transportation, Fitch, Livingston, and Fulton had recognized that steamboats could play a role in the West even more vital than on eastern rivers. Complete lack of financial resources had of course prevented Fitch from promoting steamboat travel in the West, but in 1811 Nicholas Roosevelt, acting for Livingston and Fulton, constructed the *New Orleans* at Pittsburgh, the first steamboat on western waters. The revolutionary impact of its voyage down the Ohio and Mississippi in late 1811 was not lost on enterprising businessmen of the region. By 1817 fourteen steamboats were plying the waters of the lower Mississippi, and two years later thirty-one were operating on western rivers. In 1869, 735 steamboats were serving an area half the size of the United States stretching from New Orleans to St. Paul on the Mississippi, and from Pittsburgh at the head of the Ohio to Fort Benton at the headwaters of the Missouri.

By 1824 the three or four months required by keelboats to go from New Orleans to Louisville had been lowered to ten days by steamboat, and by the 1850s fast vessels could make as much as 100 miles per day against the current. In contrast to the elongated, side wheel, oval-shaped craft on the eastern rivers, the Mississippi boats were rectangular in shape and very broad of beam in order to lighten draft as much as possible. Their characteristic stern wheels required less depth of water than side wheels, and were more conveniently located for docking and loading. Lofty superstructures were necessary to brace the flat hulls against the concentrated weight of the machinery. As the boats became more ornate and luxurious they excited admiration in Europe as well as in America, and were justly numbered among the engineering achievements of the age, the first triumph of American mechanical abilities.

The initial capital for the building of steamboats came from New York, as we have seen, but as the profit potential of the enterprise became manifest, financing in the West was taken over almost entirely by the business communities of the river towns and cities. The relatively modest amounts of capital available locally were sufficient for the purpose because the building of steamboats required a much smaller outlay than necessary for the construction of roads, canals, and railroads. On the Ohio even the largest boats cost no more than $40,000, although by the sixties the floating palaces on the lower Mississippi could cost from $200,000 to $300,000.

Construction and operation was carried on by many types of business organizations. Some boats were built and captained by single individuals, but more often construction was financed on shares in the traditional manner. Sometimes lines of boats were owned by joint partnerships, and by the end of the antebellum period an increasing number of corporations had made an appearance. Shares in individual boats were as negotiable as shares in ocean-going vessels, and for the same reasons. By holding interests in several steamboats, merchants of the river towns could not only participate in a profitable transportation enterprise but could guarantee carriage of their own goods and acquire opportunities to expand their business to distant localities. Builders, suppliers, and repairers of steamboats often became large owners as well, probably because on occasion they contributed their services for shares rather than for cash.

Despite the great economic benefits brought to the West by steamboats, because of climatic and organizational factors operations were inefficient and haphazard when compared to railroad service. During the summer months water levels over much of the Mississippi watershed fell so low that all boats except those of the "mosquito fleet" were laid up for many weeks at a time. In the northern regions ice also closed down service for a considerable period during the winter. Continuing changes in river currents and in configurations of river beds brought constant dangers of grounding and snagging.

The fact that western steamboating was carried on mostly as small-scale individual enterprise also militated against efficient operation. Most boats operated as tramps within certain "trades" such as the Cincinnati-Pittsburgh run, for example, or else wandered over a larger area of the Mississippi watershed. In the absence of marketing information, captains called at one landing stage after another, picking up whatever freight was available. Since all boats carried both freight and passengers because of the need of owners to tap all sources of revenue, passenger service was slow and unpredictable. Packet lines came into existence when groups of steamboat owners agreed to operate under uniform conditions on schedules between terminal points. Yet these lines had only a limited effect in improving service. Since the boats were usually not owned by a central organization, effective control over operations was impossible. Individual captains disregarded the terms of their agreements or pulled out entirely whenever they considered it to their advantage to do so. As a result, the life span of most lines was short. Moreover, since packet lines seldom crossed the limits of particular "trades," through service for passengers or freight was almost unknown.

Steamboat finance, in marked contrast to canal or railroad finance, was characterized by a high ratio of operating to overhead cost. By one calculation made in 1849 the annual operating expenses of a 200-ton boat valued at $9,000 amounted to $26,500. By contrast, the annual operating costs of most railroads during the nineties were about 10 percent of the capital investment. Labor, fuel, and supplies were the chief items of current expense in steamboating. Insurance costs varied widely in accordance with the conditions of boats and rivers, but rates were usually higher than for ocean-going vessels. Depreciation was heavy, amounting on some boats to as much as 25 percent per year, and maintenance was correspondingly high. The natural life span of western steamboats was estimated at no more than five years, and when the toll exacted by accidents was taken into consideration, the figure was nearer four years.

Rates varied in accordance with myriad demand and supply conditions. The stage of the rivers was an important seasonal factor. When water levels were high and all boats were afloat and operating, rates were low; but as the waters fell and the larger boats were laid up, rates rose precipitantly. Informal rate classifications were established similar to those put in force later by railroads whereby higher value, lighter goods paid more than low value commodities. In the rate schedules there was some reflection of the discrimination so loudly denounced when imposed by railroads at a later date. Because of intense competition at terminal points, charges there were often lower than charges at intermediate points or at remote landing stages on the smaller rivers. Despite rate fluctuations, however, the over-all drop in the cost of river transportation brought about by steamboats was very impressive and had an important effect in raising land values and crop prices in the Mississippi watershed. For example, before 1820 keelboat rates from New Orleans to Louisville had averaged five dollars per hundredweight; by 1843 steamboat rates for the run had fallen to about twenty-five cents per hundredweight for commodities and about thirty-three cents for groceries and dry goods.

Considering the many variables in steamboating, it is difficult to generalize about profits. In the early years they were very high, and efficiently run boats could cover their construction costs in two or three seasons. But as the number of boats multiplied and rates fell, by the forties probably few could earn the estimated 30 percent net return necessary to produce what was considered to be a normal profit. Yet, many boats remained on the rivers simply because, profit or no profit, steamboating represented a way of life for their captains. It was a prestigious occupation and satisfied the wanderlust of the footloose and fancy-free. Moreover, the constant expansion of population and growth of cities perennially promoted confidence that profits would improve in the future.

Such hopes were ultimately dashed by the railroads, however. Roads connecting terminal points were not compelled to follow the serpentine windings of the rivers and therefore cut distances and traveling time by 40 to 60 percent. Also, railroads ran on schedule twelve months of the year, rain or shine, were not immobilized by low water in summer or freezeover in winter, and could tap vast hinterlands inaccessible to steamboats. By the 1880s steamboating had lost its glamour, and the once noble vessels were reduced to carriers of heavy, low-cost commodities.

X. Specialization of Commercial Functions

As we have seen, the founding of chartered banks and insurance companies inaugurated the institutionalization of the functions previously performed by the general entrepreneur. By 1860 most of the specializations of the world of commerce which we have today were firmly established.

As markets increased in size far beyond the dimensions of the old merchants' exchanges of the seaboard towns, brokerage became necessary as a means of bringing buyers and sellers together. In the field of banking as a mounting volume of business loosened the close personal ties between banks and their clients, broker-middlemen would peddle an unknown borrower's paper among the banks of metropolitan centers. Note brokers, known as "note shavers" because of their demand for heavy discounts, served merchants and travelers by buying and selling notes issued by out-of-town banks. By 1860 some brokers were specializing in particular issues of public or corporate securities, which they sold on commission. Others wrote marine or fire insurance and sold the policies to established firms. As the consumption of cotton by New England mills increased and regular supplies at fixed prices became more vital, cotton brokers signed contracts for future delivery of cotton at agreed prices, then bought the cotton in the open market or from factors resident in southern ports. The possibility of making speculative profits by buying low led to the trading in futures which became usual in all commodity markets. At a later date futures came to perform the useful function of permitting large-scale users of commodities to protect the value of their inventories by "hedging." In this operation the hedger couples the sale of futures contracts with cash purchases. Whatever loss he might take because of a subsequent drop in the cash price is offset by a corresponding gain on the futures contracts, and vice versa.

In the South, resident cotton brokers, called "factors," evolved from the storekeepers sent out by English and Scottish mercantile houses in the late colonial period. Factors sold the cotton of their planter clients to mills in the North and in Europe and purchased goods for the planters, charging a commission of 2 percent for all transactions. They also acted as bankers, accepting bills secured by cotton shipments and often lending money on other security such as mortgages. So widespread were their activities that in 1861 Louisiana planters were estimated to be $8 million in debt to forty New Orleans factors. Factorage attracted many ambitious Yankee businessmen to the South. Some invested their profits in plantations, and thereby entered the mainstream of southern agrarian life as well. After the Civil War cotton factors increasingly lost business to competing agencies. The spread of the rail network allowed planters to ship cotton direct to northern markets, bypassing the older market centers such as New Orleans, Savannah, and Charleston, where factors were in control. Improved transportation brought to village stores much of the manufactured goods formerly purchased for the planters by factors, and an increasing number of banks, together with storekeepers, supplanted the factors as suppliers of farm credit. By 1900 this venerable type of broker had practically disappeared.

DEVELOPMENT OF THE NEW YORK STOCK EXCHANGE

Specialization of marketing facilities naturally accompanied the specialization of commerical functions. The first of the specialized markets, and the one which was to finance much of American industry and transportation, was the New York Stock Exchange. Initially, trading in securities had been carried on by merchants and auctioneers as part of their variegated business. In order to prevent the trade in the funded debt from falling completely into the hands of general auctioneers and in order to stop the competitive cutting of commissions, a group of New York brokers agreed in 1792 to conduct their business under established rules at the Tontine Coffee House, the first of many locations occupied by the Stock Exchange. The flotation of more government securities during the War of 1812 and the emissions of stock by chartered banks and insurance companies created the need for a more elaborate organization. In 1817 a Board of Brokers, consisting of seven firms and thirteen individuals, was formed under a "constitution." Speculation in the stock of the Second Bank of the United States increased the volume of trading, and during the twenties and thirties the securities issued by the states to finance internal improvements provided a large proportion of the business of the Exchange. The stocks of canal companies, and later of railroad companies, added to the list of traded shares. Industrial stocks were conspicuous by their absence. Until nearly the end of the nineteenth century even the largest manufacturing enterprises could be started with less capital than railroads and canals. Thus most initial capital was local in origin and growth could be internally financed.

The decline of Philadelphia as a financial center during the forties gave the financial primacy to New York which the city was to hold thenceforth. Good communications and facilities for fast, safe transportation of securities made the New York Stock Exchange into a national institution. Nevertheless, only a small proportion of the trading in securities was carried on there. From the very beginning the exchange had competitors in the form of a curb market and private auctions which offered a wider variety of issues and more lax trading rules. During the sixties the Open Board—a rival exchange—the Gold Exchange and the Mining and Petroleum Board continued the competition. These offered the speculator much faster operations. The Stock Exchange was still an auction in which the whole list was called once or twice a day, but the others were continuous markets in which each issue represented was traded at certain locations on the floor, as is done today on all stock exchanges. Toward the end of the antebellum period the development of a call money market made possible by the large balances deposited in New York banks by out-of-town banks facilitated quick settlements in which stock was pledged as collateral for a call loan. Thus "margin" was introduced in stock trading.

Throughout the nineteenth century the Stock Exchange was a speculator's rather than an investor's market. From the sixties through the eighties rails were the most important issues traded; industrials did not rival them until the nineties. Bonds and preferred stocks had varying degrees of investment quality, but most common stocks had very little intrinsic value and became mere instruments of speculation. The speculators themselves, according to the chronicler of Wall Street, William W. Fowler, were roughly divided into two groups. One was made up of wealthy and powerful financiers capable of directly manipulating the market. The second consisted of a shifting, transient horde of petty gamblers who merely responded to market fluctuations, and as a result almost invariably lost their shirts. The fifty to one hundred brokers occupying seats of the Exchange were all speculators themselves, and many belonged to the group of large operators. "Long" traders, called "bulls," purchased stock outright in anticipation of a rise in price. Short traders, called "bears," sold stock they did not own with the intention of purchasing it for delivery later at a lower price, thus making a speculative profit. Both sides of the market speculated in "puts" and "calls," which were options to buy or sell stock within a limited period for a stated price.

Since the total volume of shares available for purchase was much less than today, it was always possible to rig the market. Thus speculation often took the form of an intense and deadly game in which bulls tried to "corner" individual issues, i.e., purchase all the stock outstanding, and bears tried to break the corners and sell short as the stock plunged downward. As the rings of bull speculators went into action and the stocks to be cornered started to rise, bears, unaware of what was in the wind, sold short in the expectation that the stocks would soon drop back to normal prices and allow them to cover their contracts at a profit. In subsequent ploys the bulls attempted to suck more of the bears into the market by allowing downward fluctuations, but since the stock purchased by bears to cover their contracts was ultimately delivered to the bulls, the bears were only digging their own graves. If all went well for the bulls and their identities and intentions remained secret, eventually the cornered stocks reached levels at which the bears faced ruin and were compelled to settle their short contracts on whatever terms the bulls would allow, which always entailed a heavy loss. But of course the bulls were not always the winners. If, for many unforeseen reasons their resources did not permit them to purchase all stock offered regardless of the price, the corner would break. Since most bulls operated on slim margins, their brokers, acting to protect call loans, would sell them out as the stock plunged to its original level. The bears then reaped the harvest of profits by covering their short contracts at rock bottom levels. Although the game usually did not end in such a clear-cut victory for either side, it constantly and radically redistributed the wealth of the trading community. A very few of the gamesters, like Cornelius Vanderbilt, made and kept substantial fortunes, largely because heavy reserves allowed them to extricate themselves from difficulties, but most players, big and little, sooner or later lost heavily.

SPECIALIZATION IN WHOLESALE AND RETAIL MARKETING

By 1850 the general stores of the importing merchants of a half-century before had been replaced in the coastal cities by the establishment of specialized import houses, jobbers, wholesalers, and retailers. The 2,881 commission houses of New York in 1839 usually specialized in particular trades such as cotton or woolen textiles. They not only sold the merchandise of foreign or domestic manufacturers at a commission of 2½ percent, but also helped provide their clients with working capital by accepting and purchasing their bills and by outright loans. Some firms, like B. C. Ward and Company of Boston, became sales representatives and bankers for Massachusetts textile manufacturers. Not until after the Civil War did manufacturers attempt to form their own sales organizations. Jobbers were specialized wholesalers who bought goods in large lots from manufacturers or from commission merchants and put them on display for sale to retailers, many of whom came from the South and West on annual purchasing trips. Even today jobbers' establishments can be seen side by side in the various commercial areas of New York.

The primitive transportation conditions before the spread of the railroad network provided the professional opportunities for peddlers, who as a result played an important role in commercial life before the Civil War. In the spring of every year whole caravans of peddlers' wagons, loaded with a wide assortment of goods such as shoes, dry goods, tinware, clocks, and salt, departed from New England and dispersed over the West and South. Peddlers sometimes purchased their stocks from manufacturers by notes to be repaid at the end of the trading season; sometimes they got the goods under profit-sharing arrangements. Often peddlers were part owners of the little manufacturing establishments which supplied their wares. Usually they traded in kind and replenished their stock from local jobbers. Obviously this kind of marketing could provide valuable knowledge of markets and prices. For thousands of canny young Yankees peddling became a kind of apprenticeship for the jobbing trades, and many prosperous merchants could look back upon this humble traffic as an excellent introduction into commercial life. Although most peddlers were reasonably honest, as a group they acquired a reputation for sharp trading, and they were understandably disliked by most settled merchants. In 1860 there were perhaps as many as 17,000 traveling the roads, rivers, and canals of the nation.

The spread of the rail network tended to drive peddlers into the more remote areas, and as a result their number slowly declined during the second half of the nineteenth century. But the rail network also proportionally increased the number and activities of "drummers," the first traveling salesmen. Acquiring their title because of their hard-sell methods of drumming up trade, they were initially viewed with suspicion and distaste. Furthermore, since they sold goods through orders based on samples, they had many more opportunities for fraud and sharp dealing than were open to peddlers, who of necessity had to allow purchasers to examine the goods they bought. As a result of the misdeeds of many drummers, some states in the early fifties required them to purchase licenses which were sometimes prohibitive in cost. Yet because sale by sample and order allowed local merchants to acquire a much wider range of goods than could be supplied by any other means, the laws were laxly enforced. In 1871 the Supreme Court ruled that licenses on out-of-state drummers were unconstitutional. From that time forward, the number of traveling salesmen rapidly increased.

During the antebellum period there were retail outlets in the major cities for groceries, dry goods, hardware, books, drugs, and occasionally queensware. Men's clothing stores and shoe stores did not appear in significant numbers until the manufacture of uniforms during the Civil War brought into existence the ready-made clothing industry. Furniture and jewelry were retailed from artisan workshops. In rural areas general stores were not only retail outlets but also centers for barter and often sources of farm credit. Country storekeepers exchanged manufactured goods and luxuries for local produce, and usually kept accounts by much the same methods of "bookkeeping barter" used by merchants like Thomas Hancock during the eighteenth century. Often they extended long-term book credits in return for what were essentially crop liens. In the South, storekeepers acted as factors for small farmers, retaining 80 percent to nearly 100 percent of the proceeds from the sale of cotton as satisfaction of the farmers' debts on credit purchases. They also loaned money on occasion, at high rates of interest. Retail markups in country stores usually varied between 100 percent and 150 percent. In frontier areas merchants were often the junior partners or agents of established eastern concerns. Like the large planters of the colonial period, they were also the general entrepreneurs of a rapidly developing economy, engaging in land speculation, the fur trade, town planning, transportation improvement, and increasingly in manufacturing.

DEPARTMENT STORES—MACY'S, MARSHALL FIELD, AND WANAMAKER'S

The progress from specialization to integration which characterized the course of business development during the last half of the nineteenth century took place in retail marketing with the establishment of department stores, chain stores, and mail-order houses. Department stores were made possible by the combined effects of urbanization and the industrial revolution. Large cities offered a wide market of middle-class families with rising standards of living. Industrialism produced an ever-increasing quantity and variety of consumer goods. The railroad network provided regular supply from a wide range of manufacturers and jobbers. Large buildings, made possible by the use of iron beams, and later by structural steel, enabled the great emporiums to be housed under one roof, and gas light and central heating made the stores comfortable for customers.

Most department stores evolved from dry goods stores in the larger cities. During the antebellum period as the textile industry—both domestic and foreign—turned out an ever-increasing variety of fabrics, some energetic retailers multiplied their offerings and added to their floor space. The most notable of these entrepreneurs was Alexander T. Stewart, a young Irish immigrant who entered the drygoods business in New York in 1823 with a small stock of Irish linens and laces, and steadily expanded his business until he occupied an entire block between Broadway and Fourth Avenue. According to the historian of the store, Harry E. Resseguie, Stewart inaugurated many of the merchandising practices adopted by the department stores of a later date. Not only was he the first retailer in the world to erect a specially designed, functional, multi-floored building to house his "drygoods palace," but he purchased for cash from manufacturers and jobbers in every continent of the world. He organized his store by departments, took only a small retail markup, allowed merchandise returns and refunds, and offered other free services to customers. During the height of his career he was reputedly the richest man in New York, in 1863 paying tax on an income of $1,843,637. Grasping, cold, and miserly, he died in 1876 and the great business he created disintegrated shortly thereafter.

The transition from the departmentalized drygoods store to the department store of the modern type was first accomplished by Rowland H.

Macy. Born in Nantucket to a whaling family, he went to sea at an early age and upon his return engaged in a few unsuccessful retail ventures. But with the help of goods advanced by jobbers and the profits from some small-scale land speculation, he was able in 1858 to start a fancy drygoods store at Sixth Avenue and Fourteenth Street, in New York City. At the outset he followed a policy of buying for cash, selling for cash, and charging set prices which were lower than those of his competitors. All of these retailing gambits were innovations at the time. The great majority of storekeepers bargained with their customers for every article sold, and finally accepted the highest price they could get. They also bought on as much credit as they could raise, and sold on as little as they could be forced to give. Obviously all of these methods slowed the pace and volume of sales and increased both the wholesale and retail prices of the goods sold over the counter.

From the outset Macy's store was a success, doubtless largely because of his new merchandising methods. He further improved his competitive position by plowing profits back into the business, devising unique, eye-catching newspaper advertising, and adding new lines. Under the stimulus of energetic promotion and frugal management the store grew rapidly and by 1870 was selling over a million dollars worth of goods per year. At some time during this period it became a department store, stocking dry goods, china, glassware, house furnishings, luggage, toys, musical instruments, and books. The store in 1862 had eight selling divisions, each headed by a buyer who was allowed wide discretion. Operations were co-ordinated by a supervisor working under Macy himself. Macy turned over his stock about six times per year, faster than most modern stores. Gross profit margins were about 20 percent, and expenses about 14 percent, leaving a net profit of about 6 percent.

After Macy's death in 1877, the rate of growth slowed, but the firm received a blood transfusion a decade later when Isador and Nathan Straus were admitted as partners. They rigorously followed the original Macy merchandising policies, borrowed heavily for expansion, and by 1900 were selling nearly everything material a human being could want—actually a larger stock than offered by most department stores today. With a staff of about 3,000, Macy's had extensive buying agencies abroad, purchased direct from manufacturers, and was even engaged in some manufacturing itself. In 1902 the store moved to its present Herald Square location, and—like the other great department stores of the day—became a national institution.

The firm of Marshall Field came into existence in 1865 when young

Field and a partner, Levi Z. Leiter, bought a half-interest in a large Chicago dry goods store and slowly transformed it into a department store. Unlike Macy and most other retailers, Field and Leiter combined retail and wholesale operations, thus gaining a competitive advantage in purchasing not enjoyed by purely retail firms. At the outset the wholesale business was of much greater volume than the retail, and even by 1900 was three times as large despite a rapid increase in retailing operations during the intervening period. From the beginning the firm sold for set prices and purchased for cash from jobbers and manufacturers. Cash purchase gave a further competitive advantage by securing access to the best goods at the lowest prices. But on sales Field and Leiter provided a variety of credit arrangements, which in the wholesale end amounted in many cases to financing of retailers. To fulfill the famous slogan, "Give the lady what she wants"— which became a hallmark of the firm—Field and Leiter also allowed returns in retail sales with no questions asked.

Profits rose slowly from $240,000 in 1865 to about $2.5 million in 1900 on net sales of $46 million. Since department stores catered to women, who made about 80 percent of the customer purchases, stores made every effort to make shopping a pleasure. Field's had greeters, posts for cabs and messengers, facilities for the sale and reservation of theatre tickets, a telephone office and a post office, and offered delivery service. Returns proved to be a heavy expense, and, combined with the cost of services, were reflected in a steady increase in the ratio of expenses to net sales. By 1906 the store was buying back $17 of every $100 worth of merchandise sold.

By the turn of the century the firm was purchasing entire lines from foreign manufacturers, and was even submitting to the manufacturers sketches and designs for exclusive offerings. As at Macy's, the buyers for the store were allowed a wide latitude of decision making, and were evaluated by the profit performance of their departments. Actually, buyers in wholesale acted as independent merchants, borrowing their working capital from the store and receiving a portion of the profits from their operations. In the opinion of Robert W. Twyman, historian of Field's, the store owed its great success to a combination of factors: its origin in a large and successful retail enterprise, location in fast-growing Chicago, close relation of wholesale and retail operations, buying in large quantities for cash, good treatment of customers, and good quality merchandise.

The Wanamaker firm differed in several respects from Macy's and Field's, most notably, perhaps, in the person of the founder, John Wanamaker. A tireless promoter and showman, with a personality much more flamboyant than that of his two merchant contemporaries, he looked after society's business as well as his own by participation in a wide range of religious, philanthropic, and political activities. To judge from his considerable output of speeches, articles, and interviews, he felt that his great accomplishment was integrating the function of the merchant with the larger purposes of God Almighty.

He got his start by opening a small men's clothing shop in Philadelphia in partnership with his brother-in-law in 1861. The ready-made men's clothing business was then in its infancy, but was receiving a strong stimulus from the wartime needs of the Union army. By 1871 the store—Oak Hall—was the largest retail clothing business in the nation. In 1875 Wanamaker bought the Pennsylvania Railroad freight depot at Broad and Market Streets for $500,000 and converted it into a department store. At first he hoped to lease departments, but when co-operation from the city's merchants was not forthcoming, he outfitted "a new kind of store" as he phrased it—in effect a congeries of specialty shops. Little is known about its operations, but these were probably quite similar to Field's, except that Wanamaker continued to specialize in ready-made clothing. Most of it he manufactured in his own establishments, thus eliminating jobbers' profits. Even more than Field or Macy he attempted to make the store into an institution, furnishing it with an auditorium equipped to hold 1,500 people, a gigantic organ, and a succession of displays, stunts, and other promotions. In 1896 Wanamaker purchased the former A. T. Stewart store at Broadway and Tenth Street, New York, and converted it into the New York Wanamaker's.

Like Macy's, Field's, and Wanamaker's, a remarkably large number of the nation's leading department stores can trace their origins to small specialty shops and dry goods stores of the nineteenth century, among them Lord and Taylor, Arnold Constable, Best, and Altman of New York; Jordan Marsh and Filene's of Boston; The Fair, and Carson, Pirie, Scott & Company of Chicago; J. L. Hudson Company of Detroit; and Rich's of Atlanta.

CHAIN STORES

Chain stores, like department stores, represented an attempt to integrate retail marketing and attain economies of scale by volume buying and selling. Because of their specialization in a few chosen lines the chain stores could develop expert management more quickly than department stores and exercise increasing influence over the producers and distributors of goods purchased. Moreover, since individual units remained relatively small and felt no need to offer the manifold customer services performed by department stores, overhead and cost of sales could be held to a minimum.

Defined broadly as two or more stores operated under the same ownership or management, chain stores are almost as old as retailing itself. But apparently the first attempt to introduce integration into their operation occurred in the fur trade. Such Canadian organizations as the French monopolies, the Hudson's Bay Company, and the North West Company centralized the purchase of trade goods, and although the posts were operated by partners rather than salaried managers, attempts were made to achieve uniformity of prices and trading conditions. The main difference between these fur posts and modern chains was that the posts sold their goods for furs rather than for cash. But this primitive barter nevertheless necessitated a forward integration not found in modern chains; the fur companies were compelled to establish organizations for marketing their product in Europe.

The first of the modern chains was the Great Atlantic and Pacific Tea Company, which started as a tea specialty store opened in New York in 1859 by George F. Gelman and George Huntington Hartford. By 1900 scores of grocery chains operated throughout the nation. Thirteen drug chains antedated the twentieth century. But perhaps the most successful chain of any kind to begin operations during this period was the F. W. Woolworth Company.

The founder, born to a poor farm family, began his career clerking in a small general store in upstate New York. Impressed by the success of a five-cent clearance sale, he conceived the novel idea of establishing a store to sell a variety of items in volume at a single price within reach of virtually the entire population—five cents. With an initial capital consisting of a $300 inventory of goods advanced to him by his employer, Woolworth started a small store in Utica in 1879 which soon failed. Other similar misfortunes followed, but by 1881 Woolworth had two successful stores operating in Pennsylvania—one in Lancaster and the other in Scranton.

Several problems had been responsible for the initial failures. It was difficult for Woolworth to procure an adequate supply of goods within his price range. Unable to pay the high rents demanded in busy retail centers, he was compelled to locate his stores in less attractive areas. The acquisition of capital for expansion was disappointingly slow. Yet ultimately all of these problems were solved. Mass production of household goods and notions was just beginning, and as a result a progressive drop in manufacturers' prices brought scores of new items within Woodworth's price range every few months. Also, he more than doubled his inventory possibilities by selling five- *and* ten-cent items, and thereby also acquired a unique institutional status. Capital for new stores came partly from plowed back earnings, but more importantly in the early career of the business from partners recruited from among boyhood friends and relations in upstate New York. Woolworth installed the partners as managers of new stores. An increasing volume of sales made it possible to rent quarters in more promising locations, and the widening variety of goods available raised the optimum size of stores.

Woolworth early came to see that a retail business restricted to five- and ten-cent items could be successful only when carried on through a large number of retail outlets. Only volume buying could secure goods at low enough prices, and only volume selling would permit survival with the small markups at which the goods had to be sold. Convinced that the most important function within the business was purchasing, Woolworth settled in Brooklyn to be near the New York jobbers, and purchased for all of the stores. A major breakthrough came when, deciding to stock candy, he was able to bypass the jobbers and deal directly with manufacturers. Like department stores and mail-order houses, he thereby acquired a decisive advantage over the general stores of an earlier era.

Realizing the importance of retail presentation, Woolworth rapidly developed new types of window dressing and display of goods, and with his familiar red store front engraved his institutional image upon the minds of all shoppers. Although managers were given wide latitude in all matters except purchasing and store layout, Woolworth did not hesitate to shower them with advice, praise, and criticism even in areas of their own competence. Once the chain was firmly established, managers were almost never brought in from the outside but were recruited from among the successful graduates of a training program established for aspiring beginners. At the outset Woolworth paid sales girls only $1.50 to $2.50 per week, insisting that "unless we have cheap help we cannot sell cheap goods." But as the chain became larger Woolworth came to see that a courteous, efficient sales force was as important as colorful, eye-catching display, and paid higher wages in order to upgrade employee performance.

As Woolworth's resources increased he financed more of the additions to the chain himself, and by 1900 came to own a majority of the units outright. Meanwhile Kresge, Kress, and McCrory had come into the field, but Woolworth was able to stay ahead of all competitors because of an early start, good management, and an increasing volume of business. Although he was always loath to relinquish decision-making in any area, by 1905 it was plain that the magnitude of the business required extensive delegation of authority and rationalization of administration. In this year the enterprise was incorporated with $5,000,000 of preferred and $5,000,000 of common stock. Some of the preferred was offered to managers and other employees, but Woolworth and a few high officials took the entire issue of common. No stock was offered to the public. In chain stores internal financing was much easier than in heavy industry, for example, because of the low capital-output ratio of retail enterprise. F. W. Woolworth was by now one of the most successful businesses in America, and had innovated a retailing idea eventually copied around the world.

MAIL ORDER HOUSES

Department stores and chain stores represented an integration of retail marketing in an urban environment; mail-order houses constituted the same development for the rural market. The large organizations grew up in the West. Because of the growing economic distress in this region during the eighties and early nineties it might appear to have been an unpromising milieu for any new retail enterprise. Actually, the difficulties of the farmers made them more responsive to mail-order blandishments than they otherwise might have been. Much of the Populist protest was aimed at high markups at country stores and the supposedly exorbitant charges of jobbers and other middlemen. Therefore, when mail-order houses claimed that their substantially lower prices came from bypassing jobbers and accepting the slimmer profit margins of a volume business, they captured the support of farmers. In addition to political considerations, the growth of population in the rural West also increased its potential as a retail market, even in times of depression. As late as 1880, 72 percent of the American people lived in a rural environment, and agriculture was the major source of national wealth. By 1890, 27 percent of the population lived west of the Mississippi, and most Americans still got their livings from the soil.

The first important mail-order business was established by Aaron Montgomery Ward in 1872. Ward had worked among farmers and knew their needs and desires. To capitalize on western rural discontent he proclaimed his mail-order house to be the "Official Supply House" of the Grange. Furthermore, he ingratiated himself with prospective customers by guaranteeing lowest possible prices, an achievement which he explained was gained by dealing directly with manufacturers and by doing a cash business which would eliminate the expenses incurred by offering credit and carrying bad debts. In order to circumvent the advantage enjoyed by storekeepers in allowing customers to examine merchandise before buying, Ward gave a warranty with all items and allowed returns at the expense of the company if the customer was not satisfied. Examination and return was a vital, and probably an indispensable element for the success of the mail-order business. In another area besides price mail-order houses had a distinct advantage over established retail stores. Catalogues, when embellished with woodcuts and attractive layouts, constituted more effective advertising than stores could enjoy.

Ward's mail-order business was an immediate success which grew with the years. By 1883 he was publishing a 240-page illustrated catalogue listing 10,000 items.

Ward's main competitor was Richard Warren Sears, who founded the house of Sears Roebuck so often paired with Montgomery Ward. Sears was not an innovator in retailing, but he utilized all of the policies initiated by Ward to build the largest mail-order business in the United States. Coming from a farm background he entered the world of trade by selling watches C.O.D. from wholesalers while working as a freight agent in a small Minnesota railroad station. Aware that the traditionally high mark-ups of retail jewelers offered price cutters substantial profits if they could do a volume business, in 1866 Sears established in Chicago under his own name a company which sold watches by mail order. Alvah Curtis Roebuck entered the business as a partner to perform the vital task of watch repairer and assembler of movements.

During the next few years Sears elaborated the hard-sell methods which had played such an important role in the rise of Montgomery Ward. Garish displays and inflated claims in his catalogues aroused immediate interest of farmers to whom gold watches had previously been unobtainable luxuries. Lowest prices, achieved by buying in volume from manufacturers and acquiring discontinued lines where possible, placed the watches within the farmers' reach. Testimonials, guarantees, and assurance of refunds for returns gave customers confidence in the wares. And, to add to the appeal, attacks on "Combinations, Trusts, and High Prices" placed Sears in the farmers' camp politically.

As Sears's merchandising methods breached the wall of suspicion which surrounded the stereotype of the city slicker salesman, he broadened his offerings until the firm became a full-fledged mail-order house under the name Sears Roebuck and Company. He continually gave special interest to all items which would lend themselves to high pressure promotions. First it was sewing machines, then bicycles, then electric belts, then cream separators. These were all relatively new products which could be presented as adding some new dimension to the farmers' life. Moreover, as newsworthy articles of special interest in the catalogues they provided advertising for the less glamourous items.

But if Sears showed skill as a purchaser and a unique flair as a promoter and a writer of advertising copy, he exhibited much less capacity for administration, mainly because he had little interest in this prosaic aspect of the business. As a result, by 1895 the booming success of Sears Roebuck threatened to destroy the company. As gross sales rose from $296,000 in 1892 to $421,000 in 1894—incidentally, years of the deepest distress in the West—the net worth of the firm fell from $79,000 to $55,000. Deliveries sometimes could not be made as promised because Sears tended to start promotions before getting on hand a supply of goods adequate to meet the demand. Complaints mounted and returned merchandise piled up in railroad warehouses. Although Sears drove himself unmercifully from seven in the morning until ten at night, he and his small staff, working in cramped, inadequate quarters, could not keep up with the business.

Roebuck, unable to stand the pace, sold out in 1895 for $25,000, an action he must have bitterly regretted in later years. But in the same year the firm received a blood transfusion when Aaron E. Nusbaum and Julius Rosenwald, bringing fresh funds chiefly from the New York men's clothing industry, entered the firm as partners. With their financial contributions Sears Roebuck was reincorporated with a capital of $150,000. Rosenwald, much more aware of administrative needs than Sears, pulled the company together in the coming years and succeeded to its leadership after Sears retired in 1908.

As reorganized after the reincorporation, the company had twenty-four merchandise departments and kept approximately one hundred specialized buyers constantly on the road. Although Sears rather reluctantly relinquished complete oversight of administrative, financial, and merchandising affairs, he continued until his last years with the company to write the copy for the catalogue, plan layouts, and handle special promotions. Price continued to be the company's main appeal, even at the expense of quality. Men's suits at $4.98 obviously did not last long, and bedroom suites at $8.50 just as obviously lacked aesthetic charm, but the fact that Sears Roebuck could supply these items at all for the prices indicated was much more important to farming communities than quality. In any event, the fact that Sears discontinued all credit terms in 1902 and required cash with orders indicated growing public confidence in the value of the merchandise.

The company's success from 1895 to 1905 can only be described as phenomenal. Capital was increased from $150,000 to $5,000,000, the entire amount subscribed by Sears, Rosenwald, and the then secretary of the company, Albert Loeb. Of the nearly $11,000,000 in profits made during the period, representing 28 percent of sales, three-fourths stayed in the business. Volume of business reached nearly $41,000,000 by 1908, and the company by that time owned ten factories, whole or in part.

All of the attempts at integrated marketing described above had certain similarities. In the first place, all were successful responses to a burgeoning, middle-class market for consumer goods, both urban and rural. In the second place, all of the enterprises were able to secure an increasing variety of goods because of the beginnings of mass production and the spread of the rail network. In all cases the prototype retail outlets, whether department stores, chain stores, or mail-order houses, were innovations conceived by remarkably astute entrepreneurs, and in all cases the success of the individual enterprises owed much to entrepreneurial drive. The varied tasks required to run the stores created specialization in management and made marketing a discrete business career. The growth of the enterprises was financed internally out of profits or by capital contributions from other sectors of retail marketing. Finally, all depended upon intense promotion and widespread advertising, and in this respect they made great contributions to the development of advertising as another business specialty.

ADVERTISING

The innovations in retailing described above did not originate advertising; actually in one form or another it is almost as old as commerce itself. Colonial newspapers carried notices of goods offered for sale by local merchants—particularly importations from England. Among the first advertisers to experiment with "puffing," or inducements, was the celebrated printer, Benjamin Franklin. But the development of this distinguishing characteristic was delayed for a considerable period. Until around 1830 most ads continued to be simple, three- or four-line announcements, with few attempts to catch the reader's interest by pictures or special type arrangements.

Advertising entered a new phase with the appearance of the first mass circulation newspapers in the 1830s. New types of advertisers whose business depended upon the hard sell—among them patent medicine houses, lottery offices, stage coach and steamboat lines, theaters and traveling shows—experimented with superlatives and novel arrangements of type. Occasionally printing from woodcuts, the advertisers even ran display ads. P. T. Barnum, the Connecticut grocery boy who became the greatest showman of his day, was probably the first businessman to use advertising as a major implement for expansion. Rates were very low by current standards. Benjamin H. Day offered "squares" of ten lines daily in his *New York Sun* for $30 per year. During the fifties and sixties, as newspapers multiplied, the volume of advertising continued to surge forward, fed by the heavy commitment to it by the first department stores, particularly Macy's and Lord and Taylor. In 1867 the annual income of publishers from advertising was about $9.6 million per year, and one newspaper commentator called the business "the monamania of the times."

Expansion brought the advertising agent into existence. Originally merchants had written and placed their own ads with the newspaper publishers, but as the number of papers increased and the market areas of advertisers widened, the need for middlemen appeared. Solicitors, originally sent out by publishers, established themselves as independent dealers in newspaper space, buying in large quantities from a number of newspapers and reselling in smaller lots. These men were the first advertising agents.

During the years immediately following the Civil War the first important figures in the advertising field made their appearance. George P. Rowell, "the man who did more perhaps than any other man to develop advertising in the nineteenth century"—in the opinion of Frank Presbrey, historian of advertising—began publication of a newspaper directory in 1869 and distributed estimates of newspaper circulation. In 1888 he founded *Printer's Ink,* a trade journal which gave serious attention to advertising methods and agency problems. John E. Powers, sometimes called "the father of honest advertising," developed a new "reason why" style of copy writing admired for its simplicity and sincerity. Among the advertisers for whom he wrote were Lord and Taylor and Wanamaker's. J. Walter Thompson did much to develop advertising in the magazine field.

Despite the rapid expansion of advertising in the sixties, nearly half a century passed before agencies assumed responsibility for the entire process—planning campaigns, designing, writing, and placing ads—all under contract with the advertisers. The transition to modern practice is well illustrated in the career of the famous N. W. Ayer agency.

Francis Wayland Ayer, founder of the agency, was originally an advertising solicitor for *The National Baptist,* published in Philadelphia. Earning $1,200 in commissions during his first year, he determined to strike out for himself, and in 1869, at the age of twenty-one, founded N. W. Ayer and Son, named for his father. At the outset he bought space for resale in eleven religious journals, thereby operating in essentially the same manner as the other agencies of the period. Energetic and hard-working, honest, straight-forward, and deeply religious, he was a model of the "inner directed" entrepreneur of the nineteenth century. Expanding his business rapidly, he began publication of a manual for advertisers in 1874, and a quarterly magazine in 1876. Despite the increase in the Ayer firm's volume at this time, net receipts shrank. Ayer felt that this disturbing development was due in part to a conflict of interest which prevented agencies from giving their best services to advertisers. As purveyors of space, agents naturally favored the papers on their own lists whose space could be resold at the highest profit, even though these papers were often not the best outlets for the advertiser's material. Ayer's answer to the problem was the advertising contract, under which the agents worked exclusively for the advertisers and were paid by them exclusively. In January, 1876, Ayer inaugurated the new procedure.

Transition to the new relationship was carried out only slowly, and Ayer continued to deal in newspaper space long after he had begun operating under contract. But by 1900 the transition had been accomplished by the three leading firms—Ayer, Lord and Thomas, and J. Walter Thompson. Under contracts these agencies gradually expanded their functions. In 1880 Ayer inaugurated the market survey and began to prepare copy for customers, but did not hire a full-time copy writer until 1892. Meanwhile, conditions in the industry were changing. Technical advances, such as halftone prints, permitted new types of art work. Billboards and the new mass circulation magazines, such as *Ladies' Home Journal, Munsey's, Delineator,* and *Cosmopolitan,* were increasing in importance as media. Consumer products which had achieved a national market—like Sapolio (soap), Royal Baking Powder, Pears's Soap, and Ivory Soap—literally depended upon advertising for their existence. As a harbinger of the new era to come, Ayer in 1899 launched the first of the modern advertising campaigns, using different media and a variety of appeals. Conducted for the National Biscuit Company, it introduced that well-known brand name, Uneeda Biscuit.

Specialization was the common theme in the development of the diverse commercial functions dealt with in this chapter. As specialized markets appeared, beginning with the New York Stock Exchange, the number of buyers and sellers dealing in particular commodities increased rapidly, and some of the successors to the general merchants who had formerly trafficked on the merchants exchanges of the seaport towns of necessity became brokers. In all of the multiplying special markets dealt with in this book, such as the San Francisco Stock Exchange, the Chicago Board of

Trade, the Chicago Stock Yards, and the New York Cotton Exchange, speculation pitting long interests against short interests became the dynamic element which kept the markets in operation. Although many of the methods of speculation are reprehensible by modern standards, the trade in futures performed a distinct service to both buyers and sellers by permitting hedging, and the losses by unsuccessful speculators provided the capital for market operations.

The general entrepreneur's function as a wholesaler quickly developed into the jobbing trades, and jobbers also provided a portion of the capital needed by expanding industries. Retailing moved quickly into the specialized stores of the antebellum period, and after the Civil War took a long further step toward integration in the form of chain stores, department stores, five- and ten-cent stores, and mail-order houses. The course of retail development was also a cause and effect of the development of advertising into its present form. The specialization process forced a few dropouts in the world of commerce. The number of peddlers shrank as the rail network spread over the country; improved transportation and marketing facilities also brought about the demise of the cotton factor; and by the turn of the century the small retailer was entering into a battle with the chain stores the end of which is not yet.

All pervasive as specialization seems to be, it was nevertheless not a synchronous process. It started in the urban centers of the Northeast and later spread to other areas of the country wherever urbanization became a marked trend of development. But in rural areas during the nineteenth century, chiefly on the frontier, commercial functions were carried on by general entrepreneurs operating much like those in the seaboard centers during the colonial period.

XI. Reform and Specialization of Banking Services during the Antebellum Period

REFORMS IN STATE CHARTERED BANKS

Systematic reforms of the banking system were rather slow in coming, probably because of the ambivalence with which most Americans regarded the purpose of banking. Yet nearly everyone would have agreed that a serious effort should be made to obtain a uniform currency. Only the notes of the strongest banks circulated at par, and only within the immediate area of their issue. Most passed at discounts ranging from 1 percent to 30 percent depending on the reputation of the bank of issue and distance from the point of redemption.

One of the first, and most successful experiments in establishing a uniform currency, was carried out in 1818 with the founding of the Suffolk Bank of Boston. Since Boston was a market center, depreciated country notes continually gravitated to its banks. Prudence dictated that these be returned promptly; therefore the Boston banks were compelled to keep runners constantly on the roads taking the notes back for redemption. To avoid the risk and expense of handling country paper in this manner, the Suffolk offered to redeem the notes of the country banks and clear accounts between them and the Boston banks if the former would keep balances at the Suffolk of $5,000 apiece plus a sum sufficient for note redemption. Although the country banks accepted the proposal reluctantly, the arrangement was almost immediately a success, and the Suffolk operated as the first bankers' bank in the nation. By 1822 the discount on country notes had dropped to one-half of one percent.

The establishment of clearing houses in the major cities of the nation during the 1850s marked a second important step in banking control by the banks themselves. The basic procedure for settling accounts was inaugurated by the New York Clearing House in 1853. Each bank in the city sent a "specie clerk" and a "settling clerk" to the clearing house at 10 A.M. every business day. The settling clerks occupied desks side by side around a long rectangular room, each desk being regularly assigned to a particular bank. The specie clerks likewise lined up side by side, each facing a different desk. At the sound of a bell rung by the manager standing on a raised podium at one end of the room, each specie clerk stepped forward and presented for redemption to the settling clerk in front of him the checks and banknotes of the settling clerk's bank accepted by the specie clerk's bank since the last clearance the day before. The settling clerk then made the required payment in clearing house certificates, which represented deposits of specie maintained by member banks at the clearing house. At a repeated sound of the bell the specie clerks then simultaneously moved to the desk on their right and another similar settlement of accounts was made. Each bank, through its settling clerks and specie clerks was therefore constantly paying out and taking in specie certificates. In no more than six minutes the entire circuit was made and the clearance completed. When the settling clerks and specie clerks then compared their balances, each bank knew what its creditor or debtor position was for the day. In periods of normal banking activity the balances of the individual banks fluctuated back and forth, but each bank had to know just where it stood before it could make decisions on the loan applications of its clients.

The first significant governmental plan to maintain banking stability was the New York Safety Fund Act of 1829. The proposal required all banks chartered after that date to pay annually a sum equal to one-half of one percent of their capital into a fund which would be used to repay the noteholders of defaulting banks. The act also established a bank commission empowered to inspect all contributing banks and apply to the courts for injunctions and bankruptcy proceedings against those which were insolvent. The act thereby inaugurated the banking commissions which are now nearly universal in the states and established the principle of deposit insurance represented by the Federal Deposit Insurance Corporation.

In 1838 New York adopted a scheme which satisfied nearly everybody and appeared to be a specific against all the ills of banking—the Free Banking Act. Under this measure, uniform provisions for bank incorporations were established, thus making banking "free" by removing the special payments for individual charters and throwing the business open to all who wished to enter it. Second, bank note issue was secured by a 100 percent reserve in the form of state bonds. Third, a state comptroller of the currency held these bonds in pledge from the banks, printed notes against the bonds as security, and issued the notes to the banks for distribution. Fourth, banks were required to hold 12½ percent specie reserve against circulation in addition to the bonds. (This safeguard was removed in 1840, however, on the ground that it was unnecessary.)

Although free banking had much to recommend it and was therefore emulated by other states and was reflected in the National Bank Act of 1864, the implementation of the measure without additional restrictions only fed the inflationary tendencies of the period. Some enterprising bankers borrowed a large part of the money used to purchase the state bonds against which banknotes were issued, and to the degree that they did so created fictitious reserves. The precipitant decline in the value of some state bond issues during the hard times of the forties imperiled the banknotes that had been issued against them at par value. Furthermore, free banking did nothing to stop inflation through the unlimited creation of deposit account money. The lack of adequate specie reserves made inevitable in time of trouble a suspension of specie payments, which had an unsettling effect on the mercantile community and tilted the international balance of payments against the United States. Yet the lure of the magician's wand which would bring the cake and the penny too in the form of a currency that was at one and the same time stable, uniform, and inflated proved irresistible not only to New York but to the other states who inaugurated free banking and thereby poured a new sea of banknotes on an appreciative and unsuspecting population. In southern states, attempts were made to create agricultural credit without dangerous inflation through the establishment of "plantation banks." These banks were refinements of the land bank schemes of the colonial period in which land values were made negotiable through the issuance of credit instruments secured by real property. In this case the banks issued stock to planters in return for mortgages, and empowered the planters to borrow up to 50 percent of the value of their stock. The banks were capitalized by the issuance of bonds secured by the mortgages and guaranteed by the state governments. With this double guarantee the bonds sold at good prices in eastern capital markets and in Europe side by side with state improvement bonds.

Despite moves to bring greater stability, all banking experiments received setbacks during the Panic of 1837. According to the generally accepted explanation, this blow was brought about by the unwise financial policies of the Jackson administration. Supposedly, Jackson's deposit of government revenues in pet banks, the inability of the Second Bank of the United States to exercise a restraining influence over these banks because of the withdrawal of government deposits at the beginning of Jackson's second administration and the lapse of the charter in 1836, an orgy of spending by state governments on internal improvements and a sharp rise in land speculation, all conspired to promote a florid but unstable boom. The Panic of the next year was triggered by Jackson's specie circular, which required payment for government lands in gold and silver. Banks, in order to conserve dwindling supplies of specie resulting from the order, sharply contracted loans and then suspended specie payments. This action pulled the rug from under the glittering evanescent edifice of credit.

This interpretation has been challenged by Peter Temin, who offers a persuasive alternative explanation of the Panic buttressed by voluminous data and sophisticated economic analysis. According to Temin the Panic was not caused by Jacksonian policies, although these did nothing to alleviate it. Instead it was the result of forces external to the economy which caused a cycle of inflation, crisis, and deflation. Inflation was fed by increasing foreign investment in the United States during the early and middle thirties plus the retention of Mexican silver which would ordinarily have been sent to China but which was no longer in demand there because of a radically changed pattern of trade. The inflow of specie resulting from these two factors increased bank reserves and thereby led the banks to increase their currency issues faster than the rate of increase in the production and importation of goods. Crisis came when the Bank of England in 1836 restricted the outflow of specie to the United States. As the inflow of specie into the banks dropped, the banks were forced to curtail their loans and note issue, causing a crisis in commercial credit and an increasing demand for the redemption of notes. In order to husband their remaining specie the banks then suspended specie payments, and the crisis deepened until the specie value of bank notes fell to a level at which they were sustained by their claims on specie. After this point the economy went through a gradual, and not overly serious deflation in the early forties.

Throughout this painful period the political opponents of Jackson heaped the blame for the crisis on his shoulders. The public generally, with a certain amount of encouragement from the administration, singled out banks as the culprits. It seemed quite plain, of course, that it was their contraction of credit which caused so many thousands of mercantile bankruptcies. Antipathy in the West against banks grew to such an extent that Texas, Iowa, and Arkansas were later admitted to the Union with absolute prohibitions against banking in their constitutions. In Iowa the banking business was described as "a mad, untamable beast, . . . the common enemy of mankind, . . . a withering and blighting curse." Actually, the banks were caught in a situation brought about by forces which bankers could neither understand nor control. Operating within a free market economy tied to an international gold standard, and not protected by a central bank which could apply compensatory techniques, their role in precipitating the Panic was inevitable, if unfortunate.

The painful experiences of the crash did bring forth a precedent-setting reform in the form of the Louisiana Banking Act of 1842, mainly the work of Edmond J. Forstall—merchant, sugar planter, and banker. The bill drew a sharp distinction between accommodation loans, which could be made only from the bank's capital account, and ordinary commercial loans, which could be made only from deposits and note issue. Liquidity of banks was maintained by securing both deposits and notes with a reserve of $33\frac{1}{3}$ percent in specie and $66\frac{2}{3}$ percent in short-term paper. The coupling of money creation to the volume of trade brought a much needed element of elasticity to the money supply and was reflected later in the reserve requirements of the Federal Reserve Banks. The distinction between accommodation and commercial loans established an equally valuable precedent by insuring greater liquidity.

Paradoxically, the most fruitful direction of banking reform was one which after 1836 had been thoroughly discredited—the maintenance of a central bank which was national in its scope. All the reform measures described above could at best have had only limited effect because they could be applied only on the state level. The only effective stabilizer of American banking during the antebellum period had been the Second Bank of the United States. The story of its rejection is a complicated chronicle of warfare in which a valuable institution fell victim to political attack after it had appeared to conflict with some major tenets of American ideology.

THE SECOND BANK OF THE UNITED STATES

The Second Bank of the United States was chartered in 1816 under essentially the same terms as the First Bank of the United States. Capital was set at $35 million, of which the federal government subscribed one-fifth, and received, in return, the right to name five of the twenty-five directors. The bank was to make transfers of government funds and payments on the government's account without charge; in return for this service United States Bank notes were acceptable in payment of all public dues. For the valuable privilege of using government deposits as part of its working capital, the bank paid the government a "bonus" of $1.5 million for the charter. Like the First BUS, the Second Bank was an evenly weighted bargain whereby private enterprise performed valuable fiscal services for the federal government in return for a privileged position among other banks.

Because of the economic difficulties of the federal government during the War of 1812 and the surge of nationalism which swept the nation after the struggle, the chartering of the bank produced no party split or appeal to philosophy such as had characterized the inauguration of its forerunner. But the bank soon suffered a fall in public favor from which it never really recovered. Under the presidency of William Jones, a party hack and former bankrupt, persons close to the bank became involved in unsavory stock speculation in which the Baltimore branch lost $1.5 million. The Jones administration embarked upon an "enlarged and liberal policy" which allowed much of the parent bank's capital to be sucked westward where interest rates were artificially high. Riding the crest of the postwar boom, the bank by the end of 1818 had $22 million in liabilities secured by only $2 million in specie. When the government called for this specie to complete payments due on the Louisiana Purchase, the bank prevailed on the treasury to settle for bills on London, and belatedly began to retrench. By demanding an immediate settlement of accounts with the branches and the state banks, the BUS started a credit squeeze which extended down through the economy to the merchant at the crossroads store.

This action inaugurated the Panic of 1819. Ironically, the very agency designed to counter inflationary pressures had contributed to them, and by the sudden contraction which followed deepened the plunge into enforced liquidation. Naturally the outcry against the bank was tremendous. North

Carolina, Kentucky, Ohio, and Maryland all enacted taxes against its branches. But for the decision of the Supreme Court in McCulloch *vs.* Maryland (1819), which denied the constitutionality of such a tax, the Bank of the United States might have been destroyed by the combined action of the states. Jones, with the wreckage of the "enlarged and liberal policy" tumbling about his ears, fled the presidency and was succeeded by Langdon Cheves, a South Carolina attorney who had been speaker of the House of Representatives.

Cheves managed to save the bank by borrowing abroad, by insisting on the liquidation of debt, by establishing firmer controls over the branches, and by severely limiting their note issue. These policies practically drove all currency out of the South and West, and thereby greatly increased the distress in these regions. It was estimated, for example, that the bank acquired by its rigorous methods of debt collection nearly 20 percent of the real estate of Cincinnati. William Gouge was very near to the truth when he charged that "the Bank was saved and the people were ruined." Cheves was not able to save himself, however. His spartan methods aroused not only the hostility of thousands of hard-pressed debtors, but also of irate stockholders deprived of dividends. He was forced to resign and was succeeded in 1823 by Nicholas Biddle.

Scion of a wealthy Philadelphia family, intelligent, urbane, on intimate terms with leading public figures, Biddle had no practical experience to fit him for the position to which the stockholders elected him. After graduating from Princeton at the age of fifteen, the shy, studious youth with the cameo-like face served from 1804 to 1808 as secretary to the minister to France, John Armstrong, and traveled widely in Europe. Upon his return he studied law, practiced with considerable success, and was elected to the Pennsylvania House of Representatives. His only important speech was a defense of the First Bank of the United States, delivered in 1811, which brought him a reputation as an expert on banking. Prophesying quite correctly that failure to recharter would lead to a multiplication of state banks, inflation of currency, and difficulties for the federal government in raising loans, he emphasized the value of a national bank as a means of sustaining credit in times of depression. No bullionist, he pointed out that bank currency, if properly managed, was a much more flexible instrument with which to meet commercial needs than hard money.

It seems apparent from this speech that Biddle had already envisaged the outlines of a central bank of the modern type designed to regulate the flow of credit and apply compensatory force to stem inflation and deflation. Yet Biddle had at this time no personal ambitions either as a banker or as a politician. Engrossed in his model farm and in literary pursuits (he edited the journals of Lewis and Clark), he withdrew from politics, but maintained a lively interest in the affairs of the emergent Second Bank of the United States. Appointed a director in 1819, his influence increased to the point that he appeared to be a logical successor to Cheves.

The significance of Biddle's career lies primarily in his attempt to transform the Bank of the United States into a true central bank which would stabilize the economic life of the country by controlling credit. Hamilton, and later Gallatin, had conceived the First Bank's public functions to be loaning money to the government in time of need, performing services for the treasury such as making transfers and payments on the government's account, and emitting a safe, uniform currency. But the rapid expansion of the country, the reckless speculation of 1817–19, and an increasing dependence upon the London money market had shown Biddle the need for a national bank to act as a compensatory economic mechanism as well. The production, exchange, and consumption of goods and commodities in America moved in hundreds, if not thousands, of interwoven circular patterns, punctuated by the rhythm of the major crops. At every step credit was needed to keep the exchange process in motion. Most prime producers anticipated payment by discounting notes at banks or by selling to banks bills of exchange drawn upon jobbers or factors. These men in turn would send the goods on their way to wholesalers, retailers, or merchants next in the circle of exchange by again borrowing or selling bills of exchange. Merchants engaged in overseas trade used export commodities as remittances covering drafts and bills drawn on English and European merchant banking houses in payment for imported goods. The London money market was an original source of commercial credit, creating intermediate lines of credit extending westward to the crossroads store deep in the interior of the United States. Any sudden blockage in this circle of credit, whether brought about by a crop failure, overspending on imported goods, unwise investments in internal improvements, or land speculation, would eventually entail a curtailment of transactions, a fall in commodity prices, a ruinous rise in interest and exchange rates, and, after that, a swift toboggan ride toward bankruptcy.

From the outset of his career as president of the bank, Biddle exerted himself to apply compensatory techniques designed to keep the flow of credit even in pace and uniform in volume. Thus, to counter the inflationary tendencies which had come so near to destroying the bank in its first years, he set strict limits to the capital and note issue of the branches, and held over the heads of erring state banks the threat of presenting large batches of their notes for redemption. He also reduced the number of accommodation loans granted by the parent bank, and preached to the branches the wisdom of restricting themselves to commercial loans. In order to realize the ideal of a uniform currency, he decreed that the parent bank and all the branches redeem each other's notes. In order to avoid a repetition of the crisis of 1819 when so much of the parent bank's funds had been sucked westward in the form of banknotes, he began to invest a larger portion of the bank's capital in domestic bills of exchange. Since most of these bills were ultimately paid off in northeastern cities, large-scale circulation of the instruments assured an eventual repatriation of northeastern capital.

The bank's large reservoir of foreign exchange supplied credit for importers when the usual sources in England dried up, and thereby prevented an outflow of specie. For example, when in 1825 a sudden rise in exchange rates forced importers to ship specie in order to settle their accounts, Biddle sold at home and abroad a portion of the bank's large holdings of government securities and invested the proceeds in foreign bills which he made available to merchants compelled to make payments abroad. He realized that an outflow of specie would force banks in the seaport cities to contract their loanable funds in geometric ratio to the loss of specie, and thereby spread panic over the length and breadth of the country. The possibility averted, Biddle provided insurance against a repetition of the situation by keeping large balances on deposit with the Barings of London, the Hope firm of Amsterdam, and Hottinguer et Cie. of Paris, against which the bank could sell drafts to importers. The bank's large holdings of exchange and its ability to expand its loanable funds quickly by the sale of government securities also enabled it to compensate for the rapid withdrawals of government deposits when the treasury during the twenties and early thirties retired large portions of the public debt.

In his recent analysis of Jacksonian finance, Temin asserts that the central banking functions of the Second Bank have been exaggerated. He notes that the selling of government securities in the domestic market to compensate for withdrawals by the treasury to pay off government debt exerted a deflationary influence by soaking up currency. More interested in maintaining discipline over the state banks in the crisis of 1825 than in bringing aid and comfort, the Second Bank refused to lend them funds to any extent which would endanger its own position. Thus it never became a lender of last resort—a most important function of modern central banks. "Nevertheless," Temin concludes, "The Second Bank was as close to being a central bank as any bank of its day, and this judgment should not be interpreted to mean that there was no room for improvement."

Good public policy and profits went hand in hand for the Bank of the United States. Throughout Biddle's administration it paid dividends of 7 or 8 percent per year, and its stock was considered a gilt-edged security in Europe as well as in the United States. At the time of its demise it had assets worth about $80 million and liabilities of about half that amount. Its services to the government and to the people at large were immense. Its notes circulated at par and so constituted a uniform currency. Between 1829 and 1832 it engineered the retirement of about $50 million of the government debt, without disturbance to the economy. It provided about $240 million of foreign exchange, at a cost of about one eleventh of one percent. The treasury received a gross return of nearly $18 million from its original investment in the bank of $7 million. The South and West had no reason to complain that Biddle's policies tightened credit there. Note issues by the branches amounted to 70 to 73 percent of the total issued by the bank, and branch drafts (bank drafts drawn by the branches on the parent bank and endorsed to bearer) circulated locally as currency and thereby further swelled the supply of credit. Biddle himself acquired a reputation as a banking genius. Undoubtedly he was one of the best known and most admired men of his generation.

DEMISE OF THE SECOND BANK

Yet in the face of this unqualified success as a public service institution, the bank was jettisoned, to the applause of a majority of the American people, and in the process the principle of central banking was so discredited that it was not reinstated until 1913. The reason was in part the partisan political hostility fanned by Jackson and his followers, and in part a realization of latent danger to American liberties inherent in the immense potential power of the bank.

It is unnecessary to recount again the details of the Bank War in which Jackson slew the "corrupt hydra," or to enter into the controversy over which principal actor was the more responsible for the outbreak of the conflict. Given the conflicting points of view of Jackson and Biddle and their determination to win their objectives, and given the framework in which the war was conducted and the issues presented to the people, it is difficult to see how there could have been any other outcome. For Jackson the immense financial resources of the bank and its relative independence from governmental control made it a potential threat not only to his party but to any national administration. Although his specific charges of malfeasance against the bank were groundless, and his campaign against the institution an unwarranted persecution, he had a right to be concerned when in 1832 one hundred and two congressmen and senators were in debt to the bank for a total of $850,000. His own plan that the bank be deprived of the right to make accommodation loans, and be owned and directed entirely by the government, was not without merit, and anticipated similar proposals put forth well into the twentieth century. The trouble was that the Bank of the United States mingled the public function of the control of credit with the private function of supplying credit in individual instances. In a democratic nation no function such as the control of credit, which can alter the distribution of wealth, can safely be relegated to a private institution.

The failure of Biddle in 1841 proved to be an epilogue to the career of the BUS which seemed to demonstrate the correctness of all of Jackson's charges against the institution. After the lapse of the federal charter in 1836, Biddle negotiated a charter from the state of Pennsylvania which burdened the bank with heavy financial commitments. In addition to paying an outright bribe of $2 million to the state, the Bank of the United States of Pennsylvania was required to lend up to $6 million to the state upon demand and subscribe to the stock of canal and railroad companies which the state wished to encourage. Since business conditions were excellent and since the bank was augmenting its capital by the sale of its branches, these burdens did not seem too onerous at the time. Encouraged by apparently rosy prospects, Biddle tried to put into effect a grandiose scheme by which the bank would keep balances with its correspondents abroad sufficiently high to permit it to supplant British bankers as financiers of American foreign trade. Meanwhile, impressed by the efforts of the states to finance extensive programs of internal improvements, he acquired for the bank a large portfolio of state and corporate securities.

Promising as these investments seemed at the time, they reduced the liquidity of the bank. As a penalty for ignoring one of his leading precepts, Biddle was forced during the Panic of 1837 to suspend specie payments, even though the assets of the bank were higher than at any time in its history. When cotton exports fell off and exchange rates shot up and merchant failures made investment in bills of exchange precarious, Biddle formed a partnership which bought $2.3 million worth of cotton in the South and shipped it abroad for sale. This timely, though risky action helped support the cotton market and brought the partners a neat profit of $1.4 million.

With the plaudits of the business community ringing in his ears, Biddle resigned from the bank in 1839. Actually the institution was in a far from enviable position. As hard times continued, its portfolio of securities shrank in value. When another crisis forced banks to suspend specie payments again, the bank was in deep trouble. Biddle returned to the helm, but his old magic was gone. A second attempt to sustain cotton prices by direct purchase and sale failed dismally. Drained of cash and paralyzed by frozen assets, the bank was compelled to close its doors in 1841. Biddle's tremendous reputation rapidly evaporated. In the eyes of his former admirers the banking genius now became the crafty adventurer with other people's money who had been unmasked, but alas too late to avoid the ruin he had prepared for so many who were financially involved with him. Biddle retired to his farm, a bankrupt, but still wrapped in aristocratic dignity. He died three years later. The charges of fraud laid against him were unfair of course. His undoing had been brought about by a combination of adverse circumstances and shortcomings in judgment. Perhaps the most disastrous of the latter was the attempt to mix commercial and investment banking, an unhappy combination which was to bring grief to many other bankers until the two functions were permanently separated by the Glass-Steagal Act of 1933.

Nicholas Biddle embodied to a striking degree both the strength and weakness of the American entrepreneur. On one hand he was resourceful, bold, intelligent, determined, a leader who did not shrink at large undertakings, and who could face adversity undaunted. On the other hand, he gradually became intoxicated by his own success, too confident of his own powers, and allowed his judgment to be warped by dreams of grandeur. But it was as an innovator—the true test of the entrepreneur—that he stood pre-eminent among his colleagues in the banking fraternity. Ahead of his time in his understanding of the mechanisms of credit, he created a central bank capable of stabilizing the undisciplined financial condition of the nation.

BANK ADMINISTRATION

During the antebellum period country banks were managed in the informal fashion characteristic of all banks early in the century, but in the cities tasks had become much more specialized, a professional corps of bank officials and employees had come into being, the pace of business had become much faster, and the scope of operations much larger. In 1858 the fifty-three banks of New York City had an operating capital of about $66 million, were staffed by about 2,000 officers and employees, and served several hundred thousand clients.

Yet in even the largest banks, as made plain by J. S. Gibbons in *The*

Banks of New York (1858), the professionalization which had come to permeate the lower echelons had not reached the highest levels of policy making. Presidents, although much more important officials than the figureheads who occupied the position early in the century, were still general entrepreneurs who came to banking from other mercantile fields rather than from the lower ranks of a bank staff. As top decision makers they were supposed to be substantial stock holders and men of means and standing in the business community who could combine an adequate knowledge of banking procedures with a liberal education and an understanding of the larger problems facing business generally. It was considered desirable that they have no outside commercial interests which would conflict with responsibilities to their own institutions. Above all they should be impartial toward bank customers and not be borrowers themselves. Although probably few presidents possessed all of these qualifications, these officials as a whole shaped bank policies in the light of business conditions, and by their personal conduct moulded the image of the institutions held by clients and the public.

Directors, in Gibbons's view, often failed to measure up to the performance expected of them. Like presidents, their most important qualifications were prominence in the business community and large stockholdings. Although most directors seem to have met these tests, many attended discount meetings only irregularly and gave little attention to their most important function—consideration of loan applications. Many acquired their positions mainly in order to keep lines of credit open for themselves. The fact that directors served without salary probably accounted in part for the uneven nature of their performance.

In contrast to most presidents and all directors, cashiers had become highly professionalized, and—in large banks at least—gave all of their time to their jobs. As the active, day-by-day managers, they made it their business to know the banks' clients, supervised the work of the tellers, clerks, porters, and runners and consolidated their reports, opened new accounts, prepared loan applications for submission to the boards of directors, participated in discount meetings, answered letters in the name of the banks, and assisted presidents in preparing the various published reports required by law. Although appointed by the directors, cashiers were considered to be representatives of stockholders. Heavily bonded and receiving salaries up to $10,000 per year, they became, in Gibbons's words, "practically the superior officers, . . . the ears, eyes, brains, and souls of the institutions."

Paying tellers were also very important bank employees. Also heavily bonded, the sole persons in every bank empowered to pay out money, they alone held keys to bank vaults and could even refuse cashiers and presidents permission to enter the vaults. One of the most important duties of paying tellers was preparing the exchange for the daily trip to the clearing house. They were empowered to certify checks, and, surprisingly, could even issue overdrafts to be repaid on the same business day. They also kept summaries of banks' day-by-day cash positions. In large banks paying tellers had assistants and even their own clerks.

Each bank also had a deposit teller who accepted all deposits. To handle their jobs efficiently, these tellers were trained to spot counterfeit bills or bills on broken banks, and were expected to be familiar enough with credit ratings in the business community to identify bad checks as well. Note tellers received payment on all notes falling due. "Runners" served notices on debtors by personal calls on the days when obligations became payable. Porters made deliveries of specie, notes, and checks. Highly trusted employees, the porters of all the banks meeting together had made interbank settlements before the establishment of the New York Clearing House.

As far as accounting was concerned, all tellers and porters kept their own records of transactions. These were abstracted by the bookkeeper into the bank ledger—the record of every client's deposits and borrowings. A balance sheet was made up twice a week strictly for intramural perusal, and once a week the New York banks as required by law published reports of loans, specie, circulation, and deposits.

The cycle of bank operations began on "offering day" when clients called at their banks to present to the cashier their notes for discount. Virtually all businessmen used bank credit rather than attempting to accumulate working capital. The notes were for short terms—not over sixty days—and carried the names of two endorsers. Longer term paper was accepted if secured by collateral. A record of makers and endorsers was entered in the "Offering Book," which together with the notes was presented to the president and directors meeting as discount committee on the following day—the first of the biweekly "discount days." At these meetings decisions regarding the paper were reached by consensus after informal discussions centering around the credit ratings of the individuals concerned. Theoretically all loans were to be made with strict impartiality by the discount committee, but Gibbons makes it plain that accommodations of various sorts were often made privately by the presidents and cashiers to favored individuals. Final decisions on the amount of discounting to be made awaited the returns from the clearing house. Banks which showed debits then trimmed marginal paper accordingly, some notes being refused entirely and others accepted for smaller amounts than face value. Large New York banks discounted seventy-five to one hundred notes at each committee session.

The afternoons of discount days were the busiest parts of the week. Cashiers were constantly engaged in lengthy discussions with clients, some of whom were of course irate because of the trimming of their paper. Long lines formed in front of the windows of the paying and deposit tellers as borrowers stepped up to have their notes cashed or credited. The proportion of deposit credit to note issue had steadily increased in urban banks since the late eighteenth century. In the New York Clearing House operations of 1858 about $200,000 to $300,000 in bank notes were exchanged daily as contrasted to about $25 million in checks.

The contrasts between antebellum New York banks and the urban banks of today are quite plain. Most differences stem from the fact that the former were almost exclusively lending agencies and had no interest in performing deposit and transfer functions for the public generally. Also in contrast to modern bank operations was a lack of centralized management and accounting. Tellers, with their clerks, operated with a good deal of autonomy within the supervision of cashiers. Runners and porters were given a wide range of discretion. Even farther removed from modern practice was the informal procedure for making loans. Discounting committees were practically unchanged in make-up and functions from those of fifty years before. It is difficult to say just when decisions regarding loans became the province of the professional bank staff, but apparently in even the large city banks this development did not take place until nearly the last quarter of the nineteenth century.

SAVINGS BANKS

The rapid specialization of commercial life during the early nineteenth century produced several new financial institutions. Prominent among these were savings banks. Practical philanthropy and social usefulness rather than the hope of profit motivated their formation. Urbanization, by separating a larger proportion of the population from the land and subjecting it to the fluctuations of the business cycle, was decreasing the security of the laboring classes. Savings banks were considered to be a means of helping the poor to better their financial condition, and thereby lighten the load of poor relief which weighed heavily on local governments. Banks of this type established for such a purpose had been formed in Switzerland and in England at the end of the eighteenth century.

In 1816 groups of merchants and bankers with philanthropic inclinations in New York, Philadelphia, and Boston simultaneously set to work to found similar institutions in their own cities. Their efforts resulted in the formation of the New York Bank for Savings, the Philadelphia Saving Fund Society, and Boston's Provident Institution for Savings. All of the banks were mutuals which divided net profits among depositors. Boards of trustees, serving without salary, selected from among the most distinguished men in the communities, determined basic policies and nominated presidents and directors. Investment policies of the banks varied. For example, the Provident Institution of Boston, although practically unlimited by charter in its choice of investments, put most of the depositors' money into bank stock and left the remainder on time deposit with Boston banks. Most other savings banks, operating under more stringent charter restrictions, were limited in their investments to first-class mortgages and to securities of the federal, state, and municipal governments.

At the outset, individual deposits in the banks were limited to a few hundred dollars. Such a restriction was deemed necessary not only to insure that the services of the banks were reserved for the poor but also to prevent expansion of deposits beyond profitable investment possibilities. Trustees feared that such a situation would occur if wealthier people, eager for a good return on their money, used bank deposits as investment for their surplus. Moreover, such a development would greatly increase administrative costs, which were always kept as low as possible. The restrictions on individual deposits naturally inhibited growth of the banks. By 1830 total deposits in the nation's thirty-one institutions amounted to only $7 million.

Since few if any savings banks failed during the next thirty years, legislatures relaxed investment restrictions in order to provide the banks with new sources of income. At the same time, the limitations on individual deposits were gradually raised in response to pressure from the relatively wealthy. As a result of these changes, total deposits stood at $43 million in 1850 and had risen to $150 million by 1860. By this time savings banks had largely lost their original paternalistic character. Since they had become good markets for securities and depositories for reserves, their investment policies had become interrelated with those of other large financial institutions by interlocking directorates.

Savings banks by no means fulfilled the social purpose intended by their founders. Since wages at the time of their early growth were scarcely above the subsistence level, few laboring people could manage to save enough to provide a significant margin of security against accident, old age, or unemployment. Yet for their humble depositors savings banks perhaps mitigated the effect of these untoward occurrences and no doubt helped nourish a sense of social obligation among the leaders of society who promoted the banks. They also aided the growth of the economy by collecting small savings and channeling them into productive investment.

INVESTMENT BANKING

Investment banking may be defined roughly as the process by which bankers aid government and business enterprise to raise capital by selling securities on a commission basis or by purchasing the securities outright for resale to the investing public at a profit. Of much more recent origin than commercial banking, investment banking made its appearance in England when "loan contractors" formed syndicates of merchants, bankers, and wealthy titled investors which purchased portions of treasury security offerings at auction. Since the syndicates performed an important service for the treasury when it needed money in a hurry, loan contractors were able to bargain effectively and purchase at low enough figures to make profits on resale.

Loan contracting was first envisaged in the United States when the speculators William Duer and Andrew Craigie formed a syndicate with two Frenchmen—one of whom was the philosophe and luminary of the French Revolution, Brissot de Warville—which unsuccessfully attempted in 1788 to purchase from the French Crown the debt owed by the United States to France. The syndicate no doubt anticipated a funding of the debt by the federal government about to come into existence and hoped thereby to realize a fancy profit. If the plan had succeeded, the creditors probably would have formed a securities market several years before the New York Stock Market began operations. John Jacob Astor, Stephen Girard, and David Parish emerged as the first full-fledged loan contractors in the United States when they purchased for resale $10 million of a $16 million loan floated by the treasury in 1813 in order to carry on the War of 1812 (see above, p. 38). By this time loan contracting was conducted on a large scale by the leading merchant banking houses of Europe such as Hope, Baring, and Rothschild. The main problem facing contractors was lining up enough prospective "retail" purchasers for the securities they had acquired en bloc. Here merchants and bankers with international connections, like Astor, Girard, Parish, and the European banking houses, had an obvious advantage.

Investment banking entered a new era when state governments in the late twenties and thirties sought ways of marketing large issues of bonds to finance transportation improvement. Sale of government securities was handled at first by merchant banking houses and various types of brokers on a commission basis, and portions of issues found their way to the fledgling New York Stock Exchange. Prominent among the merchant banking firms engaged in selling securities were Prime, Ward and King of New York; Thomas Biddle and Company, and S. and M. Allen of Philadelphia; Alexander Brown and Sons of Baltimore; and August Belmont, German-born representative of the House of Rothschild in New York.

But by the mid-thirties commercial banks were becoming more important marketing agencies for state securities. Since many charters contained conditions that banks lend stipulated sums to state governments upon demand and purchase stated amounts of securities, the banks held improvement bonds both as collateral and as capital investments, but a larger amount they resold both in the United States and abroad. The Bank of the United States, under Biddle's leadership, and the Morris Canal Bank emerged as the most important financial intermediaries. Biddle both through his bank and as an individual was so heavily committed that he deserves the title of the nation's first investment banker. The extent to which investment banking was carried is indicated by the fact that by 1838 the total debt of the states was in the neighborhood of $225 million. Banks, brokers, merchant banking houses, and American investors held probably not more than one-third of the securities represented; the remainder had passed through their hands to English and European correspondents, who had sold them to private investors.

By 1860 the various functions of banking had all taken institutional form, but these institutions had not advanced equally far toward maturity. Commercial banks still narrowly concentrated on discounting notes, and had not expanded their deposit and transfer business to the point that they became public services. Central banking, under Nicholas Biddle's leadership, had reached a high degree of development, but for political reasons this very important aspect of banking had been abandoned. Savings banks were operating in much their present form, and were beginning to make the linkup with investment banking and trust companies which characterized their operations during the last half of the nineteenth century. Investment banking itself was still in its infancy. The function was performed primarily by commercial banks and by merchant bankers who were engaged in other types of financial enterprise as well. Federal, state, and local bonds, and the issues of canal companies and a few railroad companies constituted the bulk of the securities offered for sale. In the decades following the Civil War the great need for capital created by railroad expansion was to intensify the need for the services of investment bankers, and in the course of filling this need the bankers were to exert an increasing amount of control over the enterprises they served.

XII. Progress Toward
Modern Methods
in Insurance

SPREAD OF MUTUAL FIRE INSURANCE COMPANIES

After the larger companies, with their heavy reserves, had solved many of the more difficult problems in fire insurance and had made businessmen familiar with it, the number of local mutuals increased rapidly. Like the contemporary country banks multiplying in the early nineteenth century, these were community enterprises often started on a shoestring with a partly fictitious capitalization made up of personal notes secured by mortgages. The mutual form has always been attractive because it gives policyholders an opportunity to manage their own affairs and guarantees insurance at lowest cost plus an investment return. Nevertheless, in the early period the lack of reserves equal to those of the larger proprietary companies proved to be a serious weakness. Reinsurance, first offered by the Aetna Insurance Company, formed in 1819, gave a measure of stability to the community mutuals; nevertheless few were able to stand serious losses. Conflagrations which wiped out whole sections of towns and cities were much more common than today, and regularly bankrupted local insurance companies which had neglected to disperse the risks they insured. Even the larger companies were slow in guarding against the disastrous losses from conflagration. The great New York fire of 1834 toppled most fire insurance companies in the city and many in Connecticut as well.

After 1820 state governments began to take steps to protect the interests of policy holders at the same time that the first regulatory legislation was passed to protect bank depositors and note holders. Among other measures, maximum limits for policies were established, mutuals were prohibited from starting business until enough insurance had been subscribed to provide an adequate backlog of reserves, and a few states required companies to carry special reserve funds for the benefit of policyholders as well. After the fifties state insurance commissions made their appearance, uniform provisions for incorporation were established, and Massachusetts inaugurated standard policy forms. Aided by legal safeguards of this type, some prudently managed small companies which survived the early critical years and were not struck by conflagrations became very prosperous. A few New England mutuals returned to policyholders 95 percent to 100 percent of premium payments in years when losses were low. A few which had exceptionally good investment experience even paid back a sum larger than the premium.

A major trend in the fire insurance business becoming evident in the twenties was the formation of mutuals to insure specialized risks. Farm mutuals, appearing at about this time, spread rapidly throughout the West after the Civil War. In 1835 Zachariah Allen, engineer and author of works on solar light, gravitation, and mechanics, incorporated The Manufacturers' Mutual, the first mutual to write fire insurance for cotton mills. Allen had made a close study of fire prevention methods, and required insured mills to adhere to strict requirements in this regard and to submit to frequent and detailed inspections. His efforts in fire prevention were so successful that mill insurance rates soon dropped by 30 percent. Still in existence today, The Manufacturers' Mutual had been as much a pioneer as the Philadelphia Contributorship. After the Civil War insurance coverage spread rapidly, and by 1900 could be purchased to cover most of the risks faced by businessmen in the conduct of their affairs.

Aware of their fiduciary capacity, insurance companies in the second half of the century made extensive co-operative efforts to improve their stability and increase their services to policyholders. Competition by rate cutting, which tended to undermine companies, had almost from the beginning been a source of danger to the industry. In a move which was roughly equivalent to the formation of pools by railroads, insurance companies in 1866 established the National Board of Underwriters, designed to enforce the adoption of uniform, scientifically determined rates, and uniform policy provisions. Although this organization was no more successful in achieving its objectives than contemporary efforts to regulate competition in other fields, state underwriters' associations, working closely with local boards, did manage to bring a greater uniformity in rates, policies, and methods of adjusting claims. Companies also co-operated to improve fire protection. The National Fire Prevention Association, organized in 1896, did important work in improving the design of buildings, in devising sprinkler systems, and in developing chemical fire fighting apparatus.

SPECIAL CHARACTERISTICS OF LIFE INSURANCE

Because of its unique nature, life insurance followed a different pattern of development than that of other types of insurance. In contrast to fire and marine insurance, it is not a contract of indemnity but a contract to pay a certain benefit contingent upon the duration of one or more lives, and therefore—barring lapse of the policy—will eventually mature. Given an accurate mortality table, showing the number of individuals in a large, representative test group who die in every year of the human life span, and given a stable interest rate which can within limits be projected into the future, the risks assumed by life insurance underwriters can be reduced almost to the vanishing point. But, partially offsetting these advantages, life insurance companies must sell their product; the buyer will usually not seek the insurance voluntarily, as can normally be expected in the case of marine insurance, and to a somewhat lesser degree in the case of fire insurance. Therefore, it became apparent during the nineteenth century that the success of life insurance companies depended to a large extent on the aggressiveness of their sales forces.

A brief description of the central process of life insurance is necessary for an understanding of the institution's history. Under the level premium plan almost universal in whole life policies, an individual purchasing a policy pays a much larger premium than necessary to meet the mathematically ascertained cost of insurance at his particular age. A small part of the difference between the cost of insurance and the amount of the premium is called a "loading," that is, a charge to cover administrative costs, profit for the company, and possible adverse investment results. But the larger part of the difference constitutes a reserve which is invested by the company for the policyholder and allowed to accumulate at compound interest. When the premium payer reaches advanced age, this surplus is needed to offset the natural cost of life insurance, which by this time has advanced to a prohibitive level.

Today these policy reserves are rightly considered to be the property of policyholders, and are available to them in the form of security for loans, cash surrender value, and extended term insurance. State legislatures, quick to prevent dissipation of capital reserves, from the outset limited the investment alternatives available to life insurance companies, as had of course been done for marine and fire insurance companies. Yet public authorities were much slower to vindicate, or even recognize, the rights of policyholders to the reserves of their policies. Thus, until well past the middle of the nineteenth century, companies enjoyed an almost unlimited control over the rapidly mounting surpluses accruing from premium payments and began to transform life insurance from family protection into a device for capital accumulation.

EARLY HISTORY OF LIFE INSURANCE

From the Middle Ages onward underwriters sometimes wrote short-term insurance policies on the lives of merchants and travelers for the benefit of families and creditors, and by 1720 several mutual assessment life insurance societies had made their appearance. Upon the death of a member, these societies assessed survivors a stipulated amount to be paid to the estate of the deceased. Modern life insurance is also collaterally descended from the gambling annuities and tontines offered by necessitous European governments during the late seventeenth and the eighteenth centuries. The annuities were considered to be an abandonment of capital by the annuitant in return for stipulated payments by government made for the duration of his life. The number of payments was usually designed to coincide with the life expectancy of the purchaser, although no procedure was devised to determine life expectancy with precision. If the annuitant died before the payments had been completed, the government pocketed the remainder; if he lived beyond his anticipated span of life, the payments he collected represented pure profit.

A special type of annuity, the tontine, which offered even greater rewards, was to have a direct reflection in American life insurance. As put into effect by the French government in 1689, subscribers, upon paying 300 livres to enter the game, were divided into fourteen classes according to age. The special feature of the tontine was the continuation of all annual repayments and their division among a continually smaller group of annuitants until the last survivor of a class died. Under this plan, therefore, the income of survivors increased rapidly in their old age. The last survivor of one class in the tontine of 1689, for example, was receiving at her death an annual return of 70,000 livres on her original investment of 300 livres. The annuities and tontines of the seventeenth and eighteenth centuries were probably unfair to either governments or subscribers merely because of the lack of accurate mortality tables from which to determine the amount and number of repayments. Usually governments were the losers, because in their haste to raise cash they felt compelled to increase the attractiveness of the gambling devices by loading the odds heavily in favor of prospective customers. Tontines under private auspices continued long after governments had acquired the financial maturity to abandon them, and were even used occasionally in the colonies to raise funds for hotels and public buildings. New York's famous Tontine Coffee House, a gathering place for merchants, was an example.

In another gambling device akin to life insurance underwriters took bets on the lives of celebrities and political notables until the practice was stopped by a British law of 1773—since then universally adopted wherever life insurance is sold—invalidating insurance contracts on lives in which the insurer has no insurable interest. Without such a law life insurance paradoxically could, and did, reduce the life expectancy of the insured.

Life insurance as family protection grew in England side by side with gambling schemes. In 1762 the first modern life insurance company was founded—The Society of Equitable Assurances on Lives and Survivorships. A mutual, it granted whole life insurance on level premiums calculated on a mortality table accurate for practical purposes. It also inaugurated many of the procedures which later became standard regarding the selection of risks, the terms of policies, the handling of reserves, and the payment of dividends. By 1800 the company had 5,129 policies outstanding for a total of 3.9 million pounds in insurance. Like so many other British financial institutions it became the model for similar organizations founded later in the United States.

Understandably, life insurance was slower to develop in predominantly rural America than in Europe. The need for such protection is created by industrial society which separates most individuals from the traditional sources of security, particularly land ownership. In 1759 the Presbyterian Synod of New York and Philadelphia incorporated a mutual annuity organization for widows and children of Presbyterian ministers, which incidently is still in existence. Ten years later officials of the Church of England followed suit by establishing The Episcopal Corporation. By the end of the eighteenth century the Insurance Company of North America and other marine underwriters issued term life insurance, mostly on the lives of ship captains.

But the issuance of whole life polices did not begin until the formation of The Pennsylvania Company for Insurance on Lives and Granting Annuities, established in 1809 with a capital of $500,000 and incorporated in 1812. The company established precedents for policy terms by limiting travel to the northeast United States and Canada, canceling the contract in case of death by dueling or at the hands of justice, and appropriating all values in the policy if premiums were not paid when due. The maximum value of policies was limited to $15,000.

The sale of the simple, nongambling annuities went forward briskly, but by the end of its first year of operation the company had issued only three life insurance policies. After twelve years only thirty-seven policies were in force bringing a paltry premium income of $3,789 per year. The discouraged directors, attributing the failure of their life insurance offerings to public apathy, inserted notices in the newspapers and distributed pamphlets describing the benefits of this kind of protection. This half-hearted attempt at advertising had little effect, however. To some degree ignorance of the principles of life insurance had bred a suspicion of it fortified by a foolish religious bias that it represented an attempt to frustrate divine will. But a more fundamental reason was the subtle, psychological sales resistance to life insurance which can be overcome only by aggressive marketing methods based on personal solicitation. Annuities offered by a sound company bringing an attractive rate of interest sold themselves, for businessmen could readily recognize them as a savings investment. But without careful indoctrination the businessmen would naturally be suspicious of the long-term life insurance contract, which deferred all repayments beyond the enjoyment of the investor, brought no income, and could be quickly terminated with a loss of all invested values upon many arbitrary contingencies.

The discouraging experience of the Pennsylvania Company was repeated by the second such organization to enter the field—the Massachusetts Hospital Life Insurance Company. During the early nineteenth century state legislatures had often allowed educational and philanthropic institutions to conduct lotteries for the purpose of accumulating capital, and, as we have seen, canal and other transportation improvement companies were often granted banking privileges for the same reason. In like manner the very distinguished group of Massachusetts merchants, professional men, and politicians who founded the Massachusetts Hospital in 1811 were incorporated in 1818 as a life insurance company with the stipulation that one-third of the profits of the company were to go to the hospital. The directors chose as actuary Nathaniel Bowditch, a scholarly, self-educated ship captain who had mastered mathematics, astronomy, and several foreign languages, and had written the famous treatise on navigation bearing his name which came to be known the world over. An honorary Harvard M.A., he had been serving as president of a Salem marine insurance company. Probably realizing the poor prospect in life insurance, Bowditch upon acceptance of his new position prevailed upon the directors to obtain permission from the legislature for the company to accept and administer trusts.

The Massachusetts Hospital Life thus became one of the nation's first trust companies. The need for this type of organization was much more palpable than the need for life insurance. As we have seen, many considerable fortunes had been accumulated in Massachusetts during the Napoleonic wars, and securing capable and honest trustees to administer the funds for widows and minor children was a real problem. Bowditch was aware that a financial institution capitalized at $500,000 and administered by a board of directors containing the bluest blood in the state could perform a real service in this regard. All possible measures were taken under the revised charter to promote the stability of the company and emphasize its fiduciary nature. The stock was held entirely by first families and could be sold in the market only after having been offered at par plus interest to other stockholders. A Board of Control was appointed to examine accounts. A surprisingly wide range of investments was permitted, indicating that the legislature placed more faith in the *noblesse oblige* of the native aristocracy than in legal limitations. Beneficiaries' funds could be placed in first-class mortgages and in bank discounts and could be used for a wide range of commercial and industrial loans, including loans to the directors themselves. The legislature's faith in Massachusetts blue bloods was not misplaced. During its first thirteen years of operation the company incurred no bad debts at all, and was compelled to foreclose only five of some 3,000 mortgages.

Beneficiaries shared profits equally with stockholders, except that beneficiaries paid a yearly handling fee of one-half of one percent. Consistent with the strict fiduciary nature of the company, the only clients accepted were trustees and individuals presumably unable to handle their own affairs, such as "females, minors, clergy, instructors, charitable institutions, and navy officers."

Eminently successful, the firm by 1830 was administering 1,123 trusts with a total value of $5.5 million. It had a few accounts valued at more than $100,000, but most ranged between $500 and $1,000. Dividends paid during the antebellum period ranged between 7 and 12 percent. But the company had as discouraging an experience with life insurance as did the Pennsylvania Company, and as a result ceased offering this coverage entirely after the Civil War. Still in business today, Massachusetts Hospital Life came to be, in the words of Bowditch, "a species of Savings Bank for the rich and middle class of society," no doubt sharply to be distinguished from the philanthropically oriented savings banks of the antebellum period. Its major significance lies in its creative innovation in the trust field. Bowditch, a mathematical genius, solved most of the actuarial problems that were envisaged at the time, and worked out forms and plans which were copied by organizations founded in the years to come. The company was the direct inspiration for the New York Life and Trust, the Ohio Life and Trust, and the Girard Life and Annuity Company. Like the Massachusetts Hospital Life, these companies apparently considered the life insurance business to be rather unpromising, and therefore devoted themselves mainly to the administration of trusts.

THE COMING OF LIFE INSURANCE MUTUALS

Although many new companies were formed during the boom period between 1832 and 1837—twenty-five charters being granted in New York alone—life insurance had not become genuinely popular, nor had it made much impact upon the economy. Life insurance came of age when the mutuals, founded during the late thirties and forties, began transforming the business by aggressive new methods. The mutual form, increasingly popular in fire insurance, was particularly appropriate for life insurance. By distributing surplus above policy reserves and net cost of insurance as dividends, mutuals could present life insurance as investment. But more important, the necessity of gathering a large number of applications before companies could begin operations forced promoters to devise aggressive new marketing techniques—the dynamic element absent previously. This innovation, coming during a period in which the middle class was rapidly growing in numbers and wealth and when industrialization and urbanization were separating increasing numbers of people from the traditional sources of financial security, stimulated the rapid development of life insurance as an institution.

Although the New England Mutual was the first to get a charter, the first company to begin operations was Mutual Life of New York, founded by Alfred Pell and Morris Robinson. Pell was the wealthy New York representative of an English marine insurance firm. Robinson had been cashier of the New York branch of the Bank of the United States, and after the demise of the institution had established himself as a private banker in New York and representative of the American Life Insurance and Trust Company of Baltimore. Both men had studied the business methods of the Old Equitable while on trips to England, and Robinson in particular wanted to apply these in American organization.

The two men secured a charter from the New York legislature in 1842 often called the Magna Charta of American life insurance companies. By its terms the company was empowered to write any kind of life policies or annuities it chose. Corporate powers were to be exercised by a board of thirty-six trustees elected by policyholders for terms of three years. The trustees elected the president, and he chose the administrative staff after consultation with the trustees. Dividends were to be paid from surplus, at first every five years, but later annually. Investments were limited to grade A mortgages and the bonds of the state of New York, New York municipalities, and the United States government. Complete financial statements were to be published every five years, and the company was not to begin business until applications for at least $500,000 worth of insurance had been secured.

The opportunities confronting life insurance companies brought many new mutuals into the field. Of the twenty in operation by 1847, seven are still doing business today, among them Connecticut Mutual, Penn Mutual, New England Mutual, and New York Life. The attractiveness of mutuals did not lead to an entire abandonment of the proprietary form, however. The widespread failure of weaker mutuals shortly after founding demonstrated the value of substantial reserves above and beyond those created by policyholders at the outset of a company's career. But most stock companies eventually mutualized to the extent that they distributed as dividends to policyholders all profits above legal interest. Life insurance in force rose from $4.65 million in 1840 to $14 million in 1845 and to $96 million in 1850. By 1870 it had reached $2 billion. Proportionally the growth of the life insurance business was greater than the growth of the economy or of any other financial institution.

Many reforms were instituted by the companies after 1842 in order to protect the interests of policyholders and speed the development of the industry. Rules of selection were tightened in order to secure better insurance risks, and medical examinations were made more searching and detailed. Travel restrictions were gradually eased as the incidence of epidemics decreased. Rates were lowered several dollars per thousand below those of the life and trust companies, in part as a response to competition and in part because of improved actuarial methods and mortality tables. Policyholders were allowed to pay part of their premiums in "premium notes" which were later redeemed out of dividends. This procedure allowed a young man to buy more insurance than he could otherwise afford early in life, but by feeding dubious assets into the companies it had a detrimental effect on the quality of their reserves. Mounting criticism forced ultimate abandonment of the procedure after severe competition had led many companies seriously to undermine their stability by large accumulations of premium notes.

Another competitive policy which weakened financial structures was the payment of dividends considerably in excess of surplus. Since these were paid in scrip which could be used only to purchase more insurance, the companies suffered no immediate financial loss, but created an increasing load of future liability. Penn Mutual, for example, declared a dividend in 1849 of 80 percent of premium payments, and New York Life, between 1846 and 1867, paid from 30 to 50 percent per year. Fortunately the assets of the strongest and earliest established companies increased at a pace which enabled them to meet inflated claims, but excessive dividends drove many smaller and weaker mutuals to the wall.

Perhaps the most notable change in the life insurance business lay in marketing procedures. In contrast to the life and trust companies, the mutuals realized that staid, pedantic newspaper advertisements and booklets were not enough. From the beginning they developed aggressive agencies which sold through personal solicitation. Agents' commissions, previously about 10 percent of initial premiums and 5 percent on renewals, were doubled or tripled. During the fierce competition of the fifties companies raided each other's sales forces by offers of higher commissions, and agents "twisted" policyholders in competing companies by getting them to transfer their insurance. The techniques of modern advertising owe much to the feverish promotion programs of the mutuals during this period. Agents quickly developed the "hard sell" generally used today—the emphasis on the uncertainty of life and the dismal predicament of families adrift in a cold cruel world with no breadwinner to provide for them.

The administration of the first life insurance companies was of necessity simple and inexpensive. Their business was usually conducted in small storefronts by actuaries and a few clerks. But by 1860 the leading mutuals had developed much larger and more specialized organizations. Boards of trustees, always chosen from among leading businessmen in order to lend an air of dignity, integrity, and stability, were divided into the several committees which supervised the various departments. Among these were claims, finance, insurance, agencies, and sales. Together with the president these committees established policy. Day by day routine was carried on by the president, vice-president, secretary, and eight to ten administrative departments analagous to the trustees' committees. Because of the sharply differentiated functions in life insurance organizations, the companies soon developed specialists in investments, actuarial planning, medicine, law, and sales. Policyholders in theory had ultimate control by virtue of their power to elect trustees, but, like stockholders in modern corporations, they usually played only a passive role. Unless a major issue was at stake they regularly filled vacancies on the boards by electing slates of trustees prepared by the incumbent members.

Although much had been accomplished in the development of life insurance, the business was to achieve its greatest growth during the period following the Civil War. The changes in this era came not so much in the organization and operation of companies as in the use of reserves and in relation of companies to government, the public, and other financial institutions.

XIII. The Fur Trade

The exploitation of natural resources created some of the largest business enterprises of the nineteenth century and thereby fostered far-reaching changes in corporate finance, marketing, business organization, and technological methods. Moreover, this area of enterprise injected a dynamic element into American business growth which distinguished it from the contemporary development of business in Europe. Almost every generation of Americans during the nineteenth century was confronted by bonanzas of some sort. Fur and timber had offered rewards from the earliest colonial period. Aggressive businessmen of the nineteenth century were promised even greater gains from natural wealth of other types: lead in the upper Mississippi Valley; copper on the southern shores of Lake Superior and in Montana and Arizona; gold in the Appalachian highlands and in greater profusion in California; seas of prairie grass on the high plains capable of supporting millions of cattle; oil in Pennsylvania; silver in the Comstock Lode. Moreover, each bonanza triggered a multiplier effect in which a congeries of associated activities grew into industries, and these in turn created new opportunities for wealth.

Yet, the conquest of the continent's wealth had its unlovely aspects also —bare, eroded fields which testified to the tobacco and cotton farmer's easy assumption that land was a wasting asset; mile after mile of skinned timberland, half of it burned out by forest fires; range deteriorated by overgrazing and ruined by futile dry farming; mines caved in and water logged before half the ore had been taken out; slag piles containing a wealth of irretrievable metals. Less noticeable, but more grievous was the waste of human resources—farmers, miners, workers of all kinds broken by toil, disease, and the pathetic anomaly of poverty in the midst of riches; businessmen ruined by unwise and greedy speculation; government all too often corrupted and made to serve the interests of the most successful exploiters. But until American development was well underway its grimmer aspects were relatively unnoticed, or were shrugged off as an inevitable concomitant of progress. American optimism, supported by so much tangible evidence of success, was a durable mood, impervious to serious self-examination which would diminish its ebullience. The Protestant ethic, with its emphasis upon gain and stewardship, joined materialism and religion in holy wedlock. Success was the seal of moral approval for most acquisitive enterprises. In such a climate economic growth was fast, and the cost of speed, in the form of human and material waste, did not seem excessive to most of those who benefited from its effect.

BEGINNINGS OF THE FUR TRADE

In many ways the fur trade was unique among other American bonanzas. The very first business of any sort, along with fishing, it began when the first French and English ships touched the Atlantic coastline in the late sixteenth and early seventeenth centuries. In Canada it quickly became a state enterprise, the very *raison d'être* of that French colony. Drawing French, British, and later American traders deep into the continent and thereby hastening exploration, the trade was carried on under almost incredible hardships over an equally incredible expanse of territory. Then suddenly, in the last half of the nineteenth century, after a 250-year span of life, the trade came to an end in the United States and left behind it only romantic memories in the form of French place names and a long record of adventure. Heavily freighted with public interest and intertwined with politics and diplomacy, the traffic in furs was from the beginning closely regulated by the government, yet all legislation was nugatory because of insuperable difficulties of enforcement. This situation did not mean, however, that the fur trade was carried on under conditions of laissez-faire. Far from it. Although the trapper and Indian trader could roam at will over the millions of square miles in the center of the North American continent, a relatively small number of merchant combines such as the Hudson's Bay Company, the North West Company, and the American Fur Company monopolized the supply of trade goods and the marketing of furs. Their power was derived from their domination of the very few entrances into the fur country—Hudson's Bay, the St. Lawrence Valley, and the Mohawk Valley.

Initially the French had tried to carry on the trade through state monopolies or through licensed traders. Neither system gave controls adequate to prevent an exploitation of the Indians which resulted in savage warfare and a heavy loss of furs. Yet under the French the trade expanded greatly. Empire builders such as La Salle and d'Iberville, and lesser "fermiers" and "bourgeois" such as La Mothe-Cadillac and Daniel Duluth founded forts along the shores of the Great Lakes from which they dominated the trade over vast areas. Supplied with trade goods from state monopolies or from merchant partners in Montreal, they harvested the furs by dispatching "coureurs be bois" with the goods into remote Indian villages.

After 1763 the British carried on the Lakes trade in much the same fashion. A handful of organizations such as the North West Company tapped the sources of beaver as far west as the Rockies and as far south as the Ohio and the Missouri rivers. The companies were managed by groups of "wintering partners" established in the western forts and merchant partners in Montreal. All operations were conducted with the kind of credit arrangements common in the commodity trades of the southern colonies. The Montreal merchants received trade goods and supplies from London houses on long-term credit which enabled them to advance the goods to the wintering partners on somewhat shorter terms. The wintering partners then repacked the goods in smaller bundles and delivered them to the coureurs, again on credit. Each participant in the trade advanced the goods to the next functionary at a markup, or for a commission, which constituted his profit. Every spring, when streams and lakes opened up, beaver pelts retraced the path of the trade goods, making up debit balances all the way to London. The entire cycle took two years or more. Many of the furs were ultimately sold at the great international fur market in Leipzig. In the great basin of Hudson's Bay the fur trade was carried on in more centralized fashion by the Hudson's Bay Company. Since supplies could be shipped directly by sea to the fur posts, the middlemen of the Lakes trade were eliminated and financing was direct.

THE FUR TRADE IN THE EARLY REPUBLIC

The United States, at the beginning of its national career, labored under competitive disadvantages in the fur trade. Fur production east of the Appalachians had long since ceased to be of commercial importance.

Albany, lying at the eastern terminus of the only water level route from the seaboard to the West, had figured largely in the trade during the colonial period, but after independence its merchants had neither the financing, the ample supplies of cheap trade goods, nor the contacts with western Indians to enable them to compete effectively with traders located in Montreal. Britain, by its occupancy of forts on the southern shores of the Great Lakes, dominated the trade in the Ohio Valley, and Spain controlled it in the Southwest.

But the strong position of the merchant marine gave merchants of Boston, New York, and Philadelphia a competitive advantage in the Pacific trade which to some degree compensated for disadvantages in the Lakes and in the Mississippi Valley. In the hope of finding a domestic product besides ginseng which would sell in China, a group of Boston merchants in 1787 dispatched the ship *Columbia* and a small tender around Cape Horn to the West Coast in search of furs for the Chinese market. After spending nearly a year at Nootka Sound collecting peltry from the Indians, the *Columbia* sailed for Canton, exchanged its cargo of furs for exotic eastern goods, and came back to Boston around the world. Henceforth the China trade could be carried on without reliance on uncertain supplies of ginseng, with less drain of specie, and without lengthy tramping voyages to the West Indies and Europe in order to obtain the bullion, bills on London, and European manufactures also acceptable in the Canton market.

For at least a hundred years the staple fur of the Great Lakes and Hudson's Bay trade had been beaver, which was used in the manufacture of hats. But the pelts most in demand in China were those of sea otters, amiable creatures four or five feet long who congregated in herds off the West Coast from Alaska to Southern California. Since American Indians were unable to capture sea otters in commercially feasible numbers, large-scale trade became possible only when Captain Joseph O'Cain, of Boston, made a contract with Alexander Baranov, governor of the Russian-American Company post at Sitka, whereby Baranov agreed to supply O'Cain with Aleut Indian hunters and equipment in return for one-half of the catch of skins. This arrangement proved to be so profitable that during the period 1805 to 1812 other merchants, mostly from New England, made similar arrangements with Baranov. Jonathan Winship of Boston established a permanent hunting base off the coast of Southern California. Aleut Indians attached to the base, operating from small boats, killed the otter by rifle fire. Hawaiian swimmers, also employed by Winship, retrieved the creatures.

Meanwhile the fur trade in the Old Northwest had rebounded strongly after 1796 when the British abandoned their forts on the southern shores of the Lakes. Perhaps anticipating this development, Congress and the president had for several years been considering methods of control. During the colonial period provincial assemblies, in order to assure fair treatment of the Indians, had licensed traders, placed them under bond, and had set prices for goods and peltry. But because of the boundless expanse of Indian territory and the impossibility of effective enforcement, such measures simply had not worked. Traders regularly cheated the Indians, and as a result the irate red men wreaked bloody reprisals on the frontiers. After independence the states adopted licensing measures, but to no better effect. No doubt with these failures in mind, Washington proposed to Congress a novel and imaginative program—the establishment of a system of government "factories," or trading posts, at which trade with the Indians would be conducted under fair and uniform conditions. The system was not designed to supplant private trade, which was to be carried on under license from territorial governors, but was designed to establish standards of fair treatment which would bring peace to the frontiers and hopefully exercise a civilizing influence on the Indians. One hundred and fifty thousand dollars was initially appropriated for the project. From time to time other appropriations followed, and the number of stores was increased until ultimately twenty-eight had been in operation at one time or another. The system was administered by a superintendent of Indian trade established in the War Department who purchased goods for the stores and determined prices and policies. Retail markups ranged from 65 to 100 percent, contrasting markedly with the much higher prices usually charged by private traders.

At first this initial attempt of the federal government to compete with private enterprise appeared to be a success, but the War of 1812 brought heavy losses which continued after the coming of peace. Even more portentous, increasing condemnation came from private traders, particularly from partners in John Jacob Astor's American Fur Company. Significantly, critics never questioned the right of the federal government to go into business in competition with private enterprise; instead they disparaged the quality and variety of the goods inventoried, and accused the factors of mismanagement and waste of the taxpayers' money. Prominent western politicians came to the aid of the fur traders, and Thomas Hart Benton, after a series of denunciatory speeches in the senate in 1822, introduced the bill which abolished the "pious monster."

But death by politics came to a factory system which was already suffering from mortal economic ills. Since the purpose of the system was not profit, the factors never pursued the fur trade aggressively but merely waited in their stores for Indians to come and trade. Outfits of the major fur companies, on the other hand, restlessly probed the entire Northwest, and as a result got the cream of the fur crop at lowest prices. Moreover, since the superintendent was required by law to favor American manufactures, the inventories of the stores at this time could not have been of as good quality or variety as the English goods purchased by the fur companies. In addition, the fact that the stores could not sell liquor gave a great advantage to the independent traders who did so surreptitiously, and contrary to law. Drunken Indians could be induced to part with their furs for a pittance. In sum, the fur companies by their ruthless and more efficient methods simply blanketed the operations of the much smaller factory system. Nevertheless, the system must have offered competition to the independents; otherwise they would have had no incentive to move against it as strongly as they did.

JOHN JACOB ASTOR

The integration of the fur trade into a world-wide pattern of commerce was brought to its fullest development by John Jacob Astor and provided the impetus for the accumulation of Astor's great fortune. In the course of his trading operations, he attempted, and nearly succeeded, in monopolizing the supplies of fur from the upper Mississippi to the Pacific. In essence Astor's object was to organize the American fur trade along the lines of the Canadian trade.

Born in the village of Waldorf, Germany, in 1763, young John Jacob Astor arrived in New York in 1783 with a package of musical instruments with which he hoped to enter the life of commerce. After a few years at odd jobs, he became established in a small store where he sold musical instruments and "beat" [prepared] furs for market. By the late 1780s he was tramping the Mohawk valley of upper New York with a pack of trade goods on his back, collecting furs from Indians and country store keepers. Late in life Astor claimed that making his first thousand dollars, during this period, was the hardest task of his life. But during the nineties he rode the crest of the boom. Three weeks of every year he spent in Montreal, buying furs, shipping them to correspondents in England and the United States, and ordering trade goods for dispatch into the Indian country. In 1800 he entered the China trade, sending cargoes of specie, ginseng, and furs worth up to $160,000 apiece to Canton, with which to obtain teas, silks, and other exotic wares. These he exchanged mostly in Europe for Indian trade goods, thus keeping in motion a world-wide cycle of trade which by 1806 had brought him a fortune of nearly $1 million.

His career entered a second phase in 1808 when, with several partners, he formed the American Fur Company, the vehicle for the projected monopoly. Chartered by New York State, with nearly the entire capital subscribed by Astor himself, the organization was little more than a front to give respectability and patriotic purpose to the Astor enterprise and thus secure the co-operation of the federal and territorial governments. The company established posts from the Great Lakes to the Rockies staffed by small traders, who, in addition to trading with the Indians, sent out hunting expeditions of their own.

At the outset most of the trappers who traded with the company were independent; others, whose "outfits" were advanced by Astor, worked on a share basis and had much the same relationship to the company as did sharecroppers to landlords. Because of bitter, and often unscrupulous competition, the number of independent trappers declined over the years. Usually they fell in debt to the company, and in return for Astor's financing were compelled to deal with it exclusively, buying their supplies at prices many times those of the European market and selling their furs for a small portion of what these would bring in Montreal. All of the operations of the company were tinged with exploitation, and it was bitterly hated by most of those who were caught in its snare. It is only fair to note, however, that exploitation had from the beginning been a normal characteristic of the fur trade.

Astor naturally prospered because of his uniquely favorable position. But, although able to dominate the fur trade south of the Great Lakes and in the upper Mississippi valley, the American Fur Company was never able to acquire the desired monopoly in the Rocky Mountains. Here the company had to contend with hundreds of independent traders and with several large companies located in St. Louis.

In an attempt to capture the trade of the West Coast and its profitable connections with the Far East, Astor and several partners formed the Pacific Fur Company in 1810 and established on the Columbia River the fort Astoria, designed to be the headquarters for the trade. This truly notable feat became the most widely known and admired episode of Astor's career, largely because Washington Irving wrote a highly romanticized, two-volume account of it. Yet, somewhat paradoxically, it was also Astor's most unsuccessful business venture. The very heavy investment in the two expeditions sent out to establish the fort—one by land and one by sea—

was largely lost when Astor's garrison surrendered the entire installation to the British in 1813 for a paltry $58,000.

By 1825 overexpansion of the Far Eastern trade and a declining demand for furs in Europe and America brought about largely by a shift in fashion from beaver to silk hats induced Astor gradually to shift the bulk of his fortune elsewhere. He chose the ground under his feet. Between 1820 and 1848 he increased his already extensive holdings of New York real estate. Although he engaged in almost every type of real estate transaction, constructing many buildings, including the famous Astor House Hotel, probably the most profitable aspect of his business was buying up large tracts on the outskirts of the rapidly expanding city and subdividing these for sale as building lots. The fact that New York could expand in only one direction—northward—diminished the risks normally attendant upon urban real estate speculation. So extensive did his holdings become that in 1847 he was receiving $200,000 per year from rents alone. At his death in 1848, his fortune, from all sources, amounted to between $20 million and $30 million.

THE ROCKY MOUNTAIN FUR TRADE

The American fur trade received great impetus by the opening up of the Missouri River as a major route to the Rockies, and by the subsequent growth of St. Louis as a great fur center. The Lewis and Clark expedition of 1804–6 alerted a few men of vision in St. Louis to the new opportunities, but establishing a profitable fur trade in the Rockies entailed serious difficulties. In the first place, the traders would have to run the gauntlet of the fierce plains Indians for a distance of nearly 1,000 miles. These Indians, completely dependent upon the buffalo for their livelihood, could not be brought within the circle of the fur trade, and would most certainly look upon the white men as intruders. Secondly, many of the Indians of the Rocky Mountains, although more peaceable, were in such a primitive state that they possessed neither the techniques of trapping beaver or of making canoes. Therefore, the traders would have to plan and manage all trapping operations themselves. Finally, outfits of the North West Company of Montreal and the Hudson's Bay Company were already operating in the Rockies, and would no doubt prove to be strong competitors.

The St. Louis traders ultimately solved all of these problems. As in previous periods of development, the trade expanded not so much because of a particular system of technique, but because of the efforts of aggressive, energetic individuals. The first of these was Manuel Lisa, an enterprising

Spaniard who never learned to read or write or even to speak English or French grammatically. Stirred by the reports of Lewis and Clark, Lisa and a few partners gathered some trade goods and ascended the Missouri in 1807 to the mouth of the Yellowstone, and thence to the mouth of the Bighorn, where Lisa built a fort. Returning the next year he formed the St. Louis Missouri Fur Company, which for a short time enjoyed a monopoly of the trade. But losses of fur to Blackfeet Indians and other difficulties led to its demise about 1828.

Lisa had shown that the Rocky Mountains contained rich fur-producing areas, but it was William H. Ashley who organized trapping there on a profitable commercial basis. An immigrant from Vermont, Ashley apparently had made some money in Missouri lead mining operations which was available for other enterprises. In 1822 he advertised in *The Missouri Republican* for a hundred young men to join him in a trapping expedition to the Rockies which would last three years. In several ways his offer represented an innovation in the conduct of the fur trade. First, the party was to be much larger than those sent out by the fur companies. Second, the fur was to be obtained by trapping, not by trade with Indians; third, all operations, including menial tasks, were to be carried out by untrained, but presumably enthusiastic tyros rather than the professional "voyageurs" and "engagés" employed by the fur companies; fourth, the young men would be reimbursed on a share basis. Ashley would advance them their outfits on credit, and they in return would discharge their debts by selling him whatever beaver they secured at $3 per pound, about one-half of the market price in St. Louis. How Ashley financed the expedition is unknown, but probably funds other than his own came from St. Louis merchants.

Ashley's appeal fell upon receptive ears, and he got more than the hundred men he needed. During the spring and summer the party laboriously made its way up the Missouri River to the junction with the Yellowstone, and then broke up into parties of a dozen or so men to undertake trapping operations. These proved to be remunerative, but highly dangerous. Indians were a constant menace and stole horses at every opportunity. Gathering provisions and making preparations for the long, bitterly cold winter was difficult. In the absence of medical help any accidents could easily prove fatal. But slowly the challenges of the mountains produced a new breed of enterprisers—the "mountain men" who became the subjects of so much romantic legend—among them Jedediah S. Smith, William S. Sublette, David E. Jackson, and James Bridger.

The expedition was a financial success, and Ashley then followed the course of Montreal merchants by setting himself up in St. Louis as supplier and financier. The more energetic and resourceful of the mountain men took the road to entrepreneurship by entering into partnership arrangements with him. In 1825 Ashley introduced another innovation—the rendezvous. To enable the trappers to avoid the long, dangerous, and time-consuming trip back from the Rockies to St. Louis, in 1825 he took a year's supply of provisions and trade goods to a predetermined spot in the mountains to be exchanged for the year's crop of furs. He paid the standard $3 per pound for beaver and sold his wares at considerably enhanced, but not unreasonable prices in view of the high transportation costs. His profit came from both retail markups and resale of beaver. Since the trappers' receipts were mostly applied against pre-existing debts, they became permanently indebted and as a result locked in the mountains for most of their lifetime.

In the coming years the rendezvous became an annual event and was attended by an increasing number of trappers and St. Louis merchants. When business was concluded the traders brought out alcohol casks and the rendezvous became a scene of mass debauchery. After a few days of gambling, drunkenness, and sexual orgies with complaisant squaws and girls, the meetings broke up and the mountain men, with little or nothing to show for their year's work, moved wearily back into the mountains again for the fall hunt.

But just as the growth of fortified towns in the Middle Ages made the fairs of that period less necessary, so the building of fortified trading posts in the mountains slowly decreased the economic importance of the rendezvous. At the height of the trade, during the mid-thirties, about 150 forts and posts, all tributary to St. Louis trading firms, served the mountain men. As in New France during the colonial period, business at the posts was conducted by "bourgeois," usually partners in St. Louis houses, assisted by clerks. Voyageurs and engagés regularly attached to the posts carried out the routine tasks and provided the defensive forces. The position of bourgeois required very able men who could combine business skill with raw courage, military ability, and the capacity to exert leadership over highly individualistic and often violent trappers and Indians. The trapping "brigades" outfitted at the posts contained fifty to one hundred men and were led by "partisans"—experienced trappers who were the absolute autocrats of the expeditions. Upon arrival in beaver country— mountain valleys crisscrossed by streams—the brigades broke up into trapping parties and usually made their way back to the forts individually with the year's catch. Here the furs were traded to the merchant suppliers under much the same conditions as at the rendezvous.

OPERATIONS OF THE AMERICAN FUR COMPANY

Although Ashley had returned from the first rendezvous with $45,-000 to $50,000 worth of pelts, the great hazards of the business induced him in 1826 to sell his interests in the mountains to three of his associates, Smith, Jackson, and Sublette. These men then formed the Rocky Mountain Fur Company, which conducted both trapping and supply operations in the Rockies. Ashley continued to be the sales agent in St. Louis. During the course of the Rocky Mountain Fur Company's career, the outfits sent more than $500,000 worth of beaver to St. Louis, and lost another $100,-000 worth through Indian attacks. In 1834 the partners entered the service of the American Fur Company.

Astor had cast a covetous eye on the Rocky Mountain trade ever since the collapse of his venture at Astoria. He made several offers of partnership to leading St. Louis firms, but was rebuffed, principally because he was known to take the lion's share of profit for himself. Finally in 1827 the old firm of Bernard, Pratte and Company, of which Pierre Chouteau, Jr., was a leading figure, formed a partnership with the American Fur Company and ultimately Chouteau became the manager of the company's Rocky Mountain interests.

But by now Astor was giving little attention to the trapping end of the business, spending much time in Europe completely out of touch with the company's affairs. Ramsay Crooks had emerged as the major decision maker of day by day operations. Born in Scotland in 1787, Crooks followed the large number of his countrymen who emigrated to Canada to enter the fur trade. In the course of his service as clerk of an outfit he traveled to Mackinac, and from thence to St. Louis. Here he joined up with the Pacific Fur Company and accompanied the group which made the overland journey to the Pacific in 1811. After his return he rose steadily in the American Fur Company, and in 1817 was placed in charge of the Northern Department by Astor. After the establishment of the Western Department at the time of the partnership with Bernard, Pratte and Company, Crooks became virtual head of the company's operations.

At the peak of its career the company was a most impressive organization. General offices and warehouses were located in New York, and outfitting and departmental headquarters were established at Mackinac, Prairie du Chien, Sault Ste. Marie, and Detroit. At least a dozen substations were located throughout the West. In the Rockies the company built three forts as its base of operations, all on the upper Missouri or on the Yellowstone and Bighorn Rivers. Company factors could be found in every fur trading center on the continent, and the company had agents or correspondents around the world wherever furs were sold, from Leipzig and London to Canton. The organization represented the fullest development of the joint partnership as a form of business organization. All the major participants worked under elaborate partnership arrangements, supplied their own capital, and paid their own employees.

Determining the profits of the organization year by year is difficult because of the fragmentary nature of the books, but apparently from 1823 to 1834 net profits were in the neighborhood of $100,000 per year. From dividends and from other sources of income, chiefly from loans to the company at interest rates as high as 40 percent, Astor made about $700,-000 out of the business during this period; Crooks made about $200,000. Foreseeing the exhaustion of beaver in the Rockies and the drop in demand for the pelts because of the growing popularity of silk hats, Astor sold all of his interests to Crooks in 1834. Under the latter's administration the company continued to thrive until the hard times of the forties when Crooks failed and the company gradually dissolved.

With the rapid decline of the fur business in the early forties, in part because of style changes and in part because of the thinning out of beaver, fur posts were abandoned or became way stations for the supply of migrants on the way to Oregon or California. The St. Louis traders turned to other enterprises. Pierre Chouteau, for example, along with many others, became interested in the Santa Fe trade. By the end of his life he was a wealthy railroad promoter living in New York. The colorful mountain men, with their slouch hats, long hair, and gaily bedecked deerskin clothes, followed on the round of their toils by their squaws and half-breed children, simply disappeared. Possibly some turned to mining, others to cattle droving or lumbering, and many no doubt worked on railroad construction. As with canallers and the rivermen, their memory lingered on, nourished by artists' depictions, legend, and a thousand true adventure stories.

XIV. Lumbering

LOGGING, DRIVING, AND MILLING

The almost unbroken stand of timber which originally stretched from the Atlantic coast halfway across the continent proved to be a much richer and important natural resource than the fur bearing animals it sheltered. In the absence of structural iron and steel, lumber was even more vital as a building material than today, and the plentiful supply of white oak and pine gave the United States a competitive advantage in ship-building. Except for anthracite used in limited areas of the Northeast beginning in the 1830s, wood was the usual household heating and boiler fuel until after mid-century, and when transformed into charcoal was the major smelter fuel as well.

From the colonial period until 1900 lumbering advanced in a wave-like motion westward from Maine to Minnesota. In the beginning every settled area on the seaboard had its saw pit where two men, one above and one below, laboriously cut logs into boards with a long whipsaw. The first sawmills run by water power made their appearance shortly after the building of the first gristmills. During the late colonial period concentrations of sawmills developed on the upper reaches of the Delaware and the Hudson, where lumber was cut for the export markets of Philadelphia and New York. In Maine during the early years of the republic lumbering developed into a large industry capitalized by Boston merchants and focused on the West Indies market. But as the center of production moved westward, New York and then Pennsylvania took first place among the lumber producing states. With the opening of the Erie Canal and the development of transportation on the Great Lakes, lumber from the magnificent stands of white pine in Michigan entered the commercial market, and by 1872 Michigan produced more lumber than New York and Maine combined. But by 1900 the wave of production crested in Wisconsin and Minnesota, and from there the industry jumped to the Far West and the South.

The numerous water transportation routes in the lumber producing states of the Old Northwest played an indispensable role in the development of the industry. Until almost the last decade of the nineteenth century lumbering operations could be conducted profitably only when close to streams, rivers, and lakes, and even under these circumstances transportation costs amounted to 55 to 65 percent of the retail price of lumber. The Mississippi and its tributaries carried logs and lumber from Wisconsin and Minnesota to their natural market—the relatively treeless Midwest. The streams flowing into the lakes directed the lumber from Michigan both to the great rail hub of Chicago and to Albany and New York via the Erie Canal.

The processes and routine of the lumber industry were initially developed in Maine. Here a sharply indented coastline and a network of river systems—chief of which were the Penobscot, Kennebec, and Androscoggin—provided avenues for the driving of logs to tidewater and thus gave lumbermen direct access to ocean transportation. Bangor, near the mouth of the Penobscot, was by 1840 the largest lumber port in the world, with some 200 mills in its environs capable of turning out 1.5 million board feet daily. As developed in Maine lumbering was carried out in four operations—cruising, logging, driving, and sawing. The cycle began when timber cruisers and their parties, sometimes independent operators but more often financed by mill owners, explored areas near the headwaters of the river systems looking for clumps of white pine, the trees most desired for lumber. Cruisers were sometimes paid by fee for acreage they examined; sometimes as partners of mill owners or speculators they were allotted a percentage of land bought on their recommendation, or a percentage of the proceeds of a sale.

After receiving the reports of the cruisers and if necessary buying land or stumpage (i.e., the timber on the land), mill owners arranged to send logging crews to the area selected for operations. Sometimes the crews were employees of the mill owners; more often they were independent outfits working under contract. The work could be carried out only during the winter when the heavy logs could be dragged and sledded to the river-banks. In order to lessen the outlay for supplies, mill owners and logging companies often formed partnerships with storekeepers who advanced the provisions and took payment after the logs or lumber were marketed. Sometimes storekeepers financed the lumbering operations, took title to the logs, and paid the loggers out of the proceeds of the sale.

The earliest lumbermen in the Midwest were former coureurs de bois, but after 1860 thousands of lumberjacks from Maine emigrated to the Lake States where opportunities were more promising. An increasing number of immigrants from overseas entered the area also. Wages were low—about $18 to $30 per month with keep. Camps were ruled, in the most literal sense, by foremen who usually combined a high degree of technical skill with the ability to handle men. Most of the loggers farmed during the summers.

Operations in the woods were carried out by groups of six or eight men. These felled trees indicated by the boss, stripped them, cut them into standard lengths, and snaked them with a "go-devil" to a loading bank on the edge of a river or stream. Here logs were "scaled" and "marked" by registered and licensed professionals to determine the board feet of lumber in every log and indicate ownership. The marks were the equivalent of cattle brands, and were registered with state surveyors of logs and lumber.

The melting of ice and snow brought cutting to an end in the woods and raised the level of the rivers to the point that they could carry the logs to the mills. Sometimes driving was done by the logging crews, sometimes by independent companies. It was unquestionably the most grueling and dangerous part of all lumbering operations. Loggers had to spend hours every day in water of chilling temperature snaking logs past obstructions and doing the scores of other such tasks necessary to keep the great masses of timber moving. Yet despite the herculean efforts of the driving crews, serious losses often occurred. Low water could ground a large part of the year's log supply for the mills. Log jams four or five miles long could bring operations at the mills to a halt for weeks. Floods might disperse thousands of board feet over the river banks and often carried away booms and dams as well.

These dams were designed to raise the water level in rivers in which the supply of water was often inadequate, and were usually built by river improvement companies formed by the loggers and mill owners who used the rivers. The companies charged fees for logs passing over their spillways. Booms were the sorting establishments on the lower reaches of the logging rivers. Here, in spacious, quiet bays, the floating timber was caught and sorted according to markings in great pockets formed by logs chained end to end and attached to piles. On many rivers the booms were natural centers for the location of sawmills. On the rivers of Wisconsin and Minnesota flowing into the Mississippi, however, they were also way stations where timber was chained together in rafts destined for mills as far south as St. Louis. Before the coming of the railroads the mills of Wisconsin and Minnesota were compelled to raft their dressed lumber to market as well. Here again, as with logging operations, losses could be heavy. Despite heroic efforts of crews manning long sweeps at both ends of the rafts, the unwieldly masses of lumber often broke up after smashing against rocks and banks in swift parts of the river. Once the quieter stretches of the Mississippi had been reached the rafts of logs and lumber were consolidated into huge units pushed by tugs or steamboats. One such raft which arrived in St. Louis in 1901 was 1,450 feet long, 278 feet wide, and contained nine million board feet of lumber.

At the outset the milling was carried out in relatively small establishments, and combination never reached the degree found in the fur trade or in many heavily capitalized industries. By 1820 there were perhaps 300 sawmills in Maine, valued at between $100 and $400 apiece. Most were organized as joint partnerships divided into as many as twenty-four shares, and no doubt operated by partners who contributed their labor as investment in the enterprise. The equipment was of the most primitive kind, consisting of little more than a whipsaw mounted in a frame moved up and down by a gear connection with a waterwheel, and a movable bed on which logs were pushed against the cutting edge of the saw. As mills became larger, additional saws were mounted in "cradles" until a large log could be sawed into boards in one operation. The breakthrough from reciprocal to continuous motion came when circular saws made their appearance during the twenties in Maine and proportionally later in the mills of the Lake States.

The use of steam power made possible the mechanizing of most sawmill operations, with a corresponding increase in efficiency. In 1850 twenty-five men working with a single saw could turn out 5,000 feet daily, or 200 feet per man; twenty years later 100 men with a double rotary and a large gang saw could produce 100,000 feet daily, or 1,000 feet per man. Technological innovations also brought about a dramatic increase in the size and output of mills. During the twenties the larger mills of Maine had turned out about 2,000 feet per day. In 1873 a mill at Chippewa Falls, Wisconsin, produced 325,000 feet per day for twenty-five days. The annual cut made by Minneapolis mills rose from about 100 million feet in the seventies to 594 million feet in 1899.

FINANCING, PROFITS, COMBINATION, AND MARKETING

Throughout the early period of development the capital for commercial lumbering operations had come from eastern financial centers. The Maine industry, for example, was financed almost entirely by Boston investors. Many young men from the East, lured by newspaper reports, advertisements of land companies, or letters from friends and relatives, traveled to Michigan, Wisconsin, or Minnesota, scouted out likely timberland and mill sites, and returned to raise the money to start lumbering operations. If the quest for capital turned out favorably, they and their backers would form joint partnerships and the active partners would return to the West to build and manage the mills. As savings were built up in the lumbering centers of the Northwest such as Minneapolis, capital went out from there to new areas, particularly to the South and Pacific Coast as second or third generations of lumbermen prepared to repeat the process of expansion.

Rather surprisingly, the need to acquire capital did not promote incorporation as in other growing industries of the period. Of course, from the beginning, boom companies and river improvement companies had been incorporated because they were public services, but as long as lumbermen could raise capital under joint partnerships, they showed little inclination to incorporate mills and logging companies. For example, Knapp, Stout and Company, formed in 1846, did not acquire a charter until 1878, long after it had become a very large enterprise. Decision making tended to be a jealously guarded prerogative of kinship groups. Many lumbermen were suspicious of outsiders and were therefore reluctant to share power with boards of directors and stockholders they did not know. These considerations apparently weighed more heavily with mill owners than the enhanced security conferred by limited liability.

It is difficult to generalize on the profit aspect of lumbering. Lumber prices varied rather widely according to business conditions, but more important, the business was seasonal and subject to many hazards. During the winter, when streams and ponds froze up, operations in the mills came to a standstill, and in any event were usually not conducted for more than 190 days a year. As we have seen, the supply of logs could be curtailed by a number of causes. Under the best of circumstances there were many costs to be met, chiefly in transportation, before the manufacturer could take his profit. In Wisconsin in 1873 logs cost $3 or $4 per thousand feet to cut and bank and $1 to $1.25 to drive. Twenty cents were paid for boom service and lesser amounts for use of river improvements. In addition to the charge for sawing, lumber bore charges for sorting, piling, and drying. One Wisconsin firm estimated that lumber finished and in the market had paid total charges of about $12.15 per thousand at a time when the selling price was only $14 or $15 per thousand. Yet, although the industry suffered painful profit squeezes from time to time, the return was generally high enough to attract capital needed for expansion. In 1897 the average net return to the industry in Wisconsin was nearly 10 percent. Considering the risks at the mills, this was by no means exorbitant. Fire was a constant hazard, and once started was usually uncontrollable. Between 1885 and 1891 fire destroyed mills worth in the aggregate of $2 million in Wisconsin alone.

Profits were affected by the cost of timberland and stumpage. During the 1820s in Maine good timberland could be bought for as little as fifteen cents per acre, but during the speculative boom of 1830 to 1835 this same land rose to between $8 and $10 per acre. Western timberland, when first placed on the market, sold at the government minimum price of $1.25, but land could be located on agricultural college scrip or military warrants for as little as fifty or sixty cents per acre. When the timber in the lakes area began to thin out, however, the price of land and stumpage moved up sharply. In Minnesota, for example, stumpage which had cost fifty cents per thousand in 1880 rose to $5.17 by 1900.

Early in the development of lumbering few mill owners had the capital sufficient for large-scale investment in timberlands, nor was there any necessity for such an outlay as long as timber was plentiful and independent loggers provided enough of it to keep the mills in operation. But over the years as markets broadened and the capacity of mills increased, securing an adequate supply of logs could not be left to chance. Moreover, leading lumbermen now realized that by investment in land they could make big speculative profits and avoid a profit squeeze in mill operations. In 1882 Henry W. Sage sold lands for $817,000 near the Au Sable River which he had acquired in the 1860s at a cost of $35,000. During the eighties and nineties the possession of adequate supplies of timber came to be the most important external element of success in the lumbering business.

The decreasing supply of good timberland and mounting pressures on profits brought a movement toward combination, usually in the form of community of interest through interlocking partnerships. Affiliated mills and logging and driving companies were seldom integrated, but were conducted as independent units. All of the big lumbermen had their own logging outfits, but they also hired independent companies and on occasion bought logs if such a policy proved to be necessary. In an effort to gain self sufficiency, some of the larger mill owners moved toward local horizontal monopoly. Henry W. Sage, for example, played the part of paternalistic overlord to the town of Wenona which grew up around his Michigan mill in the same manner as southern textile mill owners dominated mill villages. By 1900 a few of the largest companies became vertical as well as horizontal monopolies. Knapp, Stout and Company, for instance, owned sales yards and finishing mills as well as vast acreages of timber. To meet the needs of lumberjacks the company also operated flour mills, truck farms, a pork packing plant, and stores doing a wholesale and retail business.

Periodic hard times from the fifties to the early seventies stimulated plans to form lumbermen's associations designed to fix prices, limit production, set up log pools and log exchange agreements, and establish standard rules for grading. But because of the intensely individualistic nature of the lumber industry, co-operative efforts were brought to an end or severely curtailed by upswings of the business cycle. The Lumber Manufacturers Association of the Northwest, formed in 1882, had little success in limiting production, but the Mississippi Valley Lumbermen's Association, founded in 1891, was effective enough to be indicated under the Sherman Act. The suit was dismissed, however, on the ground that the members of the association, although agreeing to raise prices in concert, were not guilty of a conspiracy in restraint of trade because they did not "practically control the entire commodity."

In the infancy of the lumber business, as with most other businesses, marketing was not a specialized function. The owners of mills sold to local purchasers both at wholesale and at retail, often on a barter basis. Surplus would be rafted down rivers toward commercial centers. The drivers would stop at towns along the way and sell direct from rafts at retail or at wholesale to storekeepers, jobbers, and lumber yards. But the pattern of marketing became more specialized with the rise of the great lumber centers. Bangor, and to a lesser extent other Maine ports such as Bath, Machias, and Calais shipped large amounts of lumber overseas to such widely dispersed places as Cuba, Buenos Aires, Madiera, Minorca, and even Australia in the form of sugar boxes, shingles, clapboards, laths, staves, masts and spars. Subsidiary wood-using industries such as sash, door, and furniture manufacturing always grew up in the lumbering districts.

As the lumbering industry began its movement westward, Albany became a great center, primarily because of its excellent location as far as water transportation was concerned. The city drew lumber from the Champlain region over the Champlain Canal, from the upper Hudson and the local center of Glens Falls, and from western New York via the Erie, Chemung, and Genessee Canals. New York, supplied by Albany, was an important lumber port throughout the entire nineteenth century, shipping lumber to eastern, Gulf, and West Coast ports as well as to a large number of foreign destinations. Unlike other lumber centers it did not decline with the approaching exhaustion of the great white pine forests of the Northeast and North Central United States. By 1900 nearly half of its receipts were southern pine, and much of the volume coming down the Hudson was in the form of pulpwood.

As the volume of lumber coming east from the Lake States increased, Buffalo and Tonawanda rose to prominence as lumber ports. The latter town, whose yards were handling 700 million feet per year by 1860, rivaled and finally outstripped Albany as a lumber center. Its advantage lay largely in strategic location at the western terminus of the Erie Canal where lumber was transferred from lake sloops to canal boats. But Chicago became the greatest lumber mart in the world during the nineteenth century. By 1872 it had 100 wholesale and retail yards and 45 planing mills employing in the aggregate 10,000 men and representing an investment of $60 million. For the rest of the century three-fourths of all arriving vessels carried cargoes of lumber. St. Louis had from the beginning been the market for the mills of the upper Mississippi and its tributaries.

LUMBERING IN THE SOUTH

Little has been written about lumbering in the South, which is unfortunate because it has become one of the South's major industries. The wood available for commercial purposes here was longleaf and yellow pine, which extended southwest from Virginia to eastern Texas in a belt of land 100 to 125 miles wide. In contrast to white pine, which tended to grow in clumps in the midst of other conifers and hardwoods, the longleaf pine forests stretched unbroken for hundreds of miles and the trees grew so thickly that they crowded out all underbrush. The wood was somewhat harder than white pine and more difficult to work, but it was remarkably resistant to decay and yielded quantities of resin sufficient to support a naval stores industry. The French and Spaniards had operated saw pits in the lower Mississippi Valley since the early eighteenth century, and a few Maine lumbermen had become established in the region during the 1850s. Certain natural disadvantages made expansion difficult. Fewer rivers were available for driving and for water power than in the Northeast and in the Lakes region. Lack of snow during the winters added immeasurably to the problems of logging. Distance from the marketing centers of the Northeast made it impossible for longleaf pine to compete with white pine. Finally, carpenters, finding longleaf lumber harder to work with, developed a prejudice against it.

Commercial lumbering in significant volume became possible in Mississippi only with the coming of steam power and railroad transportation. Lumbering railroads made of poles for a cost of $150 to $200 per mile helped solve the problem of transporting logs. Kiln drying reduced the weight of lumber by 25 to 30 percent, at a corresponding saving in transportation costs. The Illinois Central, sensing a fertile source of revenue, introduced yellow pine into Chicago in the late seventies and energetically promoted the new product. Markets also began opening up in the Plains states and in New York City. Agents of the big timberland speculators and mill owners of the Northeast and Lake States bought up land in large amounts which the federal government obligingly sold at $1.25 per acre or allowed to be taken for nothing through fraudulent homestead claims. By 1887 much of the land so acquired in Mississippi was selling for $15 per acre.

Lumbering in the state now appeared to have advantages not enjoyed in other parts of the country. Logging, and consequently milling, could be conducted on a year-round basis. The production of naval stores provided a natural hedge for lumbermen. The South was nearer eastern markets than the Far West—an advantage which became more important as timber in the Lake States thinned out. By 1899 in Mississippi $10.8 million was invested in 608 mills with a combined output of one billion feet per year. By 1908 the state ranked third among the lumber producing states of the union, and combination was taking place as rapidly as in the North.

LUMBERING ENTREPRENEURSHIP: FREDERICK WEYERHAEUSER

As we have seen, lumbermen tended to follow patterns of entrepreneurial behavior characteristic of the late eighteenth and early nineteenth centuries. Taking direct and personal interest in their enterprises, they preferred to work with a few trusted partners rather than within corporate structures. All the larger entrepreneurs came to combine milling with interests in logging operations, river improvements, railroads, and land and timber speculation. Just as early nineteenth-century merchants tended to retire into private banking and diversified investments, so lumber entrepreneurs, as they approached the end of their careers, tended to leave the conduct of lumbering operations to others and turned their attention to investment in the industry.

In their relations with each other lumbermen developed patterns of "antagonistic co-operation," joining forces in aspects of their business in which co-operation was plainly beneficial, such as in river improvement and the formation of boom companies. Likewise they formed combinations in the same pragmatic fashion, but avoided any organization which would limit control over their own businesses. They had no scruples against price-fixing or monopoly, but regarded organization to effect these ends without any enthusiasm because of the tendency of such associations to interfere with what they regarded as private affairs. Their attitude toward employees was paternalistic and moralistic, and they viewed labor organization with deep suspicion. In their attitudes toward company towns dependent upon them they followed what the Lynds have called "the utterly unhypocritical combination of high profits, great philanthropy, and low wage scale." Most were unable to see any connection between their private business and the larger purposes of public policy. They did not hesitate to cheat the government by collusive bidding at public land sales, and they stripped their timberlands without any regard for policies of conservation.

All of these characteristics can be seen in the careers of Henry H. Crapo, Henry W. Sage, and Philetus Sawyer, all notable lumbermen of the late nineteenth century who came to the Lake States as young men from New York or New England. But perhaps the traits of the large lumber entrepreneurs are most strikingly displayed in one of the most successful of the breed, Frederick Weyerhaeuser. Born in Germany to a substantial farm family, Weyerhaeuser emigrated to the United States at the age of eighteen, and in 1856, at the age of twenty-one, went to work in a small sawmill on the Mississippi River at Rock Island, Illinois. When the mill failed during the Panic of the following year he rented it from the creditors and in 1860 purchased it in partnership with an uncle by marriage who had considerable mechanical ability—Frederick C. A. Denkman—his lifetime colleague and friend. During the prosperous war years the two acquired interests in a second lumber mill, a flour mill, and a textile mill, and by 1869 were moderately wealthy.

But Weyerhaeuser became increasingly aware that the Mississippi mill owners were in a precarious position in regard to supply of timber and the lumber market. Since much of the timber was consumed by the mills on the tributaries where the logs were cut, he realized that in a time of relative scarcity the Mississippi mills might be starved for raw materials. Moreover, Chicago lumberyards, having a competitive advantage in railroad rates, might be able seriously to limit the marketing capacity of the Mississippi mills.

Weyerhaeuser's solution to these problems was twofold. After 1868 he traveled extensively in the forests lining the Chippewa River of Wisconsin, and in 1872 made the first of what were to become huge purchases of timberland there. Second, as a protective measure he and other Mississippi River mill owners began to acquire interests in Chippewa driving and booming operations which formed the nucleus of the widely ramified combination of a later date. Some Chippewa loggers, after sharp infighting with mill owners along the river, developed a large boom at Beef Slough, a natural sorting pond near the junction of the Chippewa and the Mississippi. When the boom company went bankrupt in 1870 after a disastrous flood, Weyerhaeuser and two partners, fearful of a curtailment of the supply of logs, leased the installation. With other Mississippi River mill owners Weyerhaeuser then incorporated the Mississippi River Logging Company to operate the boom under the lease.

From this point on, Weyerhaeuser proceeded step by step to reconcile conflicting interests in the Chippewa area, building communities of interest, integrating these within corporate forms, and combining the units into larger entities. At the outset the Logging Company was operated as a joint enterprise, each member taking control over its own logs. Matthew G. Norton, a close colleague of Weyerhaeuser's, wrote that "the members of the company were more like brothers in their intercourse with each other than would be found in most organizations for profit. . . ." In 1876 the Logging Company issued forty-three shares of stock at $25,000 apiece to thirteen members, and with part of the funds purchased the Slough itself. Meanwhile, through individual and joint purchases the company and its members controlled about 300,000 acres of timberland in the region.

The magnitude of these purchases now began to alarm the Chippewa mill owners, who anticipated a rise in the price of stumpage and a declining supply of logs as a result. Serious conflict between the two groups of lumbermen appeared inevitable until a vast flood of 1880 washed out most of the Chippewa river installations, wrecked many of the mills, and deposited a season's supply of logs for the upriver mill owners in the Slough. This catastrophe made possible the creation of a new community of interest and subsequent combination. At Weyerhaeuser's urging, the directors of the Mississippi River Logging Company credited the logs in the Slough to the upriver mills to which they had originally been destined, thus saving many mills from bankruptcy. In return the two groups formed the

Chippewa Logging Company, which operated all river installations, controlled all logging, allocated the season's cut, and was entitled by charter to hold stock in other corporations. Sixty-five percent of the stock of the new company was owned by the Mississippi River Logging Company and 35 percent by the Chippewa mill owners.

In the nineties, when the Chippewa timber began to thin out, Weyerhaeuser, the Laird-Nortons, Mussers, Denkmans, and other partners of long association, moved into the as yet dense forests of Minnesota. Through the Pine Tree Lumber Company of Iowa, they acquired an initial tract of 212,722 acres, most of it from the Northern Pacific Railroad Company. Then followed the combining of sawmills and river installation. The building of logging railroads gave access to timber formerly too far from river transportation to be economically cut, and interlocking investment and directorships in all through railroads of the region assured reasonable rates. The Weyerhaeuser group inaugurated their career in the twentieth century by purchasing 900,000 acres of Far West timberland from the Northern Pacific for $5,400,000—probably the greatest single purchase of timberland to that date.

Although most Weyerhaeuser enterprises were richly remunerative, the group followed a very conservative dividend policy, usually deferring payments entirely for a period of ten years or more until the cost of plants had been written off. The prosperity of most operations is illustrated by the fact that their White River Lumber Company between 1883 and 1905 paid $2,025,000 in dividends on an original investment of $460,000 and then was sold for $2,620,000. Rapid capital accumulation thus lessened the need to seek financing in the East.

As the pineries retreated farther and farther from the banks of the logging rivers in the Lake States after 1895 and stumpage prices rose, only those lumbermen could stay in business who possessed the heavy capital backing to make extensive purchases of land and standing timber and construct the logging railroads and tramways now necessary to transport logs to the through waterways or to trunkline railroads. But, paradoxically, as capital investment rose, production went into a swift and unrelieved decline after 1904. Thus, as the historian of log transportation, William G. Rector, has pointed out, "Lumbering became a big business only to decline as an industry." By 1920 the Lake States had the unenviable distinction of having once possessed two valuable natural resources which were exploited to extinction—furs and timber.

The lumbermen of the pine region have been heavily criticized for wasteful cutting methods and for failure to adopt conservation measures. By present-day standards their actions were indeed reprehensible, but in extenuation it should be noted that conservation was quite foreign to the American ethos of the nineteenth century, and was not effectively practiced anywhere in the country. Moreover, in a broader context the pineries were not "wasted" but were merely transformed into another and more valuable form of wealth—the building structures of Midwest cities. The historian of lumbering, George W. Hotchkiss, has estimated that it "enriched the nation" and "added to its development" by over $4 billion during the sixty years through 1897, an amount exceeding by almost 50 percent the cost of the Civil War to the North and triple the value of all gold produced in California during the nineteenth century.

XV. The First Mining Bonanzas: Lead, Copper, and Gold

LEAD MINING IN THE UPPER MISSISSIPPI VALLEY

Mining is an exciting, lustful enterprise evoking visions of wealth and power which has since antiquity stimulated the men who pursue it to sometimes superhuman exertions. Productive mines have also been a precondition of the industrial revolution. Since 1800 the world production of metals has increased more than a hundred times, and our modern industrial complexes would be simply inconceivable without a powerful and productive mining industry. Yet somewhat paradoxically mining has been less of a "business" than the other activities which are commonly listed in that category. During the nineteenth century it was essentially a gamble, and even today bears some of these characteristics. Although statistics on the point must be somewhat impressionistic, probably not more than one out of fifty mining ventures has returned the original investment, and even fewer have made a profit. Because the information upon which business judgments could be brought to bear during the nineteenth century was scanty or unavailable, most decisions to start new mining enterprises were based on nothing more substantial than hunches, and until the last pay dirt was taken out, a knowledge of the potentialities of most mines extended no farther than the tip of the miner's pick.

Even before the first English settlements on the North American continent the opening of mines had been a major element of mercantilist planning. Yet only iron was discovered in appreciable quantities, and it proved to be no magician's wand which could bring unlimited wealth. Lead was the first nonferrous metal to be found in any abundance. As early as the seventeenth century coureurs de bois had observed Indians of the upper Mississippi Valley breaking ore out of rock ledges and smelting it in wood fires atop crude hearths. Beginning in 1788 the fur trader, Julien DuBuque, conducted mining and smelting operations with Indian labor. During the following decade Americans filtered into the region in which lead mineral was found—those portions of Wisconsin, Illinois, Iowa, and Missouri lying adjacent to the Mississippi River—and began mining and smelting on a small scale. The largest of the early operators was Moses Austin, father of the American settlements in Texas, who built a shot tower in the town of Herculaneum, Missouri, which he founded.

In an effort to exercise control over what was considered a valuable and strategic natural resource, to prevent the rise of monopoly, and to open a source of revenue, Congress in 1807 withdrew from sale about 10,000 square miles of ore lands and offered to rent mining and smelting privileges on them for a royalty of 10 percent of output. The region was organized as The United States Lead Mines and was placed under the supervision of a superintendent appointed by the president. Subsequently other areas were incorporated into "the public mines."

Since lead was an indispensable metal for armaments, and was extensively used in shipbuilding and in the manufacture of paint, and since the entire national supply had previously been imported, prices were high enough to attract a considerable number of prospectors to the public mines. By 1829, 4,253 were working claims, and 52 smelters were in operation. Miners, who at the outset worked only surface diggings, could make from $1 to about $16 per day. Smelting offered opportunities of considerably greater profit to men with investment capital. Although the primitive furnaces and hearths in use could be constructed for a small outlay, the government required that smelters post a $10,000 bond to insure their payment of royalties. In 1827 smelters bought mineral from miners for about $15 per thousand pounds and smelted down the lead at a cost of about $3.60 per ton. At the prevailing price of $4.50 per hundred pounds the lead brought approximately a 24 percent profit. Larger operators, because of economies of scale, sometimes did much better. For example, John Paul Gratiot, of the St. Louis fur trading family, in 1828 made a net profit of over $28,000 on an investment, including bond, of about $11,000.

During the next decade the leasing system, which miners and smelters had originally accepted without opposition, came increasingly under fire. Falling lead prices which squeezed profit margins was one reason, but equally important was the desire of land speculators to acquire potentially valuable property. Miners and smelters fell behind in their royalty payments, and by 1835 had stopped making them entirely. When the government began selling land in the mining areas for agricultural purposes, the door was opened for fraudulent acquisition of mining properties. The large land companies of New York, Philadelphia, and Boston now added Missouri and Wisconsin mineral lands to their portfolios of western and southern properties. For example, the Boston and Western Land Company acquired through landlooker partners about 25,000 acres of lead bearing land. The small miners belatedly protested the rapid alienation of a public domain, but to no effect. Their day was drawing to a close. With most of the surface ore skimmed off, only heavily capitalized companies could afford the shafts and hoisting and ventilating equipment necessary for underground mines. By the mid-forties lead mining was becoming big business.

The capital for mine development came not only from land companies but from reinvested smelting profits and from St. Louis jobbers who marketed the metal in New Orleans and in east coast cities. The state Bank of Illinois loaned money to miners and smelters from its branch in Galena, which became the financial center of the lead region. Few mining companies attempted to conduct operations themselves. The great majority leased their works to groups of miners who operated the mines for royalties of about 20 percent of the mineral brought to the surface. In 1847 the federal government abandoned the leasing system entirely, partially because of pressure from land speculators and partially because the cost of administering the system ran far beyond the revenue it produced. A significant precedent had been established. Henceforth mining in the United States would not develop into the socialized enterprise it has become in many other countries, but instead, for better or for worse, would be carried on as private enterprise.

Rapidly rising lead prices during the Civil War led to the formation of the St. Joseph Lead Company, chartered by New York in 1864 with a capitalization of $1 million. Under the leadership of Charles B. Parsons, who had acquired experience in a smelter located in Northampton, Massachusetts, it combined important mining and smelting properties in the lead regions and greatly improved technological methods. The company entered the twentieth century in flourishing condition and eventually became the largest lead producer in the world.

A GOLD RUSH IN THE OLD SOUTH

The hopes of finding gold so strongly entertained by Spanish explorers and the first English settlers to some degree reached fruition with the opening up of gold fields in a strip of land some fifty miles wide running from Virginia to Georgia in the eastern Appalachian chain. Even before the Revolution mines had been worked in what are today Gaston, Cherokee, and Mecklenburg counties of North Carolina, and in 1799 a seventeen pound nugget had been found in a stream near Concord. During the 1820s reports of gold became an almost daily occurrence, and by the end of the decade a gold rush of considerable magnitude was under way. Immigrants poured into western North Carolina in such numbers that at the height of the rush some 30,000 men were at work in the diggings. One owner reported that thirteen different languages were spoken in his mine. In addition to immigrants, farmers working in off seasons and hired slaves contributed to the labor force. At the height of the rush Brindleton, Bissel, Capps, Jamestown, Morganton, and Charlotte became boom towns.

The methods of recovering gold quickly improved from primitive panning operations to the most sophisticated procedures used in California during the fifties. In the panning operation the prospector filled a shallow vessel the size of a large saucepan with water and with sand which he hoped was auriferous. By then swishing the water around in the pan he slowly washed the sand over the rim, and gold dust, heavier than the sand, remained in the bottom. In North Carolina some prospectors quickly advanced to the use of various kinds of "cradles" and "long Toms" and even to hydraulic mining. The cradle was a wooden box about the size and shape of a coffin with ribs on the interior of the bottom running lengthwise and holes along the side at the base. Sand was shoveled into the cradle and then slowly washed out through the holes as the cradle was tilted from side to side. Gold dust, sinking to the bottom, was trapped by the ribs. Long Toms were merely a larger variation of the cradle. In hydraulic mining jets of water under high pressure are directed against hillsides thought to contain auriferous sand and the sand washed through sluices with ribbed bottoms.

The recovery of gold found in quartz presented a quite different problem. Here the quartz had to be mined, entailing all the problems of digging, shoring, ventilating, and hoisting. The quartz was then crushed and the gold separated from it in stamp mills or in "arrastras." The latter, used for centuries in Mexico and in Europe, were merely flat pans in which ore was pulverized by rocks dragged over the bottom by horses. Gold was separated from powdered quartz by mixing the mass with water to make a sludge, and then introducing quicksilver, which has the fortunate property of uniting with gold. Once "amalgamated," the heavy metals sank to the bottom of the amalgamating pans and the rock sludge was washed out with water. Gold was separated from the amalgam by vaporizing the quicksilver in a retort. Sometimes the gold would be locked in a type of sulphide known as "sulphurets," and therefore could not easily amalgamate with quicksilver. In Georgia during the fifties the Plattner process of breaking up the sulphides by the use of chlorine gas was adopted at least a decade before chlorination made its appearance in the West. The speedy development of mining techniques serves as a qualification of the often-heard generalization that the South, devoted to agriculture, was backward in industrial technology.

Except in the placer processes gold mining requires a large capital outlay, and the opportunities in North Carolina attracted investment funds from the commercial centers of the Northeast and even from Europe. The first mines, like the first sawmills or textile mills, were operated on shares by partnership. One partner might contribute land, a second slaves, a third some cash, and so on until a going concern was in operation. But as the mine workings sank deeper into the ground, the need for additional capital was supplied by corporations formed both in North Carolina and in the eastern commercial centers. Some companies were capitalized at as much as $1.5 million. North Carolina mining shares were quoted on the New York Stock Exchange from the thirties onward, and during the forties alone it was estimated that $40 million had been invested in these securities. The Superintendent of the Charlotte Mint reported in 1840 that "many of the mines, in their most productive state, belonged to foreigners or were leased by them; and the capital, also was from abroad."

It has been estimated that during the fifty years of gold production in North Carolina ending with the Civil War about $100 million had been invested in mines and about $50 million in gold produced. The figure for investment is undoubtedly much too high, however, because it represents authorized rather than paid-in capital. Companies issued shares for a small down payment, and relied upon calls to provide future capital needs.

Doubtless much stock was forfeited for failure to meet calls, and unsuccessful companies probably never collected more than a small fraction of their authorized capitalization.

In Georgia the fact that gold was found on lands guaranteed by treaty to Cherokee Indians produced political and constitutional repercussions. Although Chief Justice Marshall validated the Indian title in the famous case, Worcester vs. Georgia (1832), President Jackson sent the Indians packing westward much to the glee of the Georgia legislature, which thereupon laid claim to the Indian lands. Prospectors then poured into the region, and by 1837 an estimated 37,000 men from the most diverse origins were at work in the mines. Governor George R. Gilmer, perhaps influenced by the federal leasing experiment in the lead regions, at first proposed that the mines be worked in similar fashion as a public enterprise. His plan got little support and mining installations eventually reverted to private ownership. By 1861 about $50 million worth of gold had been produced, about the same amount as in North Carolina.

Gold mining was carried on somewhat less extensively in Virginia than in North Carolina and Georgia, but under conditions much like those of the latter two states. More than thirty-four companies were chartered in Virginia between 1834 and 1839, and about seventy-five were chartered during the fifties. By 1860, $3,091,000 of Virginia gold had been coined by the Philadelphia mint, a small fraction of the total production.

The Civil War brought gold mining in the three states to an end. Production had been declining, and now the flow of capital from outside sources was cut off and many of the miners mustered into the Confederate armies. After the war no attempt was made to reopen the mines. No local capital was available and funds from the commercial centers of the Northeast and from England were being drawn to the West. Also, the abolition of slavery had dispersed a large part of the labor force.

MICHIGAN COPPER

As the excitement over the discovery of gold in the eastern Appalachian highlands slowly subsided, a copper boom developed on the Keewenaw peninsula jutting into Lake Superior from the Michigan shore. This small area is one of the very few places on the earth's surface where copper has been found in a pure state, unmixed with other metals. In 1765 an Indian trader, Alexander Henry, found a solid copper boulder on the peninsula weighing 6,500 pounds. Most of the copper, however, was contained in finely disseminated form in great deposits of amygdaloid and conglomerate rock. But the area was so remote and the demand for copper so small that no concerted attempt was made to start mining operations until the federal government in 1844 purchased the region from the Indians and began issuing mining permits in return for a royalty of ultimately 10 percent of gross output. Prospectors, spurred onward by optimistic reports of government surveyors, hastened to the peninsula, and a lively boom developed in the buying and selling of permits. Although copper held in soft rock was found in large amounts, little actual mining was done because of ignorance of mining techniques, scarcity of labor, but more important, the immense difficulties of getting the copper rock to the eastern seaboard where the nation's few smelters were located. Faced by such obstacles and the rigorous climate, most prospectors quickly became discouraged and the boom collapsed.

But in 1845 the great Cliff lode was found, and three years later the equally rich Minnesota lode. Now corporate enterprise backed mainly by Boston capital hastened the development of the Michigan mines. The federal government, disillusioned by the evasion of royalty payments, adopted a policy of leasing and ultimately selling copper lands, thereby repeating the solution to the similar problem faced in the lead region of the upper Mississippi Valley. By 1865, ninety-four mining companies had been formed and had made capital calls from stockholders of $13.1 million. As with most mining operations, however, a mere handful of companies were successful. Only eight paid any dividends at all, but five returned 300 percent on invested capital, one nearly 500 percent, and the Cliff Mine almost 2,000 percent. Previous to the Michigan copper strikes the United States had produced only a small fraction of the copper used in domestic manufacturing, but by 1855 the nation became a copper exporter.

One of the most long-lived of the early successful companies was Calumet and Hecla. Between 1864 and 1866 Calumet shares rose from a par value of $1 to a market value of $75, and by 1875 the company was capitalized at $2 million. Among the many notable men connected with it was its first president, Alexander Agassiz, the celebrated Harvard naturalist. Financial affairs were directed by the well-known Bostonian brothers-in-law of Agassiz—Quincy A. Shaw, Henry Lee Higginson, and H. S. Russell. From 1869 to 1876 Calumet and Hecla produced about half of the total United States output of copper. Throughout the nineteenth and early twentieth centuries it remained richly productive, and by 1930 had paid $184,027,028 in dividends.

The development of the Michigan copper fields was made possible only by the solution of many difficult problems of transportation and technology. Completion of the Sault Canal in 1855 with the aid of a land grant from the federal government enabled ore to travel by water direct from the Keewenaw Peninsula to refineries at Detroit and on the lower Lakes, and the dredging of a channel through the shallow waters surrounding the peninsula eliminated the problem of lighterage. Further improvements such as expansion of docking facilities reduced the cost of transporting ore to the smelters from $20 per ton in 1845 to $3.50 or $4.00 per ton a few decades later.

Refining was by no means the difficult problem it was to become for the copper companies of Montana or for the silver-lead smelters of Colorado. Copper mineral was separated from conglomerate rock by the familiar stamping process and the refuse was washed away over jiggling tables which precipitated and trapped the mineral. Smelting was accomplished in reverberatory furnaces, (i.e., furnaces with roofs which reflect heat directly down upon the ore to be smelted).

By far the most difficult problems were encountered in getting the copper rock out of the ground. Conglomerate was found at great depths far below the surface masses mined at the beginning of the Michigan boom. As early as 1849 the Cliff mine was down to 1,500 feet, and before the end of the century many shafts throughout the conglomerate area of seventy square miles had bottomed out at nearly a mile below the surface. Raising copper rock from these depths required elaborate and powerful hoisting machinery, and elevator and ventilation installations for the miners. Needless to say, exploration, stopeing, and mining under these circumstances necessitated heavy infusions of capital. Yet progressively higher overhead costs were more than offset by increased productivity resulting from better equipment.

Since the capital requirements for mining and smelting were much greater than similar needs in the lead mines to the south, the corporation from the outset came to be the standard form of business organization in the copper country. Issuance of stock in $25 shares, as called for by the Michigan general incorporation act for mining companies of 1850, indicated the gambling nature of the early enterprises. Even at this low par value full payment was not demanded on delivery of shares, but stockholders merely made contributions sufficient to get operations going in the hope that before the money ran out enough pay dirt would be found to justify further assessments. Thus mine development proceeded by stages, with heavy inputs of capital at the outset when little if any return could be expected. When the few successful mines began to pay, external financing diminished in volume and development was continued from ploughed back earnings at the end of periods when copper prices had been high and returns consequently substantial. During these periods ownership also contracted as larger stockholders and investment bankers accumulated shares in what now appeared to be attractive investments. In the unsuccessful mines—which of course constituted the great majority—operations merely ground to a halt when discouraged stockholders refused to pay further assessments. Forfeited stock was then accumulated at sacrifice prices by speculators or by successful companies bent on combination.

Boston continued to be the main external source of capital for the Michigan mines until the late nineteenth century. Beginning in the early fifties a section of the city's Stock Exchange was set aside for trading in mining shares. Prices fluctuated widely, and many mining companies were started purely as stock speculations with little thought of following through on mining operations. Promotion and financial management were dominated by a relatively small group which included representatives of families important in Boston's merchant capitalism back into the eighteenth century. Management was organized in much the same manner as in the New England textile industry, with corporate offices in Boston handling financial and marketing matters, and agents at the mines supervising production operations. In the antebellum period sales of copper were made through commission merchants in Boston and New York and absorbed a good deal of working capital since ice blockages and slow transportation delayed deliveries and payments long after the conglomerate had been raised from the underground beds.

Labor came initially from local sources such as lumbering and the fur trade, and from immigration. Experienced Cornish miners, leaving the aged, and now depleted Welsh copper mines, often took the entire responsibility for operating mines in return for a "tribute," or royalty of the ore produced. In the mines operated by owners the wages of most miners were paid by gang bosses operating under contract with the proprietors. To some extent this arrangement was another survival of old Cornish custom, but more directly reflected a relationship between management and skilled labor usual in the heavy industries. Contractors set a price for a given piece of work, recruited and paid the wages of their own help, and—after deduction of the cost of supplies advanced by the company—retained the remainder as payment for their services. The system was advantageous in that it stimulated incentive for the skilled contractors, but it often led to slowdowns and the fabrication of difficulties in order to create claims for higher rates on future jobs.

Since the mines were originally located in a wilderness the companies were compelled to build housing, and with the stabilizing of conditions normal community life developed. As in the textile and lumber industries, the companies exercised strict paternalistic control, but the larger ones contributed generously to community services.

The prospector found much more favorable conditions in the California gold rush of 1849 than in the early Michigan copper boom. The public lands were open to all comers, and the gold was as free for the taking as the grass of the prairies. The government made no attempt to survey the gold region, issue permits, demand royalties, or lease and sell land. All of these measures had been considered, but it was wisely decided that free prospecting, by maximizing the production of gold, would serve the best interests of all concerned. Furthermore, the previous difficulty of collecting royalties in the copper and lead districts made it plain that such measures would be widely evaded in the much larger area of California. The easy recovery of gold also favored the small prospector. A pick, shovel, and a pan was at the outset all the equipment needed. The major capital expenditure was for transportation to the gold fields and for provisions while prospecting. The labor of a few men might be required to knock together a cradle or a long Tom, but here also the expense was light. These circumstances, as well as the mere presence of gold in California, help explain the magnitude of the gold rush. Noneconomic factors were also of importance. The trip to a faraway place was attractive to the footloose, and the chance of the big payoff appealed to the fancy free.

The story of the finding of gold at Sutter's Mill and the beginning of the rush has been so often told that it is unnecessary to repeat it here. But much less has been written about the business organizations of those who came to California by sea in forty-nine. Most prospectors from New England were organized in "emigrant companies" equipped to carry on trade after arrival in the hope that trading profits would absorb the cost of transportation and perhaps provide a surplus as well. Containing from 6 to about 150 members each, the companies were made up of men who had lived in close proximity to each other or had engaged in a common occupation. Organized with full slates of executive officers and boards of directors, the companies levied assessments upon the members of from $50 to $1,000, represented by shares. Mechanics and others who had special skills which would be valuable in the diggings were taken in at a reduced rate, and sometimes outsiders bought shares, either out of a desire to support the organizations or in the expectation of profit.

After the assessments had been collected the capital sum was invested in trade goods of all kinds, provisions, and even specialities such as disassembled steamboats. A great deal of money was wasted on wildly impractical machines for gold mining. Smaller companies bought passage to California, but the larger and wealthier organizations purchased ships which they expected to sell upon arrival. After the goods had been disposed of in San Francisco, the sum realized was to be divided among the shareholders in accordance with their equities.

It would be difficult even to estimate the number of such companies which sprang into existence during the winter of 1848–49. One hundred and twenty-four sailed from Massachusetts, and others departed from New York, Philadelphia, and smaller East Coast ports. Similar organizations arrived in California from England, France, Germany, Australia, China, and Japan. Total capital investment must have been very large. The *Times* of London reported that by February, 1849, 1,250,000 pounds had been invested in English companies alone. The Massachusetts companies took about $4 million out of the state during that year.

Few of the companies achieved the financial success expected of them. Provisions and building materials brought fancy prices, but the market was soon glutted with items like calico cloth, chewing tobacco, shoes, and all kinds of Rube Goldberg inventions for mining. The lack of return cargoes and inability to find crews knocked the bottom out of the shipping market. Many thousands of dollars worth of slow selling goods were simply abandoned in San Francisco, and ships were pulled up on the beach and used for temporary living quarters. Most of the companies were able to make enough money to reduce the members' transportation costs considerably, however, and a few even showed a profit. One company paid a dividend of $2,200 on each share.

Despite occasional unwise investments and generally low returns, the emigrant companies performed useful functions. Besides lowering the cost of transportation and equipment for the members, the companies brought badly needed supplies to San Francisco. Also, the companies' demands for swift transportation stimulated the building of clipper ships and swelled shipping profits generally.

At the time of the formation of the emigrant companies it was expected that they would remain intact after reaching San Francisco and work the diggings in the same groups. Actually, however, all of the companies broke up after distribution of a dividend, and the members proceeded individually or with a few chosen companions toward the gold country. Placer mining required little co-operation, and the prospectors, therefore, could afford as much individualism as they wanted.

GOLD MINING BECOMES BIG BUSINESS

The gold fields discovered in the first few years of the rush were contained in the valleys of the Sacramento River and its tributaries—the American, the Feather, and the San Juan—and in the country lying between the Sierra Nevada mountains and the coast range, comprising a total area of about 7,000 square miles. In order to reach the gold country the prospectors proceeded up the Sacramento River to the town of Sacramento, usually by steamboat, and from thence on foot toward the diggings. The promising locations were bends in rivers or streams which contained impounded sand, or dry gullies having the same configuration. In 1849 gold was relatively plentiful. For millions of years quartz outcroppings containing gold high in the mountains had been eroding away, and the specs of yellow metal, separated from the rock, had been carried down streams and rivers, many no longer in existence.

As prospectors flooded into the gold fields and washed out the best lodes, the average return dropped from about $20 per day in 1848 to about $16 in 1849, and drifted down to approximately $3 in 1856. Nevertheless, by the late fifties there were still as many as 100,000 men prospecting for gold in California. The forty-niners contributed to the growth of the economy by injecting gold worth $80 million into the money supply of the nation during the period ending in 1852, but at a tremendous cost to themselves. Rushing feverishly from one strike to another, working themselves to exhaustion, dissipating their hard-earned gains in drink and gambling, they were exploited as cruelly by their fantasies as were Negro slaves by their masters. According to a modern mining engineer, Theodore J. Hoover, "Not one in fifty prospectors realized anything like the financial rewards that his persistent effort would have brought him in other fields."

As gold became more difficult to find and extract, mining methods became increasingly elaborate and efficient. Almost overnight gold mining became a heavily capitalized big business and the lonely prospectors produced a continually smaller proportion of the gold yield. Hydraulic systems with many miles of canal and pipe made their appearance; quartz mines hundreds of feet deep were dug, and were supplied with stamping mills and arrastras. Fortunately California also produced its own quicksilver for the amalgamation process. As placer methods spread beyond California, rivers were sometimes diverted from their channels by wing dams and canals, and mining operations were undertaken in the sand of the river bottoms.

At the outset, capital, often in the form of supplies, was provided by storekeepers, the bankers of any frontier society. They outfitted prospectors under grubstake agreements, which had legal status as contracts. In return the prospector agreed to share title to any claim he might stake out with the storekeeper, and split any finds of gold on a fifty-fifty basis. By the sixties the professional mining promoter, often a trained engineer, had made an appearance, and mining finance began to take on the form which it retained throughout the rest of the century. Now the prospector became an explorer rather than a miner. Upon making a successful strike he sold the claim to the promoter, who would work it deeply enough to get some idea of its potentialities. Satisfied that the claim was worth developing, the promoter would then seek capital from wealthy investors, organize a company, and get operations underway. Often the development process was more complicated, involving a large number of transactions until the mine was in operation. Some capitalists had promoters working for them regularly, in the same way that timberland owners like Ezra Cornell (see p. 205) employed landlookers and timber cruisers. The establishment of the San Francisco Stock Exchange in 1862 of course facilitated mine financing.

The gold rush had a profound effect upon the development of the West. In a few years it brought about a movement of population which otherwise might have taken decades to accomplish. The entrance of California into the Union, by upsetting the sectional balance, led many southern leaders to advocate secession and inaugurated the decade of controversy leading to the Civil War. Placer miners, fanning eastward from the West Coast, rapidly erased the frontier which had been a constant feature of American life since the first settlement. The eagerness to explore the bowels of the earth hastened the solution of difficult technical problems and thereby made possible a great expansion in the production of metals.

Yet, important as these developments were, from the point of view of business history they were overshadowed by the tremendous effect of gold mining upon business growth. The inrush of population created an explosive need for goods and services which could only be supplied by entrepreneurial organization. The gold dust produced by the frantic exertions of the miners was not only a medium of payment but also acted as a magnet for investment capital from all over the world. In the long run the most successful forty-niners were those who after a short time in the diggings utilized their gains (usually small) as grubstakes for the establishment of mercantile houses, banks, ranches and farms, small-scale manufacturing plants, stamping mills and refineries, and the many types of companies designed to improve water and overland transportation. In a few short years the gold rush of forty-nine was over, but, thanks to business enterprise, the material base for civilization in the Far West had been created.

XVI. Two Notable
Experiments
in Land Speculation

THE BUSINESS OF LAND SPECULATION DURING
THE ANTEBELLUM PERIOD

With the end of the land sales made to speculative combines by Congress and the state governments during the last two decades of the eighteenth century, areas on the westward moving frontier suitable for settlement were surveyed in advance by the federal government and sold at public auction. As Malcolm J. Rohrbough comments on the momentous nature of these auctions: "The process by which the public lands were brought to market through survey and public sale were known to every citizen in the western country; and a public land sale ranked with birth, marriage, and death among the most significant events in the life of any frontiersman. Here, in a few seconds, decisions were made that had a life-long impact upon the men who were present. It was invariably a moving and sobering experience, . . ." Congress made efforts to help the small farmer at the expense of the speculator by conveying land in continually smaller units. The Pre-emption Acts of 1830, 1832, 1834, and 1841 were designed to protect the interests of squatters by giving them options to purchase quarter sections of 160 acres apiece upon which they had built houses and made other improvements. The price was the government minimum of $1.25 per acre.

Although the auctions were designed to allow the little man to acquire land directly from the government without paying a middleman's profit, they generated as much fraud as had characterized the manipulations of the large land companies of the 1780s and 1790s. Most of the land sold at auction was purchased for speculative purposes. It is no exaggeration to say that the auctions were the equivalent of a national lottery rigged for the benefit of speculators large and small. Among the pre-emptors were many farmers who purchased solely to resell to larger speculators intent on combining a number of small holdings. Often pre-emptors had not fulfilled the requirements for land improvement and occupation, and therefore acquired title by fraud. Under the first three pre-emption acts if two pre-emptors laid claim to the same 160 acre tract, it was divided between them and each received in addition a "floating claim" of eighty acres which could be located in the same land district. These floats were usually sold to speculators who located them in such a manner as to box in large tracts which would eventually fall to them at depreciated prices because the speculators owned all the peripheral land.

Often farmers and local businessmen banded together in "claims clubs" which without any legal sanction whatsoever manufactured "claims" to land about to be surveyed and auctioned by the government. By selling "claims" to each other the members of the clubs arrived at an agreed upon distribution of the land at agreed upon prices. At the auctions the members by various collusive means succeeded in legally acquiring the land at prices which allowed them to make a speculator's profit. Membership in the clubs was by no means limited to the well-heeled. Often small farmers made enough money legally to purchase pre-empted plots by staking out claims elsewhere before the auctions were held and then selling the claims to other club members. In a variation of claims club operations a group of businessmen might raise a considerable sum of money through assessments of $1,000 apiece. Then, again through collusive bidding, the sum would be used to purchase land at public auction at the minimum price. Immediately, while the government auctioneer was still at work, the speculators would resell the land at a private auction of their own.

The speculators who made the largest purchases were the agents of eastern businessmen who bought land for their principals on a continuing basis. Often these men were partners in eastern banking houses like E. W. Clark and Company, and established large organizations in western cities and towns which conducted a banking business as well. The speculators they represented came from a broad spectrum of business and professional backgrounds—the same backgrounds from which come the stock market investors of today. The agents, in their capacity as bankers, often advanced purchase money under the "bond for a deed system." By this arrangement, as explained by Robert P. Swierenga, "the prospective buyer designated a desired tract, whereupon the money lender entered the land in his own name (to protect the loan), but under bond to transfer the title when the loan was paid, usually in one or two years. The standard interest rate on such transactions was 40 per cent per annum; . . ." This exorbitant rate reflected a continuing scarcity of money and banking institutions in the Midwest, but it was tolerated by purchasers because of the uniform rise in land values.

The volume of land sales was swelled by the large number of bounty warrants issued by the federal government to veterans of the Revolution, the War of 1812, and the Mexican War. These were the equivalent of the soldiers' bonuses granted after World War I and the "GI benefits" given after World War II and the Korean War. Between 1847 and 1855 almost sixty-one million acres were issued in the form of warrants. Most recipients, in need of ready cash, did not use the documents to locate land but sold them in the open market. During the forties and early fifties the warrants sold at discounts of as high as 50 percent, primarily because Congress, disapproving the stimulation to speculation and land engrossment caused by the trade, limited their use after assignment. But the pressure from the speculative fraternity could not be withstood; during the middle fifties all limitations were gradually removed and as a result the value of warrants moved upward close to the minimum land price of $1.25 per acre. Wall Street became the hub of the warrant trade, and prices were quoted in the weekly *Thompson's Bank Note Reporter*, a publication with a circulation of over 100,000. Many large warrant brokerage houses came into existence, and so extensive was the use of these documents that 52 percent of all Congress land in Iowa was located with them.

From the 1840s through the 1870s traffic in Midwest land was one of the biggest businesses in the nation. Swierenga, in his careful study of speculation in Iowa, comes to the conclusion that in the counties in the central part of the state one-fourth to nine-tenths of the land was held by nonresidents between 1865 and 1869. Moreover, "twenty-eight entrants with more than 10,000 acres apiece accounted for nearly 740,000 acres, or 12.1

percent of all Congress land in eastern Iowa." Swierenga estimates that during the fifties between one-half and three-fourths of all farmers acquired their farms from private individuals or land companies rather than from auctions of Congress land.

Extensive speculative operations were conducted by corporations formed in Eastern cities resembling modern mutual funds. For example, the American Land Company, organized in 1835 by Boston and New York capitalists, invested $400,000 of its million dollar capitalization in Mississippi cotton lands, $250,000 in Arkansas lands, and the balance in rural lands and townsites in six western states. The names of other companies, such as The New York and Mississippi Land Company, the Boston and Indiana Land Company, The Boston and New York Chicksaw Land Company, indicate particular areas of speculative interest. The holdings of the companies amounted in the aggregate to perhaps several million acres. Actually it would be impossible to estimate how much western land between 1830 and 1860 fell into the hands of speculators, and even the term "speculator" becomes so all-inclusive as to be almost meaningless. Speculation by local people was accepted as normal; it was the absentees who earned all of the opprobrium attached to the term.

INVESTMENT IN REVOLUTION: LAND SPECULATION AND
THE INDEPENDENCE OF TEXAS

One of the largest speculations of the antebellum period, and one closely connected with politics, was the traffic in Texas land during the Texas Revolution and during the subsequent decade ending with the annexation of that nation to the United States. By 1820 the farmers and planters of the lower Mississippi Valley were eying hungrily the fertile land in the Brazos and Colorado River valleys of southern Texas, now Mexican territory as a result of the Adams-Onis Treaty of 1819. The opening of Texas to American settlers was largely the work of Stephen F. Austin, a promoter of settlement who deserves a place in history beside Calvert and Penn. Following a plan envisaged by his father, Moses Austin, Stephen proposed to the Mexican government that it give him a large land grant in the fertile Gulf area in return for introducing American colonists who would swear allegiance to Mexico and nominally accept the Catholic religion. The Mexican government, anxious to develop the region, readily agreed to the proposal in 1823. As the plan was subsequently amplified, Austin was allowed to settle 300 families in Texas each of which received 177 acres for farming and a much larger area for grazing. As recompense for his efforts, the Mexican government granted Austin 65,000 acres of farming land.

Meanwhile other businessmen had seen the possibilities of profit in Austin's arrangement with Mexico. In response to their requests the state of Texas-Coahuila in 1825 established uniform provisions for settlement contracts with the "empresarios," as the sponsors of immigration were called. By 1829 the number of contracts signed had risen to fifteen, and a year later four empresarios with grants adjacent to one another pooled their resources with those of a group of New York and Boston capitalists to form The Galveston Bay and Texas Land Company. Not one of the contracts was completely fulfilled, and some were acquired solely to be resold at a profit, but the success of the empresario policy was indicated by a rapid increase in the population of Texas. By 1834 Austin alone had secured land titles for over 1,000 families.

But meanwhile the Mexican government, initially so hospitable to Americans, had come to view them as potentially dangerous. The Colonization Law of 1830, by forbidding further immigration, restricting the spread of slavery, and establishing military control over Texas-Coahuila, planted the seeds of disaffection which were to bring forth the Texas Revolution. Land speculators, in both Texas and the United States, were particularly anxious for independence. With unrestricted immigration into a new, independent nation, land values could be expected to mount precipitantly. At the 1835 session of the Texas-Coahuila legislature, now dominated by erstwhile Americans, the themes of revolution and land speculation were so combined that it was difficult to decide whether revolution was the cause of land speculation or the reverse.

Shortly after the end of the session Stephen F. Austin and William H. Wharton left Texas for the United States in order to raise money for the contemplated revolt. To New Orleans and New York capitalists they offered land scrip in a republic not yet born. Everywhere they were favorably received, and their cause was strongly aided by the Galveston Bay and Texas Land Company and the mercantile contacts of McKinney and Williams. This firm, which combined cotton factorage with a general mercantile and banking business in Galveston, performed the same service for the Texas Revolution which Robert Morris did for the American Revolution. The company advanced its own funds to the government for military purposes and managed long-term financing by the sale in the United States of cotton, land scrip, and Texas securities. "It is the prevailing opinion," wrote a Texas observer in 1836, "that but for the timely aid of McKinney and Williams, our revolution would have been a failure." By 1837, after the defeat of Santa Anna, claims to one million acres of land had come into the possession of American citizens, giving them, of course, a lively interest in the welfare of the new Texas Republic.

During the years immediately following the revolution the public debt of Texas, like the public debt of the United States some forty-five to fifty years before, came to be concentrated in the hands of large merchants and speculators, and the anticipation of annexation to the United States raised the prices of Texas securities between 1836 and 1845 to the same degree that the prospect of a new constitution raised the value of the Continental debt between 1786 and 1788. Speculators strongly supported the annexation treaty of 1844, which was narrowly defeated in the Senate. In the subsequent national election of that year, the holders of Texas paper backed Polk against Clay and were influential in securing annexation by joint resolution of Congress in 1845.

By terms of the Compromise of 1850 the United States assumed the Texas national debt and allowed Texas to retain her public lands. But as in 1790, the question of whether to pay off the debt at par or at a lesser figure promoted acrimonious debate. Finally, in 1855, Congress appropriated $6,675,000 for the purpose, which amounted to about seventy-seven cents on the dollar plus interest at up to 10 percent for some issues. Considering that the Texas securities had originally sold at about seventeen cents on the dollar and had circulated during the late thirties and early forties at about twenty to twenty-five cents, the profit to ultimate holders was very large. The concentration of debt holdings is indicated by the fact that the entire redemption fund was paid out to only 647 individuals, banks, or estates. According to Holman Hamilton, 174 payments were of more than $5,000 each, and sixteen topped $100,000.

LAND SPECULATION CREATES AN ENDOWMENT
FOR CORNELL UNIVERSITY

A notable land speculation of a somewhat later date, which had a much more beneficial social effect than the Texas operation, was the location and disposal of the pine lands which Cornell University acquired under the terms of the Morrill Agricultural College Act of 1862. The reservation of a portion of public lands for educational purposes had been an element of public land policy since the Land Ordinance of 1785, but no serious attempt had been made to effectuate it until the discussion of a homestead act began in Congress in the late 1850s. Support for education was considered to be an objective closely allied with the policy of granting free farms in the West to those who would guarantee to till them. Yet western congressmen, anxious to avoid further engrossment of public land by eastern speculators, were instrumental in inducing Congress to reject the first Morrill Act of 1857, which as a means of aiding education would have granted each state 20,000 acres of public land for each senator and representative. Under the terms of the bill western states would receive title to public land within their borders, but eastern states, which had no such lands, would be granted scrip which they would presumably liquidate in the open market. Obviously the scrip, like military warrants, would give speculators a splendid opportunity to buy up and consolidate large areas.

The South had also opposed the bill, mainly on the same constitutional and strategic grounds which led the section to oppose a homestead act, but after the southern states left the Union, enough votes could be mustered in 1862 to pass both the Homestead Act and the Agricultural College Act. Under the latter measure the amount of land given for each senator and representative was raised to 30,000 acres, and an amendment to limit scrip purchases of land to 640 acres or less was defeated. As westerners had feared, the bill proved to be a speculators' bonanza. The scrip for 7,830,000 acres of public land donated to eastern states was mostly thrown on the market and became available to speculators at prices as low as fifty cents an acre, less than half the traditional land price of $1.25 per acre. Dozens of lumbermen and mining speculators accumulated from 5,000 to 50,000 acres, and four individuals secured holdings of more than 100,000 acres apiece. One of these was Ezra Cornell, who located the some 900,000 acres of scrip allotted to the state of New York.

Cornell was a self-made businessman with engineering talents who had made about $2 million in the burgeoning telegraph industry. After this considerable achievement he devoted himself mainly to farming, politics, and civic affairs in Ithaca, New York, where he resided. But he was particularly interested in the development of the agricultural college there which he had helped to found and which later was to bear his name. With the assistance of Andrew D. White, later to become the notable president of Cornell University, Ezra Cornell succeeded in having the New York scrip earmarked for the benefit of the college at Ithaca. He then contracted to purchase the entire issue over a period of time at thirty cents per acre, locate the lands for sale, and pay the state all returns above his financial outlay minus a 7 percent charge on the capital used in the transaction. The purchase money paid by Cornell to the state and all profits upon his sales would be donated to the college.

During the late sixties lumber output in the Lake States was increasing at a fast rate, and canny speculators could easily see that timberlands in Michigan, Wisconsin, and Minnesota would undoubtedly increase greatly in price. Two speculators with an intimate knowledge of conditions in this region—Herbert C. Putnam and William A. Woodward—persuaded Cornell to join them in purchasing timberland in the upper Mississippi region by the use of the New York land scrip. It was a fortunate decision for all concerned, except perhaps the local inhabitants of the counties in which Cornell owned most of the land. By 1867 Cornell had acquired 499,126 acres of pine and farm land in Wisconsin, and additional acreage elsewhere, making himself one of the largest owners of pine land in the Northwest. The land was located by a host of landlookers working under Putnam, who was reimbursed for his efforts by a percentage of all land acquired by Cornell.

During the difficult times following the Panic of 1873 Cornell was on occasion hard pressed for cash, but was able to surmount his trouble when two lumber barons also interested in the welfare of the college—John McGraw and Henry W. Sage—took some of the land off his hands. From the original entry to final deed Cornell and his colleagues sold 512,428 acres of land and the stumpage on 190,000 acres. Allowing for taxes, interest, and other expenses, the whole operation netted about $5 million. Most states merely threw their scrip on the market for whatever it would bring, and as a result seldom got more than sixty cents an acre for it. But because of Cornell's remarkable combination of philanthropy and speculation, the New York scrip earmarked and sold for the college at Ithaca was invested in land much of which brought upwards of ten dollars per acre.

THE SOCIAL AND ECONOMIC BALANCE SHEET

It is something of a paradox that although land speculation involved wider participation and brought more capital gains to more people than any other business in American history, it continually aroused social disapproval. Critics insisted that absentee speculators added no value to the land but merely extracted their gains from the blood, sweat, and tears of the tillers of the soil. By snatching the best land in any vicinity before settlement took place they created "speculators' deserts" which dispersed population and increased the costs of roads, schools, and all other items of social overhead capital. Furthermore, by evading taxes they merely added to the already heavy burdens of the resident population. The final result of their silent depredation was an increase in tenantry as farmers, after a few years of bad crops, lost their land through foreclosures.

Although the various counts in this indictment can easily be documented, it does not follow that all of the evils allegedly flowing from land speculation were simultaneously present in areas where speculators were active. Moreover, traffic in land was not a royal road to riches for all engaged in it. The rate of increase in value varied greatly within even small areas with similar characteristics. Equally important, all speculators incurred certain costs in the form of taxes, interest on money borrowed, interest on money invested, and legal and administrative expenses. With rates varying between 10 and 50 percent, interest was the heaviest expense in frontier areas. The big question for the speculator was whether the rising value of land in which he had invested would outstrip the rising costs he was accumulating.

In the early days of the Republic, as we have seen, expenses eventually overwhelmed most of the large speculators and plunged them into bankruptcies which shook the credit of the nation. In the Midwest during the middle decades of the nineteenth century land speculation on the whole appears to have turned out more favorably for the speculators. Doubtless improved transportation, a heavier flow of immigrants, a better land marketing system, and larger capital reserves contributed to this outcome. But the few studies of speculator profits available leave some doubt as to the degree of profitability of land speculation in comparison with other types of investment. A detailed study of the profit record of five large investors from 1840 to 1885 by Alan and Margaret Bogue shows that land in central Illinois, bought in the mid-thirties and sold twenty or thirty years later, yielded a return of from 6 to 8 percent. Railroad bonds, and even farm mortgages, would have brought more. Paul W. Gates, who has studied the records of large speculative syndicates of eastern merchants, concludes that because of mounting expenses speculation in prairie lands at mid-century was on the whole not profitable.

But on the other hand, Swierenga, using computerized methods, finds that between 1845 and 1884 the average rate of return to entrymen in three groups of Iowa counties who held 1,000 or more acres apiece varied between 67.8 and 82.2 percent per year. Since land values were determined by the volume of immigration, the quality of the soil, and proximity to transportation outlets and growing urban centers, the rate varied widely in different sections of the state. In some counties it was only 30 to 45 percent; in others it was as high as 110 to 115 percent. Apart from locational factors, the rate of profit appears to have been influenced by the timing of purchases and sales, and the length of time the speculator held his land. During the fifties, by rule of thumb raw land valued at $2.50 to $3.00

per acre at the time of entry supposedly would be worth $3.00 to $5.00 within two or three years and $10 within five to ten years. Profits were at their highest during the mid-fifties, with sharp fluctuations in response to the business cycle. After 1863 they went into a sharp decline and net return dropped to about 5 percent during the seventies and eighties.

Apparently many handsome fortunes were made in Iowa during the boom days of land speculation. The net worth of a group of forty-nine resident speculators investigated by Swierenga rose from an average of $4,648 in 1850 to $31,029 in 1860, and during the period the value of one realtor-banker's real estate rose from $1,700 to $200,000. Apparently out-of-state speculators did equally well. For example, the firm of Easley and Willingham of Halifax Courthouse, Virginia, between 1853 and 1879 enjoyed a net cash income of over $500,000 which represented a return on cash expended of more than 120 percent.

Somewhat surprisingly, Swierenga finds little reflection in Iowa of the opprobrium heaped upon land speculators elsewhere, primarily because the Iowa speculators do not appear to have been guilty of many of the practices which aroused complaint. Since it was to their advantage to attract settlers, they turned over their holdings quickly, seldom keeping land off the market for more than two or three years. Speculators assumed a large part of the tax burden and paid their taxes promptly. As creditors they were indulgent with defaulting debtors, usually because it was less troublesome to wait a while for their money than institute foreclosure proceedings. This same self-interest led them to avoid promoting tenantry. The returns from land traffic were much higher than the returns from rents.

Thus it would appear that land speculation in Iowa did not lead to the disadvantageous results experienced elsewhere. Perhaps one reason was that opportunities for profit were so ubiquitous and participation in the game so widespread that both large and small speculators and farmers found themselves united in a community of interest. Further investigation may reveal that areas in which speculation aroused class conflict and led to tenantry were those in which the rise in land values was so slow that rents offered a better return than purchase and sale. In any event, in most parts of the country during the nineteenth century land speculation did not block access to land ownership on the part of the small farmer. Actually, the low crop prices, heavy load of debt, and crop failures of the early nineties were a much more dangerous threat. In the United States it has usually been harder for the farmer to hold onto his land than to get it in the first place.

XVII. The Business of Large-Scale Farming

RICE CULTURE IN THE SOUTH CAROLINA AND
GEORGIA TIDAL SWAMPS

By mid-century, large, heavily capitalized farms operating with enough attention to costs, production methods, and marketing procedures to qualify as business enterprises could be found in every section of the nation. In the Northeast they were concentrated in areas where land was fertile, high priced, and adjacent to water transportation giving easy access to marketing centers. Farming as a business enterprise was most notable in the South in the form of slave plantations and in the West in the form of large prairie farming operations.

During the first half of the nineteenth century the most striking change in the plantation system—apart from its expansion—was the shift from tobacco to rice, sugar, and particularly cotton as leading staples. After the Revolution exports of tobacco dropped off precipitantly due to a variety of factors, perhaps the most important of which was continued low prices in foreign markets because of competition and discrimination. For most years until 1840 leaf exports ran at about 60 to 90 percent of the level of 1773 and did not turn definitely upward until the fifties. Production of the popular bright leaf, flue-cured tobacco and an expanding domestic market also contributed to a rise in production. But since by 1860 tobacco was produced mainly on small farms, it had ceased to be a major plantation crop.

Rice, grown in the tidal swamps of the Waccamaw, Pee Dee, Santee, Cooper, Edisto, and Savannah rivers, suffered no such vicissitudes as tobacco but was almost continually prosperous from its introduction in the late seventeenth century until the Civil War. In contrast to tobacco the crop could be grown only within an area of some 60,000 acres, thereby decreasing the danger of overproduction. Preparation of the rice fields was a costly business. During the early nineteenth century plantations with grinding machinery could represent an investment of $50,000 upwards, and as a result the bulk of the crop was produced by no more than 500 to 600 planters. Rice was initially grown in upland swamps, but difficulties in the control of water led to the use of the lower tidal swamps. Here the marshy river edges were embanked and fitted with water gates. In March the rice grains were planted in trenches and the fields flooded by impounding water during a high tide in the river. As soon as the rice sprouted the water was allowed to drain away during a low tide. At harvest time the rice kernels were removed from the tough husks surrounding them by pounding in a pestle or in a mill. Only the larger plantations had their own mills. Many planters sent their grain to Charleston for final processing.

Once rice fields had been dyked and banked, the production of the rice crop required an investment of about $25 per acre during the antebellum period. At an average yield of about thirty-five bushels per acre, selling for an average price of one dollar per bushel, the planter could receive a return of $10 to $12 per acre, or about $140 per field hand—a good return on an agricultural operation. Most planters were able to keep the cost of maintaining their plantations at a minimum by growing vegetables and raising livestock. Not much is known about the marketing system, but it was apparently carried on in much the same manner as during the colonial period by factors representing northeastern and foreign mercantile houses.

The career of Nathaniel Heywood illustrates the possibilities of accumulating great wealth in rice planting. At his death in 1851 he owned about 2,000 slaves settled on 4,500 acres of rice land contained in fourteen plantations. His annual income was in the neighborhood of $90,000 per year, although in the period of high prices during the Napoleonic Wars it was reported to be as high as $120,000 per year. This was a handsome return on an investment estimated at about $1 million.

Rice culture in South Carolina and Georgia never recovered from the shock of the Civil War. Negroes drifted away from the plantations, and the quality of field work from those who could be induced to stay decreased markedly. Tropical storms increased in frequency and destructiveness. But the most important factor was competition from rice growers in Texas and Louisiana. Large corporations installed pumping plants in these areas and so cut losses from weather to a minimum. The remains of rice culture in the Southeast have become only a tourist attraction—a few palatial plantation houses under huge live-oak trees, magnificent reconstructed gardens, and a few reconstructed rice fields.

SUGAR PLANTATIONS IN THE LOWER MISSISSIPPI VALLEY

The production of sugar was carried on under somewhat the same conditions as the production of rice. The area of cultivation was limited—in this case to the lower Mississippi Valley and the Mississippi delta. Moreover, initial investment required for sugar plantations was high. Land was expensive and planters felt it necessary to have their own mills and boiling plants for processing sugar cane. Under these circumstances sugar could be profitably produced only in large units employing slave labor, which explains why the production of sugar doubled between 1845 and 1859 while the number of plantations dropped from 1,536 to 1,308. By contrast, the much smaller outlay required to equip a cotton plantation permitted efficient operation in much smaller units.

As in the rice country, storms and floods on the lower Mississippi periodically destroyed crops. But a perennial and more serious problem was created by the long growing season of about ten months required by sugar cane. Because freezing ruined the crop, cane planted in January had to be cut before the first frost, which could come as early as November. Since the pace at which the cane was harvested was slowed by the lengthy process of boiling down the sap, planters were engaged at every cutting season in a race against time. Their problems were aggravated by the fact that crystallization of the sugar was a tricky process which required a high degree of skill on the part of the sugar maker. Many things could go wrong during the successive boilings of sap from the crushed cane, and the final product might turn out to be a worthless, gummy mass. The introduction of vacuum pans in the 1830s speeded the boiling process and inaugurated a series of technical improvements which permitted a higher degree of quality control, but these innovations also required a greater investment. Since sugar plantations combined agricultural and industrial processes geared to a tight time schedule, greater managerial competence was required than for most other agricultural enterprises.

The profits from sugar plantations in the early years of the nineteenth century were spectacular. Net returns of from 14 to 23 percent were not considered unusual. Field hands often earned from $500 to $750 apiece per year for their masters, and in some instances even $1,000. During the 1830s, however, a cost-price squeeze began which foreshadowed an end of the bonanza. A very few planters could still achieve a net return of 30 percent per year, but high capitalization, a growing burden of debt, and declining sugar prices cut sharply into the profits of most. The sugar country nevertheless maintained its aura of prosperity. Net income was still large enough to support the luxurious life, and the capital gain on land and slaves gave an encouraging aspect to what would otherwise have been dismal balance sheets.

Sugar was marketed in a variety of ways. During the first quarter of the nineteenth century planters usually shipped to commission merchants in New Orleans, some of whom made tours of the plantation area making purchases for future delivery. Other planters, hoping to get better prices and avoid multiple commissions, dispatched their hogsheads to merchants in northeastern cities. After 1830 a daily sugar auction was held on the New Orleans levee. The West became the best market for Louisiana sugar. By 1850, 50 to 55 percent of the output traveled up the Mississippi and its tributaries for ultimate sale, while only 20 to 25 percent went to the East.

During the latter antebellum period factorage firms came to dominate the marketing process. Performing in all respects like cotton factors, they not only sold the planters' output, but advanced credit and purchased goods for the planters as well. The extensive capital needs of sugar production were satisfied by lines of credit extending to the Northeast and even to Europe. Private, commercial, and state banks extended funds to planters and factors. In 1827 the first planters' bank was formed—The Consolidated Association of the Planters of Louisiana. This organization issued stock to planters in return for mortgages used as security for bonds which were guaranteed by the state and sold in Europe. Baring Brothers of London became a principal purchaser of these bonds. Planters used their stock as collateral for long-term loans. Out-of-state funds became so important in financing the sugar crop of Louisiana that by 1837 $7 million of the state's $40 million of bank capital came from other states and $21 million from Europe. Because of the mingling of developmental and commercial loans the banks of Louisiana suffered severely during the Panic of 1837, but the painful experience did at least bring forth the Banking Act of 1842—a model of sound banking practice (see p. 135).

Although the Civil War disrupted sugar planting, it did not die out as did rice planting in South Carolina, but it faced increasing competition from Cuban production.

COTTON PLANTATIONS AS BUSINESS ENTERPRISES

Cotton was of course the greatest bonanza of the South, as we have seen, and aided the economic development of the entire nation during the antebellum period. It also perpetuated the single crop system in the South, with its heritage of destructive agricultural practices, and blighted the hopes to diversify the southern economy by widespread industrialization. Indeed, one might argue that cotton helped destroy the very society it created by aiding the growth of population and industrial power in the North and deterring similar developments in the South.

After the invention of Whitney's gin made the production of the short staple variety practical, its cultivation spread rapidly throughout the tidewater and piedmont areas of Georgia and South Carolina. Wade Hampton, for example, grew 600 bales in 1799 which brought nearly $90,000. During each decade of the nineteenth century output approximately doubled, rising from 100,000 bales in 1801 to 4.5 million bales in 1859. By 1860 the cotton exports of the United States were valued at $192 million—about two-thirds of the value of all exports—and paid for about 60 percent of the nation's imports. After 1820, as profits from cotton growing in South Carolina and Georgia began to decline, planters and farmers in large numbers began to move westward to the rich, virgin soils of the Gulf states. By 1860 the Old South produced less than one-fourth of the total crop.

As had been the case in South Carolina at the beginning of the century, the early birds in the Southwest got the big profits. It was said that the first planters in Mississippi, acquiring land at bargain rates of from $2 to $4 per acre, could make 22 percent on their capital. As the cotton belt stretched even further westward, reports of initial profits continued to be spectacular. Texans (appropriately) reported that during the 1830s plantations in the Brazos Valley were producing as much as 2,500 pounds per hand valued at between $250 and $400.

Initially high profits could generally not be maintained, however, and returns varied from time to time and from place to place. Indeed, cotton was grown under such a wide variety of conditions that it is very difficult to make generalizations on returns or point to any plantations which could be called typical. Cotton was produced on small ones with fifteen or twenty hands and on large ones with up to 1,000 hands. It was also grown by farmers with one or two Negroes or without any slaves at all. A majority of southerners owned no slaves, and the great majority of slaveholders owned fewer than ten. Yet so concentrated was slave ownership that over 50 percent of the Negroes were held on plantations with more than twenty and another 25 percent on plantations with more than fifty. The bulk of the cotton crop was produced, therefore, by a small minority of the South's white population.

Cotton plantations were characterized by as wide variations in productivity as could be found in farming generally. In the black belt planters expected a production of about 800 to 1,000 pounds per acre. In the Old South after 1820, and in upland regions generally, the yield was considerably less, and weather conditions affected output everywhere. The test for efficiency of slaves was the amount of cotton they could pick, and here also we find a wide variation in performance. Mississippi planters expected slaves to pick at least seventy-five to eighty pounds of cotton per day, but skillful hands could pick considerably more. A yearly production per hand of five to seven bales of 400 pounds apiece was considered good. With cotton at ten cents per pound, each hand under these circumstances could therefore earn between two and three hundred dollars.

In general there were two types of business problems facing the planters: those connected with the production of the staple and those relating to the market. On the surface, the institution of slavery would seem to give planters a considerable economic advantage over the nonslaveholders. The planter was able to appropriate the entire output of his labor force, the cost of maintenance was low—about $20 to $25 per year per slave— capital gains were acquired in the form of slave offspring, all members of slave families could be put to work, and slave markets enabled the planter to adjust his labor supply to his productive needs. Furthermore, slaves could be trained to all artisan tasks and so enable the plantation to achieve a high degree of self-sufficiency. But the slave system created many difficulties which in part, at least, offset these advantages. Buying labor in bulk, so to speak, soaked up much capital which could be put to other, and perhaps more profitable uses; the slave owner was compelled to support the slave during the years of infancy and old age when productivity was small or nonexistent; slave labor was unwilling labor, and often inefficient; runaways or deaths from disease or accidents caused serious capital losses which could be avoided if labor were hired.

Problems arising from the nature of the labor force were intensified by a management problem peculiar to the slave plantation system. The demands of status required that members of the planter class in good standing hire overseers to direct the Negroes at their tasks. This position required a high degree of stamina, administrative ability, and capacity to motivate unwilling laborers. Yet overseers as a class tended to be indifferent, inefficient, and given to the sins of the flesh. Low pay—$200 to $800 per year—and social stigma made the position unattractive to many men who had the requisite qualifications. Yet here, as in all aspects of the plantation system, there were many exceptions to the rule. Some overseers were able, ambitious young men from humble backgrounds anxious to rise into the planter class themselves. A few were successful planters in their own right. Often the loudly publicized failures of overseers were not due as much to their own shortcomings as to employers' frequent lack of respect and consideration for them, capricious orders, and a rate of job turnover so high that many overseers could not acquire the experience with a particular plantation necessary for efficient performance.

Methods of payment also created difficulties. When, in order to stimulate incentive, masters allowed overseers a portion of the crop, the latter tended to overwork the Negroes and equipment and overplant the cash crop at the expense of food crops. On the other hand, when overseers were placed on straight salary as a means of avoiding these eventualities, planters complained that lack of incentive eroded their efficiency. In contrast to the situation in industry, the separation of management and ownership in the plantation system did not lead to the emergence of a highly trained, intelligent managerial group; on the contrary, the peculiar juxtaposition of status and stigma on plantations tended to deprive them of effective management by owners while hindering the formation of an efficient professional managerial class.

Self-sufficiency played a varying role in the conduct of plantation affairs. Owners in fertile areas found it profitable to plant cotton intensively and purchase a larger proportion of their corn, pork, and other foodstuffs. Owners of less productive units, unable to afford this policy, conducted a more diversified agriculture and lowered maintenance cost of slaves to as little as $10 to $15 per year. When the price of cotton was high, planters tended to increase production at the expense of food crops; when prices were low, they tended to do the opposite in the conviction that net return would be benefited more by a reduction of costs than by an increase in the output of the staple.

The wide fluctuation of cotton prices necessarily brought financial instability. In 1818, for example, cotton reached thirty-five cents per pound. From there it went into an extended decline, with fluctuations upward, and touched a low of five cents in 1844. By the 1850s prices appeared to have stabilized at about eleven cents. Estimates of the cost of production necessarily varied, but were considered to be around eight cents per pound.

Planters marketed their cotton through the factorage system that moved all southern stable crops to market. Since cotton was grown so ubiquitously the system was necessarily much more ramified than rice and sugar factorage. Interior factors located in such towns as Macon, Montgomery, Nashville, Milledgeville, Augusta, and Fayetteville shipped the cotton to a second group of factors resident in seaport centers who often represented cotton supply firms and mills in the Northeast and in Europe. Before the fiber reached its destination it had passed through the hands of many middlemen and had necessarily incurred heavy charges for commissions, handling, transportation, and insurance. Since much of the financing of the crop and most of the shipping and commercial services came from New York, about one-quarter of the cotton destined for Europe was diverted to that port to pay for European imports, a large proportion of which retraced the course of the cotton into the interior parts of the South. Planters complained bitterly because of what they considered to be exploitation by New York merchants and shipowners, and commercial conventions repeatedly called for the establishment in southern seaports of commercial services and shipping lines giving direct contact with Europe. Nothing materialized from these appeals, however, simply because the bulk of capital accumulations in the South moved inexorably into the further expansion of the plantation system by purchase of land and slaves.

Cotton planters financed their crops in much the same manner as sugar and rice planters—through factors, commercial banks, and plantation banks. But since 75 to 80 percent of the crop was exported, Europe was even more important to cotton planters as an ultimate source of funds than it was to sugar and rice planters. The purchase of state bank stock and plantation bank bonds by European investors represented an indirect investment in cotton plantations. Credit extended by the large "American" banking houses of London to Liverpool cotton dealers, and through them to New York merchants and southern factors, constituted much of the commercial capital which grew and harvested the crop and moved it to market. The largest of several cotton exchanges in the South was located in New Orleans, and during the antebellum period probably did a greater volume of business than any other commodity market in the nation. The New York Cotton Exchange, founded in 1870, was almost entirely a futures market designed to serve the needs of the New England textile industry.

THE PROFITABILITY OF SLAVERY

The question of whether plantation slavery was "profitable" has been a subject of considerable discussion from the antebellum period to our own day. Both contemporary apologists and critics of slavery tended to agree that it was not, but without bringing forth much convincing evidence to support their views. Critics were no doubt influenced to some degree by their hostility toward the system; defenders may have attempted to prove unprofitability as a means of avoiding imputation that owners exploited the slaves. If the system did not make money, the paternal image which planters tried so hard to create for themselves could be more readily brought into focus. Actually, the wide variety of circumstances under which cotton plantations were operated and the many variable factors determining costs and returns make generalization difficult. It is quite apparent that well-run plantations on good land made money, and that plantations not so fortunate did not. Operating results would differ to the same degree as would be found in industrial enterprises. But perhaps a majority of investigators today believe that the plantation "system"—if such a vague term can be accepted—brought about the same return as enterprises which were considered to be profitable in other sectors of the economy. One reason for this conclusion arises from accounting methods used in the antebellum South which intentionally or unintentionally often masked profits. As already indicated, supplies for the planter and his family and the upkeep of house servants were often carried as plantation costs, and slaves and land were often overvalued, thus giving an artificially high capitalization against which to compute the percentage of profit. Profit itself was not considered to be net return, but net return minus a 5 percent charge on invested capital supposedly representing the wage due to capital. By thus magnifying costs and capitalization a net return of handsome proportions could be reduced to a small "profit" of 2 to 3 percent or even a loss.

The economists Alfred H. Conrad and John R. Meyer provide further evidence that cotton plantations could be very profitable for their owners. After compiling and analyzing elaborate statistics on slave longevity, cost, upkeep, and productivity under a "Keynsian capital-value" formula, Conrad and Meyer found that returns on cotton production varied from 2.2 percent on marginal lands to 13 percent on the best lands with 4½ to 8 percent constituting an average return. They found also that average profits of from 7.1 to 8.1 percent were gained in the raising and selling of slaves, and that this return enabled planters of the Old South with surplus slaves to achieve an adequate income from relatively unproductive plantations. Actually, the mere fact that the value of slaves was always greater than the cost of rearing and maintaining them in itself demonstrates that slavery was profitable. But, in a broader context, the question arises, profitable for whom—the slave, the slaveholder, the nonslaveholder, the South, the nation? As Harold D. Woodman writes, "With such a configuration, the . . . question 'Was slavery profitable?' becomes meaningless by itself."

Controversies over whether the slave economy was viable are closely linked to the dispute over profitability. One group of historians, citing among other factors the increasing cost of slave labor and the failure of the South to create a domestic market which could foster a diversified economy, maintains that the system was doomed. But the weight of the evidence does not support such a conclusion. Although the price of prime field hands rose from about $500 to $1,000 between 1820 and 1860, cotton exports per slave, by a contemporary computation, rose from 83 pounds in 1820 to 337 in 1850. Of course, this spectacular rise in per capita exports does not necessarily indicate a proportionate rise in slave productivity. The per capita figures probably reflect to some extent the shift of a continually greater proportion of the slave population into the cotton economy. Nevertheless, it is quite possible, and even probable, that an increase in slave productivity outpaced the rise in the price of slaves. Specialization of function on the plantations which produced the bulk of the crop had proceeded rapidly during the period in question, and must have brought considerable economies of scale.

Constantly increasing foreign and domestic demand for cotton also strengthened the southern economy. In 1860 the United States had a near monopoly of the English market, and the South had achieved an indispensable regional specialization in an international economy embracing the entire Atlantic community. Under these circumstances the failure to create a domestic market constituted no drawback. Although in 1860 southern per capita income, including maintenance of slaves, was 80 percent of the national average, it was higher than the per capita income of the North Central states. More important, the southern rate of growth of per capita income was 1.6 percent per annum compared with 1.3 percent for the nation as a whole. If slavery was indeed doomed, it was not because of economic reasons but because of the increasing moral outrage it engendered throughout the civilized world.

LARGE FARMS IN THE MIDWEST
With the coming of railroads and canals, farming in the Old North-

west during the fifties became increasingly commercialized and many farms were comparable in size and work force to large southern plantations. On one such farm in Illinois, for example, the owner, Michael Sullivant, planted 3,000 acres in corn and a lesser number in wheat and during the summer employed from 100 to 200 men. Substantial English farmers with large capital backing such as Morris Birkbeck, George and Richard Flower, and Elias P. Fordham established large agricultural enterprises on the model of English estates. In addition to improved transportation, a combination of factors made these farms profitable, at least at the outset. In the first place, since small farmers tended to avoid the prairies in favor of wooded land, farmer-businessmen could buy large open areas cheaply with military warrants, often at from fifty cents to $1 per acre. Second, the swelling immigration from abroad during the fifties supplied cheap labor. Third, the absence of trees or natural obstructions made unified farming operations possible. Fourth, increasing demand for flour created a firm market for wheat, and large-scale cattle fattening absorbed large amounts of corn. Finally, the development of farm machinery, with the tremendous advances in productivity it entailed, made possible businesslike planning of farm operations with careful separation of labor. By 1860 many different types of ploughs, reapers, threshers, corn drillers, and rakes—to mention only a few of the new machines—were in use on the prairies. The new reapers "harvested grain more thoroughly, and seven times more rapidly than the cradle, with one-half the labor force," according to one authority.

But by 1860 many of the large farms were being broken up into smaller units which were rented or sold to tenants. The precise reasons for this development are somewhat obscure, but probably owners found that large-scale operations requiring heavy overhead were risky. Also, a rapid turnover of farm labor created difficulties. Many owners probably felt that it would be easier and more remunerative to delegate operations to tenants or by selling to take capital gains and invest in lower priced lands farther west. The terms on which the land was let to tenants varied, but generally the tenant was required to plant a certain amount of wheat and corn and pay a percentage to the landlord. On conditional sale agreements the tenant paid half his crop to the landlord for a period of from three to seven or eight years and made specified improvements. Some landlords earned their tenants' respect by building houses and mills and other improvements. Others, indifferent to the farmers' welfare, were despised.

The large farmers received their developmental capital direct from eastern financial centers or even from Europe in the same circle of relationships by which land speculators located and purchased their tracts. Good farming land in the Old Northwest was usually considered an excellent investment and funds could readily be found in return for mortgages. In the fifties the Illinois Central Railroad became a financier of farmers by selling tracts in its huge land grant on time payments.

By the nineties most of the large farms had disappeared or had shrunk in size, but remnants of some exist even today. The tenant system did not prove to be the evil it became in the South. In many cases it was merely the introduction to freehold ownership and the tenant benefited greatly from the experience and equipment provided by the landlord. The system also provided an opportunity for upward mobility to the active and energetic. But perhaps more important, all of the mechanisms of the land system were tilted in favor of ownership rather than tenantry. Claims clubs, preemption, auction sales, and homesteading all made it relatively easy for the small farmer to acquire title to the acres he tilled. Furthermore, as previously indicated, railroads were eager to sell off their land quickly, and under terms favorable to the purchaser. Absentee speculators usually had little interest in establishing large farms operated by tenants simply because there was more profit to be had in selling rather than in renting land. All of these factors help explain why the large farms described above were the exception rather than the rule in the Midwest during the fifties, and diminished in number as the century advanced.

The first markets for grain and produce were the cities in the Ohio and Mississippi valleys, and the products of the Old Northwest ultimately found their way to New Orleans via a chain of commission merchants. But with the coming of canals and railroads and the opening of the Lakes trade, produce gravitated northward to the Lake ports and by a similar series of exchanges moved eastward via the Erie Canal to New York. As Chicago rose to become the greatest grain trading center in the nation, the institutions of marketing matured quickly. During the forties Chicago commission merchants sold wheat received directly from farmers or from back-country merchants to representatives of eastern millers or dealers located in the city or in Buffalo, which also became a great center of the grain trade because of its location at the point where wheat was transferred from Lake vessels to Erie canal boats. But in the mid-fifties the first grain elevators brought about a revolution in marketing methods. In the elevators grain was stored by grade, and farmers and commission merchants received warehouse receipts in return for grain deposited. These receipts circulated as currency and could be liquidated at market prices or held for the later withdrawal of wheat.

When the purchase and sale of wheat came to be carried on with warehouse receipts rather than the grain itself, the Chicago Board of Trade, formed in 1845, became the very epicenter of the grain trade. Adopting in the late fifties much the same procedures as the New York Stock Exchange, it was the scene of vast speculations involving not only spot purchases but trade in futures and options as well.

As the demand for wheat multiplied, eastern capital flowed into Chicago banks, and they performed an ever more important role in financing the grain trade. During the fifties dealers with large bank loans purchased wheat direct in interior markets. The banks also discounted bills of exchange drawn on New York dealers and even financed country banks involved in the grain trade by rediscounting their paper. Wherever grain elevators sprang up along the railroads farmers were able to sell their wheat for cash. Crop liens and crop loans became the equivalent of the advances made by factors in the South.

The capitalistic nature of American farming has left a permanent impress upon the structure of the American economy. The emphasis upon staple crops and the constant drive to increase production, the relative scarcity of labor and the abundance of land made it easy for the farmer to accept mechanization and scientific farming methods. The free alienability of land and the pervasiveness of land speculation sharpened his profit orientation and made him familiar with financial methods. The result of all these factors today is the striking paradox of high productivity in agriculture, an agricultural population large sections of which can adapt itself to work in industry, burdensome surpluses, and millions of acres of land devastated by misuse. By contrast the peasant tradition of Europe, in spite of affectionate regard for the soil, has led to the equally striking paradox of food shortages in countries which are primarily agricultural. And the communist governments of many of these countries appear at present writing to be having no more success in raising production than does our own government in reducing surpluses. No explanation of these conflicting developments can be made in purely economic terms. Industry wrenches people away from traditional habits and establishes a new set of values in which innovation, achievement, and technology play an important part, but agriculture tends to reinforce cultural patterns of the past. As time goes on, therefore, the cultural gap between peasant and industrial societies widens and it becomes progressively harder for the people of "advanced" nations to understand or help the people of the "backward" nations. But in the United States the conditions of settlement and colonial development, by separating people from a feudal past, also separated them from peasant culture. American agriculture came under the influence of the same set of values which dominated commerce and industry, and—for better and for worse—has come to share their problems. But the course of development in future decades might well bring a solution for many of these. As the pressure of burgeoning population against food supplies provided by peasant and communal agriculture increases, the problem of surpluses of both foodstuffs and farmers in America will decrease, and American agriculture, by both precept and production, may play an important role in raising standards of living everywhere.

XVIII. Construction and Operation of Canals

AWAKENING INTEREST IN CANALS

The interest in transportation improvement manifested in the turnpike movement also resulted concurrently in a mounting commitment to canal construction which produced an impressive and very expensive system of waterways. Although all of the old turnpikes in the East have now disappeared, a few vestiges of America's once splendid canal system remain, mostly in the form of short stretches of water moving slowly and quietly between overgrown banks. Here and there one finds remnants of locks, with the aged stone houses of lock keepers nearby, and occasional aqueducts still carry stretches of canals over small streams. Many of the states have interior towns with "port" attached to their names, indicating that a dry ditch in the vicinity was once a busy canal which gave the towns a reason for existence. The timeless peace of the aged waterways, and the bucolic serenity and rare natural beauty of their surroundings, give little reflection of the once mighty transportation systems they represent. The Erie locks at Lockport, New York, and the reconstructed lower portion of the Chesapeake and Ohio Canal—now a national park—give some indication of the enormous expenditure of money and labor which the building of the canals entailed.

Textbooks in economic history often treat canal building as a somewhat fumbling, convulsive prologue to the construction of the railroad network. Certainly the railroad later proved to be less expensive to build and more reliable to operate, and it offered much faster transportation. Yet these advantages could not be foreseen until the canal movement was well underway, and even until the 1880s a few canals competed successfully with railroads. But more important, perhaps, the canal network when completed represented a major advance in transportation even though few canals could be operated at a profit. As the largest financial undertakings of their time, canal companies learned valuable lessons in capital accumulation and first attracted the increasing flow of foreign funds which played such an important part later in the building of railroads. Furthermore, canal promotion made more effective the co-operation of public and private finance and management under the joint enterprise system, and thereby paved the way for extensive government aid to railroads at a later date. Many canals significantly aided regional development, and one—the Erie—proved to be possibly the most successful American developmental enterprise of the nineteenth century. Finally, canal construction provided the challenge and the training which gave birth to the profession of engineering.

The ability of canals, by greatly reducing frictional resistance, to multiply the weight which could be drawn by a horse was the technical advantage in the forefront of all canal promoters' minds. Estimating the economics in motive power provided by waterways was a favorite subject with the writers of promotional literature. According to one generally accepted rule a horse could draw twenty-five tons on a canal with the same expenditure of energy as in drawing one ton over a highway. By another calculation two men and two horses could operate a boat of eighty tons burden; moving this load on a wheeled vehicle would theoretically require forty men and sixty horses. As long as horses were the primary motive power for transportation, canal boats were undoubtedly the most efficient vehicles for the carriage of freight. The development of locomotives which could draw heavy loads over an undulating railroad of course completely altered the mechanical calculus, and consequently the economics of transportation generally, but this eventuality did not become apparent until the construction of many of the major canals was underway.

CONSTRUCTION BY PRIVATE ENTERPRISE

Despite the grandiose visions of some leading Americans of the eighteenth century, the canal movement began in a hesitant and limited fashion as an adjunct to river improvements. Since the rivers flowing from the Appalachian chain to the seacoast were the natural highways for the carriage of agricultural produce and staple commodities, most states during the years immediately following the Revolution began to charter and give financial assistance to small companies which removed rocks and stumps from navigation channels and built short canals and locks around falls and rapids. The companies were financed locally in much the same way as bridge and turnpike companies. Among the larger canals which got their start in this manner were the Erie, the Susquehanna and Tidewater, the Lehigh, the Chesapeake and Ohio, the James River and Kanawha. In order to deepen shallow stretches of river, companies sometimes constructed "slackwater systems," which consisted of series of dams bypassed by canals with locks. "Wing dams" running parallel to the riverbanks also deepened the flow of water by compressing it into a narrow channel. Despite these experiments, however, river transportation continued to be unreliable during the dry summer months, and installations were regularly damaged or carried away by spring freshets. Under these circumstances it became apparent by 1815 that adequate water transportation could only be provided by canals drawing on a controlled external source of water.

The canal system as subsequently developed can most conveniently be categorized by the major purposes for which the waterways were constructed. The earliest canals were designed, like turnpikes, to widen the hinterland of coastal cities or give access to trade routes which bypassed the cities. Thus the Middlesex and the Santee canals were designed to divert a share of the trade on the Merrimac and Santee rivers to Boston and Charleston respectively. New Haven merchants hoped that the New Haven and Northampton Canal would bring them a portion of the commerce on the Connecticut River. The Blackstone Canal was designed to extend the hinterland of Providence into central Massachusetts; the Schuylkill Navigation and the Union Canal were to perform the same service by connecting Philadelphia with the Susquehanna watershed. The Dismal Swamp Canal was Norfolk's bid for the trade of the Albemarle region. The James River and the Potomac canals were to provide better access to tidewater for piedmont farmers of Virginia and Maryland respectively.

By 1810 canal enthusiasts had raised their sights and were considering waterways as a means of giving access to the transappalachian West. The Erie and the Pennsylvania Mainline were planned for this purpose. With the same object in view the James River Company was reorganized as the James River and Kanawha Canal Company, and the Potomac Company in like manner became the Chesapeake and Ohio Canal Company.

The Delaware-Raritan and the Delaware-Chesapeake have been called "exploitative canals" because the purpose of their promoters was to profit from the traffic on heavily-traveled routes. On the other hand, the long canals connecting the Great Lakes with the Ohio and Mississippi—the Ohio and Erie, the Miami and Erie, the Wabash and Erie, and the Illinois and Michigan—were primarily developmental in purpose, although their enthusiastic promoters expected that eventually they would prove to be very profitable. Like the Erie and the Pennsylvania Mainline they were planned as the main stems of integrated state transportation systems, with feeder canals and turnpikes giving connections with all productive areas.

The anthracite canals—The Delaware Division, Lehigh, Delaware and Hudson, and ultimately the Morris and the Schuylkill Navigation—were partly exploitative and partly developmental. Reaching from the Hudson, the Delaware, and the Schuylkill rivers into the anthracite region of Pennsylvania, they became the major carriers of hard coal during the period in which it became a major furnace, forge, and household fuel in the industrial and urban centers of the Northeast.

Construction of the first canals, slackwater systems, and river improvements was supported by initial investors with great enthusiasm. No difficulty was experienced in filling the stock subscriptions for the Middlesex and Santee canals, and the stock of the Potomac Company and the Schuylkill Navigation was oversubscribed shortly after the books were opened. But it quickly became apparent that these projects would at best severely strain local savings and credit and at worst require large infusions of capital from other sources. Canal building, with its manifold unforeseeable problems, turned out to be much more expensive than the construction of turnpikes, and the enthusiasm of stockholders evaporated rapidly as assessments followed each other with monotonous regularity. Still, after seven years of work the Santee was completed in 1800 at a cost of $750,000. The Middlesex was finished by a group of wealthy Boston families in 1803 at a cost of $444,000. Work on the Schuylkill Navigation lapsed in 1795 for lack of funds. Only the infusion of public money enabled construction to be completed in 1825.

Canal building by private enterprise alone proved to be considerably easier for the companies which constructed the anthracite canals. Private capital in New York and Philadelphia was attracted by potential profits of the coal traffic and the companies' holdings of coal lands. The Lehigh

Coal and Navigation Company, after some questionable financial improvisations which included the issuance of preference shares which diluted the equity of existing common share holders, in 1838 completed a waterway which by 1860 was carrying over one million tons of coal per year. So enthusiastic was the support given by New York financiers to the Delaware and Hudson Company that it was able to finish a canal connecting Port Jervis on the Delaware with Kingston on the Hudson in only three years. Even though both canals were immediately profitable, experience soon indicated to their promoters that greater gains were to be had in the purchase of coal lands and in coal mining. As early as the sixties the canals were slipping to the periphery of the companies' attention and represented only a small proportion of their assets. When, a few decades later, the companies acquired rail networks which made the canals unnecessary, they were quietly abandoned.

The New Jersey canals were constructed by private enterprise because they were relatively short and inexpensive to build, and—more important —directly or indirectly held palpable profit potential. After a long wrangle the legislature simultaneously incorporated the Delaware and Raritan Canal Company and the Camden and Amboy Railroad, which, as "joint companies" held a monopoly of water and rail traffic across the strategic neck of New Jersey extending from New Brunswick to Trenton. In return for this privilege the companies granted the state 2,000 shares of stock and guaranteed an annual payment of at least $30,000 per year in transit duties and dividends. After a prosperous career the joint companies were eventually absorbed by the Pennsylvania Railroad, and the canal was used until the 1930s. The Morris Canal, stretching across northern Jersey from the Delaware River to New York harbor, was promoted by New York businessmen, who, like Aaron Burr and the promoters of the Manhattan Company, were much more interested in banking privileges than in the construction of a public utility. With the permission of the legislature the directors of the canal company established the Morris Canal Bank, which, during the prosperous mid-thirties, did an investment banking business second in volume only to that of the Bank of the United States. The canal, because of a small capacity which reflected the directors' indifference to matters of transportation, was never very profitable and was ultimately sold to the Central Railroad of New Jersey. The bank, because of overextension in state improvement bonds and fraudulent manipulations, followed the Bank of the United States into bankruptcy in 1841.

Although the Blackstone Canal—the only other important waterway financed entirely by private enterprise during this period—was fairly successful, experience by the late twenties seemed to indicate that private capital could only be attracted in amounts necessary to bring projects to completion if prospects of immediate profit were bright. Canals designed to widen urban hinterlands and carry agricultural products and manufactured goods were even more doubtful propositions than turnpikes. Long developmental canals required such a large initial investment and entailed such long deferred returns—if indeed any returns could be expected at all—that private enterprise could not and would not support such undertakings without direct public participation. Hence we find that the Chesapeake and Ohio and the James River and Kanawha—the major southern canals—were built by joint enterprise. The Erie, after an inauspicious start as a private venture, was taken over by the state government. New York, Pennsylvania, Ohio, Indiana, and Illinois all undertook to build canal systems as public projects.

JOINT ENTERPRISE PROGRAMS

Despite formation of the Potomac Company in 1785 and stock purchases by both Virginia and Maryland, Washington's vision of a water route to the West was far from realization by 1815. Although canals had been built around the five major falls of the river and the channel freed from obstructions, the company could not even reach its modest objective of providing reliable transportation for boats carrying fifty barrels of flour. By 1823 it was bankrupt. But in that year interest in improving the waterway was revived amid much public enthusiasm, largely due to the efforts of a distinguished group of men including Albert Gallatin, Bushrod Washington, and John Quincy Adams. The backers now proposed to build a canal six feet deep and fifty feet wide westward along the Potomac and ultimately over the Appalachians. The federal government subscribed $1 million to what Army engineers estimated would ultimately be a $22 million dollar project. Investments by the District of Columbia, Georgetown, and the state of Maryland raised public participation to $3 million. Private investors, more ready to cheer for the project than to invest in it, contributed only $600,000. Public funds were granted in the form of bond issues which the company marketed in eastern financial centers and in England.

The subsequent history of the Chesapeake and Ohio Canal Company is a record of great, but fantastically expensive achievements made against multiplying difficulties. Disaffected work crews rioted and were decimated by cholera. Controversy with the hotly competing Baltimore and Ohio Railroad, which shared the canal's route, disrupted work. Unforeseen engineering problems and frequent washouts added to the company's troubles. Financial difficulties were incessant. After the Panic of 1837, bonds could only be sold abroad at a heavy discount, and contractors often had to accept payment in scrip and post notes. Maryland poured so much money into the canal project that it was compelled to suspend payment on its debt in 1842.

The canal was completed to Cumberland in 1850, at a cost of nearly $10 million, of which Maryland had supplied three-fifths of the total. The canal was probably the most elaborate and best constructed waterway built during this period, but in its most prosperous years returned no more than 2 percent on the investment. In 1888, after a long series of losses, the company went into receivership and the canal was then operated, and eventually abandoned to the federal government, by the Baltimore and Ohio Railroad.

The history of the James River and Kanawha Company follows much the same pattern as that of the Chesapeake and Ohio Company. In both cases the private companies formed during the eighteenth century proved completely unable to reach the Appalachians. Massive public investment then in both instances drove the work to a point of completion short of the ultimate goal. But the two states administered joint enterprise in a different manner. Maryland handled the affairs of the C. and O. through the legislature; Virginia created a Board of Public Works in 1816 which supervised all transportation improvement in which the state had invested.

In 1851 the canal built by the James River and Kanawha Company reached Buchanan—a town in the shadow of the Blue Ridge—which proved to be its terminus. During the preceding fifteen years devoted to construction, the company, state, and municipalities involved in the enterprise had been harrassed by financial difficulties. In order to keep the work going, the state had been compelled to increase its already heavy commitment by taking a mortgage on the company's installations and guaranteeing interest on other obligations. Yet when construction was finally suspended the company had a line of well-built canal 196 miles long, elaborate docking and transfer facilities in Richmond, a turnpike over the mountains to the Kanawha, and minor improvements on the river down to the Ohio. The canal represented a total investment of about $8 million, more than the cost of the Erie, which was nevertheless nearly twice as long as the Virginia canal. By 1860 the system yielded a net revenue of little more than $100,000 per year—not enough to service the debt, let alone pay dividends. From a financial point of view, the Virginia canal was even less successful than the Chesapeake and Ohio.

Several other important canals were built by joint enterprise. The Chesapeake and Delaware received stock subscriptions from the federal government, Pennsylvania, Maryland, and Delaware; the Dismal Swamp Canal was aided by Virginia; the Susquehanna and Tidewater received assistance from Baltimore; the New Haven and Northampton received not only a large stock subscription from the city of New Haven but an annual subsidy as well.

STATE FINANCED CANAL SYSTEMS

The great canal systems were financed as public enterprises, chiefly because in scope they appeared to be entirely beyond the resources of private enterprise. Also, in New York there was a widely held conviction that any corporation large enough to build the Erie Canal would constitute a concentration of economic power potentially subversive to a democratic society. In this regard, construction and operation by the state was looked upon as a safeguard of the private enterprise system.

The project of connecting the Hudson with the Great Lakes by canal had been envisioned early in the eighteenth century. This route lay in the only break in the Appalachian chain and therefore constituted by far the best transportation connection between the seaboard and the West. In response to urging by the landed magnate General Philip Schuyler and other important political figures, including DeWitt Clinton, the legislature in 1792 chartered and gave financial aid to a company formed for the purpose of constructing a canal and river improvement system linking the Hudson with Lakes Ontario and Seneca via the Mohawk River. Although the company was moribund within a decade, the publication of Gallatin's *Report*, which specifically recommended a waterway between Lake Ontario and the Hudson to be built with federal funds, gave new impetus to the canal movement. A Canal Commission, formed by the legislature in 1810 and headed by Gouverneur Morris, now recommended construction of an artificial waterway terminating at Lake Erie to be financed by public funds. By bypassing Niagara Falls this route would give a much better connection with the West even though it involved building a much longer canal. On the basis of the Gallatin *Report* the commissioners confidently expected aid from the federal government. Aware of the embarrassed condition of the national treasury and the threatening nature of the international situation, they suggested assistance in the form of a large grant of western land, but the proposal was rejected by the House Committee of Ways and Means on the illogical ground that the federal government was not financially able to make any such commitment at the present time. The disappointed New York canal commissioners, however, suspected that jealousy of New York on the part of states which would derive no benefit from the canal was the root cause of the rejection. The question of constitutionality of federal expenditures for improvements within the boundaries of a single state had been raised by several congressmen, but the New Yorkers considered this issue to be a mere pretext to hide more compelling economic motives.

The coldness of the federal government proved to be no more than a temporary check to the Erie project. The commissioners now recommended that the work be undertaken by the state alone, and thereby touched off a debate which grew in intensity during the war years which followed. But as realization of the magnificent benefits to be expected from such a canal rolled over the state, leading politicians now joined the canal advocates, and with the presentation to the legislature in 1816 of a petition carrying 100,000 signatures, the impetus of the movement became irresistible. In the next year the state began building the Erie Canal.

The decision was a dramatic reversal of what were coming to be the usual procedures of joint enterprise. It is important to note that the sharp break with precedent in the Erie decision did not involve any of the modern issues in the debate over private or public construction and operation of public utilities. No one questioned the right of a state to build a canal or compete with private enterprise. Indeed, until 1852 the New York Central Railroad was compelled to pay toll to the Erie Canal for goods it carried in competition with the waterway. The suspicion and resentment aroused today by such enterprises as TVA was in 1817 directed rather toward large moneyed corporations like the Bank of the United States.

Financing as well as construction was easier than most canal enthusiasts had dared hope. When the central section of the canal, placed in operation in 1819, returned a revenue from tolls which presaged the financial success of the waterway, large investors and English banking houses began to purchase canal "stock" (bonds). When in 1825, the first year of operation, toll collections ran $100,000 ahead of the $400,000 necessary to service the debt, bonds began to sell at a premium. By 1829 more than 50 percent of outstanding securities were held abroad.

As the surplus mounted in succeeding years, the canal commissioners used it as a revolving fund not only to help finance other state canals but as capital for central banking operations as well. Revenues deposited along the line of the canal swelled bank circulation and contributed to the rapid development of the region. In 1834, in order to compensate for the financial contraction brought about by the Bank of the United States, the commissioners increased deposits in affected state banks. In order to aid the financial institutions of New York City after the fire of 1835, the commissioners siphoned deposits from upstate banks into the city banks, and during the Panic of 1837 lent canal stock to eight state banks.

Philadelphia merchants had observed the progress of the Erie Canal with mounting apprehension. New York had surpassed their city in population and in the volume of foreign trade. Baltimore had siphoned off a large proportion of the trade with the Susquehanna region, and the success of the Erie Canal might mean that Philadelphia would be largely frozen out of the western trade. As a result, the decision to build the Mainline system of canal and portage railroad connecting Philadelphia and Pittsburgh was a kind of panic reaction triggered by fear of competition and a desire to emulate the success of the Erie. Canal commissioners were appointed by the Pennsylvania legislature in 1824 and observers sent to England to gather information on canal construction there and report on the performance of Stephenson's locomotive, soon to operate on the Stockton and Darlington Railroad. The initial success of the locomotive in pulling heavy loads raised the very important question of whether a canal or a railroad would be the most feasible transportation link between Philadelphia and Pittsburgh. But without waiting for a conclusive report from the observers on the potentialities of locomotives—which, of course, they were as yet unable to give—the commissioners reported to the legislature in favor of a canal. By large majorities the legislature in 1825 and 1826 passed the enabling acts which allowed construction on the canal to begin.

The success of the Erie Canal and the rapid repayment of the national debt aided the financing of the Mainline considerably. The tide of foreign investments in this country was beginning, and the nation's banks and private banking houses were entering the investment banking business on a large scale. The Bank of Pennsylvania alone purchased more than two-thirds of state canal bonds issued up to the end of 1829, and disposed of possibly half of its holdings abroad. The appeal to state legislatures for funds to build the main stem canals in New York and Pennsylvania opened the way for much logrolling in appropriations for future building. The total investment by Pennsylvania in internal improvements came ultimately to $33.5 million. By the early forties New York's commitment was about $30 million.

The states of the Old Northwest, anxious to participate in the wave of prosperity emanating from the Erie Canal, aware of the developmental potentialities of waterways, and certain that transportation improvements would promote an immediate upward spiral of profits, plunged headlong into grandiose programs of canal construction. During the twenty-five year period from 1815 to 1840 three thousand miles of canals were built in the United States—more mileage than had been opened in Britain over the preceding fifty years.

But the tremendous expenditures produced a dangerous inflation because of the great number of borrowers converging on the rather narrow money market. As credit flooded into states building canals—60 percent of it from abroad—bank circulation increased about 75 percent between 1834 and 1839 and land values and commodity prices moved sharply upward. The foreign indebtedness of the United States rose from around $85 million in the twenties to $297 million in 1839. Banks shifted an ever increasing proportion of their reserves into long-range state securities—thereby losing liquidity. The Bank of the United States and its affiliate, the Morris Canal Bank, purchased $30 million of improvement bonds in the late thirties. London bankers, after buying issues directly from American states or from American banks, borrowed against the securities from the Bank of England in order to meet the drafts flooding in from the sellers. Convinced of the ultimate profitability of canals, some state legislatures after 1836 did not, and could not, service their obligations by taxation, but instead paid their interest bills from the proceeds of new loans. British purchasers of American securities ignored all danger signals, feeling that their investments were secure because backed by the faith and credit of the states.

Obviously the spiral could not continue indefinitely. The inevitable plunge toward bankruptcy was set in motion by the Bank of England, which raised its interest rate in order to stem a sudden outflow of specie to America following the Specie Circular. As a result a contraction of credit began in England which soon spread to the United States, increasing in severity as it moved westward. As the market for state securities shrank, quotations on leading issues fell to sixty or seventy. By 1842 not a single state with a large internal improvement program except New York could meet debt charges from current revenues, and by 1844 sixty million dollars in improvement bonds were in default.

Disillusioned by the failure of most transportation projects to pay for themselves, and appalled by the load of debt they had entailed, many former advocates were now seized by a revulsion against further internal improvements. By 1851 six states of the Old Northwest, plus Iowa, Kentucky, New York, and Maryland, bound themselves not to make loans to joint enterprises, and some states prohibited stock subscriptions as well. The legislatures of Pennsylvania, Indiana, Illinois, and Maryland attempted to relieve themselves of operating deficits by selling or leasing their public works for whatever they would bring. Pennsylvania ultimately sold its canals to private companies for about one-half of their original cost. As a result the Pennsylvania Railroad fell heir to the ill-starred Mainline. Indiana, confessing bankruptcy, turned over the uncompleted Wabash and Erie Canal to a private company for the nominal rental of $20,000 per year.

Logrolling and the failure of so many state enterprises also promoted a disillusionment with public management and led many observers to feel that private enterprise could plan, construct, and operate transportation systems with more efficiency than state appointees. Business had grown much in administrative ability and financial power since the first joint enterprise and public enterprise had been undertaken. Now, many observers felt, it was fully capable of managing even the largest projects. A committee of the Virginia House of Delegates, recommending the sale of some state works, summed up this sentiment: *"No government can manage improvements with the same prudence, foresight, and economy that characterizes those of private enterprise."* In Pennsylvania the sale of the public works was received with satisfaction by the critics of government management. "Now," wrote a Harrisburg editorialist, "the works will be run by the best businessmen of the state."

In the heat of the resentment over unwise, extravagant planning of transportation enterprises, critics often ignored the fact that many internal improvements were essentially developmental in character and could not be expected to bring profits to their builders. The smashing financial success of the Erie Canal had oversold the American people on the corollary to the transportation doctrine which held that *any* investment in transportation improvement would be self-liquidating. The reversal of attitude toward internal improvements did not mean a conversion to laissez-faire and a policy of completely separating government and business, however, but was rather a reflex action of disappointment and anger at the failure of dreams to materialize. In future years when the incurable optimism of most Americans returned, counties, municipalities, and states would vie with each other to aid the construction of railroads, and the federal government would confer on them a rich inheritance of land grants.

CANAL ENGINEERING AND CONSTRUCTION

The construction of canals presented a host of unprecedented engineering problems, more difficult, actually, than those encountered by railroad builders. The fact that solutions were worked out by self-trained engineers with little or no help from abroad constitutes a tremendous achievement. In modern underdeveloped nations local populations must be trained for long periods of time in basic technical skills before any autonomous technological advance is possible. Seen in this light the ability of so many Americans to transform artisan skills into engineering ability indicates a rare cultural trait of tremendous value.

The first task of canal building was "reconnaissance," or laying out the route. This was followed by an accurate survey to insure that canal beds and locks were level. Here at the outset the new skill of vertical surveying had to be learned. Yet Benjamin Wright and James Geddes, lawyers and property surveyors who became outstanding canal engineers, ran the "leveling" of a hundred mile section of the Erie within an error of less than one and one-half inches. Of necessity canals had to be located within reach of an ample supply of water. Canals which paralleled rivers could tap streams from the watershed, but cross-country canals had to resort to other expedients, particularly on the summit level where water supply was of the most critical importance. Water for the Delaware-Raritan, for example, was brought in a sluice many miles across New Jersey from the upper Delaware River. Pumps were used on the Union Canal, and ingenious water wheels in the Delaware River at New Hope raised river water into the Delaware Division Canal. In order to keep water in canals dug in sandy soil, the beds were "puddled," that is, plastered with successive layers of sand and clay in order to obtain a watertight surface.

On the early canals labor as well as contractors were secured from local sources. The Santee was built mostly by slaves hired out by their masters when they could be spared from tending crops. No doubt the masters took a portion of the rent in canal stock, thus reducing the cash outlay required for the undertaking. On the larger canal projects labor had to be imported, and this necessity sometimes caused unforeseen difficulties. The Chesapeake and Ohio Company, needing 10,000 laborers, not only combed the Northeast through recruiting agencies, but advertised in English and Irish newspapers as well. The company even imported 300 indentured servants in 1829. Barracks had to be built to house the labor force and an extensive supply system devised. During the late thirties at the peak of the canal building movement about 30,000 men were employed in construction, about 5 percent of the nonagricultural labor force of the nation.

The backbreaking labor involved in building a canal is hard to conceive in an age in which heavy construction is mostly accomplished by machinery. All digging and hauling were done with hand tools and carts manufactured in blacksmith and carpentry shops set up along the right-of-way. Yet on the Erie ingenious machines were devised to perform the hardest tasks. A stump puller, consisting of a large and a small drum mounted on an axle supported by wheels sixteen feet in diameter, enabled two horses hauling on a cable wound around the larger drum to pull and carry away the largest stumps. Use of the plow and scraper speeded the pace of earth moving, and one man, turning a screw-driven winch, could fell the largest trees.

The construction of locks presented many difficult problems. Wooden gates used on the earliest canals rotted quickly, and rolling mills did not exist which could turn out the large plates necessary for iron gates. Stone gates, ringed with iron, were the only answer, but the finding of a waterproof cement proved to be a major obstacle. Canvass White, an engineer of the Erie, found a type of stone near the right-of-way from which cement could be made. Henceforth the nation's first cement plants were established along lines of canal construction. Inclined planes, over which canal boats, resting in flatcars, were pulled from one level to another were sometimes used as an alternative to locks. This method of transfer was used successfully on the Morris Canal, where cast iron water wheels drove the hauling machinery.

Engineers of the Pennsylvania Mainline devised an even more elaborate scheme to get boats over the Allegheny summit between Hollidaysburg and Johnstown. By the use of inclined planes powered by stationary steam engines, and a steam railroad on the summit plateau, one hundred cars carrying canal boats in sections could be transported over the mountains in a day. Built at a cost of $1.9 million, the installation was an engineering achievement which European observers compared with the Mount Cenis tunnel. Even so, it was an economic failure, for it was expensive to operate and its speed was not great enough to prevent long lines of boats from forming in the canals on both sides of the portage waiting for service. Another feat of canal engineers were the great aqueducts which carried canals over rivers. Among the more notable were the Delaware and Hudson span across the Delaware River, the Erie aqueduct crossing the Genessee, and the Wabash and Erie aqueduct at Fort Wayne, Indiana.

Canal building produced the first professional engineers in America. Directors of the early canal projects made strenuous efforts to entice English canal engineers to the United States, but were successful only in a few cases. The figures who emerged as the nation's leading canal engineers all got their training on the job. Some of them, like Benjamin Wright and

James Geddes, were among the original promoters of canals and were led into engineering simply because no one else was available to act in that capacity. Perhaps the most notable engineer of this type was Laommi Baldwin, superintendent of the Middlesex, former storekeeper and pump maker who avidly read scientific treatises. One of his sons, Laommi II, received his training on the Middlesex and later became an outstanding railroad engineer and the alleged father of American civil engineering. James Rumsey, inventor of a steamboat, and Benjamin H. Latrobe, the noted architect and builder of waterworks who designed the national capital, also worked on plans for canals. Benjamin H. Latrobe II became the railroad engineer who constructed the mainline of the Baltimore and Ohio. The only full-fledged canal engineer who had even seen any of the great European waterways was Canvass White, a promising young man sent to study English canals by the New York Canal Commissioners. A few of the second generation of canal engineers became important railroad builders and executives. John B. Jervis, engineer for the Delaware and Hudson, built the pioneer Mohawk and Hudson Railroad, designed locomotives, and eventually became president of the Chicago, Rock Island, and Pacific. His assistant on the Delaware and Hudson, Horatio Allen, became engineer for the Charleston and Hamburg Railroad. Professional canal contractors appeared simultaneously with engineers and regularly bid on the projected new construction. Sometimes engineers were also contractors and even financial promoters. More often they rose to executive positions after canals began operations.

CANAL OPERATIONS

Since canal companies made little effort to supply transportation over their routes, operating functions were limited to maintenance, the operation of locks and planes, and the collection of tolls. For administrative purposes some long canals were divided into segments, each under the control of a superintendent, as during construction. Top management of corporations consisted of a president, secretary, treasurer, clerk, chief engineer, and superintendent of repairs. The major operating employees were lock operators, toll takers, towpath walkers, and maintenance crews. Thus a relatively small force of men could operate even the longest canals. The James River and Kanawha Company—the largest corporation in Virginia—employed only 455 men to operate its 196 mile canal. Little is known about the relative efficiency of the various canal enterprises, but political interference may well have hampered executive performance on state-owned canals. The Chesapeake and Ohio certainly suffered because its major offices were pawns in the political spoils system. Lock keepers were perhaps the key operating employees. In return for a house, an acre of land for a truck garden, and a salary of about $150 per year, they were expected to open and shut the heavy lock gates at any hour of the day or night. At the death of a lock keeper the widow sometimes fell heir to the position. Towpath walkers ranged the length of the canal looking for leaks in banks, bottoms, and aqueducts, and defective water gates.

Many of the problems of canal administrations arose from the unwillingness of companies to provide transportation, and thereby gain effective control over traffic. Anyone who wished could put his boat on a canal, provided the boat was built according to certain specifications—a rule which was often violated. As on turnpikes, freight was handled by thousands of small operators. The canalers were a restless, brawling lot who added much to the folklore and balladry of the nation, but their indifference to rules of operation posted by management and consequent misuse of canals added to the costs of maintenance. Tolls were low and rates were classified according to the principle of charging what the traffic would bear. On the C. and O. general merchandise paid one cent per ton mile, but heavy, low value commodities like coal, iron ore, and lumber were carried for as little as one quarter of a cent per ton mile. Packet lines for passenger traffic were established on the longer canals. Travel in the long, low, gaily painted boats varied from pleasant to unbearable, according to circumstances. Hulls were topped by cabins with windows running the length of the boats. In the stern was a kitchen and a bar, and forward were separate sleeping accommodations for men and women consisting of tiers of bunks along the cabin walls. In fine weather passengers could sit on the roof of the cabin and enjoy some of the finest scenery America afforded, or could walk on the towpath for exercise. But when bad weather drove passengers into the congested quarters below, and when they were subjected to the hordes of mosquitoes found in swampy areas, packet voyages became memorably unpleasant experiences.

High maintenance costs were a continual burden to the canal companies and were responsible for the abandonment of some waterways. Locks, water gates, aqueducts, pumps, and water power installations required constant repairs and frequent replacement. Many canals were drained once a year in order to remove obstructions and silt brought in by feeders and to plug leaks in the channel. But the heaviest maintenance expense was caused by the floods which regularly washed out large sections of the canals built alongside rivers. Every spring brought a certain amount of damage. In 1877 and again in 1888 long stretches of the C. and O. were totally obliterated, and repairs occasioned by the two disasters cost over $660,000. A flood of 1862 caused a million dollars worth of damage to the Lehigh, and as a result a few sections of the canal were permanently abandoned. Losses from flood damage were always increased by loss of revenue while canals were being repaired.

But the main reason for the abandonment of canals was competition from the railroads. Lower cost of construction gave them an advantage from the outset. Railroads could be built for as little as $15,000 per mile and until the sixties averaged about $25,000 per mile, while canals cost anywhere from $30,000 to as much as $120,000 per mile. Railroads operated twelve months of the year, but ice closed canals for periods varying from a few weeks for the James River to three months for the Erie. Canals could earn no profits from carriage, as did railroads. Until the 1880s canals able to carry boats of a hundred tons could offer transportation at a cheaper rate than railroads, but this advantage was largely offset by higher and unpredictable maintenance costs. Finally, railroads were able to offer much faster through service with less transfer and handling charges. The *coup de grâce* came during the 1880s when the use of steel rails enabled the roads to double their capacity and push rates below those at which most canals could afford to operate.

EFFECTS OF THE CANALS

In any discussion of canals the question naturally arises as to whether their abandonment indicated a net loss to the economy of the money spent for their construction. By 1861, $188 million had been invested in canals, $137 million of which had been provided by state and municipal governments. Of the public investment $115 million had gone directly into state projects; $22 million had been entrusted to joint enterprises. Only a handful of canals had earned enough to cover initial costs, plus interest on the investment. The Erie, however, was one of the most profitable transportation enterprises in American history. By 1836 the $7 million waterway had earned enough to repay the entire debt incurred for its construction plus that of the Champlain Canal as well. After this time the annual excess of tolls over expenditures on the two canals amounted to over $1 million.

But profits were not the sole, or even the most important criterion for judging the success or failure of canals as transportation improvements. One student of canal economics, Harvey H. Segal, has estimated that in view of the large saving they brought about in transportation costs (from about twenty-five cents per ton mile down to about two cents per ton mile), the ten most heavily utilized canals in the Northeast conferred financial benefits that exceeded the cost of the entire system. "Had there been no canals," notes Segal, "the expansion of industrial activity in the East would have been inhibited by reliance upon a much narrower domestic market and by high cost of foodstuffs produced on inferior land; and the effective development of the West, which depended upon a substantial outflow of agricultural products, could not have occurred until the coming of the railroads. By connecting the two regions the canals initiated a sequence of cumulative impacts that promoted a rapid rate of economic growth."

XIX. The Coming
of the Railroads

Railroads played an even more important role than canals in promoting economic growth, not only by lowering transportation costs, but also by stimulating many different types of ancillary economic activities. The heavy consumption of iron by railroads hastened a long overdue change in iron technology—specifically, the adoption of mineral furnace fuel, the substitution of puddling for forging, and the construction of rolling mills large enough to produce rails. Other branches of manufacturing became more centralized and concentrated because of wider markets and improved access to raw materials brought about by railroads. Many former commission merchants became jobbers, buying and selling in their own names, because faster transportation enabled them to carry a balanced stock without an inordinate outlay of capital. The massive financial needs of the railroads centralized the nation's investment market in New York City and hastened the development of investment banking toward its modern form. As the first billion dollar, nonagricultural enterprise, the railroads between 1834 and 1858 accounted for one-half of all capital importations into the United States and about 10 percent of total capital formation. Since railroad operations required careful planning and co-ordination, the railroads of necessity became pioneers in the science of business management. By the same token, construction of roads and equipment stimulated technical and engineering competence. The constantly expanding need for skilled labor provided the opportunity for the formation and development of craft unions. Problems arising out of railroad competition led to the formation of the first regulatory commissions. The contribution of railroads to the settlement of the West is so obvious as scarcely to need mention. By bringing land into production which otherwise would have been inaccessible to markets, the railroads not only greatly expanded the agricultural area of the United States but raised land values as well and tilted the terms of trade in favor of western farmers. In short, there were few aspects of the economic life of the nation which were not affected by the coming of the railroads.

THE FIRST RAILROADS

No one could have guessed in 1825 when the railroad fever first started to spread over the nation that these carriers would eventually constitute a national transportation system. The fact that a smooth rail offered less resistance to a wheel than any other roadway had been known for at least two hundred years, and horse-drawn lines had been in use in European coal mines for generations. The first individual in this country to conceive of the railroad as a means of overland transportation was apparently John Stevens, the steamboat owner and inventor of the first locomotive in America. In 1823 he received a charter from the Pennsylvania legislature to build a railroad from Philadelphia to the Susquehanna. In 1826 Gridley Bryant, with the backing of the merchant prince Thomas H. Perkins, constructed a two-mile road to carry granite blocks from Bryant's quarries in Quincy to Boston harbor. The fact that one horse could haul twelve tons of stone over this road made a deep impression upon transportation promoters. But more important, since in this same year George Stephenson's Locomotive No. 1 was hauling numerous passengers and tons of freight at a speed of twelve miles per hour over the newly constructed Stockton and Darlington Railroad in England, it was evident that railroads had acquired a new dimension, and that someday they might even supplant canals as the major carriers of transportation. During the next few years state legislatures granted some thirty-five charters to railroad companies, and by 1830 the construction of the nation's railroad network had begun.

The enthusiasm for these first railroads was a response to the same hopes and visions which had prompted the building of turnpikes and canals. In the continued effort to widen urban hinterlands railroads were built outward from coastal cities like spokes from a hub. The desire to funnel to urban centers a portion of the traffic on nearby rivers prompted the construction of the railroad from Boston to Lowell on the Merrimack and from Charleston to Hamburg on the Savannah. The desire to exploit strategic overland routes led to the building of the Mohawk and Hudson, the Camden and Amboy, and the Newcastle-Frenchtown. Massachusetts textile manufacturers invested heavily in railroads in order to improve transportation between their mills and Boston.

The charters of these companies made it evident that the railroads were at the outset considered as a special type of turnpike. Maximum tolls were usually established and turnpike gates provided for. Opposition from competing transportation interests such as teamsters, stagecoach owners, tavern proprietors, and canal investors, plus a lively fear of the monopoly of traffic which necessarily resulted from the use of locomotives, led to the elaboration of restrictions. Some charters were limited in time, contemplating ultimate reversion of the roads to the state. Sometimes earnings above 10 percent were to be paid into public treasuries, and nearly all New England roads were compelled to lower their rates if profits exceeded that figure. In several instances expensive state canals were protected from railroad competition. As we have seen, the New York Central was compelled to pay the regular tolls of the Erie Canal during the months in which the canal was in operation. Until 1861 the Pennsylvania Railroad was obliged to pay a tonnage tax to compensate for competing with the state canal system. The solicitude for canal traffic usually proved to be needless at the outset, however, for the railroads carried mostly passengers, and thereby—along with eastern steamboats— inaugurated tourism as a popular pastime. By 1847 the New York and Harlem was carrying 4,336 passengers per day, the Boston and Worcester 1,640, and the Eastern of Massachusetts 2,240. No doubt commuting, as well as tourism, was inaugurated by the railroads.

Profits on the early roads were often high, sometimes amounting to between 6 and 25 percent annually. Net returns of such magnitude were all the more remarkable considering the cost of the first railroads. New York roads were estimated in 1847 to have cost on the average $35,000 per mile; those of New England, $50,000 per mile. Probably economies of operation increased relatively faster than the drop in rates from the levels set by wagon and stagecoach companies. Also, the railroads were no doubt beginning to experience the effects of the law of increasing returns, which will be discussed below. In any event, rates were high in comparison with the levels of the 1880s, even though less than the rates for wagon and coach transportation.

THE GROWTH OF THE RAILROAD NETWORK

By the late thirties it had become apparent that railroads could compete successfully with canals and would become the preferred means of tapping the West. By 1841 the Western Railroad gave Boston direct access to the Erie Canal. Between 1850 and 1853, after years of feverish construction, the eastern trunk lines—the New York Central, the Pennsylvania, the Baltimore and Ohio—reached western waters. By 1860 the trunk lines had made connections in the Midwest with roads which gave them direct access to all of the important cities of the region. Railroad building also proceeded swiftly in the South. Interest in pushing trunk lines westward was keen among businessmen and among politicians eager to cement together the South and West in a political alliance. But this project never materialized on the grandiose scale envisaged by promoters. By 1860 only Memphis, among cities of the Old Southwest, had a direct link of eastern tidewater. Southern roads tended to radiate outward from the cotton country, and were mainly engaged in getting southern staples to seaports. Railroad building in the Old Northwest proceeded at such a pace during the fifties that by 1860 Ohio was first among the states in rail mileage and Illinois second. Many of the lines, such as the Michigan Central and the Lake Shore were in effect continuations of the eastern trunk lines. The Illinois Central, the longest railroad in the world when its main stem was opened in 1856 (700 miles), traversed in the length of the state, and, when joined with other north-south roads a few years later, provided a continuous line of track from Chicago to New Orleans. Chicago, served by eleven railroads in 1860, was soon to become the greatest railroad center of the nation.

In addition to the rapid building of individual lines the fifties witnessed the beginning of consolidation. The joining of roads end-to-end under one management offered several advantages, among them faster service, lower cost of handling freight through avoidance of breaking bulk at junction points, and a saving in wages and salaries by elimination of duplicate jobs and administrative positions. Parallel consolidation, in addition to these economies, widened the area over which a railroad exercised a monopoly of traffic and protected it from invasion by feeders sent out by competing roads. Also, promoters quickly found out that by paying themselves generous fees in the form of securities of the new combined organizations, and then watering the stock as net return mounted as the result of economies, they could make fancy capital gains out of the consolidation process.

The first important union of railroads was the joining of the Boston and Worcester with the Western of Massachusetts, thereby bringing under one management the line between Boston and the Hudson River. In a larger operation, Erastus Corning, a wealthy Albany iron manufacturer and president of the prosperous Utica and Schenectady Railroad, in 1853 joined the ten small end-to-end roads between Albany and Buffalo into the New York Central, which became the largest corporation of its day with nearly 3,000 stockholders and sensational $23 million capitalization. Somewhat later the Pennsylvania acquired the lines from Philadelphia north to Trenton and south to Wilmington, and many feeder roads in central Pennsylvania. After the Civil War both systems reached Chicago by the consolidation process. In New England the New York and New Haven eventually consolidated nearly all the railroads south of the Boston-Albany line, and to the north the Boston and Maine came to exercise a monopoly equally extensive. The South by 1861 had five major consolidations, of which perhaps the most important was the Louisville and Nashville, but combination had not been as extensively carried out as in the Northeast.

Most of the early consolidations were simple mergers in which stockholders of the roads exchanged their securities at an agreed ratio for stock in the combined organizations. But this method of consolidation, by multiplying the number of stockholders, had the disadvantage of diluting control and encouraging factional proxy battles. As a result, consolidation by lease became more popular. The stockholders and directors of leased roads gave up all control over their property in return for a guaranteed annual dividend, and therefore could in no way affect the power structure of the road holding the lease.

STATE AND MUNICIPAL AID TO RAILROAD CONSTRUCTION

Throughout the nineteenth century railroad finance developed a complex and variegated array of expedients which emphasized the conviction that transportation improvements deserved public support and testified to the pragmatic nature of American capitalism. Every possible source of credit—private, public, foreign—was eventually probed for the funds needed to undertake railroad construction. Once building was underway, the search for more capital went on unabated, and available funds were stretched to the limit in order to keep the work going.

Construction on the first railroads, as on the first canals, was financed at the outset by sales of stock. In a few instances where roads were short, costs of building rather low, and revenue quickly forthcoming, local equity capital sufficed to complete the projects. For example, the Boston and Lowell was completed in this manner. But in most instances promoters experienced the familiar evaporation of enthusiasm among investors when unexpected problems were encountered and returns delayed.

At a relatively early date, therefore, promoters turned to bond issues as a means of acquiring capital. Since these were secured by mortgages on railroad property they were obviously safer investments than common stock. Often the bonds were convertible in stock at attractive low prices, thus giving the holder an option to participate in profits. During the thirties Philadelphia was a center for railroad finance. Sometimes bonds were sold directly to investors, sometimes they were sold in London through agents, but more often they were marketed through Nicholas Biddle's Bank of the United States of Pennsylvania or through his brother's brokerage firm, Thomas Biddle and Company.

During the forties Boston rose in importance as a market for railroad securities as merchants like William Sturgis, Nathan Appleton, and Samuel Henshaw shifted an increasing amount of capital out of a foreign trade which was declining in profits into railroad stocks and bonds. When young John Murray Forbes formed a syndicate in 1846 which bought the defunct Michigan Central from the state, Boston capital started a westward march and played a vital role in the building and management of the Illinois Central and the Chicago, Burlington, and Quincy. Yet by the fifties New York surpassed Boston as a center for railroad finance. Well on its way to becoming the commercial and banking hub of the nation, it offered a much wider market for bonds than Philadelphia or Boston. The extensive contacts between New York merchants and English merchant banking houses made the city a natural funnel through which capital poured in from abroad.

During the thirties foreign investors showed little interest in American railroads, partly because of their speculative characteristics and because voting rights were sometimes denied to foreigners, but primarily because state improvement bonds, yielding high rates of interest and backed by the faith and credit of the states, appeared to be much more attractive investments. But by the forties British interest in American railroads began to increase. Such English houses as the Rothschilds, Baring Brothers, and George Peabody acquired for resale the securities of many roads, among them the B. and O., the Reading, and the Camden and Amboy. Often the securities were taken by the bankers in return for funds advanced to American promoters for the purchase of rails—as yet in short supply and very expensive in America because of small rolling mill capacity.

But since the needs of the rapidly expanding railroad network for capital were much too great to be satisfied from private sources, promoters turned quickly to state and local governments, as they had done for the construction of turnpikes and canals. The usual pressures were brought to bear on legislatures in order to obtain funds, and promoters went from town to town over projected railroad routes calling public meetings and giving glowing descriptions of the boundless prosperity which could be expected as the result of a rail connection. These appeals were usually effective. Between 1825 and 1860 most of the states and countless municipalities contributed generously to the expansion of the rail network.

The aid given to railroad companies was in the form of exchange of public securities for corporate stock and bonds, endorsement of corporate bonds, or the guarantee of interest payments. Like canal companies financed by joint enterprise procedures, the railroad companies marketed a large proportion of the public securities abroad, and thereby probably gained much more capital than by direct sale of their own stocks and bonds to English banking houses.

As with canals, there were some notable instances of construction and operation by public bodies themselves. Michigan planned four railroads as part of the state's comprehensive program of internal improvements. Two of these, partially completed, were sold at great loss and became the Michigan Central and the Michigan Southern. Georgia, in a unique experiment, built and operated the Western and Atlantic connecting Atlanta and Chattanooga in the hope that private interests could be induced to attach feeder roads to the main stem. North Carolina acquired and operated for a short time the Raleigh and Gaston Railroad and even today owns a line running between Goldsboro and Salisbury leased to the Southern Railroad. In all cases the decisions to build these roads as public enterprises were taken when private capital was not forthcoming to support the undertakings. Nearly all of the publicly built lines were later sold or leased to private interests.

The total amount of public funds devoted to internal improvements of all kinds prior to 1860 is impressive—about $400 million. Public policy varied widely from state to state. New Jersey, for example, gave practically nothing, while New York expended $79 million and Virginia $50 million. Baltimore's investment exceeded that of many states. Previous to the Civil War, governments provided 25 to 30 percent of the funds expended for railroads. Without public assistance railroad construction could never have proceeded at the pace it assumed, and most of the developmental projects entailing long delayed returns would not have been built at all.

With the sale of the great majority of publicly constructed canals and railroads to corporations the precedent became firmly established that henceforth the ownership and operation of these transportation facilities would be the province of private enterprise. It is interesting to note that in Europe, by contrast, canals and railroads originally built by private firms ultimately reverted to the state, and as a result the principle of public ownership is as firmly established there as private ownership is in the United States. The reasons for public ownership in Europe have not been adequately explored, at least by American economic historians, but as far as the United States is concerned, the decision for private ownership represented ultimately the response of a culture with strong entrepreneurial orientation to the economics of transportation as revealed by experience. Where profit prospects were bright, government had a duty to turn over the opportunity for transportation improvement to private enjoyment. Where prospects were dim, government had an equally compelling obligation to provide whatever financial expedients were necessary to improve the profit outlook, and if the transportation facility later proved to be in any degree successful, government was bound to sell it to private enterprise at any figure, however low, at which normal revenues would constitute an adequate return on the investment.

There are a few exceptions to the rule. The Erie Canal was not turned over to private ownership because any corporation capable of buying it at its capitalized value would constitute an enormous concentration of economic power dangerous to a democratic society. Conversely, turnpikes reverted to state governments because of their complete inability to produce profits. From the beginning of the turnpike movement private investment had been supported largely by the fringe benefits which the roads conferred, but when it became plain that enhanced land values and increased crop prices could be more readily secured by railroads which were also sources of profit in themselves, the last incentive for turnpike building in the East disappeared.

XX. The Textile Industry
Moves Toward Maturity

Between 1830 and 1860 the cotton textile industry underwent a phenomenal growth, spreading outward from New England to nearly all the states in the Union, and by 1850 there were about 1,000 cotton mills in the nation. In the 20 years from 1840 to 1860 the number of spindles more than tripled, the quantity of cotton textiles produced more than doubled, and employment in the industry rose by 50 percent.

Headquarters of the New England industry was Boston, home of the major stockholders and directors of the leading corporations. This relatively small group of men, sometimes loosely called "the Boston Associates," also dominated the commercial life of the city through ownership of mercantile firms, banks, shipping, and insurance companies. Commercial rather than industrial in their orientation, they carried on business in much the same manner as the general entrepreneurs of previous generations. The fact that executive heads of the textile mills assumed the title "treasurer" and resided in Boston indicates a tacit assumption that financial management, marketing, and procurement were the most important areas of the business. As in the first banks, presidents occupied

249

positions which were largely honorary and ceremonial. Chosen from the merchant aristocracy, possessing no technical knowledge of textile manufacturing and taking no responsibility for management, the presidents were expected to lend their prestige to the companies, aid in financing, and smooth the course of the companies' external relations. Many presidents held office not only in more than one textile firm, but simultaneously in banking, insurance, and transportation enterprises as well. Directors of textile companies came from the same entrepreneurial backgrounds as presidents, and were usually the leading promoters and stockholders of the mills. The degree of involvement in managerial matters was largely a matter of personal choice for directors. As in banks a small group or a single individual often assumed leadership with the tacit acceptance of other members of the board. Most directors held their positions for a variety of reasons other than participation in management. Prominent among these motives was the desire to protect an investment. Professional competence in technical matters was required only from agents and supervisors. In the large mills, at least, these men, who usually rose from the class of mechanics receiving their training on looms and spinning frames, participated little in the formulation of corporate policy.

The fact that mill operations were directed by "agents" indicates the subordinate position assigned to the function of production. The separation of top management from the mills and its indifference to technical matters entailed disadvantages which became more serious as time went on. As long as affairs at the mills on the Merrimac had been in the hands of such capable agents as Paul Moody and Kirk Boote, the disadvantages of absentee management did not become apparent, but at a later date treasurers and directors were often to be victimized by corrupt or inefficient supervision.

Also, over a period of time, top management began to lose a sense of personal responsibility for labor conditions. Under constant pressure to show profits, agents kept wages as low as possible. "Lowell girls" began to leave the mills in the thirties, and their place was taken by Irish and German immigrants for whom management felt no affinity whatsoever. The Lowell system then began a slow decline toward the industrial exploitation almost universal in England and on the Continent. Since the mills were located at water power sites often far from metropolitan centers, the owners were compelled to build houses for their workers and provide the other appurtenances of town life. Wherever possible entire families were hired, which meant that a large proportion of the workers in the mills were women and children. Although house rent was very low, wages were driven down to a level requiring all members of the family to work in order to gain a mere subsistence.

Capital accumulation in the New England companies came mostly from within the industry and from related sources, particularly from mercantile houses engaged in overseas commerce and from sales agencies. Although there was no uniformity of practice, small joint partnerships tended to plow back much of their earnings while the larger corporations, with widespread ownership, usually paid out most of their profits in dividends and relied on stock assessments and the flotation of new issues for expansion. But since a large proportion of paid-out dividends was reinvested in new textile enterprises, successful mills often indirectly produced a brood of children. Short-term funds as well as some capital for expansion came from a large assortment of organizations including commercial banks, savings banks, trust companies, insurance agencies, sales agencies, and even other mills. Treasurers and stockholders, in true entrepreneurial fashion, preferred to carry on their business with as small an outlay of cash as possible; therefore they avoided heavy financial commitments for working capital. Probably another reason for extensive borrowing to meet day-by-day needs was to provide use for the funds of creditors' firms, most of which were owned by the same group of "associates" who owned the mills.

Net profits of leading firms were large at the outset, but drifted downward as competition increased. The Boston Manufacturing Company made annual profits of about 20 percent from 1817 to 1825, but much less thereafter. Average annual dividends of leading New England firms fluctuated between an antebellum low of 3½ percent in 1842 and a high of 16½ percent in 1845. From there the course was irregularly downward to about 6¼ percent in 1859.

In their conduct of marketing, treasurers at the outset sold to general merchants on consignment or credit, but by the thirties they were often selling to specialized sales houses which acted as exclusive agents for one or more mills and often provided short-term finance. The agents gave advice on style and quality of output as well. Treasurers often held partnerships in the sales agencies which marketed the output of their firms. Mills bought cotton through agents in the southern marketing centers, who by prearrangement paid sellers in bills drawn upon the treasurers. In turn treasurers usually had to accept bills in payment for textiles sold, which they discounted at banks. The successive transactions of buying and selling carried commissions, and all delayed payments included interest charges. Treasurers were paid up to $6,000 per year—a very high salary for the times.

Although improved machinery and competition drove textile prices as well as profits down, community of interest among the large mills kept competition within bounds. Co-operative planning of production was sometimes done on an informal basis, and sometimes mills exchanged information on processes, machines, and costs. Apparently no attempt to fix prices was made in the antebellum period, nor was there any desire for consolidation. Large mills did not necessarily enjoy economies of scale denied to small mills. In contrast to the iron industry, the machinery of a small, well-equipped mill was apt to be identical with that of a large mill, and operating costs were about the same. Likewise the number of operatives per loom or spinning frame differed little, and all mills used the same type of marketing organization. Purchase of cotton in large amounts did not materially reduce the cost per bale. Since labor accounted for about 65 percent of the costs of production—a larger proportion than in many other industries—the forcing down of wages became about the only way that mills large or small could pare costs and thereby improve competitive positions. This policy accounted in large measure for the worsening of labor conditions in the industry as the century advanced, and denied the workers any share in the economies achieved by increased efficiency.

GROWTH OF THE WOOLENS INDUSTRY

The rapid growth of the cotton textile industry had somewhat obscured the less spectacular, but nevertheless substantial expansion of woolen manufacture. Throughout the nineteenth century British competition was much more severe than in cottons, primarily because British manufacturers were the beneficiaries of three hundred years of experience in the weaving of woolen cloth. Not until well past the mid-nineteenth century could American manufacturers match British quality, fabric for fabric. Moreover, preference for British woolens and worsteds, fortified by status considerations, was extremely difficult to change. Raw wool varied much more in quality than raw cotton, and not until the upbreeding of sheep after 1815 did American manufacturers have raw material available from which quality products could be made. Finally, nearly all the processes of the wool manufacture were somewhat more difficult to mechanize than those of cotton.

Like the first cotton mills, early woolen mills either spun yarn for sale or outputting, or combined mechanized spinning with hand weaving. Attempts to produce fine fabrics like broadcloth, cassimeres, and kerseymeres usually ended in failure. Like the early cotton mills the woolens industry concentrated on the production of rougher fabrics for which there was a mass market, in this case flannel and satinets. As in the cotton textile industry some capital used in foreign trade was transferred to woolen mills, and prosperous farmers and professional men contributed to local enterprises. Commission merchants who initially granted credit to mill owners often wound up as owners of the businesses. Marketing was likewise conducted by the same methods used in the cotton textile industry, and growth was similarly financed to a large extent by reinvestment of earnings. Although the great majority of mills were small and unincorporated during the antebellum period, a few had arrived at the stage of industrial feudalism exemplified by the operations of Colonel David Humphreys, who employed about 150 children at Humphreysville, Connecticut. By his experiments in sheep breeding and his production of merino wool Humphreys added an element of integration rare in the industry (see p. 381).

Growing diversity of product and improvement of quality was one of the lines of development after 1830. To a large extent this was made possible by better quality and variety of raw wools, tariff protection, and the improvement of machinery. Perhaps the most important technological advance was the automatic loom for fancy fabrics invented in 1840 by the English immigrant, William Crompton. Within a generation three-fourths of all woolen goods worn in the United States were woven on this type of loom, and by the end of the century it was used all over the world. Worsted manufacture, largely ignored during the first half of the century, got its start during the mid-fifties when the Canadian reciprocity treaty enabled domestic manufacturers to secure at reasonable prices ample supplies of long staple English wool. Combing machinery was imported from England. The dozen mills in operation in 1859 increased in number to 102 a decade later.

Tariff protection, while important in some lines of textile production, was not as vital to the growth of the industry as the many generations of protectionists have maintained. American mills, after developing technological skills in producing the rough, clean goods in which they had a cost advantage over the British producers because of lower transportation charges from mill to retail purchaser, worked their way upward, step by step, into competition with the British in the production of fine fabrics. Actually, a higher degree of protection might have slowed the advance of the textile industry, as it did the glass industry, by making it unnecessary for domestic producers to improve technological processes in order to compete with imported goods.

THE TEXTILE MACHINERY INDUSTRY

The textile machinery industry developed concurrently with the textile industry it served. In the absence of any other source of supply, the pioneer mills were compelled to establish shops to construct their carders, spinners, and looms. After successfully outfitting the mills which brought them into existence, these shops then began building machinery for other mills, and sometimes water turbines and even locomotives. At some point they were spun off as separate enterprises. A conspicuous example of this process is the Saco-Lowell Shops—still in existence—which began its career by outfitting its parent organization, the Merrimack Company. Some machinery shops evolved from the repair shops established by later mills, and still others—particularly around Providence—came into existence when traveling mechanics settled down to do business with a group of textile mills as regular customers.

The textile machinery business is not today a bellwether of change, but in the antebellum period it played a significant role in technological innovation. Until the late 1820s the industry for the most part copied the basic machinery of the British textile industry, but after that time the American shops manufactured native improvements which by 1860 enabled the American industry to lead the world in production efficiency. Yet, somewhat paradoxically, the impetus for innovation came not from the textile machine shops themselves but from the textile mills. Here could be found the conditions necessary for experiment—the wide array of operating machinery, capital, and mechanics thoroughly trained in current techniques. Such vital improvements as Tharp's ring spindle, the Scholfield card, and the Bigelow automatic carpet loom were all developed in operating mills. The textile machine shops for the most part constructed machinery to order or specialized in a few lines of apparatus they had improved.

By the mid-forties the number of firms in the field had increased markedly. Perhaps the most important was the Whitin Company of Whitinsville, Massachusetts. Originally a small textile mill, the company by 1849 offered a full line of textile machinery and today shares the leadership of the industry with Saco-Lowell. Other important companies during the antebellum period were: The Providence Machine Company, and Fales and Jenks, both of Pawtucket; E. C. Kilburn and Hawes, and Marvel and Duval, both of Fall River; and Crompton Loom Works of Worcester.

In business organization and methods the industry showed little advance over conditions of an earlier period. Most companies were family firms, usually not incorporated until a later date. The shops did primarily a local business—in part because of high transportation costs—made little attempt to develop sales organizations, and showed no interest in advertising. Most heads of firms felt that machinery in operation in a textile plant was the best advertising a company could have. Competition was not severe until near the end of the century, mainly because of the local nature of the business. Growth came mostly from plowing back of profits or from tapping local sources of new capital.

Family ties and alliances continued to be important in recruiting management and labor. There was little attempt on the part of management to specialize functions and delegate executive authority. At Whitin, for example, management was an essentially parental and hereditary function, exercised by successive generations of the Whitin family. Supervisors were originally little entrepreneurs in their own right, delivering fabricated parts to mill management at a contract price. They hired their own men, determined rates of pay, and had the power to transfer and discharge. Although this system was modified after 1860, supervisors at Whitin continued to exercise wide discretionary powers. Workmen lived in the company town, over which management's authority was as absolute as over the plant. Whitin executives received no stated salaries. They merely drew against credit accounts for their living expenses, and at the end of the year the accounts were "refreshed" with a round sum reflecting the company's profits. For the first fifty years the company had no sales force. Sales promotion was limited to correspondence and to occasional visits by Whitin executives to the plants of prospective customers. Sometimes customers inquiring about specifications of particular machines were urged to inspect the machines at textile mills where they were in operation. Bookkeeping was of the simple, single-entry variety.

The rapid technological advance of the textile industry was in part the reflection of a basic American cultural trait observable in the mechanical arts generally. But more immediately it was a response to a growing desire for labor-saving machinery fostered in part by the scarcity and high price of skilled labor but more importantly, perhaps, by the desire to reduce costs. The rise in population, the increase in agricultural income, growing urbanization, and improved transportation all widened markets while constricting the area dominated by home manufactures. Enterprising entrepreneurs proved ready and willing to shift mercantile capital into manufacturing. Ample power and raw material led American textile manufacturers to run machines faster than did the British, with a resulting increase in both the rate of production and depreciation. The consequent need for frequent repair and replacement of machinery gave opportunity for improvements in design. Finally, rapid development of machine tools made it possible to turn out components of increasing complexity and uniformity. Nearly all rising industries have an initial period of lively, and sometimes frantic experiment accompanied by rapid growth. But after the industries have established themselves the rate of growth slackens, competition becomes keener, and companies become eager to standardize technological processes. These manifestations of maturity had already become evident in the British textile industry, which by 1840 was nearly seventy-five years old. The British experience was to repeat itself in America during the late nineteenth century, and, as a result, innovation in textile machinery decreased during that period.

THE COTTON TEXTILE INDUSTRY OF THE ANTEBELLUM SOUTH

Emphasis by historians on the agrarian characteristics of the antebellum South has somewhat obscured the fact that until about 1840 that section gave promise of developing a substantial industrial establishment. All during the colonial period spinning and weaving had been carried on in plantation shops, and were firmly established as a household industry. The gospel of industrialism preached so fervently in the Northeast during the 1780s and 1790s made no impression on the South, but the Embargo revealed to many southern leaders the value of a native textile industry as a market for cotton when exports were curtailed. In 1808 a cotton mill capitalized at $500,000 was promoted in Richmond as a quasi-public enterprise by a group of first families led by Governor Cabell. Although the grandiose project never materialized, by 1810 fifteen mills with 16,900 spindles—17 percent of the nation's total spindlage—were in operation in the South.

Most of these mills went out of business immediately after the War of 1812, but the Tariff of Abominations (1828), temporarily revitalizing the gospel of industrialization, set off a flurry of investment activated largely by a desire to retaliate against northern industrialists who supported tariff protection. In this respect the movement resembled the colonial effort to expand domestic manufactures during the controversy with Britain leading up to the Revolution. Some of the mills established during the late twenties and early thirties were quite large. The Rock Fish Manufacturing Company of Fayetteville, North Carolina, was capitalized at over $100,-000 and worked 4,500 spindles and 100 looms. The Vaucluse and DeKalb mills of South Carolina were planned as elaborate enterprises vested with a large measure of public interest, somewhat like the SUM.

Capital for these enterprises came entirely from local sources. As yet the

South was not as fully committed to the production of agricultural staples as during the forties and fifties, and many planters regarded investment in cotton mills as a hedge against low cotton prices. Cheap cotton would apparently widen the profit spread of cotton mills, and the demand for cotton created by these mills would place a floor under prices when foreign demand fell off. Machinery and supervisory help came largely from New England. During the thirties and early forties the labor force consisted partially of hired slaves, mostly children. At this time the cost of slave labor was apparently as low or lower than white labor, but as more and more slaves were drawn westward into the rapidly expanding cotton belt, the price of slave labor rose. Poor whites appeared in the mills in increasing numbers, and by 1860 the slaves, now priced out of the labor market, had practically disappeared from the textile industry.

Despite the widespread building of cotton mills after 1828 the enthusiasm for industrialization gradually subsided during the coming decades as the tariff drifted downward, cotton prices rose, and the technological difficulties to be expected in new industries made their appearance. Actually, the attitude of leading southerners toward industrialization during the antebellum period was deeply ambiguous. They realized that the lack of an adequate manufacturing establishment was dooming them to economic servitude. Advocates of manufacturing like William Gregg and J. D. B. DeBow made it quite plain that by not turning southern cotton into fabrics the South was abandoning to New England the value added by manufacturing, was denying employment to the poor whites, and was allowing capital and labor to drain outward toward the West. Furthermore, advocates maintained that the South was ignoring its important competitive advantages. Water power was as plentiful as in New England, and land, white labor, and raw cotton were cheaper. Moreover, slaves could be trained to perform mill tasks and thereby provide cheaper labor than could be found anywhere in the nation. Also, with slave labor the problem of strikes and labor turnover would not exist.

But experience demonstrated that most of these hypothetical advantages were illusory. Primitive transportation and a widespread preference for the products of northern mills made marketing difficult, even though southern mills produced mostly yarn or coarse sheeting. Because of the continually heavy investment in agriculture, supplies of industrial capital were too slim to allow the building of large mills well enough equipped to produce under the same conditions as northern manufacturers. Shortage of working capital accounted for many mill failures. The fact that wage rates were 20 percent below those of the North was a real advantage, but was offset by the scarcity and high price of supervisory help. Although large planters often invested in cotton mills, their preference for plantation life prevented them from taking any responsibility for management. Because of all these disadvantages, many mills so confidently founded during the thirties had failed by 1860, including the large Vaucluse and DeKalb enterprises. On the eve of the Civil War the 181 mills in operation south of the Mason-Dixon Line turned out an annual product of about $11 million, as contrasted with the 734 mills north of the line which turned out a product valued at about $104 million.

Yet despite a generally unfavorable environment, industry collectively made strides in the South during the antebellum period and in 1860 accounted for nearly 20 percent of the manufacturing capacity of the nation—a larger proportion than in 1900. Richmond, New Orleans, and Charleston—in that order—had become important manufacturing centers and had developed some important heavy industries as well as numerous light fabricating plants. Moreover, the fact that cotton mills could flourish in the South if founded under proper conditions and carefully managed had been forcefully demonstrated by William Gregg, a successful jeweler of Columbia, South Carolina, who became an untiring prophet of the gospel of industrialization.

Gregg's attention was directed toward the cotton textile business in 1837 by misfortunes besetting the Vaucluse mill, in which he held stock. Upon investigation he was appalled by the mismanagement and waste which he found there, and the complete indifference to both on the part of the planter-directors. Although he was on the point of retiring from the jewelry business—at the age of 37—he had himself made manager of the Vaucluse and soon had the plant running temporarily at a profit. Becoming aware of the benefits which the textile industry could confer upon the South, he visited the textile regions of New England in 1844 to purchase machinery and familiarize himself with the latest practices of the industry. Upon his return he began writing the pamphlets on the advantages of manufacturing which made his name known throughout the South.

As an embodiment of his logic he founded the Graniteville Manufacturing Company in 1845, chartered by the South Carolina legislature with a capitalization of $300,000. Apparently he incorporated partly to stress the quasi-public nature of the business and partly to tap a wider range of private savings that would be possible under a partnership agreement. Two hundred thousand dollars worth of stock was quickly subscribed—

perhaps reflecting the esteem in which Gregg was already held—a water power site selected on the Vaucluse River, and construction commenced on the mill town known as Graniteville. Except for the elaborate gothic architecture of the mill, Gregg's little principality became a prototype of the many company towns built in the South at a later date.

Naturally Gregg was elected president of the company. Considering himself to be still in retirement, he expected the office to be mostly ceremonial, as it was in New England, with the active management carried on by the general agent. But because of the great difficulty of obtaining skilled help, Gregg from the outset had to manage all operations. Stockholders and directors, interested only in profits, were indifferent to the day-by-day affairs of the mill. Turning out coarse drills and sheetings, as did the Boston Manufacturing Company at the outset of its career, Graniteville had a capacity of 13,000 to 14,000 yards daily. The labor force was made up of families recruited from the poor white population of the neighborhood. Gregg had considered and rejected the Lowell plan on the ground that the family system, by making possible the employment of children, provided cheaper labor. In order to mitigate the worst effects of child labor, however, he established compulsory schooling for children of the town under twelve—probably the first such system in the South. From the purely economic standpoint Gregg preferred slave labor, which he assumed was cheaper than white labor, but his desire to help the poor whites led him to abandon this alternative which experience was soon to prove unprofitable.

Sales were handled by four commission houses. Although constantly in need of operating capital, Gregg resolutely refused to take the advances so often offered by these firms, aware that the many textile companies which did so lost their independence by being compelled to accept creditor houses as exclusive sales agencies. In times of financial stringency the commission houses sometimes ruined the mills by dumping their output on the market for whatever it would bring.

From the outset the mill made money. During the fifties earnings averaged about 10 to 12 percent, and rose to fabulous heights in depreciated Confederate currency during the Civil War. No doubt aware of the doubtful value of Confederate money, Gregg wanted to invest the returns of the war years in cotton and bills on London. The directors, by no means as far-sighted, dissipated much of the profits and surplus on extravagant dividends, but enough cotton was on hand at the end of the war to allow Gregg completely to re-equip the mill with the latest English machinery. By 1867, when Gregg died, the mill was producing in greater volume than ever before, but in order to acquire working capital it had been compelled to contract a large debt, mainly with its New York sales agency.

From the incomplete evidence available it appears that apart from mere size the antebellum textile industry of the South differed from that of the North primarily in its lack of entrepreneurial leadership and technical skills. Initial capital does not seem to have been difficult to acquire, and the mills, although somewhat smaller and less elaborate than many in the North, were operated in the same fashion. But in the South there was simply no group like the Boston Associates which could plan, build, and operate a large industry. William Gregg, tall, broad-shouldered, tireless in his drive for accomplishment, an eloquent speaker and facile writer, cut an imposing figure as a captain of industry, but he was something of an anomaly in the South. It is probably more than coincidence that his background as a hand worker was markedly different from that of the average planter. Apparently his contemporaries had greater admiration for the graces he had cultivated than for the industrial achievement he had made. In any event, his building and operation of the Graniteville mill inspired comparatively few imitators.

XXI. Technological Change in the Metals Industries

Cast and wrought iron had been produced in America since the first days of settlement. Indeed, the production of iron in the colonies had been a major objective of British mercantile planning because the tremendous consumption of charcoal by smelting furnaces caused a serious drain on British forest resources. The Iron Act of 1750, which prohibited the further erection of slitting mills, plating forges, and steel furnaces, represented only a partial change in mercantile policy. By this time the secondary processes of iron manufacture—except steelmaking—were carried on in Britian with the use of mineral fuel rather than charcoal; therefore, since the forests were not endangered, there was no reason why the general rule against colonial competition with British manufacturing industries should not be applied to the more lucrative branches of iron fabrication.

By the middle of the eighteenth century, three types of ironworks had made their appearance in America. The first, and most primitive, was represented by the numerous small country furnaces and forges which could be found in all the colonies. Situated deep in the woods wherever ore, flux, fuel, and waterpower could be found in close proximity and producing a few hundred tons of cast or bar iron per year, they served only the local farming population. Since cast and bar iron were indispensable for the manufacture of a wide variety of household utensils and farming tools, these ironworks were a form of public utility in the same class as grist mills and sawmills. Prohibitive transportation charges for all heavy goods gave the establishments a local monopoly within the quality range of their production.

The furnaces were about twenty-five feet square at the base and sloped upward to a narrow mouth about thirty feet above the ground. They were always located adjacent to a hillside, thus permitting a bridge to be built from the hillside to the mouth of the furnace over which workmen trundled the alternate loads of charcoal, flux, and ore with which the furnaces were charged. An artificial draft was supplied by a large bellows powered by a water wheel. After a furnace had been filled and the charcoal lit, the molten iron which began to trickle down on the hearth at the base of the furnace eight hours or so later was run off into moulds for cast iron shapes or was formed into "pigs"—so called because they resembled the animal—for later forging into wrought iron. If the ironworks included a forge, a "chafing hearth" and a forge hammer would be constructed adjacent to the furnace. Weighing about two hundred pounds, the hammer was lifted by cams on a wooden shaft also connected to the water wheel. Wrought iron was produced by reheating the pigs and then pounding out carbon and other impurities by repeated blows of the hammer. The resulting metal was much more malleable than cast iron. It was usually formed into bars and sold to blacksmiths and farmers for the manufacture of fabricated products such as tools, implements, wagon tires, and arms.

Raising initial capital for the construction of these ironworks was usually not an insuperable problem because local materials were used for construction and the several partners might contribute labor, land, or materials in payment of their shares. For most ironmasters it was much harder to keep an ironworks in operation than to build it in the first place. Skilled labor was scarce, and all labor was hard to keep. Cheap land enticed many workmen away, but more important, perhaps, wages were low and often infrequently paid. Moreover, since the ironmasters often had to accept commodities in payment for the iron they sold because of the scarcity of currency, they could then offer wages only in this same coin. Charcoal, ore, and flux could never be produced in quantities sufficient to keep a furnace in blast over a long period of time; therefore the average country ironworks was in operation not much more than six months of every year. Because of changing qualities of ore and the lack of metallurgical knowledge, quality control was almost impossible. For inexplicable reasons the output of furnace or forge might suddenly become almost worthless. Slowly disappearing woodlands, and the subsequent rise in the cost of fuel, limited the life span of all furnaces. Yet, despite the manifold difficulties and general unprofitability of iron manufacture, the country furnace and forge were a constant feature of the frontier economy as settlement progressed from the Appalachians to the Ozarks.

The second type of colonial ironworks was represented by "iron plantations" located mainly in eastern Pennsylvania, Maryland, and New Jersey. Larger than country furnaces and forges, they were located near enough to water transportation to be able to sell at least a part of their output in seaboard commercial centers through commission merchants. Plantations contained all of the perquisites of community life—gristmills, sawmills, slaughterhouses, barns, stables, and even tanneries. Enough bread grains were grown and livestock maintained to reduce to a minimum any reliance upon the outside world for food. The ironmasters always maintained stores, which they were able to stock because of their trade in commercial centers. Wages were paid mostly in store credit upon which the workers and their families drew to supply their daily needs. The labor supply was heterogeneous—Scotch-Irish and German immigrants, indentured servants and redemptioners, and Negro slaves. The ironmasters who ruled these little empires were on the whole energetic and able and had as much understanding of technical processes as was possible at the time. Because of the rapid obsolescence inherent in the industry, most diversified their interests by investing in shares of furnaces and forges other than the ones they supervised. Community of interest and intermarriage brought forth some important family dynasties in the iron producing regions of the Schuylkill Valley—among them the Potts, Rutters, and Savages. Some of the stone mansions once occupied by the owners of iron plantations and their families are still standing and make impressive homes for a later generation of industrialists whose interests lie far from the ruined remains of almost forgotten enterprises.

The third type of colonial ironworks consisted of a few large plantations located near tidewater which produced primarily for export. The first of these was financed by a group of English merchants who took the appropriate name, "Principio Company." In the early 1720s the company sent a partner and skilled ironworkers to America who built a furnace and forge near the head of Chesapeake Bay. Augustine Washington, father of George, was drawn into the partnership when he agreed to supply ore from his mines on the Potomac. By 1767 the company operated four furnaces and two forges, and owned 30,000 acres of land. In that year it shipped to England about 2,500 tons of pig iron and about 600 tons of bar iron. The nearby Baltimore Iron Works, founded in 1731 by five of Maryland's principal citizens led by Dr. Charles Carroll, was nearly as large. As early as 1737 it represented an investment of nearly 15,000 pounds sterling and nearly 3,000 pounds currency. Before this time Lieutenant Governor Alexander Spotswood of Virginia operated a large ironworks near the falls of the Rappahannock River manned by a force of 120 slaves and a large number of German workers imported for the purpose. During the late 1760s Peter Hasenclever, a German representing a group of London merchant partners calling themselves The American Company, built industrial complexes at Ringwood and Charlottenburg, in northern New Jersey. At Ringwood Hasenclever also constructed an imposing mansion where he lived in baronial splendor. The total investment eventually amounted to 54,000 pounds.

These export ironworks were much more systematically managed than the country furnaces and forges and the smaller iron plantations. Spotswood and Dr. Carroll planned their future operations only after careful estimates of costs and the prices which their output would bring in England. Considerable attention was devoted to marketing. Dr. Carroll, on a sales trip to England in 1735, secured a number of agents who found purchasers for Baltimore iron in London and Bristol. Much of the iron was shipped to the fabricating works owned by the Crowley family, who dominated the iron industry of northeast England. The partners of the Principio Company, devoting themselves almost exclusively to marketing and finance, held regular meetings in London, established a uniform method of accounting, and hired a full-time clerk to attend to company matters. The manager of the works in America was given complete control over production, not only because this division of labor accorded with traditional entrepreneurial procedures, but because distance and difficulty of communications would have made interference by the London partners damaging. From the scanty records available it would appear that the profit performance of the export companies was spotty, doubtless because of the many uncontrollable factors in iron production, wide fluctuations in ocean transportation costs because of wartime seizures, and variations in iron prices in England. All of the company promoters seem to have been convinced by their detailed calculations that high profits could be expected under normative conditions—a conclusion which merely begged the question. Only the American Company failed, however. Hasenclever greatly overextended himself and his partners by building ancillary facilities whose cost could not be justified by the returns from the iron produced at the company's four furnaces and seven forges.

The extent of the iron industry in colonial America on the eve of the Revolution has not always been properly appreciated. By this time 82 furnaces and 175 forges had been built, and annual output was estimated to be about 30,000 tons, about one-seventh of the world production. Exports of pig and bar iron were about 5,000 tons and 2,000 tons, respectively. Total production equaled that of England, and the colonies even contained more furnaces than England and Wales in 1788. Considering the fact that the colonies had about one-sixth of the population of the mother country, this was a remarkable record for a people 95 percent of whom were engaged in agriculture, and it augured well for the industrial development of the nation.

NEW TECHNIQUES IN THE IRON INDUSTRY

Wartime demand and financial help from state governments greatly stimulated iron production during the Revolution, but with the return of peace that segment of the industry which was commercially oriented suffered severely because of foreign competition, particularly in the finer grades of iron. Iron exports dropped precipitantly because of a protective tariff levied by Great Britain. New furnaces and forges naturally sprang up on the westward moving frontier. By 1815 Pittsburgh had become a center for heavy industry, with forges, glassworks, boat building establishments, gristmills, a textile plant, a textile machinery factory, and a machine shop. Heavy charges for transportation over the Allegheny Mountains provided an effective protective tariff against competing manufacturers from the seaboard centers, and the Ohio River was a broad avenue reaching a rapidly expanding market.

Meanwhile the English iron industry was undergoing the first important technological changes since the Middle Ages. Coke had largely replaced charcoal as a furnace fuel. Since it could support a much heavier load of flux and ore, its use permitted the construction of furnaces many times the capacity of charcoal furnaces. The refinement of pig iron into wrought iron by puddling and rolling rather than by forge hammering was an equally momentous innovation. Puddling was the process in which pig iron, kept in molten state in a reverberatory furnace, was stirred by a puddler using a long-handled rake until most of the carbon was burned out and the iron transformed into a pasty mass. The furnace, by "reverberating" heat from a fire directly onto the surface of the iron, generated much higher temperatures than could be achieved on the traditional chafing hearths. After the iron was puddled into a malleable condition it was formed directly into heavy bars and special shapes by rolling mills much larger and more complex than any in America.

American iron producers showed little interest in these innovations during the twenties and thirties, however. The main reason was that the traditional methods were entirely adequate to meet market needs as long as iron was used almost exclusively for hand tools and household utensils and artifacts. But a change in the nature of the iron market beginning in the forties ultimately forced the adoption of the new methods. A mounting demand for railroad rails and industrial equipment created an imperative need for more and cheaper iron than could be produced by the traditional techniques. Moreover, rails and many industrial components could not be manufactured at all by the old forging procedure.

Despite the spur from the demand side of the market, the necessary technological changes in iron manufacture were rather slow in coming. The reason was that the new processes were so interdependent that all had to be adopted simultaneously, and in addition to large infusions of capital, this meant experiment on many fronts and a complete redesign of all equipment. Since puddling produced wrought iron much faster than forging, iron furnaces had to be greatly increased in capacity. Increased capacity necessitated the use of coke as a fuel, and this in turn required an intensive search for bituminous coal with a low enough sulphur content to make good coke, and experiments on the methods of reducing the coal to coke. Ironmasters of northeast Pennsylvania were aware that anthracite coal burned cleanly enough to be used as a furnace fuel, but some way had to be found to raise the low combustion temperature of anthracite to the melting point of iron. The heavy, notched rolls which formed railroad rails were not too hard to build, but it was more difficult to devise a method by which the rolling process could be completed before the iron cooled and cracked.

All of these problems were solved during the forties and early fifties. Coal suitable for coking was found in large quantities in southwest Pennsylvania near Connellsville, and ovens were designed to reduce the coal to coke. The problem of raising the combustion temperature of anthracite was solved by heating the air draft in stoves and in coils at the furnace mouth. The necessary speed-up in the rolling process was accomplished with the construction of the three-high rolling mill. In this mill rails could be rolled back and forth, over and under the middle roll, without reversing the machinery, as was necessary with a single set of rolls. Adoption of these technological improvements required the integration of ironworks. Operating a rolling mill alone without a puddling furnace would have been completely impractical, and since a puddling furnace could process the output of two large smelting furnaces, it was equally impractical to purchase pig iron from an outside source. Under the spur toward integration, therefore, the size of works constructed during the forties and fifties increased dramatically. In western Pennsylvania on the eve of the Civil War the Cambria Iron Works and the Montour Iron Works had nearly 2,000 and 3,000 employees, respectively. The Trenton Ironworks, largest in the older iron-producing region of eastern Pennsylvania and Northern New Jersey, employed nearly 800. Yet, although by 1860 rolling mill capacity was capable of supplying the nation's needs for rails and industrial iron, a large volume of rails was still imported from England. The imported product was often considered to be superior in quality and was often cheaper because of the lack of adequate tariff protection for American output. Furthermore, financing arrangements could be made in England whereby a large proportion of the payments for railroad iron could be made in bonds.

Although the revolutionary new techniques of iron making accounted for a steadily increasing proportion of total output, they did not completely replace the traditional charcoal furnace and forge. As late as 1854, 46 percent of the nation's pig iron output was smelted with charcoal, and although this percentage dropped steadily during the following forty years, the tonnage of charcoal iron produced rose from 342,398 to 703,522 during the period. Its continuing popularity was apparently due to the fact that country blacksmiths, who constituted a large market throughout the nineteenth century, considered it tougher and more malleable than iron produced by other methods. Smelting with anthracite accounted for half of the pig iron output of the nation by 1860, but this method was doomed to ultimate extinction because the only large supply of this fuel was in northeastern Pennsylvania. Pittsburgh became a great center for iron production because of nearby supplies of coking coal and ore readily available by river transportation.

Initial capital came to the burgeoning iron industry of western Pennsylvania from the same sources which fed other types of manufacturing, mainly local merchants and professional men. But eastern capital built the Great Western and the Cambria ironworks, and during the fifties flowed abundantly into western Pennsylvania. Some of the profits from coal shipments down the Ohio and from the operation of canal boats on the Mainline were fed into the Pittsburgh mills. Yet during the antebellum period Pittsburgh ironmasters often experienced severe shortages of short-term funds. Banking facilities were inadequate and depreciation of banknotes eroded what credit was available. Every year the inflow of remittances for iron sold ceased and inventories piled up when low water or ice forced suspension of steamboat service on the upper Ohio for prolonged periods in midsummer and midwinter. The financial problems faced by the ironmasters were eased only by the heavy investment of the post-Civil War era, the spread of the rail network, and the expansion of the industry on a national scale with corporate headquarters in New York and in other capital markets. Disposal of the product was not the serious problem it became in the period from the early seventies to the end of the century. Demand from local engine, boiler, machine shops, and boatbuilding establishments tended to outrun supply, particularly because of the steadily increasing amounts of iron absorbed by the growing communities of the Ohio Valley.

In the South the industrial consciousness of the 1830s and 1840s was reflected in encouragement by the states to iron manufacturers in the form of donations of land and temporary exemptions from taxation. Covington, Kentucky, developed a thriving iron industry. It was here that William Kelly, the American inventor of the "Bessemer" process of steel manufacture, carried out his experiments. Small charcoal furnaces, used only as long as local wood and ore supplies held out, dotted the southern highlands, but a few regions developed a permanent industry during the antebellum period. Richmond, in particular, securing its pig iron from furnaces in the Valley of Virginia via the James River Canal, promised to become one of the nation's leading centers of heavy industry.

JOSEPH R. ANDERSON AND THE TREDEGAR IRON WORKS

Perhaps the best way to gain an understanding of the problems facing the antebellum iron industry is by an examination of two large companies of the period which have been studied by historians—the Tredegar and the Trenton Iron Works. The former, located in Richmond, was the largest industrial unit of the antebellum South and one of the most advanced works in the nation. Formed in 1838 and capitalized at $500,-000, the company was designed to exploit the burgeoning market for railroad iron products such as spikes, chairs, wheels, and axles. When hard times and technical difficulties forced the company to the verge of bankruptcy in 1843, the directors accepted with alacrity an offer from their selling agent, Joseph R. Anderson, to lease the works for five years at a yearly rental of $8,000. Anderson, who was to become one of the most successful iron manufacturers of his day, come from a family of modest means in the Valley of Virginia, graduated from West Point in 1836 near the head of his class, served briefly in the Engineer Corps, and resigned to become Tredegar's agent in 1841. Like former military personnel in our own day, he proved himself to be a valuable acquisition because of his ability to secure government contracts.

Under Anderson's management production immediately rose and the works showed substantial profits thenceforth, standing at $103,840 in 1860. Anderson owed his success to aggressive selling, diversification, and careful quality control—a happy combination of achievements for any business executive. Since Tredegar was within reach of coastal shipping, its products had a price advantage in the large cities of the Northeast over those of many firms located inland. Another favorable locational factor was the easy availability via the James River Canal of coal from mines along the upper James River and pig iron from the charcoal blast furnaces of the Valley of Virginia. Although Tredegar combined the production of wrought iron with fabrication and came to own its own coal mines, it never attempted to integrate by acquiring its own blast furnaces and ore supplies. In 1850 Anderson established a locomotive works, which served mainly southern markets, and added a boiler shop to the facilities for making wheels, axles, and other railroad iron. Tredegar constructed the boilers and other machinery for two steam frigates of the United States Navy, and turned out structural components for bridges.

In 1848 Anderson and a group of partners purchased the entire plant for $125,000, to be paid over a period of six years. The fact that some of the partners headed various production units after the purchase suggests that Anderson formed the partnership as much to get good supervisory help as to raise capital. In 1859, in order to centralize the fragmented control of the works, Anderson reorganized the plant as a family partnership. Henceforth he was chief of operations, but some of the partners participated in management as well.

If Tredegar was unusual in its business organization, it was almost unique among the large ironworks of the nation in its labor policy. Apparently at the beginning of his administration Anderson was compelled to recruit skilled labor in the North by offering wages higher than those paid in northern ironworks. In order to compensate for this and other cost disadvantages, he trained slaves as puddlers, heaters, and rollers, convinced that "all iron establishments in a slave state must come to the employment of slaves" if the industry was to survive the competition of northern and English ironworks. Anderson was not alone in employing slave labor. Hired Negroes were used extensively in the ironworks of the Valley of Virginia in all capacities, even the most skilled. Although some ironmasters of the Valley felt that Negro labor was inferior to that of white men, Anderson insisted that his Negro rollers, heaters, and puddlers were as efficient as white workers, and that their employment in 1850 reduced the labor charge per ton of iron 12 percent below the average of 1844 to 1846, when primarily white labor had been employed. Most Negroes were hired from farmers and plantation owners who for some reason had a surplus of labor, but Anderson and other partners also invested in likely young slaves who could be trained as skilled workers and rented them to the Works. Yet despite Anderson's conviction that slave labor was cheaper and at least as good as white, the number of Negroes at work in Tredegar drifted downward from about 125 in 1850 to 80 in 1860 while total employment rose from 250 to 800 during the period. The reason is probably the same which led to the virtual disappearance of slave labor from southern cotton mills during the fifties—the rising cost of slave labor.

An inability to pare labor costs was doubtless partially responsible for Tredegar's inability to meet British cost competition on some items. For example, in 1860 the Richmond press quoted Tredegar rolled iron at $85 per ton and British at $75 per ton. An equally important reason for the price differential was that Tredegar faced an insuperable problem in an inadequate raw materials base. Charcoal pig iron produced in the necessarily small furnaces of the Valley of Virginia was more expensive, if of higher quality, than Pennsylvania anthracite iron. Furthermore, the volume of production in Virginia dropped by 50 percent during the fifties. As Tredegar was forced to turn increasingly to Pennsylvania for its pig iron, the quality of its forge and rolled products declined with no compensating price advantage.

Yet despite the handicap imposed by difficulties in the procurement of base metal, Anderson not only kept the firm's head above water but expanded its operations greatly during the fifties. One reason was his constant iteration to customers that they had a duty to underwrite southern economic independence. Another reason was that Anderson knew the market better than outsiders. Producing all kinds of fabricated railroad iron in demand, except rails, he was quick to meet the needs of his customers as these needs arose. Also, he had a large share of the southern market for locomotives, and supplied stationary and portable engines for saw, sugar, and gristmills. The firm competed in bridge components even in the North. The fact that Anderson was willing to take part payment for his wares in securities and promissory notes may have been an important reason for the expansion of his sales. How he liquidated the securities is unknown, but his credit rating was excellent and he had a wide range of contacts among banks and brokers.

During the Civil War the Tredegar works became the mainstay of the Confederate heavy arms industry, and by the end of the war was the most important industry of any kind in the South. The works were not damaged during the fall of Richmond, but because of the complete financial collapse of the South were almost bereft of working capital. To facilitate the raising of funds in the North, Anderson and his partners incorporated in 1867, and by 1873 had sold $373,000 worth of stock to northern investors. Yet the company's days as an important producer were numbered because of its inability to integrate backward by acquiring its own supplies of ore and pig iron.

The Civil War brought an end to the growth of heavy industry in Virginia. Between 1850 and 1860 the manufacture of bar, sheet, and railroad iron had grown by 194 percent in the state, and Richmond, Petersburg, and Lynchburg were becoming industrial centers. After the war, the iron and steel industry of the eastern seaboard moved westward at an accelerating pace, and Birmingham became the leading center for this type of production in the South.

ABRAM HEWITT AND THE TRENTON IRON WORKS

The Trenton Iron Works was another successful iron manufacturing enterprise of the antebellum period. It was managed and partly owned by Abram Hewitt, one of the most widely known ironmasters of the day, and like his famous father-in-law, Peter Cooper, a self-trained engineer.

Cooper, beginning his career with nothing but mechanical ingenuity, entrepreneurial skill, and a capacity for hard work, had made a competence for himself by operating a successful glue factory in New York City. He patented numerous inventions and in 1830 constructed the first locomotive for the Baltimore and Ohio Railroad, the diminutive *Tom Thumb.* After building a foundry in New York, Cooper became aware that the upper Delaware Valley was an excellent location for an iron works because of its proximity to anthracite coal, iron, and water transportation links to New York and Philadelphia. In 1845 he founded the South Trenton Iron Company at Trenton, New Jersey, and offered management of it to his son Edward. Edward, somewhat overcautious and indecisive, agreed on the condition that he share the responsibility with his friend Abram Hewitt. A bright, ambitious, scholarship student at Columbia University from a background as humble as Cooper's, Hewitt had come into contact with the Cooper family when he became the tutor of his classmate Edward. Possibly because of his early involvement with the B. and O., Peter Cooper decided at the outset to construct a rail mill, an ambitious and risky undertaking in the mid-forties. Distrusting partnerships with the same intensity with which other businessmen distrusted corporations, he incorporated the works principally to obtain the protection of limited liability for his participation in an enterprise he did not intend to supervise. Hewitt, as secretary of the firm, was presumably to manage sales and finance, and Edward Cooper was to act as plant engineer. From the beginning, however, Hewitt was the dominating figure. Although without formal training in engineering but possessed of boundless energy and drive, he not only designed and superintended the building of the mill, but played a large part in the management of operations as well. An $180,000 order for rails from the Camden and Amboy Railroad got the company off to a flying start. With Peter Cooper's permission, Edward Cooper and Hewitt formed a partnership that purchased and sold for the mill, and supplied short-term credit.

In order to obtain ore of the uniform quality necessary for use in a rolling mill, Cooper and Hewitt began acquiring ore lands and eventually came into possession of the remains of the once magnificent estate built by Baron Hasenclever some eighty years before. Over the years Hewitt restored the property to something like its old magnificence and made it his summer home. He also erected two furnaces—at that time the largest in the United States—near Philipsburg at the junction of the Delaware River and the Morris Canal. Ore from the mines reached the furnaces via the Morris Canal, and Pennsylvania anthracite was available via the Lehigh Canal. Pig iron produced at the furnaces descended the Delaware Division Canal to Trenton, or to outside purchasers in Philadelphia. New facilities for fabricating spikes, wire, and other hardware were added to the Trenton mill. Thus in the space of four years the two Coopers and Hewitt had created one of the first vertical combinations in the iron industry since the colonial period.

The additional funds to finance the expansion were obtained largely from Peter Cooper, whose variegated interests had by now made him a very wealthy man. In 1847 he secured a new charter incorporating the Trenton Iron Company with a capitalization of $500,000 and subscribed for a majority of the $300,000 of stock issued. Edward Cooper and Hewitt purchased the remainder with bank loans secretly guaranteed by Peter Cooper. By 1853 the combined plant had a capacity of 35,000 tons per year—very large for the times—and was making substantial profits. By constant improvement of machinery at the Trenton mill and attention to cost cutting Cooper and Hewitt were able to reduce the cost of rails from $80 to $40 per ton, and wire rods from $120 to $60 per ton. Factors other than technological improvements must have played a part in the success of the enterprise, among them good business conditions, the financial backing of Peter Cooper, the patronage of the Camden and Amboy, the ability and energy of Abram Hewitt, and proximity to metropolitan markets for all kinds of industrial iron products.

In a remarkably short time the bookish student of a few years before became a master of every aspect of the iron manufacturing business. Hewitt regarded himself as personally responsible for sales, finance, production, technical processes, plans and projects, accounts and deliveries. Quality control and short-term finance apparently gave him the greatest difficulties. Despite the attention given to the selection of ore, wrought iron would sometimes turn brittle at the rolls. In the absence of professional metallurgists all antebellum iron operations were conducted on a rule of thumb, hit-or-miss basis. Financial problems arose when Hewitt on occasion was compelled to accept railroad stock in part payment for rails. In order to prevent dissipation of the firm's working capital he marketed the shares as quickly as possible, but often with difficulty, and no doubt sometimes at a loss.

Increasing competition from cheap English rails entering the country under the low Walker Tariff of 1846 forced Hewitt to diversify in order to protect the firm's profit margins. Increased production of wire, used for telegraph installations and for the manufacture of wire rope, helped solve the problem. But a more important solution lay in the development of the structural I beam. Because of the increasing cost of urban real estate in New York City there was a real need for buildings with a higher rise than permitted by masonry construction. Peter Cooper, in designing his beloved Cooper Union, planned to give added height to the building by using I beams to support floors rather than masonry arches and wooden beams. In order to produce the I beams Hewitt and engineers in the Trenton works constructed what came to be known as a three-high universal rolling mill, with both vertical and horizontal rolls. Working independently of Hewitt, John Fritz was developing a three-high rail mill at the Cambria Iron Works, but apparently Hewitt was the first to get such a mill in operation. Until the coming of the Civil War the Trenton Ironworks had a near-monopoly in the production of structural iron members, and these were used in most of the public buildings erected during this period.

After the Civil War, realizing that the iron industry was moving westward at an accelerating pace, Hewitt longed to enter the competitive race in western Pennsylvania. Gradual exhaustion of good ore in New Jersey, rising production costs, and movement of the rail market westward made a decline of the eastern industry inevitable. But his wife refused to reside apart from her father, the venerable, snowy-haired, much admired Peter Cooper, and Hewitt lived to see the great advances in the steel industry pass him by. After diversifying his investments he entered politics as a leader of the reform forces which ousted the Tweed Ring from power. Elected to Congress in 1874, he served as chairman of the Democratic National Committee during the bitter, contested election of 1876, and was elected mayor of New York in 1886 over Theodore Roosevelt, Republican candidate, and Henry George, candidate of the United Labor party. But his independence, outspokenness, and occasionally cantankerous personality diminished his influence in politics, and he devoted the last ten years of his life to philanthropies.

MACHINE TOOLS AND INTERCHANGEABLE MANUFACTURE

The momentous technological changes in the iron industry during the latter antebellum period were preceded by equally important innovations in the machine tool and light metal industries of southern New England. Changes in production methods for clocks, arms, locks, and brass household artifacts were much easier to effect than the comprehensive transformation of the iron industry because the problems to be solved were purely mechanical. Furthermore, since the supply of skilled artisan labor was limited and since the market for these relatively inexpensive consumer products was increasing and elastic, demand simply could not be supplied through the utilization of traditional production methods. Finally, widespread innovation in this field could be accomplished with a relatively small outlay of capital. Of course, the transition to assembly line methods required improvements in existing machine tools and the invention of many new ones. But here again the problems encountered were mechanical, and as a result the solutions were within the competence of Yankee mechanics with or without scientific knowledge.

The first reorganization of production made possible by extensive use of machine tools was interchangeable manufacture, associated in this country with the name of Eli Whitney. Actually the idea originated in Europe and experiments with the system had been made in France as early as the beginning of the eighteenth century. Several "ingenious mechanics" in New England were working independently on interchangeable manufacture concurrently with Whitney, and some of these men ultimately achieved results equally important as his. Yet since Whitney was the first dramatically to demonstrate the potentialities of the system, he deserves much, if not all, of the credit bestowed on him.

Born on a small farm in Worcester County, Massachusetts, young Whitney tinkered in a small family shop from the time he could walk. After having worked his way through Yale College by teaching school, he went south at the invitation of Catherine Greene, widow of General Nathanael Greene, and resided on Mrs. Greene's plantation apparently with the object of building a machine to separate cotton fibers from cotton seed. Here with the help of the plantation overseer, Phineas Miller, who later became his partner, he invented the cotton gin in 1793 and patented it in the following year. A simple device, the gin consisted essentially of a revolving drum covered with wire teeth which reached through the slats of an adjacent bin and pulled cotton fiber away from seed. The importance of the cotton gin for the economic growth of the South can scarcely be overemphasized. The first primitive machine, by cleaning sixty to eighty pounds of cotton per day, increased by at least fivefold the amount which could be cleaned by hand picking. The large, powered machines which soon followed the prototype multiplied output many times. The subsequent huge expansion of cotton production would have been simply impossible without the cotton gin.

Feeling unable to meet the tremendous potential demand for the machines, the partners decided not to manufacture for sale, but to locate at certain strategic spots and gin cotton for a royalty of 20 percent of the cleaned fiber—thereby following the age-old procedure of grist and flour mills. This policy proved to be a serious mistake. Planters, feeling that the royalty was exorbitant and that the whole arrangement was surrounded by an odor of monopoly, immediately began to pirate the machine. Whitney then instituted suits against the infringers of his patent, and soon found himself in a morass of litigation.

Although the partners had received from all sources a total of about $90,000 by the time the patent expired in 1807, probably all of this and more was eaten up by developmental expenses and litigation. Commenting on his discouraging experience, Whitney once remarked cogently that an invention "can be so valuable as to be worthless to the inventor." Since the cotton gin was so easy to copy, Whitney could probably never have gotten complete security for his patent rights, but he would probably have done better financially if from the outset he had sold licenses to manufacturers, and then had made improvements on the gin which could be cited as grounds for renewal of the patent. This procedure became a very common practice for inventors later in the century. Whitney's difficulties were by no means unique. The uses of patent rights brought into existence a whole new dimension of business strategy in which inventors were more often than not outgeneraled by entrepreneurs of flexible ethics.

Whitney's failure to benefit from his cotton gin directed his abilities toward precision manufacture of interchangeable components by machine tools. At the outbreak of the limited war with France in 1798 an alarmed Congress appropriated $800,000 for the procurement of arms. Whitney, despondent and loaded with debt, saw the possibility of producing muskets in large numbers by substituting machine tools for the artisan skills of the gunsmith. The English mechanics John Wilkinson and Henry Maudslay were developing tools which would make such production possible, but apparently no one had as yet organized machine processes in such a fashion as to actually mass produce on a large scale. Whitney, writing to his fellow citizen from Connecticut, Oliver Wolcott, secretary of the treasury, offered to turn out 10,000 stand of muskets by means of "machines for forging, rolling, floating, boring, grinding, polishing etc.," in place of the skilled labor which did not exist in numbers remotely sufficient to carry out such a project. Certainly the proposal must have sounded audacious to the point of insanity, for Whitney had nothing to start with—no plant, no water power, no tools, and no money. But the lack of any other alternative for supplying arms in sufficient numbers from domestic sources must have weighed heavily with members of Congress and with Wolcott. In any event Whitney was granted a contract to deliver 10,000 stand of arms to the government. The treasury agreed to help with financing by making an initial advance on the contract of $5,000 and later advances as muskets were delivered.

By September, 1801—three years later—Whitney had a shop tooled up in New Haven and had produced 500 muskets. He then took a collection of these to Washington and before an admiring group of officials dissembled the locks on several and the reassembled them from parts chosen at random from the pile. This dramatic performance was the turning point in Whitney's career, and may serve as a symbolic, if not strictly accurate, starting point for the machine tool industry in America and for the "American System" of manufacture with interchangeable parts. A revised contract and a $30,000 advance got Whitney out of debt, provided a profit of $2,500, and firmly established his arms factory. Other Yankee mechanics, equally as adept with tools as Whitney, copied and in some instances paralleled his methods. The swift adoption of the system shows clearly the close relation between precision manufacturing and labor shortage. Unfortunately there is no way of knowing what were Whitney's specific contributions to the design and manufacture of machine tools, because no adequate description of his plant remains. In producing parts for musket locks, however, it would have been necessary for him to make many of of the jigs, dies, taps, and gauges needed for the manufacture of small components.

To a large extent the development of the machine tool industry was a response to the needs of fabricators. The arms, clock, and sewing machine industries required new types of tools for small components; manufacturers of textile machinery, locomotives, and steam engines needed new tools of a heavier variety. Many second generation entrants into machine tool business came from the seminal armories of Whitney and Simeon North. North, a Connecticut manufacturer, adopted the interchangeable system almost concurrently with Whitney. Samuel Colt, a noted member of the younger generation, invented his revolver while working in the Whitney works in 1836, then moved to Hartford and built his own arms factory which, with 1,400 tools, carried interchangeable manufacture to a new level of development.

During the antebellum period machine tool firms were formed in many different ways, but the process was usually the result of a partnership between one or more mechanics trained in a seminal shop and a man of some capital. Nearly always there was a specific reason for forming the firm, such as developing a new tool or supplying a particular market. Thus, for example, the seminal firm of Robbins and Lawrence of Windsor, Vermont, was formed when Robbins provided the capital to tool up a custom gunsmith's shop so that it could fulfill a $10,000 government contract for rifles which he held. The sudden need for great quantities of arms at the outbreak of the Civil War gave Francis A. Pratt and Amos Whitney their start. Forming a partnership to manufacture arms, the two men were so successful that in 1869 they incorporated Pratt and Whitney with a capitalization of $350,000.

The rate of innovation in the tool industry continued to be swift during the second half of the nineteenth century, and the larger firms acquired international reputations not only because of the new tools they developed, but because of their ability to design and equip complete lines of production. Pratt and Whitney made tools for the manufacture of guns, sewing machines, bicycles, and typewriters, and equipped manufacturing armories in Germany. Robbins and Lawrence built the first commercially successful turret lathe and became a supplier of England's Enfield Armory. Browne and Sharpe of Providence developed the vernier caliper, which made possible a whole new generation of precision machinery.

Machine tool producers were spared many of the problems of other young, rapidly expanding industries. Initial capital requirements were light, and investment in fixed assets was proportionally less than in many other manufacturing industries. Also, the companies which manufactured arms or tools for arms manufacture under government contracts could usually count on advances to help in financing production, and to some extent the contracts could be used as security for loans. Growth came from plowing back of profits and from capital supplied by a widening circle of industries having an interest in the development of new tools. Sales did not present much of a problem. In the capital goods market the number of buyers and sellers is small and relations between them close. Buyers usually know exactly what they want, and do not have to be pressured into making purchases. The volume of patent litigation appears to have been smaller among machine tool companies than in the mass production industries. Infringement was widespread, but since it was carried out on complex machines produced in relatively small quantities offering multiple combinations of components, making up cases and bringing suits was likely to be so arduous and costly, and eventually so futile, that it was scarcely worth the effort.

The tool business was relatively immune to depression since in a period of falling prices improved tools appealed to manufacturers as a means of cutting costs. Competition was not intense, except perhaps among the relatively small number of firms which continued to innovate after coming into the business. As the number of tools in use multiplied, firms of necessity tended to specialize in a relatively small line of products. This development, while checking the drive for innovation, at least brought security. It is understandable, therefore, that failures were relatively few in the industry. Once companies acquired the skilled designers and skilled labor which were their greatest asset, and had developed firm customer relations and enough of a line to keep in operation, they could look forward to greater longevity than most businesses.

THE LIGHT METALS AND BRASS INDUSTRY OF CONNECTICUT

In Connecticut a thriving light metals and brass industry rose side by side with the textile, tool, and arms industries during the first half of the nineteenth century. In the absence of plastics and other malleable, corrosion-resistant nonferrous metals, brass was much more important for the metal fabrication industry than it is today. Until well into the twentieth century brass manufacture remained concentrated in one area—the Naugatuck River Valley—in contrast to other New England industries which migrated south and west attracted by new markets, cheaper supplies of labor and raw materials, ancillary industries, and lower transportation costs.

The poor soil which covered much of Connecticut indirectly aided industrial growth by forcing many farmers to produce items in the home which would bring added income. The boot and shoe industry was carried on in over 100 towns by outputting or in small shops, and in 1845 the state produced over 400,000 pairs of boots and 1,200,000 pairs of shoes. By 1800 the region around Danbury was producing over 20,000 hats per year, and has remained a center for hat manufacture until modern times. The manufacture of tinware began at Berlin about 1740, and by 1812 was said to consume about 10,000 boxes of imported British tinplate per year. Almost the entire output was marketed by peddlers working for the manufacturers on a wage or share basis. Probably more people were engaged in the marketing than in the manufacturing end of the business.

The brass industry was inaugurated about 1800 when tinsmiths of Waterbury began manufacturing brass buttons, which were coming more strongly into fashion about that time. Copper for the alloy (two parts copper to one of zinc) was obtained from old stills and ship sheathing; zinc was imported through New York metals merchants. Two of the largest brass firms of the nineteenth century originated from small partnerships formed during this early period—Benedict and Burnam, and Scovill Manufacturing Company. The former was merged into the American Brass Company in 1900; the latter by the 1930s was the largest independent brass company in the nation. The first small concerns had more difficulty producing the basic metal than with fabrication. Not until imported brass workers from England had built rolling mills and other installations copied after English models was it possible to equal the quality of the British metal. By 1830 sheet brass and wire was being produced in large quantities, and specialization in fabrication had begun to take place.

The entry of Phelps Dodge was an important event for the brass industry. Originally a mercantile firm engaged in general overseas trade, the company had come to specialize in metals imports by the mid-thirties. About 1837 Anson Phelps began acquiring interests in several companies of the Naugatuck Valley, partly as the result of loans advanced the firms and partly to widen the market for his metal imports. But more importantly, perhaps, Phelps's investments represented the same desire on the part of commerical entrepreneurs to share in manufacturing profits as had led the Boston Associates twenty-five years before to shift capital out of textile importing and into textile manufacturing. Increasing commitments to brass manufacture led Phelps to build the town of Ansonia, and by 1849 the Phelps interests were valued at nearly one million dollars and were returning an annual profit of about 25 percent.

Innovation in the brass industry extended only to the fabricating end of the business. By 1850 a wide variety of consumer and household goods were manufactured by mechanized processes utilizing an equally wide array of machine tools. Sheet metal, tubing, and wire was also produced for industrial purposes, and copper sheathing for ships accounted for an increasingly important proportion of output. The basic metals were smelted and compounded largely by traditional methods, however, and processes were supervised by imported workmen.

Perhaps the most spectacular success in light metals fabrication was in the production of clocks. Probably the oldest of all intricate mechanical devices, clocks had been made only by very skilled craftsmen, and as a result they were proportionally expensive. But during the 1790s Yankee craftsmen, sensing a large potential market for cheap clocks which could be reached by peddlers, began producing them with wooden works. One of the most successful of these artisans, Eli Terry of Plymouth, Connecticut, added enough drills, lathes, punch presses, and other tools to his shop so that he could produce interchangeable parts. In 1806 he acquired a mill site with water power and entered into a contract with some Waterbury merchants to produce 4,000 wooden movements in three years at a price of $4.00 per movement. Shortly thereafter he was able to produce 500 wooden movements at a time. Clocks in use stood about six feet high and weighed about 100 pounds. Between 1810 and 1812 Terry designed a shelf clock whose movement was the first important innovation in clock mechanism for centuries.

Two decades later Chauncy Jerome, by equipping a large shop in New Haven with jigs, dies, and taps for stamping gears and other parts from sheet brass, mechanized production to an even greater extent than in the most advanced arms factories. Assembly of the clocks was organized on a modern, specialized basis. Each clock passed through the hands of about sixty workers, each of whom performed a single specific function. Prices ranged down to $1 per clock, and about one-half of the plant's production was exported. Jerome's methods, unique for the time, evoked great admiration from a visiting Parliamentary Commission in 1854. It reported to the parent body that the superiority of Jerome's manufacture "is not owing to any local advantages; on the contrary labor and material are more expensive than in the countries to which exportations are made; it is to be ascribed solely to the enterprise and energy of the manufacturer, and his judicious employment of machinery." The commission might have added that the large consumer market opened up by peddlers was an important factor in making possible the economies of large-scale production.

LABOR IN THE METALS INDUSTRIES

It is difficult to generalize about the organization of labor in the metals industries, first because there is very little historical writing on the subject, and second because conditions probably varied considerably from plant to plant. It seems clear, however, that in small plants relations between employers and employees were close, and on the whole harmonious. Since small charcoal ironworks were invariably located in wooded areas often remote from commercial centers, owners had to provide housing and some community services and as a result came to exercise the paternal control over workers always associated with company towns. Yet since owners also managed the works and sometimes worked side by side with the employees, authority was exercised in a democratic rather than hierarchical manner. Also, skilled workers, because of their great value to the enterprises, enjoyed a considerable degree of autonomy within their own specialities. Moulders and forgemen directed their own crews of assistants; colliers, who produced charcoal, operated quite independently of the ironworks and often at quite a distance from them. In small machine shops the boss in all likelihood was a skilled workman himself and operations were conducted as joint enterprises without the intrusion of any hierarchical authority whatsoever. It is sometimes forgotton that American industry grew up not in the city, but in the country where water power could be found; therefore the human relations within it were characterized by rural rather than urban mores.

But despite close relationships between employers and employees, the conditions of labor seem almost barbarous by contemporary standards. Hours were usually from sunup to sundown, which meant a working day of from ten to fourteen hours. While an iron furnace was in blast it had to be tended around the clock. But an important mitigating factor was the sporadic nature of most industrial operations during the antebellum period. Ironworks lay idle for as much as several months a year, and breakdowns of machinery and adverse weather periodically shut down nearly all industries. The freezing of raceways in the winter and low water in the summer immobilized water wheels and brought all machinery to a halt for extended periods. It is impossible to generalize concerning wage levels in the metals industries because payment was often by the piece and because a large proportion of wages came in the form of store credit and commodities. The general conviction that prevailing wage rates were higher than in Europe was probably quite correct, however. Even so, wages were not far enough above the subsistence level to enable workers to accumulate significant savings.

As industries increased in size the practice of allowing skilled workers to conduct their own operations with a minimum of interference from superintendents in many instances developed into the "inside contract system." Under this arrangement the skilled workers contracted to produce components and collectively carry on all production operations. An employer and entrepreneur in his own right, the contractor supplied and paid his own labor and received his own profit out of the contract price. The employer supplied materials. The system had both advantages and disadvantages. On one hand it relieved owners and managers from production problems, but on the other hand it prevented management from ascertaining costs of production with accuracy and weakened management's control over quality. It also in many cases led to the exploitation of labor by contractors. But these disadvantages were of little moment to nineteenth-century businessmen who were mostly entrepreneurial in orientation and always anxious to delegate responsibilities in the production end of their businesses. Therefore the integration of production with the entrepreneurial functions of business did not begin on a systematic, widespread basis until the coming of "scientific management" around the turn of the century (see pp. 528–30).

The coming of the large firm and the adoption of the inside contract, coupled with the employment of increasing numbers of immigrants, all had a disadvantageous effect upon labor relations by diminishing whatever responsibility employers felt for the welfare of their workers. Two letters written by Samuel W. Collins and republished by Henrietta M. Larson give some indication of this change in employer attitude. An ax maker of Collinsville, Connecticut, and presumably proprietor of the town, Collins was responding to complaints from his workers after he had reduced wages in response to adverse business conditions first in 1833 and again in 1846. In the letter of 1833, written when the plant was small and recently organized, he addressed skilled workers of local, rural origins, representing a cohesive social group of which he plainly felt himself to be a part. As *primus inter pares* he explained the reasons for his action in an apologetic manner, begged the men's indulgence, commended them for their co-operative attitudes in the past, and promised to restore the wage cuts as soon as possible. But in the letter of 1846 he was brusque and didactic and lectured the men on the rights of capital and the duties of employees. He made it plain to them that wage levels were determined by market conditions over which he had no control, and that therefore their complaints were unjustified. The tone of the letter indicated that the close ties of mutual interest and loyalty of 1833 were a thing of the past. As Miss Larson concludes, "The relationship was now a purely commercial one, a market relationship in which one was buyer and the others sellers [of labor]." In view of evidence of dissatisfaction emanating from workingmen's societies and early labor unions, these two letters may symbolize the coming of that gulf between labor and management which characterized American industrial society of the late nineteenth century.

Part Two

From Specialization

to Combination

and Integration—

The Rise of Big Business

XXII. A New Era in Business Development

The three-quarters of a century between the American Revolution and the Civil War had brought momentous changes to business. At the beginning of the period, business existed only in the form of the undifferentiated activities of entrepreneurs, who were engaged mostly in commerce and banking. Business organization was of the simplest sort. The most effective and enduring unit was the extended kinship group, but both inside and outside of this group were shifting, temporary partnerships which lasted no longer than the time necessary to accomplish specific transactions. Because of the shortage of capital, unsuitable negotiable instruments, primitive industrial technologies and transportation facilities, and slim markets, business investment was low and limited for the most part to the supplying of commerical credit. It naturally followed that such other business functions as procurement, management, production, and marketing had no independent existence.

But at the conclusion of the Revolution the process of specialization began which by 1860 resulted in the institutionalization of all the entrepreneurial functions of the eighteenth century. Banking and commercial functions led the way, followed by transportation improvement. With the

287

coming of the Industrial Revolution, manufacturing entered the circle of entrepreneurial activities, and as the subsoil riches of the country were revealed mining became an important enterprise. As the scope of business broadened and as specialization increased, partnerships and the extended kinship group became less important as units of business organization and were increasingly replaced by corporations—organizations much better suited to the promotion, financing, and management of large enterprises. Increased stocks of capital, sophisticated financial techniques, new industrial technologies, and the beginnings of a transportation network greatly increased the effectiveness of business operating within its proliferating specialities.

Yet important as these changes were, they by no means indicated that American business had come of age. Except in transportation, organizations with over two hundred employees were rare. In 1860 the average number of employees in manufacturing establishments was only about ten. Products were mostly traditional consumer goods such as textiles, leather, paper, glass, and fabrications from wood, clay, tin, and brass. Iron was the only important basic metals industry, and producers goods were represented by machine tools, locomotives, steam engines, rolling mill products, and ships. Technological changes came mainly in the field of mechanical, labor-saving tools, and devices and did not reflect any considerable expansion of basic scientific knowledge.

Business procedures had not been radically altered during the fifty years preceding the war. Usually ownership and management were not sharply separated, and boards of directors, consisting of large stockholders, took an active part in the conduct of business. In many manufacturing industries, as we have seen, procurement and sales were handed over to outside agencies. Control over labor and methods of production were often delegated to contractors. Management usually regarded promotion, finance, procurement, and marketing as its central responsibilities. The relatively high transportation costs and the relatively thin markets in a primarily agricultural society precluded most business from operating on a national level. The local nature of business also limited competition. By 1860, then, the developments in American business were momentous primarily by comparison with the business scene of 1783. The transformation that took place by 1900 would be even more striking.

THE EFFECTS OF THE CIVIL WAR UPON AMERICAN INDUSTRY

The effect of the Civil War upon American business has become a matter of considerable debate. Until recently probably a majority of American historians have accepted the dictum of Charles A. Beard that "the second American Revolution," with its wartime profits, protective tariffs, land grants to railroads, and cheap immigrant labor, enabled northern businessmen "to march resolutely forward to the conquest of the continent." In fact, however, the war had a depressing effect upon some areas of business and industry and may actually have restricted the pace of economic growth.

Certainly when the southern states seceded the business community did not radiate confidence. The default of southern debtors on some $300 million worth of obligations owed to northern merchants and industrialists touched off a panic in some respects more severe than that of 1857. Six thousand business firms failed, as contrasted with about 2,000 in 1857. Eighty-nine of Illinois's 110 banks closed their doors. Yet the crisis was short-lived, and was followed by a florid boom fed by deficit spending, monetary inflation, and heavy purchasing for the armed forces. Prosperity in the guise of sharply rising prices and mounting bank deposits were not evenly reflected in business, however, nor did it result in an over-all increase in the pace of industrialization. Some lines of business central to army supply such as arms and ammunition naturally boomed. Need for uniforms greatly stimulated the woolens industry and established the ready-made clothing business on a firm footing. In the manufacture of shoes outputting finally disappeared and all processes were gathered together under the same roof. On the other hand, the production of cotton textiles was sharply curtailed because of the cessation of cotton shipments from the South. American shipping suffered blows from which it never recovered. Because of the depredations of Confederate raiders, transfer to British registry, and transfer of capital out of the industry, some 5,000 ships disappeared from American registry. The war retarded industrial growth in many sectors, and estimates of manufacturing output almost uniformly show a sharper rise between 1866 and 1870 than during the war years. Pig iron production increased 17 percent from 1855 to 1860; one percent from 1860 to 1865; and 100 percent from 1865 to 1870. Over eleven thousand miles of railroad track was laid between 1850 and 1855, but this figure fell to only 4,000 for the war years and then jumped to 16,000 for the period 1866 through 1870. Value added by manufacturing rose only 25 percent from 1859 to 1869, whereas, it had risen 76 percent from 1849 to 1859. After the war the high prewar rates were resumed, with a 112 percent rise for 1879 to 1889.

The effect of the war on southern industry was disastrous. Although the Confederate and state governments directly promoted and supervised the armament industries, these were of emergency nature and did not survive the struggle. The equipment of textile mills deteriorated as a result of high speed operation and lack of replacement parts. Because of the complete financial collapse at the end of the war only a few of the strongest firms, like Tredegar and Graniteville, were able to raise the capital for retooling.

The reasons why the war failed to make more of an impact upon industry are not immediately apparent. Thomas C. Cochran has suggested that the manpower drained from an industrial establishment much less automated than that of the twentieth century made advance difficult. He also feels that historians who find the Civil War to be an industrial multiplier may be projecting back to 1861–65 the experiences of World Wars I and II. During the twentieth century wartime demand filled up a good bit of unused capacity, giving an appearance of rapid growth. Actually, it would appear that none of the wars of the eighteenth or nineteenth centuries have had a permanent effect upon American industry. The Revolution caused only a temporary spurt in manufacturing, mostly of the home variety. The War of 1812 served only to continue the commercial restrictions beginning in 1807 which created a market for domestic manufactures, particularly textiles. The Mexican War and the Spanish-American war appear to have inaugurated booms, but these can be accounted for on grounds other than the conflicts themselves.

PATTERNS OF BUSINESS DEVELOPMENT FROM THE END
OF THE CIVIL WAR TO 1900

During the last third of the nineteenth century many of the conditions characteristic of antebellum manufacturing were altered. Although the number of employees per manufacturing establishment remained about the same, reflecting an increase in the number of establishments proportionate to the increase in the working force, a continually greater proportion of industrial labor was employed in the larger factories. One striking change was the development of three industries which had not even been in existence in 1850—oil, steel, and electrical equipment. These, incidentally, were the first completely new industries to appear since the colonial period. Producers of capital goods occupied an increasingly important position in manufacturing, and many of the traditional consumer industries faded into insignificance in comparison with them. The pace of technological change quickened, stimulated by a constantly increasing body of scientific knowledge. Most important industries went through technological revolutions before 1900, radically changing production methods. Accumulation and use of patents became an increasingly important aspect of business strategy in many branches of manufacturing. By the end of the century the more advanced companies in some industries were adopting research as a continuing function of their operations.

But the dominant trend, to which these innovations merely contributed, was combination and integration. In its broadest aspect it represented an attempt on the part of business to adjust to the national and increasingly urban market created by the spread of the rail and communications network and the rapid growth of cities. Starting rather slowly, and at different times in different industries, the process gathered momentum during the eighties and nineties and reached a peak in the four or five years surrounding the turn of the century. Both then and now market competition and the threat of overproduction brought about by vastly improved technological methods have been considered the major causes of the movement. These factors were of course important, but were by no means the exclusive motivations. The capital gains which so often attended stock swaps and the issuance of new corporate securities promised large profits to the financiers who engineered the combinations. The chance to exercise power on a large scale brought ego gratification to promoters who envisioned themselves as "big dealers." The failure of voluntary agreements designed to limit production formalized in trade associations stimulated a desire to find more effective means of policing the market. The need to increase and improve product lines and to gather portfolios of strategic patents was an important consideration in industries dependent upon new and sophisticated technologies, particularly the electrical industry.

Firms in new industries like steel, oil, cigarettes, and meat packing, feeling a need for their own sales agencies or control over sources of raw material, or both, tended to form first vertical and then horizontal combinations. Firms in older industries like sugar, salt, and biscuit, being in a more secure position regarding raw materials and sure of sales outlets, were more often content with horizontal combination alone. The railroads, a somewhat special case, were driven toward combination at an earlier date than any of these industries because of the particularly devastating nature of railroad competition and because of the enhanced security and profit prospects brought about by mergers.

In order fully to rationalize operations and gain economies of scale, combination should have been only the prelude to integration. Some combinations, like Carnegie Steel or Standard Oil, moved steadily toward this goal. Yet in other instances the evolutionary process stalled. Unproductive, outmoded, or unprofitable units which should have been liquidated or turned to other uses were kept alive by blood transfusions from the stronger units. Price protection, rather than efficiency, became the most important objective. In any event, regardless of the motive for combination, prices in a growing climate of oligopoly tended to be "administered" and competition shifted to other areas such as quality, completeness in lines of goods offered, and service. The pattern of competition with foreign producers changed also. Whereas before 1860 American manufacturers had competed with them on American soil, by 1900 some Americans were carrying the battle to the foreigners' home countries.

Methods of corporate finance changed radically with the coming of combination. In an earlier age, as we have seen, most types of business with the exception of transportation enterprises could be started without a large outlay of capital. Under these circumstances initial funds could be raised locally and expansion financed by internal investment and by the transfer of funds from related industries. But as industrial technologies became more sophisticated and elaborate, manufacturing establishments, like the railroads a generation before, exhausted the usual sources of capital. Also, management often desired a faster rate of growth than income would permit, and in any event a large portion of profits had to be paid out in dividends in order to satisfy stockholders and maintain the value of corporate shares on the stock exchanges. Under these circumstances industry, again like the railroads, turned to the investment bankers. The leading figures in this field as a result of their service to transportation enterprise had already mobilized capital on a national and even international scale through their contacts with the large banks, trust companies, and insurance companies of the nation and with foreign bankers.

Combination and integration forced a somewhat belated study of business management and practices. With the size of many plants increasing rapidly and with competition cutting away at profit margins, the problems of reorganization could not be avoided. As widely diffused stockholding brought about a separation of management and ownership, management in large companies became organized functionally and in some cases became professionalized within the various specialties. Loyalties and responsibilities were contained within the corporate structure rather than directed outward towards owners. Sales and procurement were regularly included among corporate functions, and many of the largest businesses by the turn of the century were eliminating the independent marketing middlemen by establishing sales agencies.

As a result of these manifold changes American business came of age during the late nineteenth century as far as organization and procedures were concerned. Products and technology would continue to evolve, but the corporate structures and their posture toward each other had attained much the same forms which we see today.

XXIII. The Institutions
of Finance Capitalism

During the period from the beginning of the Civil War to the turn of the century financial institutions proliferated in number and in the functions they performed. The beginning of the process can most readily be discerned with the formation of national banks under the National Bank Act of 1864. Federal taxation was now an obvious necessity, and the treasury stood to lose heavily through payment of taxes in depreciated banknotes and the further erosion of their value while in treasury vaults. Heavy borrowing was equally necessary, and the state banks offered uncertain markets for treasury issues. Sired by free banking, without even a distant relationship to the BUS, the Act of 1864 provided for the establishment of "national banks" under federal charters. At least one-third of their capital must be invested in United States bonds. As in free banking acts, the bonds would be deposited with the treasury and notes issued against them up to 90 percent of the value of the bonds. The system would be administered by a comptroller of the currency. Much was claimed for the new enactment. As Fritz Redlich has written, "A market would be opened for government bonds, more 'money' would be available for war loans, the interest rate would decline, investors in banks would profit, and still a great money monopoly would be avoided. Last but not least, the bonds of the union would be cemented: more people in all parts of the country would become interested in its preservation in consequence of the wide distribution of government bonds. . . ."

By 1866, 1,634 national banks had been chartered. The northern victory was naturally the most important factor in bringing success to the system. Actually, sentiment in favor of it was so strong that Congress in 1865 was able to impose a tax of 10 percent on state banknotes with the purpose of driving these out of circulation. This enactment not only accomplished this objective but nudged many state banks into the federal system as well. While the number of national banks rose sharply, the number of nonnational banks declined from 1,466 in 1863 to a low of 247 in 1868.

Although the national banks emitted a fairly uniform currency, that currency was so badly distributed throughout the country as to make the system a means of sectional exploitation. In 1866 per capita bank circulation of ten southern states and seven middle western states was $1.70 and $6.36 respectively as against a per capita average of $33.30 for New England and New York. Another aspect of the banking system's operation tended further to constrict credit where it was most needed. By the midseventies many national banks were issuing much less banknote currency than their allotments simply because lending money in this form was not as profitable as lending it through deposit accounts. Since government bonds were selling above par, and banks could issue notes only up to 90 percent of the par value, the privilege of note issue tied up more funds in low yield securities than went out over the counter to customers. This situation was made worse for bankers because they were required to pay an annual tax of one percent on their circulation. Therefore, in regard to note issue alone, banking was least profitable in the South and West where people tended to use banknotes in their transactions rather than deposit money.

The tendency of reserves to gravitate to New York also exercised an unfavorable influence on circulation in debtor regions. National banks were required to keep reserves of from 15 to 25 percent against notes and deposits, but a portion of these might be deposited with the large banks in "redemption" cities. New York was a redemption city, and the profitable business in call loans for the stock market attracted much bank capital from the South and West.

NEW INSTITUTIONS PROVIDING CREDIT FOR THE WEST

If the federal government's monetary policy did little to ease the stringency of credit in the West, during the years when the complaints of western farmers were the loudest new financial institutions were being created which facilitated the flow of investment funds westward. Western banks found that they could increase their loanable funds by "rediscounting" (selling) to eastern banks bills and notes made at the high rates of interest prevailing in the West. In this manner "cattlemen's paper" in increasing volume found its way eastward through intermediaries such as commission houses and packing houses. Beginning in the eighties, commercial paper houses, established in rapidly increasing numbers, acted as brokers in arranging for the sale of western bills to eastern investors. By 1900 the larger of these houses, employing scores of salesmen seeking purchasers in eastern financial centers, competed so actively for paper that they substantially decreased western bank rates. Mortgage loan companies performed the same service for farmers who wished long-term developmental loans. During the nineties, however, when crop failures and low prices struck devastating blows at the farmers on the high plains, most of these firms failed because they did not have the resources to carry the burden of foreclosed land for an extended period of time. As a compensating factor, life insurance companies, with their rapidly mounting reserves, became an increasingly important market for farm mortgages.

By 1900 the Old Northwest had accumulated impressive surpluses of capital and was served by strong, independent financial institutions. In contrast, the banks and financial institutions of the South did not grow at a fast enough rate to enable the region to participate adequately in interregional flows of capital. Although rediscounting was practiced, the relatively small number of banks confined their services mostly to mercantile transactions, and a commercial paper market failed to develop. Because of the scarcity of life insurance companies and savings banks, the mortgage market was much more restricted than in the West, and mortgage rates remained high well into the twentieth century. Nevertheless, as Lance E. Davis has shown, with these exceptions the innovations in the institutions designed to market commercial paper and mortgages brought into existence a national investment market.

BANKING AT THE TURN OF THE CENTURY

From the end of the war until 1900 the number of national banks tripled, but more dramatic was the resurgence of state banks. From a low of 247 in 1868, nonnational banks rose to 9,322 by 1900. Trust companies also increased sharply in number because of liberal charters (see below pp. 310–11). By the end of the century these three types of banking institutions—national banks, state banks, and trust companies—were in sharp competition with each other.

Most banks were still small, with working capitals of from $25,000 to $300,000. As late as 1912 there were only thirteen banks in the country whose capital and surplus were large enough to lend $1 million to a single customer. Bankers understood their functions much better than in the past, however, and the line between banking fraud and legitimate banking business was much more firmly drawn than in the antebellum period. Bank assets changed radically in character after the war. In 1860 the ratio of loans and discounts to securities was ten to one; after 1873 it was about two or three to one. Integrating their activities with the securities markets, large metropolitan banks established bond and savings departments, increased the number of their collateral loans, and sometimes went into the trust business.

Management changed to suit the needs of the times. Banks were no longer run by cashiers. Presidents were now full time, highly paid chief executives. The separation of ownership and management characteristic of big business generally was reflected in diminished powers of directors in large banks. Gone were the days when the directors personally considered all loan applications and directly determined management policies and procedures. In the larger institutions loan departments now handled the former function. The extent to which directors participated in decision making doubtless varied from one institution to another, but in the larger banks salaried employees exerted more authority than they had in the past. Sometimes effective control rested with outsiders—powerful industrialists or leading financiers—who retained representation on boards in the form of friends or colleagues. Sometimes boards contained important customers attached to the banks through stock ownership; sometimes big borrowers sought seats in order to secure continuing lines of credit. The fact that boards were large, numbering in some instances up to fifty members, indicates that diverse interests were represented and that the boards were inappropriate bodies to carry on management. Yet small banks undoubtedly reflected the earlier pattern of management by directors, and some do even today. New communities, at a beginning stage of development, still embark on the operation bootstrap whereby leading businessmen form and operate banks with the object of financing their own enterprises.

Competition among banks was tempered by growing co-operation, again reflecting a development common to big business generally. To some extent the element of co-operation had been present from the outset. The friendliest feelings had existed between the Bank of North America, the Bank of New York, and the Massachusetts Bank because these considered themselves regional monopolies. The coming of the inflationary country banks to some extent eroded the harmony of the earlier period, but the Suffolk system, clearing houses, and the constant need to deal with each other through interchange of notes fostered at least "antagonistic" co-operation. Financial crises exerted a powerful effect in forcing concerted action. Resumption of specie payments after the War of 1812 was the result of a series of bank conventions, and the suspension of 1837 led to the formation of committees in New York and Philadelphia to formulate common policies.

The use of clearing house loan certificates in New York during the financial panic of November, 1860, caused by sudden withdrawal of southern deposits, inaugurated collective action to save weaker members of the banking community. Banks on the verge of suspension could borrow these certificates from the clearing house, pledging securities and other assets as collateral, and use the certificates in settlement of clearing house balances. Use of the certificates prevented the sudden curtailment or stoppage of bank loans—the factor that had so often started a downward spiral of panic and multiplying bankruptcies. In the coming years banks developed an increasing awareness of responsibility toward the business community. The banks of Boston and Philadelphia adopted clearing house loan certificates, and banks in financial centers increasingly pooled resources and equalized specie reserves in time of trouble in order to keep their doors open to their customers.

The first permanent bankers' organization was the Philadelphia Board of Presidents, organized in 1853. The Association of the Banks of Wisconsin, formed in 1858, for a time operated as a cartel, claiming the right to supervise banking in the state. As a response to the movement for trade associations following the war, the American Bankers Association was founded in 1876.

The concentration of business in the nineties was reflected in banking. An estimated 600 to 800 mergers took place between 1900 and 1909. Yet, in contrast to other lines of business, the number of banks did not simultaneously decline but reached a peak in the 1920s. Concentration of interest by interlocking directorates was marked. For example, in 1912 J. P. Morgan and Company held twenty-three directorates in thirteen banks and trust companies, and the directors of the house of Morgan, the First National Bank, the National City Bank, Bankers Trust Company, and Guaranty Trust Company collectively held 118 directorships in thirty-four banks and trust companies with total resources of $2,679,000,000.

INVESTMENT BANKERS AND THE CONCENTRATION OF FINANCIAL CONTROL IN BUSINESS: JAY COOKE AND J. P. MORGAN

Before the Civil War investment bankers confined themselves to the marketing of public securities, and—to a lesser extent—corporate stocks and bonds. But after the war they increasingly turned their attention to the private sector of the economy and used their marketing function to control and combine the institutions they served. Just as the careers of Stephen Girard and John Jacob Astor illustrate the transition of the general entrepreneur to the specialized businessman, so the career of Jay Cooke illustrates the similar transformation of investment banking from a part-time activity of brokers and commercial banks to an independent and vastly important banking function.

An energetic, ebullient, deeply religious young man, Cooke served an apprenticeship in E. W. Clark and Company, and later, as a partner, participated in its variegated activities of merchant banking, sale of corporate and public securities, and lottery tickets. When the Clark house went into receivership in 1857, Cooke struck out on his own, buying and selling securities on a small scale. After the outbreak of the war, when the treasury had saturated the market available for government bonds represented by banks and other financial institutions, Cooke proposed to the secretary, Salmon P. Chase, that direct marketing to the public be undertaken, organized by Cooke himself. Although such a method had been used in Europe, it was as yet untried in America. Upon the acquiescence of Chase, Cooke organized the first of the massive sales campaigns for war bonds which have figured so largely in World Wars I and II. Creating a large distribution system throughout the country staffed by 2,500 subagents, he turned out a stream of pamphlets, brochures, and advertising emphasizing that the purchase of bonds was a patriotic duty. His several campaigns were a great success. Cooke was credited with selling $361,952,950 worth of bonds. Out of his small commission of three-eights to one-half of one percent, from which he paid all expenses, he netted only about $220,000, but gained much more in the form of reputation. By the end of the war he was a nationally known figure.

It was largely because of this reputation that he was asked to become the financial agent for the Northern Pacific Railroad. Financing the construction of a road designed to extend two-thirds across the continental United States was a task of immense proportions, by far the largest investment banking operation undertaken in this country up to this time. In 1870 Cooke agreed to sell at par $100 million of bonds which would be credited to the company at eighty-eight. But despite an advertising campaign similar to that for the Civil War bonds, banks and other investors remained apathetic, correctly regarding Northern Pacific as a highly speculative venture which could bring only long delayed returns. Yet Cooke refused to recognize the danger signals. During 1871 and 1872, while the road was being constructed at top speed and consequently top cost, Cooke made increasingly heavy advances to the company against the unsold bonds. Failing to secure an effective voice in management, he allowed his resources to be stretched dangerously thin and failed during the Panic of 1873.

Cooke's career with the Northern Pacific anticipated the role which investment bankers were to play during the last quarter of the nineteenth century— that of permanent and exclusive financial agent. Cooke's bankruptcy also made it plain that investment bankers, if only to protect their own interests, would be compelled to wield considerable influence with management. Actually, the course of business development was to make the task easier. In an era when railroads and other industries with high initial and overhead costs were rapidly expanding, growth could not be financed internally, but of necessity required recourse to the great capital markets of the world. Under these circumstances the investment bankers, as the liaison between industry and capital markets, became very important persons indeed. Moreover, through handling of mergers and reorganizations, where their services were indispensable, they in many cases moved into the potential control of the industries they served. In the course of this tidal movement of power from industrialist to financier, "industrial capitalism" became "finance capitalism," to use the terms coined by Norman S. B. Gras.

The transition is perhaps most graphically illustrated in the career of probably the most famous of the investment bankers—J. Pierpont Morgan. The son of Junius S. Morgan, who was a partner of the American-born, wealthy British banker, George Peabody, young Morgan was brought up in an atmosphere of affluence similar to that which surrounded young Nicholas Biddle. Like Biddle, Morgan traveled widely in Europe and exhibited both academic and social talents. After spending some time in England and completing his formal education by a few semesters at Göttingen, he settled in New York and in 1860 founded a firm whose principal business was acting as American correspondent for his father and Peabody. He first came to the attention of the financial community as a young man with a bright future when he helped the management of the Albany and Susquehanna Railroad conduct a successful defense against a piratical raid by Jay Gould. In 1871 the course of his career turned sharply upward when he was taken into the old Philadelphia firm of Drexel and Company as the New York partner. During the seventies he participated in many aspects of investment banking, particularly in the refunding of the Civil War debt. In 1879 he entered railroad finance, in which he was to make his great reputation, by forming a syndicate which secretly sold in England, through Junius Morgan, $25 million worth of the Vanderbilt holdings in the New York Central Railroad. For this service he received a seat on the Central board, and was soon involved in the large-scale marketing of securities for other railroads.

Morgan's overriding objective in projecting himself into railroad affairs was not merely profit—although he did well enough at that—but stabilizing the financial structure of the roads by reducing cutthroat competition. As financial intermediary between the roads and large American and English investors, he had an immediate interest in maintaining the value of railroad securities, and the constant need of the roads for new infusions of capital placed him in a strategic position to accomplish his objective. Developing a strong, awe-inspiring personality during his mature years, he became—in the view of thousands—the most powerful man in the United States. Between 1885 and 1890 he held a series of meetings at his home, famous "219" Madison Avenue, at which he persuaded leading railroad executives from all over the nation to form voluntary associations for the suppression of destructive competitive practices. Contemporaries marveled at the imperial power of the banker who could apparently at will bring railroad moguls the country over trooping to his door.

Reorganization and combinations gave Morgan a more direct access to power. Creditors of bankrupt railroads, confronted with the problem of scaling down the interest on bonded indebtedness to the point that debt service could be met by the minimum customary revenue of the roads, were usually in a state of hopeless confusion because of the conflicting claims of the different classes of securities. In the course of arbitrating these controversies Morgan insured continuation of financial control and suppression of competition by getting representation for himself or members of his firm on boards of directors, by setting up voting trusts, and by establishing communities of interest among formerly competing railroads through mutual stock purchases and interlocking directorates. Sometimes working alone and sometimes with syndicates of other bankers, Morgan reorganized many of the largest railroads in the nation, among them the B. and O., the C. and O., the Erie, the West Shore, and the Northern Pacific. Combinations such as the Southern Railway System were brought together by the usual "Morganizing" methods and eventuated in the same centralization of banker control. Beginning in the nineties Morgan took increased interest in industrial combination, and capped his career with the formation of United States Steel in 1901, the first billion dollar enterprise and the largest corporation in the world.

The generation of investment bankers, who along with Morgan exercised such great financial power, was remarkably small in numbers. According to Professor Redlich, finance capitalism "was the work of no more than half-a-dozen firms and hardly twice as many men." Outstanding among the firms were: The First National Bank and The National City Bank; J. P. Morgan and Company; and Kuhn, Loeb, and Company, all of New York; Kidder, Peabody, and Company; and Lee, Higginson, and Company, of Boston. Among the individuals were: Jacob Schiff, George F. Baker, James Stillman, Robert Winsor, Gardiner M. Lane, and James J. Storrow. Groups of these men and firms, working in syndicates, floated the securities of the largest American corporations, marketed them through allied trust and insurance companies and banking correspondents throughout the world, or fed them into the New York Stock Market and deftly manipulated the market so that they could be easily "digested." As permanent financial agents of large corporations, bankers and banking houses not only handled financial affairs but arranged mergers, combinations, reorganizations, and communities of interest. Lesser banks and trust companies in the other financial centers of the nation also participated in investment banking, sometimes perhaps as decision-making members of syndicates, but probably more often in the passive role of marketers of securities alone. In the late nineteenth and early twentieth centuries the investment bankers, as the supreme arbiters of finance capitalism, stood at the apogee of their power.

Yet the extent to which they used this power could be, and often was, exaggerated. The bankers were supreme within the financial framework they had created, and by virtue of it usually held an ultimate veto over operating management and directors of corporations regarding expansion or any change in the competitive balance of power. But the bankers had neither the inclination, nor the time, nor the specialized knowledge to participate in decision making on the level of operations. Here they felt that their responsibility was only to be sure that power did not fall into the hands of reckless or incapable men who would injure the financial stability of enterprises or repudiate the carefully drawn treaties, written and oral, limiting competition. Once "sound" operating management had been placed at the helm, the representatives of the House of Morgan on corporate boards of directors, for example, were usually content merely to keep themselves informed of what was going on. But the velvet glove contained the mailed fist; when mobilized, the power of finance capitalism could be truly awesome. It was this potential that alarmed reformers, and by its magnitude led them to exaggerate the extent to which power was actually used. With the full development of investment banking, banking as an economic function had come of age.

LIFE INSURANCE COMPANY AS INSTRUMENTS FOR CAPITAL ACCUMULATION

The Civil War proved to be a turning point in the development of life insurance as important as in the development of investment banking. Despite rapid growth, life insurance began to fall into bad repute because of the failure of weaker companies, excessive issuance of premium notes, inflated dividends or inadequate dividends, and mounting administrative costs resulting from heavy outlays for advertising and greatly increased agents' commissions. But despite public criticism and the first cautious attempts at government regulation, new types of speculative practices appeared in the late sixties which within a generation tended to pervert life insurance from family protection to a means of accumulating large amounts of capital for the operations of finance capitalism.

A leader in this development was Henry B. Hyde, organizer of the Equitable Life Assurance Society, which by the turn of the century was the largest life insurance company in the world. Since he was such a towering figure in the industry, and since his invention, the tontine policy, played such a key role in the perversion of life insurance, he deserves special mention in any survey of the institution.

Born in 1834, the son of a country merchant in Catskill, New York, who had moved to New York City to become a very successful agent for Mutual Life, Henry B. Hyde joined the company himself at the age of seventeen and by twenty-five had advanced to the very responsible position of cashier. Tall, handsome, affable, adept at cultivating people who could be of use to him, young Hyde possessed the drive and ability which early marked him as a natural business leader. In 1859 he left Mutual to found a company of his own which could write policies in excess of $10,000—a privilege denied to Mutual by its charter. By intensive promotion among wealthy men he had come to know in the course of his business and through his activities in the Fifth Avenue Presbyterian Church, he succeeded in getting the commitments for $100,000 worth of insurance as required by law, and received a charter for the Equitable from the state legislature. Although Hyde, for sales purposes, always insisted that the company was a mutual, actually it was a stock company in which policyholders as well as stockholders received dividends. Hyde did not assume the presidency, but in order to surround the company with an aura of respectability and integrity persuaded a venerable and admired New Jersey lawyer-politician to accept the position. Ever aware of the importance of the Equitable's institutional image, he selected seventeen of the company's fifty-two directors from the rolls of the Fifth Avenue Presbyterian Church. Nearly all board members were merchants and lawyers. He secured the services of Henry Ward Beecher, the celebrated Abolitionist preacher of Brooklyn, to write one of the company's first advertising brochures.

As vice president he immediately began a sales campaign of unprecedented vigor in which he often joined his agents in office-to-office, door-to-door solicitation. At the end of the first year of operation he had sold $1 million of life insurance, thus probably becoming the first million dollar insurance salesman in America. During the years of rapid growth which followed the company acquired probably the best sales force in the nation. Hyde himself lived for nothing but the Equitable. The complete autocrat, he was the head of all departments in all but name. With his salesmen he was sympathetic and appreciative, but in the office, where discipline rather than encouragement appeared to be called for, he was demanding and censorious.

When Hyde died in 1899 the Equitable had assets of $304 million, surplus of $65 million, and more than $1 billion of insurance in force. Hyde himself had made a fortune of over $50 million, mostly from his stockholdings in the company.

The success of the Equitable is attributable not only to unprecedentedly aggressive selling, advertising, and promotion, but also to the tontine life insurance policy, invented by Hyde and first issued in 1868. Holders of these policies, like participants in a tontine (see pp. 152–53), were grouped together by age, and agreed, under terms of their contracts, to forgo dividends for fifteen or twenty years. During that time reserves of all lapsed policies were added to the fund to be distributed to surviving policyholders as additional insurance or annuity at the conclusion of the period. The estates of policyholders who died before the expiration of the period received only the face value of the policies; reserves and interest accumulations were likewise added to the fund for survivors.

Because of the gambling feature tontine policies became so popular that within a decade they were issued by nearly all companies. Nevertheless the policies had certain unfortunate results which eventually forced their abandonment. In the first place, they sacrificed to the successful gamblers who collected the payoff the interests of the weaker policyholders, who were usually most in need of family protection. Moreover, by relieving the companies of the necessity of paying regular dividends they promoted irresponsibility in the handling of rapidly mounting reserves. Partly because of this effect upon management the deferred dividends, when paid, were often much smaller than the companies had predicted when the policies were written. Disappointed policyholders naturally felt in these instances that they had been victimized, and reacted accordingly.

Other practices cast increasing discredit upon life insurance companies from the late sixties onward. Forfeiture of policies upon many arbitrary contingencies, sometimes with loss of all reserves, aroused widespread resentment. As new companies flooded into the field—some 250 were chartered between 1860 and 1872 alone—agents were paid extravagant commissions and company officers received inflated salaries. Reserves against liabilities were often inadequate or illegally manipulated. A profusion of new policy plans, all so intricate as to confuse the purchaser, seemed better designed to coax away his dollar than to provide his family with real protection. In newspapers and in the insurance press leaders of the three largest companies—the Equitable, Mutual of New York, and New York Life—traded charges of malfeasance which, even if only partly true, amounted to a massive indictment of the industry. But probably the greatest grievance was the extensive losses brought about by company failures. During the depression years 1873 and 1877 alone, when competition was particularly brutal, seventy-five companies disappeared.

One result of the malodorous reputation of life insurance companies during the latter decades of the century was the rise of mutual assessment societies. These organizations, which had been prominent in England since the seventeenth century, upon the death of a member laid a small assessment upon the entire membership for the benefit of the deceased's survivors. When American companies were formed which levied annual assessments in anticipation of death claims, they thereby became in effect life insurance companies operating without benefit of reserves, marketing organizations, or actuarial planning. In their bid for public favor the companies emphasized their low costs of operation and freedom from the sins of the regular life companies. These appeals evoked such an enthusiastic response that by 1895 the assessment mutuals accounted for just over 50 percent of the life insurance in force throughout the nation. Yet many of these organizations worked as cruel deception upon their members as did the unsound life companies upon their policyholders. As the median age rose in companies which did not recruit enough new blood, assessments mounted, members were forced to drop out, and the companies finally collapsed. Since a shifting membership of assessment payers could in no way confer the security enjoyed by life insurance companies through ownership of large financial assets, the number of mutual assessment societies declined rapidly during the early twentieth century, and the principle lived on primarily in fraternal orders.

Another innovation during the latter nineteenth century was industrial life insurance. Introduced by the Prudential Life Insurance Company in 1875, this coverage was offered in small units to families too poor to afford the policies of the established life companies. The success of industrial insurance depended upon a unique marketing system developed in England. Agents were assigned a certain number of blocks in working class neighborhoods of large cities where they not only sold insurance by door-to-door solicitation but also made weekly collection of premiums, which usually amounted to about ten cents apiece. Personal collection was considered an indispensable element of the system because the poor presumably would not assume the responsibility of payment on their own volition, and in any event could not accumulate the surplus necessary to pay a yearly premium on even a small policy. The cost of industrial insurance was necessarily greater than regular life policies, but the system appeared to be the only way in which life insurance could be afforded at all by the working class.

At first industrial insurance had hard going. Most established companies were contemptuous of it, and good agents simply could not be recruited to conduct what was considered to be a nickel and dime business. In order to solve the marketing problem the Metropolitan Life Insurance Company, another pioneer in the business, imported agents from England and established the block collection arrangement as it was practiced in that country. Agents were paid by a small salary plus a 10 to 15 percent commission on each collection plus a sum representing 200 to 300 percent of all new collections. After a slow start the amount of industrial insurance in force rose rapidly. The Prudential, the Metropolitan, and the John Hancock Company came to dominate the business. By 1900 Prudential alone had written $448 million worth of this type of insurance.

Considerable changes took place in the administration of life insurance companies during the period under review. As in banks, management became more and more professionalized as the companies grew in size. Boards of directors and boards of trustees, which had originally participated in management by membership on the committees which handled the various functions of the business, now became mostly window dressing designed to enhance the status and institutional image of the companies. Ultimate decision making in the big three—the "Racers" as they were called—fell into the hands of men much more interested in capital accumulation than family protection—Hyde of the Equitable, Frederick S. Winston of the Mutual, and William H. Beers of New York Life. Although all were presumably large stockholders, the sanction for their power was not the extent of their investment but the tacit consent of complaisant directors who hoped to share in the profits generated by the master strategists. If autocratic leadership tended to be the rule in the large companies, however, exceptions could of course be found. In the Northwestern Mutual, a company which grew at a rate nearly as great as that of the Equitable, top management from the outset consisted of an executive committee of five trustees of which the president and vice-president were ex officio members.

The most important management innovation appropriately came in the field of marketing—the establishment of the general agency system. The agencies sometimes came into being when companies, anxious to cast the marketing net as widely as possible, sent men out to recruit and train sales forces in distant areas. On other occasions the general agency coalesced around an agent appointed as legal representative of the companies in foreign states as required by the laws of those states for out-of-state corporations. With the spread of the general agency system the larger companies soon did business on a nationwide basis, thereby becoming leaders in the trend toward national marketing which was to become an outstanding characteristic in the development of American business during the late nineteenth century. In 1892, for example, the Mutual had forty-one general agents in twenty-six states. Even before this time the racers, seeking new worlds to conquer, spread overseas. By 1900 the Mutual was operating in about twenty foreign nations and territories, New York Life in almost fifty, and the Equitable in nearly one hundred. At the turn of the century the big three had written $750 million of insurance abroad and had 250,000 policyholders outside of the United States.

Agents were paid by salary, or commissions, or both. A common arrangement was to give general agents 15 percent of first premiums and 7 percent of renewals, out of which they allowed 10 and 5 percent, respectively, to subagents who actually sold the policies. But under competitive conditions commissions were pushed rapidly upward. Rates of 50 percent on first premiums and 10 percent on renewals were not uncommon, and new companies seeking to break into the business sometimes allowed agents the entire first premium. Although high commissions plus widespread advertising and promotion raised the cost of doing business and weakened the financial structure of many companies, improved remuneration brought a higher caliber of businessmen into the insurance field and for the first time made it possible for the sale of life insurance to become an independent, full-time profession. With the coming of general agencies the home office agency became perhaps the most active department of the larger companies. This was where the action was, the command post where the strategies of competition were devised and put into effect.

During the period of rapid expansion in the industry the character of insurance company investment changed. In 1850 over 50 percent of the funds of all companies were invested in premium notes. Since these notes merely canceled liabilities in policy reserves, a heavy commitment to them reduced the ability of companies to purchase the income bearing securities which constituted the bedrock of the companies' financial security. Moreover, the high lapse rate of policies entailed an equally high rate of repudiation for premium notes. Essentially unsound assets, these diminished in volume and finally disappeared in the early twentieth century. Because of low yields, investment in federal, state, and municipal bonds declined along with holdings of premium notes. Conversely, investment in mortgages rose sharply, and in many companies they accounted for more than half of total assets. But perhaps the greatest change in the make-up of portfolios was brought about by increasing purchase of corporate bonds. Almost none was held by insurance companies in 1870, but by 1900 they accounted for 29 percent of company investments.

It was the capacity of the life insurance companies to absorb the large issues of railroad and industrial bonds floated by the investment bankers which drew the companies into the circle of giant financial institutions. In keeping with their new stature they formed alliances with large savings banks, commercial banks, and trust companies and became, in the words of one executive, "the bulwark and defense of large fortunes and large ventures." By the turn of the century the financial operations of the companies, plus their extravagant business methods and frequent entrapment of policyholders' funds, led to the widespread conviction that life insurance was being prostituted by the very organizations which had made it a world-wide fiduciary institution.

REFORM OF LIFE INSURANCE

Almost from the beginning life insurance companies had been subjected to the same regulations regarding investments, statements of financial condition, and initial capital which had been imposed on banks. But during the antebellum period there was distinct lack of regulation in two important areas. Legislatures had not as yet vindicated the rights of policyholders in the reserves of their policies, nor had they specified any methods of "valuation," that is, computing the present value of a company's future liabilities. Until the latter task was done there could be no standard on which to establish required reserves against policyholders' claims. In part the reason for the lack of legislation in these areas was a confusion in accounting concepts, which as yet were largely traditional and so not well adapted to the special problems of the life insurance business. The solution to the problem of valuation and the vindication of the rights of policyholders to the reserves of their policies was initially the work of Elizur Wright.

Born in Connecticut in 1804, young Wright graduated from Yale with a brilliant record in mathematics. Deeply religious, he later taught at Western Reserve College in Ohio, became caught up in the Abolitionist movement there, and moved to New York to become secretary of the American Anti-Slavery Society. Always in straightened circumstances, he took a trip to Europe to peddle his own translation of La Fontaine's *Fables*, and incidentally to gather information for the Massachusetts Hospital Life Insurance Company on the practices of British concerns. On the London Exchange he witnessed a sight which was to alter the course of his life—a life insurance auction. Dejected old men, unable to continue payments on their life insurance, mounted a platform, and speculators bid for their policies. Wright immediately saw a similarity to that most odious of all institutions for abolitionists— the slave auction. Just as good health and long life expectancy gave high value to a slave, so, inversely, advanced age and feeble health increased the value of a surrendered life insurance policy. In a slave auction the purchaser bought the freedom and the labor of the slave. In the insurance auction the speculators bought the security for a family which the policyholder had been building over the years. Equally outraged by both transactions, Wright henceforth fought for life insurance reform with the same zeal with which he battled for the abolition of slavery.

Settled in Massachusetts, he lobbied persistently in the legislature "for the widow and the orphan" in order to obtain bills which would establish legal reserves against all policy claims, set a standard method of computing these reserves, and provide for an insurance commissioner to enforce these enactments. Somewhat to his surprise, and against the bitter opposition of the insurance companies, his valuation bill became law in 1858. Even more to his surprise, he was appointed the first state life insurance commissioner, at the munificent salary of $1,500 per year. During the coming years he became a figure of national renown. Companies constantly sought his advice and retained him to work on special problems. Yet they never took him captive; during the latter nineteenth century he remained an outspoken critic of unsound practices, particularly the tontine policy which he labeled "insurance cannibalism." His greatest achievement was to make almost mathematically impossible the bankruptcy of a well-run life insurance company.

Wright also induced companies gradually to introduce into their policies liberal reforms which have become standard offerings of life insurance companies today. In 1861 the Massachusetts legislature, at his urging, passed a nonforfeiture law whereby the reserves of lapsed policy were utilized to buy term insurance which would extend the life of the policy. Once companies were forced to acknowledge the claims of premium payers on the reserves of their policies, other liberal reforms were forthcoming such as loan value, extended term insurance, paid-up insurance, cash value, surrender value, days of grace, and reinstatement.

Reform in policies, however, did little to stimulate responsibility in corporate management. The response of the New York legislature was the Armstrong Investigation of 1905. In the words of Morton Keller, a historian of life insurance, "Never before had a legislative committee subjected a group of major corporations to such a thorough and searching scrutiny." The outcome was a thorough reform of life insurance. In 1906 the New York Legislature passed a series of laws which affected nearly every aspect of the institution and established, in essentially their present form, the relations of companies to policyholders, the public, investors, financial institutions, and government. Twenty-nine of the forty-two state legislatures meeting in 1907 enacted legislation based on the New York program of regulation. Life insurance companies now ceased to be a power in politics, severed their relations with the speculative fraternity, and at last realized their potential for public service.

TRUST COMPANIES

The expanding and ever more specialized economic order created the need for a more highly organized and rationalized administration of fiduciary responsibilities as well as for life insurance. Since antiquity wardship courts and specially designated individuals had acted as trustees for minor children, widows, and others unable to look after their own affairs. Yet individual trusteeship had several shortcomings, chiefly the opportunities it provided for fraud and the misuse of funds placed in trustees' hands, and the necessity of finding replacements for trustees incapacitated or deceased. Corporations, as immortal bodies regulated by charter, had obvious advantages in overcoming these difficulties. In 1822 the Farmers' Fire Insurance and Loan Company, of New York, by obtaining an amendment to its charter empowering it to administer trusts, became the nation's first trust company. In the next year the Massachusetts Hospital Life Insurance Company received similar authorization, and the company's trust business soon overshadowed its sale of life insurance.

Over the next twenty-five years, because of the migratory character of the American people and the rapid increase in wealth and in urban population, the volume of trusts increased greatly, and their administration was carried on as a collateral function by several types of financial institutions. By 1850 there were about forty-two life and trust, fire insurance and trust, bank and trust, and savings and trust companies in the nation. Trusts accepted by these institutions were almost invariably of a personal nature, such as term deposits, endowments, and deferred annuities. A turning point was reached when trust companies began to perform services for corporations, chiefly railroads. Beginning in the fifties, railroad construction was financed to an increasing extent by the sale of bonds secured by land grants. Trust companies issued the bonds and represented the bondholders' interests under deeds of trust to the security involved. With the success of the mutuals after 1840, most of the old life and trust companies gradually abandoned the writing of insurance and expanded their services offered to corporations, often becoming agents for the issue and transfer of stock, and the payment of dividends. They also represented stockholders in corporate reorganization and consolidation.

After the Civil War, trust companies, like life insurance companies, tended to become mechanisms for capital accumulation. Because trust companies paid interest on deposits while commercial banks did not, trust company deposits increased at a more rapid rate, rising from $85 million in 1875 to $1 billion in 1900, a figure representing 22 percent of all bank deposits. The formation of these companies appealed to speculators because charters could be secured imposing fewer restrictions than those upon banks, and usually did not require the maintenance of a legal reserve. Large corporations gained trust companies as affiliates and used them as a market for issues of securities. Trust companies and life insurance companies therefore were probably the first important "institutional investors," gathering small savings and feeding them into the large corporations with which they were affiliated. Since trust companies would give much larger collateral loans than banks, they supplied much of the call money for the New York Stock Market.

Trust company regulation began during the seventies. Bankers complained of the favored position of trust companies under their blue-sky charters. Some spectacular trust company failures during the eighties, which naturally brought great pressure against the banks since trust companies were heavy bank depositors, made it plain that irresponsible management was a threat not only to widows and orphans but also to the financial structure of the nation at large. Originally responsible only to probate courts, trust companies were gradually brought under the supervision of state banking commissions where they belonged now that their functions were so closely interrelated with those of banks. By 1900 most states had general incorporation laws applicable to fiduciary organizations. As with life insurance, regulation in no way hindered the development of trust companies, but actually stimulated it by providing firmer ground for public confidence in the institutions.

XXIV. Pioneering in Western Transportation

The rapid settlement of California during the Gold Rush of '49, the subsequent advance of the mining frontier eastward over the Rockies, the blazing of immigrant trails across the prairies, and the supplying of widely scattered army posts created an immediate and unprecedented need in the West for freight and coach lines. The need was met by a group of energetic, colorful businessmen who searched out the best routes for travel, combined into regional monopolies numerous small freight and coach lines, and operated these monopolies in the face of danger and hardship with an élan which made themselves and their organizations known throughout the nation.

Freighting began with the opening of the Santa Fe Trail, which connected the communities west of St. Louis on the northern bend of the Missouri River with the Mexican town of Santa Fe. Although the feasibility of a route between these terminal points was established by the Pike

312

expedition of 1806–7, because of the hostility of Spain no trade with Santa Fe was undertaken until Mexico achieved its independence in 1821. In the next year Captain William Becknell organized a trading party in St. Louis, made his way by the Raton Pass to Santa Fe, and was enthusiastically received by the inhabitants of the town. High profits from this expedition led in the years to come to the formation of yearly caravans and the establishment of the Santa Fe Trail as an important trade route. The terms of trade were very advantageous to the Americans, for the Spanish settlers had a relative abundance of silver coin and bullion and furs, but almost no source of common cotton cloth and hardware, which was relatively cheap in St. Louis. An expedition of 1824 was able to exchange in Santa Fe $30,000 worth of such trade goods for $180,000 worth of gold and silver, plus $10,000 worth of furs. During the 1830s the value of goods sent over the trail varied from $100,000 to $250,000 per year—according to the historian of prairie commerce, Josiah Gregg—and the number of traders and their employees in the parties varied from 150 to about 225.

Trade goods were assembled in May of each year at points along the bend of the Missouri River, first at Franklin, later at Independence. The traders, numbering between twenty and sixty, purchased $100 to $600 worth of goods apiece from wholesalers in Independence or St. Louis at prices about 20 to 30 percent above those prevailing on the eastern seaboard. The large jobbers of Philadelphia were the ultimate source of the trade goods, and financed the trade by long-term credits in much the same way as English merchant bankers financed American overseas trade. St. Louis merchants were allowed twelve months for repayment, which enabled them to grant six-month credits to the traders. After the 780-mile trip to Santa Fe and several weeks spent in making the exchanges of goods, the expeditions returned to the bend of the Missouri River in October. Then started the repayment of debt which by the end of the year reached back to the Philadelphia jobbers. The trade was never very large in dollar volume, reaching a value of $450,000 in 1843, and became concentrated in the hands of not more than twenty-five or thirty individuals. During the Mexican War the trail became a path of empire—as the Spaniards of long ago had feared it would—when Colonel Stephen W. Kearney passed over it to occupy Santa Fe. After the war its romance faded, and eventually the route was followed by the Atchison, Topeka, and Santa Fe Railroad.

After the Mexican War the commerce of the prairies burgeoned rapidly. The Gold Rush brought a transcontinental wagon trail into existence, a multiplying number of army posts required a regular supply service, and the Mormons in their Utah hideaway somewhat reluctantly re-entered the world of commercial exchanges. At the outset of this period, stage lines had not yet made their appearance, and freighting was in the hands of numerous small operators none of whom owned more than ten or twelve wagons. Yet in an astonishingly short period of time the freighting business came to be concentrated in the hands of a few large concerns, and stage-coach lines were operated by a monopoly.

THE PRAIRIE FREIGHTING BUSINESS OF RUSSELL,
MAJORS, AND WADDELL

The first of the large freighting companies, which in the span of a few years built an "Empire on Wheels," was Russell, Majors, and Waddell. Russell and Waddell came from backgrounds of small-town storekeeping; Majors was a professional freighter who had got his start on the Santa Fe Trail. Throughout the life of the partnership Russell was the most active member, and ultimately the architect of its disaster. A tireless promoter with extensive contacts in the army and in the federal government, driven by grandiose visions of unlimited expansion for his enterprises, adept at negotiating the government contracts which were the lifeblood of his business and at raising the money to carry them into execution, he never appreciated the limits of the possible.

The three men began freighting operations together in 1854, and in the next year transformed their enterprise into the largest on the prairies by entering into a two-year contract with the government to haul supplies for the army from the Missouri River to outposts on the prairies and in the mountains. In order to meet their commitment they built offices, ware-houses, a blacksmith and wagon shop, and a store in Leavenworth, Kansas Territory. Within a year they had several hundred wagons in operation, alone representing an investment of from $360,000 to $400,000, and had 1,700 bullwhackers and other employees on their payroll. The funds for this rapid expansion came from loans secured by the government contract, mostly in the form of drafts payable after the payments to the partners for hauling supplies came due. Furthermore, the contract rates, varying from $1.24 to $2.15 per hundred pounds per hundred miles, were very favor-able and guaranteed a handsome profit. During the fifties and sixties wagon rates fluctuated with conditions, but were usually in the neighborhood of one dollar per hundred pounds per hundred miles. Even at this figure freighting brought impressive returns. A single wagon unit could under the best of conditions earn as much as $400 for each round trip between the Missouri River and Denver. Two and occasionally three trips could be made each year. But since a Conestoga wagon capable of carrying two and one-half tons cost at least $500, and with horses and mules represented an investment of several times that amount, and since risk and the rate of depreciation were both very high, it is doubtful whether freighting was profitable for the small operator who did not have access to government contracts.

Hauling contracts like that held by Russell, Majors, and Waddell, with inflated rates, came to represent a form of government aid to freighters comparable in a relative sense to the land grants given to railroads at a later date. Under the circumstances it is not surprising that the partners' net return from the first year of operations was about $150,000—probably not less than 35 percent of their total investment and several times the actual cash they put into the business.

In 1856 the partners made approximately the same amount of money as the year before, but in 1857 they committed an error in judgment which brought heavy losses to the firm and started it on a slide toward bankruptcy. Some time after the annual contract for hauling had been signed, the Mormon War broke out, and the army needed additional supplies in order to undertake a campaign against the saints of Salt Lake. Russell and the others should have insisted that the contract be altered to take into account additional purchases of equipment and a possible rise in the cost of transportation, but because of the pressure of time they agreed to finance additional needs by drawing drafts on Secretary of War John B. Floyd which could be used as collateral for loans. Floyd assured the partners that Congress would ultimately honor the debt to them by a deficiency appropriation. The firm then bought additional equipment at considerably higher prices because of the pressures brought to bear on the narrow market by the enhanced needs of the army. Unfortunately the campaign brought a series of disasters. The Mormons captured three wagon trains, 1,906 oxen perished in an early winter blizzard, and scores of wagons had to be abandoned. Russell set the loss at $493,553. The firm's credit now rested precariously on the drafts drawn on Floyd, as yet not honored by Congress. Events were to prove that the coming years were to bring no improvement of the fortunes of Russell, Majors, and Waddell.

THE BEGINNING OF STAGECOACHING IN THE WEST

During the fifties stagecoaching in the West became as potentially profitable a business as large-scale freighting. During the preceding decade individual operators and small companies had moved into the Midwest as feeders for the railroads, but coaching did not become a big business between the Mississippi and the Rockies until Congress undertook to establish a transcontinental mail service after the admission of California to the union. During the gold rush scores of small lines had been established in California radiating outward from San Francisco and Sacramento to the mining camps. They did a brisk business carrying not only a heavy passenger traffic but millions of dollars worth of gold dust as well. Because of mounting competition and the obvious advantages of consolidation, combination of the small lines took place quickly. In 1854 a million dollar concern, the California Stage Company, combined most of the lines in the northern part of the state and came to operate about 110 coaches over 1,400 miles of road and trail. East of the mountains coaching became a big business when Congress in 1857 granted to James E. Birch a contract to carry mail by stagecoach twice a month between San Antonio and San Diego for an annual subsidy of $149,000. Since the postal earnings from the route would obviously be small, and actually amounted to only $601 during the first year of service, the subsidy became in effect a grant-in-aid which probably covered the entire cost of equipment for the route. Henceforth the mail contracts rewarded to stage lines were to become a form of subsidy relatively as generous as any given to canal, railroad, and freighting companies.

While Birch's coaches were crawling over the New Mexico deserts, a truly transcontinental service connecting St. Louis and San Francisco was being planned by John Butterfield and a group of prominent eastern businessmen. Butterfield had entered stagecoaching at the bottom as a driver, but soon went into business for himself and eventually acquired large interests in New York lines and in many other types of business as well. In 1857 the Butterfield associates secured a New York charter for the Butterfield Overland Mail Company, capitalized at $2 million, and formulated a bid for a transcontinental mail contract the acquisition of which was the indispensable condition for the establishment of a transcontinental coach line. Meanwhile the selection of a route promoted a sharp sectional battle in Congress. Ultimately the decision in the matter was left up to Postmaster General Aaron V. Brown of Tennessee. Perhaps because of his presumed southern sympathies he rejected the direct route from St. Louis to San Francisco via Salt Lake and instead chose a route more beneficial to southern interests which dipped southward to El Paso and from there stretched westward to San Francisco via Los Angeles.

Brown then awarded a mail contract to the Butterfield company which called for a subsidy of $600,000 per year for six years and required the mails to be carried semiweekly over the nearly 3,000 mile route within an elapsed time of twenty-five days each way. In order to inaugurate the service the company purchased 250 stagecoaches, 1,000 horses and 500 mules, and built 141 way stations along the route. The company also constructed bridges and graded roadway where necessary. At the outset 800 men were needed to operate the line, but eventually the number of employees rose to 2,000. Altogether about $1 million was spent in the first year in order to get the line into operation. Fares between St. Louis and San Francisco were set at $200 exclusive of meals purchased at way stations. For organizational purposes Butterfield divided the line into an eastern and a western division, each managed by a superintendent. The main divisions were in turn divided into a total of eighteen subdivisions.

Nothing is known about the operating results of the Overland Mail, but it is probable that despite the huge mail subsidy they were not very profitable. Operating costs per passenger and depreciation were very much higher than on railroads. Any increase in speed required the building of more way stations and a heavier investment in draft animals. Profits for the company were doubtless also limited by the fact that most of the traffic over the plains to the mountains moved far to the north from the bend of the Missouri River toward Salt Lake. In any event, the Overland Mail had only a short period of time in order to test the potentialities of the southern, or "oxbow" route. Resentment of northern senators and representatives over what was deemed to be an adventure in southern imperialism, plus depradations carried out on the route by southern partisans at the beginning of the Civil War, forced Butterfield to shift operations to the northern route in 1861.

Meanwhile, William H. Russell had entered stagecoaching in the hope of extricating himself from the financial difficulties into which the freighting business of Russell, Majors, and Waddell had fallen. Without much initial planning or investigation he formed a partnership in 1859 which spent $144,000 equipping a stage line between Leavenworth and the new town of Denver, booming as a result of the Pike's Peak Gold Rush. But after the rush crested, traffic became too light to support the line, and in order to avoid bankruptcy it was taken over by its principal creditor, Russell, Majors, and Waddell, whose resources were already badly strained. Now was a time for much needed retrenchment and a liquidation of unprofitable operations. But Russell would not read the handwriting on the wall. In a last, desperate effort to avoid ruin, he induced his partners to join him in incorporating the Central Overland California and Pike's Peak Express Company, whose object was to monopolize passenger, express, and mail transportation across the northern route. In order to expedite mail service, Russell, in a move which made his name known throughout the nation, established a Pony Express to operate in conjunction with the Express Company. For a short period during 1860 the C.O.C. and P.P. operation actually enjoyed a transportation monopoly, but at the cost of operating losses of nearly $1,000 per day. Desperately Russell raced back and forth between New York and Washington, trying to raise money to keep the company going. Meanwhile Secretary Floyd by special favors had become personally interested in the tangled affairs of the partnership. The end came when the Overland Mail moved into the northern route with a million dollar per year mail contract. To stave off bankruptcy, Russell, with the connivance of a clerk in the Interior Department and perhaps with the knowledge of Floyd, embezzled $150,000 worth of bonds from the Indian Trust Fund. The end was inevitable. In December, 1861, Russell, Majors, and Waddell sold the express company for $100,000 to a successful stage line operator with whom they had formerly been associated, Ben Holladay, and shortly thereafter collapsed in ruin. Floyd, Russell, and the Interior Department clerk were indicted for the embezzlement of the Indian Trust Fund bonds, but the case was later dropped. Congress never honored the drafts which Floyd signed on behalf of the partnership in connection with the freight hauling contract of 1857.

BEN HOLLADAY, STAGECOACH KING

The heir of Russell, Majors, and Waddell's bankrupt empire, who was to remold it into one of the greatest transportation systems of the day, was a commanding personality. Tall, large-framed, bearded, darkly handsome, Ben Holladay combined with outstanding qualities of leadership an acute business judgment which was sadly lacking in William Russell. In many ways Holladay was a western Commodore Vanderbilt. The two men had the same combative personality and earthy tastes, and both used competitive tactics in an effort to gain monopoly. Circumstances, as well as superior business judgment, enabled Holladay to succeed where Russell, Majors, and Waddell had failed. While he was expanding his transportation system the West was being settled at a much more rapid rate than during the fifties; the army was extending its operations, and gold and silver strikes in the eastern Rockies were creating boom towns in inaccessible places far removed from rail connections. Equally important, the army engineers built thousands of miles of road and the Post Office Department expanded its subsidy program. During 1861, for example, the Department spent $1,228,241 on mail contracts from which it received a return in postage payments of only $296,496. In 1865, $726,065 was granted for carrying mail on the central transcontinental route alone; receipts came to $23,934.

Holladay came from a small town entrepreneurial background similar to that of Russell and Waddell. Likewise he had acquired most of his fortune by freighting for the army. Taking over the C.O.C. and P.P. for a fraction of its value and under circumstances whereby he was able to freeze out other creditors of the partnership, he accumulated mail contracts which went far toward paying the expenses of the line. He expanded his transportation system by establishing stage connections between new mining communities and the main stem, which connected Leavenworth and Salt Lake City. He also constructed roads where necessary, and built "swing stations" every ten or twelve miles along the routes, and "home stations" every fifty miles. At the same time he expanded his freighting business, in 1864 hiring 15,000 men, several thousand wagons, and 150,000 animals for transporting 100 million pounds of cargo between the Missouri River and the Rocky Mountains. In March, 1866, Holladay acquired the Butterfield interests which had been transferred to the northern route in 1861. Because of overcapitalization, Indian attacks, and management difficulties following John Butterfield's retirement from active participation in the firm, his successors could not stand the stiff competition from Holladay and were glad to sell out to him on his own terms. For a brief period Holladay now had a practical monopoly of western stagecoaching.

Although he spent most of his time in New York and Washington negotiating the fat mail and freighting contracts so vital to the success of his business, he paid constant attention to the service and equipment on his stage lines. Ultimately 3,300 miles in extent, these were organized in the divisional manner common to most railroads. Holladay incessantly urged his drivers on to new speed records which received widespread notice in newspapers throughout the country and made his name a household word. Net receipts often came to between $150,000 and $200,000 per month. A considerable portion of this naturally was represented by mail contracts, which netted him $2 million during the scant four years he was in the stage business. Shipments of treasure from gold and silver mines, carried at 1½ percent of value, were also an important source of revenue. All of his charges for transportation were extremely high, even considering currency inflation of the Civil War period and western boom conditions. Critics, of which there were many, accused him of gouging the public without mercy and of exerting a corrupting influence upon government.

Although Holladay made a large fortune from his transportation enterprises, yet the completion of the transcontinental telegraph, which brought the Pony Express to an end seventeen months after its inauguration in 1860, and the swift pace at which the Union Pacific and Central Pacific Railroads were being constructed, made it plain that the halcyon days of coaching and freighting would soon be over. In November, 1866, Holladay sold all of his holdings to Wells Fargo for $1.5 million cash and $300,000 in stock, plus a seat on the board of the company—an action somewhat similar to Commodore Vanderbilt's disposal of his steamship interests during the Civil War in order to enter railroad transportation.

WELLS FARGO AND THE EXPRESS BUSINESS

The purchase of Holladay's lines by Wells Fargo climaxed the movement toward combination in western stage transportation. This famous company, which combined coaching with banking, a private mail service, and the carrying of express, was inaugurated in 1852 when Henry Wells of Auburn, New York, and William G. Fargo of Syracuse, New York, formed a partnership to operate an express business in California. Express service had come into existence in the Northeast during the thirties with the carriage of notes, securities, and other valuables by confidential messengers. At the outset all that was needed to get into the business was a reputation for integrity and a season railroad ticket. But as volume increased, the service was carried on by companies operating under special agreements with railroads. After the start of the gold rush, express service was immediately required in California because of the need to transport, hold, buy, and sell gold dust. Furthermore, in the absence of government action, mail service had to be provided by private organizations. Therefore, scores of small express companies came into operation during the early fifties. The largest, Adams Express, was also the largest business in California at the time. Since Adams held large amounts of gold dust, it was drawn into banking by the most literal operation of the "goldsmith principle" in modern times. The "certificates of deposit" which it issued against the gold circulated as currency.

Wells Fargo expanded rapidly from the moment of its founding in California because of good management and the multiplying demand for the services of express companies. The Adams leadership, on the other hand, gradually succumbed to the speculative excesses of the times and the firm failed during the sharp, state-wide panic of 1855 because of unwise investments, over-extension, and embezzlement. The fact that Wells Fargo survived despite a run on several of its branches greatly enhanced its reputation and enabled it to move into the commanding position formerly held by Adams. By 1860 it had established 108 stations in California and had a virtual monopoly of the express business. At this time its net income had grown to about $150,000 per year and it paid a dividend for the year of 18 percent. In 1863 the company declared a stock dividend of 100 percent.

Almost from the beginning Wells Fargo separated banking from express and offered a complete banking service. It also did a lucrative business in buying and selling gold dust. As the mail carrier of California the company purchased three-cent stamped envelopes from the Post Office Department and sold them franked at its stations for ten cents apiece. The green mailboxes of Wells Fargo were as familiar a sight in California towns as the blue mailboxes of the Post Office Department in use today. The company was also the universal carrier of gold and treasure.

Somewhat surprisingly, Wells Fargo had not tried to enter stagecoaching, which outside of California was usually combined with express service. The reason may have been that the California Stage Company and the California Steam Navigation Company had acquired a monopoly of transportation before Wells Fargo was in a position to do so. In any event, these two organizations carried Wells Fargo express under carefully negotiated agreements. Outside of California Wells Fargo still had a practical option to go into stagecoaching, however. Fargo was one of the associates who had established the Butterfield Overland Mail, and he continued to maintain a large interest in the organization.

The acquisition of Holladay's properties was a bid for a monopoly of the California variety. In order to achieve it Wells Fargo increased its capital stock to $10 million and began purchasing competitors. Within a few years it controlled virtually all of the stage lines between the Missouri River and California. But with the coming of the transcontinental railroad the superior wisdom of Ben Holladay was demonstrated as Wells Fargo's revenues fell off and the price of its stock declined. Charles Crocker, one of "The Big Four" who built the Central Pacific Railroad, and Lloyd Tevis, banker and speculator in mines and California oil, then quietly bought control of the company. With Tevis as the new president Wells Fargo recovered its prosperity, transferring an ever larger amount of express from coach and wagon to rail. From the beginning express had been a very profitable business. One magazine writer claimed that as early as 1875 it had created over fifty millionaires.

Stagecoaching and freighting continued to be important enterprises until the early twentieth century. Each new strike of gold, silver, lead or copper created a new boom town, and with it an immediate and heavy demand for passenger and freight conveyance. If the ore reserves proved to be extensive enough to justify permanent mining and refining installations, a railroad spur from one of the transcontinentals soon found its way to the area, and the stagecoaches and freight wagons disappeared. But as the restless prospectors moved from place to place in the immense area of the rockies, stages and freighters followed them, and until the coming of the automobile provided the only access to the outside world for many scores of communities.

THE ROLE OF STEAMBOATS IN WESTERN TRANSPORTATION

Although steamboats necessarily served more limited areas than wagon trains, they were important as a means of transportation because of their large cargo capacity and because they penetrated for surprisingly long distances westward from the Mississippi. Nine hundred and eighty-six miles of the Red River and 984 of the Arkansas were passable for light draft stern wheelers. But the most important river for western transportation was the Missouri, which could be navigated for a distance of over 3,000 miles from St. Louis to Fort Benton, in central Montana. As steamboat service increased during the fifties and sixties, scores of landing points on the rivers became thriving entrepôts at which shipments from St. Louis were shifted to wagon trains, thus saving many hundreds of miles of overland transportation.

Steamboating on the Missouri was inaugurated by the American Fur Company, which as early as 1834 operated two boats between St. Louis and the company's main fur post at the mouth of the Yellowstone. But the extensive use of steamboats did not begin until the fifties when settlers moved into Iowa and Nebraska and westward bound wagon trains were organized at the northwest bend in the Missouri. Successful navigation of the treacherous and shallow upper Missouri had to await the building of long, light draft boats which could carry heavy cargoes and still cross the sand bars which for most of the year blocked the deeper draft vessels of the earlier era. Steamboating reached its fullest development during the late sixties when gold strikes in Montana and in the northwest Rockies and extensive military operations against the Indians created a burgeoning need for heavy mining equipment and military supplies. In 1867 seventy-one boats representing a total tonnage of 15,882 reached the upper Missouri. Thereafter traffic on the lower reaches of the river declined as railroads connecting Omaha and Sioux City with Chicago diverted much of the river traffic which had formerly passed through St. Louis. Traffic continued to be heavy on the upper Missouri, however, because of extensive wheat production in the Dakotas and the copper boom in Montana.

At the outset boats were usually owned by their captains as in the tramping trades of the Mississippi. But when St. Louis merchants established agencies for regular trade on the upper reaches of the river, they began to buy shares of boats as a means of guaranteeing transportation for their goods. Also, since insurance costs were very high—at least 10 percent— share ownership appeared to many merchants to be a cheaper way of spreading the risks on a hazardous investment in transportation. Upriver cargoes usually consisted of mining gear, military supplies, goods for Indian agencies, and general merchandise. Return cargoes during the sixties were much lighter in volume. Gold dust was the most lucrative item; five-sixths of the entire production of Montana went eastward via the Missouri. Furs and buffalo robes were also shipped in volume. As competition increased and the army and Indian agencies offered ever larger contracts for haulage, the process of combination universal in other types of western transportation took place. By the early seventies the Koontz Line, and the Northwest Transportation Company, both of Sioux City, handled most of the military and Indian agency trade under contract. The latter firm was a corporation operating nine boats, but most of the other combinations were packet lines organized on a share basis.

Because of low water levels prevailing most of the year on the upper reaches of the river, boats from St. Louis were able to make only one trip a year to the head of navigation at Fort Benton. Starting in late March as soon as the ice broke up, they unloaded their cargoes on the Fort Benton levee early in June while the spring freshets were still running and as quickly as possible reloaded for the return voyage. Even under the best of conditions the trip was laborious and dangerous. Boats continually grounded on sandbars and were literally walked across to deeper water by "sparring," a process in which stout poles set on the river bottom and lashed to the sides of the boats were worked as levers by donkey engines in order to move the boats forward.

The larger boats could carry 300 or 400 tons of cargo—about as much as 125 to 160 wagons—but in order to lighten draft were usually loaded with no more than 200 tons. Boats on the upper river that drew more than three and one half feet of water invited trouble. Because of the great need for navigational skills captains and pilots were paid up to $400 and $750 per month, respectively—at least three times the wages prevailing on the Mississippi. The almost perpetual emergency conditions required large crews of thirty to forty men. Rates between St. Louis and Fort Benton during the sixties fluctuated between $6 and $12 per hundred pounds—much more than rail rates of a later date but less than half of the prevailing wagon rates. Passenger fares were about $150 for the trip, and passenger travel was heavy. Annual earnings of boats could be very high. During the peak of the Montana gold rush in 1866 and 1867 some boats reported net earnings of from $10,000 to $40,000, and as late as 1877 earnings of $15,000 to $25,000 were not uncommon. Since the initial cost of boats was usually between $25,000 and $50,000, some could return the investment in one trip at this rate of return. Yet these earnings were extraordinary and do not reflect profits of steamboating generally over an extended period of time. Because of the rugged conditions of operation the life of steamboats was short and extensive repairs were required after visits to upriver ports. Snaggings and burnings were common, and even marauding Indians were a hazard. Although steamboating continued into the twentieth century on the upper Missouri, primarily in the grain trade, the building of the northern transcontinental railroads brought its halcyon days to an end.

In the Far West steamboats plied the Sacramento and the San Jacinto, the Columbia and the Williamette. Everywhere the pattern of development was the same—high profits for those first in the business, then increasing competition and eventual combination. The Oregon Steam Navigation Company, for example, monopolized steamboat, railroad, and coach travel in Oregon, and when purchased by Henry Villard in 1879 became part of the Northern Pacific's transcontinental empire.

Although competition was usually an important incentive to combination, in many areas governmental policies played an even more decisive role. Holders of government contracts for the carriage of military and Indian supply goods of necessity had to build large organizations in order to meet their commitments. Similarly, important mail contracts required combination of stage lines. Had there been no government subsidies it is possible that there would have been no extensive combination at this time and that freighting, steamboating, and the operation of stagecoach lines would have been carried on as in the Midwest—by numerous small entrepreneurs.

ROADS AND TURNPIKES IN THE WEST

In conclusion, a word must be said about the building of roads and turnpikes in the West. Since roads were of such crucial importance, settlers arriving in any newly opened area did not wait for governmental action but started construction themselves. At the same time aid was requested from the federal and territorial governments. The federal government responded quickly and generously, sometimes granting funds to territorial legislatures but more importantly putting appropriate agencies to work surveying and building roads. The Southern Overland route from Sante Fe to the Pacific utilized by the Butterfield stage line was explored, marked, and made passable by the army engineers. The army also explored and mapped a communication network for Texas and opened three major wagon roads to the Pacific. Actually, the western road network was constructed in pragmatic fashion by a combination of individuals, stage lines, turnpike companies, and the federal agencies. In California and Oregon roads were primarily privately owned and operated, but the federal government made important contributions also, and elsewhere it constructed all the through routes. Here again, as with freighting and mail contracts, we see an important area of governmental aid to private enterprise.

XXV. Completion of
the Railroad Network

Until 1850, the federal government played a minor role in aiding transportation enterprises, principally because of constitutional limitations and reluctance of administrations to become involved in sectional logrolling. But after this date large grants of public land became the principal form of largesse offered to railroads. In several ways land grants appeared to obviate the difficulties and expense arising from joint enterprise. First, the grants added nothing to public indebtedness yet gave railroads great potential assets; second, by granting land in alternate sections along a right of way the government's retained lands rose in value; third, grants could presumably be increased to the point where private enterprise would undertake developmental projects with initially poor profit prospects; finally, regardless of the amount of its commitment, government did not run the risk of being drawn into management always present in joint enterprise.

Congress, by an act of 1850, inaugurated the land-grant policy by donating to Illinois an ultimate 3.75 million acres to be turned over to the Illinois Central. Grants offered to western railroads were even more generous since it was obvious that the roads could not be built without massive public assistance. In 1864 the Union Pacific–Central Pacific was given aid in the form of twenty alternate sections of land per mile, and loans varying from $16,000 to $48,000 per mile depending on the difficulty of the terrain. Since the government took only a second mortgage as security for the loans, the land grant could serve as security for first mortgage bonds.

During the coming decade loans to the other transcontinental lines ceased but land grants were enlarged. Under a standard formula of forty alternate sections per mile in the territories and twenty in the states, the Northern Pacific was granted forty-four million acres, the Atlantic and Pacific twenty-three million, the Texas and Pacific thirteen million, and the Southern Pacific about seven and three-fourths million. In return the railroads were required to carry troops and government supplies at a reduced rate, ultimately set at 50 percent of normal charges. Since a portion of some grants reverted to the federal government when railroads were unable to meet construction schedules required to earn the land, and since states sometimes made donations, the amount actually received by the roads is still in dispute among historians. The net figure is often cited as 129 million acres, but it might have been as high as 180 million, an area 7 percent larger than the state of Texas.

Historians disagree also over the value of the land granted and the relative financial returns of the land-grant policy to the railroads and the federal government. Government aid probably covered the cost of constructing the Union Pacific–Central Pacific and allowed the promoters by financial manipulations to realize a profit of from $13 million to about $35 million. But the government in 1897 handsomely recouped its second mortgage investment when the railroad repaid in full the government claim of $50.4 million. Since the government continued until 1946 to use the facilities of all the land-grant roads at one-half of the usual charges, it must have recovered a considerable portion of its total investment by this means alone. According to one authority, the railroads have netted about $500 million by land sales, and the government has saved about $600 million in reduced rates. It is impossible to calculate how much value the railroads added to the government's alternate sections retained within the land grants, but it must have been of considerable proportions. All in all, it seems safe to say that the land-grant policy, even though denounced throughout the late nineteenth century as a giveaway, has proved to be very beneficial to all parties concerned.

But the long-run advantages of the land-grant policy were realized only at the cost of creating acute short-run problems. Since title to each parcel of land did not pass until the road was built past it, and since land sales were slow at best, railroads were forced into risky expedients in order to raise the funds needed for construction. Also, the pressure for speed in construction inflated costs and sometimes led to poor location of routes. The lag in bond sales, as we have seen, forced Jay Cooke and the Northern Pacific into bankruptcy in 1873. At the outset the only effective solution to the problem of marketing the bonds issued against the land grants was "construction company financing," which brought profiteering and corruption reaching upward to the highest levels of government. The land-grant policy also contributed to the overexpansion of the railroads, stimulated land speculation, and thereby accentuated the fluctuations of the business cycle.

RAILROADS AS COLONIZING AGENCIES

During the nineteenth century the misdeeds of the railroads were widely publicized and loudly denounced, but the great service the roads performed as colonizing agencies excited much less comment. In the magnitude of the colonizing operations the achievement of the railroads dwarfs the efforts of the more celebrated colonial promoters of an earlier era—the Virginia and Massachusetts Bay Companies, the Calverts, the Penns, and the Georgia Trustees.

The first railroad which undertook to encourage immigration on a large scale into its territory was the Illinois Central. Construction of the road had been financed by mortgaging the land grant, but the directors realized the traffic could only be created by settling the railroad land with farmers. The advertising department compiled a mailing list of one million eastern farmers and regularly sent out testimonial letters, maps, and brochures describing the land. Traveling agents spread the message to the countries of northern and western Europe; immigration offices of the railroad gave advice and help of many kinds to farmers setting out on the journey to the United States. The price of company land varied according to the quality and location, but averaged about $10 per acre. Payments were spread over a period of eight years, with the first three free of installments.

The results of the company's initial campaign for settlers exceeded the fondest hopes of the promoters. By 1857, only one year after completion of the road, 1.2 million acres had been sold for a sum of $15.3 million—nearly the cost of construction. The company did not forget the settler after he had bought land. It established an experimental station for the development of seeds and the improvement of stock breeding, published the results of latest research in the newspapers, and sponsored the state fair and other agricultural activities. By 1864 Illinois raised 20 percent of the wheat crop of the nation and by 1870 had taken the lead among the states in hog production. The railroad cannot take sole credit for this progress, but there can be little doubt that its enlightened policies contributed to the prosperity of the state.

The Burlington also made good use of its land grant. John Murray Forbes and the Boston group which came to control the road made it the basis of extensive real estate and land development enterprises. By 1905 the company had disposed of its entire domain for a net return of about $17 million, slightly more than the cost of the main stem from Burlington, on the Mississippi River, to Kearney, Nebraska. The Burlington sold land on a ten-year time payment plan, and charged 6 percent interest on unpaid portions of the balance. Prices during the seventies ranged from $12 to $14 per acre in Iowa and from $5 to $8 in Nebraska. Title could revert to the company in the event that a purchaser did not till or otherwise develop the land within three years—a stipulation designed to discourage speculators. The company gave free passes to land hunters, and established "immigrant homes" along the route where womenfolk might reside while the male members of families examined the offerings of the railroad.

Other western roads beginning in the seventies were making equally intensive efforts to settle their land grants. At one time the U.P. was advertising in 2,539 papers with a combined circulation of 7,250,000. Its land sales in Nebraska totaled over 300,000 acres in 1878 alone. The Northern Pacific at one point attempted to settle its lands collectively by establishing "colonies" of foreign families. In order to give shelter against the bitter prairie winters it sold at cost prefabricated houses made in company shops located in wooded areas near Lake Superior. As the West grew, the density of population was always greatest along the lines of the railroads.

The Great Northern, under the dynamic leadership of James J. Hill, was particularly successful in promoting immigration. The fact that Hill received no land grant was in some ways an advantage in that it freed him to build more slowly and at minimum cost. He located his route through the best farming areas, paced his building to the rate of settlement, and sent feeders north and south at strategic points in order to nourish the main stem and protect his territory from invasion by competitors. Like the other pioneer roads the Great Northern operated a model farm and distributed the results of agricultural experiments to farmers. Of particular help was Hill's standing offer to advance farmers 85 percent of the value of their wheat when stored in his elevators. Through an agreement with the Burlington he secured access to Chicago. The wisdom of Hill's policies as a railroad leader were revealed when the Great Northern became the only transcontinental road to avoid bankruptcy in the Panic of 1893.

By 1900 most of the railroad land suitable for agriculture had been sold off, and the settlement activities of the pioneer roads came to an end. But the remaining lands proved to be increasingly valuable for grazing or because of timber, oil, or water power resources. The Atchison between 1897 and 1952 realized about $15 million from an essentially arid domain. The Northern Pacific, after reorganization and rebuilding, became very prosperous, largely because of the great natural resources of its retained lands.

RAILROAD ENGINEERING AND EQUIPMENT

Railroad equipment was improved with the same speed and enthusiasm which characterized the mechanization of the textile industry. The first locomotive to operate in the United States was imported from England in 1829 to haul coal from the mines of the Delaware and Hudson Canal Company in northeastern Pennsylvania. It was landed, assembled, and tested at the West Point Foundry in New York, which thereafter became a pioneer producer of locomotives. In the next year Peter Cooper constructed his famous "Tom Thumb" for the B. and O. (see p. 271), and in 1832 the Philadelphia jeweler, Matthias Baldwin, built a locomotive for the Germantown Railroad. Within a decade the importation of locomotives practically ceased, principally because the swift pace of machine tool development enabled the nation's leading machine shops and textile machinery works to produce the engines as readily as shops in England. By 1837 the Baldwin Locomotive Works, which was to become the giant of the industry, was turning out forty-five locomotives per year, and by 1870 it produced one per day. Even before this time the repair shops of some of the largest railroads had been tooled up to the point that they constructed rolling stock of all kinds. In sharp contrast to the ease with which locomotives and cars were produced in America, rails continued to be imported in heavy volume until the sixties. The reason was a long lag in the build-up of rolling mill capacity. The construction of locomotives involved mechanical problems of the type Americans were already adept at solving; the rolling of rails, however, entailed metallurgical difficulties with which American engineers were not equipped to deal until the last half of the century.

The design changes in locomotives over the years were a response to the continuing need for greater pulling power. The prototypes, mounted in what were essentially wagon beds, had such short wheel bases that when pulling heavy loads they tended to drive themselves off the rails while negotiating curves. John B. Jervis of the Mohawk and Hudson solved this problem by adding a bogie truck in front to guide the driving wheels. During the thirties and forties a multitude of new designs was introduced, many quite inefficient and awkward. But, as with the development of all industrial machinery, experience brought standardization. Boilers increased in length and became the main stem of the structures. Internal cylinders and gearing gave way to outboard cylinders and drivers, with the moment of force determined by the diameter of the drive wheels. With the addition of a cab for engineer and fireman, and a cowcatcher, the distinctive "American" type of locomotive came into being by the fifties. For freight locomotives the problem of maximum traction and pulling power was solved by adding more and smaller driving wheels. Directing the steam exhaust up the smokestack greatly increased the draft on boilers, but also created a major fire hazard for towns and woodlands. The bell stack was designed to trap at least part of the cinders blasted upward. Only the replacement of wood by coal as a fuel really solved the problem, however. Seven to fifteen tons was the average weight of locomotives during the forties. Size, power, and speed increased slowly during the next three decades and then mounted rapidly with the coming of steel rails. A Baldwin locomotive exhibited at the Columbian Exposition of 1893 tipped the scales at ninety-seven tons, and in the same year Engine 999 of the New York Central made history by pulling the Empire State Express at 112 miles per hour—a record which lasted long into the twentieth century.

The first passenger cars were merely carriages fitted with flanged wheels. But the rapid increase in passenger travel brought about an abrupt change to the modern type of car with doors in the ends and an aisle down the middle. The model for this design may have been the horse-drawn omnibuses beginning to appear on the streets of New York. Four-wheeled trucks were apparently first used by the B. and O. to enable the cars to negotiate curves at street intersections in Baltimore while being drawn by horses to and from the locomotives, which were compelled as a fire precaution to remain outside city limits. It is interesting to note that cars of the American type did not make their appearance in Europe until well into the twentieth century. Even today the older European passenger cars are simply a series of carriages carried on a wagon frame. Most European freight cars are four-wheeled wagons resembling the American cars of the 1840s. European railroad management has never appeared to be as interested as its American counterpart in reducing operating costs by using heavier rolling stock which would increase the ratio of pay load to dead weight, raise train tonnage, and decrease train mileage.

The earliest rails were of wood topped by iron strips. But this makeshift arrangement was dangerous. Loose strips, called "snakeheads," often curved upwards from the wooden rails and plunged into passing trains, causing serious accidents. At the outset stone "sleepers" and even piles were sometimes utilized for roadbeds, but experience soon demonstrated the superiority of wooden ties embedded in cinders or gravel banked so as to shed water. For the first two decades of railroading iron "T" rails imported from England were attached to ties with heavy iron brackets called "chairs." Later, use of the expensive "chairs" was avoided by rolling rails with broader bases enabling them to stand upright and by attaching the rails to ties by spikes and tieplates. European railroads still use T rails buckled to ties by heavy clamps and wooden wedges. The first rails weighed only about thirty-five pounds to the yard, but as the weight of engines and rolling stock increased, the weight of rails advanced proportionally. By 1900 steel rails weighing one hundred pounds per yard were not uncommon. They lasted over twice as long as had the iron rails of twenty years before and permitted the use of larger freight cars raising the ratio of pay load to dead weight from 55 to 70 percent. Efficiency was further increased by relocating roads over more favorable terrain, by easing grades, and widening curves. The increase in tonnage which could be carried by freight trains permitted a steady drop in rates. This development delivered the *coup de grâce* to most canals by enabling railroads to carry heavy low-value commodities such as coal as cheaply as these could be shipped over the waterways.

The expansion of terminal facilities was of great importance in facilitating railroad operations. Hundreds of acres on the south side of Chicago were covered with terminals and yards, and car interchange was greatly facilitated by the construction of a belt railroad giving trunk lines direct connection with each other. Commodore Vanderbilt increased the traffic over the Central by building the great freight terminal on Manhattan's West Side and the "old" Grand Central Station. Incidentally, wags among his associates on the stock market, some of whom had no doubt suffered from Vanderbilt's financial manipulations, celebrated the gala opening of the Grand Central in 1871 by sending the Commodore a statue of himself with a watering can in his hand. The west bank of the Hudson became a continuous railroad terminal from Jersey City to Weehawken. Extensive freight terminals and docks greatly stimulated the growth of eastern seaboard cities by making them the funnels of a transatlantic trade reaching from the Great Plains to western Europe.

RAILROAD MANAGEMENT

Railroad operation occupies an important position in business history because the difficulties of co-ordinating so many different tasks and the need for efficiency, dispatch, and accuracy in carrying them out focused the attention of businessmen for the first time on the problems of management. During the last half of the nineteenth century railroad companies were by far the largest business units in the nation. As early as the mid-fifties, the Erie Railroad had over 4,000 employees and its annual operating costs topped $2.8 million. By contrast the Pepperell Manufacturing Company, of Biddeford, Maine—one of the nation's largest textile companies—had about 800 employees and annual operating costs of only $300,000. Because of their size alone railroads led the trend toward the separation of ownership and management and were among the first enterprises to give a large measure of decision making to technically trained personnel.

Railroads at the outset were unique as transportation enterprises in that they combined the building and maintenance of a transportation facility with a monopoly of carriage over it. Builders of some very early railroads assumed that as on turnpikes all users would provide their own wagons and carriages. For a few years the Philadelphia and Columbia and the B. and O. were actually operated in this fashion. But the coming of the locomotive made any such arrangement impossible and forced the railroads to monopolize traffic.

As with locomotive design and construction, the first railroad organization was copied from an English model. In 1829 as a result of an investigation of English practices, the B. and O. established three departments under, respectively, a master of transportation, a master of the road, and a master of machinery. Thus three of the four main functions of railroad management were given distinct status: operations, maintenance of way, and maintenance of rolling stock. The fourth function, traffic, was apparently handled by the secretary and the treasurer. Construction probably had its own organization under a superintendent, and the financial affairs of the railroad were no doubt handled by the president and board of directors.

In the early days of railroading presidents came almost invariably from entrepreneurial backgrounds or from law. Directors, usually elected to their positions because of large stockholdings, generally felt a responsibility to participate actively in management. The line between corporate and operating management was rather strongly drawn, and operating management had little power to make independent decisions except when no time was available for consultation. Since presidents usually made their headquarters in New York, the failure to delegate authority to management operating the lines sometimes had unfortunate effects upon efficiency. The fact that presidents often held executive positions in several lines simultaneously only made matters worse.

By the fifties, as operating units sharply increased in size, managerial difficulties became serious. Since the great majority of chief executives viewed their functions as being primarily financial, and since boards of directors began to retire from active participation in management, the owners did not manage and the managers did not own—as Henry V. Poor pointed out in *The American Railroad Journal*. What was needed, Poor felt, was a more careful separation of function, a system of reporting throughout the organization which would give top management full information on the conduct of operations, and the compiling of statistics by which the performance of railroads could be evaluated.

The B. and O., oldest of the trunk lines, became the first to systematize its operations when Chief Engineer Benjamin H. Latrobe, assisted by a committee of the board of directors, drew up an organizational manual in 1847. The road was now to be administered in two major departments, the first concerned with the working of the road and the second with the collection and disbursement of revenue. A general superintendent became the chief officer for operations, and to him reported the master of the road, the master of machinery, and the master of transportation. The treasurer, chief official of the second major branch of administration, handled external financing and such routine duties as sale and transfer of securities, and payment of dividends and interest. Under him the secretary collected and filed documents, supervised accounts, and prepared reports. Corporate policy decisions were made by the president and committees of the board of directors, of which one of the most important was the Finance Committee. A legal department, headed by the attorney, handled the wide variety of legal problems important to railroads. During the fifties this pattern of railroad organization was widely copied.

Increasing railroad mileage brought about by construction and mergers posed a major operational problem. Would the lines be operated as a unit, with all subordinate officials responsible to a functional chief at the corporate level, or would administration be decentralized into more or less autonomous units whose operations would be co-ordinated by one official alone responsible to top management? Actually both systems came into use, along with combinations of the two. The first became known as the "departmental system"; the second—much more popular and more natural for merged roads—the "divisional system." Much of the credit for the development of the latter goes to Daniel C. McCallum, who became general superintendent of the Erie in 1854. McCallum divided the road—at that time the longest in the world—into five divisions, each under the authority of a division superintendent. The superintendents were responsible for all movements of trains in their division and all maintenance. In order to integrate operations and provide at all times a clear view of performance, all officials down to conductors and stationmasters were required to submit periodic reports. When the plan was put into operation the division superintendent was able to tell at a glance the location of every car and engine on the road. Henry V. Poor was so impressed by the Erie system that he lithographed and published its organizational chart.

After the sixties, progressive reorganization made the Pennsylvania, with its very heavy traffic and thousands of employees, "in every respect the standard railroad of America"—to quote an authority of the period. Perhaps its greatest achievement was the working out of the line-and-staff concept of organization. As explained by Alfred D. Chandler, Jr.: "Its basic problem here was to define the lines of communication and authority between departmental headquarters and the field divisions in carrying out of its basic activity—transportation. In Pennsylvania's Transportation Department, the executives concerned with the moving of trains became line officers and those dealing with auxiliary or service activities, staff ones. The line of authority ran from the president to the general manager to the general superintendents and then to the division superintendents in the field. . . ."

Since railroads competed in rates rather than in service, traffic departments necessarily had to be highly centralized in order to react quickly to fluctuations in rate structures. The general traffic manager was the official who usually represented a road at rate conferences with other roads, negotiated rate sharing and car exchange agreements, and had the authority to set rates. Since the latter function was of such immediate and vital importance, the traffic manager usually exercised it in collaboration with top corporate officials. Indeed, in all of these matters decision making in practice was collective rather than individual. The traffic manager's staff consisted of general freight, passenger, and claim agents. Under these were similar officials at the divisional level who personally conducted relations with the users of the road. At the bottom of the hierarchy was a horde of traffic solicitors who fought tooth and nail for business.

Since the supplying of cars to shippers was also a matter which could immediately affect the financial condition of the road, and since it could not be handled efficiently at the division level, the function was often centered in a car service agent reporting directly to the superintendent of transportation. Purchasing and telegraph had by 1900 come to be centralized staff functions also. In the divisional system, then, decentralization was generally limited to line functions at the divisional level; lines of authority in some staff functions bypassed the divisions and ran from the corporate direct to the local level.

By the end of the nineteenth century the theoretical merits and disadvantages of the departmental and divisional systems had aroused considerable discussion. Charles Elliott Perkins probably spoke for many other railroad men when he strongly endorsed the latter: "To spread the working organization over the entire property gives heads of departments too large a field for anything like careful attention to details and makes necessary their dependence upon subordinates who are far removed from their immediate oversight, while the plan of separate and distinct units of management, on the other hand, confines the heads of departments to smaller fields and makes them directly responsible to a local head or manager." But advocates of the departmental system noted that the success of the divisional system depended to an inordinate extent on the caliber of the divisional superintendents. They asserted that personal differences and lack of co-operation among these men could hamstring a railroad, and that under the best conditions the divisional system made standardization of operations and service difficult. Actually most roads eventually adopted organizational schemes which combined elements of the two forms. Large railroads conducting operations over thousands of miles of trackage, like large nations embracing a wide geographical area, can best be administered by a judicious mixture of centralized control and local autonomy.

Until the 1860s railroad executives, with the exception of McCallum, do not appear to have made a serious effort to collect statistics, or perhaps they were reluctant for competitive reasons to divulge what information they had about operations and the condition of their property. But the fall in rates beginning in the mid-seventies and the resultant need to cut costs forced railroad management to intensify and elaborate statistical research. By this time the operating ratio—the ratio of operating expenses to gross earnings—had come to be regarded as the basic statistic giving the clearest indication of a railroad's performance and financial condition. A low ratio of 40 to 50 percent would indicate prima-facie efficient operations and low bonded indebtedness. Roads with operating ratios above 85 percent would appear to be in hazardous condition and likely to fail during a depression which would reduce operating revenues. Yet since the accuracy of the equation depended upon honest accounting, it could be misleading. When the B. and O. faced bankruptcy in 1886 it was found that for years the published operating ratio had been distorted by charging current expenditures of all kinds, but chiefly for maintenance, to the construction account.

Yet even with the best of accounting methods operating ratios could be misleading without supplementary statistics. Some roads with high operating ratios were nevertheless in flourishing condition because a large volume of business provided a satisfactory net profit even though the percentage spread between operating expenses and gross revenues seemed small. The Pennsylvania, with an operating ratio of approximately 78 percent—about 10 percent over the national average in normal times—was in this category. Operating ratios had to be evaluated, therefore, in the light of such considerations as ton miles (tons multiplied by miles carried), and traffic density (ton miles divided by miles of road). But even more figures are necessary to give an accurate picture of a railroad's performance. By the end of the century railroad management was compiling voluminous statistics in categories such as tons of revenue freight per train, percentage of loaded car mileage, average miles per car and per locomotive per day, average revenue per mile, average revenue per ton mile.

As previously indicated, efficiency of railroads increased steadily as heavier engines and cars and the easing of grades and curves permitted carriage of a larger volume of freight without a proportionate rise in operating cost. A constant effort to secure return loads and reduce the hauling of empties benefited revenue even though such "backloads" were often carried at reduced rates. By the turn of the century the average tons per train on American roads was significantly greater than the comparable figure for European railroads. Furthermore, American rates as well as capitalization were lower.

Although evaluations of human efficiency are difficult to make, it would appear that the improvements in operating performance would have been impossible without the services of alert, responsible, intelligent, and highly trained personnel. Railroading during the nineteenth century was an occupation carrying considerable prestige. Since the roads were rapidly expanding and promotions usually made from within the organizations, the profession offered the combination of challenge and opportunity which attracted young men. The fact that the number of employees per mile on American railroads was about half the figure for English roads gives some indication of the quality of employee performance.

The heavy employment by the railroads and the dependence of management upon such skilled workers as locomotive engineers, firemen, brakemen, and switchmen created a fertile field for labor organization. To quote Chandler, "As the railroad workers were among the first to form local unions and then to build a national federation of their locals, their brotherhoods quickly became the most powerful and effective unions developed in the United States before the twentieth century." Although managers somewhat reluctantly bargained with unions over purely economic matters such as wages and hours, they resisted the unions' attempt to include such issues as job classification on the ground that intrusion into this area constituted interference with management's prerogatives.

If the railroads created conditions under which collective bargaining could flourish, they also stimulated the rise of the industrial, as opposed to the craft union. In 1893 Eugene V. Debs, realizing the possibilities of tighter organization and enhanced bargaining power in the industrial form, organized the first union of this type in the nation—the American Railway Union. Although the union collapsed in the Chicago railroad strike of the next year, the precedent for industrial unionization was firmly established. The railroad labor disputes of this period also resulted in the formulation of the first procedures to mediate labor conflicts. In 1898 the Erdman Act provided for the mediation of railroad labor controversies by the chairman of the Interstate Commerce Commission and the commissioner of the Bureau of Labor.

CO-OPERATION FOR BETTER SERVICE

The substantial network of lines on a railroad map of the United States in 1865 did not mean that a railroad system existed which would permit shipment of goods between any two points without reloading. Because of competitive pressures and the lack of central planning, most roads jealously guarded their own traffic by such methods as gauge differences and refusals to allow car interchange. To add to the difficulties of through traffic there was no standardization of coupling and braking equipment and no system of time zones. In one of many similar examples of short-sighted competitive tactics, the Erie adopted a six-foot gauge in order to discourage the diversion to Philadelphia of shipments intended for Hoboken. The additional cost of reloading a shipment on the cars of a competing road terminating in Philadelphia would presumably encourage the shipper to route his goods all the way over the Erie. In many cities the freight terminals of competing roads had no rail connections with each other, thus requiring through shipments to be hauled over the city streets for reloading. The lack of terminal connections necessitated heavy forwarding charges and an army of forwarding agents.

But after the Civil War the intensity of competition was mitigated somewhat by a desire to diminish operating costs and improve service by standardization of equipment and by facilitation of car interchange. "Fast" (i.e., "through") freight lines were formed—often by railroad presidents and directors—which built and operated cars with "compromise" wheels that could be adjusted to different gauges and thereby be used on nearly all railroads. But since the operation of these fast freight lines sometimes entailed a conflict of interest for the railroad executives interested in them, they were replaced by co-operative freight lines, which were really pools of cars contributed by member railroads. Offering through bills of lading, the lines significantly reduced the cost of shipments from the Midwest to east coast ports. The use of Pullman cars simultaneously improved service for passengers.

As tonnage statistics made it plain to railroad executives after 1865 that they had more to gain than lose by adopting standardized equipment and operating procedures, railroads with end-to-end connections began to adopt the same gauge. Without fanfare during the nineties all roads shifted to the four-foot eight and one-half inch standard. The adoption of the Janney car coupler and the Westinghouse air brake, after many years of experiments with competing devices, further advanced the movement toward standardization and greatly reduced the rate of accidents from operations and among trainmen. In 1883 the nation's railroads adopted standard time zones. Signaling and switching were also standardized during this period. By the century's end manual block signals to prevent rear-end collisions had been established on many up-to-date lines, and electrical systems were well into the development stage.

The desire for co-operation in operations, even in the midst of bitter competition for traffic, brought into existence several railroad agencies which took the lead in standardization of operations and equipment. The establishment of uniform specifications for rolling stock was undertaken by the Master Carbuilders' Association and the American Master Mechanics' Association, formed in 1867 and 1868 respectively. The time zones were devised by a General Time Convention called in 1883. In succeeding years the convention standardized signaling equipment and practices. In 1891 the convention became the American Railway Association, the supreme agency which made standard rules for all operations. Meantime railroad superintendents and ticket agents had established their own organizations in order to move toward uniform practices.

One of the most important bodies of this type was the Association of Railroad Accountants, which devised the interline waybilling system allowing the free interchange of cars. Until the seventies most companies were reluctant to allow their cars to come into the possession of other roads, despite agreements which may have been made, because cars were sometimes misused and usually were not returned promptly. This situation was partially responsible for the formation of the fast freight lines. But once these pools for cars were handled efficiently by the member roads it became apparent that no real obstacle prevented the expansion of free interchange to all railroad cars, under rules universally agreed to. By co-operative effort, the railroads were then able to keep track of their cars and have them kept in repair.

By the turn of the century railroad operations had assumed most of the characteristics which they have today. In every aspect of the manifold functions performed by the leading companies competition was giving way to co-operation. At the corporate level competition was being replaced by consolidation, as we shall see in the following chapter; but the groundwork for this movement was prepared by the co-operation in operations which had preceded it by a quarter of a century.

XXVI. From Competition to Consolidation

RAILROAD FINANCE

Finance was a more difficult problem for railroads than for most other contemporary businesses because railroads had such a high capital-output ratio—that is, they required such a large initial investment before any operations could be undertaken and a profit expected. Moreover, plans for expansion always entailed a renewed search for funds in capital markets. By contrast, manufacturing enterprises such as textile mills could be started on a small scale with a relatively modest investment, and could finance expansion partially at least by plowing back a portion of earnings. As we have seen, the first small railroads, operating in densely settled areas and over strategic routes which already carried a large volume of wagon or water traffic, were able to raise their capital from local businessmen who anticipated a speedy return on their investment or benefit to other enterprises in which they were interested. But as the roads pushed westward, available local capital decreased sharply while the roads' capital requirements mounted. Under these circumstances presidents were compelled to turn to eastern commercial centers for financing. Investors increasingly preferred the security and regular return from bonds rather than the participation in putative earnings offered by stock. Henceforth the investment quality of railroad stock, particularly of western roads, decreased markedly and it came to represent primarily a claim to profits presented to bond purchasers as a bonus in order to make bonds more attractive.

In the scramble to find new lures to attract investment which would at the same time limit the obligations incurred, the railroads issued several types of bonds. Debentures represented simple debt, unsecured by specific collateral. Income bonds gave their holders claims to interest only when the railroads earned it, and in this respect resembled preferred stock, except that the bonds carried no voting rights. Convertible bonds were attractive because, in the event that a railroad proved to be a money-maker, they allowed the bondholder to shift into stock at a relatively low figure and thus get a claim to dividends and to capital gains. Collateral trust bonds, issued in large volume after the eighties, were a device utilized to effect combinations. A railroad wishing to acquire control of another would issue the bonds and exchange them for a controlling interest in the other road's stock. The stock would then be held as collateral for the bonds by a trustee named by the controlling road and empowered to vote the stock. Combination by collateral trust was often considered better than by lease because it was accomplished without an outlay of cash and allowed the purchasing road to hypothecate the purchased road's property. First mortgage bonds, because of their security and relatively high rates of interest, played an important part in stimulating foreign investment. Their attractiveness was even further enhanced because they were often accompanied by stock bonuses and could be bought at a discount, thus giving a return even higher than called for by the bond contract. By 1887 one-half of all new securities listed on the New York Stock Exchange—and a majority of these were rail issues—were also listed on the London Exchange. By 1890 foreigners had contributed about one quarter of the nation's railroad capital.

As the scale of financial operations mounted and the types of securities increased, the profits from railroad financeering rose proportionally. The career of Jay Cooke, the first great railroad financier, revealed the profit potentialities as well as the pitfalls of such undertakings. In addition to being able to pocket any surplus from Northern Pacific bond sales above the contract price of eighty-eight, he was also to receive as a bonus three-fifths of the stock issued by the road which he could keep for himself or use as a sweetener for the bonds. Cooke was also given one-half of the stock in a land company associated with the railroad. Obviously if things had turned out well Cooke stood to make a very large fortune.

The building of the transcontinental roads by "construction companies" proved to be an attractive method of finance because these organizations concentrated control of the financeering operations, construction, and the affairs of the railroad companies in the same hands. The most notorious of the companies was the Credit Mobilier of America, formed by the promoters of the Union Pacific for the purpose of building the railroad. The construction company was paid for its services in Union Pacific bonds and stock. Since the bonds could be sold only at a discount—sometimes as high as 75 percent—the company compensated for the inevitable loss by overcharging the railroad for its services. But in the long run the overcharging was carried to the point that the Credit Mobilier absorbed most of the stock and bonds of the Union Pacific, making a profit on building the road of between $13 million and $16.5 million. Although the Credit Mobilier became a symbol of corruption and although the other construction companies were equally tainted, Robert W. Fogel, who has closely studied the finances of the company, concludes that without the special profit inducements held out to investors, transcontinental railroads would have been difficult, if not impossible to build in the period immediately following the Civil War. Corruption and inflated construction costs were part of the price paid for accelerated construction schedules.

The desire to build railroads quickly, and the many possibilities of profit from financeering led to progressive watering of railroad stock—that is, "increase in the nominal capitalization without a commensurate additional investment of funds." The stock dividend became a favorite method of reaching this objective. By this means, the Erie increased its share capital from $17 million to $78 million between 1868 and 1872. Many competitive and operating practices led to overcapitalization. Extravagant building costs, mergers, and the buying of unnecessary feeder or "blackmail" roads at inflated prices often led to the same result. In a classic "blackmail" operation, Jay Gould in 1880 pressured the Union Pacific into buying a large holding of Kansas Pacific stock by threatening to extend the Kansas Pacific westward parallel to the Union Pacific. Since such "blackmail roads" were always poor money-makers, their acquisition eroded the operating profits of their purchasers. Hiding a poor performance record by paying for maintenance out of capital, or carrying maintenance charges as construction costs also required increased capitalization. Payment of dividends out of capital, the sale of securities at a discount, and the issue of stock bonuses to promote bond sales further inflated capital structures. The need to hide embarrassingly high earnings which would promote public demands for rate decreases led some very prosperous roads—notably the New York Central—to water stock as a means of avoiding a rise in the dividend rate.

Stock watering combined with "working roads up" or "down," could bring a handsome fortune. As used by Jay Gould, for instance, the technique consisted, first, of acquiring a weak road at a nominal price, which was easy to do because of the low stock prices and low proportion of stock to bonded capital characteristic of these roads. Then, by making a few highly advertised improvements in the line, by doctoring the books to show fictitious profits, and by paying high dividends out of capital, the price of the stock could be worked upward in the market. Meanwhile the insiders conducting the operation would quietly unload their holdings. When the true state of the road became known—sometimes by covert leaking of information by the manipulators themselves—the price of the stock would break and the insiders could make a second fortune by selling short as the shares plunged to their original level.

Appraisals of the amount of water in railroad securities varied, mainly because of the difficulty of estimating reasonable costs for railroad construction. Henry V. Poor, the noted railroad statistician, declared in 1884 that one-half of the current railroad capitalization was water. Another noted authority, Arthur R. Hadley, felt that one-half of all railroad stock and one-sixth of railroad bonds represented water. Returns on railroad securities certainly reflected a soggy condition. In 1891 bonds paid on an average 4.4 percent per year and stock 1.8 percent. Yet it should be noted that these returns were high in terms of actual investment. Most bonds were marketed at discounts of up to 35 percent, and so much stock was given away that it represented in the aggregate an investment of perhaps no more than ten cents on the dollar. This consideration led a leading critic of railroad practices, William Larrabee, to estimate that despite the low returns on stated capitalization the railroads were earning about 8 percent on their actual investment. Undoubtedly there was some justice to his contention, because unless railroads earned more than 5 percent, investment in them, particularly from abroad, would have slowed appreciably. Actually, the great number of fluctuating cost factors in railroad construction and operation precluded any agreement on the extent of watering. Poor estimated that the nation's railroads were capitalized at an average of about $63,000 per mile, about twice a reasonable cost figure for construction. Still, it should be kept in mind that this figure was about one-half of the cost of German and one-fourth the cost of British construction. Arthur T. Hadley may well have been correct when he insisted that regardless of the water in railroad securities the railroad network could not have been reproduced in the 1880s for the stated capitalization of all roads at that time.

RAILROAD RATES AND COMPETITION

As the recipients consecutively of unparalleled public assistance and unparalleled public abuse, the railroads were unique among American businesses. In some measure both types of attention were excessive. During the boom period from the end of the Civil War until 1873, critics usually concentrated on the railroads' reckless and often fraudulent financeering. After the Panic of 1873, however, when prices fell faster than railroad rates, the gravamen of indictment was shifted to discriminations against places and persons. In the intense competition to capture through traffic, railroads often bid down the rates for long hauls to below cost and made what profits they could by proportionally raising the rates on short, noncompetitive hauls. Examples of this practice were legion. According to one complaint, "It cost $130 to ship a carload of wheat within the state of Iowa over the same road that took the same wheat from the same point of shipment to Chicago at half the price." Charges on the twenty-one mile line from Los Angeles to the port of San Pedro amounted to half as much as those for a five- to seven-month journey by sea to Europe or Asia.

Personal discrimination appeared to be an equally glaring evil. Large shippers were usually allowed secret rebates which gave them such a price advantage in the market that they could drive less favored small competitors to the wall. Free passes, given to persons in positions of authority, were considered an insidious method by which railroads attempted to build up the political influence to subvert courts and stifle legislation designed to reform competitive practices. In the Midwest during the 1870s it was estimated that as many as one-half of the passengers on trains rode on free passes.

It was also charged that the railroads used more direct methods in politics such as lobbying, and even bribery, as the means of maintaining their exploitative practices. Actually, the fact that the railroads were common carriers and operated under charters tended to draw them into politics, but in states where one railroad was predominant, it sometimes became virtually a third house of the legislature. New Jersey as early as the 1840s was called the Camden and Amboy state. It was no secret in California that all legislative decisions regarding the Southern Pacific monopoly came ultimately from the company's offices at Fourth and Townshend Streets in Sacramento.

Defenders of the railroads replied to the indictment drawn against them by pointing to a fall in freight rates from an average of 1.9 cents per ton mile in 1867 to .8 cents in 1896—a drop of 58 percent in thirty years. During the same period freight revenue per ton mile fell from nineteen mills to a shade over seven mills. To counter the charges of profiteering railroad management cited the low returns on railroad securities. Free passes, they insisted, were exacted from them by influential politicians; combinations among shippers, playing railroads off against each other, forced carriers to grant secret rebates. Political influence, defenders declared, was necessary in order to protect railroad interests against raids by unprincipled politicians. Critics, armed with rebuttals, charged that the low return on railroad securities was the result of stock watering and other shady financial practices, and that returns on cash investments were high enough to justify even further reductions in rates.

Actually there is something to be said on both sides, and the defense put up by the railroads is not as disingenuous as it might first appear. Heavy charges for debt service and maintenance remained constant regardless of the volume of traffic, and even operating costs were not greatly affected by traffic fluctuations since train schedules were kept at a fairly constant level. Therefore in flush times railroads benefited from "the law of increasing returns" because traffic could be greatly expanded with existing facilities and without proportionally increasing costs. But in hard times as traffic fell off, sticky costs drove railroads quickly into the red. Under these circumstances management during the nineteenth century desperately tried to maintain a level of revenue adequate to meet fixed costs by lowering rates in the hope of attracting enough traffic from competitors to compensate for the lower unit profit from operations. The ability to handle an increased volume of traffic was utilized as an offset to inflexible costs. At competing points rates were forced down to the level at which goods in transit merely paid their part of the overhead, or even below. Any profit from operations, therefore, had to be made at noncompeting points. If shippers here complained of high rates, railroad apologists insisted that it was the effect of competition and not railroad policy which brought about this unfortunate situation. Users simply had the choice of purchasing transportation at the rates set by operation of market conditions or having no transportation at all. As Charles Francis Adams pointed out, among railroads competition *necessarily* created discrimination.

Railroad leaders defended the rate policy of charging what the traffic would bear as vigorously as they rebutted the charges of extortion based on discrimination against places. First, they insisted that it was the only practical way to set rates. Basing rates on cost of service, as called for by many critics of railroad practices, would be impossible because the cost of shipping any particular article in a train, and handling it in terminals, simply could not be segregated from other costs. Furthermore, railroad men pointed out, density of traffic, cost of construction, distance of shipment, and many other variables would make uniform cost figures for a large geographical area, or even for an individual road, impossible to obtain. Such factors as bulk, weight, perishability, fragility, and risk were of some importance in setting rates, and were reflected in all rate structures. But by themselves they were inadequate criteria. Any rate reasonable for drygoods would impose transportation charges on coal so high that it could not afford rail transportation at all. Conversely, drygoods would ride practically free on a rate suitable for coal. If coal and drygoods were both to move by rail, obviously they must have different rates.

Under these circumstances railroad management insisted that value of articles carried must be the major factor in rate determination. Charges obviously should be higher for expensive items, sold with a large profit margin, than for cheap, heavy goods. By a process of bargaining between producers and carriers rates would be determined by what shippers could afford to pay. This was the meaning of charging what the traffic would bear. When critics insisted that under this system the consumers of relatively expensive goods were subsidizing the transportation of cheap commodities, apologists for the railroads admitted that this was true, and they added that only by this method of ratemaking could the heavy commodities so vital to the nation's economy afford railroad transportation.

Time has vindicated the logic used to defend the traditional method of ratemaking, and rates today are established mainly on this basis. The hundreds of thousands of articles carried by railroads are grouped into five or six classes and rates are assigned proportionate to the value of the goods contained in the classes. Commodities such as coal, ore, and sand are given commodity rates much lower than the classified rates. Before 1887 nearly every railroad devised its own system of classification. The growing disposition of the railroads to suppress rate competition and provide uniform service led during the succeeding years to the adoption of regional classifications. Rates were set by committees in which all roads were represented and were binding upon all roads. By 1906 the nation was divided into three classification zones: the Official, covering the area east of the Mississippi and north of the Ohio and Potomac; the Southern; and the Western. The "Official" acquired its name because trunk line rates between New York and Chicago tended to set a standard by which rates were calculated elsewhere. Rates in the South and West were higher than in the official zone because of a variety of reasons including lighter traffic and fewer backhauls.

THE SUPPRESSION OF COMPETITION

Competition produced a sharp ambivalence of attitude on the part of the railroads. In rate wars they struggled fiercely to snatch each others' traffic, even at the expense of endangering their own solvency. The spoils of victory were certainly tempting. Competitors forced to their knees could be acquired cheaply and consolidated with the parent road, thus bringing economies of operation and a strengthening of monopoly position. But in practice rate wars were seldom so decisive, and usually ended in a standoff which left all participants exhausted. Chastened, longing for a peaceful coexistence, railway management then tried to curb competition by rate agreements and pools. But these devices bred their own dissatisfactions. Soon the wars began again, thus inaugurating another cycle of competition and the suppression of competition.

Pools eliminated rate competition by three methods. Traffic pools divided business among participants by agreement. Money pools distributed the aggregate net revenue of participating roads on a similar basis. A third type of pool divided fields of operation or business according to its nature. All pools held within them the seeds of their own destruction. Since pooling contracts were plainly designed to suppress competition they were not enforceable at common law. Also, since the last railroad into a pool and the first one out got a temporary advantage, formation was slow and dissolution fast. Finally, aggressive, expanding roads soon became dissatisfied with their quotas and were always tempted to break pools in the hope of laying claim to a quota increase in the wild melee of competition which followed.

Appearing first among stage and steamboat lines, pooling was occasionally practiced by railroads in temporary and informal fashion during the fifties and sixties. The first pool of any permanence, a revenue pool, was established in 1870 by three Granger roads—the Burlington, the Chicago and Northwestern, and the Rock Island—all of which paralleled each other and had common terminal points at Chicago and at Council Bluffs, terminus for the Union Pacific.

Serious efforts to limit competition in eastern trunk line territory did not come until after the Panic of 1873 when the carriers by desperate rate cutting tried to increase their respective shares of the rapidly diminishing western trade. At one time during this period cattle rolled from Chicago to New York at a dollar a carload, wheat paid a rate of ten cents per hundredweight, and a passenger ticket for the trip cost only $13. In 1874 losses from the rate wars became so serious that representatives of the trunk lines held a much publicized conference at Saratoga, where Commodore Vanderbilt was spending the summer, to explore the possibilities of a peace treaty.

The fact that much of the traffic from Chicago was in commodities bound ultimately for Europe posed a sticky problem. Management of the Pennsylvania and the B. and O. insisted that equality of charges over the entire distance should be the objective of any agreement, and they therefore desired somewhat lower railroad rates than roads entering New York and Boston in order to compensate for heavier ocean transportation charges paid by freight leaving for Europe from Philadelphia and Baltimore. New York and Boston merchants opposed abandoning the cherished commercial advantage of rock-bottom ocean rates. Nevertheless, in the next year the Central reluctantly gave way and agreed to a reduction from the New York-Chicago rate of 10 percent for Philadelphia and 12 percent for Baltimore. Percentages deducted from standard rates in this manner were called "differentials." Although interrupted periodically by rate wars, the agreement reached by the trunk lines was generally adhered to during the eighties.

Differentials did not create pools. Participating railroads were still free to get as much business as possible by any means that suited them. In order to achieve a more satisfactory suppression of competition than could be granted by rate agreements alone the Southern Railroad and Steamship Association, under the leadership of Albert Fink, a former vice-president of the Louisville and Nashville, worked out a more elaborate pooling scheme than any currently in force. By his plan the association formed a pool in 1875 which allotted traffic at competing points in accordance with the volume carried by participating roads under normal conditions. But each road was free to solicit more traffic on the condition that it hand over surpluses to other members of the pool who might have a deficit. Each year the quotas were revised to correspond to any increases or decreases of traffic on the roads during the previous twelve months, thus allowing a large measure of competition within the framework of quotas and agreed rates. The Southern Railroad and Steamship pool was so successful that at the request of the eastern trunk lines Fink formed a similar organization to regulate their westbound traffic. An attempt to form a gigantic pool for eastbound traffic failed, but by the mid-eighties so many regional organizations in trunk line territory and in the Midwest were in existence that traffic was pooled at nearly all competitive points.

Since its inception pooling had caused a protracted public debate. Critics charged that the device was a simple conspiracy whereby member roads exacted monopoly profits from the areas they covered. Railroad spokesmen almost unanimously defended the practice with several substantial arguments. First, they pointed out that pools did not necessarily raise rates; they only prevented their fall from normal levels. Shippers were deprived of nothing, therefore, except the ability to exploit railroads during competitive crises. Also, by enabling railroads to avoid losses at competitive points, pools made possible the reduction of discrimination against noncompetitive points. As organized by Fink, pools did not in the long run suppress competition. Finally, pooling removed much of the pressure for combination. Protected by voluntary agreements, participating roads did not feel compelled to suppress damaging competition by absorbing their competitors. Throughout the debate railroad spokesmen tried desperately to make clear that competition and not malevolence and greed was the cause of railroad "abuses." Pooling, therefore, offered a promising avenue toward reform.

RAILROAD REORGANIZATION AND CONSOLIDATION

The combination of high fixed charges from inflated bonded indebtedness, reckless expansion, and lowered revenues brought about by rate wars and other competitive practices forced railroads by the score into bankruptcy during every business recession from 1857 onward. During the four years following the Panic of 1893 no less than 40,000 miles of road representing one-fourth of railroad capitalization fell into the hands of receivers. Since a railroad was a fixed installation which could be broken up and sold to satisfy creditors only at a great loss, receivership necessarily entailed the scaling down of financial obligations to the point where they could be met from normal operating revenues. Railroad creditors were always forced to accept half a cake or no cake at all.

The first step in reorganization, after a court had appointed a receiver to continue operations of a road, was the selection of bondholders' committees to represent the holders of the various classes of securities. Since new securities would have to be issued, large investment banking firms were retained to conduct the reorganization, and in the process usually achieved policy control. All classes of securities were forced to compromise their claims, but losses fell heaviest on the holders of the junior securities—common and preferred stock, income bonds, and debentures. Fewer sacrifices were demanded from the holders of senior securities—mainly mortgage bonds—on the ground that these were acquired at higher prices than junior securities. In the final arrangement the existing 6, 7, or 8 percent bonds would be surrendered in return for new bonds bearing a lower rate of interest. Common stockholders, who had very little claim to consideration, were usually assessed from $10 to $20 per share for the privilege of participating in any future earnings. Fixed costs would be further reduced by forcing leased roads to reduce their rentals or lowering the dividends formerly guaranteed to them by the road undergoing reorganization.

Reorganizations undertaken between 1893 and 1898 nearly always reduced fixed costs—sometimes by as much as 50 percent—but did not necessarily reduce capitalization. Since security holders almost invariably wanted claims upon future earnings in order to compensate for their losses, they demanded, and received, new bonuses of common and preferred stock accompanying their bonds. Also, bankers who engineered reorganizations took most of their fees in stock and multiplied their reward by working the stock upward in the post-depression market.

We have seen (p. 300) how J. P. Morgan became a towering figure in the railroad world by presiding over the reorganization process. During the late nineties other bankers such as Edward H. Harriman and banking groups allied with railroad leaders of field rank, seeking to stifle the destructive competition which they believed had been responsible for the debacle of 1893–94, embarked on a vast plan of consolidation and the creation of communities of interest. By the time it was completed six major interests controlled 85 percent of the railroad earnings of the country. The Morgan-Vanderbilt-Pennsylvania group controlled almost every road of importance from the Atlantic coast to Chicago. In the South the Southern and the Atlantic Coast Line dominated the field. In the states of the Old Northwest the Pennsylvania and Vanderbilt lines, with their numerous appendages, were in control. Hill and Morgan dominated the trans-Mississippi Northwest, and Harriman's Illinois Central–Union Pacific–Southern Pacific group occupied a wide area adjacent. The Southwest was dominated by the Gould lines and the Rock Island.

RESTRICTIVE LEGISLATION

Critics of railroads might agree with railroad spokesmen on the diagnosis of "abuses," but they differed on the therapy to be applied. From the early seventies onward public demands for governmental regulation of competitive practices increased in intensity. To many observers the New England railroad commissions, in existence since the fifties, were promising vehicles of reform. The most notable of these was the Massachusetts Commission, which had been headed by the great-grandson of the second president of the United States, the widely respected Charles Francis Adams. His meticulous investigations and well-written, voluminous reports not only publicized abuses but also contained recommendations for the improvement of operations and services which were valuable to the railroads themselves. Since the stock of New England railroads was for the most part held locally and widely distributed, public opinion alone was usually sufficient to force management to undertake reforms. But in the West the commission method was felt to be quite inadequate. Railroads there were owned primarily by eastern capitalists who were considered to be indifferent to the plight of shippers. Farmers, dependent upon the roads for storage, grading, and sale of staple crops as well as for transportation, were more completely at their mercy.

The response of western states to railroad abuses was the direct government regulation contained in the Granger Laws, passed between 1871 and 1874 by the legislatures of Illinois, Iowa, Wisconsin, and Minnesota. Among other restrictions these enactments set maximum rates, provided commissions to enforce rate decisions, prohibited the charging of an equal or greater rate for a short haul than for a long haul, forbade the combination of competing lines, and prohibited personal discrimination and the granting of free passes to public officials. Railroad interests protested against the laws on grounds of policy and principle. Most railroad administrators professed gratitude that secret rebates and free passes had been abolished, but they felt that being subjected to frozen rates in an economy of fluctuating prices endangered their financial stability. Furthermore, they were certain that no public body could intelligently make the thousands of decisions, formerly the subject of multifarious bargaining, which ratemaking required. They also objected to the short and long haul clause on the ground that there was no necessary relation between distance traveled and railroad costs. Short hauls involving handling in terminals could be more costly than long hauls. In the matter of principle the roads contended that as corporate entities they fell under the protection of the Fourteenth Amendment. State laws which lowered rates depressed the value of railroad properties by decreasing earnings. Therefore, the railroads felt they were being deprived of property without due process of law.

The dispute over constitutionality was settled when the Supreme Court in the Granger cases upheld state regulatory legislation. In Munn vs. Illinois (1877), the Court bypassed the railroads' claims to protection under the Fourteenth Amendment, however, and instead rested the decision on the historic right of public authority to regulate common carriers.

Meanwhile, proposals for railroad legislation had been laid before Congress. Over the next decade, in response to mounting public pressure, both House and Senate worked out somewhat differing programs of government regulation. Matters were brought to a head by the Wabash Case of 1886 in which the Supreme Court partially reversed Munn *vs.* Illinois by denying states the right to regulate railroads engaged in interstate commerce. Since three-fourths of the western lines were in this category, obviously railroad regulation was now the province of federal rather than state government. The Interstate Commerce Act, passed in 1887, represented a compromise between the House and Senate programs of regulation. This notable piece of legislation required rates to be "just and reasonable," prohibited pooling and covert discrimination such as rebates, forbade "undue or unreasonable preference" in the normal railroad policies connected with competition, and contained a short and long haul clause. The bill also brought into existence the Interstate Commerce Commission, which was charged with supervision of the act. The commission did not have the power to fix rates, although it could order a carrier to abandon a given rate on the ground that it was unreasonable.

Railroad spokesmen were gratified that Congress had recognized the inability of any public body to carry out the enormous task of ratemaking. They also approved the prohibition of rebates. Although they doubted the wisdom of the general clause dealing with discrimination and the short and long haul clause, they recognized that the wording could be so construed as to leave their normal practices practically unaffected. Their strongest objection was to the prohibition of pooling. Many leading railroad economists had come to feel that pooling under government supervision offered the best hope for reform of railroad practices because it would remove the basic cause of railroad abuses—competition.

During the four or five years following the Interstate Commerce Act the railroads made a generally sincere attempt to abide by its provisions, although they tended to hold themselves aloof from the Interstate Commission and preferred to deal directly with the courts. Pools were dissolved and their places taken by "traffic associations" which set rates in much the same manner as had the Eastern Trunkline Association. Railroad men considered these organizations to be entirely within the law, and the Interstate Commerce Commission did not interfere with them as long as the rates they set were reasonable. Rate agreements had come to be indispensable for through service quite apart from any effect they might have had in suppressing competition. But the Supreme Court in the Trans-Missouri Freight Association Case of 1897 declared that all such organizations were combinations in restraint of trade prohibited by the Sherman Antitrust Act of 1890. Thus, the railroads were thrown back into the maelstrom of unlimited competition.

Seen in perspective, the effectiveness of regulation was uniformly compromised by the failure of state legislatures, Congress, and the Supreme Court to recognize that competition could be a dangerous and destructive process for railroads. The chairman of the Interstate Commerce Committee, commenting on the Trans-Missouri case, described well the dilemma in which this decision placed the railroads: "I regard the existing law as presenting this singular anomaly that it seeks to enforce competition by the mandate of the statute, and at the same time punish as criminal misdemeanors the acts and inducements by which competition is ordinarily effected." The immediate effect of the court decisions was an even greater anomaly—the stimulation of combination. Since public authority would not, and could not under existing laws and judicial decisions, provide leadership for railroads in solving their problems, they had to turn to bankers. There were of course many other inducements to combination, but to many railroad men it seemed to be the only course of safety when the federal government treated as punishable offenses activities rendered inevitable by its legislation and judicial decisions.

XXVII. Railroad Leaders

Railroad leadership attracted bold and aggressive men because, as a dynamic, expanding, hotly competitive business, it combined high financial rewards with strong challenges and placed a premium on both managerial and entrepreneurial skills. Progress up the ladder of success could be very fast for the talented and energetic, but the risks of failure were also great. As Richard C. Overton has written, "the railroad business between 1859 and 1907 was a rugged affair no matter how you looked at it. . . . Compared with industry today it was virtually devoid of security for anybody at any level." The railroad leader conducted his affairs with scant attention to the effects of his actions upon society at large. Again to quote Overton:

Quite naturally—as the first law of survival—railroad leaders sought first and foremost to fulfill the primary demand. The only effective limits on the way they did it were their own ideas of what was good for their business, and what the community would put up with, and what their individual consciences would tolerate. As [Thomas C.] Cochran points out so brilliantly, business ethics and mores did tend to crystallize as time went on, but this, I am sure he would agree, was necessarily a painfully slow process. In the meantime the prudent, far-seeing financier (and indeed there were some) had to compete all too often with the shyster and the outright crook; the efficient operator mindful of maintaining his plant and rolling stock had to match performances with the man who was willing to abuse his equipment and compromise with safety for a momentary advantage. The traffic man devoted to developing a stable market and dependable service was forever beset not only by competitors who would cut rates ruinously regardless of ultimate consequences, but by cold blooded shippers demanding special favors. A just employer might find his labor costs higher than his less scrupulous neighbor. The honorable man, to put it bluntly, had precious few safeguards, either legal or customary for his honor.

The railroad titans, who by virtue of their position seemed most capable of mastering this type of environment, were probably the best known, but not necessarily the most admired businessmen in the nation. Anecdote and folklore have invested them with the stereotyped characteristics of success, but even a cursory examination indicates that the celebrities among them shared few personality traits in common. Commodore Vanderbilt, as previously noted, was zestful, outgoing, courageous, vulgar, and somewhat vain. Jay Gould, the only opponent who ever bested him in a major contest, was by contrast retiring, secretive, and timid. James J. Hill—direct, forceful, sometimes overbearing—retained through life the earthy legacy of a youth spent as a farm hand and dock worker. Edward H. Harriman, by contrast, soon shed the naïveté of the country boy, and by his early twenties had acquired the dapper appearance, sparkling conversation, and sophistication of the clubman and social leader. Charles Crocker, who tipped the scales at 250 pounds, was boastful, stubborn, and tactless. His partner, skinny "Uncle" Mark Hopkins, practiced rigorous asceticism, reticence, and caution. Slow-thinking, slow-speaking £eland $tanford—by Ambrose Bierce's orthography—harbored illusions of grandeur. But according to one critic, he combined "the ambition of an emperor with the spite of a peanut vender." Collis P. Huntington, a compulsive worker indifferent to abuse or popularity, excited little admiration from those who knew him well. One acquaintance described him as "a hard and cheery old man with no more soul than a shark." Another capsulated this description with the comment that Huntington was "scrupulously dishonest." By contrast, Charles Elliott Perkins—so shy that he "shunned publicity like the plague"—had such a meticulous sense of honor that at a cost to himself over a period of years of from $500,000 to $750,000 he kept an insolvent bank alive because many depositors had left their money there only because they knew he was a director.

Such evaluations as those of "The Big Four" should be accepted with caution. Under sharply competitive conditions the making of a fortune necessarily entails the making of many enemies. Probably whatever faults Huntington and Stanford had would have been less noticed in men of modest means.

The qualities usually considered necessary for success were not present in any uniform configuration in the men considered above. Only Huntington and Perkins made a fetish of hard work or gave the sententious endorsement to the prudential virtues so often expected from successful men. Only Hill, Harriman, and Huntington were interested in administration. Vanderbilt, as previously noted, left this aspect of his business to subordinates, and Gould was a conspicuous failure in this regard. Yet all were energetic, with the vision to see opportunities and the perserverence to make the most of them. What most attracted railroad leaders were the opportunities for expansion and combination. Reaching these objectives represented creative, satisfying performance for them much more than technological or administrative innovation, or improvement of service. A few biographical sketches will illustrate the point.

COMMODORE VANDERBILT

Commodore Vanderbilt, although certainly not the first man to make a fortune out of railroads, was among the first to adopt the pattern of behavior which became associated with the railroad moguls. The meager returns from his ocean steamships and the dislocation of ocean traffic brought about by the Civil War induced him to sell his fleet and transfer his capital into more profitable transportation enterprises on dry land. In 1857, because of a large loan he had made to the wobbly New York and Harlem, he was made president of the road, and thereby began the career which led him from New York up the Hudson to the presidency of the New York Central. The Harlem was potentially valuable because it occupied the best entrance to Manhattan from the North and East— for the use of which the New York and New Haven paid handsomely— and held a valuable franchise to run cars between this entrance and Union Square, near City Hall in what was then central New York City.

Vanderbilt's interest in the Harlem led him to invest in the Hudson River Railway between New York and Albany, which, because it carried during the winter the freight and passengers which normally traveled on the river, had good prospects of profit. After a Wall Street skirmish in which he cornered the stock and sheared the shorts, he and a group of associates began improving the route and physical property of the road. Possibly the Commodore had his eye on the Central; in any event a series of circumstances which he brilliantly exploited delivered it into his hands. The Central regularly paid the Hudson River road a bonus of $100,000 per year for carrying its freight and passengers between New York and Albany during the winter. As a result of a series of disagreements between the two lines and pressure from steamboat interests, the Central abruptly suspended the subsidy in January, 1867. Vanderbilt in retaliation refused to accept the freight or through tickets of the Central at Albany. Since there was no alternative outlet for the Central, freight piled up in the terminal, and amid a growing public outcry passengers were compelled to trudge across the frozen river to entrain for New York. Management of the Central, afraid that the line would lose a large share of its trunkline business to its southern competitor, the Erie, capitulated and made an accommodation satisfactory to Vanderbilt. Public indignation resulted in an investigation of the incident by the legislature. When asked why he did not resort to the law to enforce any claim he might have had against the Central rather than choosing a remedy which caused inconvenience and loss to the public, Vanderbilt gave a characteristic reply: "The law, as I view it, goes too slow for me when I have the remedy in my own hands."

The skill with which the Commodore—then 73 years old—had utilized the strategic possibilities of the Hudson River road made a deep impression upon the business community of New York and Albany. At the annual meeting of the Central's board in December, 1867, he won the full fruits of victory by being elected president.

The combined Hudson River and New York Central now had a through route from New York City to Buffalo, but the Erie remained a potentially dangerous competitor for western traffic. The Commodore attempted to gain control of the road by the same method which had worked well in the previous battles—by quickly cornering the stock and driving the shorts to the wall. But Jay Gould and Jim Fiske, leaders of the Erie, frustrated the scheme by issuing convertible bonds previously authorized by the directors, which, when converted by purchasers, created more stock than Vanderbilt could buy. Consequently the attempted corner failed and he did not gain control of the Erie. If the Commodore had won, he not only would have monopolized the carriage of New York's western rail traffic, but through his possession of the Harlem's entrance into Manhattan would have exerted a considerable control over the traffic with New England as well.

Vanderbilt was more successful, however, in gaining a route to the Midwest. When the stock of the Lake Shore and the Michigan Southern declined precipitantly during the Black Friday Panic of 1869, he borrowed $10 million from Baring Brothers on his holdings in the Central and secured control of the road. At about the same time he bought a heavy interest in the competing Michigan Central. The last years of his life were spent not only in expanding his railroad investments but in improving the physical properties of his roads. Yet his ability to effect combinations was the secret of his success.

JAY GOULD

The timid, melancholy, conniving Jay Gould was personally the antithesis of the jovial, bellicose Commodore Vanderbilt. Clerking in a country store constituted most of Gould's rudimentary education. At the age of sixteen he came to New York, his mind teeming with projects for a quick fortune. He entered the railroad business by forming a syndicate which bought a small bankrupt road in Vermont, reorganized it, and sold it at a profit.

Gould was brought into the Erie by Daniel Drew, erstwhile drover, who had become a director and had gained great influence in the company by lending it a large sum of money. Following the victory over Vanderbilt in the Erie War, Gould expanded his influence in the Erie and managed to ruin and oust Drew by trapping him in one of Drew's many bear raids against Erie stock. While the physical condition of the road declined, Gould and a ring of associates ran up the debt, printed stock, and used the treasury for a wide range of speculations not only in railroads, but in coal lands, ferries, and harbor rights. Always he kept the political climate favorable by continuous bribery. Gould was finally ousted from the Erie by a "reform" group which used Gould's own corrupt methods against him. The Erie had been so thoroughly looted that a generation was to pass before the road was back on its feet. Gould's total profit from his years as president was estimated at $12 million.

Moving into western roads, Gould refined the techniques whereby railroad treasuries could be used as instruments for stock market speculations, blackmail of other roads, or for fleecing investors. He also acquired large interests in many other diverse and valuable properties, among them Western Union Telegraph (see p. 485), Pacific Mail Steamship Company, and the Manhattan Elevated Railroad. By 1881 the value of properties controlled by Gould was about $260 million, and his annual income in 1890, the year before he died, was about $10 million.

In contrast to Vanderbilt, Gould had no interest in improving service on the roads. Almost without exception they were poorly built and worse maintained. After he was through with them their financial structures were so thoroughly compromised that they suffered continual reverses during depressions. Gould owed his initial success to an almost uncanny ability to plan and execute complicated financial maneuvers centering in the stock market. By his own account his basic motivation was classically entrepreneurial. Speaking on one occasion about his sensational exploits with the Missouri Pacific Railroad, he said: "I did not care at that time about the mere making of money. It was more to show that I could make a combination and make it a success."

JAMES J. HILL

James J. Hill was in almost every respect a different kind of railroad entrepreneur than Jay Gould. An ox of a man, blind in one eye, with huge shoulders and tiny short legs, he sometimes swung a pick at the head of a construction gang with as much enthusiasm as he collected money and materials for his railroad and threatened prospective competitors with ruin. His career began when in company with Donald Smith, commissioner of the Hudson Bay Company, and George Stephen, president of the Bank of Montreal, he bought from receivers the unfinished St. Paul and Pacific Railroad. The road's physical properties were almost worthless, but it had a very valuable offer of a land grant spanning Minnesota from St. Paul to the Red River and following the rich river valley north to the Canadian border. After completing the road to a junction with the Canadian Pacific in 1879, Hill began construction of a second road westward through North Dakota which eventually became the Great Northern.

As previously noted, Hill owed his success mainly to his ability to locate roads in potentially productive areas, construct them for economical operation at minimum cost, and create traffic. His entrepreneurial talent, therefore, lay not so much in ability to combine units of transportation, as with Vanderbilt or Gould, but in the capacity to stimulate agricultural and extractive production and combine these with transportation.

HENRY VILLARD

Hill had for a time a competitor to the South, Henry Villard, who came to grief primarily because of disregard for the economics of railroad transportation combined with unbounded faith in the power of financial maneuvers to overcome all obstacles. A man of broad culture who had come to the United States at nineteen years of age from Germany and had traveled over the West as a correspondent for German newspapers, he became financial agent for groups of German bondholders in the early 1870s. Fascinated by what he considered to be the boundless opportunities of the Pacific Northwest, he acquired for himself and his backers the Oregon Steam Navigation Company, which was designed to serve as a nucleus of what would eventually become a monopoly of rail and steamship transportation in the area.

Everything seemed to be going well for the projected combination until November, 1880, when Villard heard that the revived Northern Pacific was prepared to renew its march toward Puget Sound. Hastening to New York to head off the interloper, Villard persuaded moneyed friends and associates to subscribe $8 million to a "blind pool" which would be used for a secret but highly profitable purpose. Incredible as it seems today, the fund was actually oversubscribed. With the money Villard began a campaign to buy control of the Northern Pacific, and in a short time succeeded. Money poured in from investors dazzled at the breadth of Villard's vision, the adroitness of his financial manipulation, and the apparent infallibility of his judgment. Probably no businessman in America since Jay Cooke had enjoyed such an exalted reputation.

The completion of the Northern Pacific in 1883 was an event of national importance. With a sure eye for publicity Villard had arranged inaugural ceremonies more elaborate than any since the opening of the Erie Canal. Special trains crossed the nation bearing the great and near-great to watch the spectacle of driving the last spike. In Villard's own car were President Arthur, General Grant, and cabinet members. Viscount James Bryce, also in this company, was awed. "These railway kings," he wrote later in *The American Commonwealth*, "are among the greatest men, perhaps I may say the greatest, in America. . . ."

But despite the celebration, insiders knew that Villard's house of cards was about to collapse. High cost of construction, looting by the construction company, but worst of all, the failure of traffic to materialize despite the tremendous campaign to bring in settlers, had doomed the Northern Pacific in 1884 to its second bankruptcy in a decade. But, even with due allowance for the importance of these factors, perhaps the proximate cause of Villard's failure was poor timing. If he had undertaken his scheme twenty or perhaps even ten years later, it might have been successful. Hill, pacing his building by slowly mounting traffic potential, kept the Great Northern in flourishing condition but did not reach Pacific tidewater until 1893. As we shall see later, Edward H. Harriman started reconstructing the Union Pacific in 1897 in a venture apparently as daring and even more costly than Villard's undertaking. But time was on the side of Harriman. By the turn of the century the volume of exchange between the East and the Far West was great enough to justify large expenditures on a transcontinental railroad.

THE BIG FOUR

Hill represents what might be called a creative entrepreneur; Villard may have intended to perform this function, but was forced by the course of events into the position of exploitative entrepreneur. Characteristics of both types were combined in the Big Four—Huntington, Stanford, Hopkins, and Crocker—who built and monopolized the railroads of California. Huntington was the son of a tight-fisted Connecticut tinker; Stanford helped manage an inn owned by his family in upstate New York; Hopkins clerked in a country store; and Crocker started life as an Indiana farm boy. Footloose and ambitious, all were drawn to California by the manifold opportunities accompanying the gold rush. All four rejected the visionary temptations of placer mining and instead settled down to exploit the less spectacular but more substantial opportunities offered by trade.

Their attention was drawn to railroad enterprise by a somewhat eccentric engineer, Theodore Judah, who dreamed of a transcontinental railroad. After surveying a route across the Sierras Judah incorporated the Central Pacific Railroad Company as vehicle for the undertaking. At a meeting in the vacant room over the Sacramento hardware store of Huntington and Hopkins in 1860—which eventually loomed large in local folklore—he received promises of support from a group of merchants and professional men which included Huntington, Hopkins, Crocker, and Stanford. Judah ultimately succeeded in getting the Central Pacific designated as the western section of the transcontinental railroad envisaged in the Pacific Railroad Bill. At the outset funds were hard to raise, but when government largesse in the form of land grants and loans descended upon the company, money became no problem. The Big Four increased their investments, and after Judah's untimely death found themselves somewhat unwittingly thrust into the leadership of one of the greatest construction projects in history.

Crocker, a self-trained engineer, supervised the work. The labor problem appeared insuperable until the company began importing Chinese coolies by the thousands. Supplies were scarce and high priced, and getting them to the dispersed 12,000 man work force became a major problem. For five years the work went on, under the most difficult circumstances imaginable. But the Big Four were to reap a large reward. When the last spike was driven at Promontory Point in 1869 they were the major proprietors of an immensely valuable railroad which had been constructed almost entirely at government expense.

The Central Pacific was merely the springboard from which the Big Four, by now the center of a cohesive group of aggressive businessmen, went on to achieve a complete monopoly of railroad transportation in

California. The C.P. bought up all existing roads in the state, built the California and Oregon to the North and the San Joaquin Valley road to the South. The line later became a section of the Southern Pacific. They owned the steamship line connecting Sacramento and San Francisco, monopolized docking facilities at Oakland, and formed an ocean steamship line which competed with the Pacific Mail. For nearly every type of business in California the favor of the C.P.–S.P. meant success; its disapproval, ruin.

CHARLES FRANCIS ADAMS, JR.

With the exception of Villard, who was something of an exotic on the American business scene, all of the celebrated railroad leaders mentioned previously came from lower, or lower middle-class backgrounds, had little formal education, and were interested exclusively in entrepreneurial concerns. Again with the exception of Villard, all were successful insofar as the effecting of combinations and the accumulation of fortunes constitutes success. But Charles Francis Adams, Jr., a railroad leader of equal note, differed from the pattern set by these titans in almost every respect. In birth and lineage he came from the first rank of the social aristocracy. As a Harvard man he had as good a formal education as the nation offered. As an intellectual he wrote widely and well on a variety of subjects, particularly history. As a liberal reformer and student of railroads he gained an acute, and probably unique understanding of railroad problems. And yet, withal, as a practical railroad administrator he was a failure. His problem was that his background and moral purpose in no way fitted him for success in the competitive jungle which constituted the railroad world of his day. As a patrician, brought up in affluence, he lacked the almost animalistic sense of survival which characterized railroad leaders schooled in the environment of competition rather than Cambridge. Perhaps in part because of his background his judgments were sometimes rash and his optimism unfounded. He could chase after profit as enthusiastically as any of his humbler brethren and make the accommodations necessary in an era of lax business morality, but his patrician values robbed him of much of the gratification of victory, and a consciousness of betrayal made the pains of defeat all the keener.

Marriage into a wealthy family in 1865, plus a small inheritance, relieved Adams of the necessity of working for a living. Casting about for something to do, he determined to become "a philosopher of railroads." Characteristically, he had no desire to get into the bruising warfare of railroad operations at the corporate level, but wanted to become a specialist, observing, analyzing, and criticizing from the outside. He learned by "groping," according to his biographer, Edward C. Kirkland, and registered his progress in the form of articles on railroad problems and the brilliant essay, *A Chapter of Erie.* The latter was an exposé of the massive chicanery by which Gould, Drew, and Fiske frustrated Vanderbilt's attempt to seize the Erie Railroad. Becoming convinced that the jungle warfare of the railroads could only be brought to an end by placing their operations under public scrutiny and legislative supervision, Adams strongly advocated the appointment of a railroad commission with power to investigate, issue reports, and suggest legislation. Such a proposal coming from an Adams commanded attention. In 1869, the year in which *A Chapter of Erie* appeared, the Massachusetts legislature established a Board of Railroad Commissioners, and in 1872 the governor appointed Charles Francis chairman.

In his position as superego of railroads Adams quickly earned the reputation as an expert in their problems. Among his other accomplishments he helped to codify existing legislation and draft a general incorporation act. He also got the roads to submit more detailed and accurate financial reports, prescribed a uniform system of accounting, and hastened the adoption of safety devices. His efforts to find solutions for the knotty problems of rates and discrimination were much less successful, primarily because he came to feel that any governmental action strong enough to reach the objective would constitute an oppressive force in itself.

Meanwhile as member of an investment group of eminent Bostonians headed by Henry Lee Higginson and Nathaniel Thayer, he was making a fortune. He turned a tidy profit in Calumet and Hecla, one of the many Michigan copper mines developed by Boston money (see p. 191), and undertook widespread speculations in urban real estate, particularly in "Kanzas" City. His *modus operandi* was to form land and development companies. Sometimes he managed these himself, but, in typical entrepreneurial fashion withdrew from this function as soon as the enterprises were on their feet and turned operations over to others. Money came from Boston banks and from the investors' group. Adams's excellent credit rating and wide circle of acquaintance among moneyed men gave him enviable financial muscle. Although most of his speculations turned out well, he lost heavily on occasion because of hasty, ill-considered judgments.

But the overriding failure of his life to which he was never entirely able to reconcile himself was his presidency of the Union Pacific Railroad. By the early eighties the UP was in deep trouble. Its revenues had fallen off, it had defaulted on its large debt to the federal government, and a cloud of suspicion hung over it because of the Credit Mobilier scandal and because Jay Gould was the leading figure in its management. At the behest of Liberal Republican friends Adams accepted a government seat on the board in 1883 and in 1884 was elected president. Certainly he seemed to be an excellent choice. His honesty and integrity were unquestioned, he was the nation's leading railroad expert, and he could open a pipeline to an as yet untapped source of funds in Boston.

At the outset all went well. He eased out Gould, Russell Sage, and the Wall Street crowd and replaced them with proper Bostonians. He also undertook an energetic program of expansion, buying feeders and outlets and improving the road's defensive strategy. In order to expedite a bill to fund the massive debt owed to the federal government, he reluctantly utilized tactics he had vigorously condemned as Massachusetts Railroad Commissioner by paying $20,000 apiece to the Democratic and Republican campaign funds and by offering bribes of $50,000 apiece to two senators. The funding bill was rejected nevertheless. The offer of the bribes, presumably never paid, called forth an outburst of self-abasement from Adams: "It simply wasn't in me to do it. And I knew it and they knew it, and they despised and hated me accordingly."

Securing operating management which Adams deemed adequate proved to be a serious problem. The hard-bitten westerners running the road had little sympathy for the Brahmin theorist, and he considered them for the most part to be stupid boors. Page after page of his diary is filled with epithets. Although he tried to improve management performance by bringing Harvard men into the UP, even this heroic measure did not suffice.

He denounced the discriminatory tactics of his fellow railroad generals, but he felt that as in dealing with Congress he had to play the game by the current rules: "A man who today undertook to manage a railroad on wholly correct principles would be in much the position of Don Quixote when he ran his tilt muck with the windmill."

By 1890 Adams's troubles were brought to a head by the mounting debt and falling revenues of the UP. He had expanded incautiously and too fast, attempting to dispose of floating debt by rolling it up into collateral trust bonds secured by the stock of merged roads. The large investment houses, including those of Boston, rightly became suspicious of the bonds, and the UP faced bankruptcy. Meanwhile Jay Gould had quietly been buying large amounts of stock, which sold at speculator's prices. Facing the inevitable, Adams stepped down and turned the road over to the villain of *A Chapter of Erie.*

Today it would be difficult to fully appraise the causes of the catastrophe. Debt and overexpansion, as Adams himself noted, were certainly important. Also, Adams was probably oversanguine in his hopes for increases of traffic. Finally, despite his expert analysis of railroad problems, he was not really a good manager. His entrepreneurial orientation precluded him from giving adequate attention to administration, and, in any event, he had neither the patience nor the temperament for it. His judgments of other people were so clannish and harsh that they undoubtedly limited his ability to get and keep the services of good men.

Yet despite feelings of persecution compounded by self-recrimination, Adams lived graciously until 1915, widely admired and active in civic and intellectual affairs. After 1890, however, he would have little more to do with railroads.

EDWARD H. HARRIMAN

Perhaps the most successful of the railroad tycoons of the late nineteenth century was Edward H. Harriman. Like others he initially had an entrepreneurial orientation and showed marked ability as a financier. But unlike them he had an abiding interest also in engineering problems, and a large part of his success came from his ability to relocate and rebuild roads so that they could operate more efficiently. Because of this interest in technical matters he is a transitional figure standing between the entrepreneurially oriented railroad leaders of the nineteenth century and the technically trained managers who are the major decision makers of the railroads today.

The son of an Episcopal minister, young Harriman left school at the age of fourteen to become a messenger for a Wall Street brokerage house. He grasped the techniques of the business so quickly that he was made chief clerk before reaching twenty. Two years later he borrowed $3,000 from a wealthy uncle in order to buy a seat on the Stock Exchange and open his own brokerage office. Reliability, discretion, and an acute understanding of the market soon brought him important customers, among them August Belmont and Henry B. Hyde. His entrance into the railroad field came in 1881 when he formed a syndicate which brought and rebuilt a bankrupt but potentially valuable road in central New York, and then sold it at a large profit to the Pennsylvania. Harriman was quick to see that economies of operation brought about by reconstruction of railroads could greatly increase their value. He gained prominence in the railroad field when Dutch bondholders got him a seat on the board of the Illinois Central as representative of their interests. Shortly after taking the position he persuaded the other directors to embark on a program of expansion, for which he secured the funds by marketing issues of 3½ and 4 percent bonds. Harriman's ability to secure financing at low figures by borrowing against solid security in periods when money was plentiful was one of the reasons for his success. Although Harriman's official duties were financial, he nevertheless took a large measure of responsibility for construction and operations. By 1897 he had mastered every aspect of the railroad business, including the very complex problems of ratemaking.

In that year Harriman took the step which was to project him into the top ranks of railroad leaders. With funds raised largely from the sale of an issue of Illinois Central bonds he headed a syndicate which for $58.4 million—the amount of the government's claim—bought the dilapidated Union Pacific out of bankruptcy. The property was in a sorry state of disrepair, yet Harriman could see that the road's potentialities had increased with the years and needed only an upturn in business conditions to mature into profits. The revival of the Union Pacific was a dramatic success. Branches were speedily brought back, long sections of the road were relocated in order to lower grades and widen curves, track was firmly ballasted, and structures repaired. As train tonnage increased, the operating ratio dropped from 62 to 53 percent, profits jumped from $14 million in 1899 to $20 million in 1900, and the stock began a rise which took it from about $25 in 1897 to $196 by 1906. By that time the Union Pacific was considered to be one of the most valuable railroad properties in the world.

Determined to get an absolute monopoly of western traffic, and using success to breed success, Harriman and the banking interests allied with him acquired control of the Southern Pacific in 1901 through purchase of $75 million worth of stock held by the Crocker, Stanford, and Huntington estates. The money for the stock was raised by the sale of an issue of Union Pacific convertible bonds. Again an extensive rebuilding program followed, resulting in much more efficient and profitable operations.

But the gigantic U.P.–S.P. combination was suddenly threatened when a Hill-Morgan combine controlling both the Great Northern and the Northern Pacific under a community of interest bought the Burlington, thus confronting the U.P. with competition east of Denver. Alarmed at the potential danger of the situation, the Harriman interests in 1901 attempted secretly to buy control of the Northern Pacific in the open market. Although the stock shot up to $1,000 per share when their intention became known, they succeeded in acquiring a majority of all shares outstanding, although they lacked a majority of the common stock. Unknown to them, votes of the common, under the company's charter, could retire the preferred. Theoretically, therefore, Hill and Morgan could have wrested the road from Harriman's grasp. But since this course would have involved a damaging battle, compromise seemed to be the better solution. The eventual outcome was the formation of the Northern Securities Company, a holding company for the stock of the Great Northern and Northern Pacific in which the Harriman forces were represented to the extent of their majority holdings in Northern Pacific. This community of interest guaranteed reasonable treatment of the Union Pacific by the Burlington. Large investments by the U.P.–S.P. in the Chicago and Northwestern, the New York Central, and the B. and O., to say nothing of numerous other roads, appeared to be laying the groundwork for a community of interest which might cover the nation when any such imperial project was brought to an end by the sudden death of Harriman in 1909.

The cardinal principles which Harriman followed were: bold borrowing, powerful and concentrated financial control, high operating efficiency, monopolistic rates for service, and corporate stock speculation. In 1901 alone the Union Pacific borrowed $100 million to acquire and start reconstruction of the Southern Pacific and $80 million to mount the campaign for acquisition of the Northern Pacific. Bonds issued in Harriman's financing operations carried conversion features at relatively low figures, thus attracting speculators and transforming a good bit of debt into equities on every rising market. In Harriman's hands the Illinois Central and Union Pacific became more than mere railroads; they were investment companies raising huge funds on their assets and credit for the combination of other enterprises. At all times Harriman guarded his supply lines by keeping on good terms with the large eastern banks, trust companies, and insurance companies which provided the major markets for his securities. The policy of using money raised by mortgage loans to buy corporate stock was certainly risky, and scarcely fair to creditors, but the great surge of national prosperity at the turn of the century made the policy a success—and nobody argued with success.

Harriman was widely admired at the time of his death. Even though he never even remotely approached possession of the financial power necessary to force acceptance of his proposals, the great masters of capital usually followed his suggestions gladly. Empire builder that he was, he professed that large-scale philanthropy was his only goal: "I never cared for money except as power for work," he once told a friend. "What I most enjoy is the power of creation, getting into partnership with nature in doing good, helping to feed man and beast, and making everybody and everything a little better and happier." The fact that the statement seems to reflect the advice of public relations counsel is less important than that Harriman felt constrained to make it at all. Businessmen of a generation before seldom felt a need to justify their wealth in terms of social purpose.

Formulas for entrepreneurial success constructed out of the careers of the great railroad leaders are apt to be overrationalized. Actually, luck played a large part in the outcome of their ventures. Although they usually evaluated their chances for success with more accuracy than most of their contemporaries, and kept a larger margin of reserves available for untoward contingencies, still in many instances a wrong turn of the cards would have ruined them. If business conditions had taken a sharp upturn in 1884 and had swung downward in 1897, Villard might have succeeded and Harriman might have gone down into spectacular and catastrophic bankruptcy. Had this been the case, we can be quite sure that the reputations of the two men would be quite different than they are today.

ATTITUDES AND VALUES OF RAILROAD LEADERS

Although colorful and dramatic, the careers of the great railroad tycoons, as we know them, do not necessarily reflect the personalities and values of less celebrated brethren in the business. Fortunately, Professor Thomas C. Cochran, in his *Railroad Leaders*, has analyzed the correspondence of 61 lesser known railroad men who nevertheless occupied important executive positions between 1845 and 1890, and has thereby provided a much more balanced view of group attitudes than can be gotten from biographies of the titans.

From statistics collected by Cochran it is plain that most railroad careers did not correspond to the rags-to-riches pattern so popular with nineteenth-century writers. Two-thirds to nine-tenths of the executives examined came from middle-class backgrounds, and 51 were born east of the Alleghenies and north of the Mason-Dixon Line. Twenty-one had attended college, and most had graduated from high school—proportions in both instances much higher than the national average. Despite a greater degree of educational advantages, these executives tended to deprecate the importance of formal learning as a factor leading to success. In their minds honesty, hard work, and the prudential virtues were much more important in this regard.

Until late in the nineteenth century railroad executives had little or none of the feelings of social responsibility which supposedly characterizes "business statesmanship" today. Presidents in the earlier period considered their companies to be purely private enterprises operated first and foremost for the welfare of stockholders. While management expected to treat employees and shippers with justice, it felt no responsibility to adopt more liberal policies which would shield either group from the fluctuations of the business cycle. Questions of rates, wages, conditions of employment, hiring and firing, were all to be determined by market conditions. Because of the continuation of family alliances as business entities, this spartan attitude was qualified by a tolerance of nepotism in recruitment to executive positions.

Somewhat paradoxically, in view of the veneration expressed for personal integrity, executive responsibility to stockholders was often compromised by conflict of interest. A glaring example was the Credit Mobilier. But the scandal which erupted when its operations became known discredited construction companies, and by the mid-seventies they were generally looked upon with disfavor by railroad men. Speculative purchase of other railroads, land, and townsites by railroad directors who resold at a profit to their railroad companies continued throughout the nineteenth century. Although stock watering infringed upon the rights of stockholders by diluting their equities, condemnation from the public and from all railroad experts did not suffice to suppress the practice.

Actually the operating moral code of railroad leaders was much looser than the ideal standards acknowledged by businessmen generally. As Charles Francis Adams, Jr., characterized it: "Lawlessness and violence among [the railroads], the continual effort of each member to protect himself and secure the advantage over others, have, as they usually do, bred a general spirit of distrust, bad faith and cunning until railroad officials have become hardly better than a race of jockeys on a large scale." Although Adams's description certainly did not fit all railroad leaders, it applied to so many that the charge appeared justified.

The attitude of railroad leaders toward competition was as ambiguous as the attitude toward moral standards. As we have seen, pledges of allegiance to the principle were repeatedly accompanied by attempts to suppress it in practice. Although by the 1880s railroad leaders were beginning to accept the contention put forth by experts that regardless of its theoretical beneficence competition was destructive for railroads, the change in attitude only sharpened the ambiguity. Moreover, when accompanied by the conflict between destructive competitive practices and the development of procedures for co-operation, the ambiguity produced a confusion at the level of public policy which made effective railroad legislation almost impossible to obtain.

Like most of their contemporaries in the business world, railroad leaders tended to consider government regulation a violation of economic law, the sanctity of contracts, and the rights of property. Yet they were still quite willing to accept public aid in the form of stock subscriptions, loans, and land grants. Any ambiguity in their minds resulting from this dualism of attitude was resolved by the conviction that they were helping to expand the economy and were creating wealth in other forms for the nation at large. There is a large measure of truth to this contention. Seen in perspective, the construction of the American railroad network was of much greater moment than the sometimes questionable methods by which the feat was accomplished. Reprehensible practices were usually not part of business strategies planned in advance but were defensive reactions to competition or to market crises. Although men like Jay Gould deserve condemnation by any standards, probably most railroad leaders would have preferred to have carried on their affairs in close conformity to the ideal code of business morality. Unfortunately the business conditions of the day seldom permitted them to do so.

XXVIII. Bonanza on the High Plains

THE CATTLEMEN'S FRONTIER

The raising and marketing of livestock has always been an important business in America because of favorable natural conditions and because of a large foreign market for meat. During the colonial period cattle roaming the westward moving frontier were periodically rounded up, sorted, branded, and driven to abattoirs in market centers on the east coast. Here the animals were slaughtered and the beef packed in barrels, mostly for export. In 1805 a herd was driven from the Ohio country to Baltimore, thus inaugurating the cattle trade between the transappalachian west and east coast cities. After 1815 the cattle frontier spread rapidly westward, reaching central Indiana in the 1840s.

Cattle raising permitted the Midwest to participate in the commercial economy of the Northeast before the coming of railroad transportation. Corn grown in the Ohio Valley was not of sufficient value to afford wagon transportation charges across the mountains, but when transformed into cattle its value was raised to such a point that the cost of driving a herd 700 or 800 miles to seaboard marketing centers was not excessive. Furthermore, the combination of breeding and fattening utilized both the better and poorer grades of Midwest land. Cattle were bred and brought to maturity in the rough upland regions not suitable for commercial agriculture. Fattening took place in fertile areas where both grass and corn were available. Distilling and the raising of hogs provided hedges for cattle raisers. Hogs matured earlier, were less susceptible to disease than cattle, and fattened on cattle droppings. Distilling added value to corn, and distillery slops (i.e., refuse mash) was an excellent fodder for cattle. At the outset feeding was carried on by small farmers, but the profits from the business soon attracted eastern capital and after the War of 1812 large farms with heavy investment in land and stock appeared in the Midwest.

Although some farmers drove their own cattle to eastern markets, most utilized the services of drovers, the middlemen and entrepreneurs of the cattle trade. Colorful figures ubiquitous in back-country regions, they purchased from farmers or took cattle on commission and drove the herds to the great cattle markets which grew up on the outskirts of Boston, New York, and Philadelphia. Herds from the Midwest moved eastward over through roads and turnpikes. Fodder was provided at large caravansaries called "stands" spaced along the roads. Marketing was carried on informally at the eastern centers by bargaining between drovers and butchers in an atmosphere of *caveat emptor*. One gambit supposedly inaugurated by a drover who was to become a luminary of the speculative fraternity, Daniel Drew, gave the name to a future tactic for corporate profiteering—stock watering. It consisted of keeping cattle from water for a few days until just before their sale, then allowing them to drink their fill. Obviously the purchaser then bought a heavy load of water along with his stock.

Potential profits from cattle droving were large. During the early years of the drives steers costing $25 to $45 apiece in Ohio often sold for at least double that amount in east coast cities, and in Philadelphia in 1817 brought as much as $133 apiece. The cost of driving from the Ohio country was about $10 to $15 per head, and remained at about this level throughout the antebellum period. Because of an increasing domestic and export market beef prices remained relatively high in comparison with other commodity prices, particularly in the fifties. Despite a favorable price level, there were many hazards in droving which could bring serious losses to the unlucky and the unwary. On the road cattle were lost or lamed or died of sickness. Thousand pound steers regularly "drifted" (i.e., lost) 150 pounds, and the figure could be greater if fodder were scarce. Since there was no effective way of controlling supply, unexpectedly large arrivals of cattle in individual markets would send local prices plummeting.

THE LONG DRIVE

The cattle business on the Great Plains were carried on under such favorable conditions that it blossomed into a great bonanza by the 1880s. The nutritious "buffalo grass" on which the cattle fed was as free as the air, and the cattle themselves could be acquired very cheaply. Army posts, immigrant trains, and government purchase for Indians provided markets for beef on the plains which stimulated herding and droving. The high prices of all foodstuffs in the Far West during the fifties even drew herds of Texas longhorns as far as Los Angeles and Sacramento.

The characteristic feature of the western cattle business until the disappearance of the open range—the long drives—began on the eve of the Civil War and burgeoned in the years immediately following the struggle. Groups of farm hands—many of them ex-Confederate soldiers impoverished by the war—rounded up wild longhorns, provided themselves with provisions and a cook, and started north to sell the cattle in Kansas and Missouri, or even in Chicago. As the railroads pushed westward, the points at which they intersected the trails became the sites of the famous cow towns so celebrated in western literature. The first of these was Abilene, founded by an Illinois cattle fattener, Joseph G. McCoy, in 1867. Receipts of cattle there mounted from 35,000 in 1867 to 150,000 in 1869. During the seventies Newton, Witchita, and Dodge City also became important cattle centers.

Total cost of driving a herd of some 2,500 cattle came to about $500 a month, or about $1,200 to $1,500 for a drive of 1,200 to 1,500 miles. The fact that in 1867 steers bought in Texas for $9.50 apiece sold in New York for $68 apiece might seem to indicate that profits could be large. But actually rail transportation charges, plus middlemen's commissions and the hazards of the trail might reduce net return to the vanishing point. During the drive drought could take a heavy toll; storms made streams impassable and caused stampedes; Indians and rustlers could make the trails places of terror. The fact that Texas drovers selling on government contract allowed a differential of $3 to $4 per head between the price of cattle in Texas and the delivered price perhaps gives some indication of normal profit—$2 to $3.25 per head.

All transactions in the cattle business utilized lines of credit extending back to eastern commercial centers. Drovers obtained financing from banks in the cow towns or in Kansas City in return for "cattlemen's notes." Often western banks rediscounted a portion of this paper to commercial paper houses or to eastern banks, thus drawing eastern capital into the cattle country. Interest rates, usually 10 to 12 percent, reflected a shortage of money and the inability of most cattlemen to provide adequate collateral for their loans. Yet the great majority of borrowers were trustworthy and prompt in payment. Dealers in the cow towns, financed with regular lines of credit by Chicago banks, commission houses, and packing houses, paid for cattle by drafts which drovers used to pay off their own indebtedness. They then borrowed again in order to purchase and drive other herds north.

In order to reduce the cost of doing business, draw on the savings of others, and insure continuing lines of credit, many of the larger cattlemen formed banks or participated in banking operations. Virtually all large cattlemen served as bank directors during their later years. This combination of trade and banking was typical of commercial capitalism back to ancient times.

RANCHING

The long drives reached their peak in 1871, when approximately 600,000 Texas cattle were driven north. After that time the number declined to about 250,000 per year and the cattle business entered the stage of ranching. Early western settlers had found out, to their surprise, that Texas cattle could survive the cold winters of the Northwest without special protection. Buffalo grass cured on the stem, and in the winter cattle could get at it by pawing away the snow. As early as 1866 cattle had been driven from Texas to Montana and there fattened for a year before marketing. From this procedure it was only a step for the drover to become a rancher by staking out a watercourse, knocking together a few boards to make a house, stringing wire for a corral, and acquiring a wagon and a few tools. The surrounding grasslands then became the rancher's private range. Fencing the public domain was prohibited, but until the late eighties the law was almost universally disregarded. The great advantage of the ranch was that it allowed the cattlemen to appropriate the offspring of a herd and breed the herd up by crossing Hereford bulls imported from the East with a native Texas stock. The resulting steer had both the weight of the sire and the hardihood of the longhorn. Best of all, the government supplied free of charge the greater part of the overhead in the form of range land and water.

These circumstances brought the conviction, fortified by a wave of promotional literature, that it was next to impossible not to get rich in the ranching game. For example, General James S. Brisbin, in *The Beef Bonanza*, published in 1881, asserted that an investment of $25,000 would yield a net profit of $51,278 at the end of six years, plus compound interest on the original sum at the rate of 7 percent. An even more optimistic claim was made by the author of an essay, "How Cattlemen Grow Rich" in the *Breeder's Gazette* of 1883:

A good sized steer, when it is fit for the butcher market will bring from $45 to $60. The same animal at birth was worth but $5. He has run on the plains and cropped the grass from the public domain for four or five years, and now, with scarcely any expense to his owner, is worth forty dollars more than when he started his pilgrimage. A thousand of these animals are kept nearly as cheaply as a single one, so with a thousand as a starter, and with an investment of but $5,000 at the start, in four years the stock raiser has made from $40,000 to $45,000. Allow $5,000 for his current expenses . . . and he still has $35,000, and even $45,000 for a net profit. That is all there is of the problem, and that is why our cattlemen grow rich.

Unfortunately, the author had by no means explained "all there is of the problem" of cattle ranching. Nevertheless, oversimplified descriptions of this sort, plus many authenticated cases of quick fortunes, drew a rush of would-be cattlemen into the Great Plains. Personal considerations, in many cases, fortified economic motivations. The West promised high adventure to footloose young men who could put their hands on a few thousand dollars, and the picturesque life of the cowboy appealed to many farm boys with ambitions higher than merely following the plow. The "champagne air" of the Plains was supposed to be good for weak lungs, and hundreds of sickly young men such as Theodore Roosevelt felt that the strenuous life would build a strong physique. Reconstruction and the dismal economic conditions in the South drove many energetic young men from that region into the cattle business. The roseate picture of ranching painted in 1879 by the visiting British Royal Commission on Agriculture was influential in promoting much immigration into the West from abroad. Thirteen of a group of fifty-three representative cattlemen interviewed by the historian Hubert H. Bancroft in 1885 were foreign born. The great majority of those interviewed had not been cattlemen before arriving in the West, but had come from a wide variety of occupations.

CATTLE COMPANIES

As the cattle business gathered momentum, many holdings of individual ranchers were consolidated by large corporations. By the early eighties the list of companies capitalized at over $1 million was already long. Sometimes the cattlemen accepted cash for their holdings, but more often they took part of the payments in the form of stock in the new enterprises and stayed on as managers. Some of the first organizations were quite prosperous. But the eagerness for quick profits promoted speculative and unsound business practices. Many of the companies paid more for the properties than these were worth, particularly since purchasers had to accept a "book count" (i.e., estimate made by the seller) of the number of cattle acquired. Overcapitalization was also often accompanied by payment of dividends out of capital. Often the number of steers sold in a given year was greater than the number of calves born to replace them. Under these circumstances the 15 percent annual profit reported by thirty-one cattlemen and cattle companies in New Mexico Territory in 1886 was probably inflated.

One of the most remarkable aspects of the cattle business during the eighties was the formation of land and cattle companies in England and Scotland to operate in the American West. A combination of disparate causes was responsible for the appearance and rapid growth of these organizations. Large amounts of foreign capital were seeking investment, and foreign capitalists were naturally attracted by the high interest rates of the American West and the reports of large profits to be made in the cattle business. Parliamentary legislation permitting the formation of investment trusts made possible a high degree of capital consolidation. Because of decimation of British herds by anthrax, an influx of cattle was underway, and the importation of beef, aided by the construction of refrigerator ships, rose from 1,732 tons in 1876 to more than 30,000 tons from 1878 to 1880. Large British investments in American mining enterprises also served to advertise the West.

One of the first successful British companies, and one which established a pattern for others to follow, was the Prairie Cattle Company, Ltd. Organized largely by Scots in 1881, capitalized at 200,000 pounds, the company made a contract with the Kansas City banking firm of Underwood, Clark and Company whereby the bankers, acting as agent for the English organization, purchased land and cattle in return for a three-eighths interest after the entire initial investment had been repaid. The company was an immediate success, earning 26 percent of the invested capital during the first year of operations. Investors in Dundee, Scotland, dazzled with the success of the Prairie Company, formed three similar organizations, the Texas, Matador, and Hansford Companies. Ten major British-American cattle companies were incorporated during 1882, bringing the total investment by that time to about $15.5 million. About 70 percent of the funds were used for the purchase of land and cattle.

By now the boom was underway, and lasted with undiminished intensity through 1885. As one historian of the cattle country, W. Turrentine Jackson, has described the speculative mania of the time:

Corporate ranching organizations of every conceivable variety were formed. Westerners, Easterners, and Europeans combined forces regionally, internationally, by nationality, and across such lines. They incorporated their ventures in Britain, in some eastern state, or directly in a state or territory in which they intended to operate. Some were formed for the primary purpose of selling stock to the public; others furnished all necessary investment capital from their own funds and never issued a prospectus or listed their stock for sale.

But enthusiasm for operations of this sort was not universal. Carping critics in conservative English journals labeled them "poker on joint stock principles," and cited the danger of hard winters, the possibility of fraud in book counts, and the hazard of operating on open range subject to regulation by the United States government. The separation of ownership and management by the ocean and half a continent also created problems. Managers sent over from England or Scotland sometimes had difficulty in getting their authority accepted; American managers tended to resent detailed orders and instructions as interference with their normal prerogatives. One solution, tried by several companies, was to divide authority between two boards of directors, one British and the other American.

DECLINE OF THE LARGE COMPANIES

Although British investment by 1885 stood at perhaps $25 million, serious troubles were piling up for all large cattle companies and ranches, and for the British companies in particular. Cattle prices broke sharply in that year, in part because the British government, fearing the spread of pleuropneumonia among domestic cattle, placed quarantine restrictions on the importation of American cattle. Also, the range was becoming overstocked; many cattle, weakened by undernourishment, had succumbed during the severe winter of 1884–85 and the calf crop was down. But perhaps the most difficult problem arose when President Cleveland ordered all fences on public land removed, and Texas followed suit for its own public lands. Many of the companies had sunk most of their capital in cattle, and, depending upon fenced areas of open range for grazing, had bought only small amounts of land around watercourses. Now they faced the necessity of large investments in land, or the sale of large numbers of cattle.

The terrible winter of 1886–87 brought disaster to many companies. Starving cattle, already weakened by lack of adequate forage, drifted with the winds and perished by the thousands against barbed wire fences or in sheltered hollows. Despite the loss prices fell in the spring as hard-pressed ranchers rushed half-famished beasts to market in order to meet debt payments. Scottish companies wrote off $6.6 million of capitalization and a majority of English companies were liquidated. Some of the large ranches, like the XIT of Texas, weathered the winter of 1886–87 and the hard times of the nineties and entered the twentieth century as prosperous organizations, but the day of the large absentee-owned companies was over. The open range had been a major reason for their organization and success, and once the range disappeared they had to liquidate or conduct operations on a much smaller scale. Henceforth the carefully enclosed ranch growing winter feed became the standard of the cattle country, and cattlemen became more interested in breeding good beasts than in merely increasing the size of herds.

With the disappearance of the open range came also the decline of the regional cattlemen's associations. These had been formed to police the range against rustlers and to manage the elements of the cattle business requiring collective action. The most powerful of them was the Wyoming Stock Growers Association, comprising 363 members in 1885 who owned two million head of cattle. At the height of its power, it was, for all practical purposes, the government of Wyoming. It set rules for the adopting and registering of brands and for the disposition of strays and mavericks. It had a large force of detectives at work tracking down rustlers, and as a means of identifying them posted inspectors at loading points to examine brands and check bills of sale. One of the most important functions of the association was the administration of roundups designed to separate mixed herds of cattle. But hostility of farmers, whose property rights were so often flouted by members of the associations, the losses of 1886–87, and the disappearance of the open range forced the organizations to turn over their quasi-governmental functions to territorial and state governments.

BUSINESSMEN IN TEN-GALLON HATS

Cattlemen tended to be men of action rather than of thought, impatient of restraint, and highly individualistic. To some degree, the active, risky nature of the business stimulated the development of these qualities, but more important, perhaps, it attracted men already possessing them from many other occupations. Charles Goodnight, a young Texas Ranger who with his partner blazed the Goodnight-Loving Trail and later established a huge ranch in Texas 250 miles from the nearest railhead, was attracted by the excitement of the business and even after becoming wealthy regarded it as a challenging game. George W. Littlefield, another cattle king, entered ranching in order to restore family prosperity lost during the Civil War. John W. Iliff came to Colorado as a prospector in the gold rush of 1859. Investing the modest rewards of his efforts in a store near the present site of Cheyenne, he collected lambs and footsore cattle from immigrants going west, gradually built up a large herd, and laid the basis of a fortune by selling beef to the Union Pacific for its construction crews.

Most of the wiser cattlemen early recognized the advisability of buying land and came to have a higher investment in it than in cattle. For example, Richard King, founder of the famous King Ranch of Texas, at his death in 1885 left real estate appraised at $564,784 and livestock valued at $496,700. Investment in land proved to be a wise hedge to the cattle market quite apart from the necessity of acquiring it after the dissappearance of the open range. The few corporations which weathered the crisis of the late eighties and early nineties regained their prosperity during the twentieth century in part because of rising land values.

Labor was usually not a serious problem for most cattlemen. Ranch hands tended to drift from one job to another, but the supply of labor was usually adequate. The cowboy's $30 per month wage was slightly higher than wages for unskilled farm labor, but cow punching was also a seasonal occupation. Ranches needed less hands during the winter than during the spring and summer. Ranching was not a labor-intensive industry, and the wage bill was very low in comparison with other expenses, chiefly interest on the investment in land and cattle. One hand was employed for approximately 1,000 head of cattle. During the days of the open range the fiduciary aspect of herding bred in cowboys a strong sense of loyalty to their outfits which was to some degree lost when hands became employees of large ranches performing more menial tasks such as wire stringing and fence tending.

SHEEP RAISING

Sheep were as ubiquitous as cattle in early America, and moved slowly westward with them along the cattlemen's frontier. As livestock they were in some ways more useful than cattle. Their initial cost and cost of maintenance was less; they could find a living on bare, upland pastures which could not support cattle; their heavy fleeces enabled them to survive the coldest winters; and they were valuable for meat as well as for their yearly dividend of wool. The flocks of New England provided the raw material for a woolen industry which stimulated the advance of the industrial revolution and contributed greatly to the prosperity of the region. By 1840, 5,000 to 8,000 sheep arrived daily at Brighton Livestock Market on the outskirts of Boston.

The most notable development in the sheep industry during the early nineteenth century was the introduction of merino stock and the subsequent upbreeding of herds. Merinos, originally bred in Spain, produced the fine fleeces from which the highest quality woolen fabrics were made. The Spanish government, following the instinctive mercantilist policies universal during the eighteenth century, forbad the export of merinos, but during the confusion of the French Revolutionary Wars the restrictions were relaxed and Dupont de Nemours, Colonel David Humphreys, and Chancellor Robert Livingston all managed to import breeding stock. Livingston in 1809 wrote a pamphlet on sheep breeding which was printed by the New York State Legislature. Sheep breeding aroused the interest of important men not only because of its scientific significance but also because of its wide implications for the expanding textile industry and the self-sufficiency of the nation.

Carefully bred ewes by mid-century were producing eight to twelve pounds of wool and rams up to thirty pounds, which sold at approximately one dollar per pound. Many breeders herded their own flocks but others placed them in the hands of "receivers" who took one-sixth of the wool clip as compensation for their service as herders. Rapidly rising prices for wool during the Civil War temporarily stimulated sheep raising, but falling prices and foreign competition afterwards led midwestern growers to diminish their herds. Sheep raising on any except the cheapest land simply did not pay, particularly if winter fodder had to be provided.

Since the seventeenth century millions of sheep had roamed the grazing lands of what became west Texas, New Mexico, and California, and constituted the chief source of wealth for aristocratic Spanish families in these regions. After 1848 Americans in increasing numbers entered the business of sheep raising in the former Mexican possessions. The smaller owners tended their own herds, but the larger ones followed the old Spanish custom of "partidario" in which local shepherds of Spanish and Indian descent took charge of flocks in return for a portion of the wool and lambs. As the cattle frontier moved westward during the fifties and sixties, the sheep frontier of the Southwest moved rapidly north and east. In response to brisk demand created by the gold rush, thousands of sheep were trailed into the mining country of California, where they could be sold at $10 to $12 per head, almost ten times their cost in the Southwest. The sheep were used mostly for mutton, although some fleeces were made into sheepskin coats. From 1865 to 1880 the flocks of woolies pushed steadily eastward up river valleys and over the high passes of the Rockies and entered the cattle country en masse as the boom days of the cattle business drew to a close. In Wyoming between 1886 and 1896, for example, while the number of cattle declined from 900,000 to 300,000, the count of sheep rose from 875,000 to 3,500,000. By 1900 sheep outnumbered cattle in the West.

By this time sheep raising cost much less to enter than cattle ranching and offered better hopes of profit. Moreover, it was in somewhat the same condition as the cattle business in the sixties and early seventies. The animals could be acquired very cheaply and they grazed partly on public domain. Prices for the high, rocky pastures during the nineties were about the same as the price of good cattle land a generation before. Also, since the prices of wool and mutton tended to fluctuate inversely to each other, sheepmen usually possessed a built-in market hedge. General Brisbin estimated that an average size sheep ranch could be acquired for an outlay of $15,000 to $20,000—$4,000 of which was spent for land, buildings, tools, horses, and dogs—and $10,000 to $15,000 for sheep at $2 and $3 per head. At estimated operating costs of less than fifty cents per head he calculated that such a ranch could bring a net return of 35 percent the first year, 47 percent the second year, and 60 percent the third year. Although these figures, like most of Brisbin's estimates of profit, were too optimistic, profits of 30 percent were not uncommon in the sheep country.

Marketing and finance were carried on in much the same way as in the cattle business. At loading centers along the railroads sheep destined for the table were sold to dealers representing packers and commission merchants of Chicago and Kansas City. Banks loaned freely to sheepmen to buy animals at the high rates of interest common in the cattle country, and drew eastern capital into the business by rediscounting sheepmen's paper in eastern financial centers. Sheepmen of Montana borrowed in the form of overdrafts on banks, paying 1½ percent per month for the privilege. Wool production had a separate marketing and finance organization. Professional shearers built pens in Wyoming in which forty men could shear 4,000 to 4,500 sheep daily. These pens, visited by wool buyers from all over the country, naturally became markets. Wool dealers advanced money to sheepmen under the stipulation that the clips be sent to them to discharge the debt. Wool scourers, mercantile firms, and commission merchants all on occasion figured as advancers of credit when they were in a position to handle fleeces. In contrast to the cattle business, the corporation was never important in sheep raising during the nineteenth century, perhaps because of a lack of enthusiasm for highly capitalized corporate ventures on the part of investors who had gotten their fingers burned in the cattle business.

The wars between cattlemen and sheepmen have became as permanent a part of western lore as the battles between cattlemen and "nesters."

From time to time during the nineties severe conflicts did indeed take place in Wyoming and Colorado. Wide credence was given to charges that close cropping by sheep ruined the range, and that cattle would not feed where sheep had grazed. Actually, these canards had nothing to support them, and the battles were simply contests between rival herdsmen for the shrinking open range. It was estimated that along the Colorado-Wyoming border during the decade at least twenty men were killed and sheep worth $2,000,000 destroyed. But if sheep herders stuck to the high pastures they did not get into trouble with cattlemen. Cattle raising and sheep raising were really complementary to each other because of the different range suitable for the two animals. Many cattlemen, seeking profits outside their own business after the debacle of 1886–87, invested in flocks, and some gave up cattle entirely for sheep.

MEAT PACKING

Meat packing has of course always been closely related to stock raising. Until the coming of the railroads and the focusing of the cattle trade on Chicago, the industry had been a seasonal, localized affair. During the winter when cold weather reduced the possibility of spoilage, some cattle and a large number of hogs were slaughtered in small abattoirs throughout the country and the meat salted and packed in barrels. Little use was made of by-products. Sometimes they were sold to special dealers at nominal prices; sometimes they were merely discarded. Since barreled beef and pork were important items on the list of American exports, from the early colonial period onward the Atlantic coastal ports had been slaughtering centers. The first important inland center was Cincinnati, affectionately known as "Porkopolis" during the antebellum period. The city owed its rise to the great increase in the production of corn and hogs throughout the Midwest, the coming of the steamboat and cheap transportation down the Ohio and Mississippi to New Orleans, and the desire of producers to avoid the hazards of the drive over the mountains to the eastern packing centers. By 1844 the city's packers were shipping annually to New Orleans hog products worth $2.8 million, and the packing industry gave employment to about 15,000 people. Shipments were even made up for purchasers in England and Germany.

Chicago, because of its proximity to the productive areas of so many commodities, its credit facilities, and its position as a rail hub with direct rail and water transportation to the East, naturally became a center for livestock as well as for wheat and lumber. During the Civil War the heavy influx of livestock so overflowed existing facilities that the Union Stock

Yard and Transit Company, formed in 1865, built pens and other installations capable of handling 21,000 cattle, 75,000 hogs, and 22,000 sheep. The nine railroads converging on Chicago at the time subscribed for $925,000 of the million dollars worth of stock issued. With the rapid increase in the number of commission merchants and brokers and the proliferation of credit facilities such as stockyard banks, Chicago soon became the greatest meat packing center in the world.

The growth of Chicago was accompanied by the rise of the great packers who at one time had nearly a monopoly of the business—Swift, Armour, Morris, and Hammond. Much of the history of meat packing from the end of the Civil War to 1900 can be told through biographical sketches of the two largest packers, Gustavus F. Swift and Philip D. Armour.

GUSTAVUS F. SWIFT

The son of a Cape Cod farmer, Gustavus Swift was apprenticed to a butcher at the age of fourteen. Four years later he purchased his remaining time from his master and went into business for himself. Established with a partner in a large butcher shop in Lancaster, Massachusetts, Swift specialized in purchasing, often traveling to Albany and Buffalo for the purpose. Realizing that location at the source of supply gave opportunity for wider choice of meat at lowest prices, he moved to Chicago in 1875 as a cattle buyer and in the next year, with a capital of $30,000 and a few New England butchers as colleagues, entered the packing business.

Immediately Swift became interested in the possibility of using refrigerator cars to ship dressed beef to eastern cities. Since a thousand pound steer dressed down to six hundred of meat, shipping beef would be obviously cheaper than shipping cattle on the hoof. The idea had been tried before, but was considered impractical because of inability to build refrigerator cars efficient enough to prevent meat from spoiling under all contingencies. Working with others, Swift solved the problem by designing a car which stored ice under the roof, thus cooling the meat by continuous convection currents. Since the railroads, desiring to carry the heavier loads of steers and protect their investments in cattle cars and loading stations, would not construct the refrigerator cars, Swift persuaded a car company to undertake the task and allow him to pay for the cars out of earnings. Only by hard bargaining and playing the railroads off against each other was Swift able to secure haulage rates which would render dressed beef competitive with cattle in eastern markets.

Transportation problems formed only part of the difficulties facing Swift. Butchers and cattle dealers of the East, aware of the threat which western dressed beef posed to their business, embargoed it where they could and strove to destroy its increasing popularity by spreading derogatory stories about its taste and purity. In order to meet this challenge Swift traveled widely throughout the Northeast promoting dressed beef, and wherever possible persuading doubtful butchers to accept a carload of it on consignment. When he could get no such co-operation he often sold at sharply cut prices from a car parked on a siding. These blockages in normal retail outlets forced Swift to enter marketing himself, which he did by forming partnerships with butchers which expanded into an agency system. Swift and Company thus became a leader in a major innovation inaugurated by big business in the latter part of the century—national marketing.

When in Chicago Swift worked a twelve-hour day or more and made himself familiar with every detail of the business. Always striving to cut costs, he equipped his plant with the most modern machinery and worked toward continuous process operation. Abandoning the time-honored butchering methods in which one man cut up each individual steer, Swift installed overhead conveyors which allowed each worker to perform a single cutting operation. This conveyor system was perhaps the first assembly line in America—or more properly, dissembly line. Swift also made careful use of all by-products. As he once expressed it, "We use everything of the pig but the squeal."

Short-term financing was perhaps Swift's greatest problem. Since meat packing was a business with a high ratio of operating costs to overhead costs, even in periods of rapid expansion packers had less need for the services of investment bankers than the capital-intensive industries. The successive issues of Swift and Company stock which raised capitalization from $300,000 in 1885—the date of incorporation—to $7.5 million in 1892, were readily purchased by cattle dealers and butchers of New England, among whom were many of Swift's former partners and associates. But since a considerable interim existed between the time cattle were purchased and the returns from the sale of Swift products filtered back from the East, the company needed large amounts of working capital. For this reason Swift was a constant and heavy borrower from Chicago banks. So tightly did he stretch his credit that often he could operate only on a day-to-day basis, never really being certain that he could discharge his future commitments. At the height of the Panic of 1893 his debt to Chicago banks reportedly stood at $10 million and he was in fact insolvent. But the mere size of his indebtedness, plus his excellent credit rating, saved him from bankruptcy. The banks simply could not let him go under lest they also perish in his downfall. Stockyard banks also came to his rescue, because his failure would have had disastrous reverberations in the cattle country.

In personality Swift epitomized the driving type of businessman so common today among top echelon executives. A complete specialist, he devoted his whole life to his business with fierce concentration. Unlike so many businessmen of his generation he did not gradually disengage himself from detail as he grew older in order to follow outside interests or engage in a generalized investment program.

PHILIP D. ARMOUR

Philip D. Armour resembled Swift in many ways. An equally hard worker, he had the same interest in cost reduction, mechanization, utilization of by-products, and refrigerator cars. But unlike Swift he engaged in risky commodity market speculation and at the end of his life devoted a substantial part of his fortune to philanthropy. A farm boy from upstate New York, he joined the gold rush of forty-nine and on his return to the East became established in the commission business in Milwaukee. In 1863 he joined John Plankinton in forming the pork packing firm of Plankinton and Armour. The firm prospered immediately because of the heavy orders for the supply of the Union armies. Foreseeing a sharp drop in pork prices after the war, Armour disposed of the firm's inventory at $40 per barrel in 1865 and sold contracts for future delivery at that price. Later Armour filled the contracts when pork was selling at $18 per barrel. This one speculation reportedly netted him between $500,000 and $1.5 million and was the first of many market *coups*.

During the eighties the firm expanded at a very fast rate, building beef as well as pork packing houses in several midwestern cities, acquiring a fleet of refrigerator cars, dominating banks and livestock exchanges, establishing a national marketing organization, and even extending operations to Europe. Armour plants achieved a high degree of mechanization, and in order to make the fullest use of by-products the firm even went into the manufacture of fertilizer, glue, tallow, soap, oleomargarine, and pepsin.

So fast was the growth of the packing industry generally that one executive remarked: "We never built a house big enough to hold the stuff we had to put into it five years later. The packers never caught up with the country." Gratifying as the expansion might be to the Big Four, the combination of processing, transportation, and distribution increasingly alarmed independent retail butchers, cattlemen, small packers, and self-appointed defenders of consumers. By the mid-eighties the railroads, feeling that their haulage rates for the some 6,000 cars owned by the packers were being beaten down by concerted action, joined in the mounting condemnation heaped upon the "beef trust." The result of the outcry was the appointment of a Senate monopoly investigation in 1889 headed by Senator George G. Vest. Although the committee got no firm evidence that the packers forced down the price of cattle on the exchanges by the use of "eveners," or quota buying, the committee report of 1890 found Armour, Swift, Morris, and Hammond guilty of collusion in fixing the price of beef, dividing territory and business, dividing public contracts, and bringing pressure to bear on retailers.

The passage of the Sherman Act in the same year by no means brought the monopolistic practices of the big packers to an end. In the early nineties Armour, Swift, and Morris secured practical control of the Chicago Stock Yards. Responding to the drive for combination gathering force in the late nineties, Swift, J. Ogden Armour, and Edward Morris in 1902 formed the National Packing Company designed to buy up the smaller packers and eventually to absorb the big three themselves. Dissolution of the company by the courts prevented the giant combine from ever realizing its objectives.

Apparently neither Swift nor Armour ever saw anything wrong in their attempt to combine and monopolize the packing industry. On the contrary, they were convinced that production agreements, allocations of territories and quotas, and price fixing were as beneficial to the public as to themselves. They did strenuously maintain that they never tried to beat prices down in the livestock markets—an assertion which was received with skepticism by the courts and incredulity by cattle raisers.

Failure to achieve monopoly could in no way dim the great success of the Armour enterprises. On an original investment of about $160,000 they earned about $36 million from 1869 to 1900. About $23 million of this was plowed back into the business.

Armour's chief interest outside of his business was the Armour Mission, the largest settlement house in the United States, to which he gave $200,000 and much of his time. He also founded and endowed Armour Institute, a trade school for boys much like Girard College of Philadelphia, and built nearly two hundred apartments for his employees. Like most other big businessmen of his day, he had a kindly, paternalistic, no-nonsense attitude toward labor. All of the big packers experienced severe labor troubles from time to time and were hostile to labor organizations.

In the period between the end of the Civil War and the beginning of the twentieth century, the methods of meat production and distribution underwent a revolution similar to that experienced by many other industries at the beginning of the twentieth century. Slaughtering was a business older than recorded history, and the processing, distribution, and marketing of the product changed little from the Middle Ages until after the middle of the nineteenth century. But by 1900 stock raising and packing had become entirely new industries, the result of the long drives and ranching, the centering of cattle trade in Chicago, the spread of the rail network, the use of the refrigerator car, and the rise of a great urban market throughout the western world.

XXIX. Treasure Trove
of the Rockies

From the 1850s until the eighties the mineral wealth of the West seemed as inexhaustible as the prairie grass. Gold rushes followed each other with happy regularity; depletion in one area was merely the prelude to a richer strike farther on. The opening of the Comstock Lode inaugurated a new era by revealing the wealth of silver as well as gold hidden in the Rockies. Exploitation of the discovery gave renewed impetus to the growth of San Francisco as a financial and industrial center, stimulated the development of new mining and metallurgical technologies, and elevated mining into the company of America's biggest businesses. The Lode was an "ore channel" about 22,000 feet long and from 100 to 1,200 feet wide extending across the eastern slope of Mount Davidson above the Carson River of Nevada. Some of the ore was extremely rich, assaying up to $6,000 per ton. Even more fortunate, the silver was found with gold or quartz, and not lead or other base metals; therefore it could be recovered relatively easily by the use of stamping mills and the "Washoe pan process."

Ever since 1850 placer miners had searched the area around Mount

Davidson for gold with indifferent success. In 1859 three partners, one of whom was Henry T. P. Comstock, came across large amounts of bluish ore in the gold claim they were working on the site of what was to be the rich Ophir mine. Ignorant of its content, they irritably threw it away. When another miner out of curiosity took some of the ore to California for assay, it was found to contain $1,595 in gold and $4,791 in silver per ton. The news spread like brush fire, and within a few months 20,000 men were at work on the Lode staking out claims and sinking exploratory shafts. The some 17,000 claims eventually registered became the basis of a gigantic speculation. Divided into shares known as "feet" supposedly corresponding to the footage of claims, the feet were traded in mining communities as far away as San Francisco. As one observer put it, "Everybody was a millionaire in silver claims." The speculation force fed the growth of Virginia City and Gold Hill, which had brief days of glory enriched by the wealth of the Lode.

Mining apart from speculation soon began in earnest, but as shafts reached downward toward the two hundred foot level the danger of cave-in became very great in wide veins where large masses of ore had been removed. For a short time it seemed that much of the richest ore must be left in the ground, but the problem of shoring up large underground galleries was solved by the use of "square sets," a special type of pillar devised by Philip Deidesheimer, a brilliant young German engineer. The pillars were hollow and filled with rock, and were set close enough together to support ceilings against the crushing weight above them. An equally important innovation was the "Washoe pan process" which permitted a 70 to 80 percent recovery of silver by the familiar amalgamation process used to separate gold from quartz (see pp. 188–89, 196). Adaptation of the process for silver was accomplished by a new amalgamating substance—a mixture of quicksilver, salt, copper sulphate, and iron filings.

As the mines thrust even deeper, new technical problems arose. Air temperatures at 120 degrees required elaborate blowers and ventilating systems; inrushing streams of water with temperatures as high as 170 degrees carrying poisonous wastes necessitated the design and manufacture of efficient pumps; rapid deepening of shafts made more powerful hoisting machinery necessary. Nitroglycerin, dynamite, and diamond drills were introduced from abroad. Eventually the total length of shafts and galleries on the Lode reached to between 180 and 190 miles. By the end of 1861, 76 stamping mills capable of working 1,500 tons of ore per day had been constructed. Capitalization of mining companies soared as the expense of getting mines in operation mounted. On the Comstock Lode free-lance prospectors disappeared quickly and were replaced by thousands of wage laborers employed by corporations with headquarters in San Francisco and New York.

From 1859 to 1862 several of the many mines made returns of bonanza proportions, but by 1863 output began to fall off and the price of feet on the San Francisco Exchange sagged badly. During the next several years, while the mines were in "borrasca" (i.e., depressed condition, from the Spanish word for storm), extensive interests were acquired by William C. Ralston and the Bank of California. Ralston was one of those businessmen, of whom we have seen so many, who had talent, vision, and capacity for leadership, but was brought to ruin by speculative excesses. After a series of banking partnerships in which he proved to be shrewd and daring, he organized the Bank of California in 1864, the biggest bank the state had yet seen. Through his agent in Virginia City, William Sharon—a man much like Ralston who became a very important mining promoter in his own right—Ralston began acquiring extensive properties on the Lode. After many mills fell into the hands of Ralston and Sharon by foreclosures, Sharon formed the Union Milling and Mining Company, which threatened to monopolize the milling process in Virginia City. He also sponsored the construction of a seventy-mile railroad connecting Virginia City with the Union Pacific at Reno.

But the drive toward monopoly was frustrated, partly by events, and partly by the astounding success of the Consolidated Virginia mine and its four promoters: John W. Mackay, James G. Fair, James C. Flood, and William S. O'Brien. All came from penniless Irish backgrounds, and only Fair had been even moderately successful before coming to Virginia City. Mackay and Fair were experienced miners, and Fair had served for a period as superintendent of a mine in California. Flood and O'Brien, who apparently financed operations, had been saloon keepers, and in the course of their business had doubtless grubstaked prospectors and speculated in mining claims. Suspecting that ore could be found by deepening the supposedly worthless Consolidated Virginia mine, the four acquired control in 1871, and at the 1,200 foot level came upon an ore chamber which made the mine the richest yet found in America, and perhaps in the world. By 1874 the stock valuation of Consolidated Virginia and its companion mine, the California, had risen to the incredible figure of $160 million. From 1873 to 1882 the two produced $105,168,859 in silver and between 1874 and 1881 paid $74,250,000 in dividends.

Another chapter in the romance of the Comstock Lode was written by the German-Jewish immigrant, Adolph Sutro, who conceived the idea of draining the mines in the Lode by a four-mile tunnel connecting the Carson River with the 2,000 foot level of the mines. The tunnel could also be used to bring ore to the mills on the river at a great saving of hoisting costs. Against the growing hostility of the Sharon group, who feared that Sutro would threaten their near-monopoly of milling in Virginia City, Sutro pushed his project to completion in 1878 at a cost of $4.5 million. Unfortunately the great engineering feat was accomplished just as the mines were nearing depletion. By 1881 the great bonanza was over.

Sutro unloaded his tunnel stock in time, however, made a second fortune in San Francisco real estate, and somewhat paradoxically was elected Mayor of San Francisco on the Populist ticket. Sharon, with a fortune of about $15 million, retired to a seat in the United States Senate. Mackay, Fair, Flood, and O'Brien became perhaps the richest Irishmen in the world. Ralston fared badly. His speculations led to the closing of the Bank of California and he himself was drowned in San Francisco Bay, perhaps a suicide.

From 1859 to 1882 the total yield of the Comstock mines was $292,726,310, of which the companies paid out $125,355,925 in dividends. Actually, the losses from operations on the Comstock rival the gains in magnitude. Perhaps as many as 5,000 claims were located and traded within thirty miles of Virginia City. Only 300 were ever opened, only 20 became mines, and of these only 8 or 9 ever paid dividends. Over half of the profits from the Lode came from Consolidated Virginia, California, Crown Point, and Belcher. At the outset of the "bonanza" ten companies sank $17 million in diggings without a cent of return.

Actually the chances for profit in western mining were so slim that it is hard to explain the tremendous investment on purely economic grounds. Neither costs nor net return could be predicted with any accuracy. The expense of sinking shafts and digging "drifts" varied widely according to the rock encountered and the depth required. Underground streams of sulphurous hot water would stop operations for weeks and require the installation of expansive pumping units. The silver ore assaying as high as $3,000 per ton which was so often the cause of the frantic pace and inflated costs of mine development, usually petered out at lower depths to ore of much less value. By the time the high grade ore had been taken out, so much money had been spent that the lower grade ore could not be mined at a profit. The result would be bankruptcy and reorganization. Likely as not a new company would come to the same untimely end as the assay value dropped even further. The fact that the market price of silver drifted downward during the seventies and eighties only magnified the mine owners' problems.

Working conditions and wage levels were a cause of frequent labor difficulties which harassed mine owners and caused deep resentment among miners. Many of the miners had formerly been prospectors who had organized stable communities in democratic fashion and had worked their diggings under rules they had themselves fashioned and put in force. But after the surface ore had been skimmed off and the prospectors could no longer make a daily wage working their claims, almost overnight they became the employees of absentee corporations which had very little regard for employees' welfare. The former prospectors probably felt their plight even more keenly when they were submerged by hordes of foreigners—particularly Cornishmen—brought in to meet the burgeoning need for labor. By the seventies more than 3,000 miners were at work on the Comstock alone, and the larger mines employed as many as 500 men. The mines were hot and dangerous, and the prevailing wage of $4.00 per day, while more than twice the wage for unskilled labor in the East, provided no more than a bare subsistence because of the high prices for all the necessities of life.

Residual grievances, plus resentment caused by lowered wages and layoffs during slack periods, plus an existing unity along ethnic lines among the foreigners, fostered militant labor organizations. The unions were also strong because they were industrial rather than craft, and included a large majority of the male population of the mining communities. A Miners' Union formed on the Comstock in 1867 succeeded in forcing management to keep the $4.00 wage in effect during a period when profits fell off. Other unions sprang up in newly opened areas, and when management periodically lowered wages and laid off men, the result was often strikes, dynamitings, and open warfare. The Comstock miners struck in 1869; Leadville was paralyzed by a strike in 1880; the Coeur d'Alene region was under martial law for nearly a year between 1900 and 1901. Management retaliated by compiling blacklists and inducing governors to send in the militia. Some of the strikes were broken, and the unions which called them collapsed as a result. The Western Federation of Miners was completely broken by the military suppression of the Coeur d'Alene strike. But other walkouts brought considerable gains for the miners. Those working on the Comstock won an eight-hour day in 1872. Cripple Creek miners also gained this concession and the maintenance of regular wages as well. On the other hand, management almost never acceded to demands for union shop and checkoff.

Bad mining practices, as well as labor troubles and fluctuations in development costs and in the value of ore, often caused serious losses. Some mine owners, in order to realize quick profits, started taking out ore before adequate exploration had been made, and as a result had to abandon rich deposits because of flooding or cave-ins. Sometimes when the owners of stamping mills got control of mines they would rob the mines for the benefit of stamping mills by charging exorbitant prices for refining services, in much the same way as the Credit Mobilier exploited the Union Pacific Railroad. Mills regularly appropriated perhaps as much as 8 percent over and above the customary royalty, which was 35 percent of the assayed value of the ore. Tailings, or sludge remaining after amalgamation were abandoned even though containing as much as 20 percent silver.

Litigation became a large expense. By long standing custom claimants were considered to own all "apexes," or ends of veins which could be found within the limits of claims, and were then entitled to pursue the veins to their ends regardless of whether or not these stretched outside the rectangular limits of the claims. Obviously this rule led to frequent encroachment underground which was hard to prove in court. A federal apex law of 1872 limited claimants to the pursuit of veins through the side limits of claims, and blocked off the end limits, but this was only a partial solution of the problem. The aggregate cost of litigation occurring in the first bonanza of the Comstock, during the sixties, came to about $10 million, some 20 percent of the entire product during that period.

Finally, the losses from speculation cannot be calculated. The trade in stock on the San Francisco Exchange, the main funnel through which capital flowed into western mining from all over the world, was frenzied by our standards, and entirely unregulated. Short-term fluctuations of several hundred dollars in individual issues were quite usual, and sometimes went as high as $1,500. Bulls and bears fought each other viciously with every weapon at their command. One particularly objectionable practice often used was for directors who had advance news of a strike at a listed mine to issue calls on the stock, thus forcing small holders who could not raise the money to abandon their securities. As a result of feverish speculation, a street behind the Exchange, appropriately named "Paupers' Alley," had a large population of human wrecks who had come to grief trying to beat the game.

CONSOLIDATION IN MINING ENTERPRISE

By 1885 prospectors had explored most of the mountain area. Wherever metals were found in paying quantities a uniform cycle of development took place from prospector to promoter to heavily financed partnerships and corporations. Consolidation completed the growth process. Sometimes a whole area might be merged into one corporation, or the existing companies controlled by a holding company. Usually this last stage was accomplished in New York or London by the large banking syndicates which brought about the consolidations in so many other fields of business at the end of the century. But at any point the process of development could be halted by failure of the ore. In a matter of months, if not weeks, the clattering mills would come to a stop, the work forces would thin out and nearly disappear, and towns would die. The sagging, disused mine works and the remnants of ghost towns which dot the West offer mute testimony to the untimely end of much mining operation.

For a considerable period after the first silver strikes "refractory" silver-lead ore was as often a cause of mining failure as a decline in the quantity or quality of the ore itself. Separating silver and lead, which have a natural affinity for each other, could be accomplished only by smelting. The process as applied to iron ore was almost as old as mining itself, and was easily adapted to the copper mineral of Michigan, but smelting the complex silver-lead compounds of Colorado turned out to be an enormously difficult and expensive undertaking. But recovery was substantially increased by roasting, chlorination, and by the cyanide process. Roasting burned off much of the sulphur content in refractory ores; the addition of chlorine then formed soluable gold or silver chloride, from which metal could be easily precipitated. In the cyanide process ore crushed with potassium cyanide formed a soluable compound from which metal was recovered by electrolysis.

The development of smelting in Colorado is notable in that it laid the basis for the formation of the great Guggenheim mining empire. The rise of the Guggenheim family is almost unique in the history of entrepreneurship because it encompassed in the life of its founder, Meyer Guggenheim, the transition from a mercantile capitalism of an almost medieval variety to the finance capitalism and industrial imperialism of the twentieth century. Born to a Jewish immigrant family settled in the slums of Philadelphia, young Meyer peddled notions and hardware door to door in the anthracite region of Pennsylvania. Within a few years he had learned enough to abandon the pack which had been a symbol of his race stretching back to ancient times, and concentrated on the manufacture and sale of inexpensive household products. Showing a remarkable sensitivity for consumer preferences, he added many diverse items to the list of goods he manufactured or traded, and in 1872 formed a partnership to import cheap machine-made lace from Switzerland. Meanwhile by fathering the proverbial seven sons he brought into existence what was to become one of the mightiest family dynasties of the twentieth century.

Until the early 1880s his career had been little different from that of an eighteenth-century merchant capitalist. But during the early years of the decade, it entered a new phase when, as a result of a loan to the operator of a Leadville silver mine, Guggenheim came into possession of two mining properties. Against the advice of his family he poured developmental funds into them, and was rewarded when both went into bonanza and by 1887 yielded an estimated nine million ounces of silver and 86,000 tons of lead.

Like Ralston and Sharon, Guggenheim realized that the processing of ore promised to be a more stable source of profit than digging it out of the ground. In 1888 he abandoned entirely the merchandising traditional with his ancestors and committed himself and his progeny to the production of metals by investing the bulk of his fortune in a large smelter located at Pueblo. At first the enterprise lost heavily because of the difficulty of smelting the refractory sulphite ores, but it turned the corner when Guggenheim secured the services of August Raht as superintendent. Raht, a graduate of the famous Freiburg School of Mines, was to become a major figure in the Guggenheim empire. Realizing that technical proficiency was indispensable for the success of mining and refining enterprises, Guggenheim henceforth spared no expense to get the best men available for supervisory and managerial positions.

The transformation of the few Guggenheim mines and smelters into an industrial empire came about as a result of a struggle with the smelting "trust"—the American Smelting and Refining Company. Launched in 1899 by Grant Schley, a brother-in-law of George F. Baker, and John Moore, a banker with a large interest in Western Union, the company's object (besides promoters' fees and stock speculation), was pegging smelting prices in Colorado. Although offered attractive prices for their holdings, the Guggenheims refused to sell, feeling quite able to compete with the waterlogged giant. In the same year they formed the Guggenheim Exploration Company, a new kind of mining organization which combined prospecting with the promoting, engineering, and financing of mines. They chose as the head of the company the celebrated mining engineer John Hays Hammond at the unheard-of salary of $250,000 per year. Meanwhile competition with the smelting trust was becoming more bitter. In 1901 the American Smelting and Refining Company, overcome by the usual difficulties encountered by overcapitalized combinations trying to integrate numerous operating units of varying sizes and efficiency, threw in the towel by offering the Guggenheims a controlling voice in the organization and $45 million in stock for their plants, which were worth perhaps $5 million. The Guggenheims' acceptance was the first step in the creation of a mining, smelting, and refining empire which by the 1920s stretched from Alaska to Chile and had a strong beachhead in Africa.

Mining combination was carried even farther in Montana than in Colorado and California. In the sixties and seventies the gold rushes to Bannack, Virginia City, Helena, and Butte were little different from those to California some fifteen or more years earlier. Then came silver, and by 1887 Butte, earlier on its way to becoming a ghost town, had five mills of 290 stamps treating 400 tons of ore daily. During the period of the gold rushes much copper sulphide ore had been found, but the market for copper was so small that it had been thrown aside. In 1882 Marcus Daly, an Irish immigrant who had served as foreman in a Comstock mine in which Mackay had been superintendent, made a rich strike of copper sulphide in the Anaconda region, near Butte, and induced a group of partners to back him in a mining and smelting operation. At that time, despite the output of the Michigan mines, the yearly production of copper amounted to less than three weeks' supply today; but the electrical industry was just beginning to grow, and Daly correctly foresaw that the demand for copper would increase tremendously.

During the coming decade Daly and his partners constantly expanded operations, solved difficult problems in connection with the roasting and smelting of the ore, acquired railroad transportation, and constructed a town. In 1892 they incorporated as the Anaconda Copper Company, and the organization went on to become the giant industry it is today, taking over scores of claims and copper mines, timberlands, and coal mines. Shortly after the turn of the century three-fourths of the state's wage earners were on the rolls of its various enterprises.

Phelps Dodge, another major copper producer, reached its position of eminence in the industry by the familiar process in nineteenth-century America whereby capital and entrepreneurial talent was transferred from mercantile to industrial enterprise. In the 1870s the presence of large bodies of copper ore in Arizona was confirmed. A Detroit mining promoter, attracted to the region, developed claims and started mining and smelting on a regular basis. In need of further capital, he solicited a loan in 1880 from "the last of the merchant princes," William E. Dodge, son-in-law of the founder of the firm, Anson G. Phelps. Dodge engaged a Canadian-born mining engineer, James Douglas, to investigate the properties. On the basis of Douglas's enthusiastic report, Dodge started investing in Arizona. During the coming three decades the Phelps Dodge firm committed an increasing amount of capital to copper mining and smelting enterprises there, all of which were managed by Douglas. By

1910 the company had completely abandoned the import-export business inaugurated by Anson Phelps nearly a century before and had become one of the largest copper producers of the nation.

Meanwhile, combination of copper producers had proceeded apace in the Michigan peninsula. By 1900, Calumet and Hecla, Quincy, Osceola, and six new companies had taken over the properties of some two dozen unsuccessful concerns and now produced nearly the entire output of the region. Through interest groups and interlocking directorates the large companies had integrated both backward and forward, controlling not only ore ships, smelters, and sales agencies, but even wire mills and other fabricating concerns. The turn of the century was a period of great prosperity for the industry. The phenomenal rise of electrical equipment manufacture increased the copper market by one-third between 1898 and 1900, and as copper prices rose the stock of the leading companies tripled in value. But by this time, Michigan's proportion of total copper production had begun to decline, and leadership in the movement of consolidation was taken by the great "copper kings" of Montana and a handful of leading investment bankers and industrialists who had made fortunes in other enterprises.

The growth potential of the copper industry had attracted the attention of Henry H. Rogers and William Rockefeller, former members of the Standard Oil Trust now interested in variegated enterprises in addition to their massive holding in Standard Oil. Together with other investors, Rogers and Rockefeller purchased Anaconda in 1899 with the intention of making it the nucleus of a gigantic copper combination designed to bring together properties in Michigan, Arizona, and Montana. During the late eighties American copper production and prices had been regulated by an international cartel, and during the nineties an American Producers Association was formed to negotiate quotas and prices with a counterpart European Producers Association. But in the copper industry, as elsewhere, voluntary agreements of this type were of limited effectiveness and only led to the desire for more stringent controls made possible by combination. To this end the Rockefeller-Rogers syndicate formed Amalgamated Copper Company, a holding company for the stock of Anaconda and its related companies. Although members of the combination produced three-fifths of the nation's copper at the outset, the continual opening up of new fields and the refusal of Calumet and Hecla and other important Michigan mines to join made impossible the achievement of monopoly which the syndicate sought.

The brass industry of the Naugatuck Valley was also responding to the pressures for consolidation keenly felt by other metal industries anxious for price and production controls. Between 1899 and 1902 Charles F. Brooker, energetic president of Coe Brass Company, merged all of the important companies in the area except Scovill into the American Brass Company.

Gold and silver were found in quantity in the Boise and Coeur d'Alene regions of Idaho, but the richest strike of gold since forty-nine came in the Black Hills of Dakota. As in Georgia some forty years before, the gold lay in lands reserved for Indians, and the area was opened up to white men only after a bitter struggle. General George A. Custer, in command of the troops in the Dakotas, explored the Black Hills in 1874 and confirmed the existence of gold. As prospectors entered in defiance of attempts by the army to keep them out, pressure was brought to bear on the Sioux to give up their wooded reservation. Holding the region in religious veneration, the Sioux refused, and the subsequent three-way conflict between prospectors, Indians, and army led to the famous massacre of Custer and his men in 1876. After that, the Indians were forced to give way, and gold seekers flooded into the area. It proved to be rich in both surface gold and quartz deposits. The Homestake became the most notable mine of the region. Acquired in 1876 by George Hearst, former Comstocker and founder of the family fortune, Lloyd Tevis (see pp. 321, 475) and J. B. Haggin—all of whom later became Daly's partners in developing Anaconda—Homestake likewise became a giant integrated enterprise and in some years produced as much as 90 percent of the gold output of the Black Hills. By 1931 it had taken out over $233 million in gold.

ENGLISH INVESTMENT IN AMERICAN MINING

English investors had become increasingly interested in American mining during the eighties at the same time that they were pouring money into the cattle country. American promoters, aware of the financing opportunities available in England, kept close contact with English counterparts. British agencies such as Robert O. Old's British and Colorado Mining Bureau employed engineers resident in the United States to search for likely properties in the West, and in London offices offered prospective investors dazzling promotional literature, ore displays, and high pressure salesmanship. By the nineties promotional organizations in England, nominally headed by titled tycoons capable of arousing confidence among potential investors, were formed as parents of American mining companies. The bonds of paternal affection and filial piety were welded by stock swaps, sometimes with "founders shares" giving more generous participation in profits to the American companies.

The results of this trans-Atlantic co-operation were not too encouraging. As with the cattle companies, it was almost impossible for corporate management in England to exercise adequate controls over operating management in America, whether British or American, or even establish effective communications. Litigation was a constant harrassment. Also, British companies often spent 90 to 95 percent of their capital in the purchase of properties, and in order to develop the mines had to resort to borrowing and mortgaging. Many mines were purchased at inflated prices, and overcapitalization resulting from this and other causes made payment of adequate dividends out of earnings impossible and created the temptation to dip into capital in order to make a good showing before the investing public. Because of the great distances between the mines and the British investors, frauds were common.

One of the most notorious of these was the Emma Mine swindle. The prospectors who opened and explored the mine in 1868 sold it to a group of speculators who incorporated in New York with the sole purpose of selling the property in England. British speculators then formed a parent company to purchase it, operating behind an imposing façade of notables who lent their names in return for stock. On the wave of a tremendous, largely fraudulent promotional campaign, the company sold nearly £1 million worth of stock, estimating dividends at the rate of £700,000 per year. When the first fourteen months' net return amounted to no more than £30,000, the bubble burst. Dividends of £195,000 had been paid, mostly out of capital. When it became apparent that inefficiency had hampered the operations of the mine and that stock placed in high places had evoked the warm encomiums which had induced humbler investors to plunk down their pounds and shillings, the outcry was tremendous. Much of the denunciation voiced by stockholders, the British press, and the public generally, centered on Robert C. Schenck, the American minister to England, who had lent his influence to forward the speculation in return for a privileged position at the table when the melon was to be cut. Schenck resigned his position under fire, and, after an investigation by the Committee on Foreign Affairs, was censured for his part in the promotion by the House of Representatives.

Although the Emma swindle temporarily soured the attitude of British investors toward American mining enterprises, the hope of bonanzas shortened memories of past failures. Between 1860 and 1901, 518 British companies with a nominal capitalization of about $389 million were formed to participate in American mining ventures. Actually, these figures are not very meaningful. Many of the companies never started work, many were reorganizations, and only a fraction of the capital was paid up. At least fifty-seven companies registered between 1860 and 1901 paid aggregate dividends of £11,750,000 prior to 1915, but no more than ten companies ever returned the full investment and not more than one out of nine ever paid anything at all. If losses on unsuccessful mines are taken into account in arriving at a figure for net return, profits to British investors would be much smaller, if not wiped out entirely.

In part, the spotty returns from British investments were caused by shortcomings in business judgment and by speculative practices, but more importantly the discouraging over-all profit record merely reflected the basic conditions of mining enterprise. It was simply a high risk, winner-take-all kind of business. Losses were literally incalculable. As far as the precious metals are concerned, it is questionable, according to that successful mining engineer, Herbert Hoover, whether the value of all gold and silver produced in the United States exceeded the costs of production. But the losses attending mining enterprise were more than compensated for by its multiplier effect. The mushrooming mining communities constituted markets which stimulated cattle and sheep raising and helped to bring about the transfer of a major lumber industry from the Lake States to the Far West. The market for foodstuffs promoted rapid agricultural expansion in such originally remote regions as the valleys of the Williamette, the Boise, and the Gallatin rivers. Western mining not only made San Francisco an international financial center, but because of the need for mining equipment promoted manufacturing there as well. Urbanization and railroad transportation in the Rockies was mainly a response to the needs of mining enterprise. Without the development of mining in this region, it might even today be what it was called a century and a half ago—the Great American Desert.

XXX. Patterns of Growth in the Textile Industries

Patterns of growth in the older consumer industries during the nineteenth century had many similarities. At the outset the productive units were very small and were powered by primitive water wheels. Capital came from local savings and credit, and from mercantile surpluses. Where production was mainly for local use, growth was made possible by an increase in the needs of the community. Availability of export markets also stimulated expansion in the areas geographically suited for export production. Each industry at some point had its own "take-off" in the form of a technological breakthrough which may have been a response to market demand for a greater volume, better quality of production, or for new types of product. Following the "take-off" there came in each instance a period of rapid growth and of successive mechanization of skilled tasks requiring high-priced labor. Heightened competition produced the ambiguous attitude represented by agreements on prices and production which were honored more in the breach than in the observance. Failure of these agreements to achieve their objective spurred the desire for combination. In industries containing a large number of small plants with varying degrees of mechanization turning out similar but not identical products, combination entailed little more than loose, and sometimes ineffective centralized control over finance, prices, and the volume of production. Little or no attempt was made to co-ordinate and rationalize production processes. The main object was to secure price stability. But in industries containing a small number of large plants producing an identical product, combination in some instances moved toward vertical integration. Seeking economies of scale as well as control of the market, the integrated firms invested heavily in mechanization, and reached backward to control supplies of raw materials and forward to dominate marketing.

We have already seen one type of growth pattern in the early textile industry (chapter 7). The demand factor providing a favorable environment was the widespread need for cheap clothing materials traditionally produced by hand spinning and hand weaving. Two technological breakthroughs got the cotton textile industry off to a flying start—the Arkwright spinning frame and the power loom. The growth of individual plants was financed by local savings, by the transfer of mercantile capital from commercial enterprises, and by the plowing back of profits. As the result of rapid technological improvement the American industry after the Civil War became perhaps the most efficient in the world. It had one employee for every four looms, as contrasted with one for every two looms in Britain. While the older New England centers such as Lowell and Lawrence continued to occupy an important position, many of the more modern and efficient mills came to be located in New Bedford and Fall River as steam power came into more general use. The moist climate of the two towns was particularly favorable for textile manufacture, and the mills there also enjoyed the rock bottom transportation costs prevailing in deep water ports.

Marketing methods did not change materially, although the larger firms bypassed sales agencies by selling direct to New York jobbers, large retailers, and even department stores. Purchasing was increasingly focused on the New York Cotton Exchange, a futures market utilized by mill owners primarily to hedge their cotton purchases. In hedged transactions "spot" (cash) purchases of commodities and the sale of contracts for future delivery of the commodities are made simultaneously. Since the differential between spot and futures prices tends to remain the same regardless of the fluctuations of the market, a decline in the spot price of cotton, for example, would be offset by a wider profit spread on the futures contract. Conversely, a rise in the cash price of cotton would be offset by a corresponding loss on the futures contract. The benefits of hedging are somewhat reduced by the stimulation to speculation brought about by trading in futures. On balance, the New York Cotton Market greatly aided New England mill owners by providing them with regular supplies of cotton and insulating them from fluctuations in the values of their cotton inventories. Advances or declines in the values of these inventories would entail similar, rapid changes in the prices of finished products which would have an unsettling effect upon the textile markets and alter the balance of competition.

Rising production and slowly falling textile prices during the eighties and nineties confronted the New England mills with familiar problems. Voluntary co-operation to restrict production and maintain prices was facilitated by the family alliances, interfirm stock purchases, and interlocking directorates which created strong communities of interest. The New England Cotton Manufacturers Association, one of the many trade associations making an appearance throughout American industry during these years, provided a forum for discussion of common problems, and, potentially, an agency to enforce voluntary agreements. Perhaps the most effective regulator of production was the Arkwright Club of Boston, made up of treasurers of New England mills. A permanent bureau of the club conducted lobbying activities and in many other ways promoted the common interests of the members.

The desire to form combinations as a means of meeting the problems of competition was less strong in textiles than in many other industries, probably because these offered only limited opportunities to gain economies of size. Nevertheless, four such organizations made their appearance around the turn of the century—the Consolidated Cotton Duck Company, the New England Cotton Yarn Company, the United States Finishing Company, and the American Thread Company. With the exception of the thread combine none of these groupings was very successful financially nor remotely approached a monopoly of production in its field, primarily because so many strong companies—unafraid of price competition—refused to join. The thread combine was more effective than the others because of the small number of firms in its field. Within fourteen plants it controlled one-third of the thread production of the nation in 1901 and paid dividends of between 4 and 15 percent during the first decade of the century.

Despite falling prices, stiff competition, and the effect of business fluctuations, the New England industry appeared to be fairly prosperous during the last years of the century. But little specific information is available on which to base generalizations. Directors of the closely held corporations gave out little information on financial condition, and because expansion had been financed over the years by plowing back profits against which no stock was issued, it is very difficult to ascertain the size of the investments on which returns were received. What is more plain, however, is that the youthful period of exuberant growth was over, and that as a result the industry was exhibiting many of the characteristics of the aging process. As industries in the course of their life cycle reach maturity, output levels off, the pace on innovation slackens, technology become standardized, the size of production units increases, and management become bureaucratized. Most of these characteristics were present in the New England textile industry at the turn of the century. In some sectors plants continued to increase in size and decrease in number. Spindlage in cotton textile grew only 2½ percent from 1880 to 1889, and 1 9/10 percent from 1890 to 1899. Interest in innovations practically ceased. The average age of machinery lengthened and there was little demand for the only important technological improvement of the period, the Draper loom, which changed bobbins automatically without necessitating shutdowns.

THE REBIRTH OF THE COTTON TEXTILE INDUSTRY IN THE SOUTH
One of the most notable developments in the history of business during the postwar era was the rise of the cotton textile industry in the South. It was all the more dramatic because its characteristics were remarkably similar to those of the New England industry in the youthful period during the first half of the century, and because the rebirth of the southern industry took place as the New England industry was moving toward maturity. Once slavery had been abolished, the need felt by southern leaders to protect the "peculiar institution" disappeared, and with it the paralyzing ambivalence of attitude toward industrialization. Furthermore, the Civil War had blasted into thin air the idealized agrarianism which supposedly represented the destiny of the antebellum South. Now the impassioned calls of Gregg, DeBow, and others could be enthusiastically heeded. Since during the war the British had developed new sources of raw cotton, it appeared that in the future the southern economy would have to depend for growth on factors other than staple production. Constitutional changes during Reconstruction, by bringing many long-overdue democratic reforms, had lowered the center of gravity of political power, and politicians found it expedient as well as economically beneficial to

advocate steps which would bring employment and a better standard of living to the poor whites.

Despite increasing enthusiasm for manufacturing, the confusion of Reconstruction prevented significant progress from being made until after the informal, but very important sectional treaty of 1877 placed the control of the southern social system in the hands of southern leaders. Promoters now wrote letters to moneyed Yankee businessmen describing in glowing terms the prospects for southern textile mills, and, if the Yankees could be induced to travel southward, showed promising locations to them. But the Atlanta International Cotton Exposition of 1881 proved in many ways to be the kickoff of the new campaign for industrialization. Here for the first time significant numbers of northern merchant capitalists, commission merchants, and representatives of textile machine companies had a chance to confer with the promoters of southern mills.

During the years immediately following, more such meetings were held and a wave of cotton mill building swept over the South. During the last two decades of the century the number of spindles jumped from 548,048 to 4,299,988; looms increased from 6,256 to 110,015. By 1900 the South possessed almost one-third of the cotton textile machinery in the nation, most of it late model ring spinners and power looms.

Capital for the mills came from a variety of sources. Since a major purpose was to help the poor whites, many mills were looked upon as community enterprises, and got their start by the combining of small savings. Many townspeople expected the same spiraling prosperity from cotton mills that former generations had expected from railroads. Following a plan widely publicized by the southern engineer, mill owner, publisher, and promoter—Daniel A. Tomkins—some communities financed mills by the pay-as-you-go, building and loan principle. Stock was purchased by payments of from twenty-five cents to $2 per week, and the mills were built gradually as the money came in. Sometimes the initial capital was borrowed, and repaid from the proceeds of such stock sales. The large commission merchants and jobbers of New York and Philadelphia, and lesser firms in the southern states, became important sources of capital. Northern machinery manufacturers during the nineties took stock in the mills as part payment for machinery ordered, or lent by granting long-term credit. The machinery firms were not enthusiastic about the practices, for obvious reasons, but stiff competition after the Panic of 1893 forced them to sell under terms increasingly favorable to the buyer.

Technical assistance and supervisory personnel at the outset came usually from the North. But the entrepreneurs who gave the impetus to the cotton mill movement were almost entirely southerners. Few came from the decimated ranks of the old aristocracy; most represented middle-class families with interests in banking, commerce, or railroads. Some of the most successful textile entrepreneurs, who founded enduring dynasties, were oriented toward sales. Bobo Simpson Tanner, organizer of several North Carolina mills, began his business career as a drummer. Fuller E. Callaway of Callaway Mills, Greenville, South Carolina, according to tradition started peddling spools of thread at the age of eight.

About the only promoter of this generation to have a technical orientation was Daniel A. Tomkins. Educated at The University of North Carolina and Rensselaer Polytechnic Institute, he became a draftsman for Alexander L. Holley, the Troy, New York, ironmaster who introduced Sir Henry Bessemer's process for manufacturing steel into the United States. For a brief period Tomkins represented the Whitin Textile Machine Company in the South. A versatile person with varied interests, he published the *Charlotte Observer* and drew the plans and supervised the construction of the textile school of North Carolina State College. Perhaps his greatest achievement was promoting the cottonseed oil industry. At the height of his career he also owned and managed three large cotton textile mills and was a director in many more.

The poor white families who constituted the work force of the southern textile industry were housed in drab mill villages and were usually subjected to strong paternalistic controls. But rents were low—about twenty-five cents to seventy-five cents per week, and the houses were probably better than the cabins in which the workers had been born. Also, the controls were probably necessary to protect family life and maintain efficiency in the mills. Moreover, the children got a modicum of education which would have been unavailable in the blighted areas from which the families came. Wages ranging from twenty-five cents to one dollar per day, about two-thirds of the wage levels prevailing in New England, gave the southern industry its greatest competitive advantage. Perhaps the worst aspect of the labor system was the continuing tradition of child labor it imposed upon the South and the resulting idleness and demoralization it engendered among male heads of families. In 1900 children under sixteen made up 25 percent of the labor force; in New England the comparable figure was 6 7/10 percent and falling. Appalling as these labor conditions seem to us today, they were accepted without protest by the working families, mainly because life in the mill villages was at least as good, and probably better, than on eroded hillside farms.

Built at a later date, the southern mills had the advantage of starting their careers with the most modern machinery available. The initial product, like that of the New England mills seventy-five years before, was coarse goods—unbleached sheetings, shirtings, drills, ducks, denims, and coarse yarn. But as southern manufacturers gained experience, they quickly broadened their lines and began to produce some fine fabrics. Aggressive mill men like Tomkins, responding to suggestions from commission houses, also developed an export trade of considerable importance. By the end of the century southern textiles were competing in the markets of South America and Asia.

Little need be said about developments in marketing, since these paralleled the ones in the northern industry. By 1905 a few of the largest mills had established their own sales agencies. In 1903 James W. Cannon launched his own sales affiliate, Cannon Mills, Incorporated. As in the North, family alliances, interlocking directorates, and cross holdings of stock provided strong communities of interest.

Profits from the southern mills were, on the average, larger than those in New England industry, probably because of lower wage costs and better equipment. According to one analysis, while a representative group of New England mills paid average dividends of 7.7 percent between 1889 and 1908, a comparable group of southern mills distributed earnings of from 10 to 30 percent.

WOOLENS AND WORSTEDS

The woolen and worsted industries followed a pattern of rapid expansion during and after the Civil War. The new and dynamic worsted manufacture in 1869 was carried on by 102 large, heavily capitalized corporations equipped with English machinery and employing an average of 129 persons apiece. By contrast, the 2,891 woolen mills in the nation at this time employed an average of forty-three per establishment. Because of the ubiquity of the raw materials woolen mills were more evenly distributed throughout the nation than cotton mills, but a concentration of larger mills remained in New England in the vicinity of the great Boston wool market, which supplied the many different types of wools and fleeces for the variety of materials woven on the looms of these larger companies. Between 1869 and 1919, following the pattern of the cotton textile industry, the number of mills declined, while output increased nearly sevenfold. During the course of this expansion, domestic manufacturers, with the help of generous tariff protection, left far behind the foreign competition which had so circumscribed the domestic industry during its early years. While the value of domestic production advanced from $43,207,000 in 1849 to

$292,660,000 in 1904, the value of imported goods rose only from $17,470,000 to $25,204,000 during the period.

Size offered economies of somewhat greater importance than in the cotton textile industry. Large firms with a wide variety of output lowered the cost of raw materials by purchasing fleeces, which have different types of fibers, rather than the more expensive bagged and graded wool. Large mills also saved by performing all the manufacturing processes from washing to finishing. By 1900 the larger mills were beginning to carry on their own marketing, and the worsted industry was finding a rapidly growing outlet for its products in the ready-made clothing industry.

Woolens manufacturers were more interested in combination than cotton textile manufacturers, in part because leaders of the industry felt that its prosperity depended largely on the maintenance of high tariff schedules, and in part because the industry was hard hit by a post-Civil War depression and by the hard times of the nineties. In 1899, largely under the leadership of William Wood, treasurer of Washington Mills of Lawrence, Massachusetts, the American Woolen Company was formed, ultimately combining twenty-six mills and controlling perhaps as much as 70 percent of the men's wear worsted output of the nation. Since worsted production was concentrated in a relatively small number of large plants grouped together within a limited area, it could be more easily combined than the more widely dispersed woolens industry. The company was heavily over-capitalized, largely because of inflated prices paid for its constituent parts, and as a result at the outset was able to pay nothing on its common stock. Some specialization of production was attempted, but it apparently was not carried to the level of integration.

THE CARPET MANUFACTURE

The manufacture of carpets was a sector of the textile industry growing in importance during the nineteenth century. Carpets were very rare during the colonial period, and even in upper-class homes bare, polished floors were the rule. But during the 1820s simple carpets with linen warps and woolen cloth as filler made their appearance. During the following decades, as carpets became a part of the furnishings usual in the homes of the middle class, the carpet manufacture emerged as a distinct branch of the textile industry.

The manufacture had some unique characteristics not shared by the other branches of the industry. It imported a large proportion of its skilled labor—mostly from England and Scotland—and nearly all of the short, kinky wool fiber which constituted its raw material. The few large firms which led the industry had much better machinery than the great number of small shops which produced a disproportionately large share of the output. Changing styles and weaves required heavy capital outlays for new and ever more complex looms which the smaller concerns simply could not afford. Thus, throughout the nineteenth century these firms turned out the simpler carpet weaves with looms long obsolete while the industry leaders continued to make technological improvements after the pace of innovation had slowed nearly to a halt in the cotton textile industry.

Because of the continuing need for new capital, talent, and equipment, mergers began earlier than in other branches of the textile business and by the end of the nineteenth century had produced some very large firms. Three companies survived initial competition to become early leaders in the industry—the Thompsonville Carpet Company of Enfield, Connecticut; the Lowell Manufacturing Company of Lowell, Massachusetts; and the Saxon Mill of Saxonville, Massachusetts. The last became a unit of the present Roxbury Carpet Company, and the Thompsonville and Lowell concerns amalgamated with other firms to form the Bigelow-Sanford Company. The Hartford Carpet Company also became an industry leader after absorbing two small New York concerns of E. S. Higgins and Stephen Sanford. Alexander Smith of Yonkers, New York, forged ahead to become the largest firm in the nation by 1900.

The first mechanical improvement to be adopted was the Jacquard attachment, imported from France about 1825 and used for the weaving of fancy fabrics of many kinds. The attachment consisted of an endless belt of cards fitted with wire teeth which pressed against cords which raised or lowered individual warp strings for each throw of the shuttle. The most important native achievement in technology was the invention of a power loom by Erastus Bigelow in 1839 to weave ingrain carpets. Later Bigelow built a more complicated loom with a Jacquard attachment for weaving Brussels carpets. The Skinner loom, invented in 1856, made possible the power weaving of tufted, Axminster carpets. By 1875 the carpet weaving technology of the United States was the most advanced in the world.

Between 1869 and 1904 the number of plants dropped from 215 to 139 while output of carpeting quadrupled, thus paralleling a similar development in the woolens industry. Capital came from the usual sources—from surpluses built up in foreign and domestic trade, from sales agencies, from plowing back profits, and from investment of profits made elsewhere in the textile industry. Management was unspecialized, with one or two executives in even the largest plants carrying most of the load of decision making. Marketing methods evolved somewhat faster in the carpet manufacture than in other branches of the textile industry. Since the product went unaltered from the plant to the ultimate purchaser, some firms by the end of the century were experimenting with advertising and the promotion of brand names.

The usual measures for price and product fixing had been tried, but with the meager success which usually attended these efforts elsewhere. However, the few leading firms, particularly Alexander Smith, did exercise effective price leadership—that is, the prices they set tended to become standard throughout the industry.

SILK

The manufacture of silk textiles has had a history markedly different from that of other textiles. Probably no other article of any kind produced in America has been the object of such long-continued and uniformly unsuccessful promotion by government. The production of silk was a major element of British mercantilistic planning for the colonies. But the efforts to promote the growing of mulberry trees, the culture of cocoons and the "reeling" (unwinding) of silk filaments were without exception failures. Today the reasons are obvious enough. Cocoon culture and silk reeling were processes requiring a very high degree of skill and experience which could be gained only over a period of many years, if not generations. Furthermore, even if this obstacle could have been overcome, it would not have been possible to produce silk within the price range of the oriental product. In China and Japan reelers who were the beneficiaries of thirty generations of experience were producing silk filament for wages of five to ten cents per day.

Yet even after independence the production of raw silk was still considered so important that several states granted the traditional tax exemptions and bounties to entrants into the field. In a few areas, particularly in sections of New England where there was a surplus of labor, production did gain a precarious and temporary foothold. During the 1830s silk growers and "throwsters" (i.e., spinners, from the Saxon, *thrawan*, to twist) of Mansfield, Connecticut, turned out about $50,000 worth of silk yarn per year, spinning the fibers on ordinary home spinning wheels. Several promoters in Connecticut attempted to integrate production from mulberry tree to finished silk fabric, but the corporations they founded were not successful.

By 1860 the lessons drawn from 250 years of failure in silk culture were belatedly accepted, and the attempt to produce raw silk was practically abandoned. But the weaving of silk textiles from raw material imported over the high tariff barrier proved unexpectedly successful. Mechanization gave the United States an advantage in silk weaving to offset the disadvantage in silk culture occasioned by the high price of American labor and the lack of necessary skills. Patterson, New Jersey, became a center for the production of silk fabrics after John Ryle, an English immigrant with experience in the craft, started a successful mill there in partnership with Philadelphia merchants. The largest enterprise of its type in the nation in 1857, it employed 400 to 500 operatives and consumed 2,000 pounds of raw silk per week.

After the Civil War, Congress, in recognition of the success in the manufacture of silk textiles, abandoned the duties on raw silk and replaced them with a high protective schedule for silk fabrics. Mechanical advances in reeling made possible the importation of cocoons for unwinding, thus lowering the cost of filament. Between 1870 and 1890 the annual production of silk textiles rose from $12 million to $87 million. During this period the silk textile industry went through the same cycle of rapid growth and technological progress which the cotton textile industry had experienced between 1820 and 1840. Urbanization and a rapidly growing middle class provided the expansive stimulus for the market.

XXXI. Patterns of Growth in Other Consumer Industries

The developmental traits of the textile industries were shared by many other consumer industries during the nineteenth century. But in the case of the industries discussed in this chapter the drive toward combination was more intense and the revolutionary impact of new technologies more marked. In all of the textile industries except carpet manufacturing the cards, spinning frames, and looms of 1900 were merely improved models of the machinery in use half a century before, but in each of the industries discussed below there was at least one technological innovation which, by mechanizing tasks formerly accomplished by hand, completely altered the conditions of production. In most cases these innovations were very expensive, and overnight transformed industries formerly characterized by a low capital-output ratio into capital intensive industries. By the same token the innovations sharply raised the optimum size of individual plants. Finally, the greatly increased production made possible by mechanized production methods threatened to drive down prices. All of these developments contributed to some degree to a desire for combination. Doubtless stock speculation was also a motive because expectations of high profits from merged plants which enjoyed economies of scale and could control the volume of output nearly always drove the stock of the new corporations upward in the market.

FLOUR MILLING

The wars of the French Revolution created an enhanced demand for American flour in Europe and in the West Indies, and shortly thereafter the newly independent nations of South America widened the market still further by opening their ports to the American product. By 1860 exports of flour were second in value only to exports of cotton. Yet the expanding domestic market in the cotton states, the Far West, and—most important—the large cities, provided the industry with its greatest opportunity for growth. By 1846 New York had become the largest wholesale flour center in the nation. A relatively small number of merchants there financed milling throughout the Northeast by allowing the millers with whom they did business to draw drafts for the purchase of wheat. It was estimated that during the forties these merchants advanced nearly $10 million per year for this purpose, and collected, in addition to interest, about $225,000 profit on sales. Merchants of New Orleans, Baltimore, and Philadelphia in similar fashion financed millers and sold their product, but on a smaller scale.

The first technological improvement in the milling industry was the completely automated flour mill devised in 1783 by a Delaware farm boy, Oliver Evans. This amazing, utterly unprecedented invention, utilizing conveyor systems, a screw-type elevator, and an automatic raking "hopper boy," was so far ahead of its time that it was seldom adopted in its entirety during the eighteenth century. During the first half of the nineteenth century larger mills, relying on successive editions of Evans's *Young Millwright and Miller's Guide*, constructed some of the installations, but the equipment of the smaller mills doing a custom business remained quite similar to that of the colonial period.

The problem of grinding the hard spring wheat of the Northwest, which had an oily husk resistant to conventional grinding methods for the winter wheat of the rest of the nation, stimulated further technological innovation. One solution was the "new process," using a "middlings purifier" devised from an earlier European model. By this method the middlings were ground several times until the husks were reduced to powder and could be separated from the flour by blasts of air. In 1874 John Stevens, of Neenah, Wisconsin, made an even more important innovation by using corrugated rollers instead of mill stones to crack the husk of the wheat and separate it from the kernel. This process was not only much faster but raised the proportion of top grade flour recovered from spring wheat from 25 percent to 90 percent. These two inventions were indispensable for the full development of the Northwest as a wheat growing region.

Under the impetus derived from the steadily increasing demand for flour and the spread of the new milling methods, Minneapolis became the nation's leading milling center. Location at the Falls of St. Anthony, on the Mississippi, and service by competing railroads giving good connections to Chicago and the East also aided in its growth. The average daily capacity per mill rose from 242 barrels in 1876 to 1,837 barrels in 1890, while the number of mills in the city increased only from twenty to twenty-four.

Throughout the period of growth the Minneapolis industry was dominated by a small group of families whose names became widely known throughout the nation—among them Pillsburys, Washburns, and Crosbys. At the outset construction of mills was financed largely by the transfer of capital from the lumber business after the forests had disappeared. Capital for growth came from reinvested profits, from eastern commission merchants who handled Minneapolis flour, and from eastern millers transferring their operations to what appeared to be a more favorable location. After 1888 capital in considerable amounts also came from abroad.

Economies of size multiplied after 1880. The larger mills could buy wheat over wider areas, assuring constant supplies and uniform quality. New methods and volume production reduced costs to the point that in good times leaders in the industry were making profits of two dollars to three dollars per barrel—much larger than the profits of older mills in less productive wheat areas. By sending out their own sales agents, who did business directly with eastern wholesalers and representatives of foreign houses, the larger mills could eliminate the services of the local commission merchants. Finally, volume production enabled the big mills to get larger railroad rebates than smaller competitors.

Spurred by a variety of incentives toward combination, mergers multiplied during the late eighties. By 1889 the mills owned by the Pillsbury family achieved a daily capacity of 10,000 barrels. In that year an English syndicate united the Pillsbury interests with those of their closest competitor to form the giant Pillsbury-Washburn Flour Mills Company, Ltd. The syndicate also purchased a line of country wheat elevators, a terminal elevator and control of the St. Anthony Falls water power installations. Other consolidations of large family interests followed, and by 1895 practically all of the milling capacity in Minneapolis was owned by three interest groups: the Pillsbury-Washburn, the Washburn-Crosby, and the Northwestern Consolidated. The groups also had large investments in line and public terminal elevators, and in railroads serving the wheat country.

In order to procure an adequate and continuing supply of wheat, which was difficult because of the rapid growth of the mills from the seventies onward, leading millers formed the Minneapolis Millers' Association in 1876. The organization established price schedules and rules for grading and maintained offices in the city, where wheat was bought by sample. An army of agents combed the country around Minneapolis, buying wheat and delivering it to local elevators for storage until needed. But besides antagonizing farmers, who claimed that they were exploited by artificially depressed prices and unfair grading, the Millers' Association alarmed business interests in Minneapolis not represented in it. As a result the Chamber of Commerce in 1881 established an open wheat pit similar to that of Chicago in order to provide an alternative supply of grain. Futures trading enabled millers to protect their inventories from price fluctuations and maintain stable prices for flour, but added a speculative element to market transactions which provoked a new wave of public criticism.

Paralleling marketing developments in other big businesses, the large firms by the turn of the century had largely dispensed with the services of commission merchants and independent sales agencies. In addition to employing their own salesmen they began cautiously to undertake advertising promotions. The success of brand names such as Pillsbury's Best and Ceresota led the large firms to form national marketing agencies early in the twentieth century. Foreign sales diminished relative to total sales during the nineteenth century, and the percentage of wheat exported as flour dropped from 99 percent in 1800 to 41 percent in 1900. Nevertheless, during this period total exports burgeoned from 2,980,702 barrels to 81,741,862 barrels, and the leading firms expanded their foreign marketing activities concurrently with those in the United States.

PAPER

Because of scarce raw materials and a technology behind that of Europe until the latter nineteenth century, the paper manufacture before that time could not supply domestic needs, let alone produce a surplus for export. Technological advance was more difficult than in many other fields because it involved the solution of chemical as well as mechanical problems. The paper making machines finally developed were among the most complicated and expensive machinery in use at the time.

The first improvement in technological methods was brought about by use of the Hollander "Beater Engine" which macerated rags more quickly than the stampers used previously. In order to mechanize the hand process of forming sheets a cylinder machine was constructed in 1816 similar to others used in England which picked up pulp from a vat and rolled it into long sheets. Swifter advance came with the development of the Fourdrinier machines, bulky and complicated devices originally manufactured in France which carried pulp on endless belts of wire mesh through not only the drying stage but eventually all finishing operations as well. By 1867 Fourdriniers were in use which could turn out paper at a rate of a hundred feet per minute. Today's machines, about a city block long and constructed at a cost of millions of dollars apiece, produce newsprint in endless sheets as wide as a highway at speeds up to twenty-five miles per hour.

Mechanization of the forming and drying processes focused attention on the problem of breaking the bottleneck of the industry by finding substitutes for rags in the production of pulp. After unsuccessful experiments had been carried out with straw, manila rope, and other materials, a breakthrough came in 1854 when the English process of producing pulp by boiling wood in a caustic alkali solution was introduced into this country. With the refinement of this method into the sulphite and sulphate processes the problem of raw material was solved.

The use of Fourdriniers and wood pulp completely transformed the paper industry, and at a critical moment. With the coming of the continuous action roller press and the linotype machine the newspaper industry became dependent upon a cheap and practically unlimited supply of paper which would have been inconceivable in 1850.

After 1865 size and capitalization of paper plants increased greatly. As paper making became a forest industry it moved into the woods shortly after the iron manufacture had emerged to locate in industrial centers. With increased production prices fell and paper making acquired an export sector which balanced, but never replaced the importation of fine papers during the nineteenth century.

Control of competition was attempted by the American Paper Manufacturers Association, formed in 1878, but during the hard times of the nineties the ineffectiveness of existing agreements provided incentive for two consolidations—the American Writing Paper Company, and the International Paper Company. The first of these, although combining some twenty-eight concerns and controlling 75 percent of the national production of writing paper, was not particularly successful. Its restrictive policies, variegated production, and apparent lack of co-ordination among its widely distributed plants created a situation which invited competition from small independents which could produce profitably at prices under those set by the combine. By 1940 the company had gone through two reorganizations. The International Paper Company, which controlled 70 percent of the nation's newsprint, was in a much better strategic situation. The combination was made up of thirty heavily capitalized units, all turning out the same product. International quickly transformed horizontal combination into vertical integration by simultaneously acquiring huge areas of timberland and building a national marketing organization.

GLASS

The glass industry, like the paper industry, developed slowly during the first third of the nineteenth century, held back by traditional methods of manufacture, an apparent reluctance to experiment with labor-saving machinery, and foreign competition—particularly in the finer grades of table ware. Unique labor relations had much to do with the lagging pace of innovations. Glass workers were an aristocracy of American labor, small in number, highly skilled and organized, often receiving wages which placed them on a level with professional people. Strong bargaining power, therefore, gave glass workers a considerable voice in management. The entrenched power of labor made it difficult to innovate in any area, and practically impossible to alter the functions of the labor force.

But between 1880 and 1920 the industry was revolutionized by a series of technological innovations which mechanized the methods by which window glass and common containers were produced. Leadership in the transformation was taken by a group of businessmen in Toledo, Ohio, who held large interests in the growing glass industry of the city. The most important of these men were Edward D. Libbey and Michael J. Owens, who together founded the company which became Libbey-Owens-Ford. Libbey, the son of a prosperous glass manufacturer of Cambridge, Massachusetts, moved to Toledo in 1888 when workers of his Cambridge plant struck and demanded wages equal to those of glass workers in Pittsburgh, where operating costs were lower. The Toledo area not only possessed the clay and sand necessary for glass manufacture, but natural gas for furnace fuel as well. Moreover, local businessmen, eager to promote the establishment of a strong glass industry, promised help in financing a new enterprise. Owens, the son of a penniless Irish coal miner, first achieved success as a leading official in the American Flint Glass Workers Union—an improbable origin for an outstanding businessman of the late nineteenth and early twentieth centuries. An experienced glass blower, he came to work in Libbey's Toledo plant shortly after it went into operation, and because of his ability both in expediting production and in dealing with the workers, soon rose to become plant superintendent. Libbey and Owens fortunately had capacities which were complementary. The former was an able promoter, salesman, and financier who was able to draw into his various enterprises moneyed men of courage and vision. Owens combined an intimate knowledge of traditional skills of glassmaking with the mechanical ingenuity of the self-taught engineer and a capacity for leadership seasoned in the rough school of union politics.

Libbey apparently anticipated continuing production of the glassware he had manufactured in Cambridge, and produced an artistic display of it for the Columbian Exhibition of 1893. But Owens persuaded him also to supply the bulbs used by Westinghouse to provide electric light for the exhibition, and in the course of filling the contract invented a machine which blew the bulbs. Mechanical blowing was the crucial process which inaugurated the mechanization of the industry. Appropriately, it was a response to the need for mass-producing an artifact foreign to the traditional lines of the glass manufacture, but of vital importance to a new and dynamic industry. In 1895 Libbey and Owens formed the Toledo Glass Company to hold patents and carry on developmental work. As new automatic processes and machinery were developed by the Glass Company, Libbey, Owens, and a Toledo investors' group formed companies to manufacture, license producers, or to sell equipment. A major accomplishment of this period was Owens's invention of an automatic bottle blowing machine in 1903 which revolutionized the glass container industry. Under the stimulus provided by the Toledo group the desire for mechanization radiated throughout the glass industry, and it belatedly entered into a creative period of technological development similar to like periods through which the textile industries had passed at various times during the nineteenth century.

Earnings of the Libbey and Owens enterprises were large, and about 50 percent was retained for reinvestment. Financing above and beyond retained earnings came from within the relatively small group gathered together by Libbey over the years. These men may also have acted as a funnel for additional funds coming from outside the circle. As patents ran out, the Libbey companies began the manufacture of bottles, a line of business in which they had an advantage because of accumulated experience.

Meanwhile combination moved forward rapidly in plate glass and window glass. By 1895 the Pittsburgh Plate Glass Company, founded 12 years earlier, had succeeded in absorbing all but three of the plants in this narrow field. The American Window Glass Company, a $17 million combine of 53 plants, controlled 70 percent of the nation's glass furnace capacity. Attempts to form combinations in the flint glass and tableware fields were by no means as successful as in plate and window glass. The small size, variegated production, and wide dispersal of the plants made integration impossible and invited competition from independents.

Reasons for the explosion of the glass industry into big business are not so apparent as they might seem. Tariff protection, often considered a stimulator of economic growth, was probably of little effect. It had seemingly failed to influence the industry one way or another during the first hundred years of the nation's existence, except, perhaps, to prolong the life of inefficient plants and thereby promote resistance to change. High labor costs seem rather surprisingly not to have stimulated a desire for laborsaving machinery so strongly felt at other times an in other sectors of the economy. A response to the economic trends of the day might constitute a more valid reason for the revolution in the glass industry. Urbanization, mass markets, and the needs of industry provided the opportunity for vastly increased production. Also, entrepreneurship played an important role. The fact that the revolution in glassmaking occurred in the place and at the time it did was the result of the efforts of the very talented group of Toledo businessmen led by Libbey and Owens.

RUBBER

Like the glass industry, the rubber industry experienced a rapid expansion toward the end of the century. Rubber had been introduced into Europe shortly after the discovery of America and was occasionally used for waterproofing and for the manufacture of erasers. But it was primarily a curiosity until a Glasgow chemist, Charles MacIntosh, finding naptha to be a good solvent for the gummy substance, began in 1823 to manufacture waterproof fabric by pressing a film of rubber between two strips of cloth. In this country the manufacture of waterproof fabric, and other rubber articles, was undertaken on a large scale during the early thirties. But when it became apparent that despite promising experiments it was impossible to prevent rubber from becoming soft and sticky in warm weather and brittle in cold weather, the boom collapsed as suddenly as it had risen.

It was at this point that Charles Goodyear began his long and painful attempts to stabilize rubber. An enthusiast to the point of monomania, incurably eccentric, oblivious of his economic interests, Goodyear gave his life to the promotion of rubber with the zeal of a missionary. He was one of that small, deviant, but sometimes effective group of entrepreneurs to whom the economic calculus of entrepreneurship is entirely subordinate to considerations of public welfare.

Born in 1800, the son of a hardware dealer of New Haven who manufactured tools and implements in a small shop, young Charles opened a hardware store of his own in Philadelphia, but shortly failed because of unwise extension of credit. In 1834, after inspecting some decaying rubber articles in a New York store—an encounter which he later ascribed to Divine Providence—he began his experiments to stabilize the substance. Despite repeated disappointments, dire poverty, and the ridicule of acquaintances, he grimly persevered at his task and discovered by accident in 1839 that when raw rubber was mixed with sulphur, and heat-treated, it stabilized, or became "vulcanized." But the promotion of the new product proved unexpectedly difficult. Previous failures to find a method of stabilization had left rubber in very bad repute, and therefore the manufacture of vulcanized rubber articles did not begin in significant volume until the mid-forties.

Goodyear had now to decide whether to manufacture rubber himself or license his process to others. The first alternative would probably have yielded greater financial returns and would have provided maximum protection for the patent. Unfortunately, Goodyear's chronic poverty and his desire to get funds at any cost to continue his experiments led him to adopt the policy of licensing. He thus lost control over the quality of the product produced under the patent, invited infringement by allowing others to experiment at their leisure and in secret, and failed to accumulate the mounting resources necessary to prosecute suits against infringers. But with the help of Daniel Webster as counsel he did manage to sustain the basic patent on vulcanization in a crucial and celebrated suit, Goodyear *vs*. Day (1851), known as "The Great India Rubber Case." Worldwide acclaim followed, and during the last years of his life he wrote a two-volume treatise on rubber listing nearly a thousand uses for the substance. Yet by this time he had largely lost control over the processes of rubber manufacture and played practically no part in the developing rubber industry. After his death in 1860 his estate was found to be insolvent. Never a systematic, trained scientist, he was more interested in finding new uses for rubber than in a thorough analysis of the substance itself.

Many of his proposals—such as rubber sails for ships—were visionary and impractical, but others anticipated future uses of the substance.

The Civil War gave a strong stimulus to the manufacture of rubber boots and shoes, which until the turn of the century was the most important sector of the industry. But during the nineties the industry expanded rapidly as manufacturers turned to the production of solid buggy and bicycle tires. The location of many tire companies in Akron, Ohio, started that city on its career as a rubber manufacturing center. The first of the big three—Goodyear, Goodrich, and Firestone—to begin operations was Goodrich, founded in 1879 by Dr. Benjamin Franklin Goodrich, a physician from upstate New York with an interest in rubber manufacturing. He located in Akron largely because of financial support granted by farm machinery interests which dominated the economic life of the town. Goodyear was founded by the Siberling family and at the turn of the century the company was turning out 3,000 to 4,000 tires per day. Harvey S. Firestone, one-time traveling salesman from Chicago who had constructed a small wheel and tire plant in Akron, founded the Firestone Tire and Rubber Company in 1900 with the help of local businessmen. The great boom in the pneumatic tire business of the early twentieth century projected these companies into a position of leadership.

On the surface there is some similarity between the development of the rubber tire industry at Akron and the growth of the glass industry at Toledo. In both cases initial capital was raised from a circle of businessmen who had made money in other fields. In both cases the industries were led by aggressive entrepreneurs. But the Akron group does not appear to have made important technological innovations. At the outset they made and mounted tires under license from patent holders, whereas the Libbey group from the beginning licensed others. The manufacture of rubber tires involved no important new rubber technology, nor did it result in the widespread mechanization of tasks formerly done by hand. Success for the Akron group came from the burgeoning demand for a single product which the firms were equipped to make, and not by transforming the industry itself.

In the rubber boot and shoe industry, heightened competition during the eighties had led to the usual type of associations for price and production fixing. The progression from these to a large combination was accomplished by Charles A. Flint with the formation in 1892 of the United States Rubber Company. Nucleus of the combination was nine companies producing one-third of the country's boot and shoe output. Chartered in New Jersey, it was capitalized at $50 million, making it one of the nation's largest corporations. Despite stated intentions of bringing about economies through integration, the organization during its early years was no more than a holding company. Each constituent unit retained its own identity and handled its own purchasing and selling. But merely using the leverage of stock control to fix prices and hold down production was not sufficient to bring success to U.S. Rubber. Unwelcome independents flourished under the price umbrella, and without integration the company could not lower production costs enough to drive them either into the combination or out of business. In order to achieve the economies of size, the company in 1896 embarked upon a program of consolidating purchases of raw material, reducing the number of goods manufactured, relegating production of remaining brands to the factories best equipped to produce them, and consolidating sales in a central department located in New York with branch offices throughout the United States and in Europe. Despite some progress toward integration the company was not successful during the next five years, and in 1901 wound up in red ink with a surplus of only $25,000.

The early career of U.S. Rubber provides another illustration that the mere fact of combination was no guarantee of success, particularly in industries where integration was difficult to effect. Yet the rubber "trust" came very close to achieving a monopoly. U.S. Rubber ultimately controlled, if somewhat loosely, 75 percent of the rubber boot and shoe business of the nation, and in another name—Mechanical Rubber Company —85 percent of the production of rubber goods used in industry. Another Flint combination, Rubber Goods Manufacturing Company, chartered in 1899 and successor to Mechanical Rubber, attempted to extend the combination into the tire industry. It fell short of this objective, partly because the stronger independents would not join and partly because the combination weakened its financial position by uniting tire companies with firms in less profitable lines of production.

TOBACCO MANUFACTURE

In contrast to the discouraging performance of some of the combinations we have examined, the tobacco industry produced a combination which during its rather short life was outstandingly successful—the American Tobacco Company. Founded and nurtured by James B. Duke, who stands with Carnegie and Rockefeller among the great figures of American business, it revealed new dimensions inherent in the building of big business.

Like so many consumer products which served the day-by-day needs of great masses of people, tobacco originally was manufactured in small shops and distributed locally. During the antebellum period all major cities had a number of tobacco manufacturers such as Lorillard in New York and Liggett in St. Louis—both progenitors of large firms. Yet even at this early date the industry was beginning to evolve into the pattern characteristic of business at a later period. The number of firms decreased, average size increased, and a few companies began operating on a national scale. By 1860, Richmond, with some fifty factories employing 3,400 people turning out an annual product valued at nearly $5 million, became the tobacco capital of the nation. Distribution over a wide area was doubtless facilitated by the fact that manufactured tobacco was an article of relatively high value in proportion to bulk and weight and therefore could afford to pay substantial railroad charges.

Plug and chewing tobacco, smoking tobacco, and snuff were the forms of the manufactured products. In Virginia the work forces in the factories were usually made up of hired slaves, who for purposes of incentive were allowed to make a few dollars per week. Marketing followed the familiar route from manufacturer to retailer via sales agents and jobbers. Some leading manufacturers and distributors even before the war had pioneered a technique of modern advertising by adopting image-producing brand names such as *Wedding Cake, Winesap, Rock Candy*, or—in a patriotic context—*Uncle Sam, People's Choice*, and *Daniel Webster*. On the eve of the Civil War manufacturers began to purchase their leaf tobacco at the loose leaf auctions which have become such a distinctive feature of the tobacco industry today. The system first made its appearance at Danville, Virginia, and became popular with farmers because it appeared to offer them better prices by eliminating dealers. Auction sales also made it possible to avoid the time consuming and expensive process of "prizing" tobacco (i.e., packing it in hogsheads for shipment to market).

Although the Richmond factories recovered quickly after the devastation of the Civil War, that city never again recovered its commanding position in the tobacco industry. As bright tobacco—grown in a belt between central North Carolina and the southwest piedmont of Virginia—became ever more popular, Durham and Winston, North Carolina, rose to become important manufacturing centers. The original stimulus to manufacturing in Durham came from the great success of William T. Blackwell and Julian S. Carr in marketing Bull Durham smoking tobacco. Manufactured of better quality tobacco than most contemporary brands, the Bull achieved considerable popularity among the Union soldiers who occupied Durham for a period following the war. Aided by growing popularity of pipe smoking and a sharply rising per capita consumption of tobacco, Blackwell and Carr steadily expanded their plant until by 1884, with nine hundred employees, it was the largest tobacco factory in the world.

Meanwhile in Winston, Pleasant Henderson Hanes and Richard Joshua Reynolds were conducting tobacco manufacturing enterprises which were bringing that city into prominence. During the eighties St. Louis manufacturers, headed by Liggett and Myers, raised Missouri's proportion of the nation's output from 9 percent to 27 percent, and Missouri thereupon replaced Virginia as the leading state in tobacco manufacturing.

In marketing as well as in advertising the industry was moving rapidly toward maturity during this period. An increasing number of firms built their own sales forces and dealt directly with retailers. Some independent agents, realizing the danger of being bypassed, solidified their positions by investing in the firms whose goods they handled, and thereby became a source of capital for the industry. In only one area, mechanization, did the industry make practically no advance. Actually this failure was of little importance, however, for cheap labor using specially constructed tables and foot operated tools for the production of cigars, plug, and smoking tobacco was available in quantities ample enough to meet the expanding market demand for tobacco products.

The increasing popularity of cigars and the multiplication of small manufacturing shops staffed by immigrant labor in the cities of the Northeast were important developments after 1885. But far more significant was the coming of the cigarette, which revolutionized the industry by bringing large corporations, mechanization, bitter competition, and finally the giant combination which not only controlled the tobacco industry in the United States but conducted marketing around the world as well. To a considerable degree the cigarette performed for the tobacco industry the same service which the automobile tire rendered to the rubber industry and the electric light bulb to the glass industry.

The revolution in tobacco manufacture can be traced most clearly in the career of the chief revolutionary—James Buchanan Duke. Born on a North Carolina farm near Hillsborough, James was a member of a family which had been impoverished by the Civil War. After James's father, Washington Duke, had been mustered out of the Confederate army and had arrived home with fifty cents in his pocket, the family capitalized its sole liquid asset by shredding and sifting a small store of tobacco leaf into smoking tobacco. Labeling it *Pro Bono Publico*, Washington Duke and two sons peddled the tobacco on a wagon trip within the state with such success that they decided to go into the manufacturing business. The manufacture and sale of 15,000 pounds of smoking tobacco in the next year, 1866, started the family on a successful career.

James B., showing a marked aptitude for business, turned down an opportunity to receive an education at nearby Guilford College in favor of more practical training, and graduated from Eastman Business College of Poughkeepsie, New York. With the ardor of a zealot he returned to work in a plant which his father had built in Durham. "I loved business better than anything else," he reminisced later. "I was sorry to leave off at night and glad when morning came so I could get at it again." In 1878 Washington Duke, his sons James B. and Benjamin N., Richard Wright (a local manufacturer), and George W. Watts (son of a Baltimore jobber), formed a partnership which permitted expansion of the plant. Each partner contributed $14,000 for the purpose. But despite their most intensive efforts to promote their own brands of smoking tobacco and plug, they were unable to overcome the competition of the extremely popular Bull Durham. Because of this failure the partners in 1881 decided to concentrate on the manufacture of cigarettes.

Cigarettes had been smoked in southern Europe and the Levant since the end of the eighteenth century, but did not become popular in the United States until after 1875, when Allen and Ginter began turning them out in Richmond. The bright tobacco of the North Carolina piedmont was well adapted to their manufacture, and the Dukes solved the only technical problem by importing a few skilled Russian cigarette rollers from New York who then trained a work force of local girls. The Dukes' cigarette business was so successful that in 1884 they built a large addition to their plant. Also in that year James B. moved to New York to manage a small cigarette factory on the East Side which the partners had acquired for $100,000. He was well aware that the availability of cheap immigrant labor and the proximity of marketing and advertising agencies made New York City the best location for cigarette manufacture. Now twenty-seven years old, independent of his father and brothers, James B. Duke marched forward to bring the tobacco industry of the United States under his control. Six years later his was the largest cigarette plant in the nation.

Duke ascribed his success basically to an unwearying devotion to business. From the outset in New York he spent his days at the factory and most of his evenings meeting and conferring with dealers. Actually he came to know many more of them than did any of his competitors or even his own salesmen. On the rare occasions when he had nothing to do he sat in tobacco shops listening to the comments of customers, or paced the streets counting discarded cigarette boxes. Long after his business had become a striking success he lived in a room renting for two dollars per week and took his meals in inexpensive restaurants. He spent much time on market research and knew many territories as well as his salesmen and agents. Always cost conscious, he computed the cost of manufacturing cigarettes to .00035 per thousand and pared away all unnecessary expenses. These efforts gave him the advantage of a larger margin for price cutting than enjoyed by his competitors and enabled him to reduce the price of cigarettes from ten cents to five cents for a box of ten. Although he financed plant additions out of profits, he established unnecessary lines of credit at banks merely to have contingency funds available. Spending as much as $750,000 annually for advertising while his company was still relatively small, he utilized every medium and promoted many new types of appeals. He also experimented with packaging and invented the cardboard cigarette box used by most of the manufacturers of the day.

The Duke plants acquired economies of scale by making moves toward integration beginning in the early 1880s. At that time their competitors purchased tobacco from jobbers who bought at loose leaf auctions and stored and dried the leaf in their own warehouses. In order to eliminate the middleman's profit the Dukes employed their own buyers and built their own warehouses and drying plants. At the same time they moved toward forward integration by establishing distribution centers in large cities staffed by managers and salesmen. These innovations constitute an early example of the type of integration which characterized other big business a decade later.

In 1885 the Dukes acquired a strong competitive advantage by leasing the Bonsack cigarette rolling machine under a royalty ultimately set at 25 percent less than the price offered to other cigarette manufacturers. The Bonsack was the best of several new machines which completely changed the complexion of the tobacco industry. Since up to this time all tobacco had been manufactured by hand processes, plants were small and there was little pressure for combination. But since the Bonsack could do the work of forty-eight hand rollers, it introduced economies of scale and raised the specter of damaging competition.

James B. Duke fully appreciated both the opportunities and the dangers of the situation. During the late eighties he applied unremitting pressure against his principal competitors, Allen and Ginter, Kinney Tobacco Company, William S. Kimball and Company, and Goodwin and Company. His major weapon was price cutting and a heavy volume of advertising, and his objective was a combination of the major cigarette producers. Competition during this period was greatly sharpened by the fact that the consumption of cigarettes, which had jumped from about ten million per year in 1870 to about one billion in 1885, thereafter leveled off at a slower rate of growth at the very time that machine production was greatly increasing output. Circumstances therefore indicated the wisdom of combination. But difficulties arose. The heads of the competing companies were loath to abandon the individuality of their firms; they quarreled over what should be their equities in a new combined company; and they were puzzled over what form the new combination would take now that it appeared that trusts would soon become illegal. But the pressures toward combination, plus the leadership of James B. Duke, resulted in a solution of these problems. In 1890 Duke and his four principal competitors formed the American Tobacco Company, chartered under the favorable terms offered by New Jersey.

The firm was capitalized at $25 million in common and preferred stock, of which Duke and Allen and Ginter each received $7.5 million, and the others lesser amounts down to $2.5 million. The company was outrageously overcapitalized, yet in terms of earning power the capitalization proved to be conservative. In the next five years the firm recorded annual net earnings of $4 million per year. As Richard B. Tennant, historian of the company, observes: "The subsequent history of the Tobacco Trust is one of repeated capital inflation followed, with one outstanding exception, by justifying profits. Duke and his associates had found a new philosopher's stone for changing not lead but water into gold." The water was carried on the books under the heading of "good will," which by 1908 accounted for 55 percent of all assets. The simplest definition of good will is extraordinary anticipated profits.

During the two decades from 1890 to 1910 the American Tobacco Company reached outward with the frank and unabashed intent of monopolizing the industry. At one time or another it acquired interests in 250 companies operating in the United States and abroad, and the giant combination came to be known as the Tobacco Trust (although of course without the trust form of organization, which was illegal). The Trust controlled 86 percent of all cigarette output, and from 76 percent to 91 percent of all other manufactured tobacco except cigars. The campaign to dominate the cigar industry was the sole failure in the record of the Trust's expansion, chiefly because this industry was very decentralized and was carried on by immigrant hand rollers with established patronage. The Trust also manufactured its own in-service items such as tinfoil, licorice, and boxes, and had about four hundred retail outlets organized as United Cigar Stores. Purchasing was conducted by a small army of agents who visited tobacco auctions throughout the South. Although there were complaints that these agents, acting in concert, beat down leaf prices, there is little evidence that the Trust attempted, or succeeded in doing so. Its officials were always more interested in gaining profits by superior marketing ability than by lowering the cost of raw material, which would have been a difficult and random process.

Despite its size, the Trust achieved no high degree of integration in manufacturing processes. Constituent companies continued to produce their own brands with little interference from the central organization. Of course marketing, accounting, advertising, and finance were carried on at the upper corporate level.

From the very beginning the Trust had made strong efforts to establish itself abroad. As early as 1883 Duke had sent a salesman on a round-the-world trip. In 1901 the Trust invaded Britain, but was blocked from taking over the British market by a union of thirteen large British producers organized as the Imperial Tobacco Company. After a year of costly competition American and Imperial agreed to divide the world between them. Imperial was guaranteed exclusive manufacturing and marketing rights within Britain; in return the two giants formed the British-American Tobacco Company, Ltd., which entered markets in the rest of the world with the exception of those in Cuba and the United States. Two-thirds of the British-American capitalization of 5.2 million pounds was allotted to the American Tobacco Company.

The Trust was enormously, if not to say fabulously profitable. In 1890 the ratio of earnings to tangible assets was about 55 percent, and although in the decade following they dropped to about 16 percent because of restrictive state legislation against cigarettes, by 1908 the ratio was up to about 35 percent. In that year earnings on the common stock of American Tobacco Company alone, after payment of interest and preferred dividends, amounted to 46 percent. The cumulative increase of assets was so rapid that $1,000 invested in the company in 1890 was worth $36,197 in 1908.

The basic reason for the success of the Trust was its control over a rapidly expanding market. After a slowing in the rate of growth in the late eighties, output of cigarettes doubled from 2 billion to 4.2 billion between 1890 and 1896. Duke's acquisition of the Bonsack machine under exclusive lease gave his company a great initial advantage with cumulative effects in later years. Profit margins widened as production costs fell because of mechanization. By 1900 the Trust had acquired nearly every brand of tobacco manufactured, and the American Tobacco Company alone produced one hundred brands of cigarettes. The vast sums spent for advertising created brand loyalty. The great strength of the Trust made it extremely difficult for independents to enter the field. Those who tried were usually subjected at the outset to price cutting. American Tobacco Company early found it unwise to cut retail prices because this tended to diminish brand loyalty; therefore price cutting was usually on the wholesale level. Nevertheless, the company maintained certain "fighting brands" which were used as price cutting mechanisms directed against competitors. Jobbers were often bound under contract to handle Trust goods exclusively, and were given rebates for their co-operation. In at least one case the Trust organized a secretly controlled subsidiary which bid away the labor force of an independent manufacturer.

Yet the object of the Trust in employing these tactics was not so much to destroy independents as to nudge them into the combination. Before a competitor was forced to his knees he would usually be offered an attractive price for his plant. Since the high levels of profits gave opportunity for extensive stock watering, the Trust could afford to be generous. Moreover, in the long run it was usually cheaper to buy out competitors than destroy them.

The degree to which James B. Duke was personally responsible for the success of the company is a question to which it is difficult to assign a precise answer. Because of a natural tendency to exaggerate the importance of human agency in determining the course of history, dynamic and aggressive businessmen have often been given more credit than they deserve for the success of the organizations they headed. Nevertheless, the presence of Duke was strongly felt at every stage in the development of the Trust. He was mainly responsible for maneuvering the partnership formed in 1878, with its manufacturing plants in Durham and later in New York, into the position of strength from which it could effect the combination of 1890. From this time onward the original heads of the component companies lost interest in further combination and began to retire from the Board of Directors. Their places were taken by a group of financiers including Thomas F. Ryan, William C. Whitney, A. N. Brady, and Thomas Dolan, thus reflecting a similar change of control characteristic of "finance capitalism" in other big businesses. Yet Duke remained president of American Tobacco past the turn of the century, indicating that he shared the goals of the financiers. Nevertheless it is quite possible that his personal influence waned. Certainly no one man could exercise effective control over an empire as vast as the American Tobacco Company. The fact that he made such strong efforts to recruit able executives and after 1900 devoted an increasing amount of time to other projects—particularly the development of electric power in the South—suggests that he increasingly delegated decision making to others.

Mechanization, combination, and the establishment of national marketing represented a distinct stage in the development of all consumer industries. But the American Tobacco Company, by inaugurating massive advertising campaigns and increasing the variety of goods offered, was one of the few companies to advance further toward the conditions which characterize the modern consumer goods sector of the economy. For the other producers of the nation these developments would come in the twentieth century.

XXXII. Big Steel

BEGINNINGS OF THE STEEL INDUSTRY

Impressive as were the revolutionary transformations in some of the older industries which took place during the last third of the nineteenth century, these were overshadowed in importance for most observers by the dramatic rise of three industries which were not in existence in 1850—steel, oil, and electrical equipment. Actually these industries precipitated a second industrial revolution of quite different characteristics than the first one brought about by textiles, iron, machine tools, light metals fabrication, and the initial spread of a transportation network.

The steel industry developed in the United States in an entirely different manner than the iron industry, despite the close affinity of the two metals. Iron was one of the first manufactures undertaken during the colonial period and was carried on with a technology essentially unchanged since the days of the Philistines. The produce—pig and wrought iron—was utilized for a wide variety of consumer products and farm tools. Improved technologies made their way to the United States slowly during the first four decades of the nineteenth century. By contrast steel burgeoned into a major industry within two decades—the 1870s and 1880s—and from the outset depended upon a sophisticated imported technology covered by patents originally taken out in European nations. Entrance into the industry was controlled by a small group of businessmen who acquired rights under these patents, and as a result was limited to a small number of heavily capitalized firms. From the outset the industry produced capital rather than consumer goods, and therefore had as a market a limited number of large purchasers closely allied with steel producers. Expansion in the early period was force fed by demand for a single product—steel rails. Combination in iron manufacture was rare, and integration even more infrequent, but the steel industry, because of its initial conditions, high profit potential, and the availability of economies of scale, quickly developed the largest integrated combination in the nation. Finally, steel producers secured tariff protection much more easily than had iron producers of a previous generation.

During the colonial and early national periods steel had been produced by the "blister" and "crucible" methods. Both were time consuming and yielded a small product, and as a result steel cost from $150 to $200 per ton during the early nineteenth century. About half the amount used in the United States was imported, and was bought chiefly by watch and tool makers. In 1856 Henry Bessemer patented a process in England which revolutionized the manufacture of steel by forcing compressed air into a vessel containing molten iron through jets, or "tuyeres," in the bottom. In the subsequent oxidation, which provided a dramatic display of pyrotechnics, carbon was burned out of the iron. But the process turned out to be not so simple as it seemed. Unless the oxidation were stopped in time, all the carbon would be burned out, thus transforming the pig iron into wrought iron. Moreover, the presence of more than .075 percent of phosphorous in the pig iron would destroy the effectiveness of the process. For these reasons, early experiments by Bessemer and by iron masters in America were not uniformly successful. In the early sixties the problem of controlling carbon content was solved by an Englishman, Robert F. Mushet, who first burned all the carbon out of the pig iron and then added the proper amount in the form of "spiegeleisen" or ferromanganese. At a later date it was found that lime in the lining of a "converter"—the vessel containing the molten iron—would nullify the effect of phosphorous. Whereas the refining of three tons of wrought iron in a puddling furnace required 24 hours to complete, by the Bessemer process three tons of pig iron could be transformed into steel in 20 minutes.

Even before Bessemer began his experiments, an American ironmaster, William Kelly of Eddyville, Kentucky, had used the internal combustion process for the manufacture of boiler plate, but apparently had not been able to make good steel. When he heard of Bessemer's work he hastened to take out a patent and succeeded in securing prior rights to the direct oxidation method in the United States. A group of capitalists from backgrounds in merchandising and in iron works, operating under Kelly's patent, formed the Kelly Process Company in 1863 and built an experimental plant at Wyandotte, Michigan. The group also bought the Mushet patent for the use of spiegeleisen. A second group, led by Alexander L. Holley—the distinguished ironmaster, engineer, and owner of the Rensselaer Iron Works of Troy, New York—independently acquired the right to operate under Bessemer's patents in the United States. Since Holley's group needed the Mushet patent, and since the Kelly Process Company could do little without Bessemer's machinery, the two combined in 1866, and offered to erect and license Bessemer plants.

Beginning in 1867 the patent holders advertised for licensees, asserting that the cost of Bessemer plants was no more than two-thirds the cost of crucible steel or puddling works of the same capacity. Royalties were set at about $6 per ton of steel produced, plus a charge of $5,000 for a complete set of plans drawn up by Holley. Licensors and licensees remained a tight little in-group which restricted steel making to a small number of plants in which at the outset, at least, they had mutual interests. "Of the 11 plants in operation in 1880," writes the historian of iron and steel, Peter Temin, "Holley designed six, consulted on the construction of three more, and was the inspiration for the remaining two which were copied after one of the first six." From the outset Bessemer plants were large and integrated. By 1880 some firms had capacities of over 100,000 tons, and average capacity was larger by half than the average capacity of British companies. By 1899 average investment in American plants was $967,000 and employment 412. Since Bessemer converters consumed pig iron at a much faster rate than puddling furnaces, pressures for integration were correspondingly greater and forced the building of much larger blast furnaces and the development of "hard-driving" techniques to increase the rate of production. The Bessemer process became more popular in the United States than in Europe because by good fortune the great supplies of Lake Superior ore upon which much of the steel industry came to depend were almost free of phosphorous.

Although the Bessemer process was fast and cheap and could be used with high phosphorous ores after patent rights for the limestone liner were acquired in 1881, the method was slowly supplanted beginning in the late nineteenth century by the Siemens-Martin open hearth process. By this procedure, similar in some ways to puddling, iron was held in molten state for a protracted period by the intense heat supplied by a Siemens regenerative gas furnace. Although eight to ten hours were required to make one batch of steel which could be turned out by a converter in about twenty minutes, the Siemens process came to be preferred over the Bessemer for several reasons. It could use a wider range of ores than the Bessemer with liner, and could even use scrap iron, which after 1900 was cheaper than iron ore. The saving on the cost of raw material more than compensated for the greater cost of fuel in the Siemens process. Open hearths could turn out a much wider range of steels. Like recipes, batches could be figuratively speaking cooked to taste by the addition from time to time of various chemicals necessary to produce special steels and alloys. Finally, there was a widespread belief that the controls inherent in the Siemens method made it possible to produce steel of consistently higher quality than by the Bessemer process.

Despite the rapidly growing market for rails, as early as the seventies the leaders of the industry felt the need to limit production in the interest of maintaining prices, and to that end the Bessemer Steel Association was formed in 1875. With varying degrees of success it administered pooling arrangements for the rest of the century. The Bessemer Steel Company, Ltd., the organization established by the Holley group of patent holders, now owned by 11 steel companies, also co-operated to keep the number of firms small by limiting the availability of existing patent rights to firms already in the business. During the eighties the situation was eased as patents ran out, however, and 28 new companies entered the field.

From the beginning, with allowance for cyclical fluctuations, profits in the industry were in the range of 10 to 20 percent among the firms with the technical proficiency to get into volume production. Critics of the industry to the contrary, the level of profits was relatively unaffected by the collusive agreements restricting production, because these were not very effective. Another putative aid to prosperity was the protective tariff, for which the American Iron and Steel Association had vociferously and obsessively lobbied ever since the beginning of the industry. During much of the period before 1900 the rates on rails were absolute, and not ad valorem, which meant that in periods of falling prices the tariff became increasingly protective. The reasoning behind the absolute duties was that they would give protection according to need, and thereby stabilize prices, but actually, during the eighties, they brought about the opposite effect by stimulating entrance into the field to such a degree that overproduction threatened price levels.

THE RISE OF THE CARNEGIE STEEL COMPANY

In the public mind the great achievements of the steel industry were epitomized in the history of the Carnegie Steel Company, one of the most successful enterprises of the nineteenth century. With somewhat less justification the success of the organization was attributed primarily to the substantial abilities of one of its founders, Andrew Carnegie. To many observers, Carnegie was an ideal businessman. Springing from humble origins, he built a large company which not only brought him a fortune, but conferred benefits equally great upon society at large. Resolutely rejecting the temptations toward display, self-indulgence, and the wanton use of power which come with great wealth, Carnegie devoted his fortune to philanthropic purposes which would enable men of lesser abilities to follow in his footsteps. In an age in which the Goulds, Rockefellers, Morgans, and Armours appeared to accumulate their hoards by setting up roadblocks in the paths of industry and commerce and thereby exacting toll from the people at large, Carnegie presented the reversed image of the businessman as economic builder, sociological expert, and moral leader. Certainly Carnegie was an able businessman, but he owed his greatness as much to his ability to create this very image as to the services he performed for the company which bore his name.

Born in the Scotch village of Dunfermline in 1835, the son of a cottage weaver, young Andrew grew up in an atmosphere tinged with the radicalism of the Chartist movement. When the adoption of the automatic loom signaled the end of the cottage industry, the Carnegie family emigrated to western Pennsylvania, and Andrew, at the age of thirteen, went to work as a bobbin boy in a cotton mill near Pittsburgh. The story of his rise from this point resembles Benjamin Franklin's autobiography remodeled to suit the tastes of an age which honored industrialists higher than philosophers. At sixteen he became a telegraph operator, a position requiring skill, precision, and a high degree of personal reliability. He rated so high in these characteristics that Thomas A. Scott, superintendent of the western division of the Pennsylvania Railroad, brought him into the divisional office as chief telegrapher, a position of much greater responsibility than that of the ordinary operator. When Scott, in 1859, was appointed vice-president of the railroad, he moved Andrew, now twenty-four, into his former position of superintendent. Carnegie served as a railroad executive for the next six years, and from all accounts exhibited the orderliness, attention to detail, decisiveness, and willingness to take responsibility which are the hallmarks of good managers. Yet despite his excellent performance in the organization which was at the time probably the best school of business management in the country, Carnegie apparently felt no great attachment for managerial duties and responsibilities. At a later date, as soon as he was financially independent, he divested himself of these tasks and devoted the greater part of his life to entrepreneurial activities, to the creation of an image, and to play.

Purchase of ten shares of Adams Express stock and of a one-eighth interest in a sleeping car company—both on borrowed money—projected him on his way toward fame and fortune. By the age of twenty-eight he had an income of $42,000 per year, mostly from investments. When the Pennsylvania Railroad was on the point of replacing its wooden bridges and culverts with iron structures, Carnegie persuaded several of his railroad colleagues to join him in purchasing a small metal fabrication firm which the partners expanded and incorporated as the Keystone Bridge Company, with the object, of course, of doing business with the railroad. Organization of a rolling mill for structural components and rails strengthened the position of the bridge company and offered further opportunities for profit.

From the outset Carnegie showed remarkable ability to iron out quarrels among his associates and get viable organizations under way. In contrast to Hewitt and Anderson he left technical matters to others. The role he played was entirely entrepreneurial. In 1865 at the age of thirty he resigned his position with the railroad—the last formal managerial or administrative post he was ever to hold. He thereupon took up residence in New York and thenceforth spent most of his time there or abroad. His chief business occupation was acting as salesman for the Keystone Bridge Company. Selling capital goods was a much more exacting task during the late sixties and early seventies than it is today, because in the absence of a large capital market the salesman usually had to take at least part payment in the stock and bonds of the purchasing company. Unless the salesman could resell these quickly at a good price, a prosperous, active capital goods firm could quickly be reduced to bankruptcy. The Keystone Company's market, in addition to the Pennsylvania Railroad, consisted largely of the many companies being formed to build toll bridges over the major rivers of the nation. Acting often as contractor and financial agent, Carnegie supplied the iron components and shapes necessary for bridge construction, and then sold bonds received in payment to large European banking houses. Since the bonds carried 6 to 8 percent interest—considerably higher than comparable European securities—and had excellent security in the form of bridge structures and tolls, Carnegie had little difficulty in disposing of the issues at par. He also used his entrée into European capital markets to sell American railroad bonds. Altogether from 1867 to 1872 he sold perhaps $30 million in securities and made a million dollar fortune for himself. In contrast to the businessmen represented by James B. Duke, Carnegie was never a hard worker. Actually, he often recommended that his executives emulate him in taking extended vacations.

Carnegie entered the steel business in 1872 when, in partnership with his brother Thomas, William Coleman—a leading iron master—and other Pittsburgh businessmen, he constructed a Bessemer plant at Braddock on the Monongahela River. Carnegie contributed $250,000 toward the initial capital fund, and showed a nice sense of diplomacy when he persuaded his colleagues to name the new plant after the president of the Pennsylvania Railroad, J. Edgar Thompson, whose favor and custom would count heavily in the fortunes of the steel company.

Henceforth the Carnegie enterprises grew rapidly. In 1878 the original $625,00 capitalization of J. Edgar Thompson was doubled, and Carnegie took the entire issue of new stock, paying for it in part by notes which he discharged out of dividends. In 1880 the works cleared $1,625,000 in profit. Meanwhile the various units of the business acquired since 1865, including blast furnaces and foundries, had been managed in a most informal fashion by the group of partners, and without any organic union. In some ways management resembled the manner in which the Boston Associates administered the widely dispersed enterprises under their control. Outside financing for the Carnegie firms came from loans and from new partners brought into the business. Over the years Carnegie became deeply committed to the principle that ownership and management should never be separated. In 1881, to meet the need for over-all supervision, the steel works, iron furnaces, foundries and bridge works were brought together into Carnegie Brothers and Company—still unincorporated, but the largest iron and steel combination in the nation at that time. Andrew Carnegie subscribed for $2,737,977 of the $5,000,000 capitalization.

During the early eighties, the rapid pace of urbanization, the construction of high rise buildings, and the beginnings of a revolution in naval architecture created a burgeoning market for structural beams and shapes, and armor plate. To supply the market the company acquired the nearby Homestead steel mill at its construction cost when it was crippled by a long strike and converted it into the first large, successful open hearth plant in the nation. Shortly thereafter Carnegie acquired the Duquesne Steel Works when that company, like Homestead, encountered financial difficulties. Yet Carnegie did not try to exploit the misfortunes of his neighbors. The prices he paid were certainly not lavish, but were fair under the circumstances. Also, he offered to give stock to the major owners of Duquesne, but they refused and demanded cash. No doubt they later regretted this decision bitterly.

At about the same time the company acquired an asset in some ways as important as the two steel works in the person of Henry Clay Frick. Cold and reserved, Frick was in personality the antithesis of the extroverted, ebullient Carnegie. Born and brought up near Connellsville, south of Pittsburgh on the Monongahela, grandson of the wealthy distiller, Abraham Overholt, young Frick early in his career began investing in the coking coal deposits of the region. Like Carnegie, he secured additional capital by bringing other businessmen into partnership with him. By 1882 Frick and Company owned 1,026 coke ovens and 3,000 acres of coal lands. In need of funds to pay debts, he sold a controlling interest in the company to Carnegie, and Carnegie then brought Frick into the steel combine as chief executive.

It was primarily Frick who transformed the Carnegie Company from a congeries of haphazardly acquired units into the huge, integrated combination which the company became. The first step was the consolidation in 1892 of all the holdings of Carnegie and his associates, except the Frick Coke Company, into Carnegie Steel Company, Ltd., capitalized at $25 million. The second step was to gain control over ore properties in the Lake Superior region.

The area bounding the northern and southern shores of Lake Superior near the lake's western tip contained the most valuable concentration of Bessemer ores to be found anywhere in the world. Discovered in successive ranges since the 1840s—initially the Marquette, Menominee, Gogebic, and Vermillion—the ore lay near the surface and was mined in open pits or in shallow shafts by hundreds of small operators. During the eighties the area became the focus of intense speculation. In 1891, Leonidas and Alfred Merritt discovered the Mesabi range, which, when fully explored, was found to contain as much ore as all the other ranges combined. Henry W. Oliver, a Pittsburgh manufacturer with a strong penchant for speculation who had been a boyhood playmate of Andrew Carnegie, persuaded Frick to join in acquiring extensive ore properties in the new region. Carnegie at first disapproved of the move, viewing it primarily as a speculation and preferring to continue horizontal expansion in the Pittsburgh area. But when John D. Rockefeller acquired the huge Merritt interests by foreclosure of mortgages during the Panic of 1893 and began to funnel Standard Oil profits into more ore properties, docking facilities, and ore ships, Carnegie finally "saw the light," as he explained later.

Afraid that Rockefeller might go into the steel business, or curtail the supply of ore to the Pittsburgh mills, Carnegie entered into a contract with him in 1896 which was one of the most celebrated business deals of the day. According to its terms, Carnegie leased ore properties to supply his needs from Rockefeller, and worked them at his own expense, paying a royalty of about 25 cents per ton on all ore mined. He also agreed to ship ore from Rockefeller holdings only in Rockefeller ships. Thus at a single stroke Carnegie secured his supply of ore and eliminated a potential competitor, and without the expenditure of capital. Rockefeller, on the other hand, got a guaranteed customer for his wares and services.

When the terms of the contract leaked out, many independent mine owners panicked and threw their properties on the market for whatever they would bring. Frick, Oliver, and Carnegie used the opportunity to begin purchase of extensive holdings. A wave of alarm now began to sweep through the steel industry. With the most modern and efficient plants in the nation, and with cheap and virtually unlimited supplies of coke and ore at its disposal, the Carnegie Company was getting into a position in which it could at will drive its competitors to their knees. Competitors' anxiety was not lessened when Carnegie, in order to get leverage over railroad rates, bought and rebuilt the Pittsburgh, Bessemer, and Lake Erie Railroad—which connected the Carnegie mills with the lake port of Conneaut—and began extensive expansion of the ore transfer facilities there.

Reacting to the trend of the times as well as to the Carnegie Company's expansion, competitors began to combine. Between 1898 and 1900 Wall Street syndicates launched the Federal Steel Company, the American Bridge Company, American Steel and Wire, and National Tube. At the beginning of this period covert efforts were made to get Carnegie to put a price on his own holdings. But even though in retirement and absorbed in authorship and philanthropies, Carnegie was not interested, considering any prospective combination to be mere stock speculation. When fabricators envisaged rounding out their combinations by going into the manufacture of basic steel, Carnegie checkmated by announcing plans to build a tube works at Conneaut and construct a new rail line from Pittsburgh to tidewater. But Carnegie's partners had little stomach for cutthroat competition, even when carried to the enemy from positions of strength. Negotiations began which eventuated in the formation of the trust of trusts, the largest industrial corporation in the world, with the unheard of capitalization of $1.4 billion—the United States Steel Corporation.

EXECUTIVES OF THE CARNEGIE COMPANY
In terms of profit the Carnegie Company had been a dazzling suc-

cess. During the twenty-five years from 1875 to 1900 it had paid the partners profits aggregating $133 million of which $40 million represented dividends for 1900 alone. Several reasons were put forward by contemporaries to explain the company's success. Perhaps the most often cited of these was the "genius" of Carnegie himself. This cheery little man, adept with quips and anecdotes, expert in the art of image-making, was one of the first of the "Madison Avenue" type of businessmen to score outstanding success by manipulating people rather than things. Combining a naturally warm and outgoing personality with quick perception, vision, courage, and efficiency, he had the ability to arouse the affection of intimates and the respect of competitors. Paradoxically, however, the one significant incident of failure in his life came in the area of human contacts—specifically, in his relations to Henry C. Frick, as will be discussed later.

Although his rather voluminous writings showed more than a touch of vanity, they nevertheless reveal a much greater awareness of the social implications of big business and wealth than possessed by any of his peers, and greater sympathy for the less fortunately endowed members of society than exhibited by businessmen generally. But wider interests also led him to avoid being drawn into the time-consuming details of management. Actually, except perhaps in the early days of his enterprise, Carnegie played practically no part in the formation of day-by-day management decisions. Until the coming of Frick he was a leader in the formulation of policy, but after that time he played a diminishing role even in this regard. As majority stockholder he was kept thoroughly informed about the course of business by a flow of reports sent to him in New York or in Europe, and he replied with equally voluminous criticism, praise, and requests for further information. Always cost conscious, he scrutinized financial reports most carefully, and he insisted that the executives follow his major principles for the administration and expansion of the business. But although no important decision could be made without his consent, his remoteness from the scene of operations and growing desire to retire diminished his ability to initiate policy. Although he argued spiritedly and sometimes bitterly with his partners, who were certainly not "yes men," nevertheless during the late eighties and nineties he was usually in the position of choosing between alternatives whose formulation he had only limited power to control. His position as a symbol and spokesman for what were regarded as the finest traditions of American business probably led observers to exaggerate his immediate contributions to the success of the company.

An associate of the Carnegie group, in the early days of its activities, when asked to describe Carnegie's role, replied, "Andy looked after the advertising and drove the band wagon." Another observer was more specific: "The part at first selected by Andrew Carnegie for himself was the development of outside trade and the procurement of orders. Here he displayed an originality so marked that it amounted to genius. Endowed with a ready wit, an excellent memory for stories, and a natural gift for reciting them, he became a social favorite in New York and Washington, and never missed a chance to make a useful acquaintance." More market-oriented than the iron entrepreneurs of an earlier generation, and aided by an able technical staff, Carnegie could afford to leave production problems to others, which his predecessors could not. Therefore it was natural that he should locate in the most important market center in the country—New York—and mingle with the railroad executives, representatives of the construction industries, and metal fabricators who constituted the circle of the steel companies' customers.

A marked characteristic of Carnegie's marketing policies was his cavalier attitude toward the pools which were almost constantly being formed in the steel industry during the late nineteenth century to set prices and allocate production. Initiated by overcapitalized firms which could operate profitably only under a price umbrella, they almost always suffered the early demise common to pools in other industries. Unenforceable at common law, pooling always gave an advantage to the last firm in and the first firm out, and every upward fluctuation of steel prices released groups of steel companies from the need for the protection which pooling afforded. At one time or another during the late eighties and nineties there were pools for rails, wire nails, steel billets, axles, beams, and angles. Few lasted more than a year. Although pools were conspiracies under common law, obviously contrary to public policy, and were denounced by reformers everywhere, Carnegie, for all of his moralizing, never hesitated to join them if it served the interest of the company to do so. But since the Carnegie Company was by far the strongest steel producer in the field, this need seldom arose. He outlined his basic policy regarding pools in a terse memo to company executives in 1900: "Put your trust in the policy of attending to your own business in your own way and running your mills full regardless of prices and [put] very little trust in the efficacy of artificial arrangements with your competitors, which have the serious result of strengthening them if they strengthen you."

Carnegie made it very plain on many occasions that he was in business first and foremost to make profits, and he obviously felt no responsibility for what his competitors might consider to be the welfare of the industry. As a result he abandoned and thereby broke pools with the same opportunism which had led him to join them in the first place. This unwilling-ness to co-operate led dismayed and bitter competitors constantly to accuse him of keeping the industry in chaos.

In addition to his marketing ability, Carnegie had a talent for recogniz-ing able men, and attributed the success of the company mainly to the executive staff. "Take from me all the ore mines, railroads, and manufac-turing plants," he said on one occasion, "and leave me my organization, and in a few years I promise to duplicate the Carnegie Company." Con-temporaries generally acknowledged that Carnegie had collected a superb group of executives, and many observers agreed that this staff was the major reason for the company's success. It is interesting to note that two other heads of outstandingly successful businesses, James B. Duke and John D. Rockefeller, also gave the major credit to their immediate assist-ants. To some extent this attitude might represent attempts on the part of much honored men to avoid an appearance of conceit; nevertheless, in these cases the judgments were corroborated by outside observers also.

Henry Clay Frick was probably the most fortunate of Carnegie's staff choices. Upon assuming the leadership of the company, Frick co-ordinated the loose management of the organization. Up to this time executive and supervisory personnel had been largely autonomous in their little empires, and apparently knew little about other aspects of the business than their own. Frick set out clear lines of authority and communication, set up centralized cost accounting, and established regular meetings to discuss policy. It was Frick and not Carnegie who had the vision to see the great value of the Mesabi ore lands, and it was Frick who provided the impetus for the expansion of the company into an integrated, vertical combination. Yet Frick was a strange nemesis for Carnegie. In the course of the drive for integration he contributed more than any other single individual to the de-struction of the partnership organization so cherished by Carnegie, and in the process quadrupled Carnegie's fortune.

Charles M. Schwab was a partner of abilities probably equal to those of Frick, and fortunately possessed of a much more pleasant personality. As a boy tending a country store he had been noticed by Captain Bill Jones, superintendent of the J. Edgar Thompson Works, and had been brought into the mill to drive stakes at a wage of one dollar per day. Six months later he became Jones's assistant; in five years he was made superintendent of Homestead. "Mr. Schwab," Carnegie said long after-wards, "is a genius. I never met his equal." Although the judgment no doubt reflected the strong friendship which Carnegie felt for Schwab, contemporaries would not have considered it exaggerated. After coming into the mill Schwab mastered not only the technical details of steel making, but the techniques of corporate management as well. As Carnegie's favorite partner he played the difficult role of diplomatist in reconciling the old gentleman to the demise of the partnership and to the sale of the business to United States Steel. The fact that he was then elected the first president of United States Steel showed the esteem in which he was held in the industry.

Others of the forty partners were relatives and boyhood friends. Henry Phipps, Jr., an associate from the beginning, handled financial affairs. Thomas Carnegie, a younger brother who died in 1886 at the age of forty-three, had showed great promise as an executive. George Lauder, another partner, was a cousin with whom Carnegie had played in Dunfermline. Naturally affectionate, Carnegie was influenced by emotional considerations in his choice of associates. Fortunately, nearly all of these proved worthy of his trust.

As important for the welfare of the company as the partners were a few individuals among the supervisory personnel. The critical importance of good supervisors had diminished somewhat after the Civil War when better understanding of metallurgical principles and techniques made standardized procedures possible. The early success of the Carnegie company might have been impossible without the talents of Andrew Kloman— the German immigrant whose forge constituted the birth of the Carnegie enterprises—Henry M. Curry, builder of the company's first iron furnace—and, above all, Captain Jones. One of the very few men ever to turn down an offer of partnership, Bill Jones was a direct, forceful, self-educated mechanic who supervised all steel operations until his death in 1889. Alexander L. Holley, designer of the J. Edgar Thompson Works, and William Coleman, the aristocratic ironmaster of the older generation and father-in-law of Thomas Carnegie, also deserve credit for the success of the enterprises.

Technical efficiency also contributed greatly to this happy outcome. Carnegie's first furnace was the largest in the Pittsburgh area at the time of its construction, and inaugurated a whole new generation of blast furnaces. During the eighties and nineties Carnegie Company furnaces held records for the production of Bessemer iron, in part because Carnegie was the first producer in the area to employ a full-time metallurgist, and the J. Edgar Thompson converters established similar records for steel production. Carnegie and his partners never hesitated to tear down existing facilities if new designs promised even a small reduction in production costs. During the hard times of the early seventies, when construction costs were low, the company built the Braddock plant, and almost completely rebuilt it during the mid-nineties when construction costs again hit a low point. Schwab often recounted in later life how on one occasion Carnegie ordered him to tear down a recently completed converter when Schwab pointed out how a change in design could save 50 cents per ton in the cost of steel. "What will we throw away this year," became a kind of password among the supervisory personnel. By 1900 the Carnegie firm was the most efficient producer of steel in the nation. Cost accounting was calculated to the hundredth of a cent per ton of steel. The efficiency of the company's methods is indicated by the fact that the Duquesne Works, which were bankrupt when the company acquired them, repaid their cost in one year under the new management. Achievements in the field of production may well account in part for the drop in the price of steel rails from $160 per ton in 1875 to $17 per ton in 1898.

LABOR POLICY

Labor policy was an area in which the Carnegie associates scored no successes like those of production. Perhaps as a result of childhood influences, Carnegie personally was much more liberal in his attitude toward collective bargaining and the right to strike than most employers of his generation. Yet one of the most egregious failures in labor relations during the tumultuous decade of the nineties, the Homestead Strike, took place in Carnegie's dominion. Unsurpassed in violence by any other strike in American history, it almost reached the dimensions of a domestic insurrection.

In two well-written articles in *Forum* published in 1886 Carnegie made it plain that he approved of unions and would bargain with them. Moreover, he favored wage rates geared to rising productivity, thus permitting labor to gain from industrial efficiency. In particular, he deplored the use of strikebreakers when contract negotiations broke down: "There is an unwritten law among the best workmen: 'Thou shalt not take thy neighbor's job.' " Two years later his enlightened ideas were put to the test, with a not wholly satisfactory result. Favoring a shorter work day, Carnegie persuaded his partners in 1887 to replace the two twelve-hour shifts at the plant with three eight-hour shifts. A year later, because of alleged rising production costs which injured the company's competitive position, the twelve-hour shifts were reinstated, and piecework wages were lowered slightly to compensate for the greatly increased productivity brought about by the use of new machinery. The company insisted that even with the lowered wage rates take-home pay would be greater. Nevertheless, the Amalgamated Association of Iron and Steelworkers called a strike at Braddock in protest against the changes. The plant was closed, Carnegie met with the union's committee in New York, wined and dined the members in the friendliest fashion, but refused to budge from the position. After six weeks, during which the Braddock plant lay idle, the men accepted Carnegie's terms and went back to work. Although the strike ended without violence, Carnegie was criticized on the ground that his liberality had precipitated it in the first place.

If methods like Carnegie's had been used at Homestead in 1892, violence might well have been avoided and the strike settled with a minimum of friction. But Frick, now chairman of Carnegie Steel Company, Ltd., took an entirely different approach to labor relations than his chief. Curt and autocratic, he had little sympathy and less understanding for working men, and regarded unions as thinly veiled conspiracies. When, at the beginning of contract talks in 1892, the union would not accept his proffered wage scale geared to the price of steel, he abruptly broke off negotiations and began to barricade the plant. Carnegie was in Scotland, and had placed full executive powers in Frick's hands.

Barricades meant strike breakers, and the union responded to the challenge by taking complete control of the town of Homestead. When Frick then attempted to bring a full force of Pinkerton strikebreakers into the plant at night via the Monongahela River, the "Battle of Homestead" broke out, to be ended only when state militia took possession of the town and the steel works. A few days after repossessing the company's property Frick was shot and wounded in his office by an anarchist, and the strike then achieved international notoriety. Carnegie was deeply distressed by the turn affairs had taken, and all of the persuasive powers of his partners was required to prevent him from returning to the United States on the first liner. In order to avoid an appearance of dissension within the ranks of management in a time of crisis, Carnegie felt obligated publicly to support Frick. Privately, however, he deplored the decision to bring strike breakers into the plant, and lost some of his respect for the able lieutenant's judgment. Carnegie's irritation was heightened by the fact that Frick had put him in a very embarrassing position. Some newspapers, holding Carnegie responsible for Frick's actions, were intimating in quite plain terms that Carnegie's liberal labor policies were pure hypocrisy. Loyalty to Frick and the partners stopped Carnegie from replying. The Homestead Strike marked the beginning of the steadily cooling relations between Carnegie and Frick which eventuated in the bitter quarrel at the turn of the century.

Although the strike was ended on Frick's terms, the public image of the company was scarred, and the adoption of enlightened labor policies in the Pittsburgh steel district was set back probably by decades. Many employers felt that Carnegie's liberal pronouncements only added to labor problems by making workmen more obstinate. They also insisted that by recognizing and dealing with national labor unions Carnegie abandoned his men to callous, grasping radicals who would stop at nothing to gain power. Tarred with the brush used to blacken Frick, Carnegie gained little or no support from labor to counterbalance his loss of influence among employers. Carnegie's labor policies were a casualty in the bitter relations between labor and management during the nineties. Probably no individual could have bridged the deep gap of suspicion which separated the antagonists, and Carnegie's good intentions had only gained him the worst of both worlds.

ORGANIZATION OF THE CARNEGIE COMPANIES

The organization of the Carnegie companies brought about conflicts nearly as sharp as those generated by labor relations. In an age in which the corporation had come to be accepted as the standard form for large enterprises, an age also in which management was increasingly separated from ownership, capital constantly sought from outside, and capitalization often inflated by stock watering, the Carnegie companies were something of an anomaly. From the beginning until 1900 the business had been organized as a series of joint partnerships, largely internally financed, and managed by the major partners. When purchase of additional facilities, like the Duquesne Steel Works, required extraordinary outlays of cash, the money was borrowed—sometimes in the form of bond issues which were retired out of profits. Occasionally owners of substantial interests acquired by the company were taken in as silent partners and given stock for their holdings.

Carnegie felt that a company managed by its owners was bound to be more efficient than one administerd by employees. Furthermore, a partnership with closely held stock was never in danger of losing control of its affairs to outsiders, and its financial structure would never fall victim to the bear raids of stock jobbers. Finally, such a partnership, by its ability to assign shares to promising young men, could take its pick of the business talent available and "fix a man for life" in the company. Given a situation in which a joint partnership contained men of the abilities of the Carnegie partners, and considering the anarchic conditions of the contemporary corporate world, Carnegie's position had much to recommend it.

But the partnership arrangement also contained dangers. Ever since the seventies Carnegie had been increasing his holdings, and by the mid-eighties he owned a majority of the shares. In 1886 both he and his brother Thomas fell ill, and Phipps suddenly became aware that in the event of their death the surviving partners would have to buy back the Carnegie interests or lose control of the company to outsiders. Thomas did die, and the company found the means to purchase his interests, but if Andrew had died also, the situation would have been critical. To meet an eventuality of this sort, Carnegie and the partners subscribed to the Iron-clad Agreement, which provided that at the death of any one of them the stock owned by the deceased would revert to the company treasury and be paid for in installments. No partner could sell stock except to another partner. The company would purchase the holdings of any partner wishing to retire, and the vote of three-fourths of the stock would force a partner to leave the organization and turn in his securities. Shares were assigned a book value calculated from the assets of the firm in 1887.

For the next decade the agreement worked well as far as an aid to recruitment of talent was concerned, but the older partners became increasingly restive under it. By the end of this period the appraised value of the company was three or four times the book value of the stock, and there was no bonded debt. Frick, Phipps, and Schwab were aware that if the Ironclad were dismantled they could retire as very rich men. Furthermore, the sum required to purchase the holdings of Carnegie in the event of his death was mounting. By 1897 he owned 58½ percent of the stock, Phipps 11 percent, Frick 6 percent, Schwab 2 percent, the 20 or so junior partners fractions of a share apiece, and silent partners the remainder. The book value of Carnegie's shares was about $25 million; if his heirs insisted on payment at appraised value, the purchase price might rise to above $100 million. Personal considerations also increased the dislike which the partners were coming to feel toward the Ironclad. Carnegie's interference in the management of the firm caused irritation, particularly to Frick. After "retiring" from business in 1866 Carnegie seldom attended directors' meetings and held no office or post of responsibility in the company. Yet, as a kind of Freudian superego, he scrutinized the minutes of meetings minutely and sent a constant stream of advice, criticism and commendation to the officers of the company. Although most of the older partners dearly loved the old gentleman, they resented his paternalism. Moreover, the fact that Carnegie, by virtue of his stockholding, could in all probability bring the career of any one of them to an end probably aroused feelings of insecurity as well.

Frick was naturally the partner most anxious to pry his stock out of the company treasury and liquidate it at its appraised value. With the full support of Phipps, but without consulting Carnegie, he began to fish in the murky waters of Wall Street to get an offer to purchase the company at a figure which Carnegie could not turn down. The consolidation movement was just swinging into high gear, and the Carnegie Company would seem to be a rare jewel for any trustmaster to seize. With its tremendous earning power its capitalization could be inflated several times over, with princely capital gains for insiders. The promoter's fee by itself would amount to a fortune. In 1899 Frick and Phipps found that William H. and James H. Moore, speculators of heroic stature who had engineered the Diamond Match and National Biscuit combinations, were willing to raise $330 million with which to buy and reorganize the Carnegie company and the Frick Coke Company. But since Carnegie would never have negotiated with the Moore brothers, who in his eyes represented the worst of the gambling fraternity, Frick and Phipps transmitted the offer to Carnegie without divulging their names. Suspicious that under the circumstances the offer might not be bona fide, Carnegie agreed only to grant a ninety-day option to buy at the figure stated in return for a pledge of $1,170,000 which was to be forfeited in the event the deal fell through. Frick and Phipps secretly paid $170,000 of the pledge. But because of a combination of circumstances, chiefly a temporary undigested glut of securities in the stock market, the Moore brothers were unable to raise the purchase price within the time allotted and the sale was not consummated. Carnegie was furious when a short time later he discovered the nature of the transaction. Embittered by what he considered to be an act of treachery, he would not return his partners' portion of the option payment, and had the $170,000 transferred to his own account.

A matter of a different sort brought about the permanent break between Carnegie and Frick. The Carnegie Company bought all of its coke from the Frick Coke Company at an agreed price of $1.35 per ton. When the market price of coke rose to above $3.00 in 1899, Frick wanted the steel company to pay the difference. Carnegie refused. Frick, in a passion, then threatened to shut down the coke plant, emulating, incidently, the tactics of the labor unions he so abhorred. Carnegie then let the ax fall, demanding that Frick resign both the chairmanship of the steel company and the presidency of the coke company. Frick could do nothing else than comply, since Carnegie presumably controlled enough votes in the partnership to oust him. But when Carnegie further demanded that Frick sell his Carnegie stock back to the company at book value under the terms of the Ironclad

Agreement, Frick, understandably feeling that Carnegie not only was determined to humiliate him but deprive him of his rightful equity in the company as well, refused and requested the Pennsylvania courts to enjoin the company not to set aside his stock under the terms of the Ironclad, which he now claimed was null and void.

Then began what was sometimes called the greatest trial of the century. This time Frick won his point, but by default. The lengthy complaint which his lawyers put before the court, by revealing the tremendous profits of the Carnegie Company, and by promising even more lurid revelations in the evidence, was not only damaging but provided ammunition for the numerous foes of the tariff, the Republican party, and big business generally. Therefore Carnegie called off the suit before trial and agreed to incorporation of both the steel and coke companies in a single unit. The new Carnegie Company of New Jersey was capitalized at $320 million. Carnegie's proportion of the stock amounted to $174,526,000, Phipps's $34,804,000, and Frick's $31,284,000. Schwab was elected president. At least thirteen other partners became millionaires by the new arrangement.

Able management and efficient operations had all played a part in bringing about the success of the Carnegie companies. Equally important was the multiplying demand for steel and the fact that rapid technological advance in steel making apparently lowered production costs at a faster rate than the fall in steel prices. The Carnegie Companies, then, were in the fortunate position of seeing profit margins widen as production increased. As a business organization the partnership under the Ironclad Agreement had obvious advantages, but in less able hands than those of Carnegie, Frick, Schwab, and Phipps, the company might well have run into difficulties. Also, Carnegie's position was anomalous. In a sense he was an absentee owner who exercised power without the acceptance of responsibility. A lesser man than Carnegie, in this position, could quickly have brought the organization to ruins. As it was, his position made a confrontation with Frick quite likely, and although all judgments must be tentative, it would appear that Carnegie was more responsible than Frick for the sorry manner in which the partnership was dissolved.

Death and transfiguration was to be the destiny of the Carnegie enterprises. In 1901 they became the nucleus of the United States Steel Corporation. The story of the formation of U.S. Steel is one of the great romances of business history, and was told and retold with relish by the tycoons in banking and steel at the turn of the century. On September 12, 1900, the financial and industrial elite of New York assembled at a dinner in the University Club to hear Charles M. Schwab deliver his views concerning the needs of the steel industry. Schwab envisioned a bright future, but insisted that the industry's potential could be realized only by integrating into larger units its competitive sectors. Specialization of production, under centralized control, could then bring impressive economies of scale and end the competitive chaos afflicting much of the industry. J. Pierpont Morgan, one of the assembled diners, was impressed, and with good reason, because this was the kind of doctrine he had so often preached to the railroads in the past. He had participated in the formation of several of the overcapitalized steel combines now coming under the gun of the Carnegie Company, and he realized that if Carnegie went through with his plans to branch out into steel fabrication, these companies would have hard sledding indeed.

After the dinner Morgan induced Schwab to come to a conference in early January at Morgan's home. The subject was of course merger, and the problem was getting Carnegie to merge at a reasonable price. Schwab volunteered to undertake this delicate negotiation, which turned out to be easier than expected. Actually, Carnegie was quite willing to sell. The prospect of a Napoleonic campaign against his competitors was less attractive than the opportunity to enlarge his philanthropic enterprises. The upshot was that the Carnegie Company was sold for $480 million to the nascent United States Steel Company. Andrew Carnegie himself received $225,639,000 in 5 percent gold bonds for his holdings.

At the time of incorporation, in April, 1901, United States Steel consisted of some ten major steel producers plus lake freighters, railroads, docking facilities, Mesabi ore lands, and coal lands, all capitalized at $1,403,000,000. The combined market value of the securities previously issued by the component companies was $793 million, and in 1904 John Moody, the authority on trusts, placed the value of the combination at $676 million. U.S. Steel would therefore seem to be heavily overcapitalized, but since about two-thirds of the company's assets were in fuel and ore properties constantly increasing in value, the overcapitalization diminished with the years. As Louis Hacker has expressed it: "It is difficult to assume that Morgan was grossly overestimating the value of his most impressive accomplishment. He was wagering, in effect, that the country would grow up to what the United States Steel Corporation was capable of doing. It was a bold gamble; and he turned out to be right."

OTHER COMBINATIONS IN THE IRON AND STEEL INDUSTRY

The progressive consolidation of the Carnegie companies was characteristic of developments in the iron and steel industries as a whole. One of the large combinations was the Illinois Steel Company, formed in 1889 with a capitalization of $25 million. Its original component parts—the North Chicago Rolling Mills, the South Chicago Works, the Joliet Steel Company, and the Union Iron and Steel Company, had been founded to take advantage of the rapidly growing Midwest market and the proximity to Lake Superior ore. By acquiring extensive holdings in these ore properties and in Connellsville coke lands, and by extending its activities into fabrication, the Illinois Steel Company became a vertical combination. In 1899 Illinois Steel was absorbed into Federal Steel, a vast, self-contained empire with holdings in railroads, steamship lines, and docking facilities. Horizontal combinations for the production of such articles as forgings, tin plate, steel hoops, barbed wire, pipes, and tubing also came into being during the latter part of the nineteenth century.

Although Pittsburgh and Chicago became the major steel centers, production burgeoned in other parts of the country also. Easy availability of ore and coking coal in the area where Georgia, Tennessee, and Alabama join, plus northern capital and entrepreneurial talent supplied by former Union army officers, led to the rapid growth of the Birmingham-Chattanooga iron district after the Civil War. Between 1880 and 1890 investment in Alabama blast furnaces increased from $2.7 million to $15.7 million, a greater rate of growth than could be found in any state except Illinois, and a larger absolute growth than in any state except Pennsylvania. Low cost of production plus low water freight rates enabled southern producers to sell iron and coke in New England ports in competition with the products of Pennsylvania. Steel making was slow to develop, however, because southern ores were not suitable for Bessemer converters. But during the eighties this difficulty was overcome by the use of special processes in open hearth furnaces. Combination kept pace with the movement in the North. By 1882 a cluster of several mining and manufacturing concerns had been chartered as the Tennessee Coal, Iron, and Railroad Company. The organization continued to absorb additional units until by 1892 it owned 400,000 acres of coal and iron lands, seventeen large iron furnaces, and was capitalized at $18 million. By this time the Colorado Fuel and Iron Company, also controlling vast resources as well as integrated iron and steel works, had become the largest combination in the West.

XXXIII. Standard Oil
and Its Competitors

In contrast to every other large industry of the late nineteenth century except the manufacture of electrical equipment, oil production had no roots reaching back into the past. Nearly all of the technical problems faced by the early oil industry were unprecedented. Petroleum was a rather exotic, relatively unfamiliar substance, thought to exist only in small quantities, and of unknown properties. Until analyzed in 1855 it was most commonly utilized as a medicine, a use which later was proved to be most inappropriate. Getting petroleum out of the ground, transporting, refining, and marketing it all required innovation. Although some experimental efforts in refining had been carried out in Europe, the development of refining techniques, plus pioneering and developmental work in all other sectors of the industry were carried out in the United States. The American mastery of oil technology was all the more remarkable because it took place in a field in which Americans had little experience and even less success—chemical processes. Until the mid-1880s the United States provided almost the entire world supply of oil, and throughout the remainder

453

of the nineteenth century more than half of the American production of kerosene was exported.

Use of kerosene and gas brought about a world-wide revolution in methods of illumination. The supply of tallow candles and whale oil could not satisfy the mounting demand for artificial light from the fifties onward created by factories, theaters, public buildings, and the increase of night-time activities in urban centers. Until the coming of electricity gas met the need in cities, but kerosene came to be used elsewhere, not only in the United States but eventually throughout the world. The revolutionary effect of the oil industry was felt in the sphere of business organization as well. Refining and distribution in the United States was by 1900 dominated by a single firm which had invented the "trust," and in the process helped transform the term into an epithet and fan the growing antipathy against big business which led to government regulation.

The development of mineral oil illuminants began with the discovery in Europe and North America that light oils could be distilled from bitumins and coal. Abraham Gessner, a Canadian physician who had made a geological survey of New Brunswick, distilled an oil from asphaltum which he called "kerosene" (from κέρος [oil] and the suffix ένε [volatile]). In 1856 he opened a plant, the New York Kerosene Company, to produce and market the product. In the next year Samuel Downer and Joshua Merrill established a refinery in Boston to distill a light oil from coal. In their process coal was heated to about 800 degrees, at which temperature oily vapors escaped and were condensed into a thick mass similar to the heavier types of petroleum. Redistillation of the mass recovered lighter hydrocarbons in the form of illuminating oil. After removal of impurities by treatment with sulphuric acid and caustic soda, the oil was ready for market. By 1859 inexpensive lamps designed for the new product were available. Coal oil, priced at about seventy-five cents per gallon, wholesale, proved to be immediately popular. New plants were built, and production by 1860 had reached about 30,000 gallons per day.

The feasibility of distilling kerosene from petroleum was demonstrated by Professor Benjamin Silliman of Yale, who in 1855 reported his findings in his famous *Report on Rock Oil, or Petroleum, from Venango County, Pennsylvania*. Silliman had been retained to make the study by petroleum promoters from Pennsylvania who joined a group of New Haven business-men after publication of the *Report* to form the Seneca Oil Company of Connecticut. But a major problem still remained: acquiring the raw ma-terial in commercially usable quantities. Up to this point petroleum had been skimmed off the surface of springs and pools of western Pennsylvania and southern New York, or had been found mixed with brine from salt wells. Obviously a much larger supply had to be available if a petroleum illuminating oil industry was to be created. According to an often repeated story, one member of the Seneca Company, struck by the picture of a drilling operation for salt on a handbill advertising medical petroleum, conceived the idea of drilling for oil. The story may be apochryphal, but in any event the Seneca Company dispatched one of its members, Edwin L. Drake, to western Pennsylvania to prospect on a tract of land the company had leased near Titusville. Shortly after arrival Drake began to drill for oil, to the amusement of the local inhabitants. In August, 1859, he made his famous strike, and a new industry was born.

The ensuing rush to the valley of little Oil Creek, which flows into the Allegheny River about eighty miles north of Pittsburgh, was more hectic than the gold rush of '49 because the large number of prospectors descended upon such a limited area. Frantic competition for lease and purchase of likely properties sent land values skyrocketing. Farms, which could be bought for a team of horses in 1859 brought $200,000 to $700,000 a few years later. Leases usually called for royalties of up to 50 percent of oil raised in addition to cash payments, and were often divided into fractions for speculative trading. Drilling equipment was primitive. Many wells were merely "kicked down" by foot levers rigged to drill shafting and spring poles. Since oil lay at a depth of no more than two hundred feet, the cost of drilling a well was no more than $1,000 to $1,200, and operating costs ran as low as $5 per day.

Oil City, at the confluence of Oil Creek and the Allegheny River, came into existence as an entrepôt for oil shipments to Pittsburgh, and Titusville developed into the major center for the speculative trading in leases and properties. Companies by the score were formed in New York and Philadelphia to exploit the black bonanza, and the volume of daily trading in petroleum stocks on the Philadelphia Exchange sometimes amounted to more than $200,000. By 1866 over five hundred companies representing an actual investment of as much as $100 million had been formed. Many were fraudulent and most were failures, but a few seemed spectacularly successful. The Columbia Oil Company, for example, in which Andrew Carnegie was interested, paid dividends of $300,000 during the second half of 1863 on a nominal capitalization of $200,000. Actually, since life expectancy of wells in the early period was about six to nine months, and since dry holes greatly outnumbered productive drillings, the rate of profit on producing wells had to be sky-high merely to enable the companies to break even. As we have seen in previous surveys of mining, high exploration costs and rapid depletion require the rate of return in the extractive industries to be much higher than in other lines of business.

By 1871 conditions of production had been somewhat stabilized. Life expectancy of wells had been raised to three years by deeper drilling and by torpedoing. These developments, plus a smaller proportion of dry holes—five out of eight drillings—reduced the risks of loss. It was considered that with crude selling at $2.20 per barrel an operator could break even pumping a well producing twenty barrels per day. During the sixties petroleum reached a high of $8.00 per barrel in 1864, but usually ranged between $2.25 and $5.75.

But as production methods improved and the flow of oil from the regions rapidly mounted, sharply fluctuating oil prices and transportation difficulties presented serious problems for the well operators. During the late sixties prices went into an irregular decline and by 1873 oil was selling at under $2 per barrel. Since the average yield of some 3,000 wells at this time was between four and five barrels, only the more productive wells could be operated at a profit. During the period of decline measures to restrict production were given serious consideration, but throughout the history of the Pennsylvania oil fields none was ever very effectively put into practice. When the fields were first opened, charges for barrels, drayage to rail head, and transportation to New York were so high in the aggregate that some operators could make a gross profit of only 23 cents per barrel when oil was selling in New York for $7. But by 1864 when the Pennsylvania, the Atlantic and Great Western, and the Philadelphia and Erie had extended rail lines into the oil fields, transportation conditions were much improved.

Equally important in this connection was the construction of gathering pipelines which conducted oil from the wells to storage tank depots on the railroads. The first lines, laid in 1862, greatly reduced the cost of getting oil to the railroads, and at the same time made handsome profits for the companies which constructed the networks. Teamsters, foreseeing the end of their business, often tore up the lines where they could. But with the help of Pinkerton detectives who infiltrated the teamsters' organizations, the line owners finally brought the vandals to justice. The pipeline companies gave receipts for producers' oil in the form of certificates which became a circulating medium of the regions and were traded on a curb exchange in Oil City. Railroads, realizing that control of the gathering and storage companies would play an important role in the execution of competitive strategies, formed alliances with the new organizations, but made no attempt to buy them up and integrate them into railroad systems. In view of the railroads' larger interests, the failure to do this was later revealed to be a costly mistake.

Refining proved to be the simplest of the problems facing the early oil industry. Fortunately, Pennsylvania petroleum contained little of the sulphur and other substances which made very difficult the production of a clear odorless illuminating oil from the crude found in most other parts of the nation—particularly in California and in the Lima oil fields of Ohio. Fortunately also the distilling process had been worked out by the coal oil manufacturers, and could be applied unchanged except for elimination of the first "dry distilling" step by which coal was vaporized. In 1860 a refinery designed to produce five barrels of illuminating oil per day could be erected for as little as $200, and even the large refineries of the early seventies seldom cost more than $15,000. From the outset plants were constructed in the oil fields, but Pittsburgh quickly became a center with sixty refineries by 1863 having a combined weekly capacity of 26,000 barrels. Coal oil refiners, foreseeing the speedy demise of their industry, relocated near the oil fields or converted their refineries in eastern seaboard cities to handle petroleum. Distillation of kerosene from coal cost approximately 25 cents per gallon, as compared to 6 cents per gallon from petroleum. About 80 percent of the volume of petroleum could be recovered as kerosene if the heavier fractions were redistilled. During the early days of the industry the lighter fractions—naptha and gasoline—were simply discarded, and in congested areas like Pittsburgh created a serious fire hazard. The refining of lubricating oil from the lower fractions was undertaken on only a small scale during the early period because the need for new lubricants was not so pressing as the need for new illuminants. The direct use of petroleum as a fuel developed even more slowly because crude oil was dangerous to store, gave off an offensive odor, and required special burners. Only in California, where coal was much more expensive than in Pennsylvania, did this branch of the industry make much headway until the nineties.

Thus in the short space of a decade, from 1859 to 1869, an industrial giant had come into being. Annual production of the Pennsylvania oil fields had jumped from 2,000 barrels to 4.8 mililon—a daily production of slightly more than 13,000 barrels at the end of the period. Equally striking was the advance in exports. By 1874 the nation was sending abroad nearly

6 million barrels of oil per year, and petroleum ranked third in the value of commodity exports, following cotton and wheat in that order. About 75 percent of the annual production of illuminating oil was exported.

JOHN D. ROCKEFELLER AND THE RISE OF THE STANDARD OIL COMPANY OF OHIO

Since the Standard Oil Company during the eighties came to produce 80 percent of the nation's output of refined oil, the history of the refining business is largely the history of this one company. Moreover, since Standard in the early years was largely the shadow of John D. Rockefeller, an account of his career is central to the story. The quiet, elegant, self-effacing, intense, secretive, self-disciplined little man became perhaps the most famous—or notorious depending on the point of view—businessman which the nation has produced. Admired by colleagues and the business community generally, hated by petroleum producers and by competitors in refining, regarded with deep suspicion by political and social reformers, he was forever the center of controversies the virulence of which contrasted sharply with his inoffensive demeanor, even temper, and widespread philanthropies.

Rockefeller was born in western New York in 1839, the son of a handsome, muscular, gregarious, itinerant trader, who, while secretive about his affairs, thoroughly enjoyed manipulating the strategies of his rather shady business. The mother, on the other hand, was deeply religious, reticent, and frugal. In personality young John resembled his mother, to whom he was strongly attached, but in the conduct of business he tended to follow the example of his father. At school he was a hard worker, but excelled at nothing. When asked by a young friend what he wanted to do when he grew up, he replied, "I want to be worth $100,000 and I'm going to be, too." In 1853 the family moved to Cleveland where John, now aged fourteen, went to work as an assistant bookkeeper in a wholesale produce house. Like young James Duke he threw himself into the world of business almost with rapture. "The place," he recalled much later, "was delightful to me—all the method and system of the office." At the same time he joined the Baptist Church, became a close student of the Bible, contributed regularly from his salary of $25 per month, and in a short time was appointed clerk of the church. The ordinary weaknesses of the flesh did not appeal to him. "I never had a craving for tobacco, or tea, or coffee. I never had a craving for anything," he said later in life. Apparently he did not feel that his desire for $100,000 represented a "craving."

At twenty he struck out for himself, forming a wholesale produce house with another ambitious young man, Maurice B. Clark. In their first year the two did a business of $450,000. At the outbreak of the Civil War, Rockefeller did not enlist, but outfitted several substitutes. It is notable that among other leading businessmen of this generation who avoided military service in this manner were Philip D. Armour, J. Pierpont Morgan, and John Wanamaker.

Clark and Rockefeller prospered mightily during the war years, but Rockefeller carefully kept aloof from the speculative manias of the period. Meanwhile Cleveland, with twenty refineries by 1863, was becoming a center of the rapidly growing refining industry. Pittsburgh was nearer to the oil fields, but it was served by only one railroad—the Pennsylvania. Cleveland was served by two—the Lake Shore and the Atlantic and Great Western—and had a water connection with the East via the Erie Canal as well. Under these circumstances Cleveland refiners could get rock bottom transportation rates, and because transportation accounted for a large proportion of total production costs enjoyed an advantage not shared by the refiners of Pittsburgh.

Rockefeller had watched the advance of the oil industry with great interest. He not only appreciated the advantageous location of Cleveland, but was aware that refining was in the long run a more stable and profitable end of the business than the production of the raw material. As we have seen, other bright young men had reached substantially the same conclusion after comparing the mining and refining sectors of the nonferrous metals industries. In 1862, when crude sold at the wells for twenty-five cents to fifty cents per barrel, refined oil was bringing twenty-five cents per gallon in New York. While this profit spread was unusual and temporary because of bottlenecks in transport and small refining capacity, the outlook for refiners was bright under any circumstances. With refining costs as low as five or six cents per gallon and the market for oil rapidly expanding, substantial profits seemed assured. In 1863 Rockefeller and Clark eagerly accepted the proposal of Samuel Andrews, an experienced refinery worker, that the three build and operate a refinery on a partnership basis, with Rockefeller and Clark supplying the required capital and Andrews supervising construction and operations.

From this time forward Rockefeller embarked upon a course of relentless expansion. With complete confidence in the future of oil refining, he borrowed to the absolute limit of his credit, at high rates of interest if necessary, putting every cent into facilities for the increase of production. In 1865 he dissolved the produce partnership with Clark and bought the refinery outright, operating it thenceforth in partnership with Andrews. A few months later he induced his brother William to join the business, started construction of a second refinery, and incorporated a sales agency in New York—Rockefeller and Company. Showing the same ability to secure the services of efficient men as did Carnegie, he brought Henry M. Flagler and Stephen V. Harkness into the partnership of 1867. Flagler had prospered in the grain commission business around Toledo and had married Mary Harkness, niece of Stephen, who became a financial magnate of Cleveland at the time Rockefeller was starting in the oil business. By 1869 the two Rockefellers, Andrews, Flagler, and Harkness (a silent partner), had the largest refinery in the United States, with a capacity of 1,500 barrels per day. In 1870 they incorporated as the Standard Oil Company of Ohio. The capitalization of $1 million was considerably below the market value of the firm's assets. John D. Rockefeller was elected president. With about 30 percent of the stock he was the largest single stockholder, but at no time exercised the controlling interest over Standard which Carnegie exerted over the Carnegie companies. Yet Rockefeller's influence was more direct and pervasive because he supervised the company's day-by-day operations.

Like Carnegie and his partners, Rockefeller and the Standard Oil men strove to maintain ownership and management in the same hands. Unlike Carnegie, however, Rockefeller was eager for incorporation because Standard from the outset embarked on a comprehensive program of expansion facilitated by the mechanisms for stock transfer and merger inherent in the corporate form. Since the Carnegie group at the beginning merely added units somewhat haphazardly when these became available at attractive prices, it could afford the greater security for in-group control guaranteed by the private partnership.

Combination came early to the oil industry because by 1870 the rigors of competition were becoming severe. In the steel industry, entrance was difficult because of heavy capital needs and the necessity of operating under licenses from patent holders. As a result, production was concentrated in a few large firms which could control prices and output. But, by contrast, ease of entrance into refining had resulted in a multiplication of small plants and a surge of production past the point of diminishing returns. Profit margins for refiners narrowed dangerously after 1870 as the price of refined oil fell, bringing a keenly felt need for restriction of output and price control. Since the refineries were concentrated in only a few locations—Cleveland, Pittsburgh, and the major East Coast cities—and since they all manufactured the same products, combination for effecting this objective could be brought about with relative ease. Standard of Ohio, the largest firm in the field, was the company best suited to carry out the process. There appears to have been more of a defensive element in the combination of the oil industry than in many of the combinations of the turn of the century. The Standard partners were not motivated by the desire for stock speculation and the earning of promoters' fees which characterized the trustmasters of the later period. The low capitalization of the parent company and the reasonable prices paid for its acquisitions were indicators that whatever else Standard Oil might be, it was not a mere mechanism for stock watering. Rockefeller was probably more sincere than his critics believed when he insisted that he did not put together the combination in order to enjoy monopoly profits—although this was undoubtedly an element in his thought—but rather to protect his own and other firms against the losses sure to result from unrestrained competition.

Between November, 1871, and the following March, Standard acquired the largest refinery in New York, six tar distilling plants, and eighteen other refining units. Payment was made in the stock of Ohio Standard, or cash, or both. In addition to physical properties, Standard acquired valuable assets in the form of executives of the acquired firms who were to constitute the very able management of the company in its future career—among them Oliver H. Payne, Jabez A. Bostwick, and Ambrose M. McGregor. At later dates under similar circumstances the company secured the services of Charles Pratt, Jacob J. Vandergrift, Henry H. Rogers, and the operative head after the retirement of Rockefeller—John D. Archbold.

If the objective of stabilizing the industry was defensible enough, effecting it through the mechanisms of the South Improvement Company was reprehensible even by the lax standards of the day and was a major factor in saddling Standard Oil with the notoriety under which it labored for the rest of the century. The Improvement Company, whose stock was held by the major refiners and the Pennsylvania, New York Central, and the Erie Railroads, was to act as an "evener" of oil traffic by assigning 45 percent to the Pennsylvania and 27½ percent apiece to the other two. Rates were agreed upon with rebates of from 25 percent to 50 percent to company members. If the scheme had stopped here it might have been justified according to the business practices of the day, for it was nothing more than a pool similar to many others in effect throughout the country. Even the rebates could be justified on the ground that large refiners, by contracting to ship in carload or trainload lots, lowered the cost of railroad transportation. At the present day carload rates are lower than less-than-carload rates, thus reflecting to some degree the rebates of the period before the Interstate Commerce Act. But the plan's true nature was revealed by further provisions that rebates were to be paid to members on the shipments of oil made by nonmembers, and the railroads would supply full information on the amount of such oil carried and its destination. The South Improvement Company, therefore, was in fact a weapon with which insiders could smash competition and press forward toward a monopoly, and the five or six million dollars the company was expected to earn annually was designed to be a war chest for the purpose.

Although negotiated in secret, provisions of the contract rapidly became known when the railroads attempted to raise the rates quoted to outsiders. In the subsequent torrent of condemnation, particularly from the oil producers, the members hastily backed out of the agreement and vigorously passed the buck regarding authorship. For many critics, the buck stopped in the hands of John D. Rockefeller. Although Rockefeller certainly approved of the plan, evidence indicates that it was originated by Tom Scott of the Pennsylvania Railroad. "We were willing to go with them [the other members] as far as the plan could be used," Rockefeller explained much later, "so that when it failed we would be in a better position to get their cooperation than if we had said 'No' from the start." The alternative Rockefeller apparently had in mind was combination under the aegis of Standard Oil. In any event, after the details of the South Improvement scheme had been aired, it was difficult to persuade unprejudiced observers that Rockefeller's governing motive in participating had been to pave the way for the stabilization of the oil industry. Rockefeller's motives were probably as mixed as those of most people, and he certainly would have been interested in any plan likely to redound to the benefit of his company, yet there is no reason to doubt that he regarded the South Improvement Company as only a temporary expedient to hasten acceptance of his own remedy for the damaging effects of competition.

Standard continued to insist upon rebates even after the demise of the South Improvement Company because they constituted the most important economy of scale in oil refining. Since processes were uniform throughout the industry, large refiners could not produce much more cheaply than small ones. But with railroads giving larger rebates for larger shipments, the big refiners possessed a cumulative advantage over their smaller competitors. Combination brings varying types of advantages to firms in different lines of business. It enabled the Carnegie companies to lower production costs through the progressive improvement of manufacturing facilities. Combination in glass and the subsequent mechanization of processes permitted Libbey and his associates to lower labor costs and free management from the large measure of control over production exercised by labor unions. Combination in tobacco provided James B. Duke with the financial resources to exercise controls over the market and mount the advertising campaigns so necessary for industries which cater to changing public taste.

The abortive attempt of the major refineries to suppress competition by the South Improvement Company was paralleled by ineffective efforts on the part of producers to limit production. At the outset the large number of producers made the enforcement of regulations much more difficult than in the refining end of the business. All operators were afraid that if they did not get the oil out of the ground quickly neighbors would suck it off into their own wells. Furthermore, the faster oil was pumped, the lower the unit cost of production. Finally, the terms of leases made it hard to limit production. These documents, designed to protect lessors, usually provided a time limit within which the lessee must start drilling and stipulated that if wells were not operated with "due diligence" the leases could be canceled.

After the South Improvement fiasco Standard pushed ahead with its campaign to limit competition by merger. In order to avoid the appearance of seeking monopoly, wherever possible the mergers were carried out secretly and the merged companies continued to operate in their own names and sell products under their own brands. For those companies who resisted inclusion Standard offered membership in a Central Refiners Association in which members in return for submitting to production and price controls were offered the right to subscribe to stock. Enforcement was provided by an ingenious system in which owners leased their properties to the association for one year, then took them back under a second lease as tenants-at-will subject to expulsion for violation of contractual agreements. So successful were the various ramifications of Standard's "plan" that in 1879 Henry H. Rogers could testify before the Hepburn Committee that 90 to 95 percent of the refiners in the country were working with Standard Oil. As Rockefeller's biographer, Allan Nevins, sums up: "Rockefeller ruled the empire of oil as Napoleon ruled Europe after Austerlitz, and there was no Wellington on the horizon."

Meanwhile Standard had been exerting itself to acquire pipeline companies. Not only were these very profitable, but by enabling the owners to divert crude from one railroad to another bestowed leverage which could be used when bargaining for rates. The Pennsylvania Railroad, fully aware of this situation, began to acquire gathering lines through its affiliated fast freight line, the Empire Transportation Company. Standard, in a counter move, threw together its own organizations, the American Transfer Company, and United Pipelines. Handling one-third of the crude moving from wells to railroads by 1875, Standard had acquired pipeline interests larger than those of any railroad company. Competition led to the bitter "Empire War" of 1877. When Empire, in order to forestall impending domination of the entire oil industry by Standard, moved into the refining end of the business, Standard in retaliation boycotted the Pennsylvania Railroad, diverting crude to its competitors. As losses for the Pennsylvania mounted, cries of anguish from stockholders and the destructive railroad strike of 1877 forced Tom Scott to throw in the towel. He sold Empire to Standard with a supplementary agreement that Standard would ship a minimum of two million barrels of oil per year over the road at agreed rates, and with a 20 cent per barrel rebate. Standard now had almost complete control of the transportation of oil from the fields to the railroads.

It required no great imagination to foresee that the time would soon come when both crude and refined oil would be pumped all the way from western Pennsylvania to the east coast cities. Tidewater Oil Company blazed the trail in 1874 by laying a line from the regions to Williamsport, in central Pennsylvania, from which point oil went by the Reading and Jersey Central Railroads to New York. Tidewater was soon followed by Standard Oil, whose National Transit Company had a trunk pipeline to seaboard by 1883 which was carrying the great bulk of east-bound oil at a fraction of the cost of rail transportation. Since Standard kept rates equal to those charged by the railroads, National Transit became one of the most profitable units of the Standard empire and gave the parent company an even greater advantage over the few independent refiners remaining. In view of the profitability of pipelines and their threat to railroad interests, it is difficult to understand why the Pennsylvania and other trunk railroads did not take the lead in pipeline construction. Competition and reckless expansion may have deprived the railroads of the resources with which to undertake such a program. Equally important, perhaps, Standard was such a large shipper of oil by rail that the roads, fearful of losing its business, may have delayed challenging it until the probable cost of victory in all-out warfare became greater than they could pay.

CAREER OF THE STANDARD OIL TRUST

By 1879 Rockefeller had become concerned about the lack of clear, legal centralization of authority in the now vast Standard Oil Company. Under the Ohio charter Standard had no right to operate or own stock in plants out of the state. To get around this difficulty much of the stock of component companies was held by Standard executives acting as trustees. Such a policy guaranteed secrecy, and gave the trustees control over the companies concerned, but it did not define the lines of authority within the ruling group and it was of doubtful legality. After an interim revision of this arrangement the entire combine was formally organized as a trust in 1882. This form admirably met the administrative needs of the companies and established a landmark in the evolution of business organization. Under the trust agreement, the stock of Standard as well as of its component companies was pooled and placed in the hands of nine trustees, who were the principal owners and managers of Standard Oil. Stockholders received trust certificates in return for their shares which entitled them to dividends, but to none of the rights conferred by the possession of equities. The trustees, who were to be located in New York, had a control over the combine which was absolute and unquestioned because of the power of the trustees to vote the stock of the component companies. Since the trustees could fill vacancies occurring within their own group, the trust became as eternal as the corporation.

Supposedly the brain child of Samuel C. T. Dodd, general counsel of Standard, the trust was a tour de force in the development of business organization. The fiduciary function, designed in its traditional legal sense to safeguard the interests of those who were unable to look after their own affairs, was lifted out of its original context and made a mechanism for the transfer of corporate powers from stockholders to a shadowy directorate which could exercise these powers secretly, expeditiously, decisively, and with little possibility of opposition from outside the group. From the outset the trust form aroused the suspicion and hostility of the critics of big business. Its centralization of power, abrogation of the traditional rights of stockholders, and secrecy of operation naturally offended Americans who valued democratic traditions. Furthermore, since there were no limits to the size of trusts, and since they could be operated most effectively in large units, the accumulating advantages of size appeared to put them in a position in which they could at will destroy the small businesses so vital for the nation's social as well as economic health. In short, trusts could be truly revolutionary, for they had the power to change the United States from a democracy to a plutocracy.

During the decade following the organization of the trust the expansion of Standard continued at an undiminished rate. By 1884 the some fifty-seven producing units embraced by the trust constituted 77 percent of the refining capacity of the nation, and Standard marketed about 80 to 85 percent of all oil consumed. The trust had become a completely integrated refining, transportation, and marketing organization. It produced about 150 different oil products, to say nothing of in-service items such as barrels, chemicals, and cans. With assets by 1890 of nearly $116 million and net earnings of $19,131,470, it was probably the richest business organization in the world at the time. The only sector of oil business in which Standard was not dominant was in the production of crude. Aware at the outset that production was highly speculative and nearly impossible to control, Rockefeller had stayed out of the oil fields. But as Standard's capacity grew, the danger of relying entirely upon others for the supply of crude became manifest. Therefore during the nineties the company went into the producing sector of the oil industry by buying into the Lima oil fields of Ohio, and later became even more heavily committed in California and Texas-Oklahoma.

To the critics of big business, Standard became the symbol and archetype of monopoly just as the Bank of the United States had been the symbol of the privileged corporation so widely disliked during the 1830s. The Sherman Antitrust Act of 1890 was an earnest of public feeling which caused Standard officials great concern. In 1892 came a long awaited blow when the Supreme Court of Ohio declared the Standard Oil Trust to be a conspiracy to effect monopoly, and ordered Standard of Ohio to separate from it. Without testing the decision in the federal courts the trustees dissolved the trust. But this move had little or no effect upon the actual management of the organization or upon the lines of authority by which it was held together. The some ninety refining, transportation, marketing, and producing units were merely combined into twenty large companies given the collective name, Standard Oil Interests. Policy decisions were still made by the former trustees, plus additions to the group which brought top management to about fifteen in number. Co-ordination was effected by interlocking directorates and by a widely ramified committee system. In 1899 tighter organization was effected and all of the former controls of the trust revived by the reorganization of Standard of New Jersey into a holding company. After an exchange of stock, this huge enterprise, with assets valued at about $225 million, became the parent company of forty-one operating units.

Perhaps the most striking aspect of Standard's corporate development was continuity of policy and maintenance of control by essentially the same in-group of top management despite radical changes in the form of business structure. Management had at one time or another utilized every known form of combination in order to organize the industry under Standard's leadership—merger by purchase and exchange of stock, agreements with competitors, lease of competing units, experiments with trusteeship evolving into the giant trust, interlocking directorates, committees, and finally, the holding company. It is interesting to note by way of contrast that integration in the Carnegie companies came long after the organization had achieved success. Carnegie himself inaugurated the attempt to dominate the steel industry only as a defensive riposte against combination by competitors, and the movement was brought to fruition by forces outside the company.

STANDARD'S COMPETITIVE TACTICS

Opponents and defenders of Standard Oil disagreed sharply over the reasons for the company's success. Critics insisted that the root cause was the railroad rebates which gave an unfair advantage at the outset which increased as the company grew. Once leadership in the industry was established, these critics continued, it was an easy matter for the company to use its great financial power to crush smaller competitors. Competing refiners were offered a pittance for their properties with a thinly veiled threat of ruin by price cutting and choking off of markets if they refused to sell. Critics maintained that independents daring to invade Standard's marketing territory were summarily dealt with in similar fashion.

Actually these charges were exaggerated and by themselves cannot account for the company's rise to dominance. Certainly Standard took advantage of all the weaknesses and mistakes of its opponents; such tactics are the very essence of free competition and are accepted as normal as long as no single individual or firm becomes too big a winner in the game. But Standard could exploit the shortcomings of others only *after* it had taken the lead in the industry and had become an independent power. This leadership was gained by the ability of the Standard men to envision opportunities for expansion, by the relentless drive for combination, by the capacity to manage efficiently a burgeoning empire, and by the skill in persuading competitors to join it. Combination could take place only if conditions were favorable and if a strong and widely shared incentive to combine were present. Oil refining during the seventies was an industry quite suitable for combination, and overproduction and falling prices provided the incentive. Many if not most of the firms were looking for the leadership which Standard provided.

Critics of combination often ignored the fact that its objective was not the destruction but the salvation of competing firms. As far as can be determined, Standard's competitors were offered fair prices for their plants.

The great majority joined the combination willingly enough, as illustrated by the fact that nearly all of the Standard executives except the original partners had been connected with companies subsequently absorbed. There is reason to believe that some firms competed with Standard solely for the purpose of inviting an offer of merger. It is quite likely that many of the competitors who later complained of being bludgeoned into the organization entertained exaggerated notions of the value of their properties. Had Standard paid prices high enough to satisfy all of the merged firms it would almost certainly have watered its capital structure, as did most other combinations.

Standard's treatment of competitors in the field of distribution was more rigorous. At the outset it had dealt with jobbers who sold to grocery and hardware stores as retail outlets. But occasional adulteration of oil and manipulation of prices to the company's disadvantage stimulated the desire to control marketing which was making itself felt in many other industries. In addition to defending price levels, profit margins, and the quality of products, the company no doubt also wanted to share in the profits of distribution. Standard's method was first to buy up and integrate existing distributors. Where these were lacking or were recalcitrant, Standard established its own bulk stations with railroad sidings, storage tanks, barrel plants, horses, and wagons. By 1900 the company had more than a thousand such stations in operation, and its brightly painted tank wagons, emblazoned with the Standard label, were a familiar sight in all the major cities of the nation. Standard's fleet of railroad tank cars alone gave it a great advantage because independent distributors, purchasing from jobbers who had to depend upon the railroads for cars, often had trouble getting deliveries. Assurance of regular supplies of oil was probably an important inducement to join Standard. Standard sometimes purchased independent distributors as well as refineries in order to secure the services of efficient executives, and was not niggardly in the prices offered. With some independents, Standard reached a modus vivendi which was apparently satisfactory to both parties involved. But the company usually dealt harshly with competitors who challenged it by price cutting, or who made efforts to enlarge their share of the market. Price cutters were given stronger doses of their own medicine than they could endure, and were harassed in other ways. In order to secure oil, independent distributors found that they had to order well in advance; rumors circulated that their suppliers were about to go out of business; sometimes supposedly independent refiners were secretly tied to Standard and could bring pressure to bear on jobbers which was quickly transmitted to the local distribution level. The company had an efficient and ubiquitous intelligence system which permitted the careful planning of competitive tactics. Distributing agents were required to deliver regular reports on all aspects of competitors' business. Even after the collapse of the South Improvement scheme railroads tied to the company by valuable contracts apparently continued to supply information on shipments by competitors.

But the amount of pressure brought to bear on independents varied with circumstances and with the particular Standard officials involved. Probably many instances of unfair practices occurred without the knowledge of top management. Subordinates, in competition among themselves for advancement knew that they would be judged by their performance alone. As long as they did not bring serious discredit upon the company, their attempts to enlarge their markets would be supported and top management would look the other way if any unfair practices came into view. The volume of such instances would be difficult to estimate. Quite possibly complainants, realizing that they would be speaking to a receptive audience, exaggerated both the number and the severity of the unethical tactics applied. But in any event, there were enough instances to keep alive the image of the company as a soulless monster.

TECHNOLOGICAL PROGRESS

Although technological improvements could by no means reduce costs as much as in the steel industry, Standard officials gave continuous attention to improving refining processes and to the peripheral methods of cutting costs inherent in integration. Production methods of constituent companies were under constant surveillance by the parent company, and the units were expected to compete with each other in all areas affecting profits. Standard pioneered the tower still, which by condensing the various fractions at different levels in a tall, vertical column, revolutionized refining by making it a continuous rather than a "batch" process. By 1890 the company had acquired about 150 patents, and had greatly expanded the number of its products. One of its most profitable innovations was the development of a process whereby gas could be extracted from petroleum. "Carbureted water gas" cost less to produce than coal gas, and its illuminating power was greater. But probably the company's greatest technological achievement, and one which proved very profitable, was finding a way to distill the "sour" crude from the Lima oil fields.

For more than a quarter of a century after 1859 nearly all the petroleum in the United States east of the Mississippi River came from western Pennsylvania. But the mid-eighties production began to decline and Standard executives became concerned over the possibility of future shortages. Beginning in 1885 the huge Lima field was explored and tapped, but the quality of the oil was a bitter disappointment. Because of a high sulphur content which could not be eliminated by distilling processes then in use, it produced only a murky, odorous, "polecat" kerosene unfit for illuminating purposes. Nevertheless, Rockefeller, against the advice of his associates, insisted on buying into the field. It was only a few years later that Frick began acquiring Lake Superior ore properties with the same objective of securing a source of raw material capable of supplying the voracious needs of a rapidly expanding industry.

Since a bad smell did not prevent Lima oil from serving as an acceptable fuel, Standard constructed a pipeline from the field to Chicago and promoted the use of oil as in industrial fuel. More important, as an act of faith that a process would soon be found to purify the oil for illuminating purposes, Standard began construction of a large refinery a few miles east of Chicago in a deserted sandy area near the shore of Lake Michigan called Whiting. At the same time the company bought a patent for a promising but undeveloped purification process using copper oxide invented by an immigrant German pharmacist named Hermann Frasch. In a laboratory built in connection with the plant—possibly the first industrial laboratory in the nation serving a corporation—the process was perfected and the plant completed. By 1897 Whiting was processing 27,967 barrels of Lima crude per day. Through Standard of Indiana, a marketing organization, the Whiting refinery gave the company undisputed dominance of the oil business throughout the Middle West.

By 1900 Standard Oil had become a financial success beyond the dreams of avarice, earning, in that year, approximately $7 million from crude oil production, $24 million from transportation, $20 million from manufacturing, $10 million from domestic marketing, and $3 million from foreign marketing. From 1882 to 1892 dividends had averaged $7,912,-700 per year, about 58 percent of earnings. Since expansion was thus financed internally to a large extent, the net value of Jersey Standard rose far above the valuation placed on the capital stock. From 1900 to 1911 average net value of all assets stood at about $378 million, while the capital stock was carried at only $98 million. Average earnings on this stock were $79 million, or about 80 percent per year, of which about one-half was paid out in dividends and the remainder plowed back into the business.

CHARACTERISTICS OF MANAGEMENT

Although efficiency of operations might give an impression of rigid hierarchical and bureaucratic control, actually top management was a collective function exercised in relatively informal fashion. Despite the changing forms in which the company was organized, policy was always determined by the original partners plus subsequent additions to the group, most of whom had formerly headed competing companies. John D. Rockefeller exercised the strongest influence, only partly because with about 20 percent of the stock he continued to be the largest single stockholder. In policy decisions he was no more than *primus inter pares*. Although quiet and unassuming in comparison with the more flamboyant personalities of other policy makers, he was usually able to bring others around to his point of view by his trenchant reasoning and encyclopedic knowledge of the oil business. John D. Archbold, who succeeded Rockefeller as captain of the team in 1891, was energetic, genial, kindly, well-versed in the details of Standard's affairs, and acclimated to playing the game according to the lax rules of the day. Like Rockefeller he was sincerely religious, and by his benefactions to Syracuse University paralleled Rockefeller's contributions to the University of Chicago. Others among the ruling group exhibited widely differing characteristics. Rogers was aggressive and impatient; Pratt cautious and dilatory; Payne cool and distant; Flagler daring and speculative. Most had spent their formative years in small businesses during a period in which considerations of public policy were seldom allowed to interfere with the operations of the market, which therefore largely determined the ethical standards of business. Their acceptance of so much which would be considered reprehensible today merely reflects the conditioning of a climate differing from our own in so many respects.

Their mercantile origins are perhaps also reflected in their widespread business activities outside Standard Oil. None evinced much interest in management as such or in technical and engineering matters. Instead they behaved like the entrepreneurs of an earlier generation, putting their profits into peripheral enterprises over which they exercised personal control. Thus Rogers and William Rockefeller attempted to combine and integrate the nation's copper production (above, p. 398). Flagler became the major developer of Florida real estate and built the Florida Keys Railroad, and John D. Rockefeller acquired and combined extensive iron ore properties and transportation facilities in the Lake Superior region (see pp. 439–40).

The fact that a group of men with such differing personalities as the Standard Oil executives could work together as a team for such a long period of time is unusual. Even more striking is the fact that as strong-willed men they could argue acrimoniously and at great length over questions of policy, and yet finally agree to compromises which represented creative decisions and not mere avoidance of controversial issues. Important decisions were always postponed until they could be unanimous, and once put into effect received wholehearted support. Like the Carnegie group the Standard Oil executives were considered to be among the most talented in the nation. In one respect they were superior. No controversy like the Carnegie-Frick quarrel ever arose to mar their relationships with each other and endanger the affairs of the company.

Committees were the instruments by which policies were made and carried out. The most important of these was the Executive Committee, formed in 1872 at the time of the incorporation of Standard of Ohio. The trustees of a later date were essentially the same men exercising the same functions under a different name. After dissolution of the trust they were known as "the gentlemen in 26 Broadway"—the company's office building in New York—or "the gentlemen in room 1400"—the executive suite. This group drafted general policies, supervised the local management of wells, pipelines, and refineries, and determined budgetary expenditures for new units and for expansion of existing facilities. Below the Executive Committee were eight or nine specialized committees handling specific areas of the business. Among these were committees on manufacturing, domestic trade, foreign trade, shipping, cooperage, lubricating, pipelines, case and cans. On the committees individual members of top management joined management of the second level. Membership was interlocking to such a degree that Archbold could inquire, half jokingly, as he called a meeting to order, "Gentlemen, what committee are we today?" Twenty-six Broadway also had an executive dining room where the executive group, seated at designated places at the table, thrashed out their problems with the help of visiting officials from outside the inner structure who might be in town. The raw material out of which policy was made consisted of a stream of reports coming in from the constituent organizations. Policy was carried to the companies in a reverse stream of instructions and by corporate management sitting on the boards of the companies. Yet corporate management did not try to dictate the manner in which local operations were carried out, unless corporate policy was directly involved. Local management was allowed a large measure of discretion, and constituent companies were encouraged to compete with each other in efficiency and profits. The outcome of this competition often determined promotion from the local level into the inner structure.

STANDARD'S FAILURE IN PUBLIC RELATIONS

Perhaps the company's greatest failure—somewhat analagous to the Carnegie company's failure in labor relations—was its inability to present a favorable image of itself to the public. Although there was much in the company's activities which would not bear scrutiny without further damaging its reputation, most of the facts bearing on policy and activities would have been harmless if published, and some material would have been helpful had it been generally known. Yet Rockefeller and his associates were inordinately insistent on maintaining a veil of secrecy over all of the company's operations. Under these circumstances speculation fed on itself, and in the absence of pertinent information a demonology was created which might have been avoided by candid disclosure and an attention to good public relations. This secrecy was partly the result of Rockefeller's personal reticence, and this, in turn, might have been in part a reflection of his father's close-mouthed attitude toward his business affairs. By silence in the face of attack, Standard probably added somewhat to the credence of the charges contained in Henry D. Lloyd's muckraking history of the company, *Wealth versus Commonwealth* (1894). The several legislative investigations and court trials in which the company was involved did nothing to ameliorate its public image. Occasionally the trust surreptitiously subsidized newspapers and inspired the writing of favorable articles. In 1888, after damaging admissions had been drawn from Standard officials in a trust investigation by the New York Senate, Dodd wrote a booklet in defense of the company entitled *Combinations, Their Uses and Abuses, with a History of the Standard Oil Trust*. After 1898, however, the company abandoned its policy of silence. It answered charges directly, and gave newspapers access to information about its activities.

The extensive advertising carried on by constituent companies may have improved Standard's reputation as an institution by constantly calling attention to the good quality of its products. Display ads were placed in thousands of newspapers and in trolley cars. Much attention was devoted to making up displays and exhibitions at county fairs, and Standard presented a spectacular exhibit at the Chicago World's Fair of 1893. Hundreds of thousands of dollars were spent to promote new uses for petroleum products, particularly oil as an industrial fuel and gasoline as a stove fuel.

THE INDEPENDENT OIL COMPANIES AND COMPETITION
FOR FOREIGN MARKETS

Standard's few competitors in the domestic market of the East and the Middle West had careers that were difficult and often unprofitable. Vulnerable to the company's competitive advantages and constantly in danger of losing independence because of its secret purchase of their stock, they were able to carry on largely because of support from public opinion generally and from the crude oil producers in particular. Convinced that the key to Standard's dominance and its alleged ability to depress crude prices lay in its control over transportation, producer groups periodically made efforts to establish independent pipelines to tidewater which could serve independent refineries, and—more important—give access to the growing foreign market. In its foreign operations Standard acquired a fleet of tankers and formed alliances with marketing groups around the world. But since no single organization exercised as much control abroad as did Standard at home, and since the demand for crude moved upward as foreign nations expanded their refining facilities, independents felt that they would have a reasonable chance to compete with Standard on the international level if only they could get their oil from the regions to the seaboard.

Tidewater Oil Company, whose name symbolized the objective of the independents, offered hope in the form of its pipeline to Williamsport, Pennsylvania, capable of carrying 8,000 gallons per day. But when, in 1883, Tidewater pooled its flow with National Transit, giving the Standard organization an allotment of 88.5 percent of all oil carried eastward by pipeline, producer groups and independent refiners thought it had sold out to the monopoly. Nothing effective was done to improve the independents' position until 1892, when the Producers and Refiners Oil Company was formed with the object of carrying to the coast not only petroleum but oil refined in the regions as well. Marketing was to be handled by Pure Oil Company, established a short time later with the promotional assistance of Lewis Emery, Jr., an inveterate enemy of Standard. By 1900, after a pipeline had been built, Pure Oil became an integrated organization, sending 70 percent of its product abroad.

INDEPENDENTS AND THE CALIFORNIA OIL INDUSTRY

The lengthening shadow of Standard Oil did not reach California until several independents had become firmly established in the field. Since the first days of settlement oil bitumen deposits had been noticed in the Pico-Ventura region of Southern California, near Los Angeles. Prospectors with experience gained in the Pennsylvania oil strikes entered the area as early as 1864, and Tom Scott brought in eastern capital by forming a syndicate which shortly thereafter began purchasing properties. The syndicate also retained Benjamin Silliman to analyze the oil found there and publish his findings. Ever since his epoch-making *Report* of 1855

Silliman had been considered the outstanding expert on oil in the United States. On the basis of his premature, overly enthusiastic recommendations based on a cursory examination of the terrain and its products, the syndicate leased or bought some 250,000 acres and formed three companies capitalized at an aggregate of $25 million to get out the oil. But hopes of quick fortunes were dashed when it was found that rock formations made drilling much more expensive than in Pennsylvania, and that the oil was heavy and refractory. When refined by current methods it made an opaque, evil-smelling kerosene with a dangerously low flash point. All three companies failed, and Silliman, suspected of connivance in what many believed had from the outset been a mere stock speculation, resigned from Yale under a cloud.

The presence of oil continued to attract wildcatters, however, and production got under way, but on a much smaller scale than originally anticipated. In 1879 Charles N. Felton and Lloyd Tevis formed the Pacific Coast Oil Company and over the following decade built it into an integrated organization combining production, transportation, refining, and marketing. Tevis was the ubiquitous speculator with interests in the Comstock lode and who played an important role in the affairs of the Anaconda and the Homestake mining companies and in Wells Fargo Express. Meanwhile, Standard of Ohio entered the West Coast and began to compete with PCO in marketing. The clear, safe Pennsylvania oil had a competitive advantage despite its higher price. PCO, hurt by the competition, merged its transportation and marketing organizations with Standard's in a new company—Standard of Iowa—in which PCO received three-eighths of the stock.

PCO continued as an aggressive production and refining organization, and by 1890 had come into sharp competition with Union Oil, a combination of small producing firms brought together by Lyman Stewart, a wildcatter from Pennsylvania. Because of Stewart's unremitting search for oil and his readiness to sink every dollar he could beg or borrow into leases and drilling, Union had come to control some valuable properties. Stewart actively promoted, with considerable success, the use of California crude as a fuel. When the Southern Pacific and the Santa Fe Railroads, plus some industrial firms, converted from coal to fuel oil, a valuable new market for the refractory crude opened up. Between 1896 and 1898, Twenty-six Broadway, desirous of going further into the production sector of the oil business, began negotiations for the purchase of Union. These efforts came to nothing, however, and Union thereupon entered upon a career which was to make it one of the largest and strongest independents in the nation. Developing its refining and marketing organization, it extended its operations to Hawaii and South America, and even invaded the East Coast.

Twenty-six Broadway had better luck in completing merger negotiations with PCO. When a PCO chemist, Eric A. Starke, discovered a sulphuric acid process whereby California kerosene could be rendered as clear and odorless as the Pennsylvania product, the company became more attractive to Standard Oil of Iowa, which desired a domestic source from which to supply its by now vast California market for kerosene. In 1900 Twenty-six Broadway purchased the remaining facilities of PCO and merged the entire organization into Iowa Standard.

THE OIL INDUSTRY'S SOCIAL BALANCE SHEET

By 1900 the oil industry in general and Standard in particular had made great contributions to the development of the American economy. The industry had provided a new illuminant which raised the standard of living and had developed a host of other petroleum products of great importance for industry. Oil exports, like those of gold a generation before, helped to redress the deficit position in international trade which so often afflicts nations undergoing rapid economic growth. Standard's most important specific contributions were probably the construction of a pipeline system which made possible the gathering and transportation of a much larger volume of oil than could possibly move by rail, and the development of a marketing system far more elaborate and ramified than any in existence. The company also hastened the evolution of business organization by its experiments with combination, trust, and holding company. The Whiting refinery, by making possible the production of high quality kerosene from sour crude, represented a considerable technological achievement.

It is undeniable, however, that the achievements of the oil industry in general and Standard in particular were accomplished at considerable cost. Largely ignored at the time was the wastefulness of drilling and well operations. Considering the chronic overproduction in the regions and the discarding of so many fractions of petroleum in order to get kerosene, losses caused by wasteful production must have been of large proportions. In the area of social costs, Standard's suppression of competition brought ruin to some small refiners and marketers, although, as indicated above, this aspect of the company's operations has probably been exaggerated. The trust further embittered relations between big business and the people at large and because of its many unfavorable consequences came to be the only form of business organization ever prohibited by law. Finally, Standard failed to pass on to consumers any considerable portion of the savings accomplished by its operations. Although between 1865 and 1890 the price of kerosene declined at a faster rate than prices generally—from 45 cents per gallon to about 6 cents—much of the drop was due to corresponding declines in the price of crude. To be sure, Rockefeller paid lip service to the principle of keeping prices low: "We must remember we are refining oil for the poor man and he must have it cheap and good." But Rockefeller apparently never advocated reducing prices at the expense of the company's large profits. If the company had been content with what was considered to be a normal return, it seems plain that the "poor man" could have had his oil for less. But on the other hand it must be remembered that a large proportion of the profits was plowed back into the company and so represented the cost of expansion. In the last analysis it is impossible to determine whether the social and economic costs attendant upon the development of the oil industry were inordinate, if only because there is no basis for comparison. About all that can be said is that these costs are higher in rapidly developing industries than in industries advancing at a slower pace. If Rockefeller's "poor man" did not have Standard Oil as cheaply as he might, he at least got it at an earlier date, and in greater quantities than he might have under other circumstances.

XXXIV. Electricity Brings a Revolution in Communications

DEVELOPMENT OF THE TELEGRAPH

The electrical industry, like the oil industry, was a child of the nineteenth century. Electricity as a force had been known to the ancient Greeks, who gave it the name ἤλεκτρον (amber), because when amber is rubbed with a dry cloth it generates what is known today as static electricity. But since electricity could be put to no practical use it remained a "philosophical curiosity" until the nineteenth century. When, between 1820 and 1830, Michael Farraday in England, and Joseph Henry at Princeton College discovered independently of each other that electrical energy could be transformed into mechanical energy, practical applications of electricity became apparent. The ability to energize electromagnets at a distance suggested the possibility of a magnetic telegraph to Henry and other investigators. A real need existed for a communications device superior to the few heliographs and semaphores in use at the time.

Among those working on a magnetic telegraph was Samuel F. B. Morse, son of the Massachusetts clergyman considered to be the first American geographer—Jedidiah Morse. Like Robert Fulton young Morse was an artist with a strong interest in science and mechanics. By 1837, while serving as a professor of the arts of design at New York University, Morse had developed a workable magnetic telegraph and the dot and dash code system which bears his name. Fully realizing the commercial value of the device, he made a partnership agreement with Alfred Vail, a student at New York University and son of a wealthy New Jersey industrialist, according to which Vail agreed to finance the construction of a magnetic telegraph in return for a one-fourth interest in the patent rights.

After completion of the instrument, Morse attempted unsuccessfully to induce Congress to purchase the invention and make the telegraph a public monopoly. But in 1842 the members without enthusiasm appropriated $30,000 for the construction of an experimental line connecting Washington and Baltimore. Meanwhile, in order to meet expenses Morse had been compelled to increase the number of his partners. One of the new associates was Ezra Cornell, who was to make his fortune in the telegraph business. The Washington-Baltimore line was completed just in time to rush to Washington the news of Henry Clay's nomination for the presidency by the Whig Convention meeting at Baltimore in 1844.

Although the telegraph was hailed as a great invention, so small was the appreciation of its commercial possibilities when it was placed in operation that the revenue taken in during the first four days was exactly one cent, and this sum was obtained from a visitor to Washington seeking a demonstration. The Polk administration was completely uninterested in taking over the telegraph as a government monopoly, much to Morse's disappointment, and the partners perforce had to turn to private enterprise for development. By good fortune they secured the services of Amos Kendall as promoter. A former newspaper editor in Kentucky, Kendall had become a close friend of Jackson's and had served both as a member of the "kitchen cabinet" and as postmaster general. Naturally he had a wide acquaintance in business and political circles. A member of the "Think Big" school, Kendall envisioned the country covered by a network of telegraph lines somewhat similar to the network of roads and canals proposed by Gallatin in 1808. But whereas Gallatin had advocated construction and operation by the federal government, Kendall planned for the telegraph lines to be erected by private companies licensed by the Morse patent holders in return for one-half of the corporate stock. This licensing arrangement was to become a familiar feature in many sectors of the electrical equipment business.

Exhibiting a remarkable lack of vision, New York and Philadelphia businessmen reacted as apathetically to Kendall's proposal as had Congress to Morse's. After much effort, however, Kendall in the fall of 1845 was able to raise $15,000 from a group of hesitant merchants with which to link New York and Philadelphia by telegraph. The group then joined the original partners in forming the Magnetic Telegraph Company. According to the Articles of Association $60,000 worth of stock was to be issued, $30,000 worth going to the patent holders and the remainder to the subscribers of the $15,000 construction fund. This arrangement was essentially Kendall's original licensing plan. Why joint partnership rather than incorporation was decided upon is not clear. But in any event the overcapitalization provided by the agreement established an unfortunate precedent which was to be followed almost universally in the development of the telegraph industry.

Completed one year later, the New York-Philadelphia link at the outset brought much more in the way of mechanical difficulties than profit. But slowly brokers and lottery operators began to see the helpful aids to speculation offered by the telegraph, and newspaper editors became aware of the vast potential effects of the instrument upon journalism. When a Philadelphia-Baltimore addition gave the Magnetic Telegraph Company a line stretching from New York to Washington several months later, the public at large finally awoke to the significance of the telegraph. Revenues bounded upward, and almost overnight plans were made for a network of lines stretching nearly the length and breadth of the country. All talk of urging the federal government to take over the telegraph had by this time ceased. Now that the new mechanism of communication had proved profitable to its builders, there was general agreement that its proper future lay in the field of private enterprise.

By the end of 1846, only two and one-half years after Morse had tapped out his first telegraph message, all of the major cities of the Northeast were connected by telegraph lines. This was a striking achievement, but it had touched off an unseemly scramble of extravagant promotion and jerry-built construction which weakened the nascent industry financially and cast doubt upon the reliability of the telegraph. One of the most active promoters was Henry O'Reilly, an Irish immigrant active in upstate New York politics and postmaster of Rochester. Proposing to construct a network of lines connecting the cities of the Northeast with those of the Northwest, he secured a license to use the Morse instrument. The patent holders canceled it, however, when O'Reilly failed to meet the contract date for the completion of the first of his lines. This precipitant action planted the seeds of extended litigation. Rival O'Reilly and Morse agents crisscrossed the Northwest, promising telegraph connections to towns which could raise an initial payment of as little as $2,000. In companies constructing main arteries the Morse patent holders took stock in amounts considerably less than the 50 percent interest they had originally hoped to obtain; from small feeder line companies they accepted cash payments of as low as $10 per mile.

Speed of construction was the order of the day. As F. O. J. Smith, now leading organizer for the Morse interests, wrote to Ezra Cornell, who was promoting construction in the field: "Wherever you can get money enough raised to get a line up, start it. . . . I want no pusillanimous or doubting movements made—but dash on with all the battery and thunder and lightning you can command." Hasty improvisations were made in order to obtain capital. Although construction costs averaged about $150 per mile, this figure was often greatly exceeded, and O'Reilly, for example, capitalized some lines as high as $900 per mile. To prop up his shaky empire he often pledged his stock in one company to cover payments for stock in another company, and his agents were often driven to meet expenses by exchange of racehorse notes and drafts, (i.e., notes and drafts drawn to pay other notes and drafts as the latter fell due). Rate cutting and paralleling were undertaken on a large scale. By 1852 New York and Washington were connected by three lines; New York and Boston by three; and New York and Buffalo by four.

The results of such reckless expansion might easily have been anticipated. Hastily constructed lines gave poor service and were out of commission for long periods of time. The complicated House printing telegraph and Bain electrochemical telegraph, rushed on the market to compete with the Morse instrument, were unreliable. Operators on all types of instruments were often untrained and inefficient, and garbled messages were common. It was the general unreliability of the telegraph at this time which made the railroads slow to integrate it into their operations. Although a few of the better built lines in the Northeast made money, dividends for most companies were nonexistent unless paid out of capital. Construction on some lines faltered and came to a halt when money ran out, with a loss to all concerned. Constant litigation over patents and licenses brought little benefit even to winners of court battles. Intramural quarrels wracked the Morse family, and a triangular Smith-Morse-O'Reilly feud became a focal point for general dissension in the industry. Yet by 1852 much had been accomplished. Twenty-three thousand miles of wire were in operation—more than in all of Europe—and 10,000 more were under construction. Between 450 and 500 towns and villages had been brought into communication with each other. The Morse magnetic system was supreme, in use on 18,000 miles of wire as contrasted with 2,000 to 2,500 for its two major competitors.

MERGERS AND THE RISE OF WESTERN UNION

But important as these achievements were, it was apparent that the first attempt to establish stable telegraph systems had failed, and that rationally conceived combination was necessary to improve service and reduce the losses from competition. The movement in this direction received great impetus from the entrance into the field of the New York and Mississippi Valley Printing Telegraph Company, under the leadership of Hiram Sibley, the architect of Western Union. A New England Yankee transplanted to the Genessee Valley of northern New York, active in banking, real estate, and politics, he entered the telegraph business by joining the promoters of a new line to operate west of Buffalo on the condition that combination rather than construction become the major objective of the enterprise. After raising $100,000 for the purpose from reluctant Rochester businessmen, many of whom felt that the telegraph industry was headed toward chaos, Sibley and his associates started a campaign to bring the scores of little companies in the West into larger operating units having improved connections with eastern companies.

At the outset Sibley's strategy was to offer leases or mergers under very attractive terms to lines in financial difficulties. The plans usually involved stock watering and an increase of overhead costs, but in most instances these disadvantages were overbalanced by mounting revenues resulting from economies of operation. By 1857 Sibley's campaign had achieved striking success. Western Union—successor to the New York and Mississippi Valley—had now become a telegraph system with trunk lines connecting seaboard cities with all the major centers of the Midwest, and with all towns in that region capable of supporting a telegraph office.

While the Western Union was forming, a second combination came into existence on the eastern seaboard. In 1854 Cyrus W. Field, a New York merchant who had retired at thirty-three after making a modest fortune, became interested in the project of laying a cable connecting the United States and Great Britain. With other men whose purses were as long as their vision—among them Peter Cooper, Moses Taylor, Marshall O. Roberts, and Chandler White—he formed the New York, Newfoundland and London Electric Telegraph Company. The company was capitalized at $1.5 million, a very large sum for a telegraph enterprise but obviously modest when considered in the light of the undertaking envisaged. Peter Cooper was elected president and Samuel F. B. Morse honorary electrician. The flattering gesture extended to Morse indicated that in addition to the dream of an Atlantic cable Field and his associates had something more immediately practical and profitable in mind, namely, the consolidation of telegraph companies along the eastern seaboard to form a continuous trunk line from New Orleans to Newfoundland and London. To effect this larger purpose Field and his group formed the American Telegraph Company, incorporated in 1855.

Officials of the American then began merger talks with Kendall and Morse of the Magnetic, and F. O. J. "Fog" Smith, who had large interests in New England companies. When, during the conversations, American purchased the rights to a newly developed printing telegraph, the older men suspected the beginning of a campaign against the Morse interests, and broke off the talks. Without the participation of Fog Smith and "Amos the Pious" Kendall, the promoters of American then prevailed upon most of the important companies on the seaboard to accept an agreement known as "The Treaty of the Six Nations," recalling the Iroquois confederation of seven nations. The eastern United States was divided into six districts, in each of which a combination envisaged by the treaty was dominant. Members were to refrain from further building of competing lines, and where these existed, business was to be pooled. They agreed to exchange messages exclusively with each other and to submit disputes to arbitration. Representatives of the signatory powers were to convene annually to discuss matters of common interest.

Although Magnetic at first fought vigorously to preserve its independence, it merged with American two years later. Along the seaboard American was then supreme. With 283 offices and 13,500 miles of wire, it had rights to all important patents then in use, held the best and sometimes the only routes available for trunk lines and feeders, and a flock of valuable franchises inherited from constituent companies. The economies of integration were soon reflected in earnings, and the company began paying quarterly dividends of 3 percent in 1860.

By combination and by exchange agreements the United States had acquired a fairly efficient telegraph system, but it was still rendered somewhat unstable because of the ambitions of the two leading companies—Western Union and American. Despite outward harmony Western Union was jealous of American's heady project of a transatlantic cable, and American was not overjoyed by Western Union's ambition to construct a telegraph linking San Francisco with New York.

In 1860 Congress passed a bill calling for bids to construct such a line. Governmental subsidies of up to $40,000 per year were promised, in return for rights to use the line. No land grants were included, doubtless because construction was well within the means of existing companies. Hiram Sibley, for reasons best known to himself, was the only bidder, and at the maximum subsidy. Upon award of the contract, Western Union then cooperated with the consolidated companies of California to form two companies to string lines eastward and westward, respectively, the two to meet at Salt Lake City. Within a period of four months the work was brought to completion in 1861, and, like the transcontinental railroad, constituted a dazzling feat of construction. Also, however, the feat produced the profiteering on a large scale which so discredited the Credit Mobilier. Stock watering and government subsidies brought huge rewards to insiders. The cost of constructing the eastern portion of the line—$147,000—was ultimately represented by $4 million of Western Union stock. Although the line was immediately profitable, government subsidies of $460,000 within the next decade nearly repaid the entire cost of construction conservatively estimated at $500,000.

The success of the transcontinental telegraph now fired both the American and Western Union companies with dreams of imperial conquest. Despite two failures in laying an Atlantic cable—one in 1857 and another in 1858—Cyrus Field succeeded in forming a British syndicate with large resources to back the project, and American Telegraph also gave wholehearted support. But because the vast engineering problems involved in laying the cable aroused doubt as to whether the project could ever be successfully completed, Western Union decided to seek a northwest passage to Europe by stringing telegraph lines through Canada and Russian America (Alaska), and crossing the Bering Strait by cable. From the Siberian shore a line was to be strung southward to the Amur River, where it would join a line built eastward by the Russian government. A ten million dollar stock issue to finance the project was easily floated by Western Union—the subscribers being mainly Western Union stockholders—and work began in an atmosphere of optimism which contrasted sharply with the pessimism with which the laying of the Atlantic cable was regarded. But in 1866, to the joy of the American Telegraph Company and dismay of Western Union, the cable project was successfully completed. As insiders scuttled to get out, Western Union abandoned its own plan, with a loss of $3 million.

The shock of this setback was mitigated in the next year for Western Union by its acquisition of American, a natural result of the process of consolidation underway for over a decade. At first sight it might seem that the victor was abandoning the fruits of victory to the vanquished. The explanation apparently lies in the price paid for the "abandonment." Although Western Union lines were capitalized at $485 per mile, as contrasted to less than $100 per mile for those of American, Western Union issued $11,833,100 of new securities with which to purchase the approximately $4 million of American stock outstanding. Amos Kendall's dream of a national telegraph system had at last been realized, but at the cost of a massive stock watering operation.

Although Western Union dominated the field, its position was not unassailable. Because of the company's overcapitalization the relatively few railroads which constructed their own telegraph systems could operate them profitably in competition with the giant for business outside of railroad operations. Jay Gould, the notorious wrecker of railroads, fully appreciated the opportunities offered by this situation and utilized them to make himself master of Western Union. Upon getting control of the Union Pacific in the late seventies he incorporated the railroad's telegraph department as the American Union Telegraph Company, capitalized at $13 million. Vigorously he began to parallel Western Union lines, acquired a competing Atlantic cable, and cut rates. At the same time he secretly purchased large blocs of Western Union stock after forming a bear pool which drove the stock down 20 points in the market. Emerging in 1880 as the largest single stockholder, with 90,000 shares, he offered peace. Western Union, bowing to the terms, then installed Gould as a director and purchased his American Union company at a very inflated figure. Gould had successfully adapted to the field of telegraphy the profiteering tactics he had originally applied to railroads.

But although shortly thereafter elevated to the presidency of Western Union, Gould found that turnabout was fair play, and nearly became the victim of his own methods. Within a few years several new independents were in the field, chief of which were Postal Telegraph, with lines radiating from Chicago to the Southwest, and Mutual Union Telegraph, organized by officials of the B. and O. Railroad for the same purpose for which Gould had incorporated Union Pacific's telegraph department. The newcomers, determined to bring down the giant, started a round of rate cutting which Western Union, because of its soggy financial structure, could ill afford. But Gould's proverbial good luck came to his rescue. In 1886 the B. and O., facing bankruptcy, was forced to sell Mutual Union to Western Union. Postal, weakened by this defection from the ranks of the independents, hastened to make peace in the form of rate and traffic agreements. In the new climate of co-operation Western Union recovered its prosperity, and Postal, under the able guidance of the silver king, John W. Mackay, and the banker, George F. Baker, maintained an inferior, but stable independent position.

OPERATIONS AND RATES

Consolidation of the telegraph industry, although attended by questionable business practices and arousing the ever latent fear of monopoly, was indispensable for the improvement of service. In the early days operators were poorly trained, and wages geared to the volume of traffic made it difficult to staff the stations doing a small amount of business. Messages traveling long distances had to be translated and recoded several times as they were passed from one company to another and as a result were often lost or garbled. Until nearly the turn of the century basic power was supplied by galvanic batteries spaced at intervals along routes. The use of thin copper wires made it impossible to maintain line voltage over any considerable distance. Storms, which broke the wires, and wet weather, which often made insulation on the poles ineffective, continually brought transmission to a halt. To add to these problems, performance of the complicated printing and electrochemical transmission and receiving instruments was unpredictable. Because of its simplicity the Morse instrument maintained its wide lead over competitors, but many years of experience were needed before high speed operation could be achieved.

Technical improvement came somewhat slowly, and the ability of the telegraph to handle a rapidly mounting volume of traffic was due more to increased skill of operators and the efficiencies of consolidation than to better equipment. On consolidated lines long distance transmission no longer had to be decoded and translated several times before reaching its destination, but by relays could be passed from one company to another. Improved insulation on poles and the use of iron wire, stronger than copper, also brought increased reliability. Thomas A. Edison, while working for Western Union during the early seventies, developed duplex and quadruplex transmitters capable of sending simultaneously two and four messages, respectively, over the same wire. Yet although Edison spent years trying to perfect the printing telegraph, a reliable instrument was not brought out until after the turn of the century. Despite the accumulation of knowledge regarding electricity nearly all electrical instruments except the most rudimentary developed "bugs" which mystified operators and mechanics for years, and sometimes for decades.

Because of conflicting pressures of competition, which tended to drive rates down, and stock watering, which tended to drive them up, rate-making was never established on a uniform rational basis. At best it would have been difficult to do so. Besides stock watering, the many factors influencing the levels of expenses, such as widely varying costs of construction, maintenance of facilities, volume of traffic, expenditures for patent rights, and the valuation of patents originating within companies, would affect the cost at which the service could be offered to the public. The usual charge for transmissions over short distances was twenty-five cents for ten words or less, but charges for long distance, repeat transmissions varied greatly. During the cutthroat competition of the eighties the basic rate at competitive points was sometimes lowered to ten or fifteen cents. But with the coming of peace the rate of twenty-five cents was restored. The fact that Western Union, after a generation of stock watering, was able to make profits while adhering to this rate suggests that it was higher than necessary. But since the company also wrung some of the water out of its stock by financing expansion out of profits in good times, this judgment must be tentative. The fact that British rates were many times higher than those charged in the United States makes conclusions about American rates even more difficult. British telegraph installations, like British railroads, were much more substantially constructed than those of the United States, and British land values were much higher, yet these considerations alone do not make it possible to determine whether American railroad and telegraph rates were "fair and just."

The effect of the telegraph in increasing the pace and scope of business is so obvious as to need no belaboring. Its more general effects upon national development were aptly if somewhat elaborately stated by a Boston physician, Dr. William F. Channing: "The electric telegraph is the nervous system of the nation and of modern society by no figure of speech, by no distant analogy. Its wires spread like nerves over the surface of the land, interlinking distant parts, and making possible a perpetually higher cooperation among men, and higher social forms than have hitherto existed. By means of its life-like functions the social body becomes a living whole. . . ."

THE COMING OF THE TELEPHONE

The telephone network spread over the nation in a much more orderly fashion than the telegraph network, partly because of careful planning on the part of the telephone entrepreneurs, and partly because of altered circumstances. Technological factors played an important role in this connection. The basic operative principle of the telegraph—electromagnetism induced at a distance—was unpatentable, but patents could be secured on its many applications. Therefore, competing instruments appeared from the start, and these provided a basis for competing companies and systems. Near-monopoly could be achieved only after a long struggle. But the telephone operated on a new principle unknown before the invention of the instrument, and there were only a few ways in which this principle could be used to transmit sound. Since the principle itself, and not merely an application, was patentable, the possessors of the patent were confronted at the outset with a very favorable opportunity to monopolize the industry. The first telephone entrepreneurs were quite aware of this fact, and adopted policies well designed to achieve this object. A developed and centralized capital market, which could on short notice funnel large funds into promising enterprises, also aided the efforts of the telephone promoters. Moreover, the wave of business consolidation taking place during the years when use of the telephone was rapidly increasing stimulated the drive toward monopoly.

Although several inventors converged simultaneously on the principles of telephony, credit for inventing the telephone has been accorded to Alexander Graham Bell. Bell was born in Edinburgh in 1847, the son of Professor Alexander M. Bell, a scientist and an author in the field of vocal physiology and elocution. Attracted to his father's profession, young "Graham" became the father's principal research assistant at the University of London. In 1870 the family emigrated to Canada. In the course of working on his father's system of "visible speech" for teaching the deaf, he conceived the possibility of transmitting sounds by telegraph mechanisms. In Boston where he was conducting a teacher training course in his father's methods, he formed a partnership with Thomas Sanders, a leading merchant of Haverill, and Gardiner Greene Hubbard, a wealthy Boston attorney and philanthropist, which enabled him to begin research in telephony. According to the terms of a simple, oral agreement, the two moneyed men met half of Bell's expenses and all three were to share equally in any patent rights eventuating from the research. Since both Sanders and Hubbard had deaf children who had been greatly helped by Bell, they probably regarded their financial support partly as payment of a debt of gratitude. Such was the origin of the mighty American Telephone and Telegraph Company.

In the course of his experiments Bell discovered that if a reed were made to vibrate in a magnetic field, it would generate a current, which, when transmitted to a similar magnetic field, would induce similar vibrations in a second reed of the same pitch as the first. Actually, he had stumbled upon the principle of telephony, and speculated that theoretically the human voice might become the instrument for inducing the undulating current capable of reproducing a similar pitch in a receiving instrument. Foreseeing difficulties in constructing a workable model of such a device, however, he instead applied the principle in designing a multiple "harmonic" telegraph. With this instrument he hoped to activate simultaneously reeds of different pitches, and so make possible the simultaneous transmission of more than one message. To test the idea he built two reed telegraphing devices with the help of his assistant, Thomas A. Watson. Bell located one instrument in one room of his house and the second in another, and connected the two in an electric circuit. One day in 1875, while the circuits of the telegraph were accidentally closed, Watson happened to twang a spring on the receiving instrument. The pitch, together with overtones, was transmitted to Bell working on the transmitter in the adjacent room. Because of his training in phonics, Bell immediately knew what had happened. The telegraph, with circuits closed, had become a telephone in which undulating current had reproduced the qualities of sound as well as sound itself. Several months later Bell completed a workable instrument, utilizing a membrane to activate an armature in a magnetic field so as to induce undulating current. On March 7, 1876, he patented the instrument. The invention of the telephone is worth discussing in some detail if only because this patent became one of the most valuable ever granted by the United States Patent Office.

ESTABLISHMENT OF THE BELL SYSTEM

Because the apparatus was so simple, development went forward at a rapid pace. Bell exhibited the telephone to astonished crowds at the Philadelphia Centennial Exhibition, and by August, 1876, was operating a connection between Boston and Cambridge. In order to promote the new device, Hubbard, Sanders, Bell, and Watson formed the Bell Telephone Association, in which the first three men assigned to themselves a three-tenths interest apiece, and a one-tenth interest to Watson. Capitalization was set at $500,000. Fully realizing the value of the patent, the patent holders made a decision with regard to it which profoundly influenced the development of the Bell System. Instead of licensing manufacturers to produce and sell telephones, which on the surface would seem to be the most immediately profitable way of exploiting the invention, they decided to contract with a single manufacturer to produce instruments solely for the association. The patent holders would then lease—not sell—the instruments to users. Doubtless they expected that such a course eventually would maximize the return from each instrument. Eventually subscribers would pay much more in the form of rentals than the purchase price of the telephones.

Furthermore, this policy would give to the patent the maximum protection possible under the circumstances. Patent holders who licensed others to manufacture and sell invited infringement. The melancholy career of Charles Goodyear illustrates the danger of this eventuality. Inventors desiring to undertake manufacture themselves were confronted by the need to raise large amounts of capital, build a large organization, and solve production as well as developmental problems. But the Bell Associates had neither the time nor the experience to go into manufacturing, and if they wished to avoid the dangers of indiscriminate licensing, the policy of farming out the manufacture of telephones by contract and leasing the instruments provided the best alternative for manufacture in their own factory.

The associates let the first contracts for telephones to a Chicago firm which later became Western Electric, the company which is even today a major supplier for A.T.&T. At the same time they worked out the procedures by which telephones would be offered to the public. The rental price of a telephone installation connecting two residences was set at $20 per year; for business subscribers the price was $40 per year. At the outset there were no switchboards or central offices; all connections were direct.

Over the next few years the association went through a series of reorganizations in order to meet the mounting demand for telephone service, in each instance increasing the number of stockholders and capitalization. In 1879 the New England Telephone Company and the Bell Telephone Company, successors to the Bell Telephone Association, were merged into the National Bell Telephone Company of Massachusetts. Six hundred and fifty thousand dollars worth of stock out of the new issue of $850,000 was used to retire the shares of the parent companies. By now investors were regarding the telephone with such enthusiasm that the remaining shares, offered at a par value of $100 apiece, were sold for as high as $600. At the outset Bell had hoped that the patent holders would come to control all aspects of the telephone business, including installation and the building of central stations. But since the cost and administrative problems of such a program would plainly be staggering, particularly in a period of rapidly rising demand for telephone facilities, the associates abandoned the idea and instead adopted the policy of licensing locally owned subsidiaries characteristic of the Bell System.

Infringement on the Bell patent began almost as soon as the first instruments were installed, despite the defensive strategy adopted by the associates. Elisha Gray, an inventor working for Western Union, had been conducting research on the telephone independently of Bell and had filed a caveat at the Patent Office only hours after Bell had applied for his patent. Some evidence was later brought forth indicating that Gray had filed before Bell's application, but the contention was later rejected in court. Actually in 1861 Johann Philip Reis had patented a crude telephone device in Germany. Since any mechanic could produce an instrument once the principle was understood, scores of infringers entered the field in the hope that the courts would set Bell's patent aside on the ground that prior work on telephones invalidated his claims. This situation produced litigation lasting eleven years, eventually involving about six hundred lawsuits and costing millions.

Western Union offered what appeared to be the most dangerous threat. Company officials, although originally regarding the telephone as a mere toy, quickly came to appreciate its potential as a competitor to the telegraph. They engaged Thomas A. Edison, by now recognized as an inventive genius and the world's foremost authority on telegraphy, to design a telephone different enough from Bell's to avoid outright infringement. Edison constructed an instrument in which a constant flow of current was produced by a battery and undulations created by the varying resistance of a carbon pellet in the circuit pressed against the speaking diaphragm. He also separated transmitter and receiver. Bell's telephone used no current from an outside source and the same instrument served as transmitter and receiver. By placing an induction coil in the line circuit Edison greatly increased the distance over which the telephone could transmit. Actually, therefore, it was Edison and not Bell who designed the instrument we use today, and Edison had discovered the principle of the microphone as well.

Yet Bell had patent priority on the operating principle of transmitting sound by an undulating electric current. Shortly after Western Union began producing the Edison phone the Bell interests brought suit for infringement. After eleven months of hearings, Western Union, probably anticipating failure of their defense, sold their telephone rights and properties to National Bell for $325,000 plus 20 percent of the rental on all instruments installed by Bell for a period of seventeen years. At the time it was felt by many observers that the Bell Company had paid an unnecessarily high price for peace, since the company would probably have won its suit anyway. Yet time was to prove that Bell had made a very good bargain indeed. Western Union eventually received about 7 million for its claims;

Bell removed a powerful competitor from the field, acquired the use of a superior instrument and transmission system, and—most important—cleared the way for the creation of a monopoly.

The Bell interests now faced a brilliant future. In order to obtain capital for expansion, in 1880 the officials of National Bell created the American Bell Telephone Company, capitalized at $10 million, which absorbed the parent company by paying six shares for one of National Bell. The 8,500 shares of American Bell sold in the market brought prices consistently over par. The new organization might now have embarked on a policy of purchasing the operating companies, but Bell officials still doubted whether they could find the capital for what would surely become a gigantic undertaking. Therefore, they again decided to continue the licensing policy. But in order to provide a source of income after the telephone patent expired, American Bell henceforth demanded 30 to 50 percent of the stock issued by the licensed companies. Phone rentals charged to these companies were very high—about $5.50 per month. At this figure American Bell recouped the cost of each instrument within a few months. After expiration of the Bell patents in 1893 and 1894 permitted other manufacturers to enter the field, Bell quickly lowered its phone rentals to about $1.50 per month. This move drastically altered the pattern of American Bell's income; by 1898 most of it was coming from dividends of operating companies rather than rentals. Licensed companies could operate only in areas approved by Bell, were required to use Bell-Western Electric equipment, and could make no connections with independent companies.

For strategic reasons as well as for profit, Bell officials determined to construct and operate the long distance lines which connected the licensed companies. For this purpose they created American Telephone and Telegraph Company (New York) in 1885. With this incorporation, the "Bell System" was completed. It included a company to hold patent rights and stock and grant licenses (American Bell); local licensed companies; and a construction-operating company for long distance lines.

OPERATIONS OF THE BELL SYSTEM

At the outset the Bell Associates were constantly engaged in a desperate scramble for funds. Mounting demand for telephone service required an increasing investment in telephone instruments and a widening gap between outgo and income. Time and again the associates stared bankruptcy in the face. "How on earth do you expect me to meet a draft of two hundred and seventy-five dollars without a dollar in the treasury, and with a debt of thirty thousand dollars staring us in the face?" wrote Sanders to Hubbard on one occasion. At about the same time Bell complained, "Thousands of telephones are in operation in all parts of the country, yet I have not received one cent for my invention." Hubbard hawked stock in the country's financial centers and borrowed to the absolute limit of the associates' credit. He secured much of the support needed by the company in its early, difficult years, from a group of Boston financiers with long pedigrees—among them George Z. Silsbee, George L. Bradley, Charles S. Bradley, William G. Saltonstall, Alexander Cochrane, and later Richard S. Fay and William H. Forbes. After the company began to make money and the investing public awoke to the potentialities of the telephone, capital flowed in relatively easily. Existing stockholders, given purchase rights of a fraction of a share for each share held, contributed considerably to the funds of the company. As a star performer on the New York Stock Exchange, Bell stock found buyers from a steadily increasing number of small purchasers. Generous stock dividends given at the time of corporate changes swelled capital gains acquired from rising market prices of shares. Until 1900 American Bell and A.T.&T. were distinctly Boston enterprises. During the conflict with Western Union the Boston financiers took substantial control of the company away from the original promoters as reward for financial support.

In 1899 the Bell System underwent the corporate change which resulted in the organization substantially as it exists today. At the time of the transformation American Bell was a $120 million enterprise, controlling wholly or in part 49 licensed companies capitalized at $139 million. It had a surplus from plowed back earnings of $9.5 million, paid a regular dividend of 15 percent per year, and its stock, issued at par value of $100 per share, sold at over $200. Proceeds from the issues were used to extend the long distance lines and buy more stock in licensed companies. But because the New York charter of A.T.&T. offered better opportunities for expansion than the Massachusetts charter of American Bell, American Bell sold all of its assets to A.T.&T., and in the course of the transaction doubled existing Bell capitalization by giving stockholders a 100 percent stock dividend. After 1900, therefore, A.T.&T. became an operating company for long distance lines, a holding company, and a licensor of telephone and electrical patents.

But the Bell organizations had much less success in the field of public relations than in financial affairs. As a near-monopoly, like Western Union, they were usually regarded with distrust and sometimes with hatred. Until the expiration of the basic patent in 1894 rates were set at figures sometimes tenfold above those charged for telephone services in European countries. Business subscribers in New York paid $240 per year for a line, and private subscribers $180. Since the number of instruments in use between 1885 and 1894 increased only from 330,000 to 582,506, the company appeared to be more interested in making monopoly profits than in giving the country good telephone service. Operating companies regarded the prices charged for phone rentals as exorbitant, and resented the strict limitations placed upon their operations by the license agreements.

When the patent lapsed, the Bell Company's policy of limited expansion and high charges created a promising field for independents. By 1900, 508 proprietary firms and 181 mutuals had crowded into the field. Competition was keenest in the Middle West, where farmers' mutuals using makeshift equipment had driven rates down as low as one dollar per month. Fighting the "octopus" became a civic duty repeatedly enjoined by the Populist party, and relations were sometimes so bitter that on one occasion the owner of a small independent company, who desired to make peace with a Bell organization, felt compelled to disguise himself with a false beard before meeting a Bell official to discuss the project. The Bell companies made little attempt to improve their public image. It is reported that on more than one occasion, after acquiring small independents, Bell companies piled the equipment of the independents in the streets and publicly burned it, *pour encourager les autres*.

Eventually the Bell System succeeded in snuffing out competition by exploiting two important advantages—its control over long distance lines and its portfolio of patents. By denying the use of long distance lines to independents it isolated them in small pockets of resistance and prevented the growth of rival telephone systems. Early in its career the company had established patent and engineering departments, and had progressively patented a host of small telephone improvements with the object of continuing in some measure the advantage initially given by the original patent and harassing the manufacturers of equipment for the independents. As expressed by Bell's patent attorney, constant suits for infringement kept independent manufacturers "in a nervous and excited condition," and made them change the designs of their equipment and as a result sometimes adopt inefficient forms of apparatus.

A more menacing threat to A.T.&T. than the small independents appeared in the form of the Telephone, Telegraph, and Cable Company of America, formed in 1899 by interests connected with street railways. Since the new company proposed to construct a rival network of long distance lines a bitter battle immediately began. A.T.&T. survived its challengers, but in the course of the struggle came under the control of banking groups with interests centered in Wall Street.

Probably the most important entrepreneur to be produced by the telephone business was Theodore N. Vail, by curious coincidence the nephew of Alfred Vail, first partner of Samuel F. B. Morse. Coming from a humbler side of the family than that of his uncle, young Theodore grew up on a farm, taught school, and at the age of twenty-three trained himself to be a telegraph operator—thereby entering the trade which constituted the apprenticeship of Thomas A. Edison and Andrew Carnegie. He shortly resigned his post to take a clerkship first with the Union Pacific Railroad and then in the Washington Railroad Post Office. Here he worked his way upward until in 1876, at the age of thirty-one, he was appointed general superintendent of the Railway Mail Service.

Vail first came into contact with the telephone through his acquaintance with Gardiner Hubbard, formed when Hubbard was a member of the Congressional Postal Committee. In 1878 Hubbard offered Vail the position of general manager of the Bell Telephone Associates, partly because Vail's wide acquaintance among influential men in Washington could be helpful in the desperate search for financing. Vail accepted eagerly. Entrepreneurial rather than managerial in orientation, he apparently found the routine of the Railway Mail Service too cramping for his taste. He had long been interested in mechanical devices, and had on several occasions purchased patent rights as speculations. Although many apparently farsighted businessmen considered the telephone to be little more than a toy and inadequate as a means of communication because of the poor performance of the first Bell instruments, Vail fully appreciated the telephone's potential.

Vail's greatest contributions to the Bell organization were made during the next few difficult years when the young, weak, struggling company was confronted with the problems of simultaneously raising capital in large amounts and protecting its patent rights against the attacks from the incomparably stronger Western Union Company. Although Vail canvassed all his acquaintances, money came in so slowly that when he and his colleagues formed the Bell Telephone Company of New York, designed to provide telephone services for New York City, they were compelled to offer stock for a down payment of only $2.50 per share. It was Vail who conducted the tricky, protracted negotiations with Western Union to obtain the Edison instrument. Western Union at first offered to settle if Bell would allow it to build and operate long distance lines. Coming from a very strong to a very weak company, this seemed to be an attractive offer, particularly since neither the equipment nor the methods of wiring were yet in existence to make long distance transmission possible. But Vail, foreseeing the crucial importance of long distance lines, rejected the offer and held out for the royalty arrangement which Western Union subsequently accepted.

A.T.&T., of which Vail was the first president, was largely the outcome of his constant pressure on the Bell interests to build and dominate long distance lines. For reasons still obscure, however, he resigned in 1887 after two years service to engage in a wide variety of promotions whose success steadily enhanced his reputation in the national business community. He returned to A.T.&T. as president in 1907, and two years later engineered a merger with Western Union. At the time of his retirement in 1919 he was one of the best known businessmen in the nation.

On the whole, the development of the telephone industry to 1900 was more orderly, and less marred by stock watering, than the development of the telegraph a generation before. To be sure, Bell companies aimed frankly at national monopoly, first through maintenance of patent rights, and when the basic patent ran out, through domination of long distance lines. Since Bell had no competitors with which it could make collusive agreements, and since it was not organized as a trust, it never ran afoul of the antitrust laws during the nineteenth century, but pursued its course in an entirely legal manner. Whether telephone services could have been provided more cheaply had the monopoly aspects of the industry been absent is a moot point. Had Alexander Bell not been able to patent the principle of sound transmission by undulating current, competition among manufacturers undoubtedly would have reduced the price of telephones. But there is no reason to believe that this competition would have led to better or cheaper telephone service. The telephone network might in this case have been constructed in much the same manner as was the telegraph network—with competitive losses, collusive agreements, combinations, and massive stock watering. In the end the total costs, social as well as economic, might have been greater than those incurred by the Bell pursuance of monopoly, and the quality of service more than likely would have been lower.

Actually, the Bell "federal" system of construction by licensed companies had much to recommend it. By placing full responsibility for local operations in the hands of local companies, it probably enhanced efficiency by avoiding the creation of an unwieldy bureaucracy. This arrangement probably also facilitated the collection of capital by tapping a wider range of savings, and perhaps by widening stockholding and management mitigated the resentment against American Bell.

XXXV. The Electrical Equipment Industries

The possibility of using electricity as an illuminant was first manifested when Sir Humphry Davy demonstrated to rapt audiences in lectures delivered at the Royal Institution in 1801 that a brilliant spark snapped in the air when contact between two carbon rods connected to poles of a multiple battery was broken. But until the construction of the first dynamos the demonstration could have no practical application because of the prohibitive cost of producing arcs from battery charges. By the early 1870s the appearance of the first practical, reliable generators, plus a growing realization that electric arcs would produce a much more intense light for streets and large public buildings than oil or gas, stimulated research in the development of arc lighting systems.

The pioneer of arc lighting in the United States was Charles F. Brush, a chemist with an abiding interest in electricity. Receiving financial backing and the use of factory facilities from a manufacturer of telegraphic equipment in Cleveland, Brush in 1876 constructed a dynamo and several workable arc lamps. He was able to beat competitors into the field because of a clutch electromagnetic device which separated the carbon rods in the

497

lamps when the current started to flow and kept the arc gap constant as the carbon rods slowly burned away. One of his first customers was John Wanamaker, who installed a Brush system in his Philadelphia department store. Wanamaker was always eager to adopt new methods of advertising and publicity.

Aware that street lighting would probably provide the widest market for his system, Brush in 1879 promoted the California Electric Light Company designed to illuminate the streets of San Francisco. The immediate and literally dazzling success of the San Francisco venture led to the formation of similar companies in other large cities, and by the end of 1880 over 5,000 Brush arc lights were in operation. Like the Bell Associates, Brush employed agents to promote and aid in the organization of operating companies. Since leasing arrangements like those worked out by the Bell Associates were manifestly impossible because of the much greater cost of the heavy, complex, dynamos and arc lights, Brush sold his equipment to the companies in return for 32 to 48 percent of their stock issues. In order to guarantee an income out of the earnings of the companies, Brush required them to pay out at least 30 percent of their net earnings in dividends, segregate net return from construction accounts, and grant the parent company access to their books.

Like the Bell Associates, Brush was from the outset confronted by an expanding group of imitators who entered the arc lighting field with similar equipment. Since Brush was plainly not the inventor of the dynamo nor the arc light, but only the manufacturer of a lighting system, the courts refused to uphold the patents he had nevertheless taken out. Soon nearly fifty firms were manufacturing arc lighting equipment. Competition was vigorous, and the complexity of the apparatus gave ample opportunity for product differentiation.

The strongest competitor of Brush was the Thomson-Houston Electric Company, named for Elihu Thomson and Edwin J. Houston, two teachers of science in the Central High School of Philadelphia. The company bearing their names was formed by a group of Connecticut businessmen. The president was Charles A. Coffin, traveling salesman for a Lynn shoe manufacturing firm who was later to become a leading figure among electrical entrepreneurs and the first president of General Electric.

Thomson-Houston's system was superior to Brush's because it utilized a compact dynamo of superior design which could feed more lamps than any other dynamo on the market. During the eighties arc lights were wired in series rather than in parallel, and under these circumstances the 50 volt potential required to spring an arc across one set of carbons was multiplied by the number of lights in a circuit. Therefore, more than ten arcs, by requiring more than 500 volts output from the current source, placed a heavy load on generators and created a difficult problem of heat control, particularly on the commutators which switched the natural alternating current induced in the armature windings to direct current. By directing an air blast on the commutators Thomson-Houston was able to increase the capacity of the generators, and thereby make possible the building of larger systems.

Like Brush, Thomson-Houston marketed its equipment by sponsoring the formation of street lighting companies which purchased through payments partly in cash and partly in stock. In order to separate the holding company functions from manufacturing and provide capital for expansion, the company set up trusts in 1885, 1886, and 1889 to purchase and resell the securities received from the operating companies. Since these securities often increased substantially in value, and since Thomson-Houston stockholders were given the opportunity to buy into the trusts under favorable terms, the arrangement added strength to the company's financial position. Accepting securities as part payment for equipment posed a major problem for manufacturers by reducing liquidity and forcing the firms to go into debt for expansion. Under these circumstances the management and marketing of operating company securities became a pressing problem for the equipment manufacturers.

A third company in the field of arc lighting was the Weston Electric Company, organized by Edward Weston, who was to become one of the most noted electrical engineers of the day. Since his initial system did not perform as well as those of Brush and Thomson-Houston, Weston turned to the manufacture of electrical instruments, a field in which the company acquired a leading position which it has held down to the present day.

The last of the important arc lighting firms organized during the early period was the American Electric and Illuminating Company, formed by Edward H. Goff, originally a salesman for Thomson-Houston. An energetic promoter, Goff introduced a unique element of combination in the business by establishing under his own leadership operating companies which utilized equipment manufactured by the American Company. One of his most inspired publicity stunts was to provide arc lighting for the Statute of Liberty when it was erected in 1886. Unfortunately, Goff fell victim to the temptation toward stock pyramiding inherent in the manufacturing company-operating-company relationship. Unable to withstand the blow delivered by Thomson-Houston in a successful suit against American Electric for patent infringement, Goff failed in 1888 and died practically penniless.

Mergers increased markedly at about this time. Although the market for the electrical manufacturers appeared virtually unlimited, the large number of firms in the business made competition sharp, and the need for repeated infusions of capital to finance the production of new lines of equipment became onerous, particularly for the smaller firms. The multiplication of patents, by threatening to paralyze the industry, also provided a stimulus toward combination. Costs of litigation mounted as infringements increased; avoidance of infringement became equally costly because it demanded extensive re-design of equipment. Here again the small firm was at a great disadvantage, and could be forced out of business by an unfavorable patent situation alone. Patent problems, more than any other single factor, stimulated the desire for combination in the electrical equipment industry. It is important to note that combination was not preceded by a period of price and production agreements, as in many other industries. Competition among the electrical manufacturers lay primarily in the quality and adaptability of equipment, and in new lines of production. Arc light installations were expensive and were designed to last for a long period of time. Under these circumstances initial price was by no means as important to customers as operating cost, efficiency, and longevity. Also, designs changed so rapidly that there was little incentive or opportunity to establish price agreements.

Thomson-Houston took the leadership of the combination movement by buying out a score or more of competitors, including Brush, who had made little effort to improve his equipment. Funds for the purpose were raised by the sale of stock and of trust certificates representing operating company shares purchased from Thomson-Houston. Expansion brought to Thomson-Houston multiplying advantages of size which enabled the company completely to dominate the arc lighting business. Together with its successor, General Electric, it had produced by 1900 about 300,000 of the 325,000 systems in operation. The success of Thomson-Houston was due in large measure to the superiority of its equipment at the outset, to Thomson's continued improvements, to the financial support of leading Boston capitalists such as F. L. Ames and T. J. Coolidge, Jr., and to the skillful leadership of Coffin.

The characteristics of entrepreneurs in the arc lighting industry changed as the industry advanced. The first generation, as represented by Brush, Thomson, Houston, and Weston, were technicians who showed talent for envisaging commercial uses for their apparatus and for solving the financial, marketing, promotional, and patent problems involved in the production of electrical equipment. Coffin and Goff represented a second generation of entrepreneurs who had no technical training, who left design, engineering, and production problems to others and concentrated on sales, finance, promotion, and combination. In the large concerns engineering and management were increasingly separated. Thomson, for example, left the administration of the firm he had founded to Coffin and confined himself to research.

THOMAS A. EDISON AND INCANDESCENT LIGHTING

The invention of arc lighting naturally led to a search for methods by which electricity might be used to provide illumination for homes. The bright and sometimes flickering glare of arc lamps made them entirely unsuitable for this purpose. Sir Humphry Davy, in addition to discovering the principle of the electric arc, had also noted the ability of electricity to produce incandescence, and during the sixties and seventies scientists theorized that electric lamps might be produced which utilized this principle. But the problems to be solved before a workable incandescent lamp could be created were much greater than those which had to be worked out before arc lighting became practical. An incandescent substance had to be found; to avoid swift oxidation it could be heated only in an atmosphere of nitrogen or in a high vacuum, and if this latter alternative were to be used, pumps capable of producing a higher vacuum than any currently in use would have to be developed.

Furthermore, development of the system required the solution of many difficult economic problems. Arc lights had no competition in their field, so cost was not a problem. But incandescent home lighting would have to compete with gas light and kerosene lamps, which had already greatly reduced the cost of illumination. One important cost factor was the amount of copper which would have to be used in transmission lines. In order to keep copper costs down, relatively thin wires would be required. If these were adopted, Ohm's law made it apparent that transmission voltage would have to be high in order to avoid excessive current loss in the lines. Since it was considered impossible at the time to use alternating current, stepping a high transmission voltage down to a voltage suitable for house circuits by the use of transformers was out of the question. The use of high voltage required proportionally high resistance in the incandescent filament, thus complicating the problem of finding a suitable substance. Most metals could be expected to burn away quickly under these circumstances. Resistance could be increased by hooking lamps in series, but such a circuit, in which all lamps must be turned on at once, was scarcely practical for home use. Hooking lamps in parallel circuit, the other alternative, was considered theoretically impossible by many scientists during the early seventies. In the face of all these difficulties many electrical engineers concluded that designing a practical system of incandescent lighting would require a lifetime of research, if indeed the job could be done at all.

Yet a practical incandescent lamp was invented after only fourteen months of experiment between 1877 and 1879, and an incandescent lighting system was in operation by 1882. Although many inventors were at work in the field, the accomplishment was mainly the work of one man—Thomas A. Edison—and it was not only one of the greatest scientific achievements of American history but a triumph of engineering and entrepreneurship as well.

The story of Edison's difficult childhood is too well known to need repetition. Becoming a railroad news butcher at an early age, he soon learned telegraphy and wandered over much of the northeastern United States as in itinerant operator, always poor and sometimes destitute. Yet he bought and studied books on electricity and tinkered with improvements for telegraphic apparatus, among them a printing receiver and a duplex transmitter. His initially unsuccessful attempts to market these devices made him keenly aware that successful inventions must be commercially feasible—a valuable lesson which scientists trained in laboratories sometimes did not learn. After he finally landed a permanent job in the small research department of Western Union, company officials, slowly coming to appreciate his tremendous abilities, commissioned him to undertake developmental projects. When in 1876 they offered him $500 per month to work on the "speaking telegraph," he was able to establish himself in the famous laboratory at Menlo Park, New Jersey, and go into the business of invention.

The inventor of the multiplex telegraph, the mimeograph machine, the phonograph, the microphone, the motion picture, and incandescent lighting—not to mention important developments in electrical power and other fields—Edison was a towering figure who gained world renown. But because of his slight knowledge of science and his purely pragmatic methods he also had the limitations common to most American inventors up to his own time. He owed his success primarily to an intuitive ability to find out how things worked, an almost fantastic drive to solve problems, a determination to adopt invention to commercially profitable ends, and a well-developed ego which enabled him to publicize himself and his accomplishments with no trace of embarrassment. His lack of training in basic science, however, seemed occasionally to give him feelings of inferiority which led him to deprecate the efforts of mathematicians and physicists whom he employed. His purely pragmatic methods, and perhaps to a lesser degree his occasionally hostile attitude toward scientists, provoked a rather patronizing response from the eminent electrical engineer, Nicola Tesla. "If Edison had a needle to find in a haystack," Tesla wrote on one occasion, "he would proceed at once with the diligence of a bee to examine straw after straw until he found the object of his search. . . . I was a sorry witness to such things knowing that a little theory and calculation would have saved him ninety percent of his labor." Yet at the time Edison's methods were probably better designed to yield practical results than the "theory and calculation" of Tesla, because many of the contemporary theories regarding electricity were wrong.

Despite his ability to envision commercial applications for his inventions, Edison was not a good businessman. Completely wrapped up in his experiments, he left business affairs in disarray, and was often rescued from loss and frustration by the efforts of devoted employees or friends such as his secretary—Samuel Insull—and his attorney and the promoter of the Edison Electric Light Company—Grosvenor P. Lowrey. Beginning in middle age Edison was afflicted with hardening of the concepts. For example, after designing his electrical system for d.c. current he resolutely refused to acknowledge the superior advantages in a.c. systems apparent even at the time, and prevented his organizations from experimenting with the new development.

When Edison began work on incandescent lighting, William H. Vanderbilt and other high officials of Western Union apparently thought that if anyone could invent an incandescent lighting system, Edison was the man for the job. To implement the task they formed a syndicate which included J. P. Morgan, his partner Eggisto Fabri, and Henry Villard. The group capitalized their faith in Edison at $300,000 in 3,000 shares and called it the Edison Electric Light Company. Twenty-five hundred of these shares were given to Edison in return for his agreement to assign to the company all inventions and improvements he might make in the field of incandescent lighting for a period of five years. Designed to be only a licensing agency, and not a manufacturing concern, the syndicate tempered its faith with caution by limiting the original assessment to $50,000.

The story of Edison's tedious search for a filament, during which he tested 6,000 vegetable substances, is too well known to need repetition. When he finally hit upon bamboo, and produced a lamp which burned

1,200 hours, it was evident that incandescent lighting might be made practical. Edison then persuaded his backers to build a central station as a pilot project to develop an incandescent system. To reach this objective they formed the Edison Electric Illuminating Company in 1881 and obtained a franchise to build and operate a station in New York City. Aware that in order to be competitive, electric light must cost the purchaser no more than gas or oil illumination, candlepower for candlepower, Edison and his backers planned the station with cost factors constantly in mind. The long life of the filament gave a great initial advantage in this respect. Equally important was the high resistance of the filament—100 ohms— which enabled relatively high voltage current to be employed, and this in turn permitted the use of relatively thin transmission wires without encountering the excessive current dissipation which would have taken place at lower transmission voltages. Initially, current was transmitted at 110 volts, but in 1883 Edison invented and installed the three-wire transmission system which enabled it to be generated at 240 volts and stepped down to 110 volts at the lamp circuits. The three-wire system also permitted even thinner transmission wires to be used, at a 63 percent saving in copper costs. In order to obtain public reaction to electric lighting, Edison had careful surveys made in the area of downtown New York to be served by the generating plant. Only after he was convinced that he could provide electric light at prices competitive with other forms of illumination, and that the public would be receptive to his system, did Edison proceed with construction of the central station.

In order to control the quality of his equipment, protect patents, and design improvements, Edison determined to undertake the manufacture of generators and subsidiary apparatus himself. Here he parted company with most of his backers, who wanted to limit the business to licensing and to the operation of a pilot plant designed to stimulate the construction of central stations elsewhere. Understandably, they hesitated to finance Edison's entry into a field with which he was unfamiliar, and under circumstances which would require heavy outlays of capital. Determined to go it alone, Edison raised the initial funds for his manufacturing enterprises by selling most of his stock in the Electric Light Company. He then began construction of a lamp bulb plant, a machine works, an electrical tube company, and a company to produce isolated lighting equipment for large buildings. Between 1881 and 1884 Edison was incredibly busy. Not only did he supervise the construction of these plants himself but took charge also of building the Pearl Street Station, laying transmission lines, and installing lighting equipment. The appearance of bugs in nearly all of the generating and transmission apparatus was a constant harassment. But by 1882 the Pearl Street Station was completed at a cost of $600,000— $350,000 more than anticipated. Initially it served 85 customers and carried a load of 400 lamps. Two years later the equipment companies were in operation.

Able and energetic as he was, Edison could probably not have made the great achievement of establishing a new industry without help. He found it in Samuel Insull, an English immigrant younger than himself and bursting with energy and ambition. Unfortunately Insull's brilliant career was brought to a catastrophic end during the 1930s by the collapse of his utilities empire and his subsequent flight and prosecution, and his name lingers on as a symbol of fraudulent finance—undeservedly, according to his biographer, Forrest McDonald. The son of a visionary, ineffective, and impecunious English temperance worker, young Samuel set out early in life to achieve the success so lacking in his own family. Becoming a professional stenographer, he acquired fragments of an education and distant acquaintance with the *haut monde* of fashion, wealth, and power, by serving as secretary to the editor of *Vanity Fair*, possibly the most influential and prestigious magazine in Britain during the 1860s and 1870s. The accounts of Edison's work carried in its columns fascinated Insull. When an opportunity arose in 1879 to take the post of secretary to a banker representing Edison's interests in England, Insull seized it, and in a short time became familiar with the design and operation of electrical equipment. Because of his demonstrated abilities he was called to become secretary to the great man himself two years later.

He arrived at the very moment at which Edison was starting to raise money to finance his manufacturing enterprises, and Insull was able to give him invaluable information on the most profitable way to dispose of stocks in European companies under Edison patents. Edison immediately made Insull his financial factotum. While Edison rushed from one construction site to another, ironing out bugs and solving technical problems, it was Insull who stayed home and tended the store. Without trying to systematize Edison he systematized his affairs. Edison was thus freed to do the scientific work he loved, and Insull became his alter ego in all entrepreneurial activities.

By 1884 the organizations bearing the name of Edison had a combined worth of $10 million; four years later Edison himself at the age of thirty-seven was one of the leading millionaire industrialists of the nation. By 1886 fifty-eight central stations were in operation. Like central stations for arc lighting equipment, these were formed by local businessmen. Although contract terms differed, most operating companies received a license to use Edison equipment from the Edison Electric Light Company in return for 25 to 30 percent of the capital stock and a cash payment equal to 5 percent of the company's capitalization. The Edison equipment companies sold their apparatus for cash when they could get it, but usually they had to accept part payment in notes and securities. Under these circumstances the rapid expansion of the companies' business created desperate shortages of cash and working capital. Insull's most important task by far came to be raising the money needed to carry on operations. In 1886 Edison added to Insull's already heavy responsibilities by making him head of a new manufacturing organization set up in an abandoned locomotive works in Schenectady, New York—the future General Electric Company. "Run the whole thing. Do it big, Sammy. Make it either a big success or a big failure," was Edison's injunction.

Defense of the Edison patents, particularly on the components of the incandescent lamp, was a difficult and expensive task at which Edison did not prove to be very adept. After he had completed a prototype incandescent system at Menlo Park in 1879, but before he had made the system commercially feasible, he very unwisely allowed visitors to examine the equipment. Among these were rival inventors, who shortly thereafter began to manufacture competing lamps and equipment. Chagrined at his mistake, Edison at first hoped that his head start and the superior performance of his lamps, generators, and subsidiary apparatus would enable him to suppress competition without resort to litigation. Moreover, he was too absorbed in building Pearl Street Station and his manufacturing plants to prepare suits and testimony. But his reluctance to resort to the courts merely encouraged his competitors the more, and soon they were openly infringing on all Edison patents. In 1885, with the aid of a new and more vigorous administration installed in the Electric Light Company, Edison at last took legal action. Six years later, after the expenditure of about $2 million on litigation, the crucial patent on the high resistance filament was upheld. It was largely an empty victory, however, for the patent had only four more years to run.

During the eighties competition was as brisk in incandescent lighting as in arc lighting, and similarly took place on the level of product, terms of payment, operating costs, and guarantees more than on price. Edison's prices for central station equipment were somewhat higher than those of competitors, but were offset to some degree by lower maintenance cost. Candlepower for candlepower, Edison lamps consistently outlasted those of competitors. The lamp company considered, but quickly rejected, a policy of planned obsolescence to increase sales. Believing that in the long run superior quality would bring the greatest competitive advantage, all of the Edison manufacturing companies strove to improve the performance of their products, even if it meant increased cost to the purchaser. The average production cost of lamps dropped from 70 cents in 1881 to 30 cents in 1884, while average revenue per lamp rose during the same period from 38 cents to 44 cents, indicating rapidly increasing efficiency of manufacturing operations.

Despite their prosperity, the Edison companies suffered from a lack of co-ordination, conflict of interests, and chronic shortage of working capital. In 1888, Henry Villard, recently returned from Germany where he had recovered from a nervous breakdown induced by the collapse of his transportation empire in the Far Northwest, proposed to solve the problems of the Edison enterprises by combining them into one large, integrated company. In view of Villard's dubious record of speculation and financial sleight-of-hand, one might expect that his offer would have been received with some skepticism. But apparently some of the magic which enabled him to persuade some 50 hard-headed financiers to subscribe $8 million to the blind pool of 1881 still remained. Edison directors agreed to the combination, and Edison himself acquiesced in the hope that the move would put an end to the financial difficulties which had nagged him since the beginning of his work on incandescent lighting. Eight companies, including several not among the original Edison group, found a home in the new Edison General Electric Company, capitalized at $12 million. The largest single component purchase made by the combination were the Edison patents and the stocks held by Edison Electric Light, for which an aggregate of $3.5 million was paid. Villard was elected president. Edison retired to his Menlo Park laboratory, financially secure and at last freed from his multifarious responsibilities.

FORMATION OF GENERAL ELECTRIC AND WESTINGHOUSE

During the nineties as the number of firms manufacturing electrical equipment decreased, competition became bitter between Edison General Electric and an ambitious newcomer to the field, the Westinghouse Electric Company. Its founder, George Westinghouse, was quite similar to Edison in character, personality, and abilities. Like Edison, Westinghouse was an instinctive inventor, without formal training in science and alert to the commercial possibilities of his inventions. Unlike Edison, however, Westinghouse discovered no new principles; his inventions were usually improvements on existing equipment. Also, he constantly purchased promising patents, experimented with them, and incorporated them in his electrical equipment. After his first success, Westinghouse did not retire from promotional activities, as did Edison, but pursued them ever more intensively, and by the end of his life had built a formidable industrial empire. Over the years he played some part in founding or directing the affairs of over 100 companies—scores of which bore his name—employing in the aggregate as many as 50,000 people and capitalized at about $250 million.

Born in Vermont in 1846, one year younger than Edison, Westinghouse served a hitch in the navy and returned in 1865 to work in his father's agricultural machinery shop in Schenectady. In the same year he secured a patent for a rotary steam engine, and a few years later received the first of his patents on the air brake. Few men have been more prolific inventors than Westinghouse. Between 1880 and 1890, he took out 134 patents—more than one per month—covering railroad and mechanical equipment, electrical apparatus, steam turbines, and systems of gas distribution and control.

The great success of his air brake, which was adopted almost universally on American and European railroads, provided him with the funds to enter other fields. His work on railroad signaling devices led him to electricity. Aware of the rapidly growing market for central station equipment and lamps, he purchased the patents held by William Stanley, a competitor of Edison's, and in 1885 formed the Westinghouse Electric Company to manufacture Stanley's lines of apparatus.

Feeling that experiments with alternating current under way in England and on the Continent might prove fruitful, he purchased a basic English patent and began the development of an a.c. system in his Pittsburgh plant. The most important of the several advantages of a.c. over d.c. current is that by use of transformers it can be stepped up to very high voltages and thus be transmitted over long distances with a minimum of loss. Therefore a.c. systems allow economical location of generating stations—on cheap land, adjacent to river transportation for fuel, or perhaps in water power installations. On the other hand, d.c. systems, because of inability to use transformers and the consequent necessity to transmit at much lower voltages than a.c., could serve areas of only a two-mile radius. Stations, therefore, had to be located near the center of cities, and large metropolitan centers needed more than one station. During the early days of central station operation d.c. current had an advantage over a.c. which diminished with time—greater safety because of low voltages. At the outset also, difficult problems of phase and frequency later solved by mathematical research also made a.c. less advantageous for driving motors than d.c.

With the appearance of the first Westinghouse equipment began the "Battle of the Currents," which was to end in complete victory for the a.c. system and the consequent embitterment of Edison and the tarnishing of his reputation for wizardry. When the first a.c. stations were built, Edison appeared unconcerned, apparently convinced that the greater safety of his d.c. systems would give them a competitive advantage. But as the number of a.c. installations mounted to 116 two years after they were first put on the market, and it appeared that Edison's lead was rapidly being pared down, Edison and his colleagues at EGE started a smear campaign against the competitor. A pamphlet entitled *A Warning*, bound in red, explained in morbid detail the dangers of high voltage a.c. current and listed the names of people allegedly killed by it. To provide continuing proof of its lethal character, EGE was instrumental in prevailing on the New York Legislature to adopt electric chairs for executions, and to purchase Westinghouse generators to power the first of them installed. The company then pressed unsuccessfully for legislation to ban the use of a.c. current in central stations.

Partisans of Westinghouse replied with vigor, and Westinghouse for a time considered filing a suit for defamation against EGE. He gained an important advantage when he secured the contract to provide the lighting system for the Columbian Exhibition of 1893, but this was imperiled by the final court decision upholding the Edison lamp patent. As the result of a crash program of research, however, he was able to develop a non-infringing lamp just in time to fulfill his contract. The success of his system and the spectacle of his giant alternators at work—a major part of the Westinghouse exhibit—made a deep impression on the public and did much to counteract the harmful publicity originated by EGE. Soon afterward the evident advantages of a.c. transmission, particularly in the economies of copper it permitted, won the field, and eventually 95 percent of the generating capacity of the nation came to operate on a.c. current. Yet Westinghouse's victory did not seriously injure EGE. When it merged with Thomson-Houston to form General Electric in 1892 it thereby acquired an a.c. system, and thereafter was able to offer customers both a.c. and d.c. installations.

The rather sorry part played by Edison himself in the Battle of the Currents was an embarrassment to his friends and has created a problem for his biographers. It cannot be argued that the great man acted entirely from economic considerations arising out of a desire to protect a heavy investment in the d.c. system. By the use of rotary converters a.c. current generated outside of cities could be transformed at urban central stations into d.c. current suitable for distribution by existing installations. Probably Edison was sincere in his insistence that a.c. was too dangerous to be used in cities. Subconsciously he may also have felt that the danger lay not entirely in high voltage, but in his inability to participate actively in development of the system. During the whole of his career, starting with his work in telegraphy, he had worked exclusively with d.c. current, and felt that he had come to understand it. But a.c. posed novel problems not easily susceptible to pragmatic solutions. Developmental breakthroughs were made primarily by mathematicians. Since Edison could contribute nothing in this field, he may have feared that a triumph for a.c. would mean a partial eclipse of his reputation.

By 1890 the growing confusion and litigation over patents and the desire to offer a complete line of equipment produced thoughts of merger on the part of EGE officials. Furthermore, EGE, while expanding rapidly and showing large profits, had accumulated a $3.5 million debt which it would gratefully share with a partner. Elimination of price cutting was also a factor, but probably of less importance than in many other industries in which mergers were taking place. Merger with Westinghouse was impossible because of the bitterness between the two firms, but a union with Thomson-Houston would face no such obstacle. Under Coffin's leadership TH had done little pioneering, but it had accumulated an impressive portfolio of patents which would fill out considerably the EGE line of equipment. J. P. Morgan, who had maintained a large personal as well as financial interest in the Edison organization ever since the formation of the Electric Light Company, approved of the merger.

The directors were also receptive to overtures, and negotiations proceeded smoothly during the latter part of 1891. EGE officials apparently assumed that their company, growing by leaps and bounds, a leader in the industry and a pioneer with a world-wide reputation, would receive a majority of the shares in a combine and that EGE officials would control the new organization. Events proved them sadly mistaken. Just as arrangements were about to be concluded, Coffin suddenly announced that he had changed his mind and refused to sell. Morgan summoned him to New York to explain the sudden turnabout. There Coffin pointed out that TH was making 50 percent more profit on its capitalization than EGE, that it had less money tied up in the stock of operating companies, and that it had no floating debt to match the $3.5 million obligation of EGE. Morgan, impressed, overlooked the fact that EGE was making more on the funds actually devoted to manufacturing than TH, and agreed to revise the terms of merger in favor of the latter company even though it employed fewer workers and did a smaller volume of business. The alteration of the original plans also meant that the leaders of TH, and not of EGE, would control the new combination. Morgan was becoming suspicious of the continued speculation carried on by Villard and the accumulation of outside interests which prevented him from devoting much of his time to EGE. Since the beginning, Insull, as general manager, had administered the affairs of the company, including the financing.

The bad news was broken to EGE leadership without ceremony. In the new combination, to be named merely General Electric, EGE would be valued at $15 million and TH at $18 million—the difference representing the fateful floating debt of $3.5 million which in effect became the instrument bringing about the ouster of the EGE men. Villard was informed that his "courteous resignation would be courteously received." Edison was profferred a directorship, probably as an emollient for his ruffled pride. Insull was the only EGE man offered an important post. He was requested to stay on as a second vice-president, but refused. He then turned to the public utility field in which he carved out a brilliant and tragic career. Coffin became president—a post he held until 1926—and brought with him into policy-making positions the top management of TH. Aghast at the way their company had been sold over their heads, Edison, Villard, and Insull turned against each other with bitter recriminations. But since all concerned made a handsome profit on their stockholdings, their anger was short-lived, and the three later resumed their friendship.

The precipitant drop in the value of securities held by General Electric during the Panic of 1893 made the stated capitalization of $50 million seem excessive. Yet the stock was probably not watered to a significant degree. Before the combination, EGE and TH had each valued their assets at $20 million, and the new company at the time of incorporation had issued $10 million in bonds for the improvement of production facilities. In 1891 the combined profits of EGE and TH had stood at $5 million.

Relations between GE and Westinghouse were improved by a patent sharing agreement signed in 1896. The two firms by that time possessed hundreds of patents and made it a policy to give patent guarantees with their equipment, thereby accepting responsibility for suits. But as GE and Westinghouse strove to offer full lines, the number of infringement suits pending rose to over 300 by 1896. As a result, it became increasingly risky to grant these guarantees. Potential customers tended to revise their specifications or postpone purchases until conflicting claims could be settled. Obviously both firms would increasingly hamstring each other unless the controversies were brought to an end. According to the agreement of 1896, reached after protracted negotiations, the patents of GE represented 62½ percent of the value of the pool, those of Westinghouse 37½ percent, and each firm could manufacture under the other's patents. Business in equipment lines so covered was divided in the agreed proportion, but there were no limitations on production or stipulations regarding prices. Each firm was free to exceed the allotted proportion in any line upon payment of royalties. The agreement was administered by a joint Board of Patent Control appointed by the two companies.

Contrary to what might be expected, the agreement enhanced rather than decreased competition between GE and Westinghouse. However, it bore hard on smaller firms, who found it increasingly difficult to offer patent guarantees. Thus the pool hastened the retirement of small firms from the field. By the end of the nineteenth century the electrical equipment industry appeared to be headed toward duopoly.

ELECTRIC STREET RAILWAYS

Besides being used for the creation of light and the transmission of sound, electricity was utilized toward the end of the nineteenth century for the production of motive power. Motors were put to many industrial uses, but few inventors saw that the most promising field for electric power was transportation, particularly the electrification of street railways. Utilities companies became aware also that electric traction would provide a profitable daytime load for their generating facilities.

The rapid increase in the size of American cities and the spread of population into suburbs created a need for improved urban transportation. Horsecar lines had been in existence since the antebellum period, and by 1880 it was estimated that more than 100,000 horses and mules were in service pulling 18,000 streetcars over about 3,000 miles of track. Many of the lines were very profitable, and by this time mergers had created a new transportation nobility known as "traction kings." But the cars traveled at no more than five or six miles per hour, and the lines had a sharply limited traffic capacity.

It seemed obvious to many that if cities were to continue their growth, faster transportation systems must be found. In New York, where the problem was critical because expansion could extend in only one direction—northward—construction of an elevated steam railroad over Ninth Avenue was started in 1867. By 1881 tracks had been laid over Second, Third, and Sixth Avenues, and under the guidance of the Municipal Board of Transportation the lines had been merged into the Manhattan Elevated Railway Company. But trains drawn by steam engines were smoky, noisy, and had to be relatively light in weight. Fastidious New Yorkers were appalled at the prospect of steam elevated lines stretching the length of Manhattan over all the north-south avenues.

Some cities experimented with traction systems in which cars were moved by cables sunk in trenches between the rails. Power was supplied by large stationary steam engines located in central stations. But cable systems had serious limitations also. In the first place, they were very expensive to construct. The Washington double track system, for example, cost $185,000 per mile. Cable grips, operated from within the cars, had a tendency both to lock and slip, making travel sometimes dangerous. A car with a locked grip rolled inexorably and uncontrollably over the rails, smashing everything in its path. A breakdown of any nature, occurring on the lines or in the station, required stoppage of the entire system. Yet cable systems were quiet and clean, and for this reason raised land values along their routes. Because of their large carrying capacity they could make money even though construction costs were high. But their drawbacks were generally considered to outweigh their advantages, and as a result they were installed in only fifteen cities in the nation.

With the building of the first central generating stations for arc lighting it became theoretically possible to move streetcars by electricity. Many problems appeared which could not be solved by slide rule or on the drawing board, however. Should motors be located in the trucks or in car bodies, and how should their power be transmitted to the wheels? How would motors stand up under the heating at brushes and commutators inevitably caused by starts under heavy loads? Were existing tracks and roadbeds, designed for horsecars, suitable for the much heavier electric trolleys, or would new tracks have to be laid? Not only these engineering problems but economic problems as well could only be solved by experience. Would electrical systems be competitive in operating costs with horsecar systems? One might expect that construction expenses, entailing much developmental work, would be considerably greater. But operating costs apart from servicing might be lower, and certainly increased capacity of the lines would yield greater revenues. On this level economic problems became inextricably intertwined with engineering problems.

The first experiments with electric traction were promising. Edgar M. Bentley and Walter H. Knight, manufacturing their equipment in the Cleveland plant of the Brush Electric Company, electrified a horsecar line in that city in 1884, thereby inaugurating electric trolley service in the United States. Charles J. Van Depoele, an immigrant Belgian cabinet-maker who turned to the manufacture of arc lighting equipment and motors, constructed an electric railway at the Toronto Exhibition of 1885 which carried from 6,000 to 10,000 passengers daily. This success focused the attention of some venturesome capitalists upon electric traction, and by 1887 the Van Depoele Company had installed a dozen street railways in the nation which ran nearly 100 cars over 60 miles of track. In Montgomery, Alabama, the equipment was operated at about two-thirds of the operating costs of the mule cars already in use. Difficulties in raising capital induced Van Depoele to sell his system to TH in return for royalty payments on cars equipped with his patented equipment, and he himself went to work in the railway department of the company.

The pioneer in electric traction who solved the major design problems and developed this type of transportation into something like its modern form was Frank J. Sprague. Born in Connecticut in 1857, the son of a mill superintendent, he had secured an appointment to Annapolis in order to acquire training in electrical engineering. While on a tour of duty in London, several rides on the dirty, gaseous, underground steam railway then in service turned his mind to the possibility of replacing steam power with electric power. Upon return to the United States he resigned from the navy to take a position in the Edison construction department. After designing and marketing a constant speed-variable load motor, he left Edison in 1884 and with the help of the company's president, E. H. Johnson, and several directors, formed the Sprague Electric Railway and Motor Company.

Pursuing experiments in electric traction, he tried unsuccessfully to interest officials of the Manhattan Elevated Railway in electrification. Perhaps one reason for his failure was the fact that Jay Gould, financial overlord of the line, was so badly frightened by a fuse blowout while riding in an experimental car that he allegedly tried to jump out of a window. Although Gould exhibited remarkable coolness and daring in his manifold stockmarket manipulations and in his encounters with the speculative fraternity, outside of the financial world he was a very timid man.

Sprague's opportunity to enter the traction field came in 1887 when he was offered a $110,000 contract to electrify a twelve-mile stretch of horsecar line in Richmond, Virginia. Although he had only preliminary plans for such an extensive task completed, and although the contract stipulated that the electrical equipment must be installed within ninety days, Sprague eagerly accepted the terms. The result of his work was the prototype of modern streetcar systems. Car motors were mounted on each truck rather than inside the bodies, and were geared directly to the axles. Trolleys running under overhead wires and held in place by spring poles constituted the power pickup. Controls were installed at each end of the cars. Current was supplied at 450 volts fed into the trolley wires at 1,000 foot intervals from parallel main conductors.

Despite its superior design, Sprague's system contained bugs which could be ironed out only with much expense and labor. On the Richmond line a 10 percent grade and sharp curves which made a heavy drag on outside wheels subjected motors to murderous punishment. Brushes and commutators burned with a bright blue glare under the strain and had to be replaced or machined frequently. The life span of field coils in the motors was brief. Track sank and buckled in the inadequately ballasted roadbed, and derailments were frequent. But Sprague stuck doggedly at the enormous task of making the system function efficiently. Fortunately he had the full support of the Edison organization, which supplied the generating equipment and some of the motors. Eventually Sprague solved all the major problems, although in the course of his efforts he expended $160,000 fulfilling a contract which because of delays had fallen to $90,000 in value.

Sprague's success gave great impetus to the building of other electric street railways, particularly because operating expenses on the Richmond line proved to be about 40 percent of those on the horsecar lines it replaced. By the end of 1889 one hundred and eighty systems were in operation or under construction throughout the nation. Since Sprague's company supplied the equipment for about one-third of the roads, he was to recover many times the money lost on the Richmond contract. Because of the demonstrated superiority of Sprague equipment and design, and the importance of the Sprague Company as a customer, it was absorbed in 1889 by EGE in return for a payment in stock valued at $750,000. Sprague himself accepted a post as consulting engineer with the firm.

In the next year, however, after differences with EGE management, Sprague resigned to form a company to design and manufacture elevators for the high rise buildings recently made possible by the use of structural steel construction. His work with elevator controls showed him that it would be possible to adapt these to electric railway cars in such a way that one man could operate an entire train. By making unnecessary the use of locomotives or locomotive cars, the multiple unit system could therefore handle a great increase in traffic on elevated railways without necessitating the rebuilding of the structures.

In 1897 Sprague performed a feat equal in importance to the construction of the Richmond line by designing a multiple unit system for the South Side Elevated Railway of Chicago. Again he accepted the contract before his plans were completed, but on this occasion he had no difficulty in installing the controls within the time limit allowed. He thus became the father of modern urban rapid transit. Because of the speedup in service and the increased volume of traffic carried by multiple unit trains, South Side's net earnings rose from $11 million to $45 million during the first year of operation. Market value of the company's stock advanced from $32 per share to $105 in the same period.

During the early nineties many firms began producing equipment for electric traction. But again mergers and patent purchases caused the disappearance of most small companies, and by the end of the decade the field was dominated by the two giants—Westinghouse and GE. The latter bought Sprague's patents for multiple unit controls in 1902. Despite the strengthening of the duopoly, competition between Westinghouse and GE remained brisk. Rapid changes in design of street railway equipment and expanding markets removed incentives for price and production agreements. These were to come only when the market approached saturation and designs became frozen. The fact that electrical manufacturers did not have to help finance the purchasers of equipment as a condition of making sales eased a problem which had threatened the financial stability of many companies in the past. The street railways were already in existence and many systems had large resources. Therefore operating companies assumed the entire responsibility for raising the funds to convert from horsecars to electric trolleys, and did not burden the manufacturing companies with stock.

Sprague was among the last of a line of inventor-entrepreneurs in the electrical equipment industry stretching back to Samuel F. B. Morse. Bell had left the field of electricity entirely and was devoting himself to a wide variety of other pursuits, many of them philanthropic. Edison was still working busily in his laboratory, but no longer had anything to do with the company he had founded. George Westinghouse was still a towering figure in the industry, but had largely abandoned technical work, devoting himself to the founding, financing, and combining of the many companies throughout the world in which he held interests and which bore his name. The domination of the electrical industry by the two large companies with their patent pool made it much more difficult for individual inventors to manufacture and market their innovations than in the past. Henceforth the development of new products and basic research was to become increasingly an intramural affair carried on in the laboratories of the large concerns. Whether this dampened the spirit of innovation is a moot question outside the scope of this inquiry.

Even though in the electrical industry invention came to be segregated into corporate laboratories, this development did not signal the end of the free-lance inventor himself. Most new industries in the early twentieth century went through the same initial phase as the electrical in which inventor-entrepreneurs rushed into promising new fields with a multiplicity of designs and formed small plants to manufacture their innovations. Then, as the number of companies began to decline because of multiplying patents and mergers, inventors tended to specialize in technical details, designs moved toward standardization, the rate of innovation was slowed, and the industries concerned advanced toward maturity. Let us hope, however, that American business never becomes so rigid that the inventor-entrepreneur will disappear entirely, for during the nineteenth century, at least, he was the major innovator in technology.

XXXVI. Business and Businessmen in the Latter Nineteenth Century

BUSINESS BUREAUCRATS

Among the productions of big business at the turn of the century was a new type of businessman—the business bureaucrat. The entrepreneur of the older order still dominated smaller businesses, and many of the most celebrated businessmen gloried in entrepreneurial orientations, but the pressures of organization in giant enterprises were creating the career men characteristic of modern business. As William Miller expresses it: "First among the railroads, but by the turn of the century in many other lines as well, the characteristic big business firm had become a big bureaucracy. Functions at each level of operation, supervision, and policy making had become more or less strict and specific, channels of authority and communications had been set up, and hierarchies of ascent had become articulated. Lifetime, salaried careers thus had become attainable, leading all the way to the top. . . ." In the words of Robert H. Wiebe, "The emphasis in business was shifting from the man to the company, from ingenuity to training. . . ."

An examination of the careers of 185 presidents and board chairmen of the nation's largest corporations made by Miller reveals the change which a scant fifty years had brought about in the career patterns of the business elite. Of this group only 14 percent had started or purchased their firms, but 47 percent had reached their positions by climbing the bureaucratic ladder. Twenty-six percent of the men born before 1841 were independent entrepreneurs; but only 8 percent of the men born after 1860 were in this category. In the mid-nineteenth century men of twenty-five or thirty who still clung to salaried jobs, in Miller's words, "merited as little regard in the business community as spinsters of the same age did at home." But by 1900 talented young men in increasing numbers were training for law or engineering not in order to go into independent practice of their professions but to prepare themselves for bureaucratic positions in established firms. "Captive" lawyers like Vanderbilt's Chauncey M. Depew, Harriman's Robert S. Lovett, or Rockefeller's S. C. T. Dodd—all men who made striking successes—were representative of the new breed. Service, and not status, was the key to wealth and power in an environment contrasting markedly with that in which the "merchants" of an older order had conducted their operations.

Service also introduced a new type of competition which had its effect in molding the organization man. A success novel of 1902 admonished young aspirants: "Be manly, and look it. Appear the gentleman, and be the gentleman. What's the good of unknown good? Negotiable intrinsic value must have the appearance of intrinsic worth." But "negotiable intrinsic value" included an increasing amount of extrinsic technical competence. Among Miller's executives who moved upward in the bureaucratic hierarchy, 72 percent started in manual and technical branches of business. These men changed jobs only infrequently and the majority reached the top of the ladder after careers of twenty to thirty years. Yet advancement through the ranks did not equate with progress from rags to riches. Although some executives rose from shop or mine, an increasing number went white collar all the way. Moreover, 86 percent of the group studied by Miller came from business and professional families. Forty-one percent had gone to college as against 3.3 percent of white males generally.

By the early twentieth century the "natural aristocracy" which Jefferson hoped would be recruited from among the virtuous and talented seemed to be at last becoming a reality, but in a manner which would have disturbed him profoundly. Their origins were urban and small town instead of rural, and despite the assurances of popular writers they owed their advancement much less to character than to technical proficiency. Far from desiring to maintain the agrarian ideals which Jefferson considered indispensable for the health of republics, they exerted themselves to expand the industrial system which Jefferson considered fatal to republican virtues. In their possession and manipulation of corporate securities they more resembled the "paper aristocracy" so condemned by John Taylor of Caroline. Finally, because a steadily increasing number were recruited from established families and received privileges not accorded to the rest of society, the natural aristocracy of talent began to bear some resemblance to the hereditary aristocracy whom most of the founders of the republic considered to be one of the greatest dangers to its survival.

BUSINESSMEN AND CHANGING SOCIAL SANCTIONS

The social sanctions under which businessmen operated changed nearly as much during the nineteenth century as businessmen themselves. At the outset of this period, the variety of political and social functions performed by merchants and their unquestioned status allowed them to assume the role of trustees for society at large. The social value of the entrepreneurial function and the ethical standards with which it was carried on were subjected to no hostile investigation or criticism. The profit motive was accepted as a necessary and even laudable manifestation of human nature. The uses to which a businessman put his property were considered to be his affair alone, and the more property he accumulated, the more he enhanced his reputation for astuteness. He was required only to adhere to commonly accepted standards of honesty and morality; but even here such sanctions applied much more to his dealings with business associates and correspondents than to his dealings with government.

But as the century advanced, the sanctions operating upon businessmen became more restrictive. With the adoption of democratic reforms in state government, the old landed and mercantile aristocracy lost much of its power and in governmental positions was compelled increasingly to act as the people's agent rather than a trustee of their interests. Certain types of business activity were subjected to increasingly harsh criticisms. Absentee land grabbers and the beneficiaries of lucrative corporate charters purchased from complaisant legislatures found themselves denounced as monopolists, and opprobrium was heaped upon wildcat bankers and financial intermediaries such as billbrokers—particularly if they went bankrupt. Actually, the criticism of land speculators, bankers, and brokers marks the beginning of the attacks upon business in the United States which have persisted to the present day. Yet the businessman's role was not otherwise submitted to much scrutiny, and he was judged largely in accordance with his personal qualities.

The accumulation of the first great fortunes, coinciding with the humanitarian reform movement of the antebellum period, helped to plant the idea that the possession of great wealth carried with it commensurate social responsibilities. Although this concept was not to become generally accepted until a much later date, it probably intensified post-mortem criticism of John Jacob Astor, who died in 1848 without leaving a significant amount of his fortune for public purposes. The Whig aristocrat, Philip Hone, labeled Astor "a self-invented money-making machine," and others went beyond personal criticism to challenge the close relationship of wealth and virtue and the parallelism of private wealth and public gain so often assumed in the past. The acidulous James Gordon Bennett anticipated Henry George's denunciation of unearned increment by asserting that at least one-half of Astor's fortune belonged to the people of New York, whose labors had raised the value of his vast real estate holdings.

The progress from "self-invented money-making machine" to "robber baron" was accomplished in the two decades after the Civil War during the rise of big business, and critics now concentrated their attacks on the manner in which great wealth was being made. The phrase, "robber baron" was apparently first applied to Commodore Vanderbilt about 1857. The implication was that businessmen of great wealth, particularly those who had effected combinations, performed no creative role but instead, like the *Raubritter* of the Middle Ages, preyed upon commerce and levied a heavy toll on farmers, industrial workers, consumers, and government. Actually the robber barons were to some extent at least a scapegoat for the periodic dislocation and distress caused by a rapidly growing but uncontrolled economy. It is almost axiomatic in history that the loudest complaints against existing conditions come not from the totally deprived but from groups whose situation is improving, yet not fast enough to keep pace with rapidly mounting expectations. Gross national product rose from $9.11 billion to $37.1 billion between 1869 and 1901, and per capita income tripled during the period, yet this groundswell of prosperity was much less palpable than the two major panics followed by prolonged depressions which took place between 1865 and 1914. When exaggerated expectations failed to materialize, according to John Tipple, thousands of Americans "then succumbed to their own delusions. Having identified myth as reality, they concluded that the whole structure of American political economy was breaking down, and they joined in an angry search for the wrecker."

Yet the high decibel volume of the criticism, and the harsh stridency with which it was uttered, gave an exaggerated notion of the number of individuals participating in the chorus. Actually, farmers and their organizations such as the Populist party and the Granges called the tune, and articulate, self-appointed reformers from the middle- and upper-classes drew the indictment. The image of the robber baron was kept in focus by such writers, economists, and politicians as Henry George, William J. Ghent, Robert LaFollette, Thomas Lawson, Henry D. Lloyd, Gustavus Myers, Charles E. Russell, Theodore Roosevelt, Ida Tarbell, Thorstein Veblen, and Lincoln Steffens. The muckrakers among them labored to uncover corrupt connections between business and politics.

Certainly the legislative investigations of the eighties and nineties revealed much reprehensible conduct on the part of many businessmen, but creaters of the robber baron stereotype distorted the record by treating unproved charges as fact, by employing inferences to establish intention, and by ignoring degrees of culpability. Also, critics often based their judgments on ethical standards much more rigorous than those contained in the operating code of business at the time, and condemned big businessmen for actions relatively unnoticed when perpetrated by lesser brethren of the business world. Perhaps the most misleading aspect of the robber baron concept was the inference that economic growth was an autonomous, evolutionary process which was thrown out of joint by the operations of big businessmen seeking to manipulate it for their own advantage—a concept exactly the reverse of Schumpeter's theory of economic growth. Certainly some big businessmen were mere parasites—Jay Gould is a good example—but others, while not guiltless of sharp practice, were creative builders whose financial rewards, large as these might be, were much smaller than the benefits they conferred upon the economy. But condemnation and not evaluation was the objective of most critics, and ironically, these men were indirectly aided by their victims. Businessmen under attack proved less resourceful in defending their reputations than their business interests. Anxious to maintain the privacy of their operations, they made only sporadic and usually ineffective attempts at rebuttal. Sometimes they covertly subsidized newspaper and magazine accounts giving their side of the story, and sometimes well-known champions like S. C. T. Dodd, general counsel for Standard Oil, published impressive defenses of their conduct. Down to the present day, however, this literature has never been given the attention it deserves, and has been shouldered out of history textbooks by the more flamboyant work of the critics.

Business leaders were particularly alarmed by the demands for governmental controls which often accompanied the condemnations of robber barons and the revelations of unfair competitive practices. Viewing themselves as the creators of national wealth and the engineers of progress, they resented being blamed for the sometimes harsh operation of what they considered to be natural laws over which they had no control. Periodic panics and depressions were as distressing to businessmen as to workers and farmers, but these setbacks represented merely the price of progress. Business spokesmen insisted that government intervention would at best be fruitless, since no human agency could over an extended period alter the natural laws of economics, and at worst it would bring the delicate machinery which created wealth to a stop and frustrate the remedial efforts of the only men who understood it.

Social Darwinism brought philosophy to the support of these deeply held convictions, and performed a distinct service by harmonizing two forces which on the surface were in conflict with each other—competition and combination. As John D. Rockefeller, Jr., explained to young gentlemen of the YMCA bracing themselves for their own encounters with the principle of natural selection in business: "The growth of a large business is merely a survival of the fittest. . . . The American Beauty rose can be produced in the splendor and fragrance which bring cheer to its beholder only by sacrificing the early buds which grow up around it. This is not an *evil tendency* in business. It is merely the working-out of a law of nature and a law of God." An earlier convert, Andrew Carnegie, although not professing such intimacy with the Mind of the Maker, nevertheless felt that the social implications of evolution were revealed truth: "I remember that light came in a flood and all was clear. . . . All is well since all grows better"—and, he might have added, "bigger."

This harmonization of competition and combination had its logical pitfalls. Since it seemed apparent that the purpose of combination was the suppression of competition, then the evolutionary process would lead directly toward monopoly. Indeed, this outcome was implied by Rockefeller's analogy of the American Beauty rose, which alone enjoyed the aliment of the rosebush after all the other buds had been "sacrificed." But Carnegie, the most persuasive and resourceful of the spokesmen for business of his generation, had an answer to the dilemma. Combination, when properly carried forward into integration, resulted in greater efficiency and lower prices to consumers. If the combinations utilized their positions to raise prices, or failed to bring about the economies of scale made possible by "the law of aggregation of capital," then, he asserted, smaller competitors would enter the field and ultimately force the combinations to dissolve. As a practical matter, Carnegie's forecast proved to be accurate in some areas of business at the turn of the century. As we have seen, many if not most combinations never reached the stage of integration which enabled them to realize fully their potential economies of scale, and when they attempted to raise prices they invited small competitors into the field and weakened their own position. Thus in these instances competition as well as governmental action inhibited the movement toward monopoly.

In other areas of business relations and practices where social Darwinism did not so neatly rationalize business interests, it was pointedly ignored. When the doctrinaire advocate of laissez-faire, William Graham Sumner, pointed out that to be consistent with evolutionary dogma businessmen should eschew governmental assistance like protective tariffs, the only thanks he got for his unwelcome suggestion was the near loss of his Yale professorship. Furthermore, businessmen would not grant the sanction of evolution to labor combinations which they claimed for business combinations, nor would they admit that a degree of public control should accompany public assistance to business.

If social Darwinism contained conflicting implications for public policy, its apparent justification of the widening gap between rich and poor and other social evils of the day required mollifying rationalization from business spokesmen. This task was accepted by Carnegie in his famous essay, *The Gospel of Wealth*. Acknowledging that the businessman secured wealth with the help of the community—a considerable admission for the time—he asserted that the duty of the rich man was "First, to set an example of modest, unostentatious living, shunning display or extravagance; to provide moderately for the legitimate wants of those dependent upon him; and after doing so to consider all surplus revenues which come to him simply as trust funds, which he is called upon to administer in the manner which, in his judgment, is best calculated to produce the most beneficial results for the community—the man of wealth thus becoming the mere agent and trustee for his poorer brethren, bringing to their service his superior wisdom, experience, and ability to administer, doing for them better than they would or could do for themselves." Organized philanthropy, then, dispensed in such a way as to stimulate the creative forces in society, would mitigate the harsh struggle for the survival of the fittest.

Although social Darwinism was an important current of philosophical thought during the latter nineteenth and early twentieth centuries, it is easy to overestimate its influence in the world of business because it circulated only among the very small group of businessmen interested in intellectual affairs. As Irvin G. Wyllie explains, "Guilded Age businessmen were not sufficiently bookish, or sufficiently well educated, to keep up with the changing world of ideas." For them competition was merely a fact of life which required no justification or rationalization. Vanderbilt, who read only one book in his life, and that after seventy, once remarked that if he had taken time to learn education he would not have had time to learn anything else. Daniel Drew sharpened the focus of the material preoccupation of his generation even more when he pontificated, "Book learning is something, but thirteen million dollars is also something, and a mighty sight more." Businessmen who took the time and trouble to examine the broader implications of their activities and values more often took their texts from the Bible than from Darwin and Spencer. As Wyllie further explains, "In the race for wealth they attributed little influence to native intelligence, physical strength, or any other endowment of nature, and paramount influence to industry, frugality, and sobriety—simple moral virtues that any man could cultivate. The problem of success was not that of grinding down one's competitors, but of elevating one's self. . . ." Failure was attributed to defective character rather than to deficiencies of endowment or opportunities.

Social Darwinism was hammered into the consciousness of the American people mainly by writers, educators, journalists, and the few businessmen like Carnegie who possessed the forensic skill to utilize its precepts to advantage. In the hands of the unskillful, the unpalatable aspects of social Darwinism were plainly revealed and the dogma became in effect a weapon which reformers used against the social Darwinists themselves. John D. Rockefeller, Jr., for example, had reason to regret the felicitous imagery of the American Beauty rose effusion when former competitors of Standard Oil, claiming that they had been driven out of business by the giant, greeted it as an accurate confession rather than a sermon. Whatever effectiveness social Darwinism might have had was probably negative in that it promoted complacency in the face of suffering, hindered the adoption of economic reforms, and fostered the idea that business could be carried on in its own self-contained, autonomous realm apart from the community at large. According to Edward C. Kirkland, the attempt to reach this latter objective amounted to a policy of "divide and ruin" which soured the relations of business with labor and farmers, and intensified the criticism from reformers.

SELF-DEFENSE AND SELF-CRITICISM AT THE TURN
OF THE CENTURY

In addition to their problems in foreign relations with the outside world, businessmen had many intramural problems which caused discussion and controversy. Tensions between competing segments of the business community, between business and government, and between business and labor, led to the formation of trade associations, mostly for defensive purposes. As Wiebe writes, "The businessman who after years of uncertainty had achieved a relative security and a moderate prosperity, and who was searching for ways to increase both, did not relish facing his world alone." Some regional trade associations like those of New England textile manufacturers were organized to determine wage levels, establish uniform labor policies, co-operate against unionism, and keep black lists. Another type of association was formed to exchange trade information, take measures to regulate competition, and—somewhat paradoxically—widen foreign markets and foster tariff protection. Before the turn of the century the National Association of Manufacturers, formed in 1895, stood at the apex of these organizations. After 1900 the number of associations multiplied to such an extent that they actually weakened each other by working at cross purposes. To remedy this situation an association of associations was formed in 1912—the Chamber of Commerce of the United States.

Trade journals contained many critical appraisals of current practices. Small business often voiced the apprehension with which it regarded the wave of mergers at the turn of the century, and there was serious doubt in other quarters as well that these supercorporations could be efficiently administered. Criticism of the stock watering accompanying combination was profuse, but there was no agreement on a basis for valuation which would eliminate the practice. Some critics insisted that issues of both preferred and common stock should not exceed the assessed value of physical assets, but apparently most trustmasters felt that it was enough if the preferred stock alone was secured by physical assets. They were apparently not concerned because common stock, representing only "good will and opportunity," had no investment status and became merely an instrument for stock market gambling. Some writers even suggested that capitalization be determined by earning power alone. Others noted that this would give an opportunity for combinations to hide embarrassingly high profits by spreading them out as normal dividends on watered stock. Vanderbilt's watering of New York Central shares was apparently designed for this purpose.

Agitation against watered stock was merely one aspect of an increasingly violent criticism of stock and commodity market speculation. Western Greenbackers, Grangers, and Anti-Monopolists zeroed in on futures trading, which had increased greatly in volume during the eighties. Critics insisted that futures contracts beared the wheat markets by inflating the supply side with fictitious offers to sell and drove down prices at harvest time. Furthermore, critics charged that under the best of circumstances futures only added to market instability and the range of price fluctuation. Defenders of futures denied both accusations, and of course with justice. In addition to noting the useful function of futures contracts in permitting hedging, spokesmen claimed that futures enabled commodity users to purchase over the entire year and thus avoid carrying large inventories. Casting the speculator in the improbable role of public benefactor, defenders asserted that speculators' losses supported the futures system, and thereby paid the storage charges for wheat which farmers and users would otherwise have had to pay out of their own pockets.

Yet these economically sound arguments were given little weight by farmers' organizations anxious to find scapegoats for the falling price levels of the eighties and early nineties. As early as 1879 the revised California Constitution forbade futures, and during the eighties several grain and cotton states enacted similar measures. Antipathy mounted so high that in Congress a coalition of agricultural states united in 1893 to pass the Hatch Bill by large majorities which completely cut across party lines. Key provision was a tax of 10 percent on futures contracts which would have driven them out of existence as effectively as a similar tax swept the currency clean of state banknotes after 1865. Because of a technicality, however, the Hatch Bill never became law, and with the firming of farm prices later in the nineties the futures issue faded in importance. States became increasingly lax in the enforcement of anti-futures legislation and by 1900 most of this was moribund.

Criticism of the stock market increased concurrently with the condemnation of futures. Since the market had for several decades been the very epicenter of speculation in the nation it had continually aroused righteous indignation among the keepers of public morals. But as long as the losses were sustained by known gamblers who knew all the ploys of the game, fair and foul, the criticism had been kept within bounds. But when small investors entering the market in mounting numbers during the eighties and nineties were regularly fleeced, demands for reform acquired a new urgency. Critics charged that brokers, avid for commissions, enticed the unwary by offers of low margins and that market manipulators bulled stock upward in order to attract the interest of small investors. For the same purpose fictitious activity was given to some stocks by "wash sales" and "matched orders"—simultaneous buy and sell orders which increased the volume of transactions in the stock affected. After the small investor had caught hold of what he fondly believed was the tail of a kite, it was charged that the insiders sold out after a substantial rise, broke the price, and then made a second haul by selling short during the precipitant fall which followed. To complete the melancholy cycle the broker then sold the investor out when he could not raise the collateral necessary to keep his call loan.

In contrast to the criticism of futures, the denunciation of speculative stock practices did not condense into regulatory legislation, mainly because the stock market was a voluntary market, traditionally and openly the domain of shady speculators, in which nobody was obliged to trade. The commodity markets, on the other hand, were the sole outlet for the produce of wheat farmers. Foul play here could not be avoided and could claim hundreds of thousands of innocent victims. Throughout the nineteenth century the stock market remained essentially a speculators' market. Only after the 1920s did its function as a source of useful and relatively safe investment increase markedly in importance. The only significant restriction in the area of stock trading around the turn of the century was the gradual outlawing of "bucket shops." These establishments, called "funeral parlors" in Wall Street parlance, invited customers to bet against the house in stock market quotations. Offering very low margins of around 3 percent and allowing trade in smaller odd lots than permitted on the exchanges, they did a penny-ante business with the little man who could not afford to lose his money like a gentleman in the stock market. The elimination of bucket shops suggests the same double standard applied to gambling which led to the abolition of the "policy" games connected with lottery drawings of fifty to sixty years before: gambling is a sin unless you can afford it.

SCIENTIFIC MANAGEMENT

Like cybernation today, "scientific management" was viewed at the turn of the century as a method of reorganizing production methods which had profound implications for widespread transformation of basic social and economic relationships. In its broadest meaning, according to the historian of the movement, Samuel Haber, the term had several connotations. It indicated a personal attribute of efficiency, dedication, and hard work. It also evoked a vision of machine-like, automated processes. Finally, it implied higher profits through improved commercial efficiency and a larger degree of social harmony because of more rational planning of production. For many enthusiasts scientific management became almost a cult, and its implications had palpable effect upon many leaders of the Progressive Movement seeking political and social reform along more rational and equitable lines.

But these developments belong mostly to the twentieth century. At the outset scientific management was conceived more narrowly as an attempt to increase the output of industrial workers by reorganizing shop procedures. Mainly because of the orientation of nineteenth-century businessmen toward entrepreneurial activities and away from managerial and technical functions, shop procedures as late as the eighties were practically identical with those of two generations before. Foremen determined how jobs were to be done, and the workers determined in practice if not in theory the time necessary to accomplish them. Wages were paid on either a daywork or a piecework basis. The former encouraged slowdowns and inefficiency. The latter, which allowed fast and efficient workmen to increase their incomes, did not in practice provide the incentive it was designed to create. Employers tended to reduce the piecework rate when it became apparent that a given job could be accomplished in a shorter time; workmen, in an attempt to maintain the rate, slowed their pace accordingly. The problem of improving shop procedures appeared almost insoluable because management usually did not know the most efficient procedure for each job nor the time necessary to accomplish it. The solution of the problems was largely the work of Frederick W. Taylor, and with later embellishments came to be known as "scientific management."

The son of a prominent Philadelphia lawyer, Taylor was educated at Exeter and Harvard, and hoped to follow his father's profession. A nervous breakdown forced him to change his plans, and in 1878 he went to work in the Midvale Steel Works of northern Philadelphia as a journeyman machinist. In the shop he entered a world into which gentlemen entrepreneurs scarcely ever set foot, and was apparently terra incognita even to Midvale's celebrated president, William Sellers—outstanding engineer and designer of tools, and former president of the Franklin Institute. A compulsive, dedicated worker, young Taylor rose to become chief engineer of the plant six years later, and meanwhile had earned by correspondence a master's degree in engineering from Stevens Institute. Convinced that output per worker would never rise until management took the responsibility for establishing shop procedures and planning output down to the smallest detail, Taylor determined the most efficient manner of performing every shop task. Every piece of work was ticketed with detailed specifications and instructions which workmen were to follow to the letter. In the course of standardizing work methods he found it necessary to redesign some tools and equipment.

Reforms of this type, as put into effect at Midvale, allowed piecework rate to be set at levels designed to achieve maximum efficiency of workers, and management could no longer find pretexts for lowering them. In order to stimulate incentive, Taylor worked out a differential rate system by which a fast and efficient worker could raise the piecework rate by increasing output. Taylor's system was completed by reorganizing clerical work, reports, and routing procedures in such a way that management at all times had a clear picture of all operations and therefore could provide rational and efficient supervision. Ultimate authority, binding on both management and workmen, was to reside in the planning department—in Haber's words, "the repository of a science of production [and possessor of] a new kind of authority which stemmed from the unveiling of scientific law rather than . . . arbitrary law."

The system was at first received with some suspicion by workmen, who feared the imposition of speedup and naturally resented the loss of the traditional right to plan their own work, but its effect in stabilizing the piecework rate and in permitting energetic workmen to raise their incomes reduced hostility to it over the years. Taylor stated in 1911 that no plants using his system had ever suffered a strike. Surprisingly, nine-tenths of the opposition—according to Taylor—came from management, which usually had little desire to assume responsibility for rationalizing production methods and might well have taken a dim view of the dictatorship of the planning department. Yet this resistance also diminished over the years, and after the turn of the century interest in scientific management markedly increased. No doubt one reason was Taylor's assertion that at Midvale during the decade after its inauguration the system brought about a 100 percent increase in production and a 40 percent increase in wages.

But the attention to managerial reform can easily be exaggerated. Like social Darwinism, it was the concern of a dedicated, influential, but small group of publicists and business leaders. To be sure the improvement of management performance was the focus of vital and continuing interest in some large companies like Pennsylvania Railroad where its importance was manifest, but American industrialists at the turn of the century were usually more interested in the creation of industrial empires than in redrawing organizational charts. As Alfred D. Chandler has written: "They became engrossed in planning the strategies of expansion and securing the resources—the men, money, and equipment—necessary to meet the needs and challenges of a swiftly industrializing and urbanizing economy. The powerful captains—the Rockefellers, Swifts, Dukes, Garys, and Westinghouses—and their able lieutenants had little time and often little interest in fashioning a rational and systematic design for administering effectively the vast resources they had united under their control."

THE MERGER MOVEMENT, 1898–1902

Combination was not only the most important objective of the captains of industry, but was also the most intensely debated issue within business as a whole. Between 1898 and 1902 occurred the wave of mergers which "laid the foundation for the industrial structure that has characterized most of American industry during the twentieth century"—according to a historian of the merger movement, Ralph L. Nelson. In 1899, 1,028 firms disappeared by merger, and during the four years spanning the turn of the century the average number going out of existence per year was 301. By 1904 there were 318 industrial combinations in the nation. One, the United States Steel Company, was capitalized at $1.4 billion; of the rest, ten had capitalizations above $100 million and thirty others more than $30 million apiece. With an aggregate capital above $7.25 billion the 318 industrial combinations controlled 5,288 plants.

The reasons for the mergers are by no means as evident as they may first appear. The ground often cited, both at the time and even today, was the need of competing companies to control prices and output in a saturated market. The large, heavily capitalized industries of the day—so the argument ran—faced much more serious losses from competition than had the smaller companies of a generation before, and since voluntary agreements had proved to be ineffective, combination was the only recourse. Certainly it cannot be doubted that control of competition was a major factor in the merger movement. Businessmen might chorus their conviction that competition was the benign regulator of the industrial order, but this was solely an intellectual reaction. Moves taken to suppress competition had always been responses as instinctive as the raising of an arm to ward off a blow. Even so, this consideration does not explain why the merger movement was so extensive or occurred at the time it did, because for most industries markets at the turn of the century were not saturated. Actually, this was a period of rapid market expansion.

It seems plain that the motives for the wave of combination were various, but the chance of making capital gains by stock exchanges was perhaps the trigger mechanism which started the process. The rapid build-up of investment funds in the nation at large and sharply rising stock prices made it possible for stockholders in competing firms to exchange their shares for those of a combination at a very favorable valuation. This situation may well explain why mergers have tended to take place more often in industries with high stock prices than in those with low stock prices, and in periods when prices generally were on the rise. The desire to earn promoters' fees also played an important part. The careers of

Morgan, Baker, Schiff, Higginson, and less reputable operators like the Moore brothers, John W. Gates, and Charles R. Flint made it plain that the combiners were not the least of the beneficiaries of combination.

The achievement of greater efficiency through consolidation was not an important objective in most instances. A majority of combinations were of the horizontal variety which brought few economies of scale, and in any event, in the opinion of Alfred D. Chandler, "Even after a combination had consolidated, its managers often continued to think of control of competition as its primary purpose." But because of the need to harmonize combination and public policy, promoters in their public utterances tended to ignore the reasons connected with profits and power and instead emphasized the economies of scale which they had little interest in putting into effect. As Charles R. Flint described the "benefits of consolidated management" in 1899:

The following are the principal ones: raw material, bought in large quantities is secured at a lower price; the specialization of manufacture on a large scale, in separate plants, permits the fullest utilization of special machinery and processes, thus decreasing costs; the standard of quality is raised and fixed; the number of styles reduced, and the best standards are adopted; those plants which are best equipped and most advantageously situated are run continuously in preference to those less favored; in case of local strikes or fires, the work goes on elsewhere, thus preventing serious loss; there is no multiplication of the means of distribution—a better force of salesmen takes the place of a larger number; the same is true of branch stores; terms and conditions of sales become more uniform, and credits through comparisons are more safely granted; the aggregate of stocks carried is greatly reduced, thus saving interest, insurance, storage, and shop-wear; greater skill in management accrues to the benefit of the whole instead of the part; and large advantages are realized from comparative accounting and comparative administration. . . . The grand result is, a much lower market price. . . .

After 1900 the poor performance of some combinations forced management to give more attention to efficiencies of this type, particularly in the cases where the raising of prices enabled independents to flourish under the price umbrellas involuntarily provided by the combinations. Also, the need felt by combinations using products of the soil and extractive commodities to control their own sources of raw materials gave impetus to vertical integration, which focused attention on the factors Flint had in mind. In all cases the relative ease or difficulty of rationalizing production depended partly on the composition of the individual combinations. The problem was almost insoluable for those which were hastily thrown together, overcapitalized, and contained a large number of widely dispersed plants of varying degrees of efficiency producing an extensive variety of products. As we have seen, U.S. Rubber in its early career was an example of this kind of combination. It was obviously much easier to introduce economies of scale into combinations more carefully organized in which from the outset the increase of efficiency was given as much attention as capital gains on stock swaps and control of markets. Combinations of this type in the glass and paper industries, and in baking, were able to move more rapidly toward integration.

CRITICISM OF CONCENTRATION IN BUSINESS

Responses to the merger movement in the public prints varied according to the real or fancied effect upon particular groups concerned. Hostility was most intense during the eighties when the form of combination was the trust, a device which not only seemed specifically designed to suppress competition but also deprived stockholders of any voice in the affairs of the combinations and concentrated control in a shadowy directorate with practically unlimited power. The fact that the trusts were formed among producers of basic consumer goods in wide use, such as oil, sugar, and whiskey, also probably heightened fear of monopoly and attendant price rises. Among the most bitter critics of the trusts were farmers, who saw them as a major element of an economic system which they felt was designed at every point to exploit the agricultural population.

Actually, the distresses felt by farmers were largely the outcome of overproduction, resultant low farm prices, crop failures, and competition in foreign markets. But responding to the natural human tendency to find human agency at the root of all evils, farmers held the trusts in large measure responsible for their troubles. Equally denunciatory were the reformers and muckrakers who had created the robber baron stereotype. They saw the trust movement as a kind of spiral in which suppression of competition, rising tariffs, and influence upon government worked together in unholy alliance to create monopoly. Eventually, these critics maintained, the small businessman would be driven to the wall or into combines, the mass of the people impoverished, and the trustmasters and their minions left in complete control of government.

Political economists and scholars in other fields were divided and somewhat ambivalent in their attitudes. Many agreed with John Bates Clark—perhaps the most widely read writer on economic subjects during the period—that combination was inevitable development, but most informed observers insisted that it not be allowed to create monopolies. Richard T. Ely, a liberal economist critical of laissez-faire on moral grounds, distinguished between natural and artificial monopolies. He felt that the former should be regulated or operated by government, and the latter prohibited in order to maintain competition in the private sector of the economy. Perhaps the most detailed investigation of the methods of combination was made by Jeremiah Jenks, who came to be considered a leading authority on the trusts. But like Clark, Jenks reflected the ambivalence of economists not committed primarily to some philosophical or moral ideal. After describing the chicancery which often accompanied the formation of combinations and their monopolistic behavior, he nonetheless concluded, "It is probable that few trusts are entirely evil, and none are all good." Actually, a commitment to competition accompanied by a conviction that combination was a natural, evolutionary development in business made it difficult for many economists to take a strong stand regarding trusts one way or the other. Granted their premises, regulation of trusts could easily entail interference with the operation of natural economic laws. On the other hand, if no regulation were undertaken, trusts might achieve monopoly status and bring about the manifold evils foreseen by the reformers.

Less erudite groups, whose collective voice contributed to what is called public opinion, showed the same ambivalence. Although some small businessmen were outspoken in their hostility, others appeared to be indifferent to the trust movement; indeed many must have favored it, because trusts were made up of what at one time had been independent small businesses. Although the owners of some of these may have been bludgeoned into combination, probably most went voluntarily. Such a course would in all probability increase the security of their investment and bring capital gains in the exchange of stock for trust certificates. The labor movement as represented by the A. F. of L., now divorced from the ideological considerations so important to the Knights of Labor, apparently felt that it might share in economies of size in the form of more jobs, better working conditions, and higher wages.

THE SHERMAN ANTITRUST ACT

Despite ambivalent attitudes in many quarters, hardening opposition from the public at large led several states to abolish the trust form of business organization during the eighties. By the end of the decade, in the words of Hans Thorelli—a leading student of antitrust policy—public concern "was serious enough to make immediate federal action . . . a clear desideratum if not an absolute necessity." The fact that opposition to the trusts was not primarily to bigness but to certain practices subversive of competition pointed to a solution of the problem which would satisfy a wide spectrum of both public and informed opinion. Specifically, this was to use legislative power and traditional, common-law remedies to suppress monopolistic practices, without attempting to interfere with the process of combination as long as it was not undertaken in such a way as to constitute a monopoly practice itself. Natural evolution and human measures of reform would then be harmonized; the trend toward bigness would presumably continue on its course, but under the terms of competition protected by law, and the public would presumably have its fair share of the economies of combination proclaimed by the combiners.

Under this approach to the problem trustee arrangements were particularly vulnerable because they would be interpreted easily as conspiracies to achieve monopoly. By 1885 discussion of methods for the control of combinations had begun on the federal level. The passage of the Interstate Commerce Act in 1887 stimulated the demand for similar action directed at combinations other than railroads, because most trusts were similarly engaged in interstate trade. Yet the problems were different in the two cases. Since railroads were considered to be natural monopolies there was no question of breaking them up; prescriptions extended merely to certain corporate practices. But in the case of trusts the legality of the very form itself was the issue, as had been made plain by recent state judicial decisions during the eighties.

After much discussion, redrafting, and amendment, Congress in 1890 passed the Sherman Antitrust Act. The heart of the measure was contained in the first two sections:

1. Every contract, combination in the form of trust or otherwise, or conspiracy, in restraint of trade or commerce among the several States or with foreign nations, is hereby declared to be illegal. Every person who shall make any such contract or engage in any such combination or conspiracy, shall be deemed guilty of a misdemeanor.
2. Every person who shall monopolize or attempt to monopolize, or combine or conspire with any other person or persons to monopolize any part of the trade or commerce among the several States, or with foreign nations, shall be deemed guilty of misdemeanor.

Violations could be punished by fine or imprisonment or both. Succeeding sections made it plain that "persons" included corporations and associations, declared it to be "the duty" of United States district attorneys and the attorney general to enforce the measure, and allowed individuals injured by actions prohibited by the act to sue for triple damages in federal courts. The fact that the Sherman Act in no way hindered further combination in business was not surprising in view of all of the circumstances surrounding its adoption. Only the form and the mechanism for concentrating control was changed.

The holding company was introduced to perform the functions formerly exercised by the trust. Previously corporate charters and general incorporation acts had uniformly forbade corporations to hold stock in other firms because such a procedure could lead to evasion of stated capitalization and the formation of monopolies. But the New Jersey Holding Company Act of 1888 permitted the formation of companies for the specific purpose of acquiring and holding securities. Under this arrangement holding companies could control a congeries of competing firms merely by securing slightly more than 50 percent of their voting stock. Furthermore, by "pyramiding," i.e., by setting up a hierarchy of holding companies each of which held a controlling interest in the one below it on the ladder, a small investment at the top could control a huge aggregate of securities down the line.

New Jersey's invitation was eagerly accepted by businessmen bent on combination. As we have seen, Standard Oil executives, after being ordered by an Ohio court to separate Standard of Ohio from the Standard Oil Trust, abandoned the trust form entirely and substituted for it the holding company, Standard of New Jersey. Between 1895 and 1920 combinations chartered in New Jersey accounted for 29.6 percent of the total formed in the nation, and 54.1 percent of combined capitalization.

During the nineties, following what had probably been the intent of Congress, the Supreme Court interpreted the Sherman Act solely as a prohibition of agreements in restraint of trade, and treated as irrelevant the size of companies, the percentage of the market they had acquired, and the extent of any monopoly position they enjoyed. Therefore, in the case of United States *vs.* E. C. Knight Company (1895), the Court held that acquisition of over 90 percent of the nation's sugar refining capacity by the American Sugar Refining Company did not constitute an attempt to monopolize interstate commerce of sugar, and so subject the company to the penalties of the Sherman Act. When in Addystone Pipe and Steel Company *vs.* United States (1899) the court struck down price fixing agreements between six manufacturers of cast iron pipe, its interpretation of the Sherman Act was perfectly clear. So inflexible was the Court in its rulings against such agreements that it refused even to consider whether a given restraint of trade might be "reasonable" and so perhaps justified by common law. Yet at the same time the opinions handed down during the nineties indirectly so stimulated combination that the Sherman Act became known as "the Mother of the trusts."

CONCLUSION

The turn of the century marks the end of an era in American business history. Businessmen, despite the attacks they had sustained, were in perhaps the strongest position they have enjoyed at any time before or since. Business was unquestionably the most prestigious way of life, and its leaders occupied the same relative position as those individuals in Europe who were titled owners of ancestral estates or the holders of high diplomatic and military positions. Business values associated with material success were so normative as to be almost above criticism.

After a period of development reaching back into the colonial period business had reached maturity in its basic institutions and procedures. Beginning in the late eighteenth century commercial specializations originally a part of the general entrepreneurial function had undergone a process of proliferation followed by integration into institutions forming new segments of the business world. Thus retailing had gone through the phase of multiplying specialty shops and reached the fullest stage of development in department stores. Wholesaling had become dominated by the jobbers whose establishments filled whole sections of the nation's major cities. The trade in commodities was carried on by the great exchanges for wheat, cotton, wool, and livestock which operated on a national scale, and the trade in securities came to be centered in the New York Stock Exchange. The speculative tactics of the trading fraternity associated with these exchanges had also been institutionalized as established procedures, to both the advantage and detriment of the economy at large.

The financial functions of the entrepreneur became specialized side by side with the commercial processes. Thus investment and commercial banking became separate functions, although unfortunately they were often carried on together within the same banking institution. Central banking had a brief career in the form of the Second Bank of the United States, but was abandoned when the Second Bank appeared to pose a threat as a money power which outweighed its economic usefulness. The eighteenth-century entrepreneurial functions of marine underwriting and trusteeship developed into the many kinds of insurance companies and trust companies to be found in the nation by the beginning of the twentieth century.

If specialization had been the dominant process through which development took place during the first half of the nineteenth century, combination and integration appeared to be the goal of business after the Civil War. Combination had been inaugurated by the railroads, for whom it was indispensable both for improving service to users and for effectuating new offensive and defensive competitive strategies. Combination also brought forth the new and vastly expanded financeering methods which came to be standard for big business, and forced the rationalization of business management. Finally, railroad combination became the parent of finance capitalism by stimulating the combination of the financial institutions which had achieved their separate identities in the antebellum period. So great was the power generated by this process that at century's end the great investment bankers were widely considered to be the dominant decision makers in the business world.

The coming of the industrial revolution steadily increased the importance of manufacturing as a sector of the business world. Technological progress brought new life to the older consumer industries and made possible the rapid growth of three industrial giants not even in existence before 1850—steel, oil, and electrical equipment. The use of steel wrought vast changes in transportation systems and altered the profile of American cities with high rise buildings. Oil production and refining, the only major industries ever originated and developed in the United States, began a revolution in illumination which reached its culmination with the incandescent lamp. The changes effected by electricity were so manifold that the historian, Henry Adams, characterized the end of the century as the age of the dynamo, in contrast to the age of steam inaugurated by James Watt.

For manufacturing the turn of the century was a threshold to further and even more spectacular development, but for the extractive industries it marked the end of the bonanzas which had so stimulated immigration and westward expansion since the first settlements. The search for cod and furs brought the French to the New World in the late sixteenth century, and tobacco proved to be the economic basis for the expanding English settlements in the Chesapeake region of the seventeenth century. The triangular trade sustained northern merchants and prepared them for the great trading bonanza during the French Revolutionary Wars. Land speculation, which caused spectacular business failures among the unwary, burgeoned in volume during the nineteenth century bringing a mixed harvest of profit and loss, social conflict, and corruption in government. The extent to which the finding of gold, silver, copper, and oil promoted American growth—to say nothing of the exploitation of the great stands of timber and the endless seas of grass on the prairies—is difficult to estimate, but was certainly profound.

Actually the exploitation of natural resources was a much more important element in the growth of American rather than in European business. Developmental transportation enterprises were directed toward it, and heavy industry at the stage of integration became intensely concerned with it. Even commercial banking was linked to exploitation of natural resources through overly ambitious and often unwise attempts to finance land speculation and regional development. The psychological effect of untapped resources waiting to be transformed into wealth was perhaps as important a cause of economic growth as the value of the resources themselves. During the nineteenth century the United States developed a durable and almost continuous boom mentality only temporarily deflated by cyclical panics and depressions. To energetic and aggressive businessmen the prospect of creating material abundance greater than the world had ever seen before posed a categorical imperative for the intensification of their efforts and the expansion of their enterprises.

Yet in the larger context such a response was by no means inevitable, nor can it be explained through any of the analytical methods available to the historian. Other peoples with different values than our own have sat complacently on top of rich resources with little desire to use them as instruments for the improvement of material welfare. Indeed, for these peoples material welfare has been of little importance compared with status and tradition, and in some cases the immersion in mystical, contemplative, otherworldly philosophies. In any cosmic view of the purpose of life itself such a commitment is not necessarily derogatory or inferior. Many societies of this type have achieved a high degree of culture and civilization, and these purposes have been reflected to some degree in the Christian tradition. Yet it is also true that these societies have often been indifferent to human suffering and have made little attempt to provide their less fortunate members with the means of achieving a meaningful and satisfying life.

Considered in the context of world civilizations, then, the underlying causes of American economic growth are as mysterious as immediate causes seem crystal clear. Doubtless natural resources and favorable political, social, and economic institutions have played a part, but these are so closely interwoven with indefinable cultural impulses that it is impossible to isolate any of these factors as independent causes. About all that can be said by way of conclusion is that in the United States business has been a dynamic force promoting change and abundance in a unique culture, and continues to operate with undiminished vitality in a world environment which poses greater challenges than business has ever faced in the past.

Bibliographical Note

I. ECONOMIC GROWTH AND ENTREPRENEURSHIP

The literature of American business history is by now so large that even an extended bibliographical note must be very selective. The books and articles listed below are mentioned because they have contributed in some measure to the text. Further references can be found in Henrietta M. Larson's *Guide to Business History* (Cambridge, Mass., 1948), one of the best annotated bibliographies in American historiography, but now in need of updating.

Works of synthesis in business history have been relatively few. Miriam Beard's *History of the Business Man* (New York, 1938), one of the first of such works to appear, is devoted to an examination of the richest and most famous businessmen from ancient times to the recent present. Sprightly and well-written, the book presents these men as essentially opportunistic and exploitative. A revised edition has been reissued in paperback under the title *A History of Business*, 2 vols. (Ann Arbor, Mich., 1962, 1963). Norman S. B. Gras's *Business and Capitalism: An Introduction to Business History* (New York, 1939) is the first systematic analysis of business history. A very influential book, it traces the development of business through successive stages of capitalism—mercantile, industrial, financial, and national—and devotes considerable attention to the functions and organization of business. Louis M. Hacker, surveying American history from the colonial period to the end of the Civil War in *The Triumph of American Capitalism* (New York, 1940), finds the evolving types of capitalism, particularly mercantile and industrial capitalism, to be major formative forces. Thomas C. Cochran and William Miller skillfully relate business history with social and political history in *The Age of Enter-*

prise: A Social History of Industrial America (New York, 1942). They find that business values exerted a profound effect upon American institutions. Professor Cochran's *The American Business System: A Historical Perspective, 1900–1955* (Cambridge, Mass., 1957) is a more generalized and more objective volume concentrating on the changes taking place within business and the interaction of business and the economy. Cochran's *Basic History of American Business* (Princeton, N.J., 1959) is an excellent capsulated account intended for college students. James B. Walker's *Epic of American Industry* (New York, 1949), and John Chamberlain's *The Enterprising Americans* (New York, 1963), are good, popular treatments, but if only because of limitations of space they devote attention primarily to a small number of leading businesses and businessmen.

The writings on economic growth are now so voluminous that any brief selection from them could scarcely be representative. Articles on specific aspects will be found in the journal devoted to the process, *Economic Development and Cultural Change*, published since 1952 by The Research Center in Economic Development and Cultural Change of the University of Chicago. Perhaps the best known work on the subject, and one which has had an impact on public policy, is: Walt W. Rostow, *Stages of Economic Growth: A Non-Communist Manifesto* (Cambridge, England, 1960). Surveys and anthologies designed for college students of economics are now beginning to come off the presses, and these help focus reading in the field undertaken by nonspecialists. One of the best of the surveys is: Bruce R. Morris, *Problems of American Economic Growth* (New York, 1961). Useful anthologies of representative writings are: David E. Novack and Robert Lekachman, eds., *Development and Society: The Dynamics of Economic Change* (New York, 1964); Barry E. Supple, ed., *The Experience of Economic Growth* (New York, 1963); and Thomas C. Cochran and Thomas B. Brewer, eds., *Views of American Economic Growth*, 2 vols. (New York, 1966). The historical dimensions of the subject are explored in: Bert F. Hoselitz, ed., *Theories of Economic Growth* (Glencoe, Ill., 1960). In an excellent book of great help to readers with little knowledge of quantitative economics, Stuart Bruchey has examined American economic growth in the light of recent economic research: *The Roots of American Economic Growth, 1607–1861: An Essay in Social Causation* (New York, 1965).

Entrepreneurship, like economic growth, has occupied the attention of a considerable number of scholars in economic history, and also has its own journal in which the student can follow the research of specialists: *Explorations in Economic History*, now published at the University of Wisconsin. Hugh G. J. Aitken has brought together a representative selection of articles on entrepreneurial history in: *Explorations in Enterprise* (Cambridge, Mass., 1965). Broadly categorized, the articles deal with approaches to the study of entrepreneurship, social and cultural factors in entrepreneurial behavior, portraits of leading entrepreneurs, and definitions and descriptions of entrepreneurial types. The Harvard University Research Center in Entrepreneurial History has published two volumes of essays on historical aspects of entrepreneurship: *Change and the Entrepreneur* (Cambridge, Mass., 1949); William Miller, ed., *Men in Business: Essays in the History of Entrepreneurship* (Cambridge,

Mass., 1952). Other similar studies can be found in Frederic C. Lane, ed., *Enterprise and Secular Change: Readings in Economic History* (Homewood, Ill., 1953). Articles on the subject appear regularly in all of the economic history journals, but will be found concentrated most heavily in the *Bulletin of the Business History Society* (1926–53), and its successor, *Business History Review*, both published by the Graduate School of Business Administration, Harvard University. In the face of this mass of material it is almost presumptuous to mention particular titles. However, the student will find a simple, useful introduction to entrepreneurship in: Arthur H. Cole, "An Approach to the Study of Entrepreneurship," *Journal of Economic History*, VII (Supplement, 1946). As the unofficial dean of students in entrepreneurship, Mr. Cole has summarized much recent research and added to it his own particular insights in *Business Enterprise in Its Social Setting* (Cambridge, Mass., 1959). Perhaps the most influential theorist of entrepreneurship is Joseph Schumpeter. In his *Theory of Economic Development* (Cambridge, Mass., 1934), he identifies entrepreneurship as the cause of economic development and business cycles. A more recent work producing a comprehensive theory is: David C. McClelland, *The Achieving Society* (Princeton, N.J., 1961). On the basis of psychological tests applied to societies throughout the world and to historical materials as well McClelland has come to the conclusion that "achievement motivation," an important ingredient of entrepreneurship, is the major cause of economic growth. Perhaps the most illuminating treatment of the role played by entrepreneurs in American history is: Thomas C. Cochran, "The Entrepreneur in American Capital Formation," in *Capital Formation and Economic Growth* (Princeton, N.J., 1955). A detailed treatment of entrepreneurship in American banking and in iron and steel manufacture will be found in: Fritz Redlich, *History of American Business Leaders*, 2 vols. (Ann Arbor, Michigan, 1940–51). Redlich's approach is strongly influenced by the theoretical views of Schumpeter. In addition to the above works, the student, in examining the vast literature of entrepreneurship, will find particularly helpful the work of Cole in the history of entrepreneurship, of Leland H. Jenks in role stucture, of Cochran in role and sanctions, and of William Miller in statistical studies of business backgrounds. Of particular importance in this latter connection are three articles by Miller: "American Historians and the Business Elite," *Journal of Economic History*, 9 (1949), 184–208; "The Recruitment of the Business Elite," *Quarterly Journal of Economics*, 64 (1950), 242–53; and "The Business Elite in Business Bureaucracies," *Men in Business*, 286–305. An interesting analysis of attitudes common in modern entrepreneurs is contained in: G. Herberton Evans, Jr., "Business Entrepreneurs, Their Major Functions and Related Tenets," *Journal of Economic History*, 19 (1959), 250–71.

II. COLONIAL PLANTERS AND MERCHANTS

Colonial businessmen have received a great deal of attention from historians. Important works on intellectual backgrounds are: Philip W. Buck, *The Politics of Mercantilism* (New York, 1942); E. A. J. Johnson, *American Economic Thought in the Seventeenth Century* (New York, 1932); R. H. Tawney, *Religion and the Rise of Capitalism*, 2d ed. (New York, 1926); Joseph Dorfman, *The Economic Mind in American Civilization*, 2 vols.

(New York, 1946); Louis B. Wright, *The First Gentlemen of Virginia: Intellectual Qualities of the Early Ruling Class* (San Marino, Calif., 1940). The traditional, almost medieval viewpoints of early colonial businessmen are ably described by Bernard Bailyn in *The New England Merchants in the Seventeenth Century* (Cambridge, Mass., 1955).

In connection with the problems facing southern agribusinessmen, by far the best over-all view of plantation enterprise is contained in the monumental work of scholarship by Lewis C. Gray, *History of Agriculture in the Southern United States to 1860*, 2 vols. (Washington, D.C., 1933). Avery O. Craven, *Soil Exhaustion as a Factor in the Agricultural History of Virginia and Maryland* (Urbana, Ill., 1925), is the standard work on the subject. All aspects of the tobacco economy of the Chesapeake are ably treated by Arthur P. Middleton in *Tobacco Coast: A Maritime History of Chesapeake Bay in the Colonial Era* (Newport News, Va., 1953). In two very important articles Aubrey C. Land describes the manifold entrepreneurial activities of the merchant-planter hierarchy and analyzes the wealth and property holdings of the various classes concerned: "Economic Base and Social Structure: The Northern Chesapeake in the 18th Century," *Journal of Economic History*, 25 (1965), 639–54; "Economic Behavior in a Planting Society: The Eighteenth-Century Chesapeake," *Journal of Southern History*, 33 (1967), 469–86. Jackson T. Main, working with tax and probate records, has reconstructed a picture of the economic conditions of planters and merchants throughout the colonies in his original and useful volume: *The Social Structure of Revolutionary America* (Princeton, N.J., 1965). Useful descriptions of plantation routine can be found in: Edwin M. Betts, ed., *Thomas Jefferson's Farm Book* (Princeton, N.J., 1953); Richard B. Davis, *William Fitzhugh and His Chesapeake World, 1676–1701* (Chapel Hill, N.C., 1963).

The transition from the yeoman farmer economy to the plantation system has been ably described by Thomas J. Wertenbaker in *Patrician and Plebian in Virginia* and in *The Planters of Colonial Virginia*. Both volumes have been reprinted in *The Shaping of Colonial Virginia* (New York, 1958). Wertenbaker's *The Old South: The Founding of American Civilization* (New York, 1942), gives a good account of the land-grabbing of the eighteenth-century planters. There is no study of the eighteenth-century rice plantation but material dealing with it will be found in Gray's *History of Agriculture in the Southern United States*.

The marketing of tobacco has been examined in detail. In this connection see: John S. Bassett, "Relations between the Virginia Planter and the London Merchant," *American Historical Association Report for 1901* (1902), I, 551–75; Samuel M. Rosenblatt, "Merchant-Planter Relations in the Tobacco Consignment Trade: A Study of John Norton and Sons, 1768–1775," *William and Mary Quarterly*, 3d ser., no. 19 (1962), 383–400; Robert P. Thomson, "The Tobacco Export of the Upper James River Naval District, 1773–1775," *ibid.*, 18 (1961), 393–407; Jacob M. Price, "The Economic Growth of the Chesapeake and the European Market, 1697–1775," *Journal of Economic History*, 24 (1964), 496–512; Emory G. Evans, "Planter Indebtedness and the Coming of the Revolution in Virginia," *William and Mary Quarterly*, 3d ser., no. 19 (1962), 511–33; James H. Soltow, "Scottish Traders in Virginia, 1750–1755," *Economic History Review*, 12 (1959), 81–97.

Biographical studies provide some insights into the working of the plantation economy. Nathaniel C. Hale, *Virginia Venturer: William Claiborne, 1600–1677* (Richmond, Va., 1951), and Richard B. Davis, "Chesapeake Pattern and Pole Star: William Fitzhugh and His Plantation World, 1676–1701," American Philosophical Society *Proceedings*, 105 (1961), 525–30, give a good picture of the plantation and trade economy of seventeenth-century Virginia. The sketches of William Fitzhugh and the Byrd family contained in Wright's *First Gentlemen of Virginia* show the interconnections of trade and agriculture. Louis Morton, *Robert Carter of Nomini Hall* (Williamsburg, Va., 1941), and Douglas S. Freeman, *George Washington*, 7 vols. (New York, 1948–57), contain good descriptions of the business careers of their subjects and trace the late eighteenth-century trend toward diversification in the plantation system. Halsted L. Ritter, in *Washington as a Businessman* (New York, 1931), notes the careful, painstaking manner in which Washington carried on his multifarious business activities, and also the small financial return from his enterprises. David J. Mays's excellent biography, *Edmund Pendleton, 1721–1803*, 2 vols. (Cambridge, Mass., 1952), contains the best treatment of the decline of the tobacco economy in the late eighteenth century and the trend toward diversification in the plantation system.

Freeman's *Washington* is also particularly helpful in its description of the land speculation carried on by planters. This theme is also treated in: Leonidas Dodson, *Alexander Spotswood, Governor of Colonial Virginia, 1710–1722* (Philadelphia, 1932); Aubrey C. Land, *The Dulanys of Maryland* (Baltimore, 1955); James T. Flexner, *Mohawk Baronet: Sir William Johnson of New York* (New York, 1959). The standard surveys of land speculation in the colonial period are: Clarence W. Alvord, *The Mississippi Valley in British Politics*, 2 vols. (Cleveland, 1917); and Thomas P. Abernethy, *Western Lands and the American Revolution*, 2d printing (New York, 1959). Edith M. Fox, *Land Speculation in the Mohawk Country* (Ithaca, N.Y., 1949) is an interesting case study.

Shaw Livermore, in *Early American Land Companies: Their Influence on Corporate Development* (New York, 1939), briefly traces the history of the colonial companies and analyzes their financial structure. Treatments of individual companies vary in value. One of the best is: Julian P. Boyd, "Connecticut's Experiment in Expansion: The Susquehanna Company 1755–1803," *The Journal of Economic and Business History*, 4 (1932), 38–69. Alfred P. James, *The Ohio Company: Its Inner History* (Philadelphia, 1959), is closely detailed. As with the description of plantation economy, much excellent material can be found in biographies. See particularly: Albert T. Volwiler, *George Croghan and the Westward Movement, 1741–1782* (Cleveland, 1926); Sewell E. Slick, *William Trent and the West* (Harrisburg, Pa., 1947); and John R. Alden, *John Stuart and the Southern Colonial Frontier* (Ann Arbor, 1944).

Evarts B. Greene, *The Revolutionary Generation* (New York, 1943) contains an excellent survey of urban merchants' activities. Useful accounts will also be found in the works of Carl Bridenbaugh: *Cities in the Wilderness: The*

First Century of Urban Life in America, 1625–1742, 2d ed. (New York, 1955); and *Cities in Revolt: Urban Life in America, 1743–1766* (New York, 1955).

The detailed studies available of merchants in particular localities are generally of good quality. Perhaps the best is: Virginia D. Harrington, *The New York Merchant on the Eve of the Revolution* (New York, 1935). Other merchant studies are: Leila Sellers, *Charleston Business on the Eve of the American Revolution* (Chapel Hill, N.C., 1934); Frederick B. Tolles, *Meeting House and Counting House: The Quaker Merchants of Colonial Philadelphia, 1682–1763* (Chapel Hill, N.C., 1948); Bernard Bailyn, *The New England Merchants in the Seventeenth Century* (Cambridge, Mass., 1955); Arthur L. Jensen, *The Maritime Commerce of Colonial Philadelphia* (Madison, Wis., 1963); Robert A. East, *Business Enterprise in the American Revolutionary Era* (New York, 1938); Bernard Mason, "Entrepreneurial Activity in New York during the American Revolution," *Business History Review*, 40 (1966), 190–213; Peter J. Coleman, "The Entrepreneurial Spirit in Rhode Island History," *ibid.*, 37 (1963), 319–45. Clear accounts of back-country merchants can be found in: Margaret E. Martin, *Merchants and Trade of the Connecticut River Valley, 1750–1800* (Northampton, Mass., 1938); Glenn Weaver, *Jonathan Trumbull: Connecticut's Merchant Magistrate, 1710–1785* (Hartford, Conn., 1956).

Equally important for an understanding of colonial mercantile practices are several other excellent business biographies. William T. Baxter, *The House of Hancock: Business in Boston, 1724–1795* (Cambridge, Mass., 1945), is particularly good in its description of Hancock's career as a military contractor. Three studies trace in detail the changing interests and diversification of enterprise carried on by successive generations in family businesses: James B. Hedges, *The Browns of Providence: Colonial Years* (Cambridge, Mass., 1952); Kenneth W. Porter, *The Jacksons and the Lees: Two Generations of Massachusetts Merchants, 1765–1844* (Cambridge, Mass., 1937); Philip L. White, *The Beekmans of New York in Politics and Commerce* (New York, 1956). Along with Bernard Bailyn, Byron Fairchild traces the early growth of mercantile activity in his *Messrs. William Pepperrell: Merchants at Piscataqua* (Ithaca, N.Y., 1954). See also Lawrence H. Leder and Vincent P. Carosso, "Robert Livingston (1654–1728): Businessman of Colonial New York," *Business History Review*, 30 (1956), 18–46.

For surveys of foreign trade patterns see: Richard Pares, *Yankees and Creoles: The Trade Between North America and the West Indies before the American Revolution* (Cambridge, Mass., 1956); Harold C. Bell, "The West Indies Trade before the Revolution," *American Historical Review*, 22 (1916–17), 272–87. The role of east coast ports as distributing points for imports is discussed by Curtis P. Nettels in "The Economic Relations of Boston, Philadelphia, and New York, 1680–1715," *The Journal of Economic and Business History*, 3 (1929–31), 185–215. G. M. Waller, in *Samuel Vetch, Colonial Enterpriser* (Chapel Hill, N.C., 1960), shows the extent to which some merchants violated the laws of trade. John R. Spears, *The American Slave Trade* (New York, 1900) is inadequate but about all that is available on the subject.

Oliver M. Dickerson describes the "customs racketeering" that antagonized merchants in *The Navigation Acts and the American Revolution* (Philadelphia, 1951). Dickerson argues that the Navigation Acts were of positive benefit to the colonies. This opinion is challenged by Lawrence A. Harper in several publications: *The English Navigation Laws* (New York, 1939); "The Effect of the Navigation Acts on the Thirteen Colonies," in Richard B. Morris, ed., *The Era of the American Revolution* (New York, 1939); "Mercantilism and the American Revolution," *Canadian Historical Review*, 23 (1942), 1–15. Curtis Nettels also holds that the Acts were in some ways disadvantageous to colonial development: "British Mercantilism and the Economic Development of the Thirteen Colonies," *Journal of Economic History*, 12 (1952), 105–14. The political activities of merchants from 1763 to 1776 are discussed in detail by Arthur M. Schlesinger in *The Colonial Merchants and the American Revolution* (New York, 1918). The co-operation of merchants during the Revolutionary War and their speculative activities are dealt with in East's *Business Enterprise in the American Revolutionary Era* and in Clarence L. Ver Steeg, *Robert Morris: Revolutionary Financier* (Philadelphia, 1954). The clearest description of the activities of the merchants as suppliers of the Revolutionary armies will be found in the excellent volume by E. James Ferguson, *The Power of the Purse: A History of American Public Finance, 1776–1790* (Chapel Hill, N.C., 1961).

Material bearing directly on the personalities, values, and outlooks of colonial businessmen is scanty. However, Mark Van Doren's edition of *Samuel Sewall's Diary* (New York, 1927), presents a vivid picture of the personal life and characteristics of a Massachusetts merchant of the early eighteenth century. The published works, and particularly the secret diaries of William Byrd II, do the same for a planter of this period.

There are a number of important articles dealing with specialized aspects of merchant activities. Arthur H. Cole discusses the slow pace of business in "The Tempo of Mercantile Life in Colonial America," *Business History Review*, 33 (1959), 277–98. Accounting methods are described in: William T. Baxter, "Accounting in Colonial America," in Ananias C. Littleton, ed., *Studies in the History of Accounting* (Homewood, Ill., 1956); Albert F. Voke, "Accounting Methods of Colonial Merchants in Virginia," *Journal of Accountancy*, 41 (1926), 1–11. Success and failure factors are discussed by East in "The Business Entrepreneur in a Changing Colonial Economy," *The Tasks of Economic History*, 6 (1946), 16–27; and more specifically by Stuart Bruchey in "Success and Failure Factors: American Merchants in Foreign Trade in the Eighteenth and Early Nineteenth Centuries," *Business History Review*, 32 (1958), 272–92. The "Protestant Ethic" is dealt with perceptively by A. Whitney Griswold in "Three Puritans on Prosperity," *New England Quarterly*, 7 (1934), 475–93; and by Louis B. Wright: "Franklin's Legacy to the Gilded Age," *Virginia Quarterly Review*, 22 (1946), 268–79.

The following group of articles are concerned with economic growth in early America: Gordon C. Bjork, "The Weaning of the American Economy: Independence, Market Changes, and Economic Development," *Journal of Economic History*, 24 (1964), 541–60; Jacob M. Price, "The Economic Growth of the Chesapeake and the European Market, 1697–1775," *ibid.*, 496–

511; George R. Taylor, "American Economic Growth before 1840: An Exploratory Essay," *ibid.*, 427–44.

III. COMMERCE AND COMMERCIAL INSTITUTIONS

The treatment of American commerce as an aspect of business history necessitates a different organization of material than found in histories of commerce and much greater emphasis on commercial and financial institutions. The following volumes are representative of a much larger literature in the somewhat disparate areas covered by the chapters dealing with commercial businesses.

Good general treatments of trade and commercial life will be found in: Curtis Nettels, *The Emergence of a National Economy, 1775–1815* (New York, 1962); and in: George R. Taylor, *The Transportation Revolution, 1815–1860* (New York, 1951). Nettels has material on the relatively neglected period of the 1780s; Taylor has probably the best treatment in print of the development of internal commerce. Both volumes have extensive bibliographies, but neither has a great deal to say about commercial institutions. Two volumes in the *History of American Life* series, Evarts B. Greene, *The Revolutionary Generation* (New York, 1943); and John A. Krout and Dixon R. Fox, *The Completion of Independence* (New York, 1944), deal with the life of business in the context of social history. The standard history of American commerce is: Emory Johnson et al., *History of Domestic and Foreign Commerce of the United States*, 2 vols. (Washington, D.C., 1915). The authors have little material on commercial institutions. Roy A. Foulke, *The Sinews of American Commerce* (New York, 1941), contains much material on credit and financial institutions. The book is not well written, and the treatment is often shallow. Douglass C. North, *The Economic Growth of the United States, 1790–1860* (Englewood Cliffs, N.J., 1961), is an important and original book describing the role played by commerce in the early growth of the United States. By the use of voluminous statistical material North finds that cotton exports and the greatly expanded overseas trade from 1793 to 1807 were particularly important in promoting that growth. Edward C. Kirkland, *Men, Cities, and Transportation: A Study in New England History, 1820–1900*, 2 vols. (Cambridge, Mass., 1948), while devoted mostly to railroads, has good material on water-borne commerce.

Anglo-American trade and British financing of that trade are dealt with in the following volumes: Leland H. Jenks, *The Migration of British Capital to 1875* (New York, 1927); Ralph W. Hidy, *The House of Baring in American Trade and Finance: English Merchant Bankers at Work, 1763–1861* (Cambridge, Mass., 1949); Norman S. Buck, *The Development of the Organization of Anglo-American Trade, 1800–1850* (New Haven, 1925); F. Lee Benns, *The American Struggle for the British West Indies Carrying Trade, 1815–1830* (Bloomington, Ind., 1923). The Hidy volume gives the clearest picture of commercial techniques. The opening of new trades after the Revolution is described in: Clarence L. Ver Steeg, "Financing and Outfitting the First United States Ship to China," *Pacific Historical Review*, 22 (1953), 1–12; John H. Coatsworth, "American Trade with European Colonies in the Caribbean and South America, 1790–1812," *William and Mary Quarterly*, 3d ser., 24 (1967),

242–66. Declining profits from overseas trade are dealt with in: John H. Reinoehl, "Post-Embargo Trade and Merchant Prosperity: Experience of the Crowninshield Family, 1809–1812," *Mississippi Valley Historical Review*, 42 (1955–56), 229–49. The development of trade with China is given good coverage in: Tyler Dennett, *Americans in Eastern Asia* (New York, 1941); and Foster R. Dulles, *The Old China Trade* (Boston, 1930).

Some but by no means all of the various aspects of marketing have received attention from historians. George B. Hotchkiss, *Milestones of Marketing* (New York, 1938), is a general historical survey of marketing in Britain and the United States. A good specialized study concerned with several entrepreneurs who figure in this book is: Alvin J. Silk and Louis W. Stern, "The Changing Nature of Marketing: A Study of Selected Business Leaders, 1852–1958," *Business History Review*, 37 (1963), 182–99. Fred M. Jones, *Middlemen in the Domestic Trade of the United States* (Urbana, Ill., 1937) contains material on the jobbing trades. Frontier and back-country merchants are treated in: Lewis E. Atherton, *The Pioneer Merchant in Mid-America* (Columbia, Mo., 1939); Sister Marietta Jennings, *A Pioneer Merchant of St. Louis, 1810–1820: The Business Career of Christian Wilt* (New York, 1939). Cotton factorage has been exhaustively examined by Harold D. Woodman in his excellent book, *King Cotton and His Retainers: Financing and Marketing the Cotton Crop of the South, 1800–1925* (Lexington, Ky., 1968).

The activities of drummers, and to a lesser extent of peddlers, are examined in the following articles: Lewis E. Atherton, "Predecessors of the Commercial Drummer in the Old South," *Bulletin of the Business History Society*, 21 (1947), 17–24; Lee M. Friedman, "The Drummer in Early American Merchandise Distribution," *ibid.*, 39–44; Stanley C. Hollander, "Nineteenth-Century Anti-Drummer Legislation in the United States," *Business History Review*, 38 (1964), 479–501. J. R. Dolan, *The Yankee Peddlers of Early America* (New York, 1964) is a more detailed account, but it has an antiquarian flavor, contains much irrelevant material, and adds little to our knowledge of the business activities of peddlers.

There is a surprisingly large historical literature devoted to the integration of retail marketing. The effect of such integration in promoting specialization of function is examined in: Melvin T. Copeland, "The Managerial Factor in Marketing," *Facts and Factors in Economic History* (Cambridge, Mass., 1932), 596–619. The transition from drygoods store to department store is described by Harry E. Resseguie in: "Alexander Turney Stewart and the Development of the Department Store, 1823–1876," *Business History Review*, 39 (1965), 301–23. Tom Mahoney, in *The Great Merchants* (New York, 1955), describes the founding and development of eighteen of the nation's larger retail stores. John William Ferry, *A History of the Department Store* (New York, 1960), adds material on the formation of department stores in Great Britain and contains a good analysis of the department store as an institution. Only three stores have received a detailed treatment which renders the volumes of interest to business historians—Wanamaker's, Macy's, and Marshall Field's. Material on Wanamaker's will be found in: Herbert Adams Gibbons, *John Wanamaker*, 2 vols. (New York, 1926); Joseph H. Appel, *The Business Biography of John Wanamaker, Founder and Builder* (New York, 1930). Ralph

M. Hower, *History of Macy's of New York, 1858–1919* (Cambridge, Mass., 1943), is much superior to the foregoing volumes. Written on the basis of extensive research in the company's files, the book gives a detailed and searching analysis of every aspect of the store's development and operation. It also contains a luminous chapter on the development of retailing in the mid-nineteenth century. Robert W. Twyman, *History of Marshall Field and Company, 1852–1906* (Philadelphia 1954), also written from research in company files, gives an equally good analysis of Field's operations, but is somewhat narrower in scope.

Other aspects of integration in retailing have received much less attention than department stores. Godfrey M. Lebhar, *Chain Stores in America, 1859–1962* (New York, 1963), is a brief popular account of little value to business historians. The same can be said for the only treatment of five and ten cent stores which rises above the level of short company brochures: John K. Winkler, *Five and Ten: The Fabulous Life of F. W. Woolworth* (New York, 1940). By contrast, perhaps the best historical study of a retail enterprise has been devoted to a mail order house: Boris Emmet and John E. Jeuck, *Catalogues and Counters: A History of Sears Roebuck and Company* (Chicago, 1950). Well-written, exhaustive in scope, and objective, the book differs from the other two major works in the field of retailing—Hower on Macy's and Twyman on Marshall Field's—primarily in the quality of the writing and in the incisive character sketches of entrepreneurial personalities involved in large-scale retailing.

Much material on the development of trade and commercial institutions will be found in city histories. Constance McLaughlin Green, *American Cities in the Growth of the Nation* (New York, 1957), is an excellent general study of sixteen major American cities. Robert G. Albion, *The Rise of New York Port, 1815–1860* (New York, 1939), is a pioneering study of seaport trade and commerce, and still the best in its field. The statistical materials contained in the excellent paper on New York's foreign trade by Robert A. Davison contained in: David T. Gilchrist, ed., *The Growth of the Seaport Cities, 1790–1825* (Charlottesville, Va., 1967), provides an illuminating introduction to Albion's treatment. Albion's *Square Riggers on Schedule* (Princeton, N.J., 1938), a corollary work, describes the development of transoceanic packet service in New York. Samuel E. Morison, *The Maritime History of Massachusetts, 1783–1860* (Boston, 1921), is a historical classic, broad in scope and very well-written, but contains less information of importance to the business historian. James D. Phillips, *Salem and the Indies* (Boston, 1947), describes the world-wide trade of that small seaport early in the nineteenth century. J. Thomas Scharf and Thompson Wescott, *History of Philadelphia, 1609–1884*, 3 vols. (Philadelphia, 1884), deals with the decline of Philadelphia's overseas commerce relative to that of New York. The rise of Baltimore as a commercial center has received more extensive treatment: Clarence P. Gould, "The Economic Causes of the Rise of Baltimore," in *Essays in Colonial History Presented to Charles M. Andrews* (New Haven, 1931); Rhoda M. Dorsey, "Baltimore Foreign Trade [from 1790 to 1825]," in Gilchrist, ed., *The Growth of Seaport Cities;* Hamilton Owens, *Baltimore on the Chesapeake* (New York, 1941); James W. Livingood, *The Philadelphia-Baltimore Trade Rivalry, 1780–1860*

(Harrisburg, Pa., 1947); Frank R. Rutter, *South American Trade of Baltimore* (Baltimore, 1897). The decline of Norfolk coinciding with the rise of Baltimore is well described in: Thomas J. Wertenbaker, *Norfolk, Historic Southern Port* (Durham, N.C., 1931). The failure of Charleston to fulfill its early promise as a commercial center and the economic problems of the Old Southeast brought about by New York financing of the cotton trade are treated in: John G. Van Deusen, *Economic Bases of Disunion in South Carolina* (New York, 1928); Alfred G. Smith, *Economic Readjustment of an Old Cotton State: South Carolina, 1820–1860* (Columbia, S.C., 1958). The burgeoning prosperity of New Orleans is described in a volume similar in treatment to Albion's: Harold Sinclair, *The Port of New Orleans* (New York, 1942). Inland cities have received much less attention. Richard C. Wade, *The Urban Frontier: The Rise of Western Cities, 1790–1830* (Cambridge, Mass., 1959), is a pioneering volume which gives some insight into the development of business and commerce in Pittsburgh, Cincinnati, Lexington, Knoxville, and St. Louis. Pittsburgh itself has received more detailed treatment in: Solon J. Buck and Elizabeth Buck, *The Planting of Civilization in Western Pennsylvania* (Pittsburgh, 1939), and in: Catherine E. Reiser, *Pittsburgh's Commercial Development 1800–1850* (Harrisburg, Pa., 1951). The rise of Chicago is chronicled in masterly fashion by Bessie L. Pierce in her *History of Chicago*, vol. I (New York, 1937).

Business biographies provide much important material for the study of trade and commerce. Kenneth W. Porter, *The Jacksons and the Lees: Two Generations of Massachusetts Merchants, 1765–1844*, 2 vols. (Cambridge, Mass., 1937), illustrates the coming of specialization into the business affairs of early nineteenth-century merchant capitalists, and the diversion of some capital and managerial talent into industry. Stuart W. Bruchey, *Robert Oliver, Merchant of Baltimore, 1783–1819* (Baltimore, 1956), an equally valuable book, provides an excellent account of the participation of American merchants in the syndicate which delivered Spanish silver through the British blockade to Napoleon. John C. Brown, *A Hundred Years of Merchant Banking: A History of Brown Brothers and Company* (New York, 1909), describes the evolution of this famous house from a small mercantile establishment into one of the most important Anglo-American private banks financing our overseas trade. Elva Tooker, *Nathan Trotter, Philadelphia Merchant, 1787–1853* (Cambridge, Mass., 1955), illustrates through an examination of an average merchant this progress from merchandising to banking. Richard Lowitt, *A Merchant Prince of the Nineteenth Century: William E. Dodge* (New York, 1954), describes the early development of the famous Phelps-Dodge Company from a mercantile house to a metals importer. Harry Emerson Wildes, *Lonely Midas: The Story of Stephen Girard* (New York, 1943), although not a business biography, does give some insight into the career of that famous merchant. Kenneth W. Porter, *John Jacob Astor: Business Man*, 2 vols. (Cambridge, Mass., 1931), is excellent from every point of view, and is a vital source of information on the fur trade. Historical treatments of the fur trade are cited in more detail below, (p. 566). Adele Ogden, *The California Sea Otter Trade, 1784–1848* (Berkeley, 1941), throws light on one segment closely connected with the China trade.

IV. BANKING AND OTHER FINANCIAL INSTITUTIONS

The history of American banking during the eighteenth and nineteenth centuries has been given ample and effective general coverage by two men who have made an intensive study of the subject—Fritz Redlich and Bray Hammond. Professor Redlich has been particularly interested in the origin and development of banking institutions and ideas. His *Essays in American Economic History: Eric Bollman and Studies in Banking* (New York, 1944); and *The Moulding of American Banking: Men and Ideas, Parts 1 and 2* (New York, 1947, 1951), are not easy reading, but they give valuable insights into a technical field that few historians care to enter. Mr. Hammond's Pulitzer Prize-winning *Banks and Politics in America from the Revolution to the Civil War* (Princeton, N.J., 1957), combines a rare mixture of great competence with the technical aspects of banking, a felicitous style, and a deep understanding of the part played by banking in American political life. He is something of a revisionist in that he denies that conflicts over banking always ranged the back country against the metropolis. Instead, Hammond demonstrates that such conflicts were usually between rival groups of businessmen intent upon manipulating politics to their advantage. Paul B. Trescott, *Financing American Enterprise: The Story of Commercial Banking* (New York, 1963), contains less technical detail than the above volumes, and covers a longer span of time. More sympathetic toward the shortcomings of antebellum state banks than most historians, Mr. Trescott distinguishes between their monetary policy and financial services.

The work of Redlich and Hammond has superseded all of the older general works. William Graham Sumner's *History of Banking in the United States* (New York, 1896), is marred by a strong hard-money bias, but does contain useful illustrative material. The volume by John Jay Knox, *A History of Banking in the United States* (New York, 1900), merely assembles such facts as were available at the time and makes little attempt at interpretation.

Taking the history of banking chronologically, there are many valuable studies for special periods. On the colonial land banks see: Andrew McFarland Davis, *Currency and Banking in Massachusetts* (New York, 1901); and his edition, *Colonial Currency Reprints* (Boston, 1910–11); Curtis Nettels, *The Money Supply of the American Colonies before 1720* (Madison, Wis., 1934); Theodore Thayer, "The Land Bank System in the American Colonies," *Journal of Economic History*, 13 (1953), 145–59.

William Graham Sumner's biography of Robert Morris, *The Financier and Finances of the American Revolution* (New York, 1892), again exhibits Mr. Sumner's well-known bias. A more valuable work, particularly on the founding of the Bank of North America, is: Clarence L. Ver Steeg, *Robert Morris, Revolutionary Financier* (Philadelphia, 1954). Janet Wilson, "The Bank of North America and Pennsylvania Politics," *Pennsylvania Magazine of History and Biography*, 66 (1942), 3–28, chronicles the rise of agrarian opposition to the Bank. E. James Ferguson, in *The Power of the Purse: A History of American Public Finance* (previously cited), gives the best general treatment of the finances of the late colonial period, the Revolution and the Confederation period, and describes clearly the conflict between the agrarian elements devoted to "currency finance," and the business community united behind Robert Morris and the Bank of North America.

There is a large literature devoted to the origin and development of the corporation. The student would do well to begin a study of the subject by reading the article, "Corporation," by the outstanding authorities A. A. Berle and Gardiner C. Means, in *Encyclopedia of the Social Sciences*, 15 vols. (New York, 1930–35). Charles C. Abbott, *The Rise of the Business Corporation* (Ann Arbor, 1936), is a good survey. The origin and early history of corporations is traced back to the Middle Ages in John P. Davis, *Corporations*, 2 vols. (New York, 1905). Corporations in the colonial and early national periods are thoroughly examined in: Joseph S. Davis, *Essays in the Earlier History of American Corporations*, 2 vols. (Cambridge, Mass., 1917). Edwin M. Dodd, *American Business Corporations Until 1860, with Special Reference to Massachusetts* (Cambridge, Mass., 1954), is devoted primarily to the development of corporation law. Shaw Livermore, *Early American Land Companies: Their Influence on Corporate Development* (New York, 1939), describes the formation and careers of these early speculative enterprises. Guy S. Callender, "Early Transportation and Banking Enterprises of the States in Relation to the Growth of Corporations," *The Quarterly Journal of Economics*, 17 (1902), 111–62, is probably still the best treatment of the subject. Oscar Handlin and Mary F. Handlin, in "Origins of the American Business Corporation," *The Journal of Economic History*, 5 (1945), 1–23, exposes the inadequacy of many easy suppositions about early American corporations, particularly that limited liability automatically accompanied incorporation. These last two articles are available in *The Bobbs-Merrill Reprint Series in History*.

Material on the founding of the First Bank of the United States will be found in the many biographies of Alexander Hamilton, particularly in those by Sumner and by Broadus Mitchell. John T. Holdsworth, *The First Bank of the United States* (Philadelphia, 1910), is of little value. H. Wayne Morgan, in "The Origins and Establishment of the First Bank of the United States," *Business History Review*, 30 (1956), 472–92, notes the precedents for the BUS in the Bank of North American and the Bank of England. Most of the information on the Bank's operations has been presented by James O. Wettereau in "New Light on the First Bank of the United States," *Pennsylvania Magazine of History and Biography*, 61 (1937), 263–85; and "The Branches of the First Bank of the United States," *The Tasks of Economic History*, 2 (1942), 66–101. Material on the Bank will also be found in Raymond Walter's *Albert Gallatin, Jeffersonian Financier and Diplomat* (New York, 1957), and in his *Alexander James Dallas: Lawyer, Politician, Financier, 1759–1817* (Philadelphia, 1943).

The history of the Second Bank of the United States has been treated in masterly fashion by three writers, all very favorably disposed toward the institution. Ralph C. H. Catterall's *Second Bank of the United States* (Chicago, 1903), is a classic piece of detailed research. Thomas P. Govan's *Nicholas Biddle, Nationalist and Public Banker, 1786–1844* (Chicago, 1959), is not only an excellent biographical study, but gives the clearest account available of Biddle's use of compensatory credit mechanisms. Walter B. Smith's *Economic Aspects of the Second Bank of the United States* (Cambridge, Mass., 1953), gives technical data on the Bank's operations, a good survey of antebellum commercial conditions of the United States, and an excellent critique of the various charges leveled against the Bank. None of these writers, however, appears to sense the potential danger posed by the Bank to American democratic institutions, nor are they quite fair to Jackson's position. Arthur M. Schlesinger, Jr., in *The Age of Jackson* (Boston, 1945) brings a New Deal bias to the support of Jackson, and he distorts the Bank war by viewing it in simplistic terms as a struggle of agrarian debtors and city mechanics, devoted to hard money, against the money power represented by the Bank. Kenneth L. Brown, in "Stephen Girard and the Second Bank of the United States," *Journal of Economic History*, 2 (1942), 125–48, ascribes the important role played by Girard in establishing the Bank to desire to find a market for the government securities he had accumulated during the War of 1812 in his investment banking operations. Leon M. Schur, in "The Second Bank of the United States and the Inflation after the War of 1812," *Journal of Political Economy*, 68 (1960), finds that the Bank was forced into inflationary measures by the combined pressure of the state banks and the Treasury. Peter Temin, *The Jacksonian Economy* (New York, 1969), is a sharply revisionist study. Temin ascribes the inflation, crisis, and deflation cycle from 1836 through the early forties not to Jacksonian policies but to an abnormal inflow of specie into the United States. He also feels that the role of the Second Bank of the United States as a central bank was relatively ineffective.

There is a fairly large literature on state and regional banking. The best summary is: Davis R. Dewey, *State Banking Before the Civil War* (Washington, D.C., 1910), published by The National Monetary Commission. The Commission has also published studies of the New York Safety Fund, the Sub-Treasury System, and the Origin of the National Bank System. These volumes reflect assumptions as to good and bad banking which have been somewhat outdated since the 1930s, but the books are still valuable. Callender, in "The Early Transportation and Banking Enterprises of the States in Relation to the Growth of Corporations," (as cited above), describes how states fostered banking as "joint enterprise." Redlich has an excellent article on the origin of free banking in his *Essays*. The intellectual background of the new ideas in banking is discussed in some detail by Dorfman in Vol. II of his *The Economic Mind in American Civilization*, 3 vols. (New York, 1946–49). Harry E. Miller, in *Banking Theories in the United States Before 1860* (Cambridge, Mass., 1927), notes the wide diversity and conflict in ideas about banking. J. Clayburn La Force, in "Gresham's Law and the Suffolk System: A Misapplied Epigram," *Business History Review*, 40 (1966), 149–66, denies that Gresham's Law had any relevance to the operation of the Suffolk System. Sister M. Grace Madeleine, in *Monetary and Banking Theories of Jacksonian Democracy* (Philadelphia, 1943), has a notable chapter on the Sub-Treasury system in which she sheds a good deal of light on the hard money doctrines of the time.

There are a good many histories of individual banks, but they are of uneven quality. Many are centennial volumes written to memorialize the banks in question. Useful works of this type are: Lawrence Lewis, Jr., *History of the Bank of North America* (Philadelphia, 1882); Henry W. Domett. *A History of the Bank of New York* (New York, 1884). Among the modern studies by historians which show more breadth and impartiality are: Allan Nevins, *History of the Bank of New York and Trust Company, 1784–1934* (New York, 1934); Nicholas Wainwright, *History of the Philadelphia National Bank: A Century and a Half of Philadelphia Banking, 1803–1953* (Philadelphia, 1953). More details of actual banking operations are contained in: N. S. B. Gras, *The Massachusetts-First National Bank of Boston, 1784–1934* (Cambridge, Mass., 1937); and in the work by F. Cyril James, *The Growth of Chicago Banks*, 2 vols. (New York, 1938). Beatrice G. Reubens, "Burr, Hamilton, and the Manhattan Company," *Political Science Quarterly*, 72 (1957), 578–607, is an excellent study of the political maneuvers by which the bank was brought into existence and the innovations in policy which it inaugurated. Studies of special purpose banks are: Frank P. Bennett, *The Story of Mutual Savings Banks* (Boston, 1924); Emerson W. Keyes, *A History of Savings Banks in the United States, 1816–1874* (New York, 1876); Irene Neu, "Moussier and the Property Banks of Louisiana," *Business History Review*, 35 (1961), 550–58.

Material on the operations of banks is relatively thin, but recently historians have devoted more attention to the subject. An excellent study of the operations of the early banks can be found in: Herman E. Krooss, "Financial Institutions," in David T. Gilchrist, ed., *The Growth of Seaport Cities, 1790–1815* (Charlottesville, Va., 1967). Fritz Redlich, "Bank Administration, 1780–1914," *Journal of Economic History*, 12 (1952), 438–53, is an equally good survey of the evolution of banking practices, and very central to the interests of business historians. J. Van Fenstermaker, "The Statistics of Commercial Banking, 1782–1818," *Journal of Economic History*, 25 (1965), 400–414, provides statistics which show, among other things, that bank checks were in use earlier than has been thought. Henry R. Stevens, "Bank Enterprises in a Western Town, 1815–1822." *Business History Review*, 29 (1955), 139–55, describes the community relations and functions of bankers in Cincinnati during this period. A unique and fascinating volume which gives a detailed and intimate account of how the banking business was carried on during the antebellum period is: J. S. Gibbons, *The Banks of New York: Their Dealers, the Clearing House, and the Panic of 1857* (New York, 1858).

On commercial banking after 1860, savings banks, and investment banking there is nothing that can remotely compare with Redlich's *Moulding of American Banking*, Part II, in scope, detail, understanding of technical procedures, and ripeness of judgment. Background material on the growth of financial institutions during their period is contained in: George W. Edwards, *The Evolution of Finance Capitalism* (New York, 1938). Quantitative factors are provided in the monumental volume by Milton Friedman and Anna Jacobson Schwartz, *A Monetary History of the United States, 1867–1960* (Princeton, N.J., 1963). Robert P. Sharkey. "Commercial Banking," in David T. Gilchrist and W. David Lewis, eds., *Economic Change in the Civil War Era* (Greenville, Del., 1965), brings into sharp focus the manner in which the National Banking System discriminated against the South and the West. Biographies of J. P. Morgan vary widely in their judgments of the man and the type of material they present. The volume by Morgan's son-in-law, Herbert L. Satterlee, *J. Pierpont Morgan: An Intimate Portrait* (New York, 1939), gives perhaps the clearest description of the business events in Morgan's life, but, as an official biography, is either vague or uncritically laudatory when dealing with Morgan's motivation. Lewis Corey, *The House of Morgan: A Social Biography of the Masters of Money* (New York, 1930), errs in the other direction. A portrait etched in acid, it keeps alive the Populist view of the great bankers as robber barons. Frederick Lewis Allen, *The Great Pierpont Morgan* (New York, 1949), a highly readable volume, steers a middle course between Satterlee and Corey. Henrietta M. Larson, *Jay Cooke, Private Banker* (Cambridge, Mass., 1936), is a model business biography.

The specialized financial institutions making their appeerence after the War of 1812, particularly the New York Stock Market, are described in: Margaret G. Myers, *The New York Money Market*, vol. 1 (New York, 1931). Robert Sobel, in *The Big Board: A History of the New York Stock Market* (New York, 1965), gives more information on the development of the Exchange, but devotes primary attention to the careers of the major speculators. Done in what is supposed to be a popular style, the book contains many errors of fact. Useful material on the evolution of the operations of the Exchange, written by a president of the institution, will be found in: Francis L. Eames, *The New York Stock Exchange* (New York, 1894). William W. Fowler, in *Ten Years in Wall Street* (New York, 1870), gives good, clear accounts of speculative methods. More volumes similar to the latter two can be found in the useful reprint series edited by Robert Sobel, *The Money Markets* (Greenwood Press), James E. Boyle, *Cotton and the New Orleans Cotton Exchange* (Garden City, N.Y., 1934), is mostly devoted to accounts of speculative activity, but gives some idea of the operations of the market.

Material on other financial institutions will be found in Foulke, *The Sinews of Commerce* (as previously cited), and in Albert O. Greef, *The Commercial Paper House in the United States* (Cambridge, Mass., 1938). A poorly written but useful series of articles describing the uses of checks and bills of exchange is: Joseph J. Klein, "Development of Mercantile Instruments of Credit in the United States," *Journal of Accountancy*, 12 (1911); 13 (1912). The new methods of marketing commercial paper and mortgages from the West during the latter nineteenth century are described in the excellent article by Lance E. Davis, "The Investment Market, 1870–1914: The Evolution of a National Market," *Journal of Economic History*, 25 (1965), 355–400. Atherton's *Southern Country Store* contains a good discussion of factorage. Harold D. Woodman, in "The Decline of Cotton Factorage after the Civil War," *American Historical Review*, 71 (1966), 1219–37, describes the eclipse of the factorage function brought about by the rise of centralized, urban cotton markets. Fred M. Jones's *Middlemen in the Domestic Trade of the United States 1800–1960* (Urbana, Ill., 1937), describes early brokerage activities.

The best account of the beginnings of marine insurance in America is contained in: N. S. B. Gras, *Casebook in American Business History* (New York, 1939). The volume by Lester W. Zartman and William H. Price, *Property Insurance* (New Haven, Conn., 1921), contains a short article on the origins of marine insurance by Solomon Huebner. The history of fire insurance has had little exploration. Almost the only comprehensive treatment available is an article by F. C. Oviatt in the same volume. John Bainbridge, *Biography of an Idea: The Story of Mutual Fire and Casualty Insurance* (New York, 1952), is a popular treatment which shows marked preference for mutual rather than proprietary companies. Several of the larger fire insurance companies have subsidized the writing of company histories, but these are usually designed for commemorative purposes rather than historical analysis, and so are of limited value. Exceptions to the rule, and books which give a unique insight into the early insurance business are: Marquis James, *Biography of a Business, 1792–1942: The Insurance Company of North America* (Indianapolis, 1942); Nicholas B. Wainwright, *A Philadelphia Story: The Philadelphia Contributorship for the Insurance of Houses from Loss by Fire* (Philadelphia, 1952).

In contrast to the scarcity of materials dealing with fire and marine insurance, the student will find voluminous coverage of the history of life insurance. Shepard B. Clough, *A Century of American Life Insurance: A History of the Mutual Life Insurance Company of New York, 1843–1943* (New York, 1946), is not only an excellent company history, but provides perhaps the best introduction to the subject. Another good company history, which also gives insight into the beginning of the trust business is: Gerald T. White, *History of the Massachusetts Hospital Life Insurance Company* (Cambridge, Mass., 1955). John Gudmundsen, *The Great Provider: The Dramatic Story of Life Insurance in America* (South Norwalk, Conn., 1959), is a pictorial history containing a useful glossary of life insurance terms. H. F. Williamson and O. A. Smalley, *Northwestern Mutual Life: A Century of Trusteeship* (Evanston, Ill., 1957), replete with detail and statistical analysis, provides a model for the writing of insurance company history. R. Carlyle Buley, *The Equitable Life Assurance Society of the United States* (New York, 1959), is a hastily written centennial volume of much less value than Williamson and Smalley's book, but it does give some insight into the remarkable career and innovations of Henry B. Hyde. Terence O'Donnel (compiler), *History of Life Insurance in Its Formative Years* (Chicago, 1936), is a voluminous compendium. Charles K. Knight, *The History of Life Insurance in the United States to 1870* (Philadelphia, 1920), is pedestrian, but valuable. One of the best books in the field, more inclusive in its coverage than the title would indicate, is: J. Owen Stalson, *Marketing Life Insurance: Its History in America* (Cambridge, Mass., 1942). Tontine policies and the use of life insurance for capital accumulation rather than family protection are discussed in: Burton J. Hendrick, *The Story of Life Insurance* (New York, 1907); Douglas North, "Capital Accumulation in Life Insurance between the Civil War and the Investigation of 1905," in *Men in Business*, as previously cited; and "Life Insurance and Investment Banking at the Time of The Armstrong Investigation, 1905–1906," *Journal of Economic History*, 14 (1954), 209–28. Morton Keller gives an excellent description and analysis of the operations of the large New York companies during this period in *The Life Insurance Enterprise: A Study of the Limits of Corporate Power* (Cambridge, Mass., 1963), David McCahan, *Investment of Life Insurance Funds* (Philadelphia, 1953), describes the marked changes of life insurance company assets and reserves from 1850 to 1900. The rise and changing functions of trust companies are discussed in: James G. Smith, *The Development of Trust Companies in the United States* (New York, 1927). White's *History of the Massachusetts Hospital Life Insurance Company* is valuable also in this regard. Lotteries have been given inclusive treatment in: John S. Ezell, *Fortune's Merry Wheel: The Lottery in America* (Cambridge, Mass., 1960).

V. TRANSPORTATION

The two general histories of transportation in America are: Caroline E. MacGill et al., *History of Transportation in the United States before 1860* (New York, 1917); John L. Ringwalt, *Development of Transportation Systems in the United States* (Philadelphia, 1888). Both contain a great deal of general information, but lack organization and the type of specific information useful to the business historian. The Ringwalt volume is valuable for its reflection of transportation problems as they were envisaged before 1890. D. Philip Locklin, *Economics of Transportation*, 5th ed. (Homewood, Ill., 1960), is one of the best of several volumes dealing with the subject and contains a luminous discussion of railroad economics. Seymour Dunbar, *A History of Travel in America*, 4 vols. (Indianapolis, 1915), is mainly descriptive and anecdotal. Some of the most helpful works in transportation history are regional studies. Outstanding among these are: Edward C. Kirkland, *Men, Cities, and Transportation: A Study in New England History, 1820–1900*, 2 vols. (Cambridge, Mass., 1948); Wheaton J. Lane, *From Indian Trail to Iron Horse: Travel and Transportation in New Jersey, 1620–1860* (Princeton, N.J., 1939); Oscar O. Winther, *The Old Oregon Country: A History of Frontier Trade, Transportation, and Travel* (Bloomington, Ind., 1950). Perhaps the best of several older studies is: Ulrich B. Phillips, *A History of Transportation in the Eastern Cotton Belt to 1860* (New York, 1908). Charles H. Ambler, *A History of Transportation in the Ohio Valley* (Glendale, Calif., 1932), combines a colorful, descriptive narrative with comprehensive historical treatment. William F. Gephart, *Transportation and Industrial Development in the Middle West* (New York, 1909), is thin and outdated. All of these studies are valuable as background for the business historian, but with the exception of the Kirkland and Lane volumes contain little on the formation, operation, financing, and management of business units. Curtis Nettels's volume in *The Economic History of the United States* series, *The Emergence of a National Economy, 1775–1815* (as cited), has a good chapter on business development generally but relatively little on transportation. The chapters on transportation in George Rogers Taylor's volume in the series, *The Transportation Revolution, 1815–1860* (as cited), are excellent, and contain more on the business aspect of the subject than can be found elsewhere in a single volume.

Very little has been published on road improvements and turnpikes. The best over-all study is by Joseph A. Durrenberger, *Turnpikes: A Study of the Toll Road Movement in the Middle Atlantic States and in Maryland* (Valdosta, Ga., 1931). Durrenberger deals at some length with the chartering of companies and construction of roads, but has little to say about the financing and almost nothing about the management of the turnpike companies. Frederic J. Wood, *The Turnpikes of New England and Evolution of the Same Through Virginia and Maryland* (Boston, 1919), is primarily antiquarian in interest. New light on public policy and turnpikes will be found in: Robert F. Hunter, "The Turnpike Movement in Virginia," *Virginia Magazine of History and*

Biography, 69 (1961) 278–89. Hunter's "Turnpike Construction in Ante-bellum Virginia," *Technology and Culture*, 4 (1963), 177–200, is an illuminating treatment of an almost entirely neglected subject. In order to appreciate the early nineteenth-century view of the need for turnpikes and transportation generally, the student should read Albert Gallatin's famous *Report of the Secretary of the Treasury on the Subject of Public Roads and Canals* (Philadelphia, 1808). Oliver W. Holmes, "Levi Pease: The Father of New England Stage-Coaching," *Journal of Economic and Business History*, 3 (1930–31), 241–63, is an interesting and apparently unique study of early coaching enterprise. Pease was apparently the first entrepreneur to combine many small stage lines into a transportation system.

The best general treatment of canals is: Alvin F. Harlow, *Old Towpaths* (New York, 1926). The volume contains not only detailed accounts of the building of the canals, but also discussions of canal operations, financing, and the canal versus the railroad controversy. Good historical background for American canal building will be found in: Pierre S. R. Payne, *The Canal Builders: The Story of Canal Engineers Through the Ages* (New York, 1959). Information on the construction of canals, as well as turnpikes, railroads, and railroad rolling stock, will be found in: Richard S. Kirby et al., *Engineering in History* (New York, 1956). A well-researched study describing the origin of American civil engineering in canal construction is: Daniel H. Calhoun, *The American Civil Engineers: Origins and Conflict* (Cambridge, Mass., 1960). The very important subject of public aid to canal construction is covered meticulously and exhaustively by Carter Goodrich in *Government Promotion of American Canals and Railroads, 1800–1890* (New York, 1960). Professor Goodrich, together with his former students H. Jerome Cranmer, Julius Rubin, and Harvey H. Segal, have greatly increased our knowledge of the various public policies behind canal building and the developmental effect of canals in the volume, *Canals and American Economic Development* (New York, 1961). Julius Rubin analyzes the spirited debates between canal and railroad advocates in *Canals or Railroads? Imitation and Innovation in the Response to the Erie Canal in Philadelphia, Baltimore, and Boston* (Philadelphia, 1961). An illuminating study of the developmental effect of the Erie Canal upon New York state is: Nathan Miller, *The Enterprise of a Free People: Aspects of Economic Development in New York State during the Canal Period, 1792–1838* (Ithaca, N.Y., 1962). Harry N. Scheiber, in "The Rate-Making Power of the State in the Canal Era: A Case Study," *Political Science Quarterly*, 77 (1962), 397–413, shows how Ohio manipulated the rates on the state canals in order to help domestic producers of agricultural goods at the expense of outsiders. Among the studies of individual canals one of the most comprehensive is: Christopher Roberts, *The Middlesex Canal, 1793–1860* (Cambridge, Mass., 1938). Walter S. Sanderlin, *The Great National Project: A History of the Chesapeake and Ohio Canal* (Baltimore, 1946), is excellent on the closely entwined themes of finance and politics. Ralph D. Gray, *The National Waterway: A History of the Chesapeake and Delaware Canal* (Urbana, Ill., 1967), is a well-balanced account stressing the great cost of the waterway, difficulties in construction and finance, and the ultimate unprofitability of the enterprise. The best study of an individual canal is: Ronald E. Shaw, *Erie Water*

West: A History of the Erie Canal, 1792–1854 (Lexington, Ky., 1966). Although giving adequate coverage to the building of the canal and to politics, the volume contains a detailed section on operations without parallel in the literature. Also good is the study by Wayland F. Dunaway, *History of the James River and Kanawha Company* (New York, 1922). Chester L. Jones, *The Economic History of the Anthracite-Tidewater Canals* (Philadelphia, 1908), is a good comparative study of a group of unique regional canals. A detailed history of New York canals will be found in: Noble E. Whitford, *History of the Canal System of the State of New York: Supplement to the Annual Report of the State Engineer and Surveyor of the State of New York, 1905,* 2 vols. (Albany, N.Y., 1906). A similar study for Pennsylvania canals is: T. B. Klein, *The Canals of Pennsylvania and the System of Internal Improvements* (Harrisburg, Pa., 1901). James W. Putnam, *The Illinois and Michigan Canal: A Study in Economic History* (Chicago, 1918), is inferior to the other studies of individual canals cited. Valuable as many of the above works are, there is still no independent treatment of canal companies as businesses. Material of value to the business historian is scattered widely throughout these volumes.

The ocean shipping business is given inclusive coverage in: John G. B. Hutchins, *The American Maritime Industries and Public Policy, 1789–1914* (Cambridge, Mass., 1941). John H. Morrison, *History of American Steam Navigation* (reprint, New York, 1958), is devoted mostly to the technical aspects of ship construction. Other material on ocean shipping will be found in the works by Samuel E. Morison and Robert G. Albion already cited. The beginning of steamboating on eastern waters is ably discussed in: Wheaton J. Lane, *From Indian Trail to Iron Horse* (as cited); Kirkland, *Men, Cities, and Transportation* (as cited); and in: James T. Flexner, *Steamboats Come True: American Inventors in Action* (New York, 1944). The monopolistic practices of the business and the cut-throat competition which characterized it are treated by Wheaton Lane in the excellent biography, *Commodore Vanderbilt: An Epic of the Steam Age* (New York, 1942). The quite different character of western steamboating is revealed in an equally capable volume by Louis C. Hunter, *Steamboats on Western Waters* (1949). Pertinent material will often be found in biographies. Thomas A. Boyd, *Poor John Fitch* (New York, 1935), covers the career of the eccentric who invented the steamboat. The clearest and fullest account of the Livingston-Fulton partnership is by George Dangerfield in his prize-winning *Chancellor Robert R. Livingston of New York, 1746–1813* (New York, 1960). Further details will be found in: Cadwallader D. Colden, *Life of Robert Fulton* (New York, 1817). Dorothy Gregg, "John Stevens, General Entrepreneur," in William Miller, ed., *Men in Business* (New York, 1952), is an excellent study of an early transportation tycoon.

Pioneering transportation enterprises of the West are given good comprehensive treatment by Oscar O. Winther in: *The Transportation Frontier: Trans-Mississippi West, 1865–1890* (New York, 1964). Winther's *Express and Stagecoach Days in California* (Stanford, Calif., 1936) is a valuable regional study and has a good account of the development of the express business. Winther's *The Old Oregon Country* (Bloomington, Ind., 1950), contains a section on transportation. The romance of the Santa Fe Trail has given the route a prominence in historical literature out of proportion to its economic importance. The standard treatment is: R. L. Duffus, *The Santa Fe Trail* (New York, 1931), and a good shorter account can be found in volume II of Hiram M. Chittenden's *The American Fur Trade of the Far West*, 2 vols. (New York, 1902). Henry P. Walker, *The Wagonmasters: High Plains Freighting from the Earliest Days of the Santa Fe Trail to 1880* (Norman, Okla., 1966), is a detailed study of the organization and financing of the freighting business. It also describes the traffic and the conditions of the trails, and identifies the major freighting entrepreneurs. The unhappy career of the famous freighting firm of Russell, Majors, and Waddell is traced in the excellent volume by Raymond W. and Mary L. Settle, *Empire on Wheels* (Stanford, Calif., 1949). Ralph Moody, *Stagecoach West* (New York, 1967), is a comprehensive history of stagecoaching in the West comparable in scope to Walker's study of the freighting business. Roscoe P. and Margaret B. Conkling chronicle the career of an outstanding stagecoach company in *The Butterfield Overland Mail, 1857–1869* (Glendale, Calif., 1947). J. V. Frederick, in *Ben Holladay, Stagecoach King* (Glendale, Calif., 1940), provides a biography of probably the most famous of the coaching entrepreneurs. Edward Hungerford's *Wells Fargo: Advancing the American Frontier* (New York, 1949), is a slight, popularized volume, but it is the only book devoted exclusively to a very important express business. William E. Lass, *A History of Steamboating on the Upper Missouri River* (Lincoln, Neb., 1962), is an excellent volume dealing with a neglected area—water transportation in the West. The volume contains much material on operations, financing, and entrepreneurship of value to business historians.

The best general history of American railroads is the short, but comprehensive volume by John F. Stover, *American Railroads* (Chicago, 1961). Stewart H. Holbrook, *The Story of American Railroads* (New York, 1947), is popular and anecdotal, but valuable. Alfred D. Chandler's introductory and explanatory material contained in his anthology, *The Railroads: The Nation's First Big Business* (New York, 1965) give excellent, brief coverage to many aspects of the business operations of the railroads. The important regional studies are: Robert E. Riegel, *The Story of Western Railroads* (New York, 1926); Edward C. Kirkland, *Men, Cities and Transportation* (as cited); Jules I. Bogen, *The Anthracite Railroads* (New York, 1927); John F. Stover, *The Railroads of the South, 1865–1900: A Study in Finance and Control* (Chapel Hill, N.C., 1955). Kirkland's volume is brightly written and detailed. Stover emphasizes the role of northern capital in controlling the southern roads. Two studies of railroads on the state level are: Wheaton J. Lane, as cited, for New Jersey; Cecil K. Brown, *A State Movement in Railroad Development: The Story of North Carolina's First Effort to Establish an East and West Trunk Line Railroad* (Chapel Hill, N.C., 1928). Books on individual railroads usually offer little of interest to the serious student. An outstanding exception to the general rule is the excellent volume by Richard C. Overton, *Burlington Route: A History of the Burlington Lines* (New York, 1965). Material of interest to the business historian will also be found in: Milton Reizenstein, *The Economic History of the Baltimore and Ohio Railroad* (Baltimore, 1897); and in Stuart Daggett, *Chapters on the History of the Southern Pacific Railroad* (New York, 1922). Arthur M. Johnson and Barry Supple, *Boston Capitalists and Western Railroads* (Cambridge, Mass., 1967), is an interesting study, focused on the investor, showing how a large portion of Boston's mercantile capital was drawn first into local railroads and then farther afield into midwestern railroads. The authors establish the fact that during the 1840s Boston was the most important national center for railroad finance. In a closely related study Stephen Salsbury in *The State, the Investor, and the Railroad: The Boston and Albany, 1825–1867* (Cambridge, Mass., 1967), gives a well-rounded analysis of the financing and operations of the nation's first large railroad.

The effect of railroad in stimulating economic development has been noted by Leland H. Jenks in an influential article, "Railroads as an Economic Force in American Development," *Journal of Economic History*, 4 (1944), 1–20. Robert W. Fogel, *Railroads and American Economic Growth: Essays in Econometric History* (Baltimore, 1964), is a challenging, revisionist study, questioning the generally accepted proposition, exemplified by the work of Jenks, that railroads were an "accelerator-multiplier" stimulating the growth of the West. Addressing himself to the quantitative aspect of the question, Fogel attempts to demonstrate by statistics, models, and assumptions where necessary that improved water and wagon transportation could have provided a substitute for railroads, and that the requirements of the railroad for iron and other materials were not great enough to significantly stimulate economic growth. Albert Fishlow, in *American Railroads and the Transformation of the Ante-Bellum Economy* (Cambridge, Mass., 1965), reaches different conclusions. He finds that the antebellum railroads, by lowering the cost of transportation, produced great resource savings in the form of higher commodity prices and land values. They also widened markets, promoted specialization, and enabled new land to be brought into cultivation. Because of their large capital-output ratio they hastened capital formation—partly by stimulating capital imports—and hastened the growth of ancillary industries. Contesting a point made by Jenks, however, Fishlow maintains that the pioneering function of antebellum roads has been overemphasized. They were seldom built ahead of settlement and were usually profitable from the start.

The prominence of Philadelphia, Boston, and New York successively as centers for railroad finance during the thirties, forties, and fifties respectively, is noted by Alfred D. Chandler, Jr., in "Patterns of American Railroad Finance, 1830–1850," *Business History Review*, 28 (1954), 248–63. Two articles deal with the beginning of foreign investment in American railroads: Ralph W. Hidy and Muriel E. Hidy, "Anglo-American Merchant Bankers and the Railroads of the Old Northwest, 1848–1860," *ibid.*, 34 (1960), 150–69; A. W. Currie, "British Attitudes toward Investment in North American Railroads," *ibid.*, 194–215.

The subject of government aid to railroads has been receiving increasing attention. The basic study of this type, and a volume indispensable to a business historian, is Goodrich's *Government Promotion of Canals and Railroads* (as cited). Material on government aid will also be found in: Frederick A. Cleveland and Fred W. Powell, *Railroad Promotion and Capitalization in the United States* (New York, 1909). A more specific study is: Harry H. Pierce, *Railroads of New York: A Study of Government Aid, 1826–1875* (Cambridge, Mass., 1953). Studies of public finance in various states often contain valuable material on government aid. Among the more useful of these volumes are:

Oscar Handlin and Mary F. Handlin, *Commonwealth: A Study of the Role of Government in the American Economy, Massachusetts, 1774–1861* (New York, 1947); Louis Hartz, *Economic Policy and Democratic Thought: Pennsylvania 1776–1860* (Cambridge, Mass., 1948); Milton S. Heath, *Constructive Liberalism: The Role of the State in Economic Development in Georgia to 1860* (Cambridge, Mass., 1954). Two excellent studies give accounts of the acquisition and administration of specific railroad land grants: Paul W. Gates, *The Illinois Central Railroad and Its Colonization Work* (Cambridge, Mass., 1934); Richard C. Overton, *Burlington West: A Colonization History of the Burlington Railroad* (Cambridge, Mass., 1941). Less satisfactory is: William S. Greever, *Arid Domain: The Santa Fe Railroad and Its Western Land Grant* (Stanford, Calif., 1954). Details of the Northern Pacific settlement program can be found in: Harold F. Peterson, "Some Colonization Projects of the Northern Pacific Railroad," *Minnesota History*, 10 (1929), 127–45. Material on the colonization and land policies of the Great Northern will be found in: Stewart H. Holbrook, *James J. Hill: A Great Life in Brief* (New York, 1955). Writings by Robert S. Henry, Chester McA. Destler, Robert E. Riegel and others on the still unresolved controversy over how much land the railroads actually received from the public authorities are conveniently reprinted in: Vernon Carstensen, ed., *The Public Lands: Studies in the History of the Public Domain* (Madison, Wis., 1963).

Railroad finance is dealt with most thoroughly in the admirable volume by William Z. Ripley, *Railroads: Finance and Organization* (New York, 1915). Cleveland and Powell, in *Railroad Promotion and Capitalization*, (as cited), treat the subject in somewhat shorter compass. A re-examination of construction company finance is contained in: Robert W. Fogel, *The Union Pacific Railroad: A Case in Premature Enterprise* (Baltimore, 1960). Fogel points out that the profiteering by the Credit Mobilier was necessary as an inducement for investing in a very risky enterprise. British investments after the Civil War are discussed by Jenks in "Britain and American Railroad Development," *Journal of Economic History,* 11 (1951), 375–89. For descriptions of reorganization after bankruptcy see: Stuart Daggett, *Railroad Reorganization* (Boston, 1908); E. G. Campbell, *The Reorganization of the American Railroad System, 1893–1900* (New York, 1938). Julius Grodinsky, *Railroad Consolidation, Its Economics and Controlling Principles* (New York, 1930), is the standard work on the subject.

The economic problems faced by railroads because of heavy fixed investment and overhead costs have been discussed at some length. Dionysius Lardner's *Railway Economy* (London, 1850), is surprisingly sophisticated for such an early treatment. Harry T. Newcomb, *Railway Economics* (Philadelphia, 1898), gives the views of a practical railroad man. Two volumes designed to defend the railroads from critics by explaining their predicament are: Arthur T. Hadley, *Railroad Transportation: Its History and Its Laws* (New York, 1885); Charles Francis Adams, *Railroads: Their Origin and Problems* (New York, 1888). A tremendous amount of information on the financial affairs of railroads is contained in S. F. Van Oss, *American Railroads as Investments* (New York, 1893). The populist criticism of railroad policies is eloquently expressed by William Larrabee in *The Railroad Question* (Chicago, 1893).

George R. Taylor and Irene D. Neu discuss the standardization of railroad equipment and gauge in *The American Railroad Network, 1861–1890* (Cambridge, Mass., 1956). Frank H. Spearman, *The Strategy of Great Railroads* (New York, 1904), describes railroad competitive practices.

Railroad management has been given considerable attention by Alfred D. Chandler, Jr. In "Railroads: Pioneers in Modern Corporate Management," *Business History Review*, 39 (1965), 16–41, he points out that as the first of the really big businesses in America they were forced to innovate because of their size and the complexity of their operations, and demonstrates the point by examining the early experiences of the B. and O. and the Pennsylvania Railroads. A summary of his findings will be found in Chapter I of his study of management development in the twentieth century: *Strategy and Structure: Chapters in the History of the Industrial Enterprise* (Cambridge, Mass., 1962). In his works on Henry Varnum Poor, the noted editor of *The American Railroad Journal*, Chandler analyzes the recommendations on management problems of a perceptive innovator in the field: "Henry Varnum Poor, Philosopher of Management," in William Miller, ed., *Men in Business* (Cambridge, Mass., 1952); *Henry Varnum Poor: Business Editor, Analyst and Reformer* (Cambridge, Mass., 1956). Leland H. Jenks has reprinted, with comments, a detailed analysis of the organization of the Pennsylvania Railroad appearing in *The Railroad Gazette*, December, 1882: "Early History of a Railway Organization," *Business History Review*, 35 (1961), 153–80; "Multiple-Level Organization of a Great Railroad," *ibid.*, 336–43. Valuable descriptions of railroad operations by professional railroad men familiar with practices in use about the turn of the century and shortly thereafter are: Ernest R. Dewsnup, *Railway Organization and Working* (Chicago, 1906); Logan G. McPherson, *The Working of the Railroads* (1907); Ray Morris, *Railroad Administration* (New York, 1920). The most detailed and comprehensive volume of this type is: Lewis H. Haney, *The Business of Railway Transportation,* (New York, 1924).

The problems of ratemaking have received detailed treatment in most volumes dealing with railroad management and procedures. Perhaps the clearest exposition will be found in: Walter C. Noyes, *American Railroad Rates* (Boston, 1906). Details on pooling will be found in: D. T. Gilchrist, "Albert Fink and the Pooling System," *Business History Review*, 34 (1960), 24–49; Julius Grodinsky, *The Iowa Pool: A Study in Railroad Competition, 1870–1884* (Chicago, 1950). Hadley and Adams, in the volumes cited above, also discuss pooling. A standard discussion of railroad legislation during the nineteenth century is: Henry S. Haines, *Restrictive Railway Legislation* (New York, 1906). Gabriel Kolko, in *Railroads and Regulation, 1877–1916* (Chicago, 1965), presents a persuasive but overdrawn argument that the railroads themselves were the major force working for the passage of restrictive legislation. A good study on the state level is: Lee Benson, *Merchants, Farmers & Railroads: Railroad Legislation and New York Politics, 1850–1887* (Cambridge, Mass., 1955).

Although general studies devote some attention to railroad technology, there is relatively little material of a scholarly nature on this subject—a surprising omission considering the great success of American railroad men in this field. Robert E. Carlson, in "British Railroads and Engineers and the Beginnings of

American Railroad Development," *Business History Review*, 34 (1960), 137–49, describes the attempts of early American railroad entrepreneurs to get information, techniques, and railroad equipment from England. Malcolm C. Clark, "Birth of an Enterprise: Baldwin Locomotive, 1831–1842," *Pennsylvania Magazine of History and Biography*, 90 (1966), 423–44, chronicles the very successful beginnings of the nation's leading locomotive works. William H. Brown, *The History of the First Locomotives in America* (New York, 1871), is poorly organized and often anecdotal in nature, but it contains much useful information on the design and construction not only of locomotives but of roadbeds and cars as well. August Mencken, *The Railroad Passenger Car* (Baltimore, 1957), containing many sketches and designs, gives excellent coverage to the subject.

Objective, collective biographical material on railroad leaders will be found in the works of John Moody: *The Railroad Builders* (New Haven, Conn., 1919); *The Masters of Capital* (New Haven, Conn., 1919). Matthew Josephson, *The Robber Barons: The Great American Capitalists, 1861–1901* (New York, 1934), and Gustavus Myers, *History of the Great American Fortunes,* 3 vols. (Chicago, 1907–10), contain biased and sometimes hostile accounts. Many biographies of individual railroad leaders are similarly infused with bias. Oscar Lewis, *The Big Four: The Story of Huntington, Stanford, Hopkins, and Crocker* (New York, 1938), while well-written and informative, is an acidulous portrait. Lewis Corey, *The House of Morgan* (New York, 1930), is similar in these respects to the work by Lewis. On the other hand, official biographies, even when well done, are uncritical and often ignore or extenuate questionable aspects of the subject's life. With this qualification, a very good biography of this type is: George Kennan, *E. H. Harriman*, 2 vols. (Boston, 1922). Julius Grodinsky, in *Jay Gould: His Business Career, 1867–1892* (Philadelphia, 1957), in an attempt to bring objectivity to bear on a totally discredited figure actually overcompensates in Gould's behalf. Objectivity is reached in James B. Hedges's *Henry Villard and the Railways of the Northwest* (New Haven, 1930), but at the expense of robbing Villard of all his verve and color. Two biographies that successfully combine objectivity with an interesting narrative containing much material of interest to the business historian are: Henrietta M. Larson, *Jay Cooke, Private Banker* (as previously cited); Wheaton J. Lane, *Commodore Vanderbilt: An Epic of the Steam Age* (as previously cited). Edward C. Kirkland, *Charles Francis Adams, Jr., 1835–1915: The Patrician at Bay* (Cambridge, Mass., 1965), is a perceptive, well-written account of the famous railroad reformer who became a rather unsuccessful railroad leader. Thomas C. Cochran, *Railroad Leaders, 1845–1890: The Business Mind in Action* (Cambridge, Mass., 1953), is a quite different type of book than the biographies listed above, and very valuable for the business historian. By analyzing the correspondence of 61 railroad leaders, Professor Cochran has shed much light on their motivations, values, and their conceptions of their roles as businessmen. Richard C. Overton, "Charles Elliot Perkins," *Business History Review*, 31 (1957), 292–310, is a particularly able sketch illustrating the values and intellectual orientation of an important railroad leader of the late nineteenth century.

VI. THE USES OF LAND AND SEA

There is no comprehensive treatment in print of the extractive industries in America, although some phases are touched upon by histories of American manufacturing. Short treatments will be found in two volumes of *The Economic History of the United States* series: Curtis P. Nettels, *The Emergence of a National Economy, 1775–1815* (as previously cited); and George Rogers Taylor, *The Transportation Revolution, 1815–1860* (as previously cited).

In the broadest sense the fur trade was the first "extractive industry" in America. It has received detailed and wide ranging treatment from historians, probably because of its colorful, adventurous nature and close connection with imperial and diplomatic policy. A recent comprehensive account, which brings together widely scattered materials and constantly emphasizes the political aspects of the trade is: Paul C. Phillips, *The Fur Trade*, 2 vols. (Norman, Okla., 1961). Harold A. Innis, *The Fur Trade in Canada* (New Haven, Conn., 1930), is a valuable contribution to economic history because of its perceptive analysis of the impact of the fur trade upon Canadian development. Two volumes give particularly important descriptions of the business methods of the Canadian trade centered on the Great Lakes: Gordon C. Davidson, *The North West Company* (Berkeley, Calif., 1918); and Wayne E. Stevens, *The Northwest Fur Trade, 1763–1800* (Urbana, Ill., 1928). The legislation, mostly futile, by which the American state and federal governments attempted to regulate the fur trade in order to give a square deal to the Indians is analyzed by Francis P. Prucha in *American Indian Policy in the Formative Years: The Indian Trade and the Intercourse Acts, 1790–1834* (Cambridge, Mass., 1962). The specific manner in which the federal government attempted to achieve better relations with the Indians by entering the fur trade directly is described in: Edgar B. Wesley, "The Government Factory System Among the Indians, 1795–1822," *Journal of Economic and Business History*, 4 (1932), 487–511; Ora B. Peake, *A History of the United States Indian Factory System, 1795–1822* (Denver, 1954). Ida A. Johnson, *The Michigan Fur Trade* (Lansing, Mich., 1919), is a good regional study of the fur trade during this period. The standard work on the far western fur trade is the rambling but very informative work by Hiram M. Chittenden, *The American Fur Trade of the Far West*, 3 vols. (New York, 1902). Details on the beginning of the trade will be found in the biography of a pioneer trapper by Richard E. Oglesby, *Manuel Lisa and the Opening of the Missouri Fur Trade* (Norman, Okla., 1963). The make-up and operations of trapping parties, and the business methods of the trade are described in: Frederick Merk, ed., *Fur Trade and Empire: George Simpson's Journal* (rev. ed., Cambridge, Mass., 1968); Dale L. Morgan, *Jedediah Smith and the Opening of the West* (Indianapolis, Ind., 1953). Much information on the American Fur Company is contained in Kenneth W. Porter's *John Jacob Astor, Businessman*, 2 vols. (Cambridge, Mass., 1931). Further details on the operations of the company will be found in: Grace L. Nute, "The Papers of the American Fur Company," *American Historical Review*, 32 (1927), 519–38.

The historical literature bearing on land speculation is so extensive that only a relatively small number of titles can be mentioned here. Four volumes together give a comprehensive coverage of American land policies: Marshall Harris, *Origin of the Land Tenure System of the United States* (Ames, Iowa, 1953); Benjamin H. Hibbard, *A History of the Public Land Policies* (New York, 1939); Roy M. Robbins, *Our Landed Heritage: The Public Domain, 1776–1936* (Princeton, N.J., 1942); Payson J. Treat, *The National Land System, 1785–1820* (New York, 1910). Roy H. Akagi, in *The Town Proprietors of the New England Colonies* (Philadelphia, 1924), describes the work of the town promoters and planners of colonial New England. Edith M. Fox, in *Land Speculation in the Mohawk Country* (Ithaca, N.Y., 1949), deals with the privileged speculation of the group surrounding the colonial governors of New York. Much good material on land speculation in colonial America will be found in: Thomas J. Wertenbaker, *The Old South: The Founding of American Civilization* (New York, 1942); Leonidas Dodson, *Alexander Spotswood, Governor of Colonial Virginia, 1710–1722* (Philadelphia, 1932); Charles G. Sellers, Jr., "Private Profits and British Colonial Policy: The Speculations of Henry McCulloch," *William and Mary Quarterly*, 3d ser., no. 8 (1951), 535–51. The careers of the great prerevolutionary land companies are treated in: Shaw Livermore, *Early American Land Companies: Their Influence on Corporate Development* (New York, 1939); Clarence W. Alvord, *The Mississippi Valley in British Politics*, 2 vols. (Cleveland, 1917); Thomas P. Abernethy, *Western Lands and the American Revolution*, 2d printing (New York, 1959); Albert T. Volweiller, *George Croghan and the Westward Movement, 1741–1782* (Cleveland, 1926); Sewell E. Slick, *William Trent and the West* (Harrisburg, Pa., 1947); Kenneth P. Bailey, *The Ohio Company of Virginia and the Westward Movement, 1748–1792* (Glendale, Calif., 1939); Alfred P. James, *The Ohio Company: Its Inner History* (Pittsburgh, 1959). Aaron M. Sakolski, *The Great American Land Bubble* (New York, 1932), gives a racy account of land speculation of the 1830s indiscriminately critical of the speculators.

The relationships of land speculation and politics in the early republic are discussed in the two volumes by Merrill Jensen: *The New Nation: A History of the United States During the Confederation* (New York, 1950); and *The Articles of Confederation* (Madison, Wis., 1940). Two biographies give probably the best analysis of land speculation as a business in the early United States: William H. Masterson, *William Blount* (Baton Rouge, La., 1954); Joseph S. Davis, "William Duer, Entrepreneur," in *Essays in the Earlier History of American Corporations*, 2 vols., I (Cambridge, Mass., 1917). Thomas P. Abernethy has been keenly aware of the importance of land speculation in the early period. His *The South in the New Nation* (Baton Rouge, La., 1961), contains an excellent new account of the Yazoo scandal. His *Three Virginia Frontiers* (Baton Rouge, La., 1940), and *From Frontier to Plantation in Tennessee* (Chapel Hill, N.C., 1932), lay heavy emphasis on the theme of land speculation.

Material on the methods of land speculation during the first third of the nineteenth century will be found in Malcolm J. Rohrbough's volume, *The Land Office Business: The Settlement and Administration of the Public Lands, 1789–1837* (New York, 1968). Primarily administrative history, the book nevertheless gives details on the survey and preparation of land for sale, the conduct of auctions, and the frauds and speculative practices accompanying the auctions.

A good description of the frauds perpetrated under the Pre-emption Act as a means of consolidating holdings will be found in: Everett Dick, *The Dixie Frontier* (New York, 1948). Elgin Williams, in *The Animating Pursuits of Speculation: Land Traffic in the Annexation of Texas* (New York, 1949), maintains that the annexation of Texas was primarily the result of land speculation. The prominent holders of Texas paper and the pressures they brought to bear on the federal government to insure assumption of the Texas debt are discussed by Holman Hamilton in "Texas Bonds and Northern Profits: A Study in Compromise, Investment, and Lobby Influence," *Mississippi Valley Historical Review*, 43 (1957), 579–94. However, Eugene C. Barker, in *The Life of Stephen F. Austin, 1793–1836* (Nashville, Tenn., 1925), finds land speculation to be of less importance in the Texas Revolution. Paul W. Gates, in *The Wisconsin Pine Lands of Cornell University* (Ithaca, N.Y., 1943), describes one of the most successful land speculations in American history—the sale of the college's lands acquired under the Morrill Act. Further details will be found in Philip Dorf's biography of Ezra Cornell, *The Builder . . .* (New York, 1952). Gates stresses exploitative aspects in "The Role of the Land Speculator in Western Development," *Pennsylvania Magazine of History and Biography*, 66 (1942), 314–33. Allen and Margaret Bogue, in "Profits and the Frontier Land Speculator," *Journal of Economic History*, 17 (1957), 1-24, find from case studies that speculation in prairie lands from 1840 to 1883 was about as profitable as other enterprises into which money could be invested. By far the best single volume devoted to land speculation in any period of American history is: Robert P. Swierenga, *Profits and Pioneers: Land Speculation on the Iowa Frontier* (Ames, Iowa, 1968). Swierenga identifies many of the principal land speculators and their holdings, explains in detail the business methods of speculation, and finds that speculator profits were considerably higher than most historians have thought. An excellent textbook, giving good background material on speculation is: Ray A. Billington, *Westward Expansion: A History of the American Frontier* (New York, 1949).

The student who studies agriculture as a business is fortunate in having several splendid monographic studies at his disposal. Percy W. Bidwell and John I. Falconer, *History of Agriculture in the Northern United States, 1620–1860* (Washington, D.C., 1925), is good, and Lewis C. Gray, *History of Agriculture in the Southern United States to 1860*, 2 vols. (Washington, D.C., 1933), is one of the major works of American historiography because of its breadth of scope, voluminous detail, and keen analysis. Norman S. B. Gras provides a comparative study in *A History of Agriculture in Europe and America* (New York, 1925). Two excellent volumes in *The Economic History of the United States* series cover agriculture during the nineteenth century: Paul W. Gates, *The Farmer's Age: Agriculture, 1815–1860* (New York, 1960); and Fred A. Shannon, *The Farmer's Last Frontier: Agriculture, 1860–1897* (New York, 1945). Shannon, in his very critical treatment of railroads, banks, and marketing agencies, re-echoes Populist prejudices. Joseph Schafer, in *The Social History of American Agriculture* (New York, 1936), attempts to separate and characterize the major movements in American agriculture.

Two good studies of plantation agriculture during the colonial period are: Philip A. Bruce, *Economic History of Virginia in the Seventeenth Century,* 2 vols. (New York, 1896); Richard Pares, *Merchants and Planters* (Cambridge, England, 1960). Reference should be made also to the works dealing with planters cited in Bibliographical Note II. Lewis C. Gray, "Market Surplus Problems of Colonial Tobacco," *Agricultural History*, 2 (1928), 1–35, supplements the treatment of the subject in Gray's monograph. Emory G. Evans, in "Planter Indebtedness and the Coming of the Revolution in Virginia," *William and Mary Quarterly*, 3d ser., no 19 (1962), 511–33, finds that planters' debts to British merchants were not as important a cause of the Revolution as has been generally thought. The condition of the small farmer in the Old Northwest is discussed by Beverley Bond, Jr., in *Civilization of the Old Northwest* (New York, 1934); and in: R. Carlyle Buley, *The Old Northwest: Pioneer Period*, 2 vols. (Bloomington, Ind., 1950). Paul Gates in two very important publications describes the beginnings of highly capitalized agriculture in the Midwest: "Large Scale Farming in Illinois, 1850–1870," *Agricultural History*, 6 (1932), 14–25; *Frontier Landlords and Pioneer Tenants* (Ithaca, N.Y., 1945). Harold E. Briggs, "Early Bonanza Farming in the Red River Valley of the North," *Agricultural History*, 6 (1932), 26–27, describes the first experiments in large-scale, mechanized wheat farming. An extended, more detailed account is provided by Hiram M. Drache in *The Day of the Bonanza: A History of Bonanza Farming in the Red River Valley of the North* (Fargo, N.D., 1964). More general treatments of prairie farming will be found in: Briggs, *Frontiers of the Northwest: A History of the Upper Missouri Valley*, reprint edition (New York, 1950); Everett Dick, *The Sod House Frontier, 1854–1890* (New York, 1937). Marketing difficulties are described by Henrietta M. Larson in *The Wheat Market and the Farmer in Minnesota, 1858–1900* (New York, 1926). John G. Clark, in *The Grain Trade of the Old Northwest* (Urbana, Ill., 1966), describes the rise and operations of the great grain trading centers of the Old Northwest and the revolution in marketing methods brought about by railroads, grain elevators, and the Chicago Wheat Pit.

The economics of slavery and the slave plantation is the subject of a large literature and for over one hundred years has provoked heated controversy. The very influential views of Ulrich B. Phillips are best presented in *Life and Labor in the Old South* (Boston, 1924) and in *American Negro Slavery* (New York, 1918). Phillips, relying mainly on the records of large plantations, defends slavery against the more extreme moral charges hurled against it but feels that it retarded the economic growth of the South. Kenneth M. Stampp, on the other hand, condemns the institution more strongly than Phillips on moral grounds but finds less reason to believe that it was economically disadvantageous: *The Peculiar Institution, Slavery in the Ante-Bellum South* (New York, 1956). Eugene D. Genovese, in *The Political Economy of Slavery: Studies in the Economy and Society of the Slave South* (New York, 1965), finds that slavery was particularly disadvantageous to the South because it prevented the rise of a consumer market. Because of slavery, Genovese concludes, "The southern economy was moving steadily into an insoluable crisis." Genovese's conclusions have been challenged by Stanley L. Engerman in "The Effects of Slavery upon the Southern Economy," *Explorations in Entrepreneurial History*, 2d ser., no. 4 (1967), 71–97. Using the intensive statistical analysis of the "new" economic historians, Engerman persuasively argues that on the eve of the Civil War, "Slavery was profitable to the planters, viable, and consistent with a growing economy." The controversial aspects of the slave system are presented in a more general fashion by Harold D. Woodman in his book of readings, *Slavery and the Southern Economy* (New York, 1966).

The most informative book on the commercial aspects of the slave system is probably the volume by Frederic Bancroft, *Slave Trading in the Old South* (Baltimore, 1931). Important studies of slavery in individual states are: Charles S. Sydnor, *Slavery in Mississippi* (New York, 1933); Ralph B. Flanders, *Plantation Slavery in Georgia* (Chapel Hill, N.C., 1933); James B. Sellers, *Slavery in Alabama* (University, Ala., 1950). Robert McColley, in *Slavery in Jeffersonian Virginia* (Urbana, Ill., 1964)—a persuasive revisionist study—treats as myths the contentions held by previous historians that slavery was widely criticized on humanitarian grounds before 1815 and might have disappeared but for the revival of the plantation system by cotton culture. McColley finds that despite fluctuations in the rate of returns the plantation system was never in danger of abandonment, simply because it was an established socioeconomic feature of Virginia life. Two biographies of planters cast light on the economics of the slave plantation: Wendell H. Stephenson, *Isaac Franklin: Slave Trader and Planter of the Old South* (Baton Rouge, La., 1938); Charles S. Sydnor, *A Gentleman of the Old Natchez Region: Benjamin L. C. Wailes* (Durham, N.C., 1938).

The business methods and problems of cotton planters are admirably discussed by Stuart Bruchey in the introductory and explanatory material contained in his volume of readings, *Cotton and the Growth of the American Economy, 1790–1860* (New York, 1967). David L. Cohn, *The Life and Times of King Cotton* (New York, 1956), is less detailed and useful. James E. Boyle, in *Cotton and the New Orleans Cotton Exchange* (Garden City, N.Y., 1934), gives a sketchy account of the operations of the market and speculative maneuvers. The cultivation, marketing, and manufacturing of tobacco is excellently covered in two volumes supplementary to each other: Joseph C. Robert, *The Tobacco Kingdom: Plantation, Market, and Factory in Virginia and North Carolina, 1800–1860* (Durham, N.C., 1938); Nannie May Tilley, *The Bright Tobacco Industry, 1860–1929* (Chapel Hill, N.C., 1948). Duncan C. Heyward, *Seed from Madagascar* (Chapel Hill, N.C., 1937), is a mediocre treatment of rice growing. J. Carlyle Sitterson, *Sugar Country: The Cane Sugar Industry in the South, 1753–1950* (Lexington, Ky., 1953), is a comprehensive account of the many aspects of sugar cultivation, processing, marketing, and financing. Cornelius O. Cathey, *Agricultural Developments in North Carolina, 1753–1860* (Chapel Hill, N.C., 1956), and Frank L. Owsley, *Plain Folk of the Old South* (Baton Rouge, La., 1949), describe the life of the small farmer in the South during the antebellum period. Owsley maintains that small farmers were much more important economically in the Old South than previously supposed. This view is sharply challenged by Fabian Linden in "Economic Democracy in the Slave South: A Reappraisal of Some Recent Views," *Journal of Negro History*, 31 (1946), 140–89. Linden compiles statistics to show that ownership of slaves and ownership of the most productive land was highly concentrated. Whether or not slavery was "profitable" has produced much controversy. A convenient summary of the opposing views can be found in: Harold D. Woodman, "The Profitability of Slavery: A Historical Perennial," *Journal of Southern History*, 29 (1963), 303–26. Alfred H. Conrad and John R. Meyer, in what is perhaps the most comprehensive of modern treatments, compile statistics to show that investment in plantation slave labor was probably as remunerative as any other investment which could be found in the South at this time: "The Economics of Slavery in the Ante-Bellum South," *Journal of Political Economy*, 66 (1958), 95–103. On the role of the overseer, see: John S. Bassett, *The Southern Plantation Overseer as Revealed by his Letters* (Northampton, Mass., 1925); William K. Scarborough, *The Overseer: Plantation Management in the Old South* (Baton Rouge, La., 1966).

The lumber industry has received no comprehensive treatment, but several good regional studies and biographies of lumbermen are available. James E. Defebaugh, *History of the Lumber Industry in America*, 2 vols. (Chicago, 1906–7), is the most general work in print. Very detailed, it describes most aspects of the industry, but contains nothing on lumbering in the Far West or in the South. George W. Hotchkiss, *History of the Lumber and Forest Industry of the Northwest* (Chicago, 1898), is similar of character, but is limited to the states of the Great Lakes region. Charles E. Twining, in "Plunder and Progress: The Lumbering Industry in Perspective," *Wisconsin Magazine of History*, 47 (1963–64), 116–24, notes the waste inherent in the industry, but maintains that under nineteenth-century conditions this was inevitable. William G. Rector, *Log Transportation in the Lake States Lumber Industry, 1840–1918* (Glendale, Calif., 1953), is a very important study if only because of the fact that 75 percent of the delivered cost of lumber in the mid-nineteenth century represented charges for transportation. The only adequate study of lumbering in the South is: Nollie Hickman, *Mississippi Harvest: Lumbering in the Long Leaf Pine Belt, 1840–1915* (Oxford, Miss., 1962). Several articles of uneven quality on various aspects of southern lumbering will be found in Vol. 193 of *The Southern Lumberman* (Dec. 15, 1956). John S. Springer, *Forest Life and Forest Trees* (New York, 1851), gives a delightful, first-hand account of lumbering in New England. It is supplemented by Richard G. Wood, *A History of Lumbering in Maine, 1820–1861* (Orono, Me., 1935). The two best regional studies, which together present a good analysis of lumbering as a business are: Agnes M. Larson, *History of the White Pine Industry in Minnesota* (Minneapolis, 1949); Robert F. Fries, *Empire in Pine: The Story of Lumbering in Wisconsin* (Madison, Wis., 1951). The best single work on lumbering is a history of the Weyerhaeuser Timber Company: Ralph W. Hidy, Frank E. Hill, Allan Nevins, *Timber and Men: The Weyerhaeuser Story* (New York, 1963). Much good material will be found in the following biographies: Martin D. Lewis, *Lumberman from Flint: The Michigan Career of Henry H. Crapo, 1835–1869* (Detroit, 1958); Richard N. Current, *Pine Logs and Politics: A Life of Philetus Sawyer, 1816–1900* (Madison, Wis., 1950); Anita S. Goodstein, *Biography of a Businessman: Henry W. Sage, 1814–1897* (Ithaca, N.Y., 1962). Mrs. Goodstein's book is an outstanding business biography.

Several books in the large literature devoted to cattle droving and ranching contain material of interest to business historians. Paul C. Henlein, *Cattle Kingdom in the Ohio Valley, 1783–1860* (Lexington, Ky., 1959), covers a neglected era of cattle raising and gives a good description of droving from the Midwest to East Coast marketing centers. Two good, general works on western cattle raising are: Edward E. Dale, *The Range Cattle Industry* (Norman, Okla., 1930); Ernest S. Osgood, *The Day of the Cattleman* (Minneapolis, 1929). Joseph G. McCoy, *Historic Sketches of the Cattle Trade in the West and Southwest,* reprint edition (Glendale, Calif., 1940), and General James S. Brisbin, *The Beef Bonanza: Or, How to Get Rich on the Plains* . . . (Philadelphia, 1881), are indispensable accounts of cattle raising.

The beginnings of the business are described in: T. J. Cauley, "Early Business Methods in the Texas Cattle Industry," *Journal of Economic and Business History,* 4 (1932), 460–86. A good summary of ranching will also be found in Shannon's *The Farmer's Last Frontier.* Two biographies by J. Evetts Haley are helpful: *Charles Goodnight: Cowman and Plainsman* (Boston, 1936); and *George W. Littlefield, Texan* (Norman, Okla., 1943). Lewis Atherton, in *The Cattle Kings* (1961), provides an excellent picture of the cattleman as businessman. William M. Pearce, *The Matador Land and Cattle Company* (Norman, Okla., 1964); Lester F. Sheffy, *The Francklyn Land and Cattle Company* (Austin, Texas, 1963); Tom Lea, *The King Ranch,* 2 vols. (New York, 1957); and J. Evetts Haley, *The XIT Ranch of Texas* (Chicago, 1929) are studies of business units. The volume by Maurice Frink, W. Turrentine Jackson, and Agnes W. Spring, *When Grass Was King* (Boulder, Colo., 1956), contains a year by year account of the development of the business from 1860 to 1895 by Frink; a study of British interests in the range cattle industry by Jackson; and a biographical sketch of the cattleman John W. Iliff by Spring. The standard work on the meat packing industry is: Rudolph A. Clemen, *The American Livestock and Meat Industry* (New York, 1923). Louis F. Swift, *The Yankee of the Yards: The Biography of Gustavus F. Swift* (Chicago, 1927); and Harper Leech and John C. Carroll, *Armour and His Times* (New York, 1938), give insight into the growth and centralization of meat packing as a national industry. Edward N. Wentworth, *America's Sheep Trails* (Ames, Iowa, 1948), is an encyclopedic work on the sheep industry. Charles W. Towne and Edward N. Wentworth, *Shepherd's Empire* (Norman, Okla., 1945), describes sheep driving in the Far West and Southwest.

Voluminous as is the literature devoted to mining during the nineteenth century, very little of it passes muster as good history, and even less is of help to the business historian. Thomas A. Rickard, *A History of American Mining* (New York, 1932), is full of technical data, but has little on the business of mining. This lack is supplied in part by Theodore J. Hoover, *The Economics of Mining* (Stanford, Calif., 1933). Lead mining in the Midwest is described by Joseph Schafer in *The Wisconsin Lead Region* (Madison, Wis., 1932), and by James E. Wright in *The Galena Lead District: Federal Policy and Practice, 1824–1847* (Madison, Wis., 1966). Fletcher M. Green, in three excellent articles, calls attention to the neglected story of gold mining in southern Appalachia: "Gold Mining: A Forgotten Industry of Ante-Bellum North Carolina," *North Carolina Historical Review,* 14 (1937), 1–40; "Georgia's Forgotten Industry: Gold Mining," *Georgia Historical Quarterly,* 19 (1935), 93–111, 210–28; "Gold Mining in Ante-Bellum Virginia," *Virginia Magazine of History and Biography,* 45 (1937), 228–36, 357–66. William B.

Gates, Jr., *Michigan Copper and Boston Dollars: An Economic History of the Michigan Copper Mining Industry* (Cambridge, Mass., 1951), is not only the best history of Michigan copper mining but one of the best studies of mining as a business available. Angus Murdoch, in *Boom Copper: The Story of the First United States Mining Boom* (New York, 1943), is a more popular, less useful study.

William S. Greever, *The Bonanza West: The Story of the Western Mining Rushes, 1848–1890* (Norman, Okla., 1963), contains a mass of useful information, but is repetitious and rather poorly organized. Glenn C. Quiett, *Pay Dirt: A Panorama of American Gold Rushes* (New York, 1936), is a popular treatment. By far the best historical treatment of Western mining, and one which gives considerable attention to business aspects is: Rodman W. Paul, *Mining Frontiers of the Far West, 1848–1880* (New York, 1963). Octavius T. Howe, *Argonauts of '49* (Cambridge, Mass., 1923), presents a valuable account of the emigrant companies which went by sea from Massachusetts ports to California. Arthur L. Throckmorton, in *Oregon Argonauts: Merchant Adventurers on the Western Frontier* (Portland, Ore., 1961), shows how the gold rush exerted a multiplier effect on agriculture and trade in the Williamette Valley of Oregon. Of the several accounts of the Comstock Lode, perhaps the best is: C. B. Glasscock, *The Big Bonanza: The Story of the Comstock Lode* (Indianapolis, 1931). Charles H. Shinn, *The Story of the Mine* (New York, 1897), is valuable for the insights it provides into the technical, legal, and financial aspects of mining the Comstock Lode. William J. Trimble, *The Mining Advance into the Inland Empire* (Madison, Wis., 1914), describes gold mining in Idaho, Oregon, and Montana. W. Turrentine Jackson, in *Treasure Hill: Portrait of a Silver Mining Camp* (Tucson, Ariz., 1963), presents a detailed account of the multifarious activities in a typical silver boom town, including mining, financing, legal controversies, labor troubles, speculation, and combination. George D. Lyman, *Ralston's Ring* (New York, 1937), gives us a useful account of financial manipulation of mining shares on the San Francisco Exchange. Isaac F. Marcosson, *Anaconda* (New York, 1957), is an adequate company history. Robert G. Cleland's *History of Phelps Dodge, 1834–1950* (New York, 1952), is better and supplements the biography of William E. Dodge by Richard Lowitt (as previously cited). The two books give a unique picture of the transformation of an early nineteenth-century mercantile house into a giant industry. Clark C. Spence, *British Investments and the American Mining Frontier* (Ithaca, N.Y., 1958), is a valuable addition to the scanty material on the financial aspects of mining.

VII. MANUFACTURING

The historical literature devoted to manufacturing is voluminous in some areas and virtually nonexistent in others. Furthermore, relatively few books deal with the business aspects of manufacturing. Some studies stress technological developments, others finance, and some present a record of corporate growth and change, but few give the balanced treatment of these and the other aspects of manufacturing desired by the business historian. A growing number of corporate histories and business biographies—some of excellent quality—help fill out the record, but many lacunae remain.

The standard reference work on the history of manufacturing in the United States is: Victor S. Clark, *History of Manufactures in the United States, 1607–1893*, 2 vols. (New York, 1929). J. Leander Bishop, *A History of American Manufactures from 1608 to 1860*, 2 vols. (Philadelphia, 1864), is still useful, particularly on the iron industry. Three volumes of *The Economic History of the United States* series have sections devoted to manufacturing and detailed bibliographies: Curtis P. Nettels, *The Emergence of a National Economy, 1775–1815* (New York, 1962); George Rogers Taylor, *The Transportation Revolution, 1815–1860* (New York, 1952); Edward C. Kirkland, *Industry Comes of Age: Business, Labor, and Public Policy, 1860–1897* (New York, 1961). While the treatments are uniformly good, they are not necessarily presented within the framework of business history. Textbooks on industrial economics frequently have historical material and often present clear, illustrated descriptions of technological processes not obtainable elsewhere. One of the best of these volumes is: E. B. Alderfer and H. E. Michl, *Economics of American Industry*, 3d ed. (New York, 1957). On technology John W. Oliver, *A History of American Technology* (New York, 1956) is disappointing. Perhaps the best treatment of manufacturing in the many economic history textbooks available is contained in the collaborative work edited by Harold F. Williamson, *The Growth of the American Economy* (Englewood Cliffs, N.J., 1944).

There is no adequate, complete account of colonial manufacturing, but one aspect is well covered by Rolla M. Tryon in *Household Manufactures in the United States, 1640–1860* (Chicago, 1917). The colonial iron industry has received more attention than any other of the period. A general work on the industry to 1890, mostly memorial in nature, contains material on the colonial period: James M. Swank, *History of the Manufacture of Iron in All Ages* (Philadelphia, 1892). An outstanding study extending to business relationships is: Edward N. Hartley, *Ironworks on the Saugus: The Lynn and Braintree Ventures of the Company of Undertakers of the Ironworks of New England* (Norman, Okla., 1957). These ironworks have been restored, and provide an excellent visual supplement to the book. Arthur C. Bining's two books on the colonial iron industry are probably the best works on the subject: *Pennsylvania Iron Manufacture in the Eighteenth Century* (Harrisburg, Pa., 1938); *British Regulation of the Colonial Iron Industry* (Philadelphia, 1933). For histories of individual colonial iron works see: Charles S. Boyer, *Early Forges and Furnaces in New Jersey* (Philadelphia, 1931); Keach Johnson, "The Genesis of the Baltimore Ironworks," *Journal of Southern History*, 19 (1953), 157–80; and "The Baltimore Company Seeks English Markets," *William and Mary Quarterly*, 3d ser., no. 16 (1959), 37–59; Earl Chapin May, *Principio to Wheeling, 1715–1945: A Pageant of Iron and Steel* (New York, 1945). Gerhart Spieler, "Peter Hasenclever, Industrialist," *Proceedings of the New Jersey Historical Society*, 59 (1941), 231–54, provides a valuable account of an iron tycoon of the colonial period. Kathleen Bruce, *Virginia Iron Manufacture in the Slave Era* (New York, 1930), is thin on the colonial period but contains an excellent account of the Tredegar Iron Works, largest in the antebellum South, from the 1840s through the Civil War.

On the colonial naval stores industry see: Justin Williams, "English Mercantilism and Carolina Naval Stores, 1705–1776," *Journal of Southern History*, 1 (1935), 169–85. The only work on the important potash industry is: Theodore J. Kreps, "Vicissitudes of the American Potash Industry," *Journal of Economic and Business History*, 3 (1930–31), 630–66. George L. Heiges, *Henry William Stiegel* (Manheim, Pa., 1937), is a popular account of a noted iron and glass manufacturer of Pennsylvania. Pearce Davis, *The Development of the American Glass Industry* (Cambridge, Mass., 1949), contains material on the colonial period, as do three other histories of particular industries: Charles B. Kuhlmann, *The Development of the Flour Milling Industry in the United States* (Boston, 1916); Lyman H. Weeks, *A History of Paper-Manufacturing in the United States* (New York, 1916); Blanche E. Hazard, *The Organization of the Boot and Shoe Industry in Massachusetts before 1875* (Cambridge, Mass., 1921). The last volume is particularly valuable for its illustrations of the transition from outputting into factory operations. On colonial shipbuilding see: Robert G. Albion, *Forest and Sea Power: The Timber Problem of the Royal Navy, 1652–1682* (Cambridge, Mass., 1926); Bernard Bailyn and Lotte Bailyn, *Massachusetts Shipping, 1697–1714: A Statistical Study* (Cambridge, Mass., 1959). Although covering a later period, John G. B. Hutchins, *The American Maritime Industries and Public Policy, 1789–1914* (Cambridge, Mass., 1941), is valuable because shipbuilding techniques in the early republic were practically identical with those of the earlier era.

The origin of a national policy for sponsoring manufacturing is discussed in a very important article: Samuel Rezneck, "The Rise and Early Development of Industrial Consciousness in the United States, 1760–1830," *Journal of Economic and Business History*, 4 (1932), 784–812. Harold Hutcheson, *Tench Coxe: A Study in Economic Development* (Baltimore, 1938), is valuable in this connection also.

The historical literature of textile manufacturing is extensive. Three general works, all valuable despite their age are: William R. Bagnall, *The Textile Industry of the United States*, Vol. I (Cambridge, Mass., 1893); Samuel Batchelder, *Introduction and Early Progress of the Cotton Manufacture in the United States* (Boston, 1863); Melvin T. Copeland, *The Cotton Manufacturing Industry in the United States* (Cambridge, Mass., 1917). The origins of cotton textile manufacturing are treated in a manner helpful to the business historian in the volume by Caroline F. Ware, *The Early New England Cotton Manufacture* (Boston, 1931). Robert S. Rantoul, in *The First Cotton Mill in America* (Salem, Mass., 1897), describes the building and operation of a pioneering but unsuccessful mill in Beverly, Massachusetts, in 1789. Nathan Appleton, in *Introduction of the Power Loom and the Origin of Lowell* (Lowell, Mass., 1858), gives an excellent account of the solution of initial technological and business problems by the Boston Manufacturing Company and its successor, the Merrimack Company. George S. White, *Memoir of Samuel Slater* (Philadelphia, 1836), is useful. The role of entrepreneurship and kinship groups in the expansion of the industry is discussed by Robert K. Lamb in "The Entrepreneur and the Community," William Miller, ed., *Men in Business: Essays in the History of Entrepreneurship* (New York, 1952). The first large textile enterprise is given admirable treatment by Joseph S. Davis in "The S.U.M.: The

First New Jersey Business Corporation," *Essays in the Earlier History of American Corporations*, Vol. I (Cambridge, Mass., 1917), 349–520. Further details, particularly concerning the role of Alexander Hamilton in forming and managing the company, will be found in volume II of Broadus Mitchell's *Alexander Hamilton* (New York, 1962). Evelyn N. Knowlton, *Pepperell's Progress: History of a Cotton Textile Company, 1814–1945* (Cambridge, Mass., 1948), gives a good picture of the operations of an early cotton mill.

Arthur H. Cole, *The American Wool Manufacture*, 2 vols. (Cambridge, Mass., 1926), is not only the standard treatment of the subject but also an outstanding work of business history as well. Arthur H. Cole and Harold F. Williamson, *The American Carpet Manufacture: A History and an Analysis* (Cambridge, Mass., 1941), is a similar standard treatment of real value. A more detailed study within the corporate context is: John S. Ewing and Nancy P. Morton, *Broadlooms and Businessmen: A History of the Bigelow-Sanford Carpet Company* (Cambridge, Mass., 1955). L. P. Brockett, *The Silk Industry in America* (New York, 1876), has many limitations, both in period covered and in treatment, but it is the only book on the subject available. Two urban histories contain much information on textile manufacturing: Vera Shlakman, *Economic History of a Factory Town: A Study of Chicopee, Massachusetts* (Northampton, Mass., 1935); Constance M. Green, *Holyoke, Massachusetts: A Case History of the Industrial Revolution in America* (New Haven, Conn., 1939). Two excellent histories of textile machinery companies are models for the writing of business history: Thomas R. Navin, *The Whitin Machine Works Since 1831: A Textile Machinery Company in an Industrial Village* (Cambridge, Mass., 1950); George S. Gibb, *The Saco-Lowell Shops: Textile Machine Building in New England, 1813–1949* (Cambridge, Mass., 1950).

General works on the southern cotton textile industry are: Broadus Mitchell, *The Rise of Cotton Mills in the South* (Baltimore, 1921); Ben F. Lemert, *The Cotton Textile Industry of the Southern Appalachian Piedmont* (Chapel Hill, N.C., 1933); Jack Blicksilver, *Cotton Manufacturing in the Southeast: An Historical Analysis* (Atlanta, Ga., 1959). The last volume is the best balanced of the three, containing good material on finance, marketing, and entrepreneurship. Broadus Mitchell, *William Gregg, Factory Master of the Old South* (Chapel Hill, N.C., 1928), is a good corporate study as well as a biography. Another valuable biography is: George T. Winston, *A Builder of the New South, Daniel Augustus Tomkins* (Garden City, N.Y., 1920).

A few important articles might be cited for special reference from a large periodical literature devoted to the early textile industry: George S. Gibb, "The Pre-Industrial Revolution in America: A Field for Local Research," *Bulletin of the Business History Society*, 20 (1946), 103–17; Thomas R. Navin, "Innovation and Management Policies: The Textile Machine Industry, Influences of the Market on Management," *ibid.*, 25 (1951), 15–31; Lance E. Davis, "The New England Textile Mills and the Capital Markets: A Study of Industrial Borrowing, 1840–1860," *Journal of Economic History*, 20 (1960), 1–31; John E. Sawyer, "The Social Basis of the American System of Manufacturing," *ibid.*, 14 (1954), 361–79. Frances W. Gregory, in "The Office of the President in the American Textile Industry," *Bulletin of the Business History Society*, 26

(1952), 122–34, finds that presidents exercised mostly ceremonial duties, but, coming from the mercantile aristocracy, often rendered valuable services in financing and marketing.

Several important articles relate to topics on the southern textile industry not covered in the monographic literature: Richard W. Griffin, "The Origins of Southern Cotton Manufacture, 1807–1816," *Cotton History Review*, 1 (1960), 5–13; Ernest M. Lander, Jr., "Slave Labor in Southern Cotton Mills," *Journal of Negro History*, 38 (1953), 161–73; Norris W. Preyer, "The Historian, the Slave, and the Ante-Bellum Textile Industry," *Journal of Negro History*, 46 (1961), 65–82. Difficulties faced manufacturers in other lines than textiles, but the sometimes impressive gains which were made in these industries are the subjects of several articles: Herbert Collins, "The Southern Industrial Gospel Before 1860," *Journal of Southern History*, 12 (1946), 386–402; Richard W. Griffin, "Manufacturing Interests of Mississippi Planters, 1810–1832," *Journal of Mississippi History*, 22 (1960), 110–23; Fabian Linden, "Repercussions of Manufacturing in the Ante-Bellum South," *North Carolina Historical Review*, 17 (1940), 313–31. The rise of manufacturing in Charleston but its ultimate failure to develop extensively is covered in the following articles: Ernest M. Lander, "Charleston, Manufacturing Center of the Old South," *Journal of Southern History*, 26 (1960), 330–51; Lander, "Manufacturing in South Carolina, 1850–1860," *Business History Review*, 28 (1954), 59–67; Leonard P. Stavisky, "Industrialism in Ante-Bellum Charleston," *Journal of Negro History*, 36 (1951), 302–22.

Two recent books provide good background for a study of light metals manufacture and "The American System." H. J. Habakkuk, in *American and British Technology in the Nineteenth Century* (Cambridge, England, 1962), analyzes the subjects in depth and in general confirms the thesis that the shortage and high price of labor in the United States stimulated the development of manufacturing with laborsaving devices. This conclusion is questioned by Peter Temin, however, in "Labor Scarcity and the Problem of Industrial Efficiency in America in the 1850's," *Journal of Economic History*, 26 (1966), 277–98. W. Paul Strassman, in *Risk and Technological Innovation: American Manufacturing Methods During the Nineteenth Century* (Ithaca, N.Y., 1959), finds that in general American entrepreneurs would not accept high business risks and were often slower to adopt technological innovations than has previously been thought. Joseph W. Roe, *English and American Tool Builders* (New York, 1926), is the standard history of a basic industry often neglected by historians. The more recent work by L. T. C. Rolt, *A Short History of Machine Tools* (Cambridge, Mass., 1965), adds little to Roe's account. Nathan Rosenberg, in "Technological Change in the Machine Tool Industry, 1840–1910," *Journal of Economic History*, 23 (1963), 414–43, stresses the changing needs of industry as a determinant of tool innovation. Constance M. Green, *Eli Whitney and the Birth of American Technology* (Boston, 1956), is the best biography of the man credited with originating interchangeable manufacture in the United States. Robert S. Woodbury, in "The Legend of Eli Whitney," *Technology and Culture*, 1 (1960), provides a useful corrective, however, by pointing out that Whitney was only one of several mechanics working independently on interchangeable manufacture. Greville and Dorothy Bathe, in

Oliver Evans: A Chronicle of Early American Engineering (Philadelphia, 1935), follow the career of an early American engineer who invented the automatic, continuous process flour mill.

The development of the brass and light metals industries in Connecticut may be traced in the following: Grace P. Fuller, *An Introduction to the History of Connecticut as a Manufacturing State* (Northampton, Mass., 1915); Clive Day, *The Rise of Manufacturing in Connecticut* (New Haven, Conn., 1935); William G. Lathrop, *The Development of the Brass Industry in Connecticut* (New Haven, Conn., 1936); Richard Lowitt, *A Merchant Prince of the Nineteenth Century: William E. Dodge* (New York, 1954). John J. Murphy, in "Entrepreneurship in the Establishment of the American Clock Industry," *Journal of Economic History*, 26 (1966), 169–87, in effect describes the beginning of mass production for consumer durables in America.

Material on labor policy can be found in most of the monographs devoted to manufacturing in the antebellum period, but the subject has been given little special study by historians. Theodore F. Marburg, in "Aspects of Labor Administration in the Early Nineteenth Century," *Bulletin of the Business History Society*, 15 (1941), 1–10, deals with labor conditions in the Connecticut button industry. He finds that because of the great scarcity and high price of native skilled labor, the manufacturers imported many skilled metal workers from abroad. Henrietta M. Larson, in "An Early American Industrial Capitalist's Labor Policy and Management," *ibid.*, 18 (1944), 132–41, presents a case history showing how close personal relations between a Connecticut ax maker and his employees during the 1830s became much more distant and hostile a decade later after the plant had expanded. John Buttrick, "The Inside Contract System," *Journal of Economic History*, 12 (1952), 205–21, is an important article. In it Buttrick describes the labor system common in the metals industries whereby supervisors contracted with management to perform specific operations, and hired and paid the necessary working force.

Although there are several good corporate histories in the rubber industry, they have so little material bearing on the nineteenth century that they are not worth citing for the purposes of this book. Nearly all the material in print on the earlier period is contained in: Howard and Ralph Wolf, *Rubber: A Story of Glory and Greed* (New York, 1936); and in: Ralph F. Wolf, *India Rubber Man: The Story of Charles Goodyear* (Caldwell, Ind., 1939). The authors write primarily for popular consumption, and have obvious biases in favor of Goodyear and against the large rubber companies.

General discussions of tobacco manufacturing are contained in two books cited under VI: Joseph C. Robert, *The Tobacco Kingdom: Plantation, Market, and Factory in Virginia and North Carolina, 1800–1860* (Durham, N.C., 1938); Nannie May Tilley, *The Bright Tobacco Industry, 1860–1929* (Chapel Hill, N.C., 1948). Meyer Jacobstein, *The Tobacco Industry in the United States* (New York, 1907), contains material on the American Tobacco Company gained from legislative investigations. The author is influenced somewhat by the muckraker point of view. Richard B. Tennant, in *The American Cigarette Industry: A Study in Economic Analysis and Public Policy* (New Haven, Conn., 1950), provides a more detailed study of the company and is less biased in his judgments. Patrick G. Porter, in "Origins of the American Tobacco Company," *Business History Review*, 43 (1969), 59–76, sheds further light on the formation of the great combination and notes the attempts to introduce a certain amount of vertical integration into it. John W. Jenkins, *James B. Duke, Master Builder* (New York, 1927), is a biography of the founder of American tobacco and one of the most important businessmen of the nineteenth century.

The far-reaching changes in the glass industry at the end of the nineteenth century are covered in a model volume that investigates all of the aspects of an industry of interest to the business historian: Warren C. Scoville, *Revolution in Glassmaking: Entrepreneurship and Technological Change in the American Industry, 1880–1920* (Cambridge, Mass., 1948). Similar developments in the paper manufacture are described by Weeks in *A History of Paper-Making* (cited above), and in Louis T. Stevenson, *The Background and Economics of American Paper-making* (New York, 1940).

The best volume on the growth of the iron industry, is: Peter Temin, *Iron and Steel in Nineteenth-Century America: An Economic Inquiry* (Cambridge, Mass., 1964). Devoted primarily to the production aspect of the industry, Temin gives a clear description, with voluminous statistics, of the interrelated technological and economic problems that were encountered and solved during the formative period. Fritz Redlich, *History of American Business Leaders: Theory, Iron and Steel, Iron Ore Mining*, Vol. I (Ann Arbor, Mich., 1940), skillfully combines description of technological processes with biographical studies of the chief iron entrepreneurs. Allan Nevins, *Abram S. Hewitt, with Some Account of Peter Cooper* (New York, 1935), is an excellent biography of one of the foremost ironmasters of the era. Perspective on the period can be enlarged by comparing the career of Hewitt with that of Joseph R. Anderson, a leading southern ironmaster, as treated in the biography by Charles B. Dew, *Ironmaker to the Confederacy: Joseph R. Anderson and the Tredegar Iron Works* (New Haven, Conn., 1966). Material on Tredegar and on the southern iron industry generally will also be found in Kathleen Bruce's *Virginia Iron Manufacture in the Slave Era* (as previously cited). *The Autobiography of John Fritz* (New York, 1911), gives insight into the career of a third ironmaster of the period. Two articles by Louis C. Hunter throw light on special aspects of the iron manufacture by Western Pennsylvania: "Influence of the Market upon Technique in the Iron Industry in Western Pennsylvania, up to 1860," *Journal of Economic and Business History*, 1 (1928–29), 241–81; "Financial Problems of the Early Pittsburgh Iron Manufacturers," *ibid.*, 2 (1929–30), 520–44. Lester J. Cappon, in "The Trends of the Southern Iron Industry Under the Plantation System," *ibid.*, 353–78, describes the development of iron manufacture in the southern back country. S. Sidney Bradford, in "The Negro Ironworker in Ante-Bellum Virginia," *Journal of Southern History*, 25 (1959), 194–206, reveals that Negroes were extensively used in Virginia ironworks in all capacities except management. James D. Norris, *Frontier Iron: The Maramec Iron Works, 1825–1876* (Madison, Wis., 1964), is an excellent, detailed study of a large iron works in the Ozarks.

The best accounts of the rise of the steel industry are contained in: Redlich, *Business Leaders* and Temin, *Iron and Steel*, as cited above. Stewart H. Holbrook, *Iron Brew: A Century of American Ore and Steel* (New York,

1939), and Douglas Alan Fisher, *The Epic of Steel* (New York, 1963), are the best of several popular treatments. Much information on the Carnegie steel companies is contained in the well-written, comprehensive biography by Burton J. Hendrick: *The Life of Andrew Carnegie*, 2 vols. (Garden City, N.Y., 1932). A valuable contemporary treatment, presenting a somewhat hostile appraisal of the man and the companies is: James H. Bridge, *The Inside History of the Carnegie Steel Company* (1903). Louis M. Hacker, in *The World of Andrew Carnegie* (Philadelphia, 1968), leans more toward the evaluation of Carnegie by Hendrick than that by Bridge. The volume adds valuable detail to the information available regarding Carnegie personally and the operation of the Carnegie companies. It also provides insight into Carnegie's attitude toward pooling and contains a good, short description of the formation of United States Steel Company. Because of very recent appearance, use could not be made of the excellent new biography by Joseph Frazier Wall, *Andrew Carnegie* (New York, 1970). George Harvey, in *Henry Clay Frick: The Man* (New York, 1926), gives useful information on Frick's career in the companies, but defends Frick uncritically in the Frick-Carnegie quarrel. Eugene G. Grace, *Charles M. Schwab* (Bethlehem, Pa., 1947), is a short personal memoir of a figure of equal importance to Frick in the industry. The various biographies of J. P. Morgan contain accounts of the formation of United States Steel. Perhaps the most useful in this regard is the biography by Frederick Lewis Allen, *The Great Pierpont Morgan* (New York, 1949). The acquisition of iron ore properties by the Carnegie companies is described in: Henry R. Mussey, *Combination in the Mining Industry: A Study of Concentration in Lake Superior Iron Ore Production* (New York, 1905). Much material on the development of Mesabi and Vermilion ore fields will also be found in Hal Bridges's *Iron Millionaire: The Life of Charlemagne Tower* (Philadelphia, 1952). Tower was a large-scale mining operator in the region.

Some of the most valuable works in the field of business history are devoted to the oil industry, which has attracted considerable attention from historians. Harold F. Williamson and Arnold R. Daum, *The American Petroleum Industry: The Age of Illumination, 1859–1899* (Evanston, Ill., 1959), is solidly researched with a multitude of statistics and tables covering all aspects of the industry. Ralph W. and Muriel E. Hidy, *Pioneering in Big Business, 1882–1911: History of Standard Oil Company (New Jersey)* (New York, 1955), a model of corporate history, is the objective study of Standard Oil so long needed. The Hidys absolve the company from many, but not all of the charges brought against it during the late nineteenth century. Allan Nevins, *John D. Rockefeller: The Heroic Age of American Enterprise*, 2 vols. (New York, 1940), is a sympathetic, but searching and objective biography which also provides a good external history of Standard Oil. Arthur M. Johnson, *The Development of American Petroleum Pipelines: A Study in Private Enterprise and Public Policy, 1862–1906* (Ithaca, N.Y., 1956), covers a unique and very important aspect of the industry. The beginnings of the industry are described by Paul H. Giddens in *The Birth of the Oil Industry* (New York, 1938), a book in part superseded by the later work of Williamson and Daum. Giddens, *Standard Oil Company (Indiana): Oil Pioneer of the Middle West* (New York, 1955); and Gerald T. White, *Formative Years in the Far West: A History of Standard*

Oil Company of California and Predecessors Through 1919 (New York, 1962), are good corporate histories. Frank J. Taylor and Earl M. Walty, *Black Bonanza: How an Oil Hunt Grew into the Union Oil Company of California* (New York, 1950), and Carl C. Rister, *Oil! Titan of the Southwest* (Norman, Okla., 1949), are popular but nevertheless helpful treatments.

Since the magnetic telegraph was the first piece of electrical equipment to be manufactured for commercial purposes, the history of the electrical equipment industry logically begins with the revolution in communications brought about by the use of the telegraph. Robert L. Thompson, *Wiring a Continent* (Princeton, N.J., 1947), is an excellent, comprehensive treatment of the building of the telegraph network. Frederick L. Rhodes, *Beginnings of Telephony* (New York, 1929), is primarily technical in nature and gives the clearest account of Bell's invention of the telephone. J. Warren Stehman, *The Financial History of the American Telephone and Telegraph Company* (Boston, 1925), provides a useful and factual account of the formation of the Bell System. Noobar R. Danielian, *A. T. & T.: The Story of an Industrial Conquest* (New York, 1939), although somewhat biased and critical of the Bell companies' drive for monopoly from the outset of their career, gives illuminating insights into corporate policy. Arthur W. Page, *The Bell Telephone System* (New York, 1941), is a strong defense of the company by a former vice-president. It does not deal with the Bell companies' early years, however. Albert B. Paine, *In One Man's Life: Being Chapters from the Personal and Business Career of Theodore N. Vail,* (New York, 1921), follows the career of the first President of A. T. & T., throughout his life a leader in the development of telephone service.

The electrical industry for the manufacture of apparatus for lighting and power has received excellent, comprehensive treatment by Harold C. Passer in *The Electrical Manufacturers, 1875–1900* (Cambridge, Mass., 1953). Malcolm MacLaren, *The Rise of the Electrical Industry during the Nineteenth Century* (Princeton, N.J., 1943), covers a wider time span, but is devoted mainly to scientific and technological developments and has little else of interest to the business historian. Arthur A. Bright, Jr., *The Electric-Lamp Industry: Technological Change and Economic Development from 1800–1947* (New York, 1949), devotes considerable attention to corporate developments as well as to technological matters. Matthew Josephson, *Edison* (New York, 1959), the best biography of the great inventor, emphasizes his career as an entrepreneur. A business biography of George Westinghouse, perhaps the most important of the electrical entrepreneurs, still remains to be written. Henry G. Prout, *A Life of George Westinghouse* (New York, 1922), deals with his career as an inventor and as a developer of electrical apparatus. Harold C. Passer has written a short but well-balanced biography of a third important inventor-entrepreneur: "Frank Julian Sprague, Father of Electric Traction," in William Miller, ed., *Men in Business* (New York, 1962), 212–38. Some information on the development of streetcar lines can also be found in: John A. Miller, *Fares, Please: A Popular History of Horse-Cars, Street-Cars, Elevateds, and Subways* (New York, 1960). Forrest McDonald's *Insull* (Chicago, 1962), an eloquent, partisan, but nevertheless, persuasive defense of a man often considered a symbol of speculative, corrupt financeering, calls attention to the contributions to the success of the Edison enterprises made by Insull as Edison's secretary and as manager of Edison General Electric. Louis Stotz, *History of the Gas Industry* (New York, 1938) is an inadequate treatment of the major competitor faced by the electric light industry.

VIII. BUSINESS AND BUSINESSMEN DURING
THE LATTER NINETEENTH CENTURY

Historians have generally believed that the Civil War had a stimulating effect upon the economic growth of the North. Thomas C. Cochran throws considerable doubt upon this conclusion in a persuasive but controversial article, "Did the Civil War Retard Industrialism?" *Mississippi Valley Historical Review*, 48 (1961), 197–211. Stanley L. Engerman, in "The Economic Impact of the Civil War," *Explorations in Entrepreneurial History*, 2d ser., no. 3 (1966), 176–200, brings further statistical evidence to the support of Cochran's view. In a similar vein Stanley Coben denies the often repeated conclusion that northern business interest tried to use Radical Reconstruction as a means of gaining control of southern business and industry: "Northeastern Business and Radical Reconstruction: A Re-examination," *Mississippi Valley Historical Review*, 46 (1959), 67–91. The Cochran and Coben articles are reprinted, together with others of interest to business historians, in the volume edited by Carl N. Degler, *Pivotal Interpretations of American History* (New York, 1966).

There is no comprehensive examination of American business at the turn of the century in print. Alfred D. Chandler, Jr., describes changes in management brought about by the rise of supercorporations in his *Strategy and Structure: Chapters in the History of the Industrial Enterprise* (Cambridge, Mass., 1962). William Miller notes the tendency toward bureaucratization in business at this time in "The Business Elite Bureaucracies: Careers of Top Executives in the Early Twentieth Century," William Miller, ed., *Men in Business* (New York, 1952), 286–305. In a companion article, "The Recruitment of the Business Elite," *Quarterly Journal of Economics*, 64 (1950), 242–53, Miller reveals how the business elite was being increasingly recruited from the privileged ranks of society. Marion V. Sears, in "The American Businessman at the Turn of the Century," *Business History Review*, 30 (1956), 382–444, discusses the major issues facing businessmen as revealed in the business press for the year 1900. The business setting of 1900 is outlined in the introductory chapters of Thomas C. Cochran's volume, *The American Business System: A Historical Perspective, 1900–1955* (Cambridge, Mass., 1957). The merger movement at the turn of the century is examined by Ralph L. Nelson in *Merger Movements in American Industry, 1895–1956*. (Princeton, N.J., 1959). Revisionist in his point of view, Nelson feels that the desire to make capital gains in rising markets through exchanges of stock was a more important motive for merger from 1897 to 1905 than the desire to control competition, which has generally been considered the dominant motive. Cedric B. Cowing, in *Populists, Plungers, and Progressives: A Social History of Stock and Commodity Speculation, 1890–1936*, (Princeton, N.J., 1965), describes speculative gambits and attempts at legislative reform.

The businessman at the turn of the century has been subjected to much more scrutiny than business itself. The philosophical background for the strong objection to governmental interference with business is ably discussed by Sidney Fine in *Laissez-Faire and the General Welfare State: A Study of Conflict in American Thought, 1865–1901* (Ann Arbor, Mich., 1956). Robert H. Wiebe, in the opening chapters of *Businessmen and Reform: A Study of the Progressive Movement* (Cambridge, Mass., 1962), reveals the complex pattern of fears and rivalries among businessmen during the late nineteenth century and the response by business to these threats in the formation of trade associations. The studies of businessmen's attitudes and values by Edward C. Kirkland are particularly sharp and revealing. In *Dream and Thought in the Business Community, 1860–1900* (Ithaca, N.Y., 1956), Kirkland discusses attitudes toward cyclical fluctuations, education, governmental intervention, laissez-faire, and social Darwinism. In *Business in the Gilded Age: The Conservatives' Balance Sheet* (Madison, Wis., 1952), he explores business values through a comparison of Charles Francis Adams, E. L. Godkin, and Andrew Carnegie. In "Divide and Ruin," *Mississippi Valley Historical Review,* 43 (1956), 3–17, he finds that one of the most fertile sources of conflict between businessmen and the community arose from businessmen's delusion that they could carry on their business affairs in isolation from public concerns. Sigmund Diamond, in *The Reputation of the American Businessman* (Cambridge, Mass., 1955), through a comparison of the postmortem reputations of Stephen Girard, John Jacob Astor, and Cornelius Vanderbilt, explores the changing social sanctions brought to bear on businessmen during the nineteenth century. Irvin G. Wyllie describes the great admiration for the self-made man and the identification of success and virtue in *The Self-Made Man in America: The Myth of Rags to Riches* (New Brunswick, N.J., 1954). In "Social Darwinism and the Businessman," *Proceedings of the American Philosophical Society,* 102 (1959), 629–35, Wyllie points out that although social Darwinism was important for the relatively small number of business leaders with intellectual interests, it exercised little or no effect on the outlook and values of most businessmen.

The "robber baron" concept has provoked considerable controversy among historians. The first comprehensive treatment of big businessmen as exploiters of society was made by Gustavus Myers in his *History of the Great American Fortunes,* 3 vols. (Chicago, 1910). Myers got most of his material, which he used in an uncritical fashion, from muckraking articles and from legislative investigations. Matthew Josephson, in *The Robber Barons: The Great American Capitalists* (New York, 1934), is somewhat more objective, but nevertheless sees the big businessman as the manipulator of the economy to his advantage. Interest in entrepreneurial history beginning in the late forties, and the end of the "depression mentality," fostered a more favorable reevaluation. Thomas C. Cochran, in "The Legend of the Robber Barons," *Pennsylvania Magazine of History and Biography,* 74 (1950), 307–22, labels the robber baron concept "a pathological approach" and points out that the growth of the economy was not autonomous but largely the result of businessmen's decisions. John Tipple, in "The Anatomy of Prejudice: Origins of the Robber Baron Legend," *Business History Review,* 33 (1959), 510–21, finds that the legend was accepted by the public in the late nineteenth century because of a general belief, fortified by reformers, that big businessmen were responsible for the economic distress of the period. Hal Bridges, tracing the progress of the robber baron stereotype in "The Robber Baron Concept in American History," *Business History Review*, 32 (1958), 1–13, concludes that happily it is fading into oblivion. The chief modern defender of the concept has been Chester McArthur Destler. In "Entrepreneurial Leadership among the Robber Barons: A Trial Balance," *The Tasks of Economic History*, 6 (1946), 28–50, he attempts to isolate creative and destructive activities of a test group of forty-three outstanding businessmen of the turn of the century. He maintains that the term robber baron is justified because of the strong penchant for promotional and speculative profits exhibited by many of the group. His argument is not very persuasive, because his data are too imprecise to admit of much generalization, and because he fails to take into consideration the background and environments of the men concerned and the social sanctions operating on them. In "The Opposition of American Businessmen to Social Control during the Gilded Age," *Mississippi Valley Historical Review*, 39 (1953), 641–72, Destler further justifies the robber baron concept by describing the means by which businessmen tried to frustrate the public controls placed upon them. He does not take into account the more usual situations in which businessmen tried to accommodate themselves to legislative control, nor does he note the sincerity of the widespread conviction that such legislation was wrong in principle.

From the late nineteenth century to the present there has been a great deal of writing on the trust problem. One of the best of the older works by an acknowledged and impartial expert in the field, is: Jeremiah Jenks, *The Trust Problem* (New York, 1917). The best of the modern treatments and work of scholarship which explores in detail the entire background of the antitrust movement is: Hans B. Thorelli, *The Federal Anti-Trust Policy: Origination of an American Tradition* (Baltimore, 1955). Material on "scientific management" will be found in: Horace B. Drury, *Scientific Management: A History and a Criticism* (New York, 1918); Frank B. Copley, *Frederick W. Taylor, Father of Scientific Management*, 2 vols. (New York, 1923); Frederick W. Taylor, *The Principles of Scientific Management* (New York, 1911); Taylor, *Shop Management* (New York, 1911). Samuel Haber, in *Efficiency and Uplift: Scientific Management in the Progressive Era, 1890–1920* (Chicago, 1964), has shown how the principles of scientific management became a means of promoting reform in political and social relationships as well as in business management.

Index